Courtesy Ronald Reagan Library

Ronald Reagan

{ 108TH CONGRESS, 2D SESSION . . . HOUSE DOCUMENT NO. 108–227 }

MEMORIAL SERVICES IN THE
CONGRESS OF THE UNITED STATES
AND TRIBUTES IN EULOGY OF

Ronald Reagan

LATE A PRESIDENT OF THE
UNITED STATES

Compiled Under the Direction of the
Joint Committee on Printing
Chairman Robert W. Ney
Vice Chairman Saxby Chambliss

UNITED STATES GOVERNMENT PRINTING OFFICE
WASHINGTON : 2005

Senate Concurrent Resolution No. 135

(Mr. FRIST submitted the following concurrent resolution)

IN THE SENATE OF THE UNITED STATES,
July 22, 2004.

Resolved by the Senate (the House of Representatives concurring),

SECTION 1. COMMEMORATIVE DOCUMENT AUTHORIZED.

A commemorative document in memory of the late President of the United States, RONALD WILSON REAGAN, consisting of the eulogies and encomiums for RONALD WILSON REAGAN, as expressed in the Senate and the House of Representatives, together with the texts of the state funeral ceremony at the United States Capitol Rotunda, the national funeral service held at the Washington National Cathedral, Washington, District of Columbia, and the interment ceremony at the Ronald Reagan Presidential Library, Simi Valley, California, shall be printed as a House document, with illustrations and suitable binding, under the direction of the Joint Committee on Printing.

SEC. 2. PRINTING OF DOCUMENT.

In addition to the usual number of copies printed, there shall be printed the lesser of—

(1) 32,500 copies of the commemorative document, of which 22,150 copies shall be for the use of the House of Representatives and 10,350 copies shall be for the use of the Senate; or

(2) such number of copies of the commemorative document that does not exceed a production and printing cost of $1,000,000, with distribution of the copies to be allocated in the same proportion as described in paragraph (1).

A compilation of addresses and tributes as given in the United States Senate and House of Representatives plus such additional materials, including the texts of eulogies, messages, prayers, and scriptural selections delivered at the funeral services held in Washington, DC, and in Simi Valley, CA, on the life, character, and public service of the late President Ronald Reagan.

Contents

	Page
Biography	vii
Funeral Services for the Late Ronald Reagan, Held at—	
U.S. Capitol Rotunda	xiii
Washington National Cathedral	xxiii
Ronald Reagan Presidential Library	xlix
Memorial Tributes in the House of Representatives of the United States	1
Memorial Tributes in the Senate of the United States	177
Index	323

Ronald Reagan
(1911–2004)

RONALD WILSON REAGAN was born on February 6, 1911, in an apartment above the general store in Tampico, IL. His family consisted of his parents, John and Nelle, and his older brother Neil.

After a series of homes in Chicago, Galesburg, Monmouth, and Tampico, IL, the Reagans moved to Dixon, IL, in 1920. RONALD REAGAN considers Dixon his boyhood home. There he attended high school where he became involved in school football, basketball, and track. He served as student body president, participated in school plays and worked on the yearbook. For 7 summers he was employed as a lifeguard at Lowell Park, and is credited with saving 77 lives.

REAGAN graduated from Eureka College with a bachelor of arts degree in economics and sociology. At Eureka College he was also involved in extra-curricular activities including football, swim team, drama, yearbook editor, school newspaper reporter and student body president.

After graduating college REAGAN became a radio sportscaster, first at WOC in Davenport, IA, later a full-time staff announcer at WHO in Des Moines. While reporting on spring training with the Chicago Cubs in California, he made a screen test for Warner Bros. They liked the easy-speaking, handsome REAGAN and signed him to a 7-year contract. REAGAN worked in Hollywood for the next 27 years and appeared in 53 films.

His military career began in 1935 with enlistment in the Army Reserve. Two years later he was promoted to second lieutenant in the Reserve Corps of the Cavalry. In the Cavalry he learned to ride horses, which became a love he enjoyed throughout his life. In 1942 he was called to active duty in World War II. His eyesight made him ineligible for overseas duty, and he was assigned to the U.S. Army Air Corp's First Motion Picture Unit attaining the rank of captain. There he appeared in numerous training films and starred in films selling war bonds.

In 1940 he married Jane Wyman, an actress he met while filming *Brother Rat*. Maureen Reagan was born, and Michael Reagan was adopted before their divorce in 1949. He then met actress Nancy Davis, they fell in love, and were married in 1952. They had two children, Patti and Ronald Reagan. REAGAN and Davis appeared together in only one film, *Hellcats of the Navy*, made in 1957. In 2002 they celebrated their 50th wedding anniversary.

After World War II, REAGAN returned to Hollywood. His interest in the entertainment industry waned and he became increasingly more focused on political matters. He was president of the Screen Actors Guild for 5 years, and toured the country giving speeches as General Electric's celebrity spokesman. In 1960 REAGAN campaigned for Richard Nixon as a Democrat for Nixon. In 1962 he switched political parties from Democrat to Republican. He co-chaired the California campaign for Barry Goldwater for President, and launched his political career with a televised speech, "A Time for Choosing," which raised a record $8 million for the Goldwater campaign. In 1964 REAGAN appeared in his last film, *The Killers*. In 1966 he was elected Governor of California, where he served for 8 years from 1967 through 1975.

In 1975 he announced his candidacy for President of the United States, but failed to win his party's nomination. In 1980 he won the Republican nomination for the Presidency, was overwhelmingly elected, and was inaugurated as the 40th President of the United States in 1981. President REAGAN was the oldest man to be inaugurated as President, the first two-term President since Eisenhower, and the longest living President of the United States.

During his 8 years in office, REAGAN was wounded by an assassin's bullet, appointed the first woman to the Supreme Court, worked to cut inflation and reduce government spending, improved the military, negotiated reduction of nuclear weapons with the Soviet Union, defeated the takeover of Grenada, and called upon Soviet Leader Mikhail Gorbachev to tear down the Berlin Wall.

At the age of 79 he left the Presidency and returned to California. In 1991 the Ronald Reagan Presidential Library was dedicated. In 1994 President REAGAN released a letter to the American people announcing that he had Alzheimer's disease, concluding his letter with, "I now begin this journey that will lead me into the sunset of my life. I know that for America there will always be a bright dawn ahead. Thank you my friends. May God always bless you."

RONALD REAGAN died on June 5, 2004, and is buried at the Ronald Reagan Presidential Library in Simi Valley, CA.

Courtesy Ronald Reagan Library

Speech at the Berlin Wall, June 12, 1987

Courtesy Ronald Reagan Library

Official family photograph following the inauguration, January 20, 1981

FUNERAL SERVICES FOR

Ronald Reagan

1911–2004

With Gratitude for
Your Expression of Sympathy
in Honoring the Life of

Ronald Wilson Reagan

February 6, 1911

to

June 5, 2004

Ronald Reagan Presidential Library
Simi Valley, California

——————— ———————

RONALD WILSON REAGAN

FORTIETH PRESIDENT OF THE UNITED STATES

February 6, 1911–June 5, 2004

Wednesday, the 9th of June, 2004
The Rotunda
United States Capitol
Washington, D.C.

ROTUNDA SERVICE
United States Capitol

PRELUDE	"Battle Hymn of the Republic" "America" "God of Our Fathers" U.S. Army Brass Quintet
INVOCATION	The Reverend Daniel P. Coughlin *Chaplain, U.S. House of Representatives*
EULOGIES	Senator Ted Stevens *President pro tempore, U.S. Senate* Representative J. Dennis Hastert *Speaker, U.S. House of Representatives* Richard B. Cheney *Vice President of the United States*
HYMN	"America the Beautiful" U.S. Air Force Singing Sergeants
WREATHS PLACED	Senator Ted Stevens Representative J. Dennis Hastert Vice President Richard B. Cheney
BENEDICTION	Dr. Barry C. Black *Chaplain, U.S. Senate*
POSTLUDE	"God Bless America" U.S. Army Brass Quintet

{Air Force One plane lands at Andrews Air Force Base.}
{The color guard representing all branches of the U.S. military gets into position.}
{The honor cordon and the Army band march into position.}
{The color guard carries the casket from the plane.}
{Mrs. Reagan disembarks. Mourners disembark.}
{"Hail to the Chief." 21-gun salute. "America the Beautiful."}
{The color guard carries the casket to the hearse.}
{The hearse carrying the casket of RONALD REAGAN and the motorcade leave Andrews Air Force Base.}
{The motorcade travels from Suitland Road to Suitland Parkway, picks up I295 north to the 11th Street Bridge, then I395 south into Virginia to the George Washington Memorial Parkway north and back into Washington, DC, at the Memorial Bridge, to Henry Bacon Drive and Constitution Avenue.}
{The motorcade stops at the Ellipse at 16th and Constitution.}
{The casket is transferred from the hearse to the caisson by military pallbearers.}
{The funeral procession is comprised of the Honor Cordon; 16 marching units of 89 people each; 3 marching bands with 100 pieces each; 3 Commanders with staff; the cortege—Special Honor Guard, Honorary Pallbearers, and the National Color Guard; Clergy; horse-drawn carriage; caisson; riderless horse with the boots in the stirrups facing backward; personal color bearer; and members of the family. The caisson is followed by the honor guard, the color guard, the marching bands, and the cortege, the procession of mourners.}
{The procession starts at the Ellipse on Pennsylvania Avenue, and travels up Constitution Avenue to Capitol Hill.}
{God Bless America.}
{Flyover of 21 F–15 aircraft at Fourth and Constitution. 21 U.S. military F–15 aircraft from the Fourth Fighter Wing, Seymour Johnson Air Force Base in South Carolina fly over the Capitol and look like a giant V. A single plane flies in the lead position followed by five waves of four plane formations at 10-second intervals. At the very end, as the last part of the formation, one of the F–15s performs the missing man maneuver where that aircraft shoots straight up and leaves the others behind.}
{Military band plays.}
{Two 105mm howitzers sound the traditional 21-gun salute.}
{"Battle Hymn of the Republic."}
{Procession reaches Capitol Hill.}
{The casket is removed from the caisson and carried up the stairs by the honor guard and placed inside the Capitol rotunda on the catafalque.}

REV. DANIEL P. COUGHLIN, HOUSE CHAPLAIN: Let us pray. The poet T.S. Eliot wrote, "neither does the actor suffer nor the patient act, but both are fixed in an eternal patience, an eternal act. And the wheel turns. The wheel turns and is forever still." RONALD WILSON REAGAN had many roles to play in life: husband, father, Governor, but the most notable role on the world stage was that of the 40th President of the United States of America. With his style and grace he made it seem easy. With his compassion and sense of timing, he brought strength of character to the Nation and enkindled hope in a darkened world. As the patient, he brought humility to greatness and presided over embracing life to its natural end and dying with dignity surrounded by love. To you, oh Lord, ever patient with all of us, ever active in all of us, be praise and thanks for the life and impact RONALD REAGAN has had upon us all. Support with your grace the Reagan family, and especially Mrs. Nancy Reagan, who stood by him in memorable moments of history and never left him in the long moments of difficult performance when the wheel turned, ah so slowly. Inspired by President REAGAN, empower all of us, Lord, to employ our part in crumbling the walls of separation and in opening the gates to a globalized world. May our stillness here help us to remain faithful and patient with those suffering and to make decisions that will renew faith in the future. All powerful God, fix America in your eternal patience, in your eternal act, as the wheel turns now and forever. Amen.

⸨Salutes.⸩

SENATOR TED STEVENS, PRESIDENT PRO TEMPORE: Mrs. Reagan, Patti, Ron, Michael, distinguished guests, members of the Reagan family, and friends of RONALD REAGAN in America and throughout the world:

Tonight, President RONALD REAGAN has returned to the people's house to be honored by millions of Americans who loved him.

Since 1824, under this rotunda, our Nation has paid final tribute to many dedicated public servants. President Abraham Lincoln was the first President to lie in state under this Capitol dome. In the coming days, thousands will come to these hallowed halls to say goodbye to another son of Illinois who, like Lincoln, appealed to our best hopes, not our worst fears.

In the life of any nation, few men forever alter the course of history. RONALD REAGAN was one of those men. He rose from a young boy who didn't have much to a man who had it all, including the love of a faithful partner and friend he found in his wife Nancy.

The true measure of any man is what he does with the opportunities life offers. By that standard, RONALD REAGAN was one of America's greatest.

He first proved that as Governor of California and later as President of the United States.

When RONALD REAGAN was sworn in as our 40th President, this Nation was gripped by a powerful malaise. Inflation and unemployment were soaring, and the Soviet Union was winning the cold war.

By the time President REAGAN left office, he had reversed the trend of ever-increasing government control over our lives, restored our defense capabilities, guided us through the worst economic downturn since the Great Depression, and set in motion policies which ultimately led to the collapse of the evil empire.

His integrity, vision and commitment were respected by all. But history's final judgment, I believe, will remember most his ability to inspire us.

President REAGAN put it best when he said, "The greatest leader is not necessarily the one who does the greatest things. He is the one that gets {the} people to do the greatest things."

This President inspired Americans by reaching out far beyond what he could attain. Like a good coach, he understood the value of a goal isn't always in achieving it; sometimes it's enough to simply look out into the future and remind people what is possible. And often, President REAGAN achieved the impossible.

He reminded us that "government is not the solution." The solution lies in each of us. True American heroes are ordinary people who live their lives with extraordinary character and strength.

President REAGAN showed us freedom was not just a slogan. He actually brought freedom to hundreds of thousands of people around this globe by opposing oppressive regimes. Those of us from the World War II generation looked up to him for his moral courage. In him we saw the leadership of great men like Eisenhower who led the way and moved us to follow.

On a wintry day in 1981, RONALD REAGAN stood on the steps that lie just behind these doors to deliver his first inaugural address. He spoke of a journal written by a young American who went to France in 1917 and died for the cause of freedom. From that journal he read these words: "I will work, I will save, I will sacrifice, I will endure, I will fight cheerfully and do my utmost, as if the issue of the whole struggle depends on me alone."

Throughout his life, RONALD REAGAN bore our burdens as if the outcome did depend on him alone. We will all remember him as an unparalleled leader and an exceptional man who lifted our Nation and set the world on a new path.

President REAGAN achieved greatness in his life. Some might even argue he transcended it. He could not have accomplished this without Nancy. Nancy is one of the finest First Ladies these United States have ever known. And the love RONALD and Nancy REAGAN shared touched the hearts of people everywhere.

In 1989, President REAGAN delivered his farewell address from the Oval Office. In that speech, the President spoke of the "shining city on a hill" that, "after 200 years, two centuries ... still stands strong and true on the granite ridge." Now it is our turn to thank RONALD REAGAN for making us believe in that shining city. As we say farewell, his last words as President echo across this great Nation. If we listen, we will hear him whisper the humble words he used to sum up his revolution: "All in all, not bad, not bad at all."

REP. DENNIS HASTERT, HOUSE SPEAKER: Mrs. Reagan, Mr. Vice President, Members of Congress and distinguished guests:

RONALD REAGAN's long journey has finally drawn to a close.

It is altogether fitting and proper that he has returned to this Capitol rotunda, like another great son of Illinois, Abraham Lincoln, so the Nation can say goodbye. This Capitol Building is, for many, the greatest symbol of democracy and freedom in the world. It brings to mind the "shining city on the hill" of which President REAGAN so often spoke. It is the right place to honor a man who so faithfully defended our freedom, and so successfully helped extend the blessings of liberty to millions of people around the world.

Mrs. Reagan, thank you for sharing your husband with us—for your steadfast love and for your great faith. We pray for you and for your family in this time of great mourning.

But as we mourn, we must also celebrate the life and the vision of one of America's greatest Presidents. His story and values are quintessentially American. Born in Tampico, IL, and then raised in Dixon, IL, he moved west to follow his dreams. He brought with him a midwestern optimism, and he blended it with a western can-do spirit.

In 1980, the year of the Reagan revolution, his vision of hope, growth, and opportunity was exactly what the American people needed and wanted. His message touched a fundamental chord that is deeply embedded in the American experience.

President REAGAN dared to dream that America had a special mission. He believed in the essential goodness of the American people and that we had a special duty to promote peace and freedom for the rest of the world.

Against the advice of the timid, he sent a chilling message to authoritarian governments everywhere, that the civilized world would not rest until freedom reigned in every corner of the globe.

While others worried, President REAGAN persevered. When others weakened, President REAGAN stood tall. When others stepped back, President REAGAN stepped forward. And he did it all with great humility, with great charm, and with great humor.

Tonight, we will open these doors and let the men and women whom RONALD REAGAN served so faithfully, file past and say goodbye to a man who meant so much to so many. It is their being here that I think would mean more to him than any words that we may say, because it was from America's great and good people that RONALD REAGAN drew his strength.

In the years ahead, we will tell our grandchildren about this night when we gathered here to honor the man from Illinois who became the son of California and then the son of all America. And then our grandchildren will tell their grandchildren, and President REAGAN's spirit and eternal faith in America will carry on.

RONALD REAGAN helped make our country and this world a better place to live. But he always believed that our best days were ahead of us, not behind us. I can still hear him saying with that twinkle in his eye, "You ain't seen nothing yet!"

President REAGAN once said, "We make a living by what we get; we make a life by what we give." Twenty years ago, President REAGAN stood on the beaches of Normandy to honor those who made a life by what they gave. Recalling the men who scaled the cliffs and crossed the beaches in a merciless hail of bullets, he asked, Who were these men—these ordinary men doing extraordinary things? His answer was simple and direct: They were Americans.

So I can think of no higher tribute or honor or title to confer upon RONALD REAGAN than just to simply say, he was an American. Godspeed, Mr. President. God bless you, and God bless the United States of America.

DICK CHENEY, VICE PRESIDENT OF THE UNITED STATES: Mrs. Reagan, members of the President's family, colleagues, distinguished guests, members of the diplomatic corps, fellow citizens: Knowing that this moment would come has not made it any easier to see the honor guard and the flag draped before us, and to begin America's farewell to President RONALD REAGAN. He said goodbye to us in a letter that showed his great courage and love for America. Yet for his friends and his country, the parting comes only now. And in this national vigil of mourning, we show how much America loved this good man and how greatly we will miss him.

A harsh winter morning in 1985 brought the inaugural ceremony inside of this rotunda. And standing in this place for the 50th Presidential inauguration, RONALD REAGAN spoke of a Nation that was "hopeful, big-hearted, idealistic, daring, decent and fair." That was how he saw America, and that was how America came to know him. There was a kindness, simplicity, and goodness of character that marked all the years of his life.

When you mourn a man of 93, no one is left who remembers him as a child in his mother's arms. RONALD WILSON REAGAN's life began in a time and place so different from our own, in a quiet town on the prairie, on the 6th of February, 1911. Nelle and Jack Reagan would live long enough to see the kind of man they had raised, but they could never know all that destiny had in store for the boy they called "DUTCH." And if they could witness this scene in 2004, their son, taken to his rest with the full honors of the United States, they would be so proud of all he had done with the life they gave him, and the things they taught him.

President REAGAN once said, "I learned from my father the value of hard work and ambition, and maybe a little something about telling a story." That was the RONALD REAGAN who confidently set out on his own from Dixon, IL, during the Great Depression, the man who would one day speak before cameras and crowds with such ease and self-command.

"From my mother," said President REAGAN, "I learned the value of prayer. My mother told me that everything in life happened for a purpose. She said all things were part of God's plan, even the most disheartening setbacks, and in the end, everything worked out for the best." This was the RONALD REAGAN who had faith, not just in his own gifts and his own future, but in the possibilities of every life. The cheerful spirit that carried him forward was more than a disposition; it was the optimism of a faithful soul who trusted in God's purposes, and knew those purposes to be right and true.

He once said, "There's no question I am an idealist, which is another way of saying I am an American." We usually associate that quality with youth, and yet one of the most idealistic men ever to become President was also the oldest.

He excelled in professions that have left many others jaded and self-satisfied, and yet somehow remained untouched by the worst influences of fame or power. If RONALD REAGAN ever uttered a cynical, or cruel, or selfish word, the moment went unrecorded. Those who knew him in his youth and those who knew him a lifetime later, all remember his largeness of spirit, his gentle instincts, and a quiet rectitude that drew others to him.

Seen now at a distance, his strengths as a man and as a leader are only more impressive. It's the nature of the city of Washington that men and women arrive, leave their mark, and go their way. Some figures who seemed quite large and important in their day are sometimes forgotten, or remembered with ambivalence. Yet nearly a generation after the often impassioned debates of the REAGAN years, what lingers from that time is almost all good. And this is because of the calm and kind man who stood at the center of events.

We think back with appreciation for the decency of our 40th President and respect for all that he achieved. After so much turmoil in the sixties and seventies, our Nation had begun to lose confidence, and some were heard to say that the Presidency might even be too big for one man. That phrase did not survive the eighties. For decades, America had waged a cold war, and few believed it could possibly end in our own lifetimes. The President was one of those few. And it was the vision and the will of RONALD REAGAN that gave hope to the oppressed, shamed the oppressors, and ended an evil empire. More than any other influence, the cold war was ended by the perseverance and courage of one man who answered falsehood with truth, and overcame evil with good.

RONALD REAGAN was more than a historic figure. He was a providential man who came along just when our Nation and the world most needed him. And believing as he did that there is a plan at work in each life, he accepted not only the great duties that came to him, but also the great trials that came near the end. When he learned of his illness, his first thoughts were of Nancy. And who else but RONALD REAGAN could face his own decline and death with a final message of hope to his country, telling us that for America there is always a bright dawn ahead? Fellow Americans, here lies a graceful and a gallant man.

Nancy, none of us can take away the sadness you are feeling. I hope it is a comfort to know how much he means to us, and how much you mean to us as well. We honor your grace, your own courage, and above all, the great love that you gave to your husband. When these days of ceremony are completed, the Nation returns him to you for the final journey to the West. And when he is laid to rest under the Pacific sky, we will be thinking of you, as we commend to the Almighty the soul of His faithful servant, RONALD WILSON REAGAN.

{Music}

DR. BARRY C. BLACK, CHAPLAIN, U.S. SENATE: Let us bow for the benediction. O giver of every good and perfect gift, accept our gratitude for the life of your servant, President RONALD REAGAN, whose love for freedom summoned our Nation to embrace our best hopes and not our worst fears. Thank you for his ability to plant seeds of confidence and not doubt and to lift liberty's lamp until totalitarian towers tumbled. In the days to come, remind us of America's opportunity to remain a "shining city on a hill." Continue to comfort those who mourn. In a special way, be near to Mrs. Nancy Reagan and the family. May the death of this beloved leader prompt us to see you more clearly, to love you more dearly, and to follow you more nearly day by day. Now fill us with your peace, as we trust you, so that we may overflow with hope by the power of your spirit. Amen.

{Music}

[Mrs. Reagan, accompanied by Mr. Cheney, says goodbye to her husband at the casket. Michael Reagan also says goodbye. Family and friends file out.]

---- ----

RONALD WILSON REAGAN

FORTIETH PRESIDENT OF THE UNITED STATES

February 6, 1911–June 5, 2004

Friday, the 11th of June, 2004
Eleven thirty o'clock in the morning
Washington National Cathedral
Washington, D.C.

CELEBRANT
The Reverend John C. Danforth

PARTICIPANTS
The Right Reverend John Bryson Chane
Bishop of Washington and Dean of the Cathedral

The Right Reverend A. Theodore Eastman
Vicar, Washington National Cathedral

His Eminence Angelo Cardinal Sodano
Secretary of State, Personal Representative of Pope John Paul II

His Eminence Theodore Cardinal McCarrick
Catholic Archbishop of Washington

His Eminence Archbishop Demetrios
Primate of the Greek Orthodox Church in America

Imam Mohamed Magid Ali
Imam and Director of the All Dulles Area Muslim Society

READERS
Rabbi Harold Kushner
Temple Israel, Natick, Massachusetts

The Honorable Sandra Day O'Connor

TRIBUTES
The President of the United States
The Honorable George H.W. Bush
The Right Honourable The Baroness Thatcher, L.G., O.M., F.R.S
The Right Honourable Brian Mulroney

HONORARY PALLBEARERS
The Honorable Michael K. Deaver
Mr. Merv Griffin
Brigadier General John E. Hutton, MC U.S. Army, Retired
The Honorable Frederick J. Ryan, Jr.
The Honorable Charles Z. Wick

Funeral Services

MUSICIANS

Ronan Tynan
Irish Tenor

The United States Marine Chamber
Orchestra
Colonel Timothy W. Foley, Director

The Armed Forces Chorus
Lieutenant Colonel John Clanton,
Director

The United States Coast Guard Band
Captain Lewis J. Buckley, Director

The Cathedral Choir of Men,
Boys, and Girls
Michael McCarthy, Director of Music

Erik Wm. Suter
Organist and Associate Choirmaster

Scott Hanoian
Assistant Organist and Choirmaster

The Reverend Canon
W. Bruce McPherson
Director for Worship and Liturgy

The Cathedral Vergers
Stephen Lott, Head Verger

The Cathedral Ushers
Michael Heid, Head Usher

ORDER OF THE SERVICE

PRELUDE	U.S. Marine Chamber Orchestra
"Faire is the Heaven"	
"Bring Us, O Lord God"	
"And I Saw a New Heaven"	
"Ave Maria"	Ronan Tynan
RECEPTION OF THE BODY	
Musical Honors	U.S. Coast Guard Band
"Ruffles and Flourishes"	
"Hail to the Chief"	
"Navy Hymn"	
tune: Melita	
Prayers	The Right Reverend John Bryson Chane attended by The Reverend John C. Danforth, The Right Reverend A. Theodore Eastman, and Stephen Lott
ANTHEM IN PROCESSION	The Reverend John C. Danforth
COLLECT FOR BURIAL	The Reverend John C. Danforth
A READING FROM THE HEBREW SCRIPTURES	Rabbi Harold Kushner
READING	The Honorable Sandra Day O'Connor
"We shall Be as a City Upon a Hill," by John Winthrop	
ANTHEM	
"O Love of God, How Strong and True"	Cathedral Choir
INTRODUCTION OF REMEMBRANCES	The Reverend John C. Danforth
TRIBUTES	The Right Honourable The Baroness Thatcher, L.G., O.M., F.R.S
	The Right Honourable Brian Mulroney
	The Honorable George H.W. Bush
	President George W. Bush
ANTHEM	Armed Forces Chorus
"Battle Hymn of the Republic"	U.S. Marine Chamber Orchestra
GOSPEL	His Eminence Theodore Cardinal McCarrick
HOMILY	The Reverend John C. Danforth
ANTHEM	
"Amazing Grace"	Ronan Tynan
THE LORD'S PRAYER	The Reverend John C. Danforth
PRAYERS OF THE PEOPLE	The Right Reverend A. Theodore Eastman
HYMN	
"Sing with All the Saints in Glory"	
THE COMMENDATION	The Reverend John C. Danforth
THE BLESSING	The Right Reverend John Bryson Chane
THE DISMISSAL	The Right Reverend A. Theodore Eastman
ANTHEM	
"The Mansions of the Lord"	Armed Forces Chorus
	U.S. Marine Chamber Orchestra

The congregation is asked to remain at their seats until directed by an usher. A full peal, half-muffled, will be rung on the Cathedral bells at the conclusion of the service.

⸪{The Color Guard moves up the stairs toward the rotunda, to begin the process of transferring the casket of RONALD REAGAN from the rotunda to the hearse.}⸫

⸪{21-gun salute as the casket is carried down the House steps and loaded into the hearse.}⸫

⸪{As the hearse carrying President REAGAN's casket leaves the Capitol, the bells begin to peel.}⸫

⸪{The drive to the National Cathedral.}⸫

PRELUDE
U.S. Marine Chamber Orchestra
    "Faire is the Heaven," *William H. Harris*
    "Bring Us, O Lord God," *William H. Harris*
    "And I Saw a New Heaven," *Edgar L. Bainton*
    "Ave Maria," *Franz Peter Schubert; sung by Ronan Tynan, Irish tenor*

⸪{The motorcade arrives at the National Cathedral. The casket is removed from the hearse.}⸫

⸪{The chimes continue to ring once a minute. Afterward there will be a much, much louder and sustained chiming of those bells.}⸫

RECEPTION OF THE BODY
    Musical Honors, *U.S. Coast Guard Band*
        "Ruffles and Flourishes"
        "Hail to the Chief"
        "Navy Hymn," *James Sanderson (tune: Melita)*

Prayers
The Right Reverend John Bryson Chane attended by The Reverend John C. Danforth, The Right Reverend A. Theodore Eastman, and Stephen Lott

    With faith in Jesus Christ, we receive the body of our brother RONALD for burial. Let us pray with confidence to God, the Giver of life, that he will raise him to perfection in the company of the saints.

    Deliver your servant RONALD, O Sovereign Lord Christ, from all evil, and set him free from every bond; that he may rest with all your saints in the eternal habitations; where with the Father and the Holy Spirit you live and reign, one God, for ever and ever. *Amen.*

    Let us also pray for all who mourn, that they may cast their care on God, and know the consolation of his love.

    Almighty God, look with pity upon the sorrows of your servants for whom we pray. Remember them, Lord, in your mercy; nourish them with patience; comfort them with a sense of your goodness; lift up your countenance upon them and give them peace; through Jesus Christ our Lord. *Amen.*

⸪{The People stand.}⸫

⸪{The Celebrant is led to the center of the rood screen landing; all others to their seats. When at about the midnave cross-aisle, the Celebrant begins.}⸫

ANTHEM IN PROCESSION
The Reverend John C. Danforth

> I am the resurrection and the life, saith the Lord;
> he that believeth in me, though he were dead, yet shall he live;
> and whosoever liveth and believeth in me shall never die.
>
> I know that my Redeemer liveth,
> and that he shall stand at the latter day upon the earth;
> and though this body be destroyed, yet shall I see God;
> whom I shall see for myself and mine eyes shall behold,
> and not as a stranger.
>
> For none of us liveth to himself, and no man dieth to himself.
> For if we live, we live unto the Lord;
> and if we die, we die unto the Lord.
> Whether we live, therefore, or die, we are the Lord's.
>
> Blessed are the dead who die in the Lord;
> even so saith the Spirit, for they rest from their labors.

{The Celebrant reaches the rood screen landing and faces the congregation. The casket is put in position and the bearers depart. The family is shown to their seats. President Bush accompanies Mrs. Reagan to her seat.}

COLLECT FOR BURIAL
The Reverend John C. Danforth

> Let us pray. O God, whose mercies cannot be numbered: Accept our prayers on behalf of thy servant RONALD, and grant him an entrance into the land of light and joy, in the fellowship of thy saints; through Jesus Christ our Lord, who liveth and reigneth with thee and the Holy Spirit, one God, now and for ever. *Amen.*

{The People are seated.}
{The Celebrant goes to his stall as the first and second readers are led to the lectern. The first reader steps up to the reading desk.}

A READING FROM THE HEBREW SCRIPTURES
Rabbi Harold Kushner
Isaiah 40:28–31

> Where does a person find the strength to persevere in difficult times? Many people find that strength from the pages of the Bible. Turning to the Book of Isaiah, the 40th chapter:
>
> > Hast thou not known? hast thou not heard
> > That the everlasting God, the Lord,
> > The Creator of the ends of the earth,
> > Fainteth not, neither is weary?
> > There is no searching of his understanding.
> > He giveth power to the faint:

And to him that hath no might He increaseth strength.
Even the youths shall faint and be weary,
And the young men shall utterly fall;
But they that wait for the Lord shall renew their strength;
They shall mount up with wings as eagles;
They shall run, and not be weary;
They shall walk, and not faint.

{The first reader steps down to the landing and the second reader steps up to the reading desk.}

READING
The Honorable Sandra Day O'Connor
"We Shall Be as a City Upon a Hill," by John Winthrop

This is a reading from a sermon delivered in 1630 by the Pilgrim leader John Winthrop, who was aboard the ship the *Arabella* on his way from England to the Massachusetts Bay Colony. "The city on the hill" passage was referenced by President REAGAN in several notable speeches.

Now the only way ... to provide for our posterity, is to follow the counsel of Micah, to do justly, to love mercy, to walk humbly with our God. ... We must delight in each other, make others' conditions our own; rejoice together, mourn together, labor and suffer together, always having before our eyes our commission and community in the work, as members of the same body. ... The Lord will be our God, and delight to dwell among us, as His own people ... For we must consider that we shall be as a city upon a hill. The eyes of all people are upon us. So that if we shall deal falsely with our God in this work we have undertaken, and so cause Him to withdraw His present help from us, we shall be made a story and a by-word through the world.

{The second reader steps down, and both readers are led back to their seats.}
{A lectern is placed on the rood screen landing center for Mr. Mulroney.}

ANTHEM
"O Love of God, How Strong and True"
Tune: Jerusalem
C. Hubert H. Parry, 1916
arr: Michael McCarthy, 2004
text by: Horatio Bonar, 1858
Cathedral Choir

O love of God, how strong and true
Eternal and yet ever new,
Uncomprehended and unbought,
Beyond all knowledge and all thought!

O love of God, how deep and great,
Far deeper than man's deepest hate;
Self-fed, self-kindled like the light,
Changeless, eternal infinite.

O heav'nly love, how precious still,
In days of weariness and ill,
In nights of pain and helplessness,
To heal, to comfort and to bless!
O wide-embracing, wondrous love!
We read you in the sky above,
We read you in the earth below,
In seas that swell and streams that flow.

We read you best in him who came
To bear for us the cross of shame;
Sent by the Father from on high,
Our life to live, our death to die.
We read your pow'r to bless and save,
E'en in the darkness of the grave;
Still more in resurrection light
We read the fullness of your might.

O love of God, our shield and stay
Through all the perils of our way!
Eternal love, in you we rest
Forever safe, forever blest.
We will exalt you, God and King,
and we will ever praise your name;
We will extol you ev'ry day,
and ever more your praise proclaim

⸫Toward the end of the anthem, Mr. Mulroney is led to the landing lectern for his tribute.⸬

INTRODUCTION OF REMEMBRANCES
The Reverend John C. Danforth

⸫The Celebrant stands at his stall, faces the congregation, and introduces Baroness Thatcher's videotaped tribute, then takes his seat again.⸬

President REAGAN's deepest long-held wish was that Lady Thatcher should participate in this service. But as the years have passed, Lady Thatcher's health, too, has suffered its ups and downs. Eighteen months ago, her doctors advised her to give up all formal public speaking. But she was determined to record her tribute to President REAGAN come what may, and this she has done. She was equally determined, on learning of the President's death, to be with us today. The next voice you will hear will be Lady Thatcher's.

TRIBUTE

Margaret Thatcher, former Prime Minister of the United Kingdom

We have lost a great President, a great American and a great man, and I have lost a dear friend. In his lifetime, RONALD REAGAN was such a cheerful and invigorating presence that it was easy to forget what daunting historic tasks he set himself. He sought to mend America's wounded spirit, to restore the strength of the free world, and to free the slaves of communism. These were causes hard to accomplish and heavy with risk.

Yet they were pursued with almost a lightness of spirit, for RONALD REAGAN also embodied another great cause, what Arnold Bennett once called "the great cause of cheering us all up." His politics had a freshness and optimism that won converts from every class and every nation, and ultimately from the very heart of the evil empire.

Yet his humour often had a purpose beyond humour. In the terrible hours after the attempt on his life, his easy jokes gave reassurance to an anxious world. They were evidence that in the aftermath of terror and in the midst of hysteria, one great heart at least remained sane and jocular. They were truly grace under pressure.

And perhaps they signified grace of a deeper kind. RONNIE himself certainly believed that he had been given back his life for a purpose. As he told a priest after his recovery "Whatever time I've got left now belongs to the big fellow upstairs."

And surely it is hard to deny that RONALD REAGAN's life was providential, when we look at what he achieved in the 8 years that followed.

Others prophesied the decline of the West; he inspired America and its allies with renewed faith in their mission of freedom.

Others saw only limits to growth; he transformed a stagnant economy into an engine of opportunity.

Others hoped, at best, for an uneasy cohabitation with the Soviet Union; he won the cold war—not only without firing a shot, but also by inviting enemies out of their fortress and turning them into friends.

I cannot imagine how any diplomat, or any dramatist, could improve on his words to Mikhail Gorbachev at the Geneva Summit: "Let me tell you why it is we distrust you." Those words are candid and tough and they cannot have been easy to hear. But they are also a clear invitation to a new beginning and a new relationship that would be rooted in trust.

We live today in the world that RONALD REAGAN began to reshape with those words. It is a very different world with different challenges and new dangers. All in all, however, it is one of greater freedom and prosperity, one more hopeful than the world he inherited on becoming President.

As Prime Minister, I worked closely with RONALD REAGAN for 8 of the most important years of all our lives. We talked regularly both before and after his Presidency. And I have had time and cause to reflect on what made him a great President.

RONALD REAGAN knew his own mind. He had firm principles—and, I believe, right ones. He expounded them clearly, he acted upon them decisively.

When the world threw problems at the White House, he was not baffled, or disorientated, or overwhelmed. He knew almost instinctively what to do.

When his aides were preparing option papers for his decision, they were able to cut out entire rafts of proposals that they knew "the Old Man" would never wear.

When his allies came under Soviet or domestic pressure, they could look confidently to Washington for firm leadership.

And when his enemies tested American resolve, they soon discovered that his resolve was firm and unyielding.

Yet his ideas, though clear, were never simplistic. He saw the many sides of truth.

Yes, he warned that the Soviet Union had an insatiable drive for military power and territorial expansion; but he also sensed it was being eaten away by systemic failures impossible to reform.

Yes, he did not shrink from denouncing Moscow's "evil empire." But he realised that a man of good will might nonetheless emerge from within its dark corridors.

So the President resisted Soviet expansion and pressed down on Soviet weakness at every point until the day came when communism began to collapse beneath the combined weight of those pressures and its own failures. And when a man of good will did emerge from the ruins, President REAGAN stepped forward to shake his hand and to offer sincere cooperation.

Nothing was more typical of RONALD REAGAN than that large-hearted magnanimity. And nothing was more American. Therein lies perhaps the final explanation of his achievements. RONALD REAGAN carried the American people with him in his great endeavors because there was perfect sympathy between them. He indeed loved America and what it stands for: freedom and opportunity for ordinary people.

As an actor in Hollywood's golden age, he helped to make the American dream live for millions all over the globe. His own life was a fulfillment of that dream. He never succumbed to the embarrassment some people feel about an honest expression of love of country. He was able to say, "God bless America" with equal fervour in public and in private. And so he was able to call confidently upon his fellow countrymen to make sacrifices for America and to make sacrifices for those who looked to America for hope and rescue.

With the lever of American patriotism, he lifted up the world. And so today, the world—in Prague, in Budapest, in Warsaw, in Sofia, in Bucharest, in Kiev and in Moscow itself—the world mourns the passing of the "great liberator" and echoes his prayer: "God bless America."

RONALD REAGAN's life was rich, not only in public achievement, but also in private happiness. Indeed, his public achievements were rooted in his private happiness. The great turning point of his life was his meeting and marriage with Nancy.

On that we have the plain testimony of a loving and grateful husband: "Nancy came along and saved my soul." We share her grief today. But we also share her pride—and the grief and pride of RONNIE's children.

For the final years of his life, RONNIE's mind was clouded by illness. That cloud has now lifted. He is himself again—more himself than at any time on this Earth. For we may be sure that the Big Fellow Upstairs never forgets those who remember Him. And as the last journey of this faithful pilgrim took him beyond the sunset, and as Heaven's morning broke, I like to think—in the words of Bunyan—that "all the trumpets sounded on the other side."

We here still move in twilight. But we have one beacon to guide us that RONALD REAGAN never had. We have his example. Let us give thanks today for a life that achieved so much for all of God's children.

TRIBUTE
Brian Mulroney, Former Prime Minister of Canada

In the spring of 1987, President REAGAN and I were driven into a large hangar at the Ottawa Airport to await the arrival of Mrs. Reagan and my wife Mila prior to departure ceremonies for their return to Washington. We were alone except for the security details.

President REAGAN's visit had been important, demanding and successful. Our discussions reflected the international agenda of the times: the nuclear threat posed by the Soviet Union and the missile deployment by NATO, pressures in the Warsaw Pact, challenges resulting from the Berlin Wall and the ongoing separation of Germany, and bilateral and hemispheric free trade.

President REAGAN had spoken to Parliament, handled complex files with skill and good humor, strongly impressing his Canadian hosts. And here we were waiting for our wives.

When their car drove in a moment later, out stepped Nancy and Mila looking like a million bucks. And as they headed toward us, President REAGAN beamed. He threw his arm around my shoulder. And he said with a grin, "You know, Brian, for two Irishmen, we sure married up."

In that visit, in that moment, one saw the quintessential RONALD REAGAN: the leader we respected, the neighbor we admired, and the friend we loved, a President of the United States of America whose truly remarkable life we celebrate in this magnificent cathedral today.

Presidents and prime ministers everywhere, I suspect, sometimes wonder how history will deal with them. Some even evince a touch of the insecurity of Thomas D'Arcy McGee, an Irish immigrant to Canada who became a father of our confederation.

In one of his poems, McGee, thinking of his birthplace, wrote poignantly,

"Am I remembered in Erin?
I charge you speak me true.
Has my name a sound, a meaning
In the scenes my boyhood knew?"

RONALD REAGAN will not have to worry about Erin because they remember him well and affectionately there. Indeed they do.

From Erin to Estonia, from Maryland to Madagascar, from Montreal to Monterey, RONALD REAGAN does not enter history tentatively. He does so with certainty and panache.

At home and on the world stage, his were not the pallid etchings of a timorous politician. They were the bold strokes of a confident and accomplished leader.

Some in the West, during the early eighties, believed communism and democracy were equally valid and viable. This was the school of moral equivalence.

In contrast, RONALD REAGAN saw Soviet communism as a menace to be confronted in the genuine belief that its squalid underpinnings would fall swiftly to the gathering winds of freedom, provided as he said, "that NATO and the industrialized democracies stood firm and united." They did. And we know now who was right.

RONALD REAGAN was a President who inspired his Nation and transformed the world. He possessed a rare and prized gift called leadership, that ineffable and magical quality that sets some men and women apart so that millions will follow them as they conjure up grand visions and invite their countrymen to dream big and exciting dreams.

I always thought that President REAGAN's understanding of the nobility of the Presidency coincided with that American dream.

One day in Brussels, President Mitterand, in referring to President REAGAN, said, "Il a vraiment la notion de l'Etat"; rough translation: "He really has a sense of the state about him." The translation does not fully capture the profundity of the observation.

What President Mitterand meant is that there is a vast difference between the job of President and the role of President.

RONALD REAGAN fulfilled both with elegance and ease, embodying himself that unusual alchemy of history and tradition and achievement and inspirational conduct and national pride that defined the special role the President of the United States of America must assume at all times at home and around the world.

La notion de l'état; no one understood it better than RONALD REAGAN. And no one could more eloquently summon his Nation to high purpose or bring forth the majesty of the Presidency and make it glow better than the man who referred to his own Nation as "a city on the hill."

May our common future and that of our great nations be guided by wise men and women who will remember always the golden achievements of the Reagan era and the success that can be theirs if the values of freedom and democracy are preserved, unsullied and undiminished until the unfolding decades can remember little else.

I have been truly blessed to have been a friend of RONALD REAGAN. I am grateful that our paths crossed and that our lives touched. I shall always remember him with the deepest admiration and affection.

And I will always feel honored by the journey that we traveled together in search of better and more peaceful tomorrows for all God's children everywhere.

And so in the presence of his beloved and indispensable Nancy, his children, his family, his friends and all of the American people that he so deeply revered, I say au revoir today to a gifted leader, a historic President and a gracious human being.

And I do so with a line from Yeats, who wrote, "Think where man's glory most begins and ends, and say, 'My glory was that I had such friends.'"

{Choir singing}

{Mr. Mulroney returns to his seat. Mr. Bush is led to the pulpit for his tribute.}

TRIBUTE

George H.W. Bush, former President of the United States

When Franklin Roosevelt died in 1945, "The *New York Times*" wrote, "Men will thank God 100 years from now that Franklin D. Roosevelt was in the White House." It will not take 100 years to thank God for RONALD REAGAN. But why? Why was he so admired? Why was he so beloved?

He was beloved, first, because of what he was. Politics can be cruel, uncivil. Our friend was strong and gentle. Once he called America "hopeful, big-hearted, idealistic, daring, decent and fair." That was America and, yes, our friend.

And next, RONALD REAGAN was beloved because of what he believed. He believed in America so he made it his "shining city on a hill." He believed in freedom so he acted on behalf of its values and ideals. He believed in tomorrow so the Great Communicator became the Great Liberator. He talked of winning one for the GIPPER and as President, through his relationship with Mikhail Gorbachev with us today, the GIPPER, and yes Mikhail Gorbachev, won one for peace around the world.

If RONALD REAGAN created a better world for many millions it was because of the world someone else created for him.

Nancy was there for him always. Her love for him provided much of his strength, and their love together transformed all of us as we've seen—renewed seeing again here in the last few days.

And one of the many memories we all have of both of them is the comfort they provided during our national tragedies.

Whether it was the families of the crew of the *Challenger* shuttle or the USS *Stark* or the Marines killed in Beirut, we will never forget those images of the President and First Lady embracing them and embracing us during times of sorrow.

So, Nancy, I want to say this to you: Today, America embraces you. We open up our arms. We seek to comfort you, to tell you of our admiration for your courage and your selfless caring.

And to the Reagan kids—it's OK for me to say that at 80—Michael, Ron, Patti, today all of our sympathy, all of our condolences to you all, and remember, too, your sister Maureen home safe now with her father.

As his Vice President for 8 years, I learned more from RONALD REAGAN than from anyone I encountered in all my years of public life. I learned kindness; we all did. I also learned courage; the Nation did.

Who can forget the horrible day in March 1981, he looked at the doctors in the emergency room and said, "I hope you're all Republicans." [*Laughter*]

And then I learned decency; the whole world did. Days after being shot, weak from wounds, he spilled water from a sink, and entering the hospital room aides saw him on his hands and knees wiping water from the floor. He worried that his nurse would get in trouble.

The Good Book says humility goes before honor, and our friend had both, and who could not cherish such a man?

And perhaps as important as anything, I learned a lot about humor, a lot about laughter. And, oh, how President REAGAN loved a good story.

When asked, "How did your visit go with Bishop Tutu?" he replied, "So-so." {Laughter}

It was typical. It was wonderful.

And in leaving the White House, the very last day, he left in the yard outside the Oval Office door a little sign for the squirrels. He loved to feed those squirrels. And he left this sign that said, "Beware of the dog," and to no avail, because our dog Millie came in and beat the heck out of the squirrels.

But anyway, he also left me a note, at the top of which said, "Don't let the turkeys get you down."

Well, he certainly never let them get him down. And he fought hard for his beliefs. He led from conviction, but never made an adversary into an enemy. He was never mean-spirited.

Reverend Billy Graham, who I refer to as the Nation's pastor, is now hospitalized and regrets that he can't be here today. And I asked him for a Bible passage that might be appropriate. And he suggested this from Psalm 37: "The Lord delights in the way of the man whose steps he has made firm. Though he stumble, he will not fall for the Lord upholds him with his hand."

And then this, too, from 37: "There is a future for the man of peace."

God bless you, RONALD WILSON REAGAN and the Nation you loved and led so well.

{Mr. Bush is led back to his seat as President Bush is led to the pulpit.}

TRIBUTE

George W. Bush, President of the United States

Mrs. Reagan, Patti, Michael and Ron, members of the Reagan family, distinguished guests, including our Presidents and First Ladies, Reverend Danforth, fellow citizens, we lost RONALD REAGAN only days ago but we have missed him for a long time. We have missed his kindly presence, that reassuring voice and the happy ending we had wished for him. It has been 10 years since he said his own farewell, yet it is still very sad and hard to let him go. RONALD REAGAN belongs to the ages now, but we preferred it when he belonged to us.

In a life of good fortune, he valued above all the gracious gift of his wife, Nancy. During his career, RONALD REAGAN passed through a thousand crowded places, but there was only one person, he said, who could make him lonely by just leaving the room. America honors you, Nancy, for the loyalty and love you gave this man on a wonderful journey and to that journey's end. Today, our whole Nation grieves with you and your family.

When the Sun sets tonight off the coast of California and we lay to rest our 40th President, a great American story will close.

The second son of Nelle and Jack Reagan first knew the world as a place of open plains, quiet streets, gaslit rooms and carriages drawn by horse.

If you could go back to the Dixon, IL, of 1922, you'd find a boy of 11 reading adventure stories at the public library or running with his brother Neil along Rock River, and coming home to a little house on Hennepin Avenue. That town was the kind of place he remembered where you prayed side by side with your neighbors. And if things were going wrong for them, you prayed for them and knew they'd pray for you if things went wrong for you.

The Reagan family would see its share of hardship, struggle and uncertainty. And out of that circumstance came a young man of steadiness, calm and a cheerful confidence that life would bring good things.

The qualities all of us have seen in RONALD REAGAN were first spotted 70 and 80 years ago. As the lifeguard in Lowell Park, he was the protector, keeping an eye out for trouble. As a sports announcer on the radio, he was the friendly voice that made you see the game as he did. As an actor he was the handsome all-American good guy, which in his case required knowing his lines and being himself.

Along the way certain convictions were formed and fixed in the man. RONALD REAGAN believed that everything happens for a reason and that we should strive to know and do the will of God. He believed that the gentleman always does the kindest thing. He believed that people were basically good and had the right to be free. He believed that bigotry and prejudice were the worst things a person could be guilty of. He believed in the Golden Rule and in the power of prayer. He believed that America was not just a place in the world, but the hope of the world. And he believed in taking a break now and then, because, as he said, "there's nothing better for the inside of a man than the outside of a horse."

RONALD REAGAN spent decades in the film industry and in politics, fields known on occasion to change a man. But not this man. From Dixon to Des Moines to Hollywood to Sacramento to Washington, DC, all who met him remembered the same sincere, honest, upright fellow.

RONALD REAGAN's deepest beliefs never had much to do with fashion or convenience. His convictions were always politely stated, affably argued, and as firm and straight as the columns of this cathedral.

There came a point in RONALD REAGAN's film career when people started seeing a future beyond the movies. The actor Robert Cummings recalled one occasion. "I was sitting around the set with all these people and we were listening to RONNIE, quite absorbed. I said, 'Ron, have you ever considered some day becoming President?' He said, 'President of what?' 'President of the United States,' I said. And he said, 'What's the matter? Don't you like my acting either?'" [Laughter]

The clarity and intensity of RONALD REAGAN's convictions led to speaking engagements around the country, and a new following he did not seek or expect. He often began his speeches by saying, "I'm going to talk about controversial things." And then he spoke of communist rulers as slave masters, of a government in Washington that had far overstepped its proper limits, of a time for choosing that was drawing near.

In the space of a few years he took ideas and principles that were mainly found in journals and books and turned them into a broad, hopeful movement ready to govern.

As soon as RONALD REAGAN became California's Governor, observers saw a star in the west, tanned, well-tailored, in command and on his way. In the sixties his friend Bill Buckley wrote, "REAGAN is indisputably a part of America and he may become a part of American history."

RONALD REAGAN's moment arrived in 1980. He came out ahead of some very good men, including one from Plains and one from Houston. What followed was one of the decisive decades of the century as the convictions that shaped the President began to shape the times.

He came to office with great hopes for America. And more than hopes. Like the President he had revered and once saw in person, Franklin Roosevelt, RONALD REAGAN matched an optimistic temperament with bold, persistent action. President REAGAN was optimistic about the great promise of economic reform, and he acted to restore the rewards and spirit of enterprise. He was optimistic that a strong America could advance the peace, and he acted to build the strength that mission required. He was optimistic that liberty would thrive wherever it was planted, and he acted to defend liberty wherever it was threatened.

And RONALD REAGAN believed in the power of truth in the conduct of world affairs. When he saw evil camped across the horizon he called that evil by its name. There were no doubters in the prisons and gulags, where dissidents spread the news, tapping to each other in code what the American President had dared to say. There were no doubters in the shipyards and churches and secret labor meetings where brave men and women began to hear the creaking and rumbling of a collapsing empire. And there were no doubters among those who swung hammers at the hated wall that the first and hardest blow had been struck by President RONALD REAGAN.

The ideology he opposed throughout his political life insisted that history was moved by impersonal tides and unalterable fates. RONALD REAGAN believed instead in the courage and triumph of free men and we believe it all the more because we saw that courage in him.

As he showed what a President should be, he also showed us what a man should be. RONALD REAGAN carried himself, even in the most powerful office, with the decency and attention to small kindnesses that also define a good life. He was a courtly, gentle and considerate man, never known to slight or embarrass others. Many people across the country cherish letters he wrote in his own hand to family members on important occasions, to old friends dealing with sickness and loss, to strangers with questions about his days in Hollywood.

A boy once wrote to him requesting Federal assistance to help clean up his bedroom. {Laughter} "Unfortunately, funds are dangerously low." {Laughter} He continued, "I'm sure your mother was fully justified in proclaiming your room a disaster ..." {Laughter} "... therefore you are in an excellent position to launch another volunteer program in our Nation." {Laughter} "Congratulations." See, our 40th President wore his title lightly, and it fit like a white Stetson.

In the end, through his belief in our country and his love for our country, he became an enduring symbol of our country. We think of the steady stride, that tilt of the head and snap of the salute, the big screen smile, and the glint in his Irish eyes when a story came to mind. We think of a man advancing in years with the sweetness and sincerity of a scout saying the pledge. We think of that grave expression that sometimes came over his face, the seriousness of a man angered by injustice and frightened by nothing.

We know, as he always said, that America's best days are ahead of us. But with RONALD REAGAN's passing, some very fine days are behind us. And that is worth our tears.

Americans saw death approach RONALD REAGAN twice in a moment of violence and then in the years of departing light. He met both with courage and grace. In these trials, he showed how a man so enchanted by life can be at peace with life's end.

And where does that strength come from? Where is that courage learned? It is the faith of a boy who read the Bible with his mom. It is the faith of a man lying in an operating room who prayed for the one who shot him before he prayed for himself. It is the faith of a man with a fearful illness who waited on the Lord to call him home.

Now death has done all that death can do, and as RONALD WILSON REAGAN goes his way, we are left with the joyful hope he shared. In his last years he saw through a glass darkly. Now he sees his Saviour face to face. And we look for that fine day when we will see him again, all weariness gone, clear of mind, strong and sure and smiling again, and the sorrow of this parting gone forever.

May God bless RONALD REAGAN and the country he loved.

{Mr. Bush is led back to his seat.}

ANTHEM
"Battle Hymn of the Republic"
William Steffe
arr: Peter J. Wilhousky
text by: Julia Ward Howe, 1862
Armed Forces Chorus
U.S. Marine Chamber Orchestra

>Mine eyes have seen the glory
>Of the coming of the Lord;
>He is trampling out the vintage
>Where the grapes of wrath are stored;
>He hath loosed the fateful lightning
>of His terrible swift sword;
>His truth is marching on.
>
>*Glory! Glory! Hallelujah!*
>*Glory! Glory! Hallelujah!*
>*Glory! Glory! Hallelujah!*
>*His truth is marching on.*
>
>I have seen Him in the watchfires
>Of a hundred circling camps
>they have builded Him an altar
>In the evening dews and damps;
>I can read His righteous sentence
>By the dim and flaring lamps;
>His day is marching on.
>
>*Chorus*
>
>In the beauty of the lilies
>Christ was born across the sea,
>With a glory in His bosom
>That transfigures you and me;
>As He died to make men holy,

Let us die to make men free;
While God is marching on.

Chorus

{During the last chorus, the third reader is led to the lectern for the Gospel lesson.}

{The people stand.}

GOSPEL

His Eminence Theodore Cardinal McCarrick

Matthew 5:14–16

A reading from the Holy Gospel according to Matthew.

Jesus said, You are the light of the world. A city built on a hill cannot be hid. No one after lighting a lamp puts it under the bushel basket, but on a lampstand, and it gives light to all in the house. In the same way, let your light shine before others, so that they may see your good works and give glory to your Father in heaven.

Reader: The Gospel of the Lord.

People: Thanks be to God.

{As the reader returns to his stall, the Celebrant goes to the pulpit for the homily.}

HOMILY

The Reverend John C. Danforth

May I speak in the name of one God, who created us, who redeemed us, who comforts us. Amen. This is a service about RONALD REAGAN, and it is a religious service. We've gathered to celebrate the life of a great President in a church where believers profess their faith. So this is not only about a person, but about faith. And the homily is the place to connect the two. For President REAGAN, the text is obvious. It's from the Sermon on the Mount. "You are the light of the world. A city set on a hill cannot be hid." It was his favorite theme, from his first inaugural address to his final address from the Oval Office.

For him, America was the "shining city on a hill." His immediate source was the sermon preached by John Winthrop just read by Justice O'Connor. Winthrop believed that the eyes of the world would be on America because God had given us a special commission, so it was our duty to shine forth. The Winthrop message became the Reagan message. It rang of optimism, and we longed to hear it, especially after the dark years of Vietnam and Watergate. It was a vision with policy implications. America could not hide its light under a bushel. It could not turn in on itself and hunker down. Isolationism was not an option; neither was protectionism. We must champion freedom everywhere. We must be the beacon for the world.

What RONALD REAGAN asked of America, he gave of himself. The great American theologian Reinhold Neibuhr wrote "The Children of Light and the Children of Darkness." If ever we have known a child of light, it was RONALD REAGAN. He was aglow with it. He had no dark side, no scary, hidden agenda. What you saw was what you got. And what you saw was that sure sign of inner light, the twinkle in the eye. He was not consumed by himself. He didn't need to be President to be a complete person. The only thing he really needed was to be with his wife. Mrs. Reagan, you shared him with us, and for that we will always be grateful. He shined the light, but not upon himself.

Personally modest, he disclaimed the title the "Great Communicator," and claimed only to communicate great things from the heart of a great Nation. He liked to laugh, especially at himself. There was nothing petty or mean-spirited about him. Even his opponents liked him. I recall sitting at a table with President REAGAN and Speaker O'Neill listening to their jokes. It was the opposite of negative politics. He inspired devotion more than fear. Mike Deaver wrote, "There was something about him that made you want to please him and do your best. This applied to everybody." It certainly applied to those of us who served in Congress.

His most challenging test came on the day he was shot. He wrote in his diary of struggling for breath and of praying. "I realized that I couldn't ask for God's help while at the same time I felt hatred for the mixed-up young man who shot me," he wrote. "Isn't that the meaning of the lost sheep? We are all God's children and therefore equally loved by him. So I began to pray for his soul and that he would find his way back to the fold." He was a child of light. Now consider the faith we profess in this church. Light shining in darkness is an ancient biblical theme. Genesis tells us that in the beginning darkness was upon the face of the deep. Some equate this darkness with chaos. And God said, "Let there be light," and there was light. And God saw that the light was good. Creating light in darkness is God's work. You and I know the meaning of darkness. We see it on the evening news: terror, chaos, war. An enduring image of 9 11 is that on a brilliantly clear day a cloud of darkness covered Lower Manhattan. Darkness is real and it can be terrifying. Sometimes it seems to be everywhere.

So the question for us is what do we do when darkness surrounds us? St. Paul answered that question. He said we must walk as children of light. President REAGAN taught us that this is our mission, both as individuals and as a Nation. The faith proclaimed in this church is that when we walk as children of light, darkness cannot prevail. As St. John's gospel tells us, "The light shines in the darkness and the darkness did not overcome it." That's true even of death. For people of faith, death is no less awful than for anyone else, but the resurrection means that death is not the end. The Bible describes the most terrible moment in these words: "When it was noon, darkness came over the whole land until 3 in the afternoon." That was the darkness of Good Friday. It did not prevail. Very early on the first day of the week when the Sun had risen, that's the beginning of the Easter story. The light shines; the Lord is risen.

In this service of worship, we celebrate the life of a great President and we profess the resurrection faith of this church. It is faith in God's victory over darkness. It is faith in the ultimate triumph of light. We believe in this victory every day of our lives. We believe it as individuals. We believe it as a Nation. There is no better time to celebrate the triumph of life than in a service for RONALD REAGAN. Amen.

{As the homilist returns to his stall, the orchestra and soloist begin the anthem.}

ANTHEM
"Amazing Grace"
Tune: New Britain
text by: John Newton; st. 5 John Rees
Sung by Ronan Tynan

> Amazing grace! how sweet the sound,
> that saved a wretch like me!
> I once was lost but now am found,
> was blind but now I see.
>
> 'Twas grace that taught my heart to fear,
> and grace my fears relieved;
> how precious did that grace appear
> the hour I first believed!
>
> The Lord has promised good to me,
> his word my hope secures;
> he will my shield and portion be
> as long as life endures.
>
> Through many dangers, toils, and snares,
> I have already come;
> 'tis grace that brought me safe thus far,
> and grace will lead me home.
>
> When we've been there ten thousand years,
> bright shining as the sun,
> we've no less days to sing God's praise
> than when we'd first begun.

⸨During the last verse, the Vicar is led to the bottom of the lectern steps.⸩
⸨The people stand for the remainder of the service, as they are able.⸩
⸨From his stall, the Celebrant leads the Lord's Prayer, said by all.⸩

THE LORD'S PRAYER
The Reverend John C. Danforth

Let us stand and say together the Lord's Prayer.

Our Father, who art in heaven, hallowed be thy name. Thy kingdom come, thy will be done, on earth as it is in heaven. Give us this day our daily bread and forgive us our debts as we forgive our debtors. And lead us not into temptation, but deliver us from evil. For thine is the kingdom, and the power, and the glory, for ever and ever. *Amen.*

⸨The Vicar steps up to the lectern reading desk to lead the prayers.⸩

PRAYERS OF THE PEOPLE
The Right Reverend A. Theodore Eastman

In peace, let us pray to the Lord.

Almighty God, who hast knit together thine elect in one communion and fellowship, in the mystical body of the Son Christ our Lord; Grant, we beseech thee, to thy whole Church in paradise and on earth, thy light and thy peace. *Amen.*

Grant that all who have been baptized into Christ's death and resurrection may die to sin and rise to newness of life, and that through the grave and gate of death we may pass with him to our joyful resurrection. *Amen.*

Grant to us who are still in our pilgrimage, and who walk as yet by faith, that thy Holy Spirit may lead us in holiness and righteousness all our days. *Amen.*

Grant to thy faithful people pardon and peace, that we may be cleansed from all our sins, and serve thee with a quiet mind. *Amen.*

Grant to all who mourn a sure confidence in thy fatherly care, that, casting all their grief on thee, they may know the consolation of thy love. *Amen.*

Grant us, with all who have died in the hope of the resurrection, to have our consummation and bliss in thy eternal and everlasting glory, and, with blessed Peter and Paul and all thy saints, to receive the crown of life which thou dost promise to all who share in the victory of thy Son Jesus Christ; who liveth and reigneth with thee and the Holy Spirit, one God, for ever and ever. *Amen.*

⸨As the Vicar is led back to his stall, the organ begins the hymn introduction.⸩
⸨During this hymn, those who are required for the departing ceremonies outside are unobtrusively escorted from the Cathedral.⸩

HYMN

"Sing with All the Saints in Glory"
Tune: Ode to Joy
text by: William Josiah Irons, 1873
{Sung by all.}

>Sing with all the saints in glory, sing the resurrection song!
>Death and sorrow, earth's dark story, to the former days belong.
>All around the clouds are breaking, Soon the storms of time will cease;
>In God's likeness, we awaken, Knowing everlasting peace.
>
>O what glory, far exceeding. All that eye has yet perceived!
>Holiest hearts for ages pleading, Never that full joy conceived.
>God has promised, Christ prepares it, There on high our welcome waits;
>Ev'ry humble spirit shares it, Christ has passed th' eternal gates.

{During the last verse, vergers lead the Bishop of Washington, the Vicar, and the Celebrant to the foot of the casket, the Celebrant at the foot, the Vicar to his left, and the Bishop to his right, where they face the congregation.}

{The Celebrant then says the commendation responsively with the people.}

THE COMMENDATION

The Reverend John C. Danforth

>Give rest, O Christ, to thy servant with thy saints,
>
>*All:*
>
>>where sorrow and pain are no more,
>>neither sighing, but life everlasting.
>
>Thou only art immortal, the creator and maker of mankind; and we are mortal, formed of the earth, and unto earth shall we return. For so thou didst ordain when thou createdst me, saying, "Dust thou art, and unto dust thou shalt return." All we go down to the dust; yet even at the grave we make our song; Alleluia, alleluia, alleluia.
>
>*All:*
>
>>Give rest, O Christ, to thy servant with thy saints,
>>where sorrow and pain are no more,
>>neither sighing, but life everlasting.

{The Celebrant faces the body.}

>Into thy hands, O merciful Saviour, we commend thy servant RONALD. Acknowledge, we humbly beseech thee, a sheep of thine own fold, a lamb of thine own flock, a sinner of thine own redeeming. Receive him into the arms of thy mercy, into the blessed rest of everlasting peace, and into the glorious company of the saints in light. *Amen.*

THE BLESSING
The Right Reverend John Bryson Chane

      The God of peace, who brought again from the dead our Lord Jesus Christ, the great Shepherd of the sheep, through the blood of the everlasting covenant, makes you perfect in every good work to do his will, working in you that which is well-pleasing in his sight; and on this day may the blessing of God Almighty, the Father, the Son, and the Holy Spirit, be with you, and remain with you forever. *Amen.*

THE DISMISSAL
The Right Reverend A. Theodore Eastman

    Vicar: Let us go forth in the name of Christ.
    People: Thanks be to God.

{As the introduction to the anthem begins, the three clerics are escorted back to their stalls.}

{During the last verse, the acolytes take their positions at the rood screen, and vergers take positions by their charges.}

ANTHEM
"The Mansions of the Lord"
Nick Glennie-Smith
text by: Randall Wallace
Sung by the Armed Forces Chorus with the U.S. Marine Chamber Orchestra

    To fallen soldiers let us sing
    Where no rockets fly nor bullets wing
    Our broken brothers let us bring
    To the Mansions of the Lord.

{The pallbearers come from the north transept, rotate the casket, and prepare to take it out.}

    No more bleeding, no more fight
    No prayers pleading through the night
    Just divine embrace, eternal light
    In the Mansions of the Lord.

    Where no mothers cry and no children weep
    We will stand and guard though the angels sleep
    through the ages safely keep
    The Mansions of the Lord.

{Procession of clergy leaving cathedral. The casket is taken out of the cathedral. Mourners follow casket.}
{"Ruffles." "Hail to the Chief." "God Bless America."}
{The hearse drives to Andrews Air Force Base.}
{Solo bagpipe performance of "Amazing Grace."}
{Bells toll around the country.}

{The casket is taken out of the hearse, and escorted aboard the Presidential aircraft.}
{21-gun salute.}
{Air Force band plays the spiritual "Going Home."}
{Applause as the plane takes off.}

IN HONOR OF

Ronald Wilson Reagan
FORTIETH PRESIDENT OF THE UNITED STATES

FEBRUARY 6, 1911 TO JUNE 5, 2004

★ ★ ★

RONALD REAGAN PRESIDENTIAL LIBRARY
SIMI VALLEY, CALIFORNIA

Ronald Reagan

Interment Services

FRIDAY, JUNE 11, 2004
AT SIX O'CLOCK

*W*HATEVER ELSE HISTORY MAY SAY ABOUT ME WHEN I'M GONE, I HOPE IT WILL RECORD THAT I APPEALED TO YOUR BEST HOPES, NOT YOUR WORST FEARS; TO YOUR CONFIDENCE RATHER THAN YOUR DOUBTS. MY DREAM IS THAT YOU WILL TRAVEL THE ROAD AHEAD WITH LIBERTY'S LAMP GUIDING YOUR STEPS AND OPPORTUNITY'S ARM STEADYING YOUR WAY.

—RONALD REAGAN
AUGUST 1992

I KNOW IN MY HEART THAT MAN IS GOOD, THAT WHAT IS RIGHT WILL ALWAYS EVENTUALLY TRIUMPH, AND THERE IS PURPOSE AND WORTH TO EACH AND EVERY LIFE.

—RONALD REAGAN
NOVEMBER 4, 1991

Order of Services

Instrumental Prelude	U.S. Air Force Band of the Golden West
Musical Honors	U.S. Air Force Band of the Golden West
"Amazing Grace"	Solo Bagpiper, Eric Rigler
Invocation	The Reverend Doctor Michael H. Wenning
"Battle Hymn of the Republic"	U.S. Army Chorus
	U.S. Air Force Band of the Golden West
Words of Remembrance	Michael Reagan
	Patti Davis
	Ronald Prescott Reagan
Scripture: Psalm 23	The Reverend John C. Danforth
Musical Honors	U.S. Air Force Band of the Golden West
"My Country 'Tis of Thee"	U.S. Air Force Band of the Golden West

Guests should stand and remain at their seats.

Brief Witness on Life, Death, and Everlasting Life	The Reverend Doctor Michael H. Wenning
21-Gun Salute	11th Marine Artillery Regiment
Benediction	The Reverend Doctor Michael H. Wenning
Three Volleys of Musketry	U.S. Army Firing Party
"Taps"	U.S. Army Band Bugler
Flyover	U.S. Navy
"America the Beautiful"	U.S. Air Force Band of the Golden West
Flag Presentation	Capt. James A. Symonds, Commander
	USS *Ronald Reagan* (CVN–76)
"God Bless America"	Congregation and U.S. Army Chorus
	U.S. Air Force Band of the Golden West

Guests are invited to file by the casket to pay final respects and attend a reception in Albritton Hall.

•{The Presidential jet flies over the Presidential library in Simi Valley on its way to Point Mugu Naval Air Station.}•
•{The funeral party arrives at Point Mugu Air Station Airport.}•
•{"Hail to the Chief." 21-cannon salute. Marine band plays "God Bless America."}•
•{Honor guards carry the casket to the hearse.}•
•{The motorcade leaves the naval air station at Point Mugu, to travel to the Ronald Reagan Presidential Library.}•
•{The casket is removed from the hearse and transported through the courtyard of the library, through the library itself, and out into the backyard for the ceremony.}•
•{Instrumental Prelude, U.S. Air Force Band of the Golden West, "Hail to the Chief."}•
•{Musical Honors, U.S. Air Force Band of the Golden West.}•
•{"Amazing Grace," solo bagpiper, Eric Rigler.}•

REV. MICHAEL H. WENNING: Please pray with me. Eternal and Almighty God, we began this day and it seemed the heavens were weeping as we paid our farewell to your servant RONALD REAGAN. We eulogized him. We worshipped under the arches of that stately cathedral. We have come from sea to shining sea to this soil, which he loved so much, and where his body will remain. Gracious Lord God, turn our tears of sorrow into the hope of the resurrection. Comfort our hearts and especially the Reagan family and the Nation for we celebrate his life and we do it through Jesus Christ our Lord. Amen.

•{"Battle Hymn of the Republic," U.S. Army Chorus, U.S. Air Force Band of the Golden West.}•

MICHAEL REAGAN, RONALD REAGAN'S SON: Good evening. I'm Mike Reagan. You knew my father as Governor, as President. But I knew him as Dad. I want to tell you a little bit about my dad. A little bit about Cameron and Ashley's grandfather because not a whole lot is ever spoken about that side of RONALD REAGAN. RONALD REAGAN adopted me into his family 1945. I was the chosen one. I was the lucky one. In all of his years, he never mentioned that I was adopted either behind my back or in front of me. I was his son, Michael Edward Reagan. When his families grew to be two families, he didn't walk away from the one to go to the other. But he became a father to both. To Patti and then Ronnie, but always to Maureen, my sister, and myself. We looked forward to those Saturday mornings when he would pick us up, sitting on the curve on Beverly Glenn as his car would turn the corner from Sunset Boulevard and we would get in and ride to his ranch and play games and he would always make sure it ended up a tie. We would swim and we would ride horses or we'd just watch him cut firewood. We would be in awe of our father. As years went by and I became older and found a woman I would marry, Colleen, he sent me a letter about marriage and how important it was to be faithful to the woman you love with a P.S.—"you'll never get in trouble if you say I love you at least once a day," and I'm sure he told Nancy every day "I love you" as I tell Colleen. He also sent letters to his grandchildren. He wasn't able to be the grandfather that many of you are able to be because of the job he had. And so, he would write letters. He sent one letter to Cameron, said, "Cameron, some guy got $10,000 for my signature. Maybe this letter will help you pay for your college education." He signed it, "Grandpa. P.S., your grandpa's the 40th President of the United States, RONALD REAGAN." He just signed his sign. Those are the kinds of things my father did. At the early onset of Alzheimer's disease my father and I would tell each other we loved each other and we would give each other a hug. As the years went by and he could no longer verbalize my name, he recognized me as the man who hugged him. So when I would walk into the house, he would be there in his chair opening up his arms for that hug, hello, and the hug goodbye. It was a blessing truly brought on by God. We had wonderful blessings of that nature. Wonderful, wonderful blessings that my father gave to me each and every day of my life.

I was so proud to have the Reagan name and to be RONALD REAGAN's son. What a great honor. He gave me a lot of gifts as a child. Gave me a horse. Gave me a car. Gave me a lot of things. But there's a gift he gave me that I think is wonderful for every father to give every son. Last Saturday, when my father opened his eyes for the last time, and visualized Nancy and gave her such a wonderful, wonderful gift. When he closed his eyes, that's when I realized the gift that he gave to me, the gift that he was going to be with his Lord and Saviour, Jesus Christ. He had, back in 1988 on a flight from Washington, DC, to Point Mugu, told me about his love of God, his love of Christ as his Saviour. I didn't know then what it all meant. But I certainly, certainly know now. I can't think of a better gift for a father to give a son. And I hope to honor my father by giving my son Cameron and my daughter Ashley that very same gift he gave to me. Knowing where he is this very moment, this very day, that he is in Heaven, and I can only promise my father this. Dad, when I go, I will go to Heaven, too. And you and I and my sister Maureen that went before us, we will dance with the heavenly host of angels before the presence of God. We will do it melanoma and Alzheimer's free. Thank you for letting me share my father, RONALD WILSON REAGAN.

PATTI DAVIS, RONALD REAGAN'S DAUGHTER: Many years ago, my father decided to write down his reflections about death, specifically his own, and how he would want people to feel about it. He chose to write down the first verse of an Alfred Lord Tennyson poem "Crossing The Bar" and then he decided to add a couple of lines of his own. I don't think Tennyson will mind. In fact, they've probably already discussed it by now. Tennyson wrote, "sunset and evening star and one clear call for me. And may there be no moaning of the bar when I put out to sea." My father added, "we have God's promise that I have gone on to a better world where there is no pain or sorrow. Bring comfort to those who may mourn my going." My father never feared death, he never saw it as an ending. When I was a child, he took me out into a field at our ranch after one of the Malibu fires had swept through. I was very small on the field, looked huge and lifeless, but he bent down and showed me how tiny new green shoots were peeking up out of the ashes just weeks after the fire had come through. "You see," he said, "new life always comes out of death. It looks like nothing could ever grow in this field again, but things do." He was the one who generously offered funeral services for my goldfish on the morning of its demise. We went out into the garden and we dug a tiny grave with a teaspoon and he took two twigs and lashed them together with twine and formed a cross as a marker for the grave. And then he gave a beautiful eulogy. He told me that my fish was swimming in the clear blue waters in Heaven and he would never tire and he would never get hungry and he would never be in any danger and he could swim as far and wide as he wanted and he never had to stop, because the river went on forever. He was free. When we went back inside and I looked at my remaining goldfish in their aquarium with their pink plastic castle and their colored rocks, I suggested that perhaps we should kill the others so they could also go to that clear blue river and be free. He then took more time out of his morning, I'm sure he actually did have other things to do that day, and patiently explained to me that in God's time, the other fish would go there, as well. In God's time, we would all be taken home. And even though it sometimes seemed a mystery, we were just asked to trust that God's time was right and wise.

I don't know why Alzheimer's was allowed to steal so much of my father before releasing him into the arms of death, but I know that at his last moment, when he opened his eyes, eyes that had not opened for many, many days and looked at my mother, he showed us that neither disease nor death can conquer love. He may have in his lifetime come across a small book called "Peace of Mind" by Joshua Loth Liebman. If he did, I think he would have been struck by these lines, "then for each one of us, the moment comes when the great nurse, death, takes man, the child, by the hand and quietly says, it's time to go home, night is coming. It is your bedtime child of Earth."

RON REAGAN JR., RONALD REAGAN'S SON: He is home now. He is free. In his final letter to the American people, Dad wrote, "I now begin the journey that will lead me into the sunset of my life." This evening, he has arrived. History will record his worth as a leader. We here have long since measured his worth as a man. Honest, compassionate, graceful, brave. He was the most plainly decent man you could ever hope to meet. He used to say, a gentleman always does the kind thing. And he was a gentleman in the truest sense of the word. A gentle man. Big as he was, he never tried to make anyone feel small. Powerful as he became, he never took advantage of those who were weaker. Strength, he believed, was never more admirable than when it was applied with restraint. Shopkeeper, doorman, king or queen, it made no difference, Dad treated everyone with the same unfailing courtesy, acknowledging the innate dignity in us all. The idea that all people are created equal was more than mere words on a page, it was how he lived his life. And he lived a good, long life. The kind of life good men lead. But I guess I'm just telling you things you already know.

Here's something you may not know, a little RONALD REAGAN trivia for you, his entire life, Dad had an inordinate fondness for earlobes. Even as a boy, back in Dixon, IL, hanging out on a street corner with his friends, they knew that if they were standing next to DUTCH, sooner or later, he was going to reach over and grab ahold of their lobe, give it a workout there. Sitting on his lap watching television as a kid, same story, he would have a hold of my earlobe. I'm surprised I have any lobes left after all of that. And you didn't have to be a kid to enjoy that sort of treatment. Serving in the Screen Actors Guild with his great friend William Holden, the actor, best man at his wedding, Bill got used to it. They would be there at the meetings, and Dad would have a hold of his earlobe. There they'd be, some tense labor negotiation, two big Hollywood movie stars, hand in earlobe.

He was, as you know, a famously optimistic man. Sometimes such optimism leads you to see the world as you wish it were as opposed to how it really is. At a certain point in his Presidency, Dad decided he was going to revive the thumbs up gesture. So he went all over the country, of course, giving everybody the thumbs up. Dory and I found ourselves in the Presidential limousine one day returning from some big event. My mother was there and Dad was of course, thumbs upping the crowd along the way, and suddenly, looming in the window on his side of the car was this snarling face. This fellow was reviving an entirely different hand gesture. And hoisted an entirely different digit in our direction. Dad saw this and without missing a beat turned to us and said, you see? I think it's catching on.

Dad was also a deeply, unabashedly religious man. But he never made the fatal mistake of so many politicians wearing his faith on his sleeve to gain political advantage. True, after he was shot and nearly killed early in his Presidency, he came to believe that God had spared him in order that he might do good. But he accepted that as a responsibility, not a mandate. And there is a profound difference. Humble as he was, he never would have assumed a free pass to Heaven. But in his heart of hearts, I suspect he felt he would be welcome there. And so he is home. He is free. Those of us who knew him well will have no trouble imagining his paradise. Golden fields will spread beneath a blue dome of a western sky. Live oaks will shadow the rolling hillsides. And someplace, flowing from years long past, a river will wind toward the sea. Across those fields, he will ride a gray mare he calls Nancy D. They will sail over jumps he has built with his own hands. He will at the river carry him over the shining stones. He will rest in the shade of the trees. Our cares are no longer his. We meet him now only in memory. But we will join him soon enough. All of us. When we are home, when we are free. {Applause}

{Scripture: Psalm 23, The Reverend John C. Danforth.}

{Musical Honors, U.S. Air Force Band of the Golden West. "Star Spangled Banner." "Amazing Grace."}

{Procession.}

{Casket is moved. Flag is lifted.}

{U.S. Air Force Band of the Golden West.}

REV. MICHAEL H. WENNING: Mrs. Reagan, members of the Reagan family, distinguished and honored guests, it is a wonderful, awesome responsibility for me to be able to give these final parting words on this long journey of this week of sadness. I want to thank you for the privilege of being your pastor and chaplain to the President. Little did I think that four and a half decades ago, when Frieda and I came to this country to study in college, that one day I would end up as the chaplain to the President of the United States—only in America. Dear Nancy, thank you for bearing your grief so nobly. Thank you for the dignity that you have shown this week. Our hearts have gone out to you. So many people have commented on the picture where you and I are together as we began this week. And I think the reason for its poignancy was that the whole American Nation was putting its arms around you. And so we love you and care for you. Thank you for caring for the President in his declining years. Thank you for the wonderful example of your marriage that you modeled throughout your life together and especially in the White House years. Yours was truly a glorious friendship, based on mutual love and respect. And we love you for it. And thank you for it. To you, Michael, and Patti, and Ron, thank you for those very, very touching and moving words, a little humor, but the heartfelt love of children who loved their father and respect him so much. We gathered at the beginning of this long day in the National

Cathedral and heard so many wonderful words from the Nations' leaders and also from a beloved friend. I have never heard Lady Margaret Thatcher speak more eloquently in all her life. The last time I heard her speak, I had the privilege of being present as she was awarded the Ronald Reagan Freedom Award. And I remember her saying particularly, "when RONNIE spoke about the Soviet Union as the evil empire, even I blanched." Thank God that neither she, nor your husband, shirked in the face of communism, but saw its demise. He touched us all. When I went back to the land where I was born in South Africa, I went to see my aging father. And, as I sat in his study, he pointed to a huge picture behind me framed. It was of your husband. And he said, "This is my President"; 10,000 miles away, he identified, as we all do and shall do through time to come. It now remains for me to talk about the man and his faith. Indeed, he was a gift from God to us all. He made us feel good and confident about ourselves, about our country, and about our future. And I believe it's because he gained his confidence from the psalm which I read at the beginning of this week, Psalm 46. The psalm says, "God is our refuge and strength, a very present help in the time of trouble." When you attended church, so many people noticed that he could sing the hymns without looking at the hymnal. He loved hymns. And it was appropriate that it was sung in the cathedral this morning and played on the bagpipes this evening. That hymn speaks about God's amazing grace. And RONALD REAGAN knew of the grace of his Lord, Jesus Christ, for he lived with and on and in that grace. I think of that one particular stanza of that hymn which says, through many dangers, toils and snares, I have already come. 'Tis grace hath brought me safe thus far and grace will lead me home. Grace has led him home this day. He was a man who exhibited graciousness with all that he met, from the highest in the land to the lowliest.

On one occasion, when Alzheimer's was beginning to rob that beautiful mind and he no longer came to Bel Air Presbyterian Church, you know that I came to the office regularly and brought the church to him and then to your home. And, on one occasion, his secretary said, Mr. President, your pastor is here. Come and sit in the corner of his office. And he said, "No, I think I'll just sit here at the desk." I looked at her. She looked at me. We knew he wasn't going to budge. So I sidled up and sat on the edge of the desk. And I said, "Mr. President, you're still boss. I'll sit where you are." And so I read scripture and prayed. Shortly afterward, his secretary ushered in my wife and he stood up immediately and went over to her and shook her hand. You see, the gentleness, the kindness, the love, the gifts, the fruit of the holy spirit was deeply embedded in his DNA.

As Ron has already said, in 1994, he wrote that letter saying, "I now begin my journey into the sunset of my life." But I believe that, last Saturday, he began a new journey into the glorious presence of Almighty God, and he is basking in the sunshine of his love. And I believe he's touching the face of God, as he said during the *Challenger* disaster. And the Lord is saying to him, "Well done, my good and faithful servant." Let me close with just one thought. In the ancient nation of Israel, when the Temple had been built, the Lord appeared to King Solomon and said to him these words: "If my people who are called by my name humble themselves and turn from their wicked ways and pray and seek my face, I will hear from Heaven and forgive their sin and heal their land." God was reminding his ancient people that the glory of the Nation was not in power or prestige, in wealth or in might. RONALD REAGAN knew that as a cardinal truth, that ultimately, our strength is not in our might, but it is as we depend upon Almighty God and trust in him and walk humbly before God. RONALD REAGAN lived and believed that. And thank God that he did. Mr. President, I salute you.

NANCY REAGAN, FORMER FIRST LADY: Thank you.

{21-gun Salute, 11th Marine Artillery Regiment.}

REV. MICHAEL H. WENNING: Please pray with me. Now, Eternal God, we commend into your hands the spirit of your servant, RONALD WILSON REAGAN. We commend him into your care and keeping. And as we do so, we commit ourselves afresh into your love and care. Teach us to so live that we shall never, ever be afraid of death, nor ever ashamed to see you face to face, but grant that your love and peace may rest with us now and always. The Lord bless you and keep you. The Lord make his face to shine upon you and be gracious unto you, the Lord lift up the light of his countenance upon you and grant you his peace now and forever more, in the name of the father and of the son and of the holy spirit. Amen.

{Three volleys of musketry, U.S. Army Firing Party.}

{"Taps," U.S. Army Band bugler.}

{Flyover, U.S. Navy, missing man formation.}

{"America the Beautiful," U.S. Air Force Band of the Golden West.}

{Flag Presentation, Capt. James A. Symonds, Commander, USS *Ronald Reagan* (CVN–76).}

{"God Bless America," Congregation and U.S. Army Chorus, U.S. Air Force Band of the Golden West.}

Memorial Tributes

IN THE

House of Representatives
of the United States

IN EULOGY OF

Ronald Reagan

In the House of Representatives of the United States

Tuesday, June 8, 2004

Hon. David Dreier

OF CALIFORNIA

Mr. Speaker, not 24 hours after RONALD REAGAN had passed away, I had the opportunity to talk to a great American, Ronald Reagan's Secretary of State, George P. Shultz. He already by Sunday afternoon had penned a statement, which was so moving that I asked him if I could share it with my colleagues. Secretary Shultz agreed, so I would like to do that at this point, Mr. Speaker.

He entitles this "Remembering RONALD REAGAN." It reads as follows:

REMEMBERING RONALD REAGAN

(By George P. Shultz)

We have lost RONALD REAGAN, but his ideas remain with us, as vital as ever. We can remember the gifts he gave us, his advocacy of freedom, his contributions to our security, his belief in America and his restoration of our belief in ourselves.

When he took office as Governor of California, RONALD REAGAN took responsibility for a State that was in rocky shape; when he left office, California was golden again. When RONALD REAGAN took office as the President of the United States, the country was adrift, inflation was out of control, the economy was in the doldrums, and the cold war was as cold as it had ever been. When he left office, inflation was under control, the economy was expanding, the cold war was all over but the shouting, and America once again stood tall.

RONALD REAGAN brought so much to this country. He started with carefully thought out ideas and he put them to work effectively. He had a strong and constructive agenda, much of it labeled impossible and unattainable in the early years of his Presidency. He challenged the conventional wisdom: On arms control, on the possibility of movement toward freedom in the communist-dominated world, on the need to stand up to Iran in the Persian Gulf, on the superiority of market- and enterprise-based economies. The world learned when RONALD REAGAN faced down the air traffic controllers in 1981 that he could dig in and fight to win. The world learned in Grenada that he would use military force if needed. He did not accept that extensive political opposition doomed an attractive idea. He would fight resolutely for an idea, believing that, if it was valid, he could persuade the American people to support it. He changed the national and international agenda on issue after issue. He was an optimist; he spoke the vocabulary of opportunity. He had a vision of what he stood for and what we aspire to as a nation.

RONALD REAGAN had and could express a clear and simple view of a complex world. Every Sunday, he brought acorns down from Camp David to feed the squirrels outside the Oval Office. The squirrels at the White House hadn't had it so good since Ike cleared the area to put in a putting green. His most endearing aspect was his fundamental decency. He appealed to people's best hopes, not their fears; to their confidence, rather than their doubts.

RONALD REAGAN was a doer, a pragmatist, a man who enjoyed hard physical tasks, as in the ranch work he loved to do. But that brush clearing and fence fixing was a symbol, too; he wanted to be doing it himself because from the land came not only strength and clarity, but a vision, the vision of the West and the endless horizon. The American people liked RONALD REAGAN and reelected him in one of the biggest landslides in history because he trusted them and he conveyed to them that they need not be bound, tied down by class or race, or childhood misfortune, or poverty, or bureaucracy. They, the people, could make something of themselves; indeed, they could remake themselves endlessly.

But beneath this pragmatic attitude lay a bedrock of principle and purpose with which I was proud to be associated. He believed in being strong enough to defend our interests, but he viewed that strength as a means, not an end in itself. RONALD REAGAN had confidence in himself and in his ideas and was ready to negotiate from the strength so evident by the mideighties.

He was a fervent anticommunist who could comprehend and believe that people everywhere would choose to throw off the communist system if they ever had the chance. And he worked hard to give them that chance. He favored open trade because he had confidence in the ability of Americans to compete, and he had confidence that an integrated world economy would benefit America. He stuck to his agenda.

The points he made, however consummate the delivery, were unmistakably real in his mind and heart, an American creed: Defend your country, value your family, make something of yourself, tell government to get off your back, tell the tyrants to watch their step. RONALD REAGAN conveyed simple truths that were especially welcome because "nowadays everything seems so complicated." What he said ran deep and wide among the people.

REAGAN as President was a Republican, a conservative, a man of the right. But these labels will mislead historians who do not see beyond them, for Americans could see some of RONALD REAGAN in themselves. You couldn't figure him out like a fact, because to REAGAN, the main fact was a vision. He came from the heartland of the country, where people could be down-to-earth, yet feel the sky is the limit, not ashamed of or cynical about the American dream.

Not far from RONALD REAGAN's small town of Dixon, IL, is Jane Addams' small town of Cedarville; not far from Cedarville is Ulysses Grant's small town of Galena. And not far from Galena is Carl Sandburg's Galesburg. REAGAN had something of them all: His heart going out to the people; his will ready to fight for the country; his voice able to move the Nation. And, as Carl Sandburg wrote it, "The republic is a dream. Nothing happens unless first a dream."

Hon. Jim Ryun
OF KANSAS

Mr. Speaker, there are few leaders who we can look to who truly embody the characteristics of what a leader should be. RONALD REAGAN embodied them all.

He was a man of principle; he was a man of action. Unlike many who just talk about their convictions, he was a man who acted upon them. As a man of deep faith, he brought conviction to the Presidency, knowing what he believed and why he believed it. Yes, he was "Mr. President;" and indeed a role model, a man of conviction and courage.

He once said:

> A leader, once convinced a particular course of action is the right one, must have the determination to stick with it and be undaunted when the going gets rough.

It was this conviction and courage that enabled him to lead the world out of the cold war into an age when communism no longer thrived. As he put it, "We did not seek the role of leadership that has been thrust upon us. But whether we like it or not, the events of our time demand America's participation."

My wife Anne and I had the privilege of meeting President REAGAN at the White House for a St. Patrick's Day event in 1982. As we chatted for a few minutes, I remember being in the presence of someone great. I told him that we were praying for him. He shook my hand, and in a genuine, soft-spoken voice, he thanked us.

His convictions guided him on social issues as well. In 1983, on the 10th anniversary of *Roe* v. *Wade*, he wrote a 9 page article to the American people laying out his opposition to the abominable practice of abortion. In it he wrote:

> {W}e cannot survive as a free nation when some men decide that others are not fit to live and should be abandoned to abortion or infanticide. My Administration is dedicated to the preservation of America as a free land, and there is no cause more important for preserving that freedom than affirming the transcendent right to life of all human beings, the right without which no other rights have any meaning.

Our Founders believed in the idea of America. It was an idea of freedom and justice for all. REAGAN believed in America, and, more significantly, he believed in the American people. Rather than simply imposing his principles upon others, he redefined the mainstream by giving them something to believe in. It was this quality of principled, caring leadership that inspired many, including me, to act upon our convictions, believing that the American way was just and right.

As we mourn the passing of our 40th President, we must not allow his legacy to die with him. His legacy is a continued belief in the idea of America. To carry it on, we must not only look to what has been, but we must look forward to what will be. Because of the work of RONALD REAGAN, the idea has prevailed. It is up to us to ensure that we continue his optimism for the future. President REAGAN left us a legacy to uphold.

PRAYER

The Reverend John Boyles, National Capital Presbytery, Washington, DC, offered the following prayer:

O Lord God, we come before You on this day to ask that You would be with all here today as servants of Your will, and that of this Nation's people, in giving honor for service to country, this land of the free. And strengthen all here today in the work of this body, to establish steadfast and righteous rules of law to guide and direct the way of this Nation.

O Lord God, that here would be frontiers of freedom just as there were in foreign fields on beachheads of liberation which are remembered and honored in these days.

O Lord God, before You, and gathered here, we are met to lift up to You and remember those who have given of themselves in highest service to this Nation. O Lord, You have been our dwelling place in all generations and now this House, this Chamber would prepare to receive under its dome, a hallowed place of honor for one who served as highest leader of this Nation. Prepare here now, O Lord, those assembled to give honor for service and dedication to America of RONALD REAGAN, that in honoring his service, that the service to Nation given by those here in this House might be rededicated and strengthened; that in honoring the grace and goodness of a man who served his Nation's people, that all here would be renewed in their dedication to the good of all, and the building up of all, and even then knowing, before You, O God, that if this earthly house of a tabernacle were desolved that there is a building of God, a house not made with hands, eternal in the heavens. May you, O God, bless the work of our hands here today. Amen.

MESSAGE FROM THE SENATE

A message from the Senate by Mr. Monahan, one of its clerks, announced that the Senate has passed a concurrent resolution of the following title in which the concurrence of the House is requested:

S. Con. Res. 115. Concurrent resolution authorizing the use of the rotunda of the Capitol for the lying in state of the remains of the late RONALD WILSON REAGAN, 40th President of the United States.

Hon. Frank R. Wolf

OF VIRGINIA

Mr. Speaker, I join with others in the House in expressing the deepest condolences to Nancy Reagan and the Reagan family on the passing of RONALD WILSON REAGAN, the 40th President of the United States of America, and in paying tribute to President REAGAN as we remember his Presidency and what he meant to our country and, indeed, to the world.

I deeply admired and respected President REAGAN. I had the good fortune to run for the 10th Congressional District of Virginia seat in Congress in November 1980 when he was elected to his first term. Some called my victory then "on REAGAN's coattails." I have no doubt that I am in Congress today because of President REAGAN.

I will always be grateful that after my two successful bids for Congress RONALD REAGAN led the ticket I was on and I became a member of the class of 1980. I am sure all members of the class of 1980 would agree, President REAGAN made us feel good again. He gave us hope. He inspired us. He gave us optimism because he was an optimist. His legacy belongs not only to America but to the world.

I saw a woman in California being interviewed. She was holding a bouquet of flowers and tears were streaming down her face. She had a broken English accent and identified herself as a Russian immigrant. She said she had to come to the makeshift memorial outside the funeral home where President REAGAN was resting because, "I owe my life to President REAGAN."

Mr. Speaker, I will close by sharing his own words spoken in August 1992 about how he wanted to be remembered. President REAGAN said:

{W}hatever else history may say about me when I'm gone, I hope it will record that I appealed to your best hopes, not your worst fears, to your confidence rather than your doubts....

May all of you as Americans never forget your heroic origins, never fail to seek divine guidance, and never lose your ... God-given optimism.

Mr. Speaker, we thank God for the life of RONALD WILSON REAGAN.

Hon. Joseph R. Pitts

OF PENNSYLVANIA

Mr. Speaker, last week as I reflected on the anniversary of D-day, I recalled President

REAGAN's speech on the 40th anniversary of that first day of liberation of Europe on June 6, 1984. President REAGAN spoke of "the men of Normandy" who "had faith that what they were doing was right, faith that they fought for all humanity, faith that a just God would grant them mercy on this beachhead or on the next."

As he so often did, his conviction and passion, his grace and sincerity connected a distant event to the struggle each and every human being faces every day, fighting to know what we are doing is right.

Later that day he told a different audience, "We will always remember. We will always be proud. We will always be prepared, so we may always be free."

Newsweek called this freedom, which President REAGAN mentioned in 1984, the freedom "from self-doubt, from the Soviet threat, from uneasiness about our national power and capacity to do great things."

This was REAGAN's gift to his country. He knew that America was great and that our greatness had not come without a price. Indeed, we will always remember, Mr. President. We will always remember so that we may always be free.

Hon. Nick Smith
OF MICHIGAN

Mr. Speaker, I was farming and in the Michigan Legislature when RONALD REAGAN took office. With President REAGAN, he not only led the country but restored America's confidence. He renewed our sense of America's goodness and America's greatness. And with that assurance, the American people achieved great things.

When RONALD REAGAN came into office, we had Watergate, defeat in Vietnam, we surrendered control over the Panama Canal. Vietnam fell to communism and Cambodia soon followed. The Sandinistas took control of Nicaragua. The Ayatollah Khomeini held 52 American hostages for more than 1 year at our Embassy in Tehran.

Inflation stood at 13.5 percent and interest rates reached 21 percent. People in America had lost their optimism and pride in our country, and it was RONALD REAGAN that brought us back.

It was RONALD REAGAN who turned it around. He never lost faith in the American people, and he had enough optimism to restore our lost confidence and get America back on its feet.

That is what impressed me so much in those days, that tremendous turnaround from so many being down to being proud again of America. He believed that we could cut taxes and restore our economy, and we did. By the end of his term, the U.S. economy had grown by a third.

He believed we could stand up proudly for American values around the world and stand up to the Soviet Union, and we did. It was President REAGAN's resolve that halted the march of communism in Central America and Afghanistan. It was REAGAN's resolve that nurtured the Solidarity movement in Poland, and gave heart to the dissidents of the Soviet bloc.

Ultimately, it was President REAGAN's faith in American ideals and his steadfast determination that led to the fall of the Berlin Wall and the liberation of Eastern Europe.

In conclusion, Mr. Speaker, it was that leadership and vision for America that made RONALD REAGAN special. And now the country mourns and the world remembers in the death of a great world leader.

COMMUNICATION FROM THE CLERK OF THE HOUSE

The SPEAKER laid before the House the following communication from the Clerk of the House of Representatives:

OFFICE OF THE CLERK
U.S. HOUSE OF REPRESENTATIVES
Washington, DC, June 8, 2004.

HON. J. DENNIS HASTERT,
The Speaker, U.S. House of Representatives, Washington, DC.

DEAR MR. SPEAKER: Pursuant to the permission granted in Clause 2(h) of Rule II of the Rules of the U.S. House of Representatives, I have the honor to transmit a sealed envelope received from the White House on June 8, 2004 at 2:37 p.m. and said to contain a message from the President whereby he notifies the Congress of the death of RONALD REAGAN.

With Best wishes, I am
    Sincerely,

JEFF TRANDAHL,
Clerk of the House.

MESSAGE FROM THE PRESIDENT OF THE UNITED STATES

The SPEAKER laid before the House the following message from the President of the United States; which was read:

To the Congress of the United States:

By this Message, I officially inform you of the death of RONALD REAGAN, the fortieth President of the United States.

RONALD REAGAN was a great leader and a good man. He had the confidence that comes with conviction, the strength that comes with character, the grace that comes with humility, and the humor that comes with wisdom.

Through his leadership, spirit, and abiding faith in the American people, President REAGAN gave our Nation a renewed optimism. With his courage and moral clarity, he enhanced America's security and advanced the spread of peace, liberty, and democracy to millions of people who had lived in darkness and oppression. As America's President, he helped change the world.

The sun has now set on RONALD REAGAN's extraordinary American life. Just as he told us that our Nation's best days are yet to come, we know that the same is true for him.

GEORGE W. BUSH.
THE WHITE HOUSE, *June 8, 2004.*

EXPRESSING PROFOUND REGRET AND SORROW OF THE HOUSE ON THE DEATH OF RONALD WILSON REAGAN FORMER PRESIDENT OF THE UNITED STATES OF AMERICA

Mr. DeLAY. Mr. Speaker, I offer a privileged resolution (H. Res. 663) and ask for its immediate consideration.

The Clerk read the resolution, as follows:

H. RES. 663

Resolved, That the House of Representatives has learned with profound regret and sorrow of the death of RONALD WILSON REAGAN, former President of the United States of America.

Resolved, That the House tenders its deep sympathy to the members of the family of the former President in their bereavement.

Resolved, That in recognition of the many virtues, public and private, of one who served with distinction as President, the Speaker shall appoint a committee of the House to join with such Members of the Senate as may be designated, to attend the funeral services of the former President.

Resolved, That the Sergeant-at-Arms of the House be authorized and directed to take such steps as may be necessary for carrying out the provisions of these resolutions, and that the necessary expenses in connection therewith be paid out of the applicable accounts of the House.

Resolved, That the Clerk communicate these resolutions to the Senate and transmit a copy of the same to the family of the former President.

Resolved, That when the House adjourns today, it adjourn as a further mark of respect to the memory of the former President.

Hon. Tom DeLay

OF TEXAS

Mr. Speaker, he was a gift to us: the healthy, hearty child handed down from God to John and Nelle Reagan in Tampico, IL, in 1911; the strong, athletic young man handed up from the bustling, laughing, big-shouldered Midwest of his youth; the underrated actor, the underrated labor leader, the underrated politician; and the visionary who foresaw America's victory in the cold war and brought about that victory with wit, will, and undaunted valor for 8 heroic years.

Everything that America is, and everything that mankind can be, was in our 40th President: wisdom, mercy, humor, honesty, honor, and courage.

In an hour of doubt and fear, RONALD REAGAN rose in the West, reminded his Nation of its unique mission in history, and with the help of a few million friends, worked the great miracle of the age. And he did it all smiling through the condescending insults of his critics, who, bless their hearts, could never quite get past his infuriating optimism.

They said RONALD REAGAN could ruin the economy, but in fact he led it to heights of strength and prosperity never before witnessed in history.

They said REAGAN would provoke our enemies to war, but in fact he bent our enemies to surrender without firing a single shot.

They said RONALD REAGAN was an "amiable dunce," but in fact he was a fearless intellectual warrior, who marshaled words like soldiers to fight battles of ideas across a table or across a continent, and won.

Which is why his death, even after a decade of slow, agonizing decline, comes as a shock to all of us. For RONALD REAGAN was not just a man. He was the personification of an idea. And not just an idea, but the idea: the irreducible American idea that this Nation, founded by a generation of heroes upon the self-evident truth of equality under God, is possessed of a special commission in the affairs of men.

According to RONALD REAGAN, and according to Washington, Lincoln, Roosevelt, and Kennedy before him, America is not just another nation. Instead, we are the "last, best hope of man on Earth"; "the torch of freedom" guiding mankind through the darkness; the living promise to all times and men that despite the relentless march of tyranny, the ultimate victory of liberty is assured.

And people wonder where he got his optimism. Of course RONALD REAGAN was an optimist. He was an American. In his life, the United States pulled the world through the Great Depression, two great world wars, and back from the brink of nuclear holocaust. And all the while, despite all the hardship, indeed perhaps because of it, America got stronger, richer, and, as far as he was concerned, better.

REAGAN's confidence and optimism in his country were simply extensions of his confidence and optimism in his countrymen. He knew the things Americans had done, repelling the British, freeing the slaves, settling the West, liberating Europe, shooting for the Moon, and simply could not see this arc of history as anything but the irresistible advance of freedom against oppression; or as REAGAN sublimely put it: "We win, and they lose."

"We" are those who seek to defend human dignity, and "they" are those who seek to stifle it. This was not a mere political calculation. To RONALD REAGAN, the innate dignity of man was a spark of the Divine, a light created in God's image that the darkness could not overcome. He saw it as his role in our Nation and America's role in the world, for that matter, to liberate people from the shackles of government, so that they might first enjoy their right of self-determination, and then share with their neighbors the blessings of faith, hope, and charity.

REAGAN knew these were the virtues that built our Nation and remain the essential ingredients of American achievement, the tonic that has sustained the United States for more than 200 years, in Emerson's words, as "the country of tomorrow."

REAGAN loved that quote, and the idea behind it; that even as we stand today as the oldest democracy on Earth, we remain the youthful champion of liberty and justice, best poised of all nations to lead mankind in the uncertain future. He believed it was true because he knew it had to be.

He knew that without the American Nation, that is without the American people and their steadfast adherence to the true and the good, the West could fail in the cold war and fail the cause of freedom around the world. And so he never let failure become an option.

From the earliest days of his administration, President REAGAN stood before the world and proclaimed the United States' commitment to freedom. He called the Soviet Union the evil empire and declared that "regimes planted by bayonets do not take root." He met with Pope John Paul II and pledged to assist and equip the Solidarity movement in Poland. He called the Soviet's bluff at Reykjavik and went to the Brandenburg Gate to challenge Soviet Leader Mikhail Gorbachev to "tear down this wall!"

Around the world, his words and deeds filtered down to the oppressed citizens behind the Iron Curtain who knew, for the first time, that the American President and his people were coming to the rescue; that the truth about the evils of communism was being exposed to the world, and that the West had made a conscious decision that the cold war was not to be managed, but fought and won.

To RONALD REAGAN, the answers to the world's problems were not simplistic, but they were simple. In foreign policy, evil must be confronted. Domestically, more government is not the solution; it is the problem. Publicly, honesty is the best policy. And privately, follow the golden rule.

This was not merely the recipe for a spectacular career, which dominated and forever altered the map of the world, or for the national pride he restored to an America that, under his watch, became freer, stronger, and more prosperous than any nation in history. It was also the recipe for a full life of love and friendship, an ineffable romance with his wife, Nancy.

In short, he left the world a better place than he found it and left his country with policies in place to solve problems great and small. It is for us, then, who inhabit the world he shaped, to finish the work he began. For we honor him best not by our words today, but our deeds tomorrow, and the next day and the next, to do right by each other, right by our Nation, and right by our responsibilities to history.

Though he may no longer be with us, Mr. Speaker, we still live in an Age of Reagan. Come Friday afternoon, he will be laid to rest, after making one final journey home to his beloved California coast. But even as we say our tearful goodbyes that evening, and the Sun sets out West over the Pacific, we will find in ourselves the strength to carry on without our hero.

We will simply do as REAGAN did at the end of any long and difficult day. We will turn and look to the East with anticipation and wonder, and wait for another hopeful dawn.

Hon. Nancy Pelosi
OF CALIFORNIA

Mr. Speaker, with the death of RONALD REAGAN and the dignity with which he left us, there is truly mourning in America. If the meaning of a life can be measured by the hearts touched by one's death, the outpouring of grief at the death of our 40th President speaks to the distinctly American life that was RONALD WILSON REAGAN.

We Californians mourn RONALD REAGAN as our Governor; all Americans mourn RONALD REAGAN as our President; and people the world over mourn RONALD REAGAN, the passionate voice for freedom.

Today a grateful Nation remembers RONALD REAGAN the man. We remember his indomitable optimism and abiding love of country. RONALD REAGAN understood the greatness of America has always been the character of the American people. As Americans, we have always dared to dream. And so President REAGAN appealed to the enduring belief that sustains us as a people: That America's best days are yet to come.

We remember his leadership. Those of us on this side of the aisle may not have always stood with him on matters of policy, but we always knew where he stood, as he did us, when it came to matters of principle. And though firm in his convictions, President REAGAN was not afraid of compromise. Indeed, the lifelong crusader against communism will be remembered for signing the first agreement with the Soviet Union to actually destroy nuclear weapons.

We remember his eloquence. After the loss of our *Challenger* astronauts, President REAGAN consoled a grieving Nation. And whether in front of the Berlin Wall, or overlooking the beaches of Normandy, he echoed the democratic aspirations of freedom-loving people everywhere.

We remember his grace and humor. This is a story that perhaps our colleague, the gentleman from California (Mr. Lewis), understands and appreciates better than most in the Chamber. When RONALD REAGAN was Governor of California, he came to the legislative chamber to deliver the State of the State Address. Because it was near the time of his birthday, they wheeled in a birthday cake and sang "Happy Birthday" to then-Governor REAGAN. I have to add at that time, the speaker of the Assembly of California was a giant of a man, Jess Unruh, and who sometimes did not see eye to eye with then-Governor REAGAN. They sang "Happy Birthday," and Governor REAGAN blew out the candles. Someone said, "Governor, did you make a wish?"

Mr. Speaker, the Governor looked up and said, "Yes, I made a wish, but it did not come true; he is still there," as he spoke to the then-Speaker.

At the end of the day, though, President REAGAN knew whatever may divide us by party is dwarfed by what unites us as Americans. Speaker Tip O'Neill famously told of how he and the President clashed by day, but were friends after 6 p.m., prompting the President to begin his phone calls, "Tip, is it after 6 p.m.?"

We remember RONALD REAGAN's faith in his country, in his family, and in his God. In that poignant letter 10 years ago announcing his battle with Alzheimer's disease, President REAGAN wrote:

When the Lord calls me home, whenever that may be, I will leave with the greatest love for this country of ours and eternal optimism for its future.

... I know that for America there will always be a bright dawn ahead.

That dawn was referenced by the gentleman from Texas (Mr. DeLay).

We remember RONALD REAGAN's dignity, the dignity with which he lived and led our country, and the dignity with which he died, turning the long goodbye of his final years into a lesson for all of us.

And all Americans, and I know everyone who serves in the Congress of the United States for sure, have been touched by the dignity, private strength and public grace of Nancy Reagan and the Reagan family to whom we offer our prayers and deepest condolences. Our Nation is in your debt for the care and love you gave our President and the dignity with which you held his hands at the end.

I hope it is a comfort to Mrs. Reagan and the Reagan family that the whole world mourns their loss and is praying for them at this sad time.

For his eloquent defense of freedom, for his leadership style of conviction and compromise, for his eternal optimism for the future, America pays tribute to President RONALD WILSON REAGAN.

May God bless RONALD REAGAN, may God bless this country that he loved and led, may RONALD REAGAN rest in peace.

Hon. J. Dennis Hastert

OF ILLINOIS

Mr. Speaker, I rise today to honor the life and the legacy of our Nation's 40th President, RONALD WILSON REAGAN.

He was born in the small town of Tampico, IL, which is in my congressional district, and grew up in Dixon, another town some of my constituents call home. It was there that he learned the common-sense values and virtues that helped him reshape not only our Nation, but also the world.

When I first ran for public office in 1980, for the Illinois Legislature, RONALD REAGAN was running for President. Back then people did not have a lot of faith in America and what America could do. What made him so special was his willingness to step forward at a time when the rest of the world was stepping back and remind us what made America the "shining city on the hill." He restored our faith in America, and he made us proud to be Americans again.

His easygoing personality and a sense of humor endeared him to the people he served. His word was his bond. It was genuine. His honesty and sincerity were the foundation of his strength while working with Democrats and Republicans in both Houses of Congress.

The world struggled against communism, but our country stood tall as RONALD REAGAN's perseverance led the world to freedom. As a former history teacher, I have taught students about George Washington and Thomas Jefferson. I have taught them about our fellow Illinoisan, Abraham Lincoln, and I have taught them about FDR and JFK. History has now called RONALD REAGAN to take his place alongside the most noble of our countrymen. Here in the People's House, thousands of Americans will file in the Capitol rotunda to honor the people's President.

He will be remembered as a symbol of "peace through strength," but most of all we will remember him for the hope he gave to the rest of the world that freedom was possible. His grit, his sheer willpower made it possible for more people to walk in freedom today than at any other time throughout history.

Not only was he an ambassador of the American people and the American way of life, President REAGAN was an ambassador of faith. He reminded us of his faith when America grieved the loss of the seven astronauts of the *Challenger* space shuttle. He said:

> We will never forget them, nor the last time we saw them, this morning, as they prepared for their journey and waved good-bye and "slipped the surly bonds of earth" to "touch the face of God."

Tonight, as we honor the man who believed America was a "shining city on the hill," we should remember his words to the students of his alma mater, Eureka College in Illinois. He said:

> Live each day to the fullest. Live each day with enthusiasm, optimism and hope. If you do, I am convinced that your contribution to this wonderful experiment we call America will be profound.

With Godspeed, Mr. President. God bless RONALD REAGAN. God bless America.

MOURNING THE PASSING OF PRESIDENT RONALD REAGAN

Mr. LEWIS of California. Mr. Speaker, pursuant to the order of the House of today and as designee of the majority leader, I call up the resolution (H. Res. 664) mourning the passing of President RONALD REAGAN and celebrating his service to the people of the United States and his leadership in promoting the cause of freedom for all the people of the world, and ask for its immediate consideration.

The Clerk read the resolution, as follows:

H. RES. 664

Whereas President RONALD REAGAN reminded us that our great Nation was founded and built by people with great dreams and the courage to take great risks;

Whereas President REAGAN reminded his countrymen of the Nation's calling in world history: "From our forefathers to our modern day immigrants, we've come from every corner of the earth, from every race and every ethnic background, and we've become a new breed in the world. We're Americans, and we have a rendezvous with destiny.";

Whereas President REAGAN championed freedom and democracy throughout the world, bringing courage to millions of people suffering the bondage of tyranny and oppression;

Whereas on June 12, 1987, President REAGAN stood at the Brandenburg Gate, the symbol of communism's brutal oppression, and demanded: "General Secretary Gorbachev, if you seek peace, if you seek prosperity for the Soviet Union and eastern Europe, if you seek liberalization: Come here to this gate. Mr. Gorbachev, open this gate! Mr. Gorbachev, tear down this wall!";

Whereas on November 9, 1989, the Berlin Wall was torn down, signifying the end of the Cold War;

Whereas President REAGAN, and his wife Nancy, brought dignity and respect to the White House and dedicated their lives to promoting national pride and to bettering the quality of life in the United States and throughout the world;

Whereas on May 16, 2002, Congress bestowed the congressional gold medal in recognition of their service to the Nation;

Whereas RONALD REAGAN's eloquence united Americans in times of triumph and tragedy;

Whereas on January 28, 1986, President REAGAN comforted a grieving nation as Americans mourned the death of seven American astronauts who "slipped the surly bonds of earth to touch the face of God";

Whereas President REAGAN spent the twilight of his life as he always lived, leading a fight against Alzheimer's disease with faith, courage, and dignity, with the greatest love for the Nation and eternal optimism for its future;

Whereas by opening his heart to the Nation about his affliction with Alzheimer's disease, President REAGAN promoted greater awareness of this condition; and

Whereas President REAGAN appealed to the best hopes of the American people, not their worst fears, and to their confidence rather than their doubts: Now, therefore, be it

Resolved, That the House of Representatives—

(1) expresses its deepest appreciation for the profound public service of President RONALD REAGAN;

(2) expresses its condolences to Nancy Reagan and to Patti, Michael, Ron, and the entire Reagan family;

(3) calls on the people of the United States to reflect on the record of President REAGAN during this national period of remembrance and to remember always his encouraging words: "We have every right to dream heroic dreams."; and

(4) directs the Clerk of the House of Representatives to transmit a copy of this resolution to the family of President REAGAN.

Hon. Jerry Lewis

OF CALIFORNIA

Mr. Speaker, through the years of having the opportunity to know President RONALD REAGAN, one could go down many a pathway in recalling his greatness. My first recollection of RONALD REAGAN, I can recall clearly I was lying on the living room floor, and he was giving this speech on behalf of Barry Goldwater. The remarks in that speech entitled, "A Time for Choosing," never to forget:

You and I have a rendezvous with destiny. We will preserve for our children this, the last best hope of man on earth, or we will sentence them to take the first step into a thousand years of darkness.

I will never forget rolling over on the floor and saying to my family, "This guy ought to be Governor of California." And, by golly, just 2 years later, he was: Governor RONALD REAGAN, elected in 1966 by the people of California.

Two years after that, a group of seven Republican freshmen legislators were invited to the Governor's home for a little dinner. They had a set of card tables in the living room, a couple sat down at one card table, I sat on an extra chair, and, lo and behold, the Governor sat down beside me. The gentleman from California (Mr. Waxman) may remember that I was a bit more brash in those days than I choose to be now.

And so almost immediately, I raised the subject of interest to me to the then-Governor REAGAN. I asked him what he thought about preschool and child care. It did not take 30 seconds for me to begin to understand that I had asked the right question, for Governor REAGAN knew an awful lot more about preschool and child care than I ever thought of knowing. He and Nancy had been thinking about this subject for some time. And indeed, as a result of that beginning point of working together in this very special area of education, the Child Development Act was signed in 1972 by Governor REAGAN and became the first major State quality day care programming that included health components and education components and involved parental responsibilities as well.

The Governor was way ahead of the curve, as one might see; for some 25 years later, Washington discovered the importance of child care.

Another illustration of an interesting side of the Governor who by many was considered to be some way out there, far out on the right; but quickly those who would observe carefully recognized that this Governor was looking out for the benefit of all people of California and because of that, he soon became very well known as an environmental Governor. He joined quickly with Governor Laxalt of Nevada, and together hand in hand they literally saved Lake Tahoe.

A leader way ahead of his time, it was my privilege to spend so much time in those early days with Governor RONALD REAGAN. At another time in this evening's discussion I would like to spend a moment discussing with all of you my first experience with Governor REAGAN when he became President of the United States.

Hon. Henry A. Waxman

OF CALIFORNIA

Mr. Speaker, I rise today to pay tribute to President RONALD REAGAN. President REAGAN has been a part of my entire political life. President REAGAN got his start in politics when he was elected Governor in 1966. Two years later, I got my start in politics when I was elected to the California Legislature. I served in the State legislature until 1974, the last year of Governor REAGAN's term. And, of course, I served in the Congress of the United States for the entire 8 years of his Presidency.

I knew from those early days that President REAGAN had remarkable political skills. He is known as the Great Communicator and, truly, he was. President REAGAN knew how to connect with people. And he could articulate values and resonate across America and around the world with his ideals. He was also likable and charming.

For many years, President REAGAN was actually my constituent. Hollywood, the place and the industry associated with it, had a great impact on his life. It refined his communication skills and honed his sense of drama and delivery. And it gave him something that many people do not fully appreciate—an understanding that in America, with hard work and honest values Hollywood endings really can come true.

President REAGAN thought our Nation should be a shining example to the world. And under his leadership, we were really admired and respected around the world. He viewed America as a "city on the hill," a beacon for freedom and a model for democracy.

And here is another thing many people do not fully appreciate: President REAGAN was a pragmatic leader. He had strong convictions, but if he learned that those convictions were taking America in the wrong direction, he had the confidence and the wisdom to change course.

As everyone knows, President REAGAN was afflicted with Alzheimer's disease in the last 10 years of his life. President REAGAN struggled with this terrible condition with great dignity. And with great courage he and his wife Nancy shared his struggle with the American people. It is a true tragedy that this country lost the opportunity to have this elder statesman involved and seek his advice and leadership in the last years of his life.

I know that all of us in this body would like to find a fitting way to honor President REAGAN's life. For my part, I can think of no better tribute than an accelerated effort to address the horrific disease known as Alzheimer's. Mrs. Reagan, the President's beloved wife, bravely spoke out about this just last month. In her moving words she said:

> Science has presented us with a hope called stem cell research which may provide our scientists with many answers that for so long have been beyond our grasp. We have lost so much time already. I just really cannot bear to lose any more.

Well, it is past time for us to seize the potential that Nancy Reagan identified. There could be no important or more lasting legacy to her husband.

America has lost a devoted citizen and a dedicated leader. I want Mrs. Reagan and the Reagan family to know they are in my heart and in my thoughts. President REAGAN's passing is truly felt among Democrats and Republicans, by all Americans, and people of goodwill all around the world. We will certainly miss him.

Hon. Jerry Lewis

OF CALIFORNIA

President REAGAN came to Washington at a moment when our country was in great malaise. Interest rates had risen as high as $21^1/_2$ percent. Inflation was raging the country. Jobs were very, very difficult to come by. And in typical RONALD REAGAN fashion, the President for whom the glass was always more than half full, he began setting forth policies that reduced interest rates, that impacted inflation, and created jobs. He set a stage for tomorrow that would lead us all to believe in America again and have new hope and opportunity within our country.

Hon. Roy Blunt

OF MISSOURI

Mr. Speaker, I want to thank the gentleman from California (Mr. Lewis) for yielding this time to me and leading this important recognition today.

I also want to thank you, Mr. Speaker, for your special understanding of President REAGAN from your work in the military serving alongside him in his days in the White House.

What all of those that served with the President or watched him from afar were able to see was how his optimistic leadership reinvigorated the American spirit and how it redefined the politics of his time. Born in a small town near the middle of America, this son of a shoe salesman rose to heights of gigantic proportion and lifted his countrymen along with him.

After facing his last great challenge with courage and patience, RONALD REAGAN now takes his place where his vision is once again clear, his faith rewarded, and his storied sense of humor returned. He placed his faith in God along with economic and permanent freedom. And the world is a better place because of those beliefs.

President REAGAN helped raise individuals up and helped tear down the Berlin Wall. He inspired us, and he was inspired by us. President REAGAN's leadership inspired more current members of our conference on my side of the aisle than any other political figure in the 20th century.

When I became the majority whip in this Congress, I named the conference room in the whip's office the Reagan Room for the brief time I am privileged to make that designation. And I hope many of my colleagues come by that room during this week on the third floor of the Capitol and view the photographs there chronicling the life of this remarkable man from his days as a radio announcer to those that foreshadowed the end of the Soviet Union.

President REAGAN said:

> We are a powerful force for good. With faith and courage we can perform great deeds and take freedom's next step, and we will.

America is taking freedom's next step, and we are doing so in large part because of President RONALD WILSON REAGAN.

Today America's light shines a little dimmer because he is gone, but, Mr. Speaker, it shines much brighter than it would have if he had not been here. He made a difference in America. He made a difference in the world. Today people all over the world are remembering and recognizing that difference.

Hon. Danny K. Davis

OF ILLINOIS

Mr. Speaker, I rise today to join with my colleagues as we pay tribute to the life and legacy of President REAGAN. A bigger-than-life screen actor and television personality, RONALD REAGAN moved from being Governor of California in the sixties to President of the United

States and dominating American politics in the eighties. He was the first President to be reelected to a second term since Dwight D. Eisenhower.

Media-made and media-presented, President REAGAN got millions of Americans to feel proud of their Nation. America's 40-year cold war with the Soviet Union cooled considerably and perhaps actually ended during REAGAN's Presidency. Many Americans credit him with having achieved that significant outcome.

Born the son of a shoe salesman in smalltown Illinois, President REAGAN's impoverished but loving parents instilled in him a sense of optimism that carried him through college as an average student. After graduation, he worked for a few years as a sports broadcaster in midwestern radio before landing a film contract with Warner Brothers, which took him to Hollywood in 1936.

Over the next 30 years, President REAGAN made scores of films, including Army films produced during World War II. He hosted two popular television series and was actively engaged in politics as president of the Screen Actors Guild.

In the fifties, President REAGAN changed from being a Roosevelt New Deal Democrat to a conservative Republican. In 1966, he became Governor of California and was reelected in 1970. Using his popularity in California, he unsuccessfully challenged President Gerald Ford for the Republican nomination in 1976. He tried again and won the nomination in 1980 and thereafter defeated the incumbent Democrat Jimmy Carter. With his 1984 reelection victory, President REAGAN became the most politically successful Republican President since President Eisenhower.

In his last years, as President REAGAN battled Alzheimer's disease, our Nation went from having zero drugs for this devastating disease to today having five new prescriptive drugs to help manage and treat the progression of Alzheimer's. Today it is even possible to diagnose Alzheimer's with more than 90 percent accuracy. It is clear that Alzheimer's does not discriminate on whom it affects, regardless of gender, ethnicity, socioeconomic status, political ideology or if one worked in the fields, in the factories or in the Oval Office.

With now more than 4.5 million people suffering from this disease, the upsetting effects of Alzheimer's are growing faster than modern medicine can manage. This is only likely to become more complicated with the aging of the baby boomers, boosting the number of Alzheimer's patients to an astounding 11 to 16 million people by the middle of the century.

As a way to honor President REAGAN, let us make the greatest commitment that we can to real investment in research for Alzheimer's disease and follow through with clinical trials to translate the research into treatments. We must now act to make the lives of all Alzheimer's patients more comfortable with a better quality of life, while hopefully being able to prevent this disease in the future.

Mr. President, as one might say in a western movie, you had a good ride and our country is proud to say, "Much obliged."

Hon. Elton Gallegly

OF CALIFORNIA

President REAGAN's impact on America and the world is immeasurable. He ended the cold war and restored America's confidence. His Republican administration rebuilt our economy with the help and support of a Democratic House of Representatives.

President REAGAN achieved such successes because when you sat in a room with him, there could be over 1,000 people in the room, yet you felt like there was only the 2 of you, and his wonderful wit would put you at ease. That was a tremendous gift.

That is why some of his biggest political enemies were among his closest personal friends. It is why a staunch anticommunist could negotiate with the President of the Soviet Union. President REAGAN reached across and connected with people.

President REAGAN is now at rest. We mourn his passing, but we are grateful for the gifts he gave us: a safer world, a strong economic base, and a renewed belief in America's greatness.

Mr. Speaker, President REAGAN will be laid to rest at his Presidential library in Simi Valley,

CA. It is where I began my political career as mayor and city councilman. It has been my home for more than 35 years.

President REAGAN often spoke about a "shining city on a hill." The Ronald Reagan Presidential Library is such a place. President REAGAN will be laid to rest at the edge of a high hill where his library stands. His grave overlooks the farmlands, ranches and chaparral of the Tierra Rejada Valley. On a clear day, one can see the Channel Islands in the Pacific Ocean more than 30 miles away. It is a fitting place for America's greatest son.

Mr. Speaker, it is the end of an era, but it is the beginning of a legacy that will last forever. We will miss him.

Hon. David Scott

OF GEORGIA

Mr. Speaker, today we remember a true leader, a statesman and a great man who led our country with dignity, with grace and with strength. President REAGAN was the quintessential American who exemplified unbridled optimism, a strong sense of faith and the idea that our Nation was a true beacon for the world.

There is no doubt that among his greatest achievements was his resolve to end the cold war so that other Nations could experience the glory of freedom and the power of democracy. His combination of political strength and personal appeal, his ability to communicate set the forces in motion for the walls of communism to crumble, and for this he will always be remembered.

However, President REAGAN should also be remembered, especially in this House, for his willingness to fight in the political arena with dignity, with respect for his opponents, and his strong belief that democracy was for all of our citizens, even those with whom he might have disagreed. President REAGAN exemplified civility and honor in an arena that is often lacking in both, and because of that he earned the goodwill not only of his supporters, but often of his friendly adversaries. In the end we remember a man, RONALD REAGAN, not only as a great leader, but as a good and decent man.

My condolences and prayers are with his family and with his wife Nancy, who shared him with our country.

Mr. Speaker, we are all called by God for a special purpose with this turn at light that he gives us. Some nobility of purpose is embedded in each of us with that calling, and as it is the case with RONALD REAGAN, there will be on his tombstone 1911–2004, but the most important thing on his tombstone will be the dash in between. For the fundamental call from God is always what we will do with the dash.

RONALD REAGAN did great things with his dash. For those 93 years in that dash was actor, head of a union, the breakdown of the barriers of communism, the star wars defense system, and his legacy of rebuilding the Republican Party.

Yes, RONALD REAGAN was a great man, and he, as so many of us, have heeded the call, and as I think of RONALD REAGAN, I am reminded of the great prophet Isaiah who said in that great conversation when God called and said, who will go for us and whom shall we send, that great prophet Isaiah said, at no hesitation, Here I am, Lord, send me.

RONALD REAGAN responded the same way. I can almost see it. When the Lord called and said, who will go for us and who will we send to perform that nobility of purpose in life that RONALD REAGAN did, which is the legacy of his Presidency, I can see him standing at attention and saying, Here I am, Lord, send me.

God bless RONALD REAGAN.

Hon. William M. Thomas

OF CALIFORNIA

Mr. Speaker, we are all going to talk about President REAGAN, Commander in Chief REAGAN, leader of the free world REAGAN. Some of us were privileged to know him in a different context. My friend from California (Mr. Lewis), the chairman, has talked about his relationship with him when he was Governor of California.

I knew him in a number of different contexts, and I was always amazed at one thing, and that was he was the same person regardless of the context in which you met him, worked with him or were led by him.

In 1974, I decided that I would run for public office. He was then in the last year of his governorship, and he decided to come to Bakersfield, and so I planned an event for the Governor. We decided that we would charge what seemed to be an appropriate amount, $25 a head, and almost 500 people came to see the Governor. I had no doubts about why they were coming.

We picked him up at the airport, and when we got in the car, he started quizzing me about myself, and so I was visiting with him. But as we got closer, I said, "Well, do you want to take just a little time now so that you can get ready for the event?" He said, "Bill, if I am not ready now, 5 minutes will not make any difference."

He was always prepared. He was always on time, whether it was a minor event or a debate with other leaders of the world.

And you see him in a bunch of different contexts and you say, well, of course, because he was a movie star and he is supposed to carry himself. And the point I want to make, if I do not make any other point, is he was that way because of who he was, not because of what he did. Because, frankly, if you tried to write a script and went to Hollywood on RONALD REAGAN's life, you would last about 2 minutes in the room. Because people are willing to suspend belief, but not that much.

And what I like most about the juxtaposition of RONALD REAGAN and his career, which was kind of molded out of the context that he found himself in, was that the American people were wise enough, first of all to choose him as Governor of California for the traditional two terms, had he chosen to run for a third term he probably could have gotten elected; and the American people chose him for two terms as President, a now constitutionally limited period of time. Were it not for that constitutional limit, he may have been elected again.

And so when you watch people recognizing RONALD REAGAN as they pass the casket, as they did in California, many people will have an individual memory, perhaps a general shared one, and perhaps a personal one. For me, RONALD REAGAN's life means that any American can do anything any American wants to do. For RONALD REAGAN, the public person, it means he made sure that he set up a structure which allows any American to do whatever any American wants to do; and his justification and enabling of that is, he would tell you, "because I did."

You are going to hear him called the Great Communicator a lot. What you also need to know was he was a great compromiser. It can be put no more clearly than a comment he made when he was Governor of California, because he became Governor with an enormous debt at that time for the State of California. California did not have a withholding tax, and he needed to create a frontload for money to solve the problem that he was facing. He had, however, made a statement earlier that his feet were in concrete over not having a withholding tax. Once he looked at the options in front of him and he realized he did not have any options other than instituting a withholding tax, having worked with the legislature, he then went to the microphone and said, "That cracking sound you hear is the cement breaking away from my feet."

And so when you wonder why RONALD REAGAN could get along with so many different people in so many stages of life, whether small or great, it was because RONALD REAGAN was the same person regardless of the job the American people gave him. He was always prepared, he was always on time, and he was a very, very sincere man. He was also quite smart, in ways that many people never understand.

So what I want to do tonight is to just share briefly the memoirs of someone who, if you are looking for an example, he certainly stands out, not just in what he did but the way in which he lived his life and the way in which he recognized his condition later in life and the way in which he concluded his life. All of us should pause and remember that he was an amazing person. He was an American.

Hon. Steny H. Hoyer

OF MARYLAND

I am particularly pleased that the gentleman from Texas is managing the time, because I think if RONALD REAGAN were here, he would say Charles Stenholm was one of those who stood with me on principle, who believed that we needed to get this country moving, and believed that we needed to have sound policy; and Charles Stenholm stood with me. And as the gentleman from California (Mr. Thomas) just related, for RONALD REAGAN the concrete cracked again, frankly, when he viewed the program adopted and thought that perhaps some changes needed to be made.

Mr. Speaker, like every Member of this House, I offer my sincere condolences to the family and friends of former President REAGAN, particularly, of course, his beloved wife, Nancy, and his children. What a wonderful example Nancy Reagan set for our country. RONALD REAGAN and Nancy Reagan clearly loved one another deeply and cared for one another, and Nancy Reagan has shown extraordinary courage and fidelity not only throughout the course of their marriage but particularly in the course of RONALD REAGAN's final illness.

Mr. Speaker, RONALD REAGAN loved this Nation and served it with distinction; and he will ever be remembered for his humor, his grace, his irrepressible optimism which mirrored the American spirit and buoyed it in periods of difficulty.

The last decade, when this man who had lived life with such physical vigor slowly slipped away, was an especially cruel blow. However, let us be comforted today that he has been summoned to a far better place.

Having been elected to Congress just 4 months after he took office, and just 6 weeks after an assassin's bullet nearly claimed his life, I had a front-row seat during President REAGAN's 8 years in Washington. He was a man I both liked and respected. I liked him for his warmth and for the respect that he accorded others, and I respected him for the honesty of his convictions and the intellectual integrity that he displayed in pursuing them.

After signing into law what was then the largest tax cut in American history in 1981, President REAGAN had the fortitude to face fiscal reality, just as the gentleman from California (Mr. Thomas) reflected upon. His policies caused yawning deficits and spiraling debt, consequences that he subsequently tried to address, although not as successfully as I am sure he would have hoped. Without question, RONALD REAGAN held strong ideological beliefs. But one of his real strengths was his willingness to put pragmatism above ideology, to make sure that his country had programs that were working.

I also remember him as a person who early in life committed to equality and justice for all, and later in life to the success of freedom and democracy around the world. I believed he was right in that endeavor, and like the gentleman from California (Mr. Lewis), supported his efforts to build up our defenses, to deploy those Persian and cruise missiles, to, yes, even provide for multiple warheads on the MX missile, and say to the Soviet Union, if you want to compete, we are prepared to compete; but we would rather seek peace together. And he had the courage to build up, and he had the courage to make peace.

While Democrats disagreed with and strongly opposed much of his domestic agenda, our political differences never hardened into paralyzing personal animosity on his side or on ours. We were blessed by the fact that we were led by two great Irishmen, RONALD REAGAN and Tip O'Neill. They were friends. And they had a third friend, his name was Michel, Bob Michel, an extraordinary leader of this House. And they, together, believed that country was more important than partisanship and party.

For the most part, they worked together. On those matters that they disagreed on, they took their own separate ways. But when they could agree, they did. The Social Security reform of 1983 was probably the most stark example of that cooperative spirit. It was good for the country, it was good for Social Security, and they came together, worked together, and succeeded together.

That was due in great measure to the leadership styles and personalities of President REAGAN and Speaker O'Neill. These two men, the most powerful political figures in our Nation in the eighties, one a Republican, the other a Democrat, demonstrated to all Americans that our elected leaders could disagree politically without being disagreeable personalities or personally. They reminded all of us that cynicism and mean-spiritedness are inimical to American democracy, and that our real adversaries lie beyond our shores, not here.

The surest tribute that we can pay to RONALD REAGAN today is to commit ourselves to recapture the generosity of spirit that always guided him. In a very real way, RONALD REAGAN's life was the embodiment of the American dream. Both President REAGAN and President Clinton, like Harry Truman, gave credence to the promise that in America neither privileged birth nor economic advantage is necessary to enable one to become the President of the United States of America. It was, for them, and for millions to follow their example, the land of opportunity.

President REAGAN's leadership renewed the conviction that the future would be better, better than the past, and that America's best days were still ahead. That is a philosophy that all of us should embrace and convey to our fellow citizens. I believe it is the case, RONALD REAGAN believed it was the case, and may God bless his soul and comfort his beloved wife, Nancy.

Hon. Dana Rohrabacher

OF CALIFORNIA

Mr. Speaker, it is a blessing that RONALD REAGAN did not die immediately after leaving office in 1989. In these last 16 years that we have had RONALD REAGAN with us, it has given America a chance to take a look at who RONALD REAGAN was and what he meant to our country. And now, with 16 years that have passed, we can look back and see what an enormous difference RONALD REAGAN made not only to our lives as Americans but to the entire world.

Let me note that RONALD REAGAN was 56 years old when I first met him, and that was when he was running for the first time for public office. And all of these things we are talking about, a man who accomplished so much and changed the world for the better, happened after he was 56 years old. He had already had a successful life, a full career.

And he did come from a relatively poor family. I know his first job was being a lifeguard. That affected his way of looking at things his entire life. He saved 77 people's lives as a lifeguard. And having gotten to know him as President and also during his campaigns, I think he always had that consciousness, that he was there to save the day for the people who were in some type of a crisis.

He was a sports broadcaster, and he was a moderately successful film actor. But all of that seemed to be over when he was 50 years old. And then, when he was 56, he jumped into political life. Now, why did he do that? Because California was a mess in 1966.

And he came and stepped forward because he felt he had a contribution to make. He jumped into the political waters to save the day.

I was a youth volunteer in that first campaign, and I got to meet him personally, and it was one of the joys of my life.

Let me note that years later after I got finished with school, I became a journalist, and I covered RONALD REAGAN's last 2 years as Governor as a journalist. I remember that he had a press conference one day, it was near the end of his term, where he was announcing the findings of his law and order task force. One of their findings was an expanded use of the death penalty. And just as I am now, I was then always trying to get to the heart of the matter and ask the tough questions, and I asked President REAGAN, who was then Governor, well, how can you be in favor of expanding the use of the death penalty when you are a committed Christian? And, you know, he sat forward, and he leaned forward to the mike, and said:

> I take that question very seriously. I prayed about this, about using the death penalty more frequently and taking people's lives. I have sought help. I have read the scripture, and I have talked to other people about this, and I have come to the conclusion that if we are executing people for revenge, that it is inconsistent with the principles that Jesus Christ taught us, but if we are executing murderers in order to deter people from killing other human beings, we are doing it then to save people, to save innocent people, and that is totally consistent with Christianity.

At that point Evelle Younger, who was the attorney general of the State, reached over and grabbed the mike and said, "oh, this religious and philosophical stuff does not mean anything. The voters of this State voted for the death penalty, and they are going to get it." Well, in my opinion of RONALD REAGAN's sword, I knew that he was a man who did not take these things lightly, a man of strong conviction, but a man who deeply cared about people enough to think about it and to pray about decisions like this. He was not just a Great Communicator, and I worked for him as a speechwriter for 7 years in the White House. He was, yes, someone who understood the fundamentals of communication, but that is not what made him great. He was not the Great Communicator. He was America's great leader. He had ideals that helped direct his decisions.

We have heard about his strong convictions. We know today that most people with strong convictions are not very pleasant to be around. When they talk about people with philosophies, there is a saying that you cannot change somebody's mind, and he will not change the subject. RONALD REAGAN was a person who taught me that you can have strong principles and have a solid philosophy, but be a pleasant person and care about people at the same time. It was that type of humane approach that permitted RONALD REAGAN to capture the hearts of the American people and inspire us.

When our country was in such terrible peril economically and in retreat internationally, and our spirit had been destroyed, people were not even waving the American flag back in the late seventies, RONALD REAGAN dove into the political waters again to save the day. And he saved us. He was the lifeguard who saved us, and he saved the world.

Jim Bruelte, a political person in California, noted on D-day the American soldiers liberated half of Europe. RONALD REAGAN liberated the other half of Europe and did it without firing a shot.

We live in a more prosperous country, a safer country, and hundreds of millions of people now live in relative freedom than if he had not been here. We are so grateful to RONALD REAGAN for having dove in to save us, and he did. He saved America, and he saved us personally.

I am now 56 years old, the same age RONALD REAGAN was when he first entered politics. I am so grateful that he spent those years of his life making this a better world for my children. I just had three children, and I am so grateful that he made it a better world for them.

Hon. Rodney Alexander
OF LOUISIANA

Mr. Speaker, it is with great sadness that we devote this week to honor the memory and the contributions of our 40th President RONALD REAGAN. My thoughts and prayers are with President REAGAN's family and all of the Americans who grieve this week.

Mr. Speaker, President REAGAN was a true patriot, committed to the ideals of a democratic nation, and dedicated to maintaining the strength of America as a world power. His abilities as a strong leader and a communicator gave Americans confidence and strength during a time of economic hardship and struggling with the Soviet Union.

President REAGAN once said, "There is no limit to what a man can do or where he can go if he does not mind who gets the credit." We should follow this example and remember that public service is not about partisan battles or taking credit, it is about serving the American people to the best of our ability.

I am honored to be here in Washington during this week of memorial services. I am grateful to all of those involved with arranging the safety and logistics during a week when thousands of Americans will journey to our Nation's Capital to pay their respects to President REAGAN.

Mr. Speaker, as we face a new decade and new challenges, let us honor the life and contributions and remember the debt of gratitude we owe our 40th President, RONALD REAGAN.

Hon. Randy "Duke" Cunningham
OF CALIFORNIA

Mr. Speaker, we rise to honor and mourn RONALD REAGAN.

But first I would like to thank Mrs. Nancy Reagan. The wisest of men knows it takes a good woman to make a good man, and what a good wingman she has been, both in sickness and in health. This Nation also owes Nancy Reagan a debt of gratitude; both of them good and decent people. RONALD REAGAN was one of the most respected and effective Presidents in American history.

Mr. Speaker, the Irish have a toast, and it goes like this. It is to those who support RONALD REAGAN, and everybody lifts their glass; to those who may support RONALD REAGAN, and everybody lifts their glass; and to those that will never support President RONALD REAGAN, may God strike them in their shins so we shall know them by their limping. But there are not many of those, Mr. Speaker.

President REAGAN said:

> You know, the United States was never meant to be a second-best nation. ... {W}e set our sights {high for} ... the stars, and we're going for the gold.

He said that back in the eighties. He came to the job with one underlying goal, and that was freedom. Freedom for you, Mr. Speaker, and people all over the world, much to the same challenges that we have today; the freedom in Bosnia, in Kosovo, in Afghanistan and in Iraq, and with the United Nations signing a resolution today following in suit much as RONALD REAGAN guided us through troublesome times when he was President.

RONALD REAGAN restored the economy of a double-digit inflation, interest rates the same thing. He gave this Nation tax relief, much as President Kennedy and President Bush did. He increased the coffers by three times the amount. Unfortunately, it was Congress that spent a lot of that money.

He followed his pledge to restore our military. RONALD REAGAN believed in "peace through strength," and I think it showed through. He eliminated an entire class of nuclear weapons. He is responsible for bringing down the Berlin Wall, ending the cold war, and challenging governments to have a new way of life to bring freedom to their people, also a task that we face today in this body and in this Nation.

For his imprint on history, for his legacy which will be felt for generations to come, this Nation owes President REAGAN and Nancy Reagan a debt of gratitude.

One of the President's many legacies is the Navy's newest nuclear carrier, the USS *Ronald Reagan* which will reside in San Diego. That aircraft carrier will travel all over the world, much as RONALD REAGAN did, and serves as a symbol of the respect and elegance of his family. Throughout his political career, President REAGAN always concluded his campaign in San Diego. He called it his lucky city. We feel fortunate that he considered San Diego so. It is only fitting that this great new "shining city on the hill," San Diego, will be called the home of the USS *Ronald Reagan*, our latest and newest nuclear aircraft carrier.

Mr. Speaker, we bid RONALD REAGAN adieu and thank the Reagan family for what they have given to this Nation. God bless you, Nancy Reagan, and your family and the President.

Hon. Sheila Jackson-Lee
OF TEXAS

I imagine this time is the reason why so many of us, in fact I would say this entire House, cherishes this body and cherishes this institution, because it allows us to come at a time like this and shed our Democratic and Republican labels and simply approach this tribute as Americans. I would imagine that is what these times, although sad, allow us to do.

I am proud as an American to come forward and to salute an American President, and to be able to join the millions of Americans mourning the passing of President RONALD REAGAN and celebrate his service to the people of the United States and his leadership in promoting the cause of freedom for all of the people of the world.

Protest has its place, protest is good in life, but protest has no place in death, and so this opportunity is to acknowledge the principles by which this President lived and stood for during his Presidency. The love that President REAGAN had for this Nation was infectious to the point that it reflected on everyone who listened to him, here in America and abroad.

Even when his actions did not agree with the policies and initiatives of many of us who wear a different political hat, he maintained himself with integrity and engaged in honest and open debate. We have heard repeatedly over these last couple of days that despite partisan disagreements, former President REAGAN followed the tenet that when the day ends, we are no longer

Democrats or Republicans; rather, we are Americans, families and friends.

I am reminded of the stories told about him and Speaker of the House Tip O'Neill, who shared in their Irish heritage a bit of good conversation and maybe a little bit of drink.

The differences may have been real; but because of the way President REAGAN led, he taught us that there is a big difference between strong beliefs and bitter partisanship. As the Commander in Chief, he was the voice of America in imparting both good news and bad news. As we mourned the loss of our brave astronauts in the *Challenger* tragedy, it was President REAGAN who reminded us, "Nothing ends here; our hopes and our journeys continue." We in Texas at that time appreciated his strong leadership and that in fact even in spite of the *Challenger* tragedy at that time, we would prevail and we would go forward.

President RONALD WILSON REAGAN was an American who will always be remembered. He will be forever remembered for the warmth and the respect with which he accorded others. Furthermore, our thoughts and prayers are with Nancy and his children at this difficult time.

Strong beliefs and a love of our country are the only way to bring this country forward as we face a costly and difficult war in Iraq and a budget that is struggling to survive. Strength and leadership is what we need now. Strength and leadership will be required to bring this Nation back to the standards by which we have always been known.

President REAGAN himself admitted that he was an optimist and he believed that this Nation had an optimistic future, and so he was always able to rise to the occasion and share words of encouragement. President REAGAN always stressed that America is a can-do country. I would say to you that we Democrats agree. We can and will get back on the right track, largely through his legacy of integrity and hard work. With strong leadership and a real commitment to confronting the problems facing American families, we can improve upon our weaknesses.

It was interesting to hear over these last couple of days the number of young people, then young people, who were amazed that they had the opportunity to work in President REAGAN's administration. Sixty-nine years old when he took office, it seemed that he gravitated toward young people. Now being able to recite their wonderful experiences again, a tribute to a man who had a great history.

We will always remember him as the man who tore down the Iron Curtain. He did it with a kind of leadership and integrity but sternness and determinedness. I will simply say no one will ever forget him challenging Mr. Gorbachev by saying, "open this gate!" and, "Mr. Gorbachev, tear down this wall!" We are better for it. He did it with a sternness but also with an attitude of peace.

I am grateful also for the shining example of the wonderful relationship between him and his wife Nancy, the great love that they shared and the fact that they were married for some 52 years. Might I share with you some words that he wrote in 1983 on their 31st wedding anniversary as he was riding on Air Force One, and might I commend to you Nancy's book, "I Love You, RONNIE," published in 2000, but hear these words. He wrote:

> I more than love you, I'm not whole without you. You are life itself to me. When you are gone I'm waiting for you to return, so I can start living again.

That is a true testament to the value of marriage and partnership and they did it unabashedly and without fear.

Mrs. REAGAN wrote in 1989, "Some of the reporters who wrote about me felt that our marriage was at least partly an act. But it wasn't and it isn't." And I believe her.

Finally, in 1998 she told *Vanity Fair*:

> Our relationship is very special. We were very much in love and still are. When I say my life began with RONNIE, well, it's true. It did. I can't imagine life without him.

Mr. Speaker, I started by saying that is why I cherish this institution, because it allows us now to come together again, not wearing any partisan hat but simply saying that we are Americans. I do not know if she would mind me saying this, but my daughter is now 24, I remember her as a small girl, very small, and she always used to refer to RONALD REAGAN as the grandfather. I had to kind of clarify that for her, but it was out of the mouth of a child that described him as such.

And so I simply leave you with the idea of why we have come today to be able to honor this American President. It is because he did leave us with a sense of optimism and an ability to go forward, to look at the troubles that we might be facing both to the left and to the right and forward and back but yet to say that we are determined to succeed. I would only say that in his passing, let us maintain the legacy of optimism for this country. "We are the showcase of the future. And it is within our power to mold that future, this year and for decades to come. It can be as grand and as great as we make it. No crisis is beyond the capacity of our people to solve, no challenge too great," the words of RONALD REAGAN on January 5, 1974.

With that, Mr. Speaker, I simply say, farewell. And though we say farewell to a great and wonderful American President, his legacy will live on—that America's future is founded on our optimism, our belief in freedom and democracy and, certainly this day on our understanding that we all are Americans.

So when we return to work next week, I hope this House will be inspired by the leadership of RONALD REAGAN instead of mired in the partisan politics and a lack of integrity that have too often affected our work as of late. We should be inspired by his patriotism and devotion to our country. Moreover, we should remember his faith, his optimism, and his unwavering commitment to his convictions as we do the work of the American people.

President REAGAN had a calm speaking voice and forceful diction that earned him the title of the Great Communicator. This task was surely the work of a leader of fortitude and commitment to the betterment of our diplomatic relations with that Nation.

Mr. REAGAN's efforts and tenacity contributed greatly to the end of the cold war. His policies included strong support of the U.S. military and the doctrine of "peace through strength."

In a few days it will be exactly 17 years to the day that President REAGAN stood at the Brandenburg Gate in what was then West Berlin, Germany, in which he famously proclaimed:

General Secretary Gorbachev, if you seek peace, if you seek prosperity for the Soviet Union and Eastern Europe, if you seek liberalization: Come here to this gate! Mr. Gorbachev, open this gate! Mr. Gorbachev, tear down this wall!"

The speech was made to the free people of West Berlin, but it was clearly audible on the East side of the Wall, and soon those words would help make it possible that the people of East and West Berlin could finally hear each other. For all of his achievements and acclaim, I am certain that President REAGAN's greatest accomplishment will be the demise of the Soviet Union. As Margaret Thatcher said, he was the man who "won the cold war without firing a shot."

The world President REAGAN faced when he came into office in 1981 was very different from the world we see today. Today the United States is the unquestioned superpower of the world, but two decades ago this world was dominated by the struggle between two superpowers: the United States and the Soviet Union. President REAGAN came into office with his own vision on how this great struggle could be dealt with. He succeeded in maintaining the standoff with the Soviet Union so that the world did not have to witness the consequences of a brutal nuclear war. He fought the Soviet Union indirectly wherever they sought to threaten the freedom of the world's people. In Afghanistan he mobilized our allies and our resources in the region to ensure that the Soviets would not have a stranglehold on the continent of Asia. The Reagan doctrine succeeded in a time where grave danger not only threatened our Nation, but indeed the fate of the world as we know it.

President REAGAN used his great communication skills to help end the cold war without the necessity of another world war. As with his speech at the Brandenburg Gate, President REAGAN inspired people throughout the world to believe that freedom and prosperity were indeed possible.

President REAGAN made Americans believe again that our Nation was the greatest on Earth and that we would indeed be victorious. Finally, his words made the leadership of the Soviet Union believe that they were fighting from a side of weakness, that the good of our beliefs and our national system would prevail. His words were inspirational two decades ago, but today they have been proven true. The Soviet Union no longer threatens our world, and we must always pay tribute to President REAGAN for that accomplishment.

At a time when war and bloodshed are one of the biggest thoughts on the minds of Americans, the history of President REAGAN's relationship with his wife is a refreshing thought that has restored a feeling of compassion in our hearts.

Relationships—whether they be diplomatic, spousal, or platonic, have not been placed in the greatest light as of late in America. We have been marred by accounts of human rights abuse and other examples of a disregard for the rights and personhood of our neighbors.

In contrast, the relationship between RONALD and Nancy Reagan was one of the greatest love stories in U.S. Presidential history. The two were utterly devoted to each other, and Nancy was said to have been a key adviser and confidante during her husband's two-term Presidency from 1981 to 1989. Though they were married 52 years, Nancy has told with great pain how her husband did not recognize her during the final years of his struggle with Alzheimer's disease.

Mr. Speaker, I support the resolution offered by my colleague, Representative Lewis of California, saluting a leader whose influence and positive legacy will live on with not only the American people but the entire international community. Thank you, Mr. President, and may you rest in peace. May your family find strength and courage through these very difficult days.

I conclude now by reciting some of President REAGAN's spirited words to us as Americans:

> The house we hope to build is ... not for my generation, but for yours. It is your future that matters. And I hope that when you're my age, you'll be able to say as I have been able to say: We lived in freedom, we lived lives that were a statement, not an apology.
>
> The challenge of statesmanship is to have the vision to dream of a better, safer world and the courage, persistence, and patience to turn that dream into reality.
> —March 8, 1985

> We have every right to dream heroic dreams. Those who say that we're in a time when there are no heroes, they just don't know where to look.
> —January 20, 1981

> We are the showcase of the future. And it is within our power to mold that future—this year and for decades to come. It can be as grand and as great as we make it. No crisis is beyond the capacity of our people to solve; no challenge too great.
> —January 5, 1974

Again, farewell, Mr. President. May your optimism live on.

Hon. Jerry Lewis

OF CALIFORNIA

Mr. Speaker, the eloquence of our colleagues from both sides of the aisle reflects the best of RONALD REAGAN. His leadership indeed recognized that there was little partisanship when you were really working toward solving problems for America's people.

Hon. Wally Herger

OF CALIFORNIA

Mr. Speaker, some of my first impressions of RONALD REAGAN were back in the fifties when I was yet in grammar school, and I observed him as he hosted "General Electric Theater." And then again I remember him just after graduating from high school in 1964 when he campaigned and spoke out for Barry Goldwater. RONALD REAGAN stood for ideals that simply were not being expressed anyplace else.

The appropriately named "Reagan revolution" was precisely that. He was one of the main reasons I ran for political office. In the late seventies, we heard our leaders talk about lowering expectations and that the good times were over and that our Nation was in a "general malaise." This was mirrored in high inflation that reached 10 to 12 percent, unemployment rates that were over 10 percent, and a prime interest rate that reached as high as 21.5 percent.

But then in stepped RONALD REAGAN saying America could do better and America would do better. When RONALD REAGAN said it, you believed it. His vision of the "shining city on the hill" gave hope to countless millions of Americans. Back then, for me, as a small business owner who grew up on a ranch, the American dream appeared endangered by high taxes and big government. In California, property taxes were doubling and tripling. With RONALD REAGAN, there was someone we could rally around. His hope, his direction, and his moral clarity gave us all renewed energy. RONALD REAGAN had the great ability to say what so many of us were thinking, what we were thinking about our national budget, about our national defense, about taxes; and, yes, about a better America.

The first time I ever met RONALD REAGAN was in 1980 when I was running for the State assembly in California and I journeyed to Simi Valley to get my picture taken with him. I can remember growing up hearing my mother talking about President Franklin Roosevelt, how she would listen to President Roosevelt on the radio during the Great Depression and during World War II. President Roosevelt gave hope to her generation. RONALD REAGAN was to my generation what FDR was to my parents.

In Congress I had the privilege of meeting RONALD REAGAN six or seven times. Just being around President REAGAN was inspiring. He lit up the room. To those of us who believed strongly in the American dream, in traditional values and the Judeo-Christian faith, RONALD REAGAN was indeed a shining light in the city when there seemed to be none. His spirit will live on in the hearts of Americans. He was truly one of our Nation's greatest Presidents.

RONALD REAGAN, thank you for all you have done for me. Thank you for all you have done for our great Nation.

Hon. Steve Israel

OF NEW YORK

Mr. Speaker, I rise in joining my colleagues on both sides of the aisle in mourning the loss of President REAGAN. I did not agree with the President on every issue, but there were three values that he exuded which I do share deeply: first, a respect for the democratic process and the building of consensus to move us forward and to make us safer; second, a fundamental belief in a strong military and a strong defense; and third, as we have heard before, a boundless optimism about America's capacity and our potential and our role in making the world safe for democracy.

I never had the privilege of personally meeting President REAGAN, but I did work here in Congress during his administration for a former Member of Congress, and I have a sense that even tonight, President REAGAN and former Speaker Tip O'Neill are looking down upon this House with rather wry and proud smiles wishing us the best as we join together—as they joined together—to move our country not to the left, not to the right but forward, and they guide us not from the left, not from the right, they guide us from above.

Several months ago, I had the privilege of participating in an issues forum in New York with Ronald Reagan, Jr. Tonight my thoughts and prayers are with him and the entire Reagan family as they mourn the loss of a father and a husband and as America mourns the loss of a President.

Hon. David Dreier

OF CALIFORNIA

Mr. Speaker, let me say at the outset I think it is extraordinarily appropriate that the gentleman, the former mayor of Simi, CA, the home of the Ronald Reagan Library and what will be the final resting place for Nancy and RONALD REAGAN, is presiding over this institution at this moment. I would also like to thank my friend, the true dean of our California congressional delegation, for yielding me this time.

A generation was inspired by RONALD REAGAN is what we have been hearing, but it was really a generation, and then some, inspired by RONALD REAGAN. The gentleman from California (Mr. Lewis) heard RONALD REAGAN's speech on behalf of Barry Goldwater in 1964. Two years later, RONALD REAGAN was elected Governor of California, and 2 years after that the gentleman from California (Mr. Lewis) was elected to the California State Assembly, serving 6 of the 8 years that RONALD REAGAN was Governor of California. In fact, he is the only Republican Member here who did serve while RONALD

REAGAN was Governor of California. He went on to inspire many others. I am among them.

I was pleased this morning to be able to include in the *Record* very thoughtful remarks that were provided by a great American, George Shultz, who Sunday afternoon read his statement to me and I read it into the *Record* this morning, and I would like to commend it to my colleagues because it talks about the vision and the perspective that RONALD REAGAN offered in a wide range of areas. RONALD REAGAN made it very clear that the Republican Party is the party of ideas. We constantly hear about RONALD REAGAN being the Great Communicator, but he had a message to communicate. Members on both sides of the aisle have talked about that message.

To me it embraced four very simple points: his commitment to a free economy, limited government, a strong national defense, and personal freedom. Those are the bases from which RONALD REAGAN made his decisions on public policy issues, but he had those deeply rooted principles. And because they were so deeply rooted, he was able to communicate them extraordinarily well. Why? Because it came right from the heart. It came right from his heart.

We have heard a lot of very serious statements made about RONALD REAGAN; but, of course, one of the most memorable things as people talked about his ability to communicate was his ability to communicate with that amazing sparkle, that twinkle in his eye. There were some wonderful things that he said that were able to, in fact, break the ice and really entertain all of us. Remember, it was RONALD REAGAN who said, "Hard work never killed anybody, but I figured, why take the chance?" It was RONALD REAGAN who after he had been hit by that bullet, right up Constitution Avenue here at the Washington Hilton when the statement was made to him shortly thereafter that the government was working as usual and he looked up and said, "Why would that make me happy?"

There was, of course, his last speech which really stuck with me. It was February 3, 1994, and the Republican National Committee was having a dinner over here at the Pension Building, and RONALD REAGAN was obviously quite elderly then, and the speech was delivered literally months before he wrote his famous letter in November of that year to the American people stating that he had Alzheimer's. So when he stood up at this meeting, I remember that Bill Clinton had been elected President of the United States the year before, and as we Republicans were gathering, we were poised to win our majority, and RONALD REAGAN stood up without a great deal of strength for this speech.

He stepped up to the lectern, and he looked out at the audience, and he said:

> Well, I flew into town today to give this speech this evening, and as we came in, we circled the White House, and as I looked out the window, I looked down there, and there was everything just as I remembered it, the South Lawn, the Rose Garden, David Gergen.

David Gergen was at that moment working for President Bill Clinton. And we knew then that even though the President was obviously not in the most robust of health, that sparkle continued. He still had that amazingly wonderful sense of humor.

I see my friend from San Diego, Mr. Lowery, here on the House floor. I was very pleased to, along with Bill Lowery and 51 others, be part of the Reagan revolution. We came here to the House of Representatives, elected in November 1980, and we made RONALD REAGAN an honorary member of our class in 1980, and that is because he was leader of the revolution that brought all of us here and allowed us to vigorously pursue those goals that we shared in common.

We stand on his shoulders. George W. Bush stands on his shoulders. The similarities, to me, are so striking. The "ism" that RONALD REAGAN stood up to was communism. The "ism" that George W. Bush is standing up to is terrorism. RONALD REAGAN had broad, across-the-board tax cuts to stimulate economic growth. That is exactly what we have done. He did it in 1981. George W. Bush started it in 2001. The party of ideas is strong and vibrant. It is doing extraordinarily well, and it is the vision that RONALD REAGAN put forward.

I thank my friend for taking this time, and I thank my colleagues on the other side of the aisle who are joining in this very important recognition of one of our Nation's greatest leaders.

Hon. Charles W. Stenholm
OF TEXAS

Mr. Speaker, it is not just nostalgia that makes us remember President RONALD REAGAN especially so fondly upon the occasion of his death. Politics, ideology, geography aside, there is a mark of leadership and charisma which undeniably stamps some men and women.

RONALD REAGAN was one of those men whose leadership was felt by all who encountered him. When President REAGAN first came to office, he quickly understood that enacting his economic agenda would require bipartisan support in Congress, which was under Democratic control, 242 to 192 and 1 absent. It took 52 bipartisan votes to enact anything, and President REAGAN understood that.

I met with the President on several occasions as he sought to build that bipartisan coalition to pass his legislation. I met with President REAGAN one on one in the Oval Office as well as on Air Force One, and for a second-termer in 1981 that was pretty tall cotton for a Jones County cotton farmer.

In 1981, I was just in my second term and was a member of the Conservative Democratic Forum better known as the Boll Weevils, the precursor to today's Blue Dogs. In the very first month REAGAN was in office, he had to pass into law an increase in the debt limit, and so he invited me to meet with him. Now, mind you, this was the first major piece of legislation of the Reagan administration. In the past, prior to President REAGAN's being elected, Republicans had always opposed increasing the debt limit. Republicans had denounced Democrats for voting to increase the debt limit. So here was the first Republican President in many years coming to ask conservative Democrats for support in passing this very thing into law, something members of his own party had opposed on many occasions in the past.

We had a lengthy talk. The twinkle in the eye that many of those who had known him much better from California was there, and we finally struck a deal. We had an understanding that if the President could deliver 100 votes from Republicans, then we would do our best to deliver the necessary Democratic votes. President REAGAN more than held up his end of the bargain. He ultimately delivered 150 Republican votes. So in the spirit of bipartisanship and on a very tough issue, REAGAN successfully secured the votes he needed, from Democrats and Republicans, and got the increase in the debt limit, just as he and we needed it.

I was proud to have several opportunities to work with the President in the months and years ahead to build bipartisan coalitions, especially on his economic agenda. I still proudly display a picture in my home in Abilene, TX, of President REAGAN signing the 1981 tax bill. I got one of the pens and it's one I treasure.

REAGAN had very strong principles and very strong values. We know what they were. But he also understood that in order to govern, it was important to find a middle ground. And I was lucky enough to be in the middle of many of those compromises.

One of his greatest strengths was his ability to communicate, a skill that he used to great effect when courting votes in Congress. His courting of Members of Congress was the best of any President I have served with, and I have now been privileged to serve with five. If the Members can imagine a second-termer sitting in the Roosevelt Room in the White House talking about some issues with the President's Cabinet members and others and having the President walk in unannounced and put his hands on his shoulder; some telephone calls that we had many times when there was a vote and the President had to work the phones like no President that I have seen since, rounding up the votes, and he was very effective at doing that.

President REAGAN's private and public demeanors were the same. What one saw was what one got. That is the mark of a great leader.

RONALD REAGAN was a very decent man, and he understood how he could use his office to make a difference in countless lives. This aspect of his personality was always very clear to me because it was this decency, this understanding of the power of the office that gave me the most rewarding opportunity I had to work with President REAGAN.

The context was very personal. In May 1983, I was contacted by the grandfather of Ashley Bailey, a baby girl in Abilene, TX, who needed a liver transplant to survive. At that time organ donations and organ transplants were not as common as now, and the organ donation system was not organized to the extent it is today.

I spoke to President REAGAN's folks about it to ask for his help in getting the baby girl a new liver. Shortly after receiving my letter, President REAGAN used his weekly radio address to publicize Ashley's situation and encourage all Americans to fill out organ donor cards. He also called Ashley's mother, Annette.

Unfortunately, the President's plea did not result in finding a liver in time to save Baby Ashley, but it did end up saving the lives of dozens of other babies who needed liver transplants. President REAGAN later started a national organ donor awareness program, which led to the designation of National Organ Donation Awareness Week every April. To this day I consider this one of the highlights of my 25 years in Congress.

REAGAN knew how to disagree without being disagreeable, to rise above politics, and these qualities, unfortunately, are rare today. President REAGAN and House Speaker Tip O'Neill, the Massachusetts liberal, were good friends who got along very well during their years of service together. They never lost their philosophical convictions, and they never let those philosophical convictions hijack their understanding that America's democracy requires respect for all opinions and a practical determination to work out our differences for the good of the country.

President REAGAN spoke of hope and a better tomorrow. He reminded us that we live in the greatest country in the world, and he made us believe it and believe in ourselves. He believed that we, as Americans, had a special duty to promote peace and freedom for the rest of the world. He always told us that for America, the best was yet to come.

It is good for all of us to remember RONALD REAGAN's optimism, his kindheartedness, and his cordiality. As we remember this great man this week, it would do us good to remember how we should behave today and in the future.

Hon. Darrell E. Issa

OF CALIFORNIA

Mr. Speaker, on this second week of June, 17 years ago, President RONALD REAGAN stood in the then-divided city of Berlin and called on Soviet President Mikhail Gorbachev to "tear down this wall!" Then, as perhaps now, critics did what they so often do. They cast aside the genuineness of his statement and, in fact, said that his speech was a publicity ploy. The Soviets and East Germans called it an infringement of East German sovereignty, an unwarranted meddling by the American President.

Two years later the wall came down.

Mr. Speaker, President REAGAN was a leader with the foresight and strong conviction to get things done. He believed in America so much that he made America believe in itself again. He valued freedom, especially for those who had none. He understood that for America to be great, it first had to be good. He understood that America's problems, the malaise of the years preceding his Presidency, were simply America's not understanding how great it was and how great it could be.

Mr. Speaker, I was just a soldier during the period leading up to Mr. REAGAN's becoming President REAGAN, but I was a businessman starting a business from scratch when President REAGAN came to office, and I recognized overnight that this was a special time to be an American, a time when we had a President who was saying that an American hero was somebody who took chances, who made a difference for the world, but particularly somebody who cared enough to work those extra hours and to care enough about his country.

RONALD REAGAN knew America. He knew what was right about our Nation. What was right about our Nation and what was right about America would set the world in a better direction. RONALD REAGAN led America, and the rest of the world became a freer place. Under his leadership we headed toward more than 400 million people in 27 countries finding a freedom they did not have. Today the soldiers of some of those democracies now fight side by side in Iraq and Afghanistan.

President REAGAN showed us that our freedom and our determination can tear down walls.

Many Speakers will come here tonight, and they will talk of how profoundly President REAGAN affected them, and I would be no different, but perhaps I can be slightly different tonight by saying that the only way to honor President REAGAN's legacy is to take it to the next step. Today we are trying to do that for people in the Arab and Muslim world, and we have not finished that job. Today communist China still denies rights to the people of its own country and is attempting to stifle the freedom and independence of Hong Kong. Today Cuba, to our south, is still a communist nation, having little or no respect for the rule of law and for its people.

All of these and more need to be part of the American struggle because, Mr. Speaker, only if we determine that America's greatness will be in our willingness to set a course for the world in a positive way, not to dominate, but, in fact, to liberate, I think that is the legacy that Mr. REAGAN would want.

And if I can take a personal liberty on behalf of Mrs. Reagan, I believe that continuing to look for a cure to the terrible illness that plagued President REAGAN for his last 10 years of life and promote and continue stem cell research consistent with what this body has passed would also be a tremendous addition to the Reagan legacy.

I am determined to work for both of these, and I ask this body to take those steps to free those who were not freed under President REAGAN, and to commit itself to the research to end the terrible illness that the Reagan family has suffered under for 10 long years.

Hon. Melissa A. Hart

OF PENNSYLVANIA

I think like most of us, we all have our own different, but very similar, inspirations from President REAGAN. I first heard about RONALD REAGAN probably around the dinner table when I was a kid when he was Governor of California and when he first decided to run for President. But I had grown up in an era that was pretty difficult. I grew up thinking assassinations were normal, remembering the assassinations of Martin Luther King and Robert Kennedy; that government corruption was normal, remembering Watergate; and that a failure of government to properly serve its people was normal. Very high inflation, for example.

But I remember also the things that my dad and my mom and my grandfather, who was an immigrant, told me about America. They were patriotic people. RONALD REAGAN was a patriotic man. And I heard his message, and it resonated with me, because it was something that I had always heard at home, but, unfortunately, had not seen much in practice in government. I became interested, and, as I guess somewhat of a precocious seventh-grader, wrote an editorial in my middle school newspaper supporting RONALD REAGAN for President. He did not win that time, but it was not because I did not try. But that legacy and what he stood for stuck with me.

My family paid attention. I was very fortunate. Our normal dinner conversation often dealt with politics. So when I turned 18 in 1980, RONALD REAGAN was running for President, and I volunteered. I found out that politics is a means of achieving a greater good and could be respected. I was hooked. He showed for us the America that we all knew could exist. It was the America that my parents believed in. It was the America we knew we could get back.

RONALD REAGAN said:

{I}t's not my intention to do away with government. It is rather to make it work—work with us, not over us; to stand by our side, not ride on our back. Government can and must provide opportunity, not smother it; foster productivity, not stifle it.

Government is to walk with us. That is the most important thing, and it is important because it is the American dream.

After 10 years of volunteering on campaigns, and after RONALD REAGAN was elected that first time, through law school, through the private practice of law, I took part in the process in a big way, to dream big dreams, and to take some risks. So at 28 I ran for the State senate, unseated an incumbent, and had the opportunity to pursue the same dream.

RONALD REAGAN said America is too great for small dreams. There are many of us here in

Congress today who agree with him. Let us in government remember him and his legacy and act on that legacy.

Hon. Ralph M. Hall

OF TEXAS

Mr. Speaker, I came to the U.S. Congress in 1981, the same year President REAGAN was sworn in as our President. I examined the brochures that he ran on and looked at the brochures that I ran on, and I found them to be almost identical: jobs and security, and jobs meant dignity; a strong military; a concern for the unborn; strong second amendment rights. All of those things we totally agreed upon. At that time I was a Democrat. I was a member of the Boll Weevils and the Conservative Democratic Forum.

We have heard others speak here before us tonight and know of the respect and admiration that we all had for President REAGAN. I had the pleasure of going out to Camp David with him and spent times and hours, and had the opportunity for discussions, and we discussed everything from the problems of the day to his times in the movies. He was a good, down-to-earth guy that you could talk to.

I just know that he knew of our needs. He knew that our military had atrophied away. He knew that we needed to have an injection there, and that United Airlines could employ one of our pilots the minute they graduated and had spent their time. He knew that the enlisted men, 35 percent of them were eligible for food stamps, and he knew something had to be done there. I think he is responsible for the strong position that we have, the strong financial position we have, the strong geopolitical position we have in the world.

I know that I have had a lot of occasions to visit with him. Jim Baker was in his Cabinet at that time, and Jim and I had been longtime friends when I was 10 years in the Texas Senate. I knew Jim Baker, Hines Baker, Rex Baker and all of his folks. That gave me access to President REAGAN. I had been a Navy pilot with George Bush. He was his Vice President, so I had access to the President, and I enjoyed that access, enjoyed visits with him over there.

One time I went in and the President said, "Congressman Hall, what would it take to get you to vote for my budget cuts?" I said, "Well, Mr. President, I have a brother who always wanted to be a Federal judge." He said, "Well, that should not be any problem." He turned to George Bush and he turned to Jim Baker and said, "Can you get one of Ralph's brothers approved by the Senate and go through confirmation there?" They said, "I think we can." I said, "Well, wait just a minute, Mr. President; he is not a lawyer." And the President got a big kick out of that. He never really forgot that. Any time he would see me out in a group, he would come shake hands with me. But he liked me. Sometimes he really could not think of my name, but he would say, how is your brother. He liked my brother because he was not a lawyer.

I just think that this country is stronger today and this country is great today because of the gifts of RONALD REAGAN, for the time he gave us, for the honesty that he brought to the office, for the common man background that he had, that he understood frailty of men and women and their need for help.

I am honored to have known him. I am very lucky to have been a friend of RONALD REAGAN.

Hon. Jerry Lewis

OF CALIFORNIA

Mr. Speaker, we appreciate the comments of our colleague from Texas. I am reminded of that tragic day when RONALD REAGAN, shortly after he became President in March 1981, and the assassination attempt took place. As they rolled him on a gurney into the emergency room, he looked up and said to his wife, "Honey, I forgot to duck." RONALD REAGAN, a man who was always ready to try to calm down the other person and make sure they felt OK, our President.

Hon. Bob Goodlatte
OF VIRGINIA

Asked in 1980 what Americans saw in him, RONALD REAGAN replied, "Would you laugh if I told you that I think maybe they see themselves?" Mr. Speaker, hardly would we laugh.

A few years ago I had an opportunity to visit Rancho del Cielo, President REAGAN's beloved "Ranch in the Sky." The home reflects the man. It does not feel like a museum; quite the opposite, with Nancy's and his TV trays still standing by their respective recliners, both facing the old black-and-white television. It seems they have just gone out for an afternoon ride and will return at any moment.

At purchase the ranch was a mere 600 square feet. REAGAN labored diligently with his own hands to remodel and expand it. Even so, the only grand thing about it is the natural surroundings. Asked once to explain the ranch's almost magnetic appeal for him, REAGAN replied with a quote from Psalms: "I look to the hills from whence cometh my strength."

Mikhail Gorbachev, Margaret Thatcher, and Queen Elizabeth were among the notables that he hosted there. Gorbachev is said to have been disappointed by the humble ranch, knowing the lavish palaces of European leaders. However, it is fitting that the place at which REAGAN felt most at ease disarmed the world's dignitaries.

He always related best with the common man, yet he was far from ordinary. To the contrary, he lived an extraordinary life which had a profound impact on the landscape of our Nation and the greater span of human history.

He left us on the eve of the 60th anniversary of the D-day liberation, and almost 20 years ago to the day of one of his most beloved speeches on the cliffs overlooking the beaches of Normandy. Looking out at faces wizened by time, calling them the "boys of Pointe du Hoc," REAGAN offered a compelling picture of how these young men, freedom's army, struck a death knell to the nazism and fascism which had a stranglehold on formerly-free Europe.

He extended this same moral clarity to the great conflict of his day, possessing a steadfast commitment not just to containing communism, but to transcend it, and transcend it he did.

Bursting on the national political scene during the 1964 Presidential campaign with his now famed "A Time for Choosing" speech, he spoke to a divided and searching Nation:

> You and I have a rendezvous with destiny. We will preserve for our children this, the last best hope of man on earth, or we will sentence them to take the first step into a thousand years of darkness. If we fail, at least let our children and our children's children say of us we justified our brief moment here. We did all that could be done.

These words reflected his eternal optimism not just in America, this great experiment in self-governance, but in Americans.

In 1979, we were in the throes of a nationwide recession, the Soviets had invaded Afghanistan, and the hostage crisis in Iran dominated the nightly news. Yet REAGAN saw us as a "shining city on a hill," the hope of the world.

Reflecting on his death, may we find consolation in his own words spoken to a grieving Nation in the wake of the *Challenger* disaster, whose crew perished on his watch. They, and now he, has "'slipped the surly bonds of earth' to 'touch the face of God.'"

In his farewell address from the Oval Office, a place where he refused to remove his suit jacket out of a humble respect for the post he held, REAGAN described how he envisioned the shining city he had invoked countless times. He went on to observe this of his time in office:

> We weren't just marking time. We made a difference. We made the city stronger. We made the city freer, and we left her in good hands. All in all, not bad, not bad at all.

"Not bad" reflects the modesty of the man, but not the magnitude of his accomplishments. In rebuilding the military and facing down the tyranny of communism, calling the Soviet Union the evil empire that it was, and calling on President Gorbachev to tear down the Berlin Wall, in restoring our faith in the free enterprise system through cutting taxes and encouraging innovation, and, most important, in raising our spirits, he made us proud to be Americans.

He set this Nation on a new course that still inspires us today. We have a right to dream great dreams, he said, because after all, we are Americans. Yes, Mr. President, we do see ourselves in you. We still dream great dreams of freedom and opportunity around the world. And I am honored to pay tribute tonight to President REAGAN, the greatest President of the last century.

Hon. Jerry Lewis
OF CALIFORNIA

Mr. Speaker, I very much appreciate my colleague from Texas joining with us in this discussion this evening of perhaps America's greatest President, RONALD REAGAN. In his words, RONALD REAGAN said:

> Some argue that we should encourage democratic change in right-wing dictatorships, but not in Communist regimes. Well, to accept this preposterous notion—as some well-meaning people have—is to invite the argument that once countries achieve a nuclear capability, they should be allowed an undisturbed reign of terror over their own citizens. We reject this course.

As RONALD REAGAN rebuilt America, his defense budget designed to restrengthen our country's ability to defend itself, he stared down the evil empire and negotiated a nuclear arms treaty with Gorbachev. As two enemies became close friends, think of that, two enemies became close friends, Gorbachev was heard to say, "Who would have thought it?"

Hon. Dave Weldon
OF FLORIDA

Mr. Speaker, I was a young intern in 1984. I had been through medical school and college and had not really followed politics much, but I was rotating through the cardiologist service. And I remember asking one of our attendees who he was going to vote for in the 1984 election. RONALD REAGAN was running against Walter Mondale. He said he was voting for RONALD REAGAN because he had a wife and three kids at home and the tax cuts that REAGAN had put through were putting about $200 a month more in his pocket. And it was just making it easier for him to take care of his family.

I had not followed politics much, but I was very much impressed by Rick Monsor's comments and began to read more and more about the policies of RONALD REAGAN. And over time I came to realize, like millions of other Americans, that his economic policies had been reducing taxes on Americans, actually had precipitated a great economic recovery. It had resulted in a doubling of revenue into the Federal Treasury, a dramatic reduction in unemployment. It was essentially the right economic policy. And it is an economic policy that we still follow to this day.

Of course, RONALD REAGAN is most well-known for ending the cold war, precipitating the breakup of the Soviet Union, and allowing millions of people in Eastern Europe to taste freedom—freedom of speech, freedom of religion, freedom of assembly—for the first time in their lives. Millions of people besides those of us here in America were positively affected by the policies of RONALD REAGAN.

But what is most dear to my heart about RONALD REAGAN was his indefatigable optimism, belief in the power of American ingenuity, the American spirit, the can-do attitude. At the time that he took office, we were facing, as many of us know, terrible problems with inflation and a declining economy and as well our defenses were in decline. It was not only his policies that moved us in a positive direction but his attitudes and beliefs that lifted our Nation and helped us to move on to better things.

And he once said the following:

> {W}hatever else history may say about me when I'm gone, I hope it will record that I appealed to your best hopes, not your worst fears, to your confidence rather than your doubts. My dream is that you will travel the road ahead with liberty's lamp guiding your steps and opportunity's arm steadying your way.

President REAGAN, your desire has become a reality. You did appeal to our best hopes and not our worst fears. And your confidence in us is leading us in the right direction today. We salute your great accomplishments.

Hon. Sherwood Boehlert
OF NEW YORK

Mr. Speaker, earlier today I joined my colleagues in voting for a resolution expressing the profound regret and sorrow of the House of Representatives on the death of Ronald W. Reagan, former President of the United States of America. I did not cast that vote as one Member of this, the people's House, nor as a Congressperson for 654,000 New Yorkers who it is my privilege to represent here in our Nation's Capital. Rather, that vote reflected the profound regret and sorrow felt far beyond the borders of one district, one State, one Nation.

It is illustrative of the sincere sentiment of a world community in collective mourning. President Reagan was so much more than a head of state. He was an inspiration to all whose lives he touched, not just by his words, which reached across the great divides that separate people, but by his deeds which always sought to bring people together in common cause.

The President's noble achievements, and there were so many, have been and will continue to be chronicled by historians for time immemorial.

So many of my colleagues who preceded and those who will follow have been and will be eloquent in their tributes to the lasting legacy of this great man, and deservedly so. For my part, I simply want to add a listing of the words which come immediately to mind when recalling President Reagan: words like integrity, conviction, honor, faith, grace, dignity, friendship, humor, values, honest, humble. The list of positives in the life of this man of principle and character is endless.

To President Reagan and his beloved partner, Nancy, who was always at his side and in his heart, I am but one of so many who say a heartfelt thank you for leading by example and serving so many so well for so long. You will always be an inspiration and you will always be in our thoughts and prayers.

Hon. Joe Barton

OF TEXAS

Mr. Speaker, I was driving down to Corpus Christi last Saturday afternoon with my wife, Terry, and her daughter Lindsey and her cousin Jackie and Terry's family for a brief family vacation when my staffer Andy Black called me on the telephone and asked, "Have you heard the news that President Reagan died this afternoon?" And I said, "No, I have not heard that," but we immediately switched on the radio; and sure enough, there was a news bulletin from California that President Reagan had passed away.

And so as we continued to drive down to Corpus, I began to reminisce about the President. My mind went back to the late seventies when this country was mired in recession and interest rates were sky high and we had hostages in Iran and there was a spirit of pessimism that America could not be great anymore. And Governor Reagan came out of California and announced for the Presidency and said that there was hope, that not only could we be great, but we would be greater again. And that inspired me to campaign for him to be President of the United States in the 1980 election.

And the night that he won in November 1980, I dusted off an old White House Fellows application and changed the date and signed it and mailed it in. White House Fellows is a program that takes young men and women from all over the country and puts them in positions to observe the workings of the Federal Government either in the White House or in the Cabinet agencies. The year that I applied there were about 1,600 applications, and I was fortunate enough to be 1 of like 15 or 16 that got selected.

I worked in the Department of Energy as a White House Fellow for Secretary of Energy James P. Edwards. In spring 1982 the Secretary called me into his office and said, "Joe, I am going over to the White House this afternoon for a Cabinet meeting. Would you like to go with me?" I said, "Mr. Secretary I would love to go with you." He said, "There is one thing: you cannot say anything. You can only sit in the back of the room and listen." So I said, "I promise."

We went to the White House, and they walked us into the Cabinet room, and I was seated directly behind Vice President Bush, who was seated directly across from President Reagan. The President came in from the Oval Office and shook hands with his Cabinet, and he reached over and got a handful of jellybeans out of a jar in the middle of the Cabinet table and ate the jellybeans and asked if anybody wanted them.

Then he said, "Gentlemen, what is the agenda for the day?" And a Cabinet Secretary said, "It is the Caribbean Basin Initiative and what to do about sugar quotas." The Secretary of Agriculture Jack Block raised his hand, he said, "Mr. President, you have tasked me to try to help the American farmers and we are doing the best that we can, but sugar prices are low in the world market. And I think it would be disastrous for American farmers if you let more sugar into our country." And the President said, "Thank you, Mr. Secretary."

Then the Secretary of State, I think it was General Haig, raised his hand and said, "Mr. President, I am the Secretary of State and you have tasked me with creating this Caribbean Initiative to help the emerging democracies in the Caribbean. Their largest export crop is sugar. It would really help my job as Secretary of State if you allowed more sugar to come into the United States." And the President said, "Thank you, Mr. Secretary."

He said, "Is there any other discussion?" The rest of the Cabinet just sat there. The President said, "Well, what we ought to do is take American wheat and Caribbean sugar and create cookies and create a cookie export, cookies for peace program maybe, to the Third World." The Cabinet chuckled about that; but he said, "Really, I have heard what is best for the State Department and I have heard what is best for the Agriculture Department, now I want you gentlemen to tell me what is best for America." And there were no cameras and he really said that.

And I just was absolutely inspired when he said it. I was sitting directly across from him behind Vice President Bush. Of course, I had been told I could not say anything, but when the President said that, "Gentlemen tell me what is best for America," it kind of jumped out from me, I said, "Right. That is why I voted for you." And, of course, the Secretary of Energy was aghast that I had said something. But the President looked over and he looked around the Vice President, he looked at me with a twinkle in his eye, did not say anything, he just smiled. And I knew then that that is why the American people trusted him, because he wanted to do whatever the issue was, what was right for America.

So when I finished my White House Fellows Program, I went back to Texas. And in 1984, John Tower announced that he was not going to run for the U.S. Senate, and Congressman Phil Gramm of the Sixth District announced that he was going to run for the Senate and Joe Barton announced that he was going to run for the Sixth District as a Republican. I wanted to be a part of the Reagan revolution in Washington.

I was very fortunate that I got elected that year. I primarily got elected because my entire campaign was Reagan-Gramm-Barton. And when people went to vote for President REAGAN and Senator Gramm, they also voted for me.

So now as a senior member of the majority in the House of Representatives, I simply hope that I can do what little I can to help foster the Reagan vision for America, which is always do what is right for America.

Hon. Earl Blumenauer
OF OREGON

As we observe the news, we have commentators rushing to give an assessment of the legacy of RONALD REAGAN. Conservative commentators will credit him with the fall of the former Soviet Union, new approaches to the economy, especially with tax-cutting strategies. And, in large measure, the rise of today's Republican Party can trace its roots to his leadership. His was a strong voice for the conservative perspective from corporate spokesperson to the governorship of our country's largest State, to two terms as our President.

There were, of course, areas of policy disagreement, some of which I had strong feelings about. There were also areas of mistakes, blunders for which President REAGAN characteristically and clearly assumed personal responsibility.

Balanced commentary will spotlight his pragmatic approaches as Governor and President; his ability to reach across party lines, to listen, to work, to add a human touch. There was his willingness to protect the economy and work with moderates, for instance, in both parties, even to the point of significant tax increases when he was faced with spiraling budget deficits and felt that it was important for our country.

I personally am content for history and the passage of time to sharpen the focus and place his entire career in perspective, but I am thinking this evening of how he became a leader and a symbol in his last years as he made a stark admission that he suffered from Alzheimer's disease. His wife Nancy became a champion in this great struggle to help lead the fight against Alzheimer's.

At a time when there are some who would put ideology ahead of meeting the needs of victims and families, Nancy Reagan stood tall and spoke out forcefully on the needs and benefits of stem cell research. Because of the affection for President REAGAN and the strength of Nancy Reagan, millions will someday be spared this suffering.

My personal memory of President REAGAN will be dominated by his almost magic ability to reach out and touch the American people. Along with Franklin Roosevelt and John Kennedy, RONALD REAGAN stands out as someone who could truly communicate with the American people. Would that the American public today be able to hear his calm, confident, friendly voice.

He has earned our respect and our thanks. The American people send their condolences and best wishes to Mrs. Reagan and the entire family.

Hon. Tom Osborne

OF NEBRASKA

I would like to express my appreciation to President REAGAN for his adherence to principle rather than to expediency; for standing firm against America's enemies when so many urged containment and conciliation; for displaying a sense of humor when events were grim; for being decent when indecency was so common; for realizing that an offensive strategy is superior to defense when confronted by grave danger; for restoring a troubled economy by putting more resources in the people's hands and less in the government's hands; for promoting optimism when many were discouraged; for his capacity to disagree without being disagreeable; for his willingness to reach out to members of both parties in uniting, rather than dividing, this country; for showing kindness in the face of hostility; for communicating so clearly with words from his own heart and mind, written by his own hands; for inspiring courage in others through his own courage; and finally, for displaying trust in God, rather than human institutions, through an unwavering faith in God's sovereignty and mercy.

Hon. Phil Gingrey

OF GEORGIA

Mr. Speaker, I am humbled to be one of the many Americans from all across our Nation who is paying tribute to President RONALD REAGAN this week.

Members of Congress, including myself, came to this floor in February to celebrate President REAGAN's 93d birthday, but it is with a sad heart tonight that we come to the floor of the House of Representatives to eulogize one of our greatest Presidents.

It was appropriate that RONALD REAGAN, a smalltown American from Dixon, IL, would make a career and a home in California, would represent the very best of American life. As Governor of California, President REAGAN became adept at representing the diverse nature of our country and cared deeply for all Americans.

As he is laid to rest, RONALD REAGAN's legacy for America will carry on eternally in the annals of history. Not since Lincoln and Roosevelt has one man touched the core of what it means to be an American: Through unity and strength, we can achieve peace; and through self-determination, responsibility and character, we can live the American dream.

RONALD REAGAN restored faith in America during one of our darkest hours of self-doubt. He gave us hope and promise when we needed it most. REAGAN's true legacy is the restoration of the dream that is America. Even with his passing, REAGAN's sense of hope and strength lives on.

As someone who has been inspired by his leadership and courage in the face of the evil empire of the Soviet Union, I deeply thank President

REAGAN for restoring our Nation's confidence and our hope.

God bless you, RONALD REAGAN, and may God continue to bless the America whose spirit of eternal optimism you helped renew.

Hon. John Linder
OF GEORGIA

On an October evening in 1975, before he announced that he would seek the Republican nomination for President, RONALD REAGAN addressed the 20th birthday celebration of the *National Review*. It was an uplifting and humorous speech until the end, when he somberly quoted Whittaker Chambers. Two decades earlier, Chambers had written:

> It is idle to talk of preventing the wreck of Western civilization, it is already a wreck from within. That is why we can do little more now than snatch a fingernail of a saint from the wrack, or a handful of ashes from the fagots, and bury them secretly in a flower pot against that day, ages hence, when a few men begin again to dare to believe that there once was something else, that something else is thinkable, and need some evidence of what it was, and the fortifying knowledge that there were those who, at the great nightfall, took loving thought to preserve the tokens of hope and truth.

Chambers spent 13 years in the service of the Soviet Union as a spy. He always believed that the world was engaged in a battle between the two great religions, communism and freedom. He believed that communism could not survive in a world where people believed in a higher power. Freedom, on the other hand, could not survive in a world where people did not. A nascent faith took hold in Chambers, and in 1937 he left communism for freedom. As he did so, he told his wife that he feared they were moving to the losing side.

This is what RONALD REAGAN was thinking of in October 1975. Communism was ascendant, and free people were losing their confidence, becoming fearful and timid of the future, and over the following 4 years, the Soviet Union increased its influence in 14 sovereign nations around the globe.

I was privileged to travel in his campaign plane in 1976 when he was in the Southeast, and in several meetings thereafter, with large numbers of people or small numbers of people, he always spoke less than anyone else in the room, enjoyed watching others have it out, and indeed, the next day he may not have remembered the name of everyone in the room, but he never forgot who he was.

Michael Deaver tells a wonderful story about walking on a street with RONALD REAGAN in 1978. By this time, he was easily recognized. A fellow kept inching close to him on the street wanting to say hello. REAGAN saw him, looked over, reached out his hand and said hello. The man said, "May I have your autograph, Mr. Milland?" REAGAN wrote Ray Milland on his paper and walked on. Michael Deaver said, "Why didn't you tell him who you were?" REAGAN said, "I know who I am. He wanted to meet Ray Milland."

That was pure RONALD REAGAN. He was not interested in making sure a stranger knew of his importance. He cared about making this one stranger happy.

Four years later he was President. He faced a military where one-third of our fleet was in dry dock, one-third of our planes could not fly for lack of spare parts. Our soldiers were practicing with pretend bullets. The economy had a 21 percent interest rate and a 14 percent inflation rate, and we were in trouble.

On January 20, 1981, President REAGAN addressed these challenges and then said this:

> [T]ogether with God's help we can and will resolve the problems which now confront us. And after all, why shouldn't we believe that? We are Americans.

Over the next 8 years, his economic policies took an economy from $2.5 trillion to $5 trillion. Revenues to the Federal Treasury went from $519 billion to $1.054 trillion. We created 20 million new jobs, and on the foreign front REAGAN was the first President since 1917 to ignore the bureaucracy and speak truth to evil. Eight years later the evil empire was crumbling, and the cold war was over.

I always thought that the biggest missed opportunity of the past 60 years was to not have celebrated the end of the cold war. RONALD REAGAN deserved that, and now he takes his leave.

It has been a very difficult decade for Mrs. Reagan and the family, but for those of us who love freedom, we remember a man who dared to believe that there once was something else, that something else was thinkable. He gave us evidence of what it was in the fortifying knowledge that he would be there at the great nightfall to take loving thought to preserve the tokens of hope and truth, and he was there. Not a bad final act for a B actor from Dixon, not bad at all.

Hon. Joe Wilson

OF SOUTH CAROLINA

Mr. Speaker, the world is grieving this week over the loss of a true American hero, President RONALD WILSON REAGAN. Words cannot describe the admiration and respect that I have for this great man. He led a revolution for free enterprise, for victory of democracy over communism and for national political realignment.

For many Americans in mourning, including myself, RONALD REAGAN was not just a good President, he was our President. He defined the honor and dignity of the Office of the Presidency, and he lifted the spirit of a Nation with his hope and joyfulness that sprang from an abiding faith in God and deeply held belief in the American dream.

I am grateful to have lived the Reagan revolution as a foot soldier promoting his vision of a dynamic economy, creating jobs through tax cuts and free markets, his support of America's military to achieve success in liberating millions by victory in the cold war, and his transformation of developing the Republican Party which today holds the majority of State legislative seats across America for the first time since 1952. He reinvigorated the Republican Party with optimism and vision.

He entered office during a time of doubt and despair and malaise, with the economy sputtering in a looming cold war that threatened our families. With these seemingly insurmountable problems he faced, many critics underestimated the former California Governor. Yet President REAGAN brought with him his conservative principles of individual freedom, limited government, personal responsibility, and "peace through strength." He also brought an optimism that America's greatest days were ahead of us.

Proving all of his detractors wrong, President REAGAN won the cold war, spurred the economy to robust growth and restored our national confidence and patriotism. As author and former Presidential staffer Peter Robinson said recently, "RONALD REAGAN was great, because RONALD REAGAN was right."

His straightforward speeches began to change minds across America, and many became Reagan Democrats. Today in my home State, Republicans hold most statewide offices, a complete turnaround that has occurred throughout the South thanks to the leadership of RONALD REAGAN.

He started a revolution where in 1980 Republicans in South Carolina held only 16 seats in the statehouse, and now there is a Republican supermajority of 76 out of 124 members. In the State senate, Republicans soared from 3 members in 1980 to now a supermajority of 27 of 46 members.

For 2 years I was honored to work in the Reagan administration as Deputy General Counsel to the Secretary of Energy Jim Edwards. I am a proud REAGAN alumni association member, and in 1990, because of his efforts to win the cold war and bring freedom to the oppressed people of the Soviet Union, I was asked by former Republican National Committee Chairman Lee Atwater to observe the first democratic elections in Bulgaria.

I saw first-hand the REAGAN legacy of peace and freedom, as Central and Eastern Europe rose from the ashes of communism to become strong democracies and American allies. The people I have met over the years from Bratislava, Slovakia, to Novosibirsk, Russia, regard President REAGAN as their own hero, a man who was unafraid to tell the truth about the evil empire.

While we mourn his passing, President RONALD REAGAN will never be forgotten. Children will read for centuries to come about the "Happy Warrior" who helped liberate tens of millions from totalitarian communism and restored America's position in the world as the "shining city on a hill."

Democracy is more widespread today in the world than any time in history due to President REAGAN's success of "peace through strength."

We cannot help but be reminded of his legacy as America faces similar battles today against the oppression of terrorism, and his critics deride our President, much as they did President REAGAN 20 years ago. America is under attack because we are a symbol of liberty in the world, and we must meet this challenge with the same courage and conviction that RONALD REAGAN had.

As he said in the 1964 Goldwater campaign in what has simply become known as "The Speech" and was earlier referenced by Chairman Lewis:

> You and I have a rendezvous with destiny. We will preserve for our children this, the last best hope of man on Earth, or we will sentence them to take the last step into a thousand years of darkness.

May God bless the REAGAN family, God bless our troops, and may God continue to bless America.

Hon. Jerry Lewis

OF CALIFORNIA

Mr. Speaker, I thank the gentleman from South Carolina (Mr. WILSON) very much for those very eloquent comments. I am reminded of the fact that in very simple form, RONALD REAGAN challenged the world on behalf of liberty, on behalf of peace. He had this remarkable relationship that developed over time with Mikhail Gorbachev. After he described the evil empire in straightforward terms, they began to communicate as leaders of two great countries. Indeed, together over time they reduced the nuclear threat by coming to agreement with one another.

It has been said earlier, but let me repeat the words of RONALD REAGAN:

> {Mr.} Gorbachev, if you seek peace, if you seek prosperity for the Soviet Union and Eastern Europe, if you seek liberalization: Come here to this gate! ... open this gate! Mr. Gorbachev, tear down this wall!

And indeed, within a couple of years, that wall came down. The East-West confrontation began to thaw; and between these two leaders, the world has seen a different kind of opportunity for peace. Today we face the challenge that involves the war on terrorism; and, indeed, that struggle is bound to last for years to come. It was the legacy of RONALD REAGAN that laid the foundation for America to best be prepared to defend itself for liberty and for freedom.

Hon. Ken Calvert

OF CALIFORNIA

Mr. Speaker, I rise today to pay tribute to one of the greatest Presidents in the history of our Nation, RONALD WILSON REAGAN, the 40th President of the United States.

He was a leader when our country needed it most, at a time when many Americans, including myself, had found ourselves disaffected by politics. His optimism gave our Nation the confidence and motivation to resume its place as a world leader.

I well remember the seventies after President Nixon's resignation and the pessimism that followed, when many Americans disassociated themselves from public service. RONALD REAGAN came onto the Presidential scene and reminded us that the "best was yet to come," that we are not to blame for the world's problems; and yet, as a great Nation, we had a place of responsibility and a role to play.

President REAGAN believed, as our Declaration of Independence states, "all men are created equal, that they are endowed by their creator with certain unalienable rights, life, liberty and the pursuit of happiness." Additionally, he knew better than most that strength comes from within, from the people. Therefore, first and foremost, REAGAN used his first term as President to bring these rights back to Americans starting with what was then known as Reaganomics.

He sought to restore America to the people by giving them back control of their pocketbooks. Uncle Sam was put on a diet of lower taxes, sound money and fewer regulations, allowing us the benefits of hard work. By the time that REAGAN left office, only two income brackets existed, with a top rate of 28 percent, compared to the 14 income brackets, with the top rate of 70 percent, that existed when he took office. Additionally, government was scaled back and redtape eliminated, allowing Americans to take care of themselves. As REAGAN was apt to say. "Government is not the solution to our problem; government is the problem."

He saw the rebuilding of America's military. After years of low morale and interest in the armed services, President REAGAN made a return to the pre-Vietnam days of faith and professional appeal in our military. As Commander in Chief, he oversaw the largest peacetime buildup of military spending in history, leading to the collapse of the Soviet Union and the end of the cold war. His revolutionary policies regarding investment in military technology, good training, and pay laid the foundation for a strong military that later claimed victory in Operation Desert Storm and continues to protect our national security well into the 21st century and, now, in the war on terror.

RONALD REAGAN lived a life worth living. He saw both the birth and death of communism. He won the hearts of Americans and world leaders. How? He believed in "peace through strength," and he lived his convictions based on experience, intuition, and love of life.

I will end with one of my favorite quotes:

> Above all, we must realize that no arsenal or no weapon in the arsenals of the world is so formidable as the will and moral courage of free men and women.

Thank you, President REAGAN. May God bless you and your family, and may God bless America.

Hon. Chris Chocola

OF INDIANA

Mr. Speaker, I thank the gentleman for yielding me this time, and I join my colleagues tonight and rise in tribute to a great man, President RONALD REAGAN.

In 1980, I turned 18, and the first person I ever voted for was RONALD REAGAN. With that vote, the world changed. It changed because President REAGAN clearly understood that the greatest strength of this Nation is the American people. He believed in us so much that he inspired us to believe in ourselves.

And in his typical humble fashion, during his last speech from the Oval Office, he said:

> I wasn't a great communicator, but I communicated great things, and they didn't spring full bloom from my brow, they came from the heart of a great nation.

Mr. Speaker, President REAGAN captured the hearts of the American people and he unleashed the power, the hope, and the optimism that comes with a sincere understanding and love of freedom and democracy. President REAGAN changed the world by simply reminding us all of exactly who we are. He inspired us to become the Nation we were all along. He always saw the "shining city on the hill," and he gave us the vision to see it with him.

Although we deeply mourn his passing, RONALD REAGAN's life was a gift to the world, a gift that will never be forgotten by all who love freedom and the shining example he gave us.

Thank you, Mr. President, and God bless RONALD REAGAN.

Hon. Robin Hayes

OF NORTH CAROLINA

Mr. Speaker, first let me thank my dear friend and colleague, the gentleman from California (Mr. Lewis), for his leadership tonight in honoring such a wonderful man. President RONALD REAGAN was a good man who became a great President. His leadership has inspired me throughout my career in public service, as I am sure REAGAN inspired many folks presently serving in the public arena.

One of my favorite RONALD REAGAN quotes comes from his 1986 State of the Union Address:

> Government growing beyond our consent had become a lumbering giant, slamming shut the gates of opportunity, threatening to crush the very roots of our freedom. What brought America back? The American people brought us back with quiet courage and common sense, with undying faith that in this nation under God the future will be ours; for the future belongs to the free.

That is one of my favorite REAGAN quotes for a number of reasons. First, it addresses one of the main reasons I switched parties. Like President REAGAN, I began my career not as a Republican but as a Democrat; and, like REAGAN, I switched parties because I felt that big government was "slamming shut the gates of opportunity, threatening to crush the very roots of our freedom."

RONALD REAGAN's conservative principles, put into successful action, changed our Nation's attitude on the role of government and personal responsibility. Without President REAGAN, there would not have been a bipartisan effort to reform welfare and end that vicious cycle of government dependency.

The other thing I like about this quote is that it reveals so much about the character of RONALD REAGAN: his unbridled optimism, his belief in the American people, and his humbleness. He was too humble to take sole credit for the United States' return to greatness, even though had his measures failed he would have assumed the blame. Instead, he gave the credit to the American people, because he believed in the American people.

One of his favorite quotes was: "There is no limit to what you can accomplish if you don't care who gets the credit." And he lived that quote on a daily basis.

One of the other things I admired about RONALD REAGAN was his steadfast determination to stand up to communist aggression. Even though he knew such a determined view may not be popular, he never backed away from his firm belief that communism was wrong. In 1982, speaking before the British Parliament, REAGAN said:

> It is the Soviet Union that runs against the tide of history. ... {It is} the march of freedom and democracy which will leave Marxism-Leninism on the ash-heap of history as it has left other tyrannies which stifle the freedom and muzzle the self-expression of the people.

No truer words have been spoken. I believed it then, and I believe it now. We all saw REAGAN's words validated when the Soviet Union fell apart shortly after President REAGAN left office.

Finally, even when facing a devastating diagnosis, President REAGAN still delivered the news with his typical optimism for America and his belief for the American people. On November 5, 1994, he wrote a letter to the American people announcing that he had Alzheimer's disease:

> In closing let me thank you, the American people for giving me the great honor of allowing me to serve as your President. When the Lord calls me home, whenever that may be, I will leave with the greatest love for this country of ours and eternal optimism for its future.
>
> I now begin this journey that will lead me into the sunset of my life. I know that for America there will always be a bright dawn ahead.

I do believe that the United States does face a bright dawn. And President REAGAN and his leadership can take a large part of the credit for that fact. While I am saddened that President REAGAN is no longer with us, I rejoice knowing that he has met his Maker, and his Maker is looking him in the eye and saying, President REAGAN, the GIPPER, you are a good and faithful servant.

He is now in a far better place. He is looking down on the country and the people that he loved. May God bless and protect America and the vision that was RONALD REAGAN's for us and our future; that freedom belongs to the free.

Hon. Duncan Hunter

OF CALIFORNIA

Mr. Speaker, I thank the gentleman from California (Mr. Lewis) for yielding me this time, and I want to thank my great friend also for not only helping to preside over this special tribute, but for everything that he did in helping to lead the California delegation to be a source of strength for President REAGAN when he put forth those monumental changes in the direction of our government.

I have listened to his statements and just now to the statement of the gentleman from North Carolina (Mr. Hayes), and many others, in talking about this wonderful American, RONALD REAGAN; and I thought I might just touch on a couple of the things he did in the way of national security.

We have short memories, Mr. Speaker; and President REAGAN was not always popular, especially with the media and often with our European allies. I can remember in the eighties, when he responded to the Soviet Union's ringing Western Europe with the SS–20 missiles and he started to move those Persian missiles and ground launch cruise missiles into Europe to offset the Soviet strength of their strategic programs and their intermediate range ballistic missiles that they were moving in. And there were massive demonstrations against RONALD REAGAN and against those who supported him in Europe and lots of sniping by the press in this country.

And yet because of that strength and because he rebuilt national security, especially after the Reykjavik summit, he refused to give up the Strategic Defense Initiative, that is, missile defense, the right of Americans to defend themselves against incoming ballistic missiles. After he did that, there was lots of hand wringing among the elite media and lots of our European allies who said, there it goes, the last chance for peace, and lo and behold, the Russians picked up the phone and said, Can we talk?

RONALD REAGAN at that point started to negotiate with the Soviet Union, and not just to negotiate a peace, but to negotiate the disassembly of the Soviet empire, the tear-down of the Soviet empire, which is manifest today in numerous free states where once there was one state ruled by tyranny.

Mr. Speaker, I remember the gentleman from California (Mr. Lewis) was present as one of our senior Members, and the gentleman from California (Mr. Herger) had not been elected yet, along with the gentleman from California (Mr. Thomas) and the gentleman from California (Mr. Dreier), and Bob Lagomarsino, and John Rousselot, and Chip Pashayan, and my colleague Bill Lowery, and Bobby Fever, new Republicans who had come in in the Reagan win of 1980, and the President invited us to Blair House even while President Carter was still in the White House. We were standing in the foyer, celebrating this victory of our Commander-in-Chief-to-be because he had not been sworn in yet, and the President-elect came down the stairs, and he talked to us about being up on his ranch in Santa Barbara and killing an especially big rattlesnake the day before while he was cutting brush. We had a great time talking with the President-elect. After a while he said, "I am tired, I am going to go upstairs and hit the hay." He said, "you guys turn off the lights when you leave." He went right upstairs; we continued to have a good time. That represented that western hospitality, that great charm that RONALD REAGAN had that brought so many people, attracted so many people, even people of very different political persuasion.

My son Sam was not even born in those days when we first came in. I remember the picture of the cowboy that the President drew for my other son Duncan, who is now a U.S. Marine and deployed overseas.

I think the one thing that this President sold in boatloads was inspiration. He was great at inspiration. He realized a little secret, and that is this country runs on inspiration. Whether it is the markets or the economy or people deciding whether or not they are going to join the uniformed services, inspiration is the fuel that this country runs on, and that is something that RONALD REAGAN had an endless supply of.

He was tough during the tough times. You have to have good endurance to be a good President, and he had great endurance. He was able to handle the difficult times, the times when he was not real popular, and outlast his critics. It has been kind of fun in the last couple of days to watch people who criticized him very severely to seem now to remember that he was not such a bad guy after all. Not only was he not such a bad guy, but he brought this country together as a family. He was, of course, the head of the family.

It is a time for us to mourn this President, but also to celebrate his great life and the big piece of this life that he gave to our Nation. I will never forget when I was first running for Congress, I was practicing law on behalf of a barbershop on the waterfront in San Diego. My dad came in and said, "You can be a Member of Congress." He said, "RONALD REAGAN is running. He is going to run on a platform of national defense and jobs, and in San Diego that is the same thing." I said, "What do I need to start running?" He said, "We need one thing; you need a picture with RONALD REAGAN, and we are going to go up and get it." And we went up and got it in Los Angeles. That launched my foray into politics. So many of us won that year who had no chance of winning because we were riding along with a guy named RONALD REAGAN.

Let us take a message and a lesson from this great American and proceed ahead with optimism and with dedication to the idea that you get "peace through strength." That was a trademark of RONALD REAGAN's foreign policy. I think we are following it with this President. I think we need to stay the course and stay steady.

Hon. Jerry Lewis

OF CALIFORNIA

Mr. Speaker, the gentleman from California (Mr. Hunter) reminds me of another time when RONALD REAGAN was trying to bring together Republicans to form a majority. It was 1969, and there was a majority for approximately 2 years in the California lower house for the assembly, and RONALD REAGAN was then Governor of California. He came into this room, and here were 41 members of the new majority sitting there in front of him. He was sitting at a table in front of us, his legs dangling from the table, and he had argyle socks on.

He said:

> I was trying to think about what I should say to you all. We have not had a majority before. We have to govern ... it is possible from time to time we may disagree with each other as we go about making decisions on public policy.
>
> As I was thinking about what to say to you, I was reminded of my father-in-law, who is a dentist. It seems he had this fellow sitting in the chair, and the guy had an abscessed tooth which had to come out. And my father-in-law began to put this needle in his jaw. About that time my father-in-law felt kind of a groping at the lower part of his abdomen. He looked down startled, and the fellow looked back up and said, "we are not going to hurt each other, are we, Doc?"

For those who knew RONALD REAGAN, he would get just to the edge of color, but nonetheless, he knew how to make a point to bring people together in a very special way; a man never to be forgotten, recognizing how important it is that we work together.

Hon. Jeb Hensarling

OF TEXAS

Mr. Speaker, this week millions of Americans and people around the globe mourn the loss of one of our Nation's greatest heroes, RONALD REAGAN. From the time that he took the oath of office until he left the White House, few American Presidents ever enjoyed the popularity, support and love that RONALD REAGAN engendered. He developed a special bond with the American people, and one can see from the tremendous outpouring of sympathy and support across our great Nation that that special bond still endures today.

More than any other person, President REAGAN is responsible for winning the cold war. He engaged his communist adversaries in the battle of ideas and achieved victory by winning the war for the hearts and minds of people. In his heart he knew these people. He knew the Bulgarian student who was never allowed to read Thomas Jefferson. He knew the East German mother who wanted a better life for her children. He knew the Polish factory worker who longed to be free of Soviet subjugation.

One 65-year-old Czech who lived under the Soviet regime said:

> For us, REAGAN was important because we knew he was really anticommunist, emotionally anticommunist. For us, he was a symbol of the United States' genuine determination to bring communism to an end.

A Romanian man who was recently interviewed struggled to find the words to describe President REAGAN's legacy, and then he simply said, "It is due to him that we are free."

Thanks to RONALD REAGAN's determined leadership, untold millions were liberated from communist tyranny and from the palpable fear of nuclear annihilation.

America was fortunate to have RONALD REAGAN. At a time when our country needed a hero, RONALD REAGAN was able to rekindle the American spirit. He inspired us with his powerful words and unwavering optimism. He had a steadfast belief in the goodness of America. No amount of pessimism, strife or tragedy could discourage that thinking or blur his vision of America as a "shining city on a hill."

I was one of perhaps hundreds of thousands of people that had the privilege to shake the hand of the former President, look him in the eyes and thank him for all he did for America. Frankly, next to my marriage and the birth of my children, it was one of the most profound moments in my life. An earlier generation was inspired to public service by Barry Goldwater. Many in my generation were inspired to serve by RONALD REAGAN.

A woman in Santa Monica recently stated, "When I think of him, I think of America. What is that saying, American, like Mom and apple pie. He should be in that, too, because he represented what this country is all about."

President REAGAN was what this country is all about. He believed in the American dream. He believed in the power of free men and free markets. He championed less government, lower taxes and lifting regulation. He believed in our country's ability to produce boundless possibilities and limitless opportunity. His policies ushered in a new age of entrepreneurship and innovation, and led to one of the greatest economic expansions in our Nation's history.

We believed in President REAGAN because he believed in us. He always saw the best in us, and he never stopped believing in the decency and ingenuity of the American people. He believed deeply in the strength of democracy and never lost hope of America realizing its "rendezvous with destiny."

Our Nation will deeply miss RONALD REAGAN. Undoubtedly future generations of Americans will remember him among the pantheon of America's great leaders, among the names of Washington, Jefferson and Lincoln, but there will never be another President REAGAN.

Let us remember his words the way he wished to be remembered:

{W}hatever else history may say about me when I'm gone, I hope it will record that I appealed to your best hopes, not your worst fears, to your confidence rather than your doubts. My dream is that you will travel the road ahead with liberty's lamp guiding your steps and opportunity's arm steadying your way.

Mr. Speaker, today should serve more than just a memorial, it should serve as a reminder. As President REAGAN also said, "there's much work before us: ... Not easy tasks perhaps. But I would remind you ... they're not impossible, because, after all, we're Americans," and perhaps none more so than RONALD REAGAN.

Hon. Judy Biggert
OF ILLINOIS

Mr. Speaker, unlike many other Members of this body, I never had the great privilege of serving with RONALD REAGAN. When President REAGAN was elected in 1980, I was raising my four children and running a law practice out of my home in Hinsdale, IL. Back then I did not follow world events or political developments like I do now. In those days, it was all I could do to keep up with kids' soccer games, make it to the school board meetings on time, and ensure that I did not miss a court deadline for an important client.

This week, like most Americans, I revel in the stories that my colleagues and others who knew him well have recounted about their special moments with our 40th President. Like most Americans, I cannot get enough of RONALD REAGAN.

What strikes me as I think back through the years of those REAGAN times of the eighties are two very important things. They are the things that he said that touched my life and my interests as a busy mother and a died-in-the-wool Republican.

First is what later became known as the REAGAN 11th commandment. RONALD REAGAN said, and practiced this principle, "Speak no ill of a fellow Republican."

Second was the REAGAN rule for success: "There is no limit to the good a man can do in this world if he does not care who gets the credit."

Mr. Speaker, tonight my thoughts and prayers go out to the REAGAN family. It is true I never met him, but they will never know how much his words, his deeds and his common sense have influenced and will continue to positively affect the generations of leaders that will follow him.

Hon. Roger F. Wicker

OF MISSISSIPPI

Mr. Speaker, I too rise and join so many of my colleagues on both sides of the aisle in paying tribute to RONALD WILSON REAGAN, the 40th President of the United States. I agree with so much of what has been said here today and throughout the Nation in the past few days about the incredible legacy of RONALD REAGAN and what he left to America and to the world. RONALD REAGAN will always be larger than life to millions of people around the world who were freed from the shackles of communism because he stood firm against what he so correctly called the evil empire. RONALD REAGAN's determination and leadership forced an end to the cold war. His philosophy of cutting taxes and easing Federal regulations brought about one of the largest periods of economic growth in American history. And his eternal optimism and hope for a brighter day lifted the spirits of a Nation.

Much has been said about RONALD REAGAN's charisma, quick wit and ability to put people at ease. He was also blessed with a great asset for anyone in public life, a sense of timing. Whether it was one of his famous one-liners or the ability to do just the right thing at the right time, he always seemed to disarm a tough national press corps or defuse a difficult political issue.

Mr. Speaker, I had the privilege of witnessing an example of his instinctive timing and humor in 1980 in Mississippi when then-candidate RONALD REAGAN and his wife, Nancy, came to the Neshoba County Fair in Philadelphia, MS. The Neshoba County Fair is called Mississippi's largest house party and has been the premier gathering for political speeches during the hot Mississippi summers for more than a century. RONALD REAGAN's visit was the first ever by a Presidential candidate to this most celebrated political event in my home State.

One of the issues that had surfaced in Mr. REAGAN's Presidential campaign was the question of his age. He was 69 years old. Some questioned whether he might be too old for the job. At the Neshoba County Fair an incident occurred which could have potentially exaggerated the issue of his age. After Mr. REAGAN's speech, a local craftsman, Gary Harkins of Mississippi, presented Mr. REAGAN with a rocking chair. I am sure some of the candidate's advisers and staff were horrified to think of the prospect that the one image coming from this appearance was a picture of the 69-year-old former Governor sitting in a rocking chair. But without hesitation, RONALD REAGAN sat down in the chair, grabbed his wife, Nancy, by the hand and pulled her onto his lap. They appeared at that moment to be the very picture of vitality and energy. The widely distributed photograph and film footage which followed went around the Nation and nobody seeing that image thought RONALD REAGAN was too old to be President.

Mr. REAGAN's quick thinking probably boosted his candidacy and dispelled doubts in the minds of some voters. The incident also changed the life of Greg Harkins, the craftsman who made the rocking chair and whose fledgling business was energized by his short encounter on the national stage. Mr. Harkins soon began receiving hundreds of requests for chairs from across the Nation and around the world. His business is still going strong today nearly 25 years later, and RONALD REAGAN provided the spark for that little bit of business success. Harkins was quoted recently as saying, "What they did was give me a foothold on something that I can be able to carry on for the rest of my life."

Mr. Harkins represents just one small example of how RONALD REAGAN touched the lives of people in ways that are hard to quantify. We may not know all of their names or their unique stories, but his fellow citizens gained inspiration from RONALD REAGAN's leadership and his attitude that it really was "morning in America."

Whether it was a young American answering a call to public service or becoming involved in the growing conservative movement or simply taking the initiative to exercise their rights and register to vote for the first time, RONALD REAGAN energized many Americans to action. They followed him because they trusted this man of principled beliefs and because he captured their imagination, and they simply liked him.

RONALD REAGAN, some people said, would be limited because he was only an actor. He was perhaps the best example of an actor turned politician; but he ended up being the real thing, the true article, the genuine American; and, Mr. Speaker, I believe he will be recorded as being the greatest President of our time.

Hon. Virgil H. Goode, Jr.
OF VIRGINIA

The death of President REAGAN reminded Americans and many around the world of the achievements of his 8 years in office. A significant part of his legacy is that he helped the United States to feel good about itself again and the tax cuts that he advocated in the early eighties stimulated the economic boom that lasted until the end of the century.

History may well show that President REAGAN's greatest accomplishment was reestablishing our military strength and bringing about the collapse of the Soviet Union, which had been the principal adversary of the free world in the cold war that had raged since the close of World War II. The strengthened military was the one that waged Desert Storm successfully and laid the foundation for the U.S. military that is leading the war on terrorism. President REAGAN rekindled the American spirit and patriotic fervor in this country. We shall never forget the grace and style with which President and Mrs. REAGAN represented America. Our country will always remember RONALD REAGAN.

Hon. Zach Wamp
OF TENNESSEE

Mr. Speaker, I thank the gentleman for taking the leadership tonight. The previous speaker, the gentleman from Virginia (Mr. Goode), myself, and President REAGAN all shared one thing in common as many do in this House and that is we used to be Democrats and now we are Republicans. That brings me to what I want to share tonight, which is the change in the political landscape brought about by the life and service of RONALD WILSON REAGAN; but I want to start by saying that I believe, and I think this honors his memory, that neither party has an exclusive on integrity or ideas, neither party always has it right or always has it wrong, and the two-party system continues to serve our country extremely well.

I am proud of the first half of my life when I was a Democrat and proud of the second half of my life as a Republican, but the story in my life as a southern conservative Democrat goes way back for generations. My father's great-great-grandfather, Enoch Alldredge, served in the 19th century in the Alabama General Assembly for over 40 years. My mother's great uncle Reuben Alldridge served in the 20th century in the Alabama General Assembly for a number of years, both very prominent political figures from the northern part of Alabama, all as Democrats. So I grew up honestly as a southern conservative Democrat.

As a matter of fact, my first real memory of it all as a young person was watching my parents be involved in local campaigns and then, in fall 1976, going to Woolen Gym at the University of North Carolina at Chapel Hill as a 19-year-old freshman and voting for Jimmy Carter as President of the United States and then having my parents attend the inaugural in Washington here with Franklin and Emmy Haney, two of the biggest Democrats in the State of Tennessee and being proud that my parents were here and saluting the new President, Jimmy Carter.

But the years that followed in my formative years certainly gave me an opportunity and hope when I saw RONALD REAGAN. I saw the malaise we were in. Let me say that Jimmy Carter has proven what a fine and outstanding man he is over these last 24 years since leaving office. It was a low point in our country's history, but he is a good and decent man; and frankly I will stand by that vote as a Democrat at that time, but over those next 4 years at the University of North Carolina, we saw a real low in our country's history and then all of a sudden there was a new day in 1980, and it seemed like someone came from the West and actually kind of showed us the hope and opportunity that you heard repeated on this floor over and over and over again.

I can remember as the campaign generated momentum in 1980 at UNC, my fraternity, the Sigma Nu house, got real energized about the campaign and by the convention when they had that strong conservative Governor from the West team up with maybe the best person on paper that had run in 100 years, George Herbert Walker Bush. It was like that did it. That sealed the deal. What a great team. And on election night in fall 1980 we loaded up in cars from UNC. It was Lee Ives and Tom Nesbit and Tony Floyd and Allen Miller and Lyn Thornburg and a group of us, and we drove to Washington, DC, and we were here that night in 1980 when RONALD REAGAN was elected President of the United States.

I was a southern conservative Democrat who became a Republican. Our entire family shifted from our party identification over the hope, the opportunity, the fresh start that RONALD REAGAN brought to the political process. That changed the political landscape in the United States of America, and it moved our country from what was more left of center to slightly right of center.

The Founding Fathers did not want things to change dramatically. This is like a big ship of state. If you turn it one degree, you arrive at a different destination. The country went from being left of center to right of center over the leadership, the strength and what I would say is the constancy of RONALD REAGAN. He stood for something, and he simply articulated to this country what he stood for, and he never wavered. When people elect a President, they want a strong leader who can make a decision, who will stand his ground. When the wind blows, he stands firm. RONALD REAGAN did that.

That is why the 8 years is a legacy beyond measure. As the previous speaker said, in our lifetime, the model, the great leader is RONALD REAGAN. I salute him. He made a Republican out of me, and I have been in the House of Representatives as a Republican elected official for 10 years. I ran once and lost to get here, and I am proud of the whole story. I am very typical of a lot of southern boll weevil conservatives that believed in that simple limited government, personal responsibility, traditional values, strong national defense, lower taxes, take care of yourself and your family first and your extended family, look to the government last, but do it with a smile on your face and love in your heart. He is like a father, a big brother, a great leader who we could trust and have confidence in. Today we remember a truly great American President, RONALD WILSON REAGAN.

Hon. Kay Granger

OF TEXAS

Mr. Speaker, I am tempted to begin by saying that I come to honor the life of RONALD REAGAN; but the truth is nothing I can say, nothing anyone can say can speak more loudly than do REAGAN's own achievements. His legacy will endure and his memory will remain.

Many leaders have changed history. RONALD REAGAN changed the future. How soon we forget the environment he inherited in 1981, double-digit inflation, high interest rates at home, and Soviet aggression combined with American malaise abroad. Yet through his conviction, his courage, and his commitment, RONALD REAGAN changed the Nation and the world.

The story of RONALD REAGAN is the story of America. He was an ordinary man who led a most extraordinary life. Born in poverty, REAGAN rose to the greatest political office in the world. Along the way he did not merely argue for American values, he lived them. His determination was matched only by his decency, his leadership equaled only by his love of country.

He was a great President who was also a good man, and he was a man so unlike any other in politics. Politics is filled with people who go with the flow, change with the times, and exchange principles for polls. These politicians are like tugboats, pushed back and forth by the waves. Not REAGAN. He was like a battleship, always moving forward in its destination, always certain of victory.

Though he has now left us, his impact never will. Every time we see a free person in a foreign land vote in a democratic election, RONALD REAGAN is there. Every time we see a new job created through innovation and creativity, RONALD REAGAN is there. And every time we see an American taking pride in his country, RONALD REAGAN is there.

Ultimately we mourn for ourselves, not for REAGAN, for his life was one of victory. Like few other leaders in history, he lived to see his vision vindicated. Just as he had predicted, he saw communism repudiated and freedom spread across the globe.

RONALD REAGAN always knew who he was and what he believed. He knew why America was great and why America must lead. We recognize tonight his achievements and his legacy, but also let us also remember his style and his self-deprecating humor. We give him the credit he did not seek or think important.

At the end of his Presidency, REAGAN was asked if he objected to all the favorable press coverage that Mikhail Gorbachev got. "Good Lord, no," REAGAN responded. "I co-starred with Errol Flynn once."

Hon. Trent Franks

OF ARIZONA

Mr. Speaker, tonight it is my deepest heartfelt honor to remember and to celebrate the life of RONALD WILSON REAGAN. President REAGAN was a man of unfettered principle. He was not afraid to do what was right. And not only was he not afraid, he was tenaciously committed to doing only that what he thought was right in his own heart.

Mr. Speaker, President REAGAN warned us all "to beware {of} the temptation ... to ignore the facts of history and the aggressive impulses of an evil empire, to simply call the arms race a giant misunderstanding and thereby remove {ourselves} from the struggle between right and wrong and good and evil." Mr. REAGAN understood that some things were worth fighting, even dying, for, and he was resolute about them in his heart.

President REAGAN made us all believe that America still had what it takes to be victorious, to rise above and out of difficult circumstances, and to face devastating challenges. He said:

> Every promise, every opportunity is still golden in this land. And through that golden door our children can walk into tomorrow with the knowledge that no one can be denied the promise that is America.
>
> Her heart is full; ... her future bright. She has arms big enough to comfort and strong enough to support.

By the grace of God, those words are still true today.

Mr. Speaker, President REAGAN on so many occasions simply shared his wisdom and experience with us. He stated that "The future doesn't belong to the fainthearted; it belongs to the brave." I believe he would want us to continue to make this Nation great by preserving its goodness. He would want us to continue in the struggle between right and wrong and good and evil.

Mr. Speaker, RONALD REAGAN's life was a transformed one, one that reflected the light from within, and he shared that light with all of us in the brightness and warmth of his smile and in his grace and good humor.

Mr. REAGAN said this of his Saviour: "He promised there will never be a dark night that does not end. And by dying for us, Jesus showed how far our love should be ready to go: all the way." RONALD REAGAN's dark nights on this Earth have ended, and he is at this moment in the presence of his precious Saviour. And now for Mr. REAGAN each day has a bright new dawn and a shining sunset, and while he was here, he went all the way. And, Mr. Speaker, if he could speak to us one last time, I truly believe that he would tell us the same message that he told us so many times before when he said:

> You and I have a rendezvous with destiny. We will preserve for our children this, the last best hope of man on earth, or we will sentence them to take the first step into a thousand years of darkness. If we fail, at least let our children and our children's children say of us we justified our brief moment here. We did all that could be done.

Thank you, Mr. President, for your life, and thank you for reminding us all of our rendezvous with destiny.

Hon. Marsha Blackburn

OF TENNESSEE

It is an amazing thing to join our colleagues tonight and to thank President REAGAN and his family for their decades of service. And as I have listened to our colleagues tonight, I thought about the first time I had the opportunity to see and hear President REAGAN, and this was back in the early seventies, and he had come into Jackson, MS, for a Republican Party event. And I attended that event with my parents and was absolutely amazed at several things as I listened to and watched RONALD REAGAN. It was his warmth, his ability to communicate, the way he used simple words for a very strong message, one that really showed his principle and his commitment in those still convictions that never ever wavered.

And one of the things that really impressed me was that this was a man who really loved America. He loved everything that America stood for. And I think that it is fitting that we have a world that stands in awe today as they look back and they remember those commitments and accomplishments.

Mr. Speaker, I had the opportunity to return today with some of my colleagues from being in Normandy to celebrate and to commemorate the 60th anniversary of D-day and the fight for freedom that was so important to our allies and also to our Nation, and to have an opportunity to share with so many of those individuals their love of President RONALD REAGAN. And I think they all saw in him something that we appreciated and maybe could not always put into words. But he promised a renewal of American spirit for us, and by sheer willpower, he made that happen. And I think, yes, that he believed in us more than we believed in ourselves as he became the President of this great country, and he taught us how to enact that belief.

He also taught us that tax relief would make our economy boom, and that indeed happened with an unprecedented economic expansion. He also showed us how one could say, I am not going to hide behind diplomatic platitudes, and I am not going to allow the Soviet Union to slowly eat away at the West. He simply communicated the truth about communism and exposed it for what it was: a cruel system built by thugs and murderers.

And President REAGAN truly was the quintessential American hero, the smalltown boy with the can-do attitude who set out with a dream and ended up changing the world. He had courage, he had wisdom, and he believed in the best that there was with America. God bless, RONALD REAGAN. He was a true American original.

Hon. Jerry Lewis
OF CALIFORNIA

Mr. Speaker, from the days I knew RONALD REAGAN as Governor, and he was a key leader who sponsored early development of child care in our State, recognizing the importance of quality daycare in terms of the future of America's children, the environmental Governor who saved Lake Tahoe, to the days that I had a chance to watch him rebuild America's strength by building our defense, he always was straightforward, candid with the American people.

And not so long ago he was heard to say:

> In closing let me thank you, the American people for giving me the great honor of allowing me to serve as your President. When the Lord calls me home, whenever that may be, I will leave with the greatest love for this country of ours and eternal optimism for its future.
>
> I now begin this journey that will lead me into the sunset of my life. I know that for America there will always be a bright dawn ahead.

God bless you, RONALD REAGAN. To Nancy and their family, all of us share with you our prayers for our great President, RONALD WILSON REAGAN.

Hon. Jim Saxton
OF NEW JERSEY

Mr. Speaker, I rise today to support this resolution, a fitting tribute to a personal hero of mine, the 40th President of these great United States, President RONALD WILSON REAGAN.

Mr. Speaker, President REAGAN was, and is today, the personification of all that is good in America. All that knew him have commented on the eternal optimism he exuded, much like the hope America presents to the rest of the world.

He was a beacon of light for freedom and for freedom-loving people everywhere. The fact is that today there are not hundreds, not thousands, but millions of people in the world who live in freedom, and these people are free because of the leadership of President RONALD REAGAN. He had a vision that set this Nation down a path of greatness that historians shall look back on as a vital turning point for not only this country, but indeed the world as well.

There is an old military axiom that there are no bad battalions only bad leaders. As a corollary, I propose that there are no great nations, only great leaders.

President REAGAN was indeed one of this country's greatest leaders. During the 8 years he was President, he turned this country around militarily, economically and diplomatically. And as a result, he stands with many of the great leaders of our country's past—like George Washington, Abraham Lincoln, Franklin Roosevelt, and Dwight D. Eisenhower.

What he left most importantly was a legacy of optimism and a restored faith in the American Presidency. In 1984, the year I was elected to Congress, President REAGAN said while speaking to students at Fudan University in Shanghai, China, "We're an optimistic people. Like you, we inherited a vast land of endless skies, tall mountains, rich fields, and open prairies. It made us see the possibilities in everything. It made us hopeful." He made us hopeful even in the face of adversity.

Who can forget that cold, grim day the hours after the *Challenger* disaster, when our Nation was stunned and weeping? He comforted us with these words:

> We will never forget them, nor the last time we saw them, this morning, as they prepared for their journey and waved good-bye and "slipped the surly bonds of earth" to "touch the face of God."

And today we, as American people, are comforted for it is most certain that as he heads on his final journey, we wave goodbye to our 40th President as he " 'slip{s} the surly bonds of earth' to 'touch the face of God.'" Well done, Mr. President. I will miss you and America will miss you, but we will never forget you.

Hon. Madeleine Z. Bordallo

OF GUAM

Mr. Speaker, I rise today to pay tribute to RONALD REAGAN—a beloved President who changed America and the world.

I first want to express my deepest condolences to Former First Lady Nancy Reagan and the Reagan family. An entire Nation shares your sadness over the loss of our former President, a man of humble beginnings who rose to capture our hearts and minds, our hopes, and our aspirations.

RONALD REAGAN embodied the spirit of what it means to be an American. As much as he was a leader of the people, he was also a product of the people, which helped him to relate with people from all different backgrounds. He was born to a working family in a small rural town, and brought up to respect traditional values such as family, hard work, God and country. Blessed with an unmistakably entrepreneurial spirit, he set out to pursue the American dream.

RONALD REAGAN lived through and endured tremendous economic hardship during the Great Depression. Despite these challenges, he put himself through college by earning a scholarship, washing dishes, waiting tables, all while sending some of his earnings home to his parents to help support his family. His strong character was forged by hard work.

Driven by the belief that all people should be able to live freely, RONALD REAGAN joined the American people and the world community to rally against the tyrannical oppression of the Axis powers and to defeat Nazism in Europe. United behind the many brave soldiers fighting for freedom in Europe and the Pacific, RONALD REAGAN volunteered his talents to create instructional videos critical to the training of Army recruits during World War II. A staunch defender of freedom and democracy, RONALD REAGAN would, after the defeat of the Axis powers, turn his attention to vanquishing from the world another threat to liberty: communism.

RONALD REAGAN began his political ascendancy in 1966 during his campaign for Governor of California. He would go on to win the first of two terms as California's Governor before reaching the White House in 1980. His conservatism appealed to many across political and cultural lines. We will always remember his optimism and confidence in America's future.

From "sea to shining sea," President REAGAN recognized the importance and value of every individual and every community to our country's strength. On two separate occasions, President REAGAN visited Guam, America's most distant territory. On these occasions, I had the honor of hosting President REAGAN as First Lady of Guam along with my husband Governor Ricky Bordallo, experiences I remember fondly. Donning island wear rather than more formal business attire, President REAGAN was approachable and personable and put those around him at ease. His charm and grace left a lasting impression on those he came into contact with. He was as genuine and real in person as he was behind the podium or in front of the camera.

He recognized the importance of Guam in promoting American values in the region, calling our island "America's flagship in the western Pacific." President REAGAN declared:

> It's said that it's here on Guam each morning that the Sun first casts its rays upon the Stars and Stripes. Well, my friends, I can't think of a more beautiful way for America's day to begin.

While these words are recorded in history, it is the grace and sincerity with which he delivered those words that are remembered by the people of Guam.

The outpouring of love and affection President REAGAN has received from family, friends and the entire American family is a testament to his life and all of those he touched. Through courage, clarity and compassion, he led the people of this great Nation and the entire world from the perils of the cold war to the hope of liberty, freedom and dignity. His spirit will continue to live in the hearts and minds of all of us for whom he dedicated his life of public service. The advent of freedom in the former Soviet bloc and the spread of democracy throughout the world will forever be linked to his famous challenge, "Mr. Gorbachev, tear down this wall!" On behalf of myself and the people of Guam, I want to say "*Adios, esta ki.*" Goodbye until we meet again.

Hon. Gene Green

OF TEXAS

Mr. Speaker, Americans and people across the world respect and admire RONALD REAGAN. My greatest admiration is for his steadfast opposition to communist threats to our national security and the security of our allies.

Many credit RONALD REAGAN for winning the cold war, a bipartisan war begun under President Truman and lasting 45 years under bipartisan U.S. Governments. When President REAGAN spoke out against the evils of communism, as he often did, he spoke out for all Americans: Republican, Democrat, and Independent.

In this long-running struggle, President REAGAN excelled by working with America's strong belief in freedom and our patriotic love for our country.

He was instrumental in keeping the Nation united against the threat that Soviet communism posed to our national security, an important and difficult task after the domestic and foreign policy conflicts of the sixties and seventies.

President REAGAN's ability to lead a united America during 8 years of bipartisan government is conclusive proof that he was a natural leader who knew to treat all Americans with dignity and respect. The sincerity of his patriotism and his beliefs were crucial for uniting America against the threats of communism. Any American leader could learn from him.

REAGAN was also inspiring for an America hit by tragedy. His underlying faith in America and Americans shone through in a powerful speech after the *Challenger* tragedy.

He made it clear, when directly addressing the millions of American schoolchildren who had watched the disaster, that tragedy was a painful setback, but was no reversal. The President said on January 28, 1986: "The future doesn't belong to the fainthearted; it belongs to the brave. The *Challenger* crew was pulling us into the future, and we'll continue to follow them." That also applies today.

By bringing America to common terms during international tyranny and national tragedy reinforced the strong, shared goals of the American people: to live in freedom, to excel in technology, and to believe in something larger than ourselves.

Today we mourn the passing of an American giant.

Hon. Tim Holden
OF PENNSYLVANIA

Mr. Speaker, this weekend marked the passing of one of the most influential Presidents of our era. Our thoughts and prayers are with his wife, Nancy, and his children at this difficult time.

President REAGAN was an American icon. No matter what your politics, he had a special way of making every citizen feel good about their country. He made us proud to be Americans. He will be forever remembered for his warmth and the respect he accorded others.

Even when he disagreed with those who did not share his political philosophy, President REAGAN lived by the noble ideal that at the end of the day, partisanship ended and we are all fellow Americans and friends. He taught us that there is a big difference between strong beliefs and bitter partisanship.

President REAGAN is credited with many great accomplishments, not the least of which is ending the cold war. In spite of all he achieved, he once said, "that the greatest leader is not the one who does great things—it is the one who gets the people to do the greatest things." RONALD REAGAN's glass was always half full. His optimism, his patriotism and his sense of duty inspired several generations of Americans to do great things.

In life, President REAGAN enjoyed the affection of a grateful Nation. We all join together to mourn the passing of this great American.

Hon. Joe Baca
OF CALIFORNIA

Mr. Speaker, I rise to honor the life of RONALD REAGAN, the 40th President of the United States. I am proud to be a co-sponsor of Congressman Lewis' resolution. Today, Republicans and Democrats alike honor in unity the life of a man who left a permanent mark on the history of our Nation and the world.

Today we praise the life and accomplishments of the Great Communicator, and we give our condolences to Nancy, and the entire Reagan family. President RONALD REAGAN was a man who meant much to all free peoples in the world through his many noble accomplishments. President REAGAN's policies, many of which I disagreed with, were nevertheless motivated by a commitment to preserve and enhance our Nation's greatness. I remain firm in my admiration of this great leader whose intellectual integrity was always unquestioned.

As the oldest serving President in American history, President REAGAN was an inspiration for seniors. He showed us that youthfulness can be found in people of all ages, and that life does not expire at 65. When President REAGAN was diagnosed with Alzheimer's disease, he brought awareness and understanding to an illness that is too often ignored.

President REAGAN will be remembered for his dedication to the American dream. Although many Americans may have disagreed with his policies, they were still inspired by his enthusiasm and optimism.

President REAGAN should be remembered not just for his role in Washington, but for his hard work in the State of California as well. As Governor of California for 8 years, he led the State with dedication and commitment to his convictions. As an actor, he provided us with entertainment in over 50 motion pictures.

On behalf of myself, the residents of the 43d Congressional District in California, and a grateful world that is safer and freer, I pay homage to President RONALD REAGAN—leader, statesman, actor, father, husband and American hero.

And now, let's make this resolution "one for the GIPPER."

Hon. Lincoln Diaz-Balart
OF FLORIDA

Mr. Speaker, I rise today to honor a man whom I believe to be the greatest President of the 20th century.

President RONALD REAGAN succeeded in defeating the most powerful and dangerous military empire in the history of humanity without firing a single shot. REAGAN knew instinctively that, despite the imperfections inherent in every human enterprise, the United States of America represents good and communism represents evil.

President REAGAN never wavered in his conviction that freedom is the birthright of all mankind. His firm belief that freedom is the inalienable right of all people changed the world, and is his most enduring legacy. However he also realized the liberties we hold sacred must be constantly protected against the forces of tyranny and oppression. President REAGAN proved that when one fights for justice, for human rights, and for the liberty of those suffering under repression, one must persevere in spite of the strength of the opposition and the apparent magnitude of the obstacles one must confront.

The enemies of the United States never forgave him for his firmness, for his character, for his faith in the people of the United States and in the cause of liberty. Even in his death they continue to attack him. This hatred is evidenced by the declaration made by the tyrannical regime in Havana yesterday, "He, who never should have been born, has died." That monstrous statement illustrates the ultimate evil of the tyrant who has enslaved the Cuban people for over 45 years. President REAGAN knew that Castro, and every communist tyranny, represents the antithesis of liberty, freedom and human dignity.

At home, RONALD REAGAN forever changed the political landscape of America. He was a union leader. In fact, he was the only President in the history of the United States to have been a union leader. He was also at first a member of the Democratic Party, having campaigned for Franklin Roosevelt and Harry Truman. However, ideas and times change. When he became a Republican at the age of 52, he convinced millions of members of his former party that the superior ideas and the better reforms of our age belonged to the Republican Party. Inspired by his leadership and his example, my brother, Congressman Mario Diaz-Balart and I proudly became Republicans.

May RONALD WILSON REAGAN, apostle of freedom, democracy and human rights, rest in peace.

Hon. Darrell E. Issa
OF CALIFORNIA

Mr. Speaker, on this second week of June, 17 years ago, President RONALD REAGAN stood in the then-divided city of Berlin, and called on Soviet Leader Mikhail Gorbachev to, "tear down this wall!" President REAGAN's critics at home called his speech a publicity ploy. The Soviets and East Germans called it an infringement of East German sovereignty—unwarranted meddling by the American President. Two years later, the wall came down.

President REAGAN was a leader with foresight and strong conviction. He believed in America—then he made America believe in itself again. He valued freedom—so he brought it to those who had none.

Through wise policies, force of will, and a kind demeanor, President REAGAN conveyed strength and determination alongside reason and optimism to America and those who yearned for freedom behind the Iron Curtain. He never doubted what America could do—and he wouldn't let us doubt ourselves. When tragedy struck, he told us to move forward—and we listened.

RONALD REAGAN knew America. He knew what was right about our Nation, what was right for our Nation, and what America could set right in the world. RONALD REAGAN led America and the rest of the free world against communism. When his work was finished, the free world had expanded by over 400 million people in 27 countries.

Today, soldiers from these new democracies fight side by side with Americans against the new enemies of freedom in Iraq and Afghanistan. President REAGAN showed us that freedom can tear down walls. He reaffirmed for us that America is a force for good in the world, and that our proudest achievements will never come without criticism or sacrifice.

I never had the opportunity to meet RONALD REAGAN, but knew him, like most Americans, as someone who had faith in our ability to achieve great things for ourselves and the world.

Mr. Speaker, history will remember RONALD REAGAN for bringing freedom to more people throughout the world than has ever been done before. The America and the world RONALD REAGAN leaves behind is a better place because of him.

President REAGAN, we still carry the confidence you gave our Nation and will never forget what we accomplished together. A grateful Nation thanks you.

Hon. Steve King

OF IOWA

Mr. Speaker, I rise today to honor the memory of President RONALD REAGAN.

RONALD REAGAN leaves an enduring legacy of character and a dedication to the American ideal of liberty. His philosophy and values were not political calculation; they were inscribed in his heart.

I recognize RONALD REAGAN as a true leader that remained true to American principles of the individual over government, sense of duty toward neighbors, and expansion of freedom.

Moreover, REAGAN was a man with vision on a grand scale. He knew America's greatest achievement was spreading democracy throughout the world. He was resolute in this endeavor and faced each challenge with both vigilance and grace. No American did more to spread the gift of liberty and respect for human dignity to people who had never enjoyed them. No American did more to persuade our Nation that the contribution of democracy and human rights to all is the proper goal of the United States.

Throughout our history, when evil and iniquity has been the common enemy, Americans have displayed a resolve to create a better country and a better world. RONALD REAGAN personified that American trait. REAGAN's service is considered recent in history's timeline, but his character and deeds are a model of leadership for all time. We need to remember in our hearts the dedication to higher purpose. We are dutybound to advance each society to RONALD REAGAN's "shining city on the hill."

Thank you Mr. Speaker. I conclude by saying that this week's passing should not be seen as the loss of a man but rather the beginning of a legend.

Hon. Ginny Brown-Waite

OF FLORIDA

Mr. Speaker, I rise today to add my voice to the chorus extolling the life of RONALD REAGAN. On a similar occasion over a century ago, Lincoln said of Washington, "How do you add glory to the Sun?" And I must confess, I feel the same futility at trying to add my few words to a life and legacy that shines so bright.

RONALD REAGAN came to the stage when it appeared that America was grasping at the complexities of modernity. Inflation, recession, and unemployment appeared permanent and the light of freedom appeared to be dim. Europe was enthralled with socialism and communism and the American exception was denounced as arrogant and on the edge of failure. Much like today, we were told what we needed was more government not less; higher taxation, not less; more regulation, not less. REAGAN saw all of this and he smiled.

I was at his inauguration. When he said "It is time for us to realize that we're too great a nation to limit ourselves to small dreams," my spine stiffened. I got goose bumps when he called out "that peace is the highest aspiration of the American people. We will negotiate for it, sacrifice for it; we will not surrender for it, now or ever."

From that day, I knew America was back. You see many people speak of the Reagan revolution. I like to think of it as the Reagan restoration. REAGAN restored our optimism, our belief in our ability to create, and the belief that God put man on this Earth to be free and made America to prove it.

I was in Washington the day REAGAN was shot. I held my breath and was glued to the television. The humor, strength and courage that were REAGAN's came through and, along with the rest of America, I laughed when he said, "Honey, I forgot to duck."

RONALD REAGAN changed the paradigm. He changed America's foreign policy from one of benign containment to active confrontation and for the first time since communism began extending its sinister reach, we saw its hand pushed back, and that gave us hope.

REAGAN confronted the evil he saw in the world and he did it without apology. He battled communism. He armed the resistance in Afghanistan; he sent troops to Grenada; Lebanon; and Pershings to Europe. In a courageous move he walked away from negotiations at Reykjavik. To the cries of the left and chattering classes he held firm to the belief that America never should and never would surrender her right to defend herself. Mikhail Gorbachev has said Reykjavik was the turning point. His strength broke the back of the Soviets.

Before the British Parliament, REAGAN envisaged that the last pages of communism were being written and in those famous words predicted that totalitarianism would be consigned to the "ash heap of history." He was derided. Yet few could know how prophetic his words would be, or how fast the fall would come.

In 1989, Soviet citizens voted for the first time. Prodemocracy demonstrations were held in Tiananmen Square. Lech Walesa was elected president of Poland. Shortly thereafter, the Eastern European Soviet bloc closed the door on communism for democracy. In November, the Berlin Wall was opened and, as REAGAN would have it, an anonymous German struck the first blow at tearing down the wall. The following year, free elections defeated the communist Sandinistas and the Soviet Union was dissolved. The light of freedom extended its reach.

REAGAN has been so often called the Great Communicator, but I like to think about his time in office and his legacy in a different way. His victory was not of communication, but a triumph of content—the content of his ideas. He reignited the light of freedom. He cut taxes and regulation and in 8 years created 19 million jobs. He reminded us that the path to prosperity was one of individual freedom and personal responsibility. As REAGAN has said, these were not his ideas, but they were American ideas. REAGAN thought his revolution was "more like the great rediscovery, a rediscovery of our values and our common sense."

So, as we honor President REAGAN let us remember his humility, his dignity, his kind words and most of all his courage. Let us honor the legacy of President REAGAN with a renewed commitment to the exceptionalism that makes us American. Let us renew freedom's promise to those who live in oppressive tyranny. Let us renew our determination, our courage, and our strength. And let us renew our faith and our hope.

There are many who stand against freedom and peace. There are many who criticize and compromise, but let us honor RONALD REAGAN by standing firm, with resolve, in this time of war.

We can do it. Why? As REAGAN would say, "after all, ... {we} are Americans."

Hon. Nick Smith

OF MICHIGAN

Mr. Speaker, I share with my colleagues a poem by Albert Carey Caswell.

AND TO THIS END

(By Albert Carey Caswell)

And to this end
Approach Heaven, our True American Hero ... America's finest of all true friends
Rest now ... our Great American Patriot ... as up to Heaven your magnificent soul as so ascends.
And to this end
And oh, what to this our Country you have so been
With that, your warm smile and that thick brown hair ... and what your heart of gold has so meant.
And to this end
The promise, and your gift ... the pride and the respect ... believing in us as if ... as you'd begin
Bringing your Nation back to shore, our savior ... rescuing & seeing the light that others so ignored.
And to this end
Breaking down walls, hearing the children's calls ... wearing your heart on your sleeve
To believe ... In God and Country, and in all of those things which made us free ... all in you we see.
And to this end
To dream ... to start from nothing, as it would so seem
As was yours ... this The Great American Dream ... as is this, our Nation's greatest of all themes.
And to this end
Returning and The Pride and The Respect ... to America's greatest of all assets

Her fighting Women & Men ... her one true fine reason why we all can dream, you'd not let us forget.
And to this end
As you brought the light, into that battle against the darkness ... this your courageous fight
As you have brought us hope, where there was none ... as your journey begun ... for what was right.
And to this end
Yes, RON ... there are jelly beans up in Heaven my dear friend
And to you, I so salute ... this one's for you GIPPER ... as the swollen tear drops so roll down my chin.
And to this end ... "Well, There You Go Again"
And now, and forever ... whenever, I look into our flag ... I'll see your face
For such men of heart, such men of warmth & character & grace, Heaven ... so surely holds a place.

Mr. Speaker, people say that a truly great athlete is not only gifted himself, he makes those who play with him better. The same is true of President REAGAN, who not only led the country, but restored America's confidence. He renewed our sense of America's goodness and America's greatness. And with that assurance, the American people achieved great things.

When REAGAN came into office, America was demoralized. President Carter had even spoken of our malaise. Watergate and our defeat in Vietnam shook our self-confidence. We surrendered control over the Panama Canal which we had built.

The Soviet Union was at the height of its power and communism seemed to be on the march. After Vietnam fell to the communists, Cambodia followed. The Sandinistas took control in Nicaragua and communist insurgencies were under way in Ethiopia, Angola, and Mozambique. The Soviets invaded Afghanistan in 1979 and were in the process of suppressing the Solidarity movement in Poland.

At the same time, the Shah fell in Iran, and supporters of Ayatollah Khomeini held 52 Americans hostage for more than a year at our Embassy in Tehran. Worse, the American military expedition to free them failed in the desert, with the crash of two helicopters and the death of eight servicemen.

The economic situation was just as dire. In 1980, inflation stood at 13.5 percent, and interest rates reached 21 percent. The turmoil in the Middle East sparked gasoline shortages. People waited for hours in line just to fill up their cars and worried about people stealing the gas out of their tanks.

People lost their optimism. America no longer seemed special, or a world leader. It felt like the divine spark at the center of the American experiment had gone out.

It was RONALD REAGAN who turned it around. He never lost faith in the American people. And he had enough optimism to restore our lost confidence and get America back on its feet.

He believed we could restore our economy—and we did. By 1990 the U.S. economy had grown by a third, or roughly the size of the entire German economy. And 35 million jobs were created.

He believed we could stand up proudly for American values around the world and stand up to the Soviet Union—and we did. It was President REAGAN's resolve that halted the march of communism in Central America, and in Afghanistan. It was REAGAN's resolve that nurtured the Solidarity movement in Poland, and gave heart to the dissidents of the Soviet bloc. Ultimately it was President REAGAN's faith in American ideals that led to the fall of the Berlin Wall and the liberation of Eastern Europe and the Soviet Union.

It was that leadership and vision for America that made RONALD REAGAN special. Like FDR during the Depression, he taught us that there was nothing to fear but fear itself. Like Winston Churchill during World War II, he spoke for an entire nation at a time of stress. It restored our confidence, and that made all the difference.

Let us remember RONALD REAGAN. Let us remember what RONALD REAGAN wanted for America. He wanted us always to be that "shining city on a hill." And he wanted us to know that America's best days always lie ahead.

May God bless RONALD REAGAN and Mrs. Reagan and may God bless America.

Hon. Frank R. Wolf

OF VIRGINIA

Mr. Speaker, I join today with others in the House in expressing deepest condolences to Nancy Reagan and the Reagan family on the passing of RONALD WILSON REAGAN, the 40th President of the United States of America, and in paying tribute to President REAGAN as we remember his Presidency and what he meant to our country and indeed to the world.

I deeply admired and respected President REAGAN. I had the good fortune to run for the 10th District of Virginia seat in Congress in November 1980 when he was elected to his first term. Some called my victory then "on REAGAN's coattails." I have no doubt I'm in Congress today because of him.

I will always be grateful that after my two unsuccessful bids for Congress, RONALD REAGAN led the ticket that I was on and I became a member of the class of 1980.

As we remember President REAGAN today, I have been moved by the outpouring of love and support we have been seeing over the past few days across our Nation and especially in California, where he served the Golden State as Governor for two terms.

"Thank you, President REAGAN. You made us proud again."

That was the sentiment on one of the many posters and other mementos in memory of President REAGAN placed outside the entrance to his Presidential library in Simi Valley, CA, the day after his death on June 5. And that sentiment could well sum up the legacy of President REAGAN, who lost his 10-year battle with Alzheimer's disease at age 93.

He was the leader of our Nation when Americans needed to know and more importantly to believe that indeed it was "morning again in America," and the best was yet to come for our great country—that we could be proud to stand up and be called Americans. He made us feel good again. He gave us hope. He inspired us. He gave us optimism because he was an optimist.

And when we needed to be comforted at a time of our own Nation's mourning in the wake of the space shuttle *Challenger* disaster in 1986, he was there for us, speaking to us much like a father, telling us it would be all right:

> It's all part of the process of exploration and discovery. It's all part of taking a chance and expanding man's horizons. The future doesn't belong to the fainthearted; it belongs to the brave. . . . Nothing ends here; our hopes and our journeys continue.

The June 7 edition of *National Journal's Hotline* headlined, "RONALD WILSON REAGAN," described Mr. REAGAN's Presidency well:

> The optimism of Morning in America left little room for mourning in America. So instead of grief, there is respect for the man, celebration of his boldness, relief for his widow, and memories of leadership with purpose, grace and humor.
>
> He literally disarmed his enemies aboard with his tenacity. He gently disarmed his political enemies at home with his modesty. If he was overestimated as an actor, he was underestimated as a political leader. Because he never quite fit in with official Washington, he stayed connected inseparably with the people. And for an entire generation of Americans, he defined the Presidency.
>
> He dreamt, acted out, and embodied the American dream. He was a leader. Those who agreed with his policies cherished his principles. Those who doubted his capacities wondered at his accomplishments.
>
> Friend and foe have come to see him as an American icon, whose light may forever shine from his city on the hill.

In many ways, President REAGAN's profound conviction that every human being had the right to live in freedom inspired my work for humanitarian and human rights causes. While he didn't always outwardly show it, he was a man of deep faith. He said in a speech before the House of Commons in 1982:

> We must be staunch in our conviction that freedom is not the sole prerogative of a lucky few, but the inalienable and universal right of all human beings.

I saw a poignant television news report from southern California on Sunday evening which also reminded me that another crucial part of his legacy belongs not only to America, but to the world. A woman was interviewed. She was holding a bouquet of flowers. Tears were streaming down her face.

She had a broken English accent and identified herself as a Russian emigrant. She said she had to come to the makeshift memorial outside the funeral home where President REAGAN was resting because, "I owe my life to President REAGAN."

I was also reminded of how President REAGAN gave hope to the persecuted peoples of the world when I read an opinion article from the June 6 edition of the *Jerusalem Post* written by former Soviet political dissident Natan Sharansky. I will insert the entire text of that article for the *Record*. Mr. Sharansky wrote:

> In 1983, I was confined to an eight-by-ten-foot prison cell on the border of Siberia. My Soviet jailers gave me the privi-

lege of reading the latest copy of Pravda. Splashed across the front page was a condemnation of President RONALD REAGAN for having the temerity to call the Soviet Union an "evil empire." Tapping on walls and talking through toilets, word of REAGAN's "provocation" quickly spread throughout the prison. We dissidents were ecstatic. Finally, the leader of the free world had spoken the truth—a truth that burned inside the heart of each and every one of us.

Who will ever forget RONALD REAGAN calling the Soviet Union an evil empire and his challenge to then-Soviet Premier Mikhail Gorbachev outside the Brandenburg Gate in Berlin: "Mr. Gorbachev, tear down this wall!"

And who would ever have imagined the relationship President REAGAN forged with Mr. Gorbachev which ultimately led to the fall of communism and indeed, the tearing down of the Berlin Wall. Mikhail Gorbachev will honor that legacy of President REAGAN by his attendance at Mr. REAGAN's funeral service at the National Cathedral in Washington on Friday, June 11.

RONALD REAGAN was a remarkable man and I believe will be remembered by history as one of the greatest Presidents of our Nation. I will close by sharing his own words spoken in August 1992 about how he wanted to be remembered:

{W}hatever else history may say about me when I'm gone, I hope it will record that I appealed to your best hopes, not your worst fears, to your confidence rather than your doubts. ... May all of you as Americans never forget your heroic origins, never fail to seek divine guidance, and never lose your natural, God-given optimism.

We thank God for the life of RONALD WILSON REAGAN.

Republican Members who were elected in 1980 on the ticket with President REAGAN:

Wendell Bailey, Missouri; Cleve Benedict, West Virginia; Tom Bliley, Virginia; Hank Brown, Colorado; Greg Carman, New York; Gene Chappie, California; Dan Coats, Indiana; Jim Coyne, Pennsylvania; Larry Craig, Idaho; Hal Daub, Nebraska; Larry DeNardis, Connecticut; David Dreier, California; Jim Dunn, Michigan; Bill Emerson, Missouri; T. Cooper Evans, Iowa; Bobbi Fiedler, California; Jack Fields, Texas; Steve Gunderson, Wisconsin; and Judd Gregg, New Hampshire.

James Hansen, Utah; Tommy Hartnett, South Carolina; Bill Hendon, North Carolina; John (Jack) Hiler, Indiana; Duncan Hunter, California; Gene Johnston, North Carolina; John LeBoutillier, New York; Bill Lowery, California; Bill McCollum, Florida; Bob McEwen, Ohio; Ray McGrath, New York; David Martin, New York; Lynn Martin, Illinois; Guy Molinari, New York; Sid Morrison, Washington; John Napier, South Carolina; and Jim Nelligan, Pennsylvania.

Mike Oxley, Ohio; Stan Parris, Virginia; Clint Roberts, South Dakota; Pat Roberts, Kansas; Hal Rogers, Kentucky; Marge Roukema, New Jersey; Claudine Schneider, Rhode Island; Clay Shaw, Florida; Mark Siljander, Michigan; Joe Skeen, New Mexico; Albert Lee Smith, Alabama; Chris Smith, New Jersey; Denny Smith, Oregon; David (Mick) Staton, West Virginia; Ed Weber, Ohio; Vin Weber, Minnesota; Frank Wolf, Virginia; and George Wortley, New York.

{From the *Jerusalem Post*, June 6, 2004}
THE PRISONERS' CONSCIENCE

(By Natan Sharansky)

In 1983, I was confined to an eight-by-ten-foot prison cell on the border of Siberia. My Soviet jailers gave me the privilege of reading the latest copy of Pravda. Splashed across the front page was a condemnation of President RONALD REAGAN for having the temerity to call the Soviet Union an "evil empire." Tapping on walls and talking through toilets, word of REAGAN's "provocation" quickly spread throughout the prison. We dissidents were ecstatic. Finally, the leader of the free world had spoken the truth—a truth that burned inside the heart of each and every one of us.

At the time, I never imagined that three years later, I would be in the White House telling this story to the president. When he summoned some of his staff to hear what I had said, I understood that there had been much criticism of REAGAN's decision to cast the struggle between the superpowers as a battle between good and evil. Well, REAGAN was right and his critics were wrong.

Those same critics used to love calling REAGAN a simpleton who saw the world through a primitive ideological prism and who would convey his ideas through jokes and anecdotes. In our first meeting, he told me that Soviet premier Brezhnev and Kosygin, his second-in-command, were discussing whether they should allow freedom of emigration. "Look, America's really pressuring us," Brezhnev said, "maybe we should just open up the gates. The problem is, we might be the only two people who wouldn't leave." To which Kosygin replied, "Speak for yourself."

What his critics didn't seem to understand was that the jokes and anecdotes that so endeared REAGAN to people were merely his way of expressing fundamental truths in a way that everyone could understand.

REAGAN's tendency to confuse names and dates, something I, too, experienced first-hand, also made him the target of ridicule. In September 1987, a few months before a summit meeting with Gorbachev in Washington, I met with REAGAN to ask him what he thought about the idea of holding a massive rally of hundreds of thousands of people on behalf of Soviet Jewry during the summit. Some Jewish leaders, concerned that if the rally were held Jews would be accused of undermining a renewed hope for peace between the superpowers, had expressed reservations about such a frontal challenge to the Soviet premier.

Seeing me together for the first time with my wife Avital, who had fought for many years for my release, REAGAN greeted us like a proud grandparent, knowing he had played an important role in securing my freedom. He told us about his commitment to Soviet Jewry. "My dear Mr. and Mrs. Shevardnadze," he said, "I just spoke with Soviet Foreign Minister Sharansky, and I said you better let those Jews go."

Not wanting to embarrass the president over his mistake, I quickly asked him about the rally, outlining the concerns raised by some of my colleagues. His response was immediate: "Do you think I am interested in a friendship with the Soviets if they continue to keep their people in prison? You do what you believe is right."

REAGAN may have confused names and dates, but his moral compass was always good. Today's leaders, in contrast, may know their facts and figures, but are often woefully confused about what should be the simplest distinctions between freedom and tyranny, democrats and terrorists.

The legacy of president REAGAN will surely endure. Armed with moral clarity, a deep faith in freedom, and the courage to follow his convictions, he was instrumental in helping the West win the Cold War and hundreds of millions of people behind the Iron Curtain win their freedom.

As one of those people, I can only express my deepest gratitude to this great leader. Believe me, I will take moral clarity and Shevardnadze any day.

Hon. Eni F.H. Faleomavaega

OF AMERICAN SAMOA

Mr. Speaker, I rise today to pay tribute to former President RONALD REAGAN who passed away on Saturday June 5, 2004. At this time, I extend my deepest condolences to his loving wife, Nancy, and his children, and I join with our Nation in mourning the loss of a great leader.

RONALD WILSON REAGAN was born in Tampico, IL, to Nelle Wilson and John Edward "Jack" Reagan. In 1928, RONALD REAGAN graduated from Dixon High School where he served as student body president. From 1928 to 1932, REAGAN attended Eureka College, a small liberal arts institution in Illinois. He majored in economics and sociology.

In 1937, REAGAN enlisted in the Army Reserve as a private and was soon promoted to second lieutenant in the Officers Reserve Corps of the Cavalry. While in the Army, an agent for Warner Brothers discovered RONALD REAGAN. In 1940, REAGAN wed Jane Wyman.

In 1942, the Army Air Force called REAGAN to active duty. He was assigned to the First Motion Picture Unit in Culver City, CA, where he made over 400 training films. REAGAN was discharged from the Army in 1945 at the rank of captain.

After the war, REAGAN resumed his acting career and in 1952 wed Nancy Davis. In 1956, REAGAN campaigned as a Democrat for Eisenhower. In 1960, he campaigned for Richard Nixon. In 1962, he officially changed his party registration to Republican.

In 1966, REAGAN was elected Governor of California and was reelected in 1970. On November 4, 1980, RONALD WILSON REAGAN became the 40th President of the United States.

RONALD REAGAN wished to be remembered as the President who wanted Americans to believe in themselves. We will remember him for much more.

We will remember RONALD REAGAN as a political leader who worked diligently to stimulate economic growth, increase employment and strengthen national defense. He was the Great Communicator whose words and actions spoke of honor and peace.

Through his convictions, we witnessed the fall of the Berlin Wall and the end of the cold war. "Peace through strength" is what he sought and achieved.

In his own words taken from 1986 as he sought to comfort us after the *Challenger* disaster:

> We will never forget {him}, nor the last time we saw {him} ... as {he} prepared for {his} journey and waved good-bye and "slipped the surly bonds of earth" to "touch the face of God."

Hon. Randy "Duke" Cunningham

OF CALIFORNIA

Mr. Speaker, I rise to honor and mourn the passing of one of the greatest Presidents in American history—RONALD WILSON REAGAN. This leader was a man of clear vision, principle and conviction, a Great Communicator, and an individual who had perhaps one of the greatest influences on my life.

An eternal optimist with a can-do spirit, President REAGAN once said in my hometown of San Diego:

> You know, the United States was never meant to be a second-best nation. ... we set our sights on the stars, and we're going for the gold.

He also believed that this forward-looking superpower Nation could transform the global picture.

He came to the job armed with one underlying philosophy: Freedom. Freedom for the economy, for individuals, our Nation, and people around the globe.

RONALD REAGAN brought our economy back to life. It was his policies that ultimately put Congress on a course to the fiscal discipline that spurred a balanced budget and economic growth.

President REAGAN followed through on his pledge to restore our military, and he brought back the pride associated with serving this Nation.

Despite the rhetoric and good intentions of those on the other side of the political spectrum, it was RONALD REAGAN who actually initiated the disarmament of whole classes of nuclear weapons. Perhaps his greatest legacy will be that of bringing an end to the cold war. Staring down repressive governments and challenging them to a new way of life, he brought freedom to millions of people around the globe.

Using old Navy terms to describe his first term, President REAGAN once said, "We've taken control of the ship of state and changed direction. And what are we going to do now? Well, the way I see it, it's all ahead full, no turning back."

For his imprint on history, for his legacy which will be felt for generations to come, this Nation owes President REAGAN a debt of gratitude.

I am pleased that one of the President's many legacies is the Navy's newest nuclear carrier, the USS *Ronald Reagan*. That ship recently set sail from Norfolk for its rightful home in San Diego.

Throughout his political career, President REAGAN always concluded his campaigns in San Diego. He called it his lucky city. It is only fitting that our "shining city on the hill," San Diego, will be called home to the USS *Reagan*. This ship is perhaps the most fitting tribute to RONALD REAGAN's legacy of strength and security, to the imprint he had on our past and the promise that we hold for the future.

We anxiously await the arrival of the *Reagan*, and welcome it to the lucky city. The way I see it, it's all ahead full, no turning back.

Hon. Jim Kolbe

OF ARIZONA

Mr. Speaker, RONALD REAGAN's passing gives this Nation an opportunity to reflect on the can-do attitude that he exuded and the greatness of the American people that he believed in. He was the essential American, a President born in mid-America, instilled with solid midwestern values. He had a deep love affair with the American people, and they with him. Like Franklin Roosevelt, he was an American icon, and like Roosevelt, he had an uncanny ability to connect and communicate with common people.

Today we salute four tenets of President REAGAN's legacy: economic growth, deregulation, "peace through strength," and patriotism though a return of the American dream.

The father of Reaganomics launched the boldest economic plan since FDR that promoted lower taxes, sound money, and less regulation. REAGAN unveiled a "program for economic recovery" to a joint session of Congress calling for $41.4 billion in tax cuts—the largest in history.

REAGAN was an advocate for deregulation and free trade pacts. He worked to tear down barriers to enterprise and encourage a spirit of self enterprise. His commitment to deregulation was evident when in 1981 he took decisive action to carry out this promise to fire 13,000 air traffic controllers for an illegal strike.

After years of crumbling defense spending, President REAGAN increased defense spending 35 percent during two terms and promoted "peace through strength." He called the Soviet Union for what it was—an evil empire—and by standing firm against it hastened the end of the cold war and the return of Russia to the family of nations.

Influenced by his humble beginnings, REAGAN's patriotism and optimistic spirit exemplified the American dream. He restored America's can-do creed. We will always remember the words of his farewell address, when he said those of his generation "were taught, very directly, what it means to be an American. And we absorbed, almost in the air, a love of country and an appreciation of its institutions."

He never trimmed his sails or compromised his values. We will remember him as a President who understood the balance between pragmatism and partisanship. We will remember him as the Great Communicator who united Americans toward common goals. But most of all we will remember him as a great President who brought honor and respect to the Office of President. I join with all Americans in expressing our sympathy to Nancy Reagan and his family for the loss of this great American.

Hon. Peter Hoekstra

OF MICHIGAN

Mr. Speaker, today I rise in honor of RONALD REAGAN, the 40th President of the United States and one of the greatest leaders and statesmen of the 20th century.

America has long known that President REAGAN was ill, but his death came as a shock to a country that continued to feel his presence. He touched millions of lives during his tenure as Governor of California and two terms in America's highest office. Although long anticipated, his passing marks with finality the end of the Reagan era.

President REAGAN's commitment to freedom altered the course of modern history. He brought the United States through the end of the cold war with strength and resolve, and he led the U.S. economy to heights once unimaginable through his sound domestic policies.

He possessed a vision for America that reflected its devotion to individual liberty, that every person is born with the intrinsic right to achieve their dreams through their own labors and determination.

He will forever be remembered as a champion of promoting peace and prosperity throughout the world with a strong faith at the core of his principles and values. He was a great man elected to take charge of a great country at a time when strong leadership was sorely needed.

President REAGAN's infectious optimism inspired many Americans to become involved in the political process, and his influence and vision will continue to live throughout the ages.

My prayers and those of my family are with the family and hundreds of millions of friends of President REAGAN, knowing that the Lord has preserved a very special place for him in Heaven.

Hon. Patrick J. Tiberi

OF OHIO

Mr. Speaker, folks from across the country came to Washington this week to mourn the passing of President RONALD REAGAN. Even in death, the former President continued his fascinating connection with Americans of all types.

Although I never met RONALD REAGAN, he was one of my inspirations for entering politics. I was 18 at the time of his 1980 Presidential campaign and it was the first big election to which I really paid attention. I remember being drawn to what this man, a half a century older than me, was saying about having faith in our country, its people and their future. He was optimistic, cheerful and came across as a thoroughly likable guy.

It was simply astounding how he could establish a bond with even the most unlikely audience. In 1984, I was a senior at the Ohio State University and a member of the marching band. We were asked to play at a rally that President REAGAN would be holding at St. John Arena. At first we all thought it would be an official band appearance, but then we were informed that since the President's visit was actually a campaign event, we could not appear as the Ohio State University Marching Band. If we wished, though, we could volunteer on our own, and appear without our uniforms. There were roughly 200 members in the band at that time and, as I recall, roughly 200 of us jumped at the opportunity to play at the President's campaign event. Think of it. A couple of hundred college kids were treating the appearance of a 73-year-old Republican President as enthusiastically as the Michigan game—we would not have missed it for the world.

President REAGAN could connect with college kids and he could connect with Democrats, particularly those like my dad, an Italian immigrant who worked as a machinist. He came to America so he could have a better life and his kids' lives would be better still. He knew exactly what RONALD REAGAN was talking about.

He was the Great Communicator. President REAGAN swept aside the filters and "analysis" of the news media and spoke from the Oval Office directly with the American people. He had the gift of explaining issues and his positions on them in simple, effective terms—a gift all too few of us in politics today possess. President REAGAN spoke in a way that made Americans feel like they were almost partners with him.

Perception is reality, and RONALD REAGAN knew that. His message of hope and optimism put a new face on the Republican Party, and brought an end to the dour Nixonian era of GOP politics. Young people like me began looking at the Republican Party in a different way. Because of RONALD REAGAN, we could take pride in being Republicans.

I was struck by the attitude I saw in Washington this week. Certainly, there was sadness and grief over the loss of one of the giants of our time. But in keeping with the makeup of the man himself, there was more. As often as not, people also smiled when they spoke of RONALD REAGAN, often displaying that same sense of hope and good cheer that he himself had radiated throughout his life. For all his accomplishments, it's that same sense of hope and optimism that I'll think of whenever I remember RONALD REAGAN.

Hon. Michael R. Turner
OF OHIO

Mr. Speaker, I'm honored to join my colleagues in support of H. Res. 664, honoring the late Honorable RONALD WILSON REAGAN, the 40th President of the United States. As is the case for so many speaking in this Chamber today, RONALD REAGAN was one of my personal heroes.

Although we are all deeply saddened by the passing of President REAGAN, Americans today are still touched by his legacy and his steadfast belief in the promise of this great Nation. By using his famous wit, he knew how to make us believe in ourselves again. Each of us has our favorite examples of the Reagan wit. My favorite quote is:

{G}overnment's view of the economy could be summed up in a few short phrases: If it moves, tax it. If it keeps moving, regulate it. And if it stops moving, subsidize it.

To RONALD REAGAN:

America is a shining city upon a hill for all to see and to follow and reach to, something toward which mankind should strive.

REAGAN brought convictions and determination as well as a genuine, hopeful and optimistic outlook to the Office of President. RONALD REAGAN never doubted his convictions. He never lost faith in America. His reassuring tones were comforting even in difficult times. With REAGAN as President, it was indeed morning again in America.

Just prior to RONALD REAGAN assuming the Presidency, many people wondered whether this country's best days were behind us. REAGAN insisted that America's best days lie ahead. By the time he left office, the United States was enjoying the longest peacetime economic expansion in our history. President REAGAN's most long-lasting legacy is his role in winning the cold war. While the common doctrine of the time called for containing communism, REAGAN boldly predicted it would soon be "left on the ash heap of history."

During the journey that was the Reagan revolution, he restored prosperity, confidence, optimism, faith and pride in America. While we will miss RONALD REAGAN, his contributions to the world will be felt for generations to come. He came to Washington to change the country and ended up changing the world. As he said in his farewell address to the Nation from the Oval Office:

{A} final word to the men and women of the Reagan revolution, the men and women across America who for eight years did the work that brought America back. My friends: We did it. We weren't just marking time. We made a difference. We made the city stronger. We made the city freer, and we left her in good hands. All in all, not bad, not bad at all.

Summing up an American icon, a giant, like RONALD REAGAN is an enormous task. I am grateful for the vision RONALD REAGAN taught me and the lessons about the power of convictions, the value of principled leadership, and the goodness and the decency of the human spirit. We'll miss the twinkle in his eyes and affable smile which have left this Earth. However, the contributions he made to his country and to mankind remain with us, as vast as the great continent that the United States spans, and God willing, will outlast us all.

As an American, I want to join in offering my support of H. Res. 664, honoring the late Honorable RONALD WILSON REAGAN, the 40th President of the United States.

Hon. Jane Harman

OF CALIFORNIA

Mr. Speaker, I join my colleagues in offering a tribute to former President RONALD REAGAN. He is rightly remembered as a larger-than-life figure—a man who conquered first Hollywood, then California, and then Washington, DC, and whose message of freedom and democracy spread around the world. Though I did not know him well, I did know his daughter Maureen very well, and she is also missed.

President REAGAN was naturally possessed of the qualities that make a great leader. As Governor of California and later as President, he used a blend of humor, kindness and boldness to communicate with the American people, to challenge and defeat the Soviet adversary, and to promote his uniquely American vision of how things should be.

While I disagreed with a number of his policies, I always admired his ability to convey his ideas and his power to persuade.

The enormous outpouring of emotion and love for this man comes as no surprise. When we think of RONALD WILSON REAGAN, we will remember his infectious optimism and grace, and his belief that there is always a better day ahead for America.

Hon. Eliot L. Engel

OF NEW YORK

Mr. Speaker, along with all of my colleagues here today, I rise to honor President RONALD REAGAN. I was first elected to Congress in 1988, on the same day that President George H.W. Bush was elected. Because Members of Congress officially take office on January 3, while a new President does not take office until January 20, my first 17 days as a Congressman were during the last 17 days RONALD REAGAN served as President. So when people ask me who was the President when I first came to Washington, I reply that it was RONALD REAGAN. I had the opportunity to see RONALD REAGAN in person only one time, with his wife Nancy, during the inauguration of President George H.W. Bush. I remember thinking that together they had a larger than life presence.

Although I differed with RONALD REAGAN a great deal on domestic policy, I nevertheless admired him for the strong leader that he was. He had an affable manner that allowed him to interact well with people who both supported and opposed his policies. He was a strong leader who had a lot of charm, strength and enthusiasm.

The gulf between the Republican and Democratic policies can sometimes seem vast. But the bridge that spans that gulf is our common heritage as Americans and belief in this great Nation. RONALD REAGAN had the gift to make that bridge seem very small. I am pleased to honor him today.

Hon. Anne M. Northup

OF KENTUCKY

Mr. Speaker, our Nation honors the life of one of the most beloved, and most important, Presidents of the 20th century. During the eighties, President REAGAN did what many considered the impossible.

As we faced great challenges at home and abroad, he helped us believe that it was "morning in America," and that we would overcome our difficulties. With the will of the Nation behind him, President REAGAN's steadfast leadership led to the defeat of communism and a robust economic recovery.

When President REAGAN took office a quarter century ago, communism was on the march, threatening to bring the free world to its knees.

But President REAGAN's policy of "peace through strength" starved the Soviet bloc and made it safe for freedom to flourish in new nations. "No weapon in the arsenals of the world is so formidable as the will ... of free men and women," he said.

Here at home, our country was in the worst recession since the Great Depression, with high unemployment, inflation, and interest rates. But President REAGAN trusted the entrepreneurial spirit and cut taxes from 70 percent to 28 percent, creating 19 million new jobs and 20 years of growth. His economic policies formed the foundation upon which American families prosper. "We believe that no power of government is as formidable a force for good as the creativity and entrepreneurial drive of the American people," he said.

By rallying the will of our country, by reminding us of our remarkable abilities—of what it means to be Americans, President REAGAN reunited us as a confident and hopeful Nation. And with a focused vision, he set us on a course that preserved our liberty and allowed our domestic economy to prosper again.

In life, President REAGAN was a guiding light for our Nation. Even when times were tough, he rejected the idea that America's best days were past, insisting that there is no limit to what our Nation and our people can endure—or accomplish. And he was right.

Today we face a new enemy of liberty, in the war on terror. It is my hope, Mr. Speaker, that the confident optimism and clear vision that President REAGAN gave to this Nation will light our path.

May God bless President RONALD REAGAN.

Hon. Tom Davis

OF VIRGINIA

Mr. Speaker, I was deeply saddened to learn of the passing of President REAGAN over the weekend. My thoughts and prayers go out to Nancy and to the Reagan family and friends. This is an extraordinarily difficult time for any family, but I hope they can find some comfort in the joy and inspiration that President REAGAN brought to so many around the globe.

RONALD REAGAN was a true American original, a midwestern boy of humble beginnings who chased his dreams of stardom in Hollywood and evolved into one of the foremost political leaders of the 20th century.

His legacy is so profound and pervasive that it's easy to take for granted. But we should not forget that it was RONALD REAGAN who restored strength to the Office of the President. It was RONALD REAGAN who reshaped the Federal Government and ushered in two decades (and counting) of lower taxes and economic growth. It was RONALD REAGAN who bolstered America's strength as a world military power. And it was RONALD REAGAN who reminded us that America was indeed that "shining city on the hill," and we had bountiful reasons to be proud to be Americans.

His love of country was a guiding force throughout his life and his political career—he knew America was great because America was free, and he sought to shine the light of freedom on corners of the globe darkened by the stain of totalitarianism. His demand for Mikhail Gorbachev to "tear down this wall!" is not only a seminal moment into cold war history, but a reminder that America's democratic ideals are ultimately stronger than any barriers erected by forces of oppression.

Quite simply, President REAGAN's words and actions helped change the world for the better. And I can't think of a greater accomplishment than that.

We lost more than a man on Saturday, when President REAGAN ended his long journey into the sunset.

We lost a true giant, and a great American.

Hon. Rob Simmons

OF CONNECTICUT

Mr. Speaker, I rise to commemorate the passing of RONALD REAGAN, the 40th President of the United States of America.

As a Vietnam veteran and an officer with the CIA from 1969 to 1979, my world was changed dramatically and for the better when RONALD REAGAN won his historic Presidential race in November 1980.

At the time I was serving on the staff of Senator John H. Chafee (R–RI). Politically, it was a watershed year. Not only did the Senate go from Democrat to Republican control for the first time in 26 years, but also some very well-known Democratic Senators were swept from office in the Reagan revolution. They included Senator Frank Church, former chairman of the Committee to Investigate the Intelligence Activities of the United States, and Birch Bayh, second chairman of the newly established Senate Select Committee on Intelligence.

The Senate Intelligence Committee, where I went on to serve for 4 years as staff director, gained new leadership under Chairman Barry Goldwater and Vice Chairman Daniel Patrick Moynihan.

Goldwater had a long-standing and close political relationship with RONALD REAGAN. In fact, many have said that a speech delivered by REAGAN during Goldwater's historic 1964 Presidential campaign propelled REAGAN into the national political spotlight.

Goldwater was excited to work with President REAGAN and CIA Director William Casey to institute a new approach to intelligence oversight. First, it focused on bipartisan consensus in intelligence where Vice Chairman Moynihan was a valued partner.

It also departed from the adversarial process of Senators Church and Bayh, and focused on rebuilding the morale and intelligence capabilities of American intelligence. Rather than adopting Church's belief that the CIA was a "rogue elephant," Goldwater expressed his supportive feelings by talking about the "intelligence family."

Sadly, in 1984 these positive developments were disrupted when the CIA was discovered to have been covertly involved in the mining of Nicaraguan harbors without proper notification to Congress. In the ensuing firestorm, Barry Goldwater wrote a pointed note to CIA Director Casey expressing his concern over the lack of communication. The letter was quickly leaked to an eager press, excited that Senator Goldwater was at odds with the Reagan administration.

At the time these events were unfolding, President REAGAN was scheduled to appear at the Washington Hilton for the White House Correspondents Association annual black-tie dinner. Many observers felt that the press would use the opportunity to embarrass the President over the intelligence "flap." But, in what was to become a classic response of the President to a difficult situation, RONALD REAGAN opened his remarks by saying:

> What's all that talk about a breakdown of White House communications? How come nobody told me? {Laughter.} Well, I know this: I've laid down the law, though, to everyone there from now on about anything that happens, no matter what time it is, wake me, even if it's in the middle of a Cabinet meeting. {Laughter.}[1]

It was to the point. It was funny. It was self-deprecating. It defused for a moment what was a gathering storm for the administration. It gave everyone the opportunity to step away from a potentially explosive moment and get on with the challenging business of government.

Mr. Speaker, under the leadership of President REAGAN, the United States rebuilt her intelligence and national security structure from 1980 to 1988. This was not done without controversy, but it was done. Morale was restored at the Central Intelligence Agency and elsewhere in the intelligence community. Capabilities were improved.

The military, too, regained a new pride and strength following the disasters in Vietnam and Iran. Members of the Armed Forces felt their service was respected by the Commander in Chief, and they valued his support. They loved his patriotic speeches, and were eager to follow his lead.

And yet for all of his accomplishments as a national and world leader, President REAGAN never lost the personal touch. When I departed Washington, DC, in early 1985, I left with a personal letter of thanks signed by the President.

This letter hangs in my office even today as a proud reminder of what President REAGAN and Congress were able to accomplish during those difficult but historic years. It is also a clear symbol of a man who never allowed the trappings

---

[1] Bob Woodward, Veil: The Secret Wars of the CIA 1981–1987, p. 333. The official presidential documents recorded that the President received 26 more laughs.

of high office to obscure his view of the "little people" who constitute the strength of our government and Nation.

Now, as we remember the life of RONALD REAGAN, and as his casket lies with honor under the Capitol dome, it is my turn to thank him for his distinguished service to our country and to the world. He left us a better people and he left the world a better place.

The man will be missed, but the memory lives on in all of us who were touched by his life and his leadership.

ADJOURNMENT

Mr. LEWIS of California. Mr. Speaker, I move that the House do now adjourn.

The motion was agreed to; accordingly (at 10 o'clock and 29 minutes p.m.), pursuant to House Resolution 663, the House adjourned until tomorrow, Wednesday, June 9, 2004, at 10 a.m. in memory of the late Honorable RONALD WILSON REAGAN, former President of the United States.

PUBLIC BILLS AND RESOLUTIONS

Under clause 2 of rule XII, public bills and resolutions were introduced and severally referred, as follows:

By Mr. MILLER of Florida (for himself, Mr. Bishop of Utah, Mr. Bradley of New Hampshire, Mr. Doolittle, Mr. Foley, Mr. McCotter, Mr. Pence, Mr. Rogers of Alabama, Mr. Souder, Mr. Weldon of Florida, Mr. Feeney, Mr. Lincoln Diaz-Balart of Florida, Ms. Harris, and Mr. Jones of North Carolina):

H.R. 4525. A bill to require the Secretary of the Treasury to redesign the half dollar coin to commemorate RONALD WILSON REAGAN, and for other purposes; to the Committee on Financial Services.

By Mr. NEY (for himself and Mr. Larson of Connecticut):

H. Con. Res. 444. Concurrent resolution authorizing the use of the rotunda of the Capitol for the lying in state of the remains of the late Honorable RONALD WILSON REAGAN, the fortieth President of the United States; to the Committee on House Administration.

By Mr. DeLay:

H. Res. 663. A resolution expressing the profound regret and sorrow of the House of Representatives on the death of RONALD WILSON REAGAN, former President of the United States of America; considered and agreed to.

By Mr. LEWIS of California (for himself, Mr. Waxman, Mr. Dreier, Mr. George Miller of California, Mr. Cox, Mr. Thomas, Mr. Hunter, Mr. Gallegly, Mr. Herger, Mr. Rohrabacher, Mr. Cunningham, Mr. Doolittle, Mr. Calvert, Mr. McKeon, Mr. Pombo, Mr. Royce, Mr. Farr, Mr. Radanovich, Ms. Loretta Sanchez of California, Mrs. Bono, Mrs. Capps, Mr. Gary G. Miller of California, Mr. Ose, Mr. Issa, Mr. Nunes, Ms. Lofgren, Mr. Schiff, Mr. Cardoza, Mr. Sherman, Ms. Pelosi, Mr. Costello, Ms. Harman, Mr. Berman, Mr. Neugebauer, Mrs. Davis of California, Mr. Lantos, Mr. Filner, Mr. Shadegg, Ms. Eshoo, and Mr. Matsui):

H. Res. 664. A resolution mourning the passing of President RONALD REAGAN and celebrating his service to the people of the United States and his leadership in promoting the cause of freedom for all the people of the world; to the Committee on Government Reform.

Wednesday, June 9, 2004

Hon. Mark Foley

OF FLORIDA

Mr. Speaker, I come to the floor as my colleagues have before me saddened by the death of one of our Nation's greatest leaders and humbled by the far-reaching impact his life has had on millions of people throughout the world. He was a great man and a gentle spirit. Optimistic, cheerful in service and buoyed by the confidence that comes with unwavering conviction, President REAGAN reignited the feeling of promise for this country.

RONALD REAGAN is the reason I became a Republican. And for many Democrats, he was the pathway to the Republican Party. He reminded us all that government cannot replace individual empowerment and told us in 1995 that every dollar the Federal Government does not take from us, every decision it does not make for us will make our economy stronger, our lives more abundant, and our future more free.

We join together with people across the globe in mourning the loss of RONALD REAGAN. His decisive leadership during the twilight years of the cold war indeed made him a beacon of hope for freedom-loving people throughout the world.

Our thoughts and prayers and our love go out to Mrs. Reagan and the entire family. Because of RONALD REAGAN our Nation is stronger and our future is more free. Here we honor him and are continually working toward the dreamed-of-day he spoke of when no one wields a sword and no one drags a chain.

Hon. Shelley Berkley

OF NEVADA

Mr. Speaker, I rise today to express my sincere condolences to former First Lady Nancy Reagan and the entire Reagan family. And I join our Nation in expressing profound sorrow at the loss of our 40th President.

RONALD REAGAN had a special place in the hearts of Nevadans. Long before he came to the White House, RONALD REAGAN in another life headlined on the Las Vegas Strip as an entertainer in the early fifties. Later as Governor of California, he worked with his counterpart from Nevada, former U.S. Senator and Governor Paul Laxalt, to address environmental threats to Lake Tahoe.

While in the White House, RONALD REAGAN would often turn to his old friend from Nevada, Senator Laxalt, who was one of his closest advisers during his time in our Nation's Capital.

RONALD REAGAN served our Nation with honor and distinction. He will long be remembered for his warm wit, his quiet strength, and ability to inspire through his words and his deeds. His actions as President reshaped the course of the 20th century, and his unbridled optimism helped restore America's faith in itself.

Today we also remember RONALD REAGAN for his leadership and for his unwavering vision that America remains for all a land of hope, promise, and opportunity.

Hon. Joseph R. Pitts

OF PENNSYLVANIA

Mr. Speaker, a few years ago I had the privilege of visiting with Natan Sharansky, a former Soviet dissident who is now an Israeli cabinet minister. I asked him what his reaction was, as he was in the Soviet gulag at that time, to the "Evil Empire" speech. Here is his reaction as expressed in a recent quotation:

In 1983, I was confined to an eight-by-ten-foot prison cell on the border of Siberia. My Soviet jailers gave me the privilege of reading the latest copy of Pravda. Splashed across the front page was a condemnation of President RONALD REAGAN for having the temerity to call the Soviet Union an "evil empire." Tapping on walls and talking through toilets, word of REAGAN's "provocation" quickly spread throughout the prison. We dissidents were ecstatic. Finally, the leader of the free world had spoken the truth—a truth that burned inside the heart of each and every one of us.

At the time, I never imagined that three years later I would be in the White House telling this story to the president. When he summoned some of his staff to hear what I had said, I understood that there had been much criticism of REAGAN's decision to cast the struggle between the superpowers as a battle between good and evil. Well, REAGAN was right and his critics were wrong.

There is no doubt that Natan Sharansky speaks for millions of people who today are free. A great President, with a great legacy, RONALD WILSON REAGAN.

Hon. Joe Wilson

OF SOUTH CAROLINA

Mr. Speaker, the world is grieving this week over the loss of a true American hero, President RONALD WILSON REAGAN. RONALD REAGAN defined the honor and dignity of the Office of the Presidency, and he lifted the spirits of a Nation with his hope and joyfulness that sprang from an abiding faith in God and a deeply held belief in the American dream.

President REAGAN entered office during a time of doubt and despair and malaise with the economy sputtering and a looming cold war that threatened our families. Yet he brought his conservative principles of individual freedom, limited government, personal responsibility, and "peace through strength."

President REAGAN led a successful revolution to promote tax cuts, recognizing taxes are the people's own money. He achieved victory in the cold war, expanding democracy worldwide. And he realigned America's political process with an open door especially for young people.

His legacy lives on today as America unites to fight the war on terror liberating millions from tyranny to protect American families as our economy is booming through tax relief.

May God bless the Reagan family. May God bless our troops. And may God continue to bless America.

Hon. Joel Hefley
OF COLORADO

Mr. Speaker, I rise today, as so many others have, to pay tribute to one of our Nation's finest sons and political leaders. Former President RONALD REAGAN is worthy of respect and admiration both as a man and world leader, and his passing this weekend leaves each of us with a sense of loss and sadness.

His lasting mark on American politics is unquestionable. At a time when it was fashionable to declare one's political moderation, REAGAN fearlessly changed the face of American politics by standing up and boldly declaring himself to be a conservative. He fought for principles and causes that, before his Presidency, were considered heresy. Balanced budgets, tax cuts, smaller government, and a robust national defense were the hallmarks of his ideology, and he never shied away from articulating and fighting for those views.

He proudly became the father of political conservatism and made it possible for people like me to become Members of Congress. In the late seventies and early eighties, those who espoused conservative political views had few outlets from which to share their philosophies, but REAGAN ushered in an era of conservatism whose tide has yet to wane. The makeup of today's political world is due, in large part, to the legacy of RONALD REAGAN.

Hon. Cliff Stearns
OF FLORIDA

Mr. Speaker, what distinguished President REAGAN among American Presidents in the last century? Where many Chief Executives saw gray and moral relativism on the international landscape, he saw good and evil, right and wrong.

What relationship should we in the United States have with the Soviet Union, a tyranny that trampled freedom, starved its people, imprisoned dissidents, choked its economy and wrapped its tentacles around its neighbors? Do we engage them? Do we fight them in one corner of the world while doing business with them in the other? Can we co-exist under the constant threat of mutual destruction and endless arms races? Do we practice detente, containment?

RONALD REAGAN was the President who said, "Americans cannot live like this, and I do not think the world's other citizens should." The day he stood at the Berlin Wall and defiantly challenged the Soviet tyranny with the unforgettable words, "Mr. Gorbachev, tear down this wall!," was the beginning of the end of the cold war. God bless President REAGAN.

Hon. Michael C. Burgess
OF TEXAS

Mr. Speaker, I rise this morning with so many of my friends to pay tribute to the 40th President of the United States, RONALD WILSON REAGAN, and to extend my condolences to his wife Nancy and to his family.

President REAGAN will always be remembered as the architect of policies that ended the cold war—"peace through strength." He more than anyone else was directly responsible for giving us the possibility of a world that could live in peace. He ended the cold war. He ended the threat of hostilities between the United States and Russia, and he brought an end to the Soviet domination in Eastern Europe.

He unleashed the power of the American economy. Yes, it cost money to defeat the Soviet Union. It cost money to defeat Soviet tyranny, but in the long run, was it worth it? You bet it was, for this generation and for the generations to come.

Hon. John J. Duncan, Jr.
OF TENNESSEE

Mr. Speaker, President RONALD REAGAN was an inspiration to me and millions of others throughout the United States and even all over the world. He saw the American dream come true in his life, rising from humble beginnings and achieving great, great success in almost every way.

He will certainly go down in history as one of our greatest Presidents, but his greatness may have been achieved in large part because, as one of his closest friends said a couple of days ago, he did not worry about how history would view him.

It has been said his greatest legacy will be leading us to victory in the cold war, but his domestic achievements were great, too, especially in lowering taxes and helping curb the greed of government.

I had the privilege of meeting President REAGAN on many occasions, starting when he was Governor of California. He was always so kind to me and to everyone, and possibly one of his greatest attributes may have been in showing us that you can have strong views on important issues, but still treat opponents with kindness, compassion and even good humor.

We are all better people, Mr. Speaker, because of the life and example of President RONALD REAGAN.

Hon. Vernon J. Ehlers
OF MICHIGAN

Mr. Speaker, for many years I have heard comments about the power of ideas. I learned as a youngster that the pen is mightier than the sword and that there is nothing so powerful as an idea whose time has come. President RONALD REAGAN demonstrated that these and similar statements are true. He was living proof that ideas win battles.

He was not regarded as an intellectual, but yet he understood the importance of the basic, simple ideas that this country is founded upon, the ideas of peace and freedom, freedom to worship, freedom to speak, freedom of the press, but he also went beyond that. He recognized that these are not ends in themselves, but these are means to an end, and freedom to worship is meaningless unless you use it to worship. Freedom of the press is meaningless unless you use it to print ideas that are for the betterment of the Nation.

Simple ideas, valiantly fought for. With grace, charm and a twinkle in his eye, he succeeded where others had failed. He inspired a troubled Nation. He brought us together. He conquered the symbolic Iron Curtain and brought it down, along with the very real Berlin Wall. He led to nuclear disarmament, the greatest threat to humanity during his tenure.

I rise today to thank President REAGAN for what he did for this country, for the ideas he fought for and the transformation he made in the culture and the attitudes of this Nation.

Hon. Bill Shuster
OF PENNSYLVANIA

Mr. Speaker, we rise today with solemn hearts for the loss of an American hero, a man with an optimistic vision of this country that was infectious. I stand as an individual who felt the energy of the Reagan era.

As a 19-year-old in 1980, I attended my first Republican Convention where RONALD REAGAN accepted the GOP nomination for President. My first vote for President was for RONALD REAGAN, and I spent the beginning of adulthood under the spirit of a man who defined the American dream.

Today we stand in awe of a life of passion and accomplishment. RONALD REAGAN crumbled walls of oppression in Europe and rebuilt the American spirit. He was forever the gentleman statesman, a man who thought that politics, no matter how tough the battle with your opponent, should never leave scars.

In the end he bore no ill will to anyone, and in that mold he was the definition of a leader, a leader who inspired confidence in those around him and who led by example.

He feared not an assassin's bullet or political setback because he always looked to tomorrow, always believed the best days of America were ahead beyond the horizon, and that he would chart the course to take us to a better tomorrow. We stand here as a testament to that simple, yet powerful, truth.

Hon. Mario Diaz-Balart

OF FLORIDA

Mr. Speaker, I am here to really just first express my sorrow and my gratitude to the Reagan family.

Through President REAGAN's optimism and courage and strength, he carried this country from a state of what some people said was a state of malaise to further greatness. He understood and never apologized for his understanding that the United States was a source of good around the world, a source of freedom around the world.

I recall when he said his famous remark about the evil empire how all of the experts said he could not say that, that he was wrong, that they were not bad. Well, he was right, and he tried and fought hard and worked hard to spread freedom across the globe, to strengthen the United States and, therefore, also strengthen our allies to spread freedom.

He succeeded by tearing down the Berlin Wall, by tearing down the evil empire, by spreading freedom to millions of people around the globe.

Mr. Speaker, I am here again in awe of the life of President RONALD REAGAN, his achievements, his success in spreading freedom, his success in making this country what it is today. The greatness that we have achieved today, in great part, is due to the optimism, the greatness, the spirit of RONALD REAGAN. We can never thank him enough.

AUTHORIZING USE OF ROTUNDA OF THE CAPITOL FOR LYING IN STATE OF THE REMAINS OF THE LATE HONORABLE RONALD WILSON REAGAN, 40TH PRESIDENT OF THE UNITED STATES

Mr. EHLERS. Mr. Speaker, I move to suspend the rules and agree to the concurrent resolution (H. Con. Res. 444) authorizing the use of the rotunda of the Capitol for the lying in state of the remains of the late Honorable RONALD WILSON REAGAN, the 40th President of the United States.

The Clerk read as follows:

H. CON. RES. 444

Resolved by the House of Representatives (the Senate concurring), That in recognition of the long and distinguished service rendered to the Nation and the world by RONALD WILSON REAGAN, the 40th President of the United States, the rotunda of the Capitol is authorized to be used for the lying in state of the remains of the late Honorable RONALD REAGAN from June 9 until June 11, 2004. The Architect of the Capitol, under the direction of the Speaker of the House of Representatives and the President pro tempore of the Senate, shall take all steps necessary for carrying out this event.

Hon. Vernon J. Ehlers

OF MICHIGAN

Mr. Speaker, this may seem like a routine resolution because we must pass these resolutions to allow the use of the rotunda of the Capitol for certain events, but frankly, this is a very auspicious moment.

By statute, we have defined how state funerals are to proceed in this Nation's Capital. We have very few of them. I believe the last one was at the time of the death of President Lyndon Johnson of Texas. It is a great honor to host an event such as this in the rotunda, and today I rise to present a resolution which will grant permission to have the body of President RONALD REAGAN rest in state in the rotunda of the Capitol so that the Members of Congress and members of the public may join in honoring him by viewing the casket.

This is, as I said, a very auspicious event, and fortunately, we do not have to do this often. But it inspires in us, again, respect for the ideals of our Nation and for the things that we do and that we believe in.

When President REAGAN's body will arrive, the casket will be placed on a caisson, according to tradition and law, and that horse-drawn procession will proceed from near the White House to the Capitol. It will be followed by a black, riderless horse, indicating a fallen leader. The boots on that horse will be placed in the stirrups backward, indicating the fallen leader reviewing the troops behind him. When that arrives at the Capitol, with great pomp and circumstance, an honor guard will present the casket and the body and carry them inside the Capitol, displaying the casket in the rotunda.

This evening we will have a memorial ceremony, restricted to the Members of Congress, in the rotunda. Following that, the people of this Nation, anyone who wishes, may stand in line and view the casket and give their respects to our fallen President.

It is my pleasure to be able to present this resolution honoring President RONALD REAGAN and providing the opportunity for the Members of Congress and for the public to view the casket and to pay their respects to this great man. It is the least we can do, and I wish we could do more because he did a marvelous job of leading this Nation in a very troubled time. When we had a broken economy and a dispirited people, he restored their spirits with grace, charm and a twinkle in his eye and eventually helped us prevail over the Soviet Union, which had threatened us for decades with nuclear weapons.

The world is a far better place because of RONALD REAGAN, what he did, and the leadership he provided, and it is my pleasure to present this resolution and honor him in this way.

Hon. Juanita Millender-McDonald

OF CALIFORNIA

Mr. Speaker, it is with great sorrow that I join the distinguished chairman, or the appropriate person in his place, in support of this legislation to authorize use of the Capitol rotunda for this very sad occasion.

There can be no more proper use of the rotunda, the center of the temple of our democracy, than to honor the late former President RONALD REAGAN with a state funeral and lying in state.

With this observance, President REAGAN will take his proper place in the pantheon of American heroes who have lain in state in this temple, befitting their vast contributions to the fabric of our national political life.

Although I did not have the honor to serve in the Congress during President REAGAN's term, I greatly admired him as a statesman, and his skills as the Great Communicator, and am grateful for everything he did for our country.

Mr. Speaker, it is especially fitting that Congress and the Nation pay their respects to our 40th President in this temple because several memorable events of his 8 years in office took place here. Of course, he delivered all of his State of the Union Messages right here in this Chamber, including the one in which he dropped several pounds of paper onto the rostrum and urged Congress not to send him any more massive, catch-all spending bills.

In 1985, President REAGAN returned from a Geneva summit meeting with Soviet Leader Mikhail Gorbachev, flew directly from Andrews Air Force Base to the Capitol by helicopter, and addressed a joint session, reporting hopeful progress on arms control and reassuring the Nation and the world.

Perhaps more relevant to the resolution before us, many Americans will recall that the bitter cold of January 21, 1985, forced President REAGAN's second inaugural ceremony to come indoors and take place in the rotunda itself in order to protect the multitudes attending and participating in the inauguration, who would otherwise have been at great risk from the elements and frostbite.

Throughout his life and career, President REAGAN was always considerate of others. And like others who have preceded him in the Nation's highest office, RONALD REAGAN hailed from a humble background. Born in 1911 in Illinois, REAGAN grew up in the town of Dixon, was active in sports, drama, and student politics, all of which would serve him well later. In 1932, the future President graduated from Eureka College with a degree in economics and sociology. He embarked on a radio career that eventually led him to Hollywood, where he worked in the entertainment industry for two decades, principally in motion pictures.

He appeared in over 50 movies, including one of my favorites, the 1940 "Knute Rockne: All American." In the film, REAGAN portrayed the legendary Notre Dame athlete George Gipp, who set numerous football records during a 5-year career before succumbing in 1920 to an infection that struck 20 years before the discovery of antibiotics. In the movie's climax, REAGAN earned his lifelong nickname when the dying Gipp asked Coach Rockne to urge his teammates to go out there and "win one for the Gipper." For us football fans, especially one who has a son who played football, the scene is priceless. My son loved the movie, and he certainly loves football as well. And I have little doubt that today, for millions of Americans, the legends of George Gipp and the man who portrayed him on film have become inextricably linked.

In the sixties, when the GIPPER became active in politics, he generally supported Republican candidates, including Richard Nixon and Barry Goldwater. Like Nixon and Goldwater, REAGAN became known as an ardent anticommunist. In 1966, he became a Republican candidate himself, winning the first of two terms as Governor of California.

Two years after leaving office in Sacramento, Governor REAGAN challenged President Gerald Ford for the GOP nomination for the Presidency, and nearly won it. In 1980, he won both the Republican Presidential nomination and the general election, where he received nearly 51 percent of the popular vote and carried 45 States and 489 electoral votes.

Of course, we all recall that in 1981 an assassin nearly ended our new President's life in a hail of gunshots here in Washington. Fortunately, the would-be assassin failed to achieve his demented purpose, and the President went on to survive not only gunshot wounds but also colon cancer.

The President also survived the bruising political battles so common in this Capital City. He did so simply by refusing to take politics personally. President REAGAN's ability to build and maintain a lasting friendship with House Speaker Tip O'Neill, with whom he disagreed on many political issues, exemplified an approach to politics and to governing which I greatly admire, and one that I wish others would emulate.

In 1984, President REAGAN won reelection, with nearly 59 percent of the popular vote, the electoral votes of 49 States, and completed his two momentous terms. By the time he left office in 1989, he was, despite large budget deficits and the Iran-Contra scandal, one of our most beloved Presidents.

The massive outpouring of grief seen across this country and the world since his death on Saturday is abundant proof of the esteem Americans hold for their 40th President throughout every city, suburb, and hamlet in this land.

Mr. Speaker, the state funeral and the lying in state authorized in the rotunda this week will be solemn state occasions whose purpose is to provide the public with an opportunity to view the body and mourn the passing of a head of state. Ceremony, history, and protocol will permeate these rites.

Among them, it is worth noting, that when President REAGAN's body lies in state in the rotunda, his remains will rest upon the historic catafalque constructed for the funeral of our 16th President, Abraham Lincoln, another son of Illinois. All those who have lain in state in the Capitol rotunda have rested on the Lincoln catafalque, made of simple pine boards and draped in black velvet.

It is fitting that this relic, built for one who became, if not in life, one of the most cherished and beloved Presidents, will now be used to support the body of our 40th President, a cherished and beloved successor to Lincoln. As a people, we are truly grateful for President REAGAN's long service to our country and for the opportunity to honor him and his memory in this way.

Mr. Speaker, I am honored to play a role in these proceedings by managing this resolution for the minority, in the absence of our ranking member. I hope that all my colleagues will join in paying tribute to our 40th President by supporting this very important resolution.

Hon. Christopher Cox

OF CALIFORNIA

Mr. Speaker, I thank the gentleman for yielding me this time, and it is entirely fitting that we pass this resolution authorizing the remains of President REAGAN to lie in state in the Nation's Capital.

It was in this building that President REAGAN took the oath of office in January 1981. Eight years later, he yielded his authority as President and Commander in Chief in this building, in that quiet peaceful transfer of power that is the hallmark of our democracy.

Many of the shining moments of his two Presidential terms took place right here in this Chamber. None are more thrilling than that 1982 State of the Union that marked his triumphant return shortly after he was shot by a would-be Presidential assassin.

And some of his greatest challenges have close associations with this Chamber as well. In his second term, after President REAGAN had won Senate passage of his request for aid to the freedom fighters in Nicaragua, the challenge he faced was in this House. The President asked permission to address the House, but Speaker O'Neill said no. I served then as legal counsel in the White House, and I was asked whether the Speaker of the House could deny the President the opportunity to come and address the Congress in the people's House. And my answer, swiftly delivered, was "absolutely."

President REAGAN did not mind the legal advice. He asked, "They all have televisions, don't they?" And he addressed the Nation from the Oval Office. As a result of that magnificent address, intended for all of us here but absorbed equally by the American people, this Congress did the right thing and democracy did move forward in Nicaragua. The Soviet Union was not able to establish a beachhead in our own hemisphere. And whereas upon President REAGAN's assumption of office there were only 56 electoral democracies in the world, today there are 117, and over 1 billion people now live in democracies that otherwise would not.

When President REAGAN took the oath of office here in this building, he was facing west. The west front of the Capitol was the staging area for that inauguration. He was the first President to do so. He thought it was important to face west, because not only was he a westerner, not only was he a Californian, but the history of our country moving westward signified the spirit of frontier, the pioneer spirit, and entrepreneurship that President REAGAN thought was the genius of America.

When his body is placed in the rotunda later today, it will come to the Capitol up those same steps on the west front and all of us will be looking west to his beloved State of California thinking about what President REAGAN meant by that symbolism.

So it is entirely appropriate that we pass this resolution we address now. I know that each of us will take personal pride in recalling his contributions to our country, to our sense of patriotism as we observe the ceremonies in the rotunda later today and as we have our own personal moment to walk by that casket.

Hon. John B. Larson

OF CONNECTICUT

Mr. Speaker, I join with the distinguished gentleman from Michigan (Mr. Ehlers) and the distinguished gentlewoman from California (Ms. Millender-McDonald) in support of this motion to suspend the rules and pass the resolution to authorize the use of the Capitol rotunda to honor President REAGAN and I would urge all Members to do likewise.

Mr. Speaker, this is a very sad occasion for our country. Last Saturday, June 5, 2004, RONALD WILSON REAGAN, the 40th President of the United States, departed this life, and now belongs to the ages.

Since I was first elected to this House in 1998, I did not have the privilege of serving with President REAGAN. But I certainly wish I had known him. President REAGAN's engaging smile, his reassured demeanor, and his boundless optimism about America, her people and her future, were literally contagious.

And the contagion surely did spread, Mr. Speaker. The overwhelming grief since President

REAGAN's death reflects the American people's respect for the man, and their gratitude for what he accomplished for present and future generations. While he may now be gone, he will never be forgotten.

Mr. Speaker, as the Congress and the Nation mourn our 40th President in the Capitol rotunda, we might recall the many memorable moments that occurred under this great dome during his 8 years in office. Indeed a harbinger of things to come, President REAGAN asked that his inauguration take place for the first time on the west front of the Capitol, so he could look out across The Mall toward the west. Not only did this vista accommodate more people attending the ceremony in person, it symbolically shifted the ceremony's focus toward the vast reaches of the country, where most Americans live.

Of course, President REAGAN delivered all of his State of the Union Messages, and addressed other joint sessions of Congress, from right here in the House Chamber. Once, after Congress had wrapped an entire year's worth of appropriations bills into one mammoth measure, he dramatically plopped a huge stack of paper—not even printed, but instead, Xeroxed copies—onto the desk with a "thud." He implored lawmakers never to repeat the practice. Unfortunately, it has done so repeatedly in the years since that speech. It was a bad practice in President REAGAN's time, and it is a bad practice today.

President REAGAN's second inaugural took place in the rotunda, driven inside by the cold winter of 1985. While some television viewers might have been disappointed at the cancellation of the outdoor inaugural and the accompanying parade, I am sure many parents of high school students scheduled to march in the festivities were relieved. In another thoughtful gesture, the President paused during his inaugural address to note the passing of a Democratic Representative, Gillis Long of Louisiana, who had died hours before.

Throughout his life and career, President REAGAN was always considerate of others. Perhaps this attribute reflected the midwestern values of his native Illinois, and the fact that RONALD REAGAN came from humble beginnings.

Born in 1911 in Tampico, IL, REAGAN's family soon moved to the town of Dixon, where he was active in swimming and other sports, drama, and the student government at the local high school. In 1932, the future President graduated from Eureka College, with a degree in economics and sociology. Popular among his peers and clearly blessed with a radio announcer's voice, after graduation REAGAN embarked on a radio career. A journey to Los Angeles to cover a sporting event led to a Hollywood screen test, which in turn led to a contract at Warner Brothers Studios.

REAGAN made more than 50 movies, including "Knute Rockne: All American," from which he earned his lifelong nickname for playing the famous Notre Dame athlete George Gipp. In the last reel of the film, legendary Notre Dame football coach Knute Rockne inspired his 1928 team, who was losing a game to Army, by telling them George Gipp's dying remarks, which were:

> Some time, Rock, when the team is up against it, when things are wrong and the breaks are beating the boys, tell them to go in there with all they've got and win just one for the Gipper. I don't know where I'll be then, Rock, but I'll know about it, and I'll be happy.

Needless to say, the inspired Fighting Irish went on to win the game despite their numerous injuries and underdog status. Today, millions remember REAGAN as "the GIPPER," and far fewer remember George Gipp. REAGAN became even better known in the fifties by working in television, appearing on such early programs as "Death Valley Days" and "General Electric Theater."

Reagan lived the rest of his life in California, where in the sixties, he became active in politics. Though a Democrat, even becoming president of the Screen Actors' Guild, he supported Richard Nixon in 1960 and Barry Goldwater in 1964. In 1966, as a Republican, REAGAN won the first of two terms as Governor of California. In the tumultuous year of 1968, Governor REAGAN briefly sought the Republican Presidential nomination, but lost to his fellow Californian, Richard Nixon.

In 1976, the Governor challenged President Gerald Ford for the GOP Presidential nomination, and nearly won it at the Kansas City Convention. In 1980, he won the nomination and the election, where he received nearly 51 percent of the popular vote and carried 45 States. Of course, we were all stunned on March 30, 1981, when an assassin shot the President and several others outside the Washington Hilton. Little did we know at the time how close the President came to dying of his wounds. The President went on to survive not only his 1981 gunshot wound, but also, in 1985, a bout with colon cancer.

President REAGAN was, and his memory is, beloved in this town. He readily agreed with House Speaker Tip O'Neill's admonition, at an early meeting, that "after 6 o'clock, we're all friends." President REAGAN worked to make friends not only with Speaker O'Neill, with whom he often disagreed on policy matters, but with countless others in Congress and around the country. The President's willingness to reach across the aisle and work in a constructive way, refusing to take politics personally, was a hallmark of his approach to governing. I wish others would follow his example in today's poisonous political environment in this city.

In 1984, President REAGAN handily won reelection with over 58 percent of the popular vote carrying 49 States. By the day he left office in January 1989, he was, despite massive budget deficits and the Iran-Contra arms-for-hostages scandal, one of our most beloved Presidents.

Mr. Speaker, the solemn state occasion authorized in this resolution will provide an official opportunity for the American people to mourn our former head of state. This ceremony will be rich in history, and include the use of the Lincoln catafalque, originally built for the state funeral of our 16th President in 1865. This observance will enable Americans, through the Congress and others able to attend, to bid an official, fond farewell to President REAGAN for his long career and many contributions to the rich fabric of our Nation.

I am honored to play a role in these proceedings in my position as ranking minority member of the Committee on House Administration and to represent the many residents of Connecticut who revere President REAGAN and his memory. On their behalf, and mine, I offer Mrs. Reagan and the entire Reagan family the condolences and the thanks of a grateful Nation for the President's service. I would like to close by joining our Committee on House Administration's vice chairman in urging our colleagues to pass this resolution and win one last victory for the GIPPER.

Hon. Robert W. Ney

OF OHIO

Mr. Speaker, I rise today to introduce House Concurrent Resolution 444, to allow the use of the rotunda of the Capitol for the late Honorable RONALD WILSON REAGAN, the 40th President of the United States of America, to lie in state.

More than any leader in my lifetime, RONALD REAGAN embodied the noble ideals and irrepressible optimism of the American spirit. As President, he led our country into an era of renewed faith in the American dream. RONALD REAGAN guided the United States to victory over communism in the cold war, and his domestic policies ushered in an age of unprecedented prosperity. As we stand in the wake of RONALD REAGAN's recent passing, we mourn his loss, but we celebrate the remarkable legacy he leaves to the country he loved and served so faithfully.

RONALD REAGAN was born into humble circumstances in the small town of Dixon, IL. It was in this quintessential midwestern setting that RONALD REAGAN recognized the near-limitless opportunities that flow from liberty, and consequently developed his deep and abiding appreciation for the founding ideals of our great country.

Rising from these modest origins, RONALD REAGAN set off on a life journey that was both rich and diverse in experiences. As a young man, he spent seven summers as a lifeguard on a hazardous section of river near his hometown where he saved the lives of 77 swimmers. He went on to become a college athlete and then traveled to Hollywood, where he became one of the most popular actors of the fifties and early sixties. But it was in the realm of politics where RONALD REAGAN would make his most meaningful and lasting impact, first as a two-term Governor of the State of California and then, most significantly, as the President of the United States from 1981 through 1989. Quite simply, RONALD REAGAN changed the world, and we are all the better for it.

RONALD REAGAN, more than any other individual, was responsible for winning the cold war, the epic struggle that pitted the United States and its allies against a communist force armed with enough nuclear weapons to threaten the existence of humanity. Relying on his deeply held beliefs of the supremacy of liberty and democracy, REAGAN assumed the Office of President and sought not to accommodate or merely contain communist expansionism, but to defeat it. He had the courage to speak the truth about the former Soviet Union, to accurately label it as an evil empire that would ultimately be consigned to the ash heap of history. He realized that for democracy to prevail in this twilight struggle of differing ideologies with monumental consequences, he had to become a relentless warrior on behalf of the American ideals of liberty, free enterprise, and the primacy of the individual in society. His fortitude provided the American people with purpose and victory over communism.

RONALD REAGAN buoyed up our Nation not only with his ever-present smile, his genial nature, and his self-deprecating humor but also with the substance of his ideas: his enduring faith in the innate goodness and creativity of the American people; his steadfast belief in the exceptionalism of our constitutional democracy and economic order; and his unyielding conviction that freedom and democracy will triumph over oppression and tyranny. RONALD REAGAN was, and will always remain, a giant on the stage of history, a commanding presence and respected leader whose commitment to freedom and democracy will inspire generations to come. Truly it can be said that RONALD REAGAN lifted the spirits of the American people by appealing to our best hopes, not our worst fears, and because of that, he will remain forever in the hearts of the American people.

Walking side by side with RONALD REAGAN through his life's journey was his wonderful wife and best friend, Nancy. Her dignity and grace as First Lady were exemplary, but even more inspiring has been the strength and resiliency she has demonstrated since her husband was diagnosed with Alzheimer's disease 10 years ago. Nancy's devotion to the former President has been nothing less than heroic, and our prayers and the prayers of a Nation are with her during this time.

Though our hearts are heavy as we mourn the loss of a beloved leader, we are comforted knowing that RONALD REAGAN has gone on to a better place. To borrow the words he used to comfort the Nation following the *Challenger* disaster, RONALD REAGAN has "'slipped the surly bonds of earth' to 'touch the face of God.'"

Passage of this resolution will allow us to pay tribute to this great man and his legacy. It will allow all those who loved and admired RONALD REAGAN a final opportunity to say a final goodbye. As he lies in state, the American people will have the opportunity to pay their respects by coming to the Capitol rotunda. I expect that many thousands will do so.

AUTHORIZING THE USE OF THE CAPITOL ROTUNDA FROM JUNE 9 UNTIL JUNE 11, 2004, FOR THE LYING IN STATE OF THE REMAINS OF THE LATE RONALD WILSON REAGAN, 40TH PRESIDENT OF THE UNITED STATES

Mr. EHLERS. Mr. Speaker, I ask unanimous consent to take from the Speaker's table the Senate concurrent resolution (S. Con. Res. 115) authorizing the use of the rotunda of the Capitol for the lying in state of the remains of the late RONALD WILSON REAGAN, the 40th President of the United States, and ask for its immediate consideration in the House.

The Clerk read the title of the Senate concurrent resolution.

The SPEAKER pro tempore. Is there objection to the request of the gentleman from Michigan?

There was no objection.

The Clerk read the Senate concurrent resolution, as follows:

S. CON. RES. 115

Resolved by the Senate (the House of Representatives concurring), That in recognition of the long and distinguished service rendered to the Nation and to the world, by the late RONALD WILSON REAGAN, the 40th President of the United States, his remains be permitted to lie in state in the rotunda of the Capitol from June 9 until June 11, 2004, and the Architect of the Capitol, under the direction of the President pro tempore of the Senate and the Speaker of the House of Representatives, shall take all necessary steps for the accomplishment of that purpose.

The Senate concurrent resolution was concurred in.

A motion to reconsider was laid on the table. A similar House concurrent resolution (H. Con. Res. 444) was laid on the table.

Hon. Henry J. Hyde
OF ILLINOIS

I have given much thought to what I might usefully contribute to the chorus of those thousands who will be called upon or be moved to voice their respect and their sadness at the death of President REAGAN. His accomplishments will be rightly celebrated, his humanity and character justly praised, his passing mourned in words of elegance and emotion. How large a stone can one hope to add to this touring mountain?

President REAGAN was the oldest person to be elected President in our history, and this is proof that you get the sweetest music from the oldest violins.

In the play "Camelot," King Arthur says, "We are all of us tiny drops in a vast ocean, but some of them sparkle." President REAGAN was never a tiny drop in a vast ocean, but he did indeed sparkle.

By his life and service he put the "sacred" back in honor. Not through exhortation, but by example, REAGAN's gentle leadership reminded a country disoriented by doubt of its enduring beliefs. In this, his guiding principle was that of George Washington's, "Let us raise a standard in which the wise and honest can repair. The event is in the hand of God."

He was a rare and subtly powerful speaker, able to instill in others a confident belief in their own capacities and goodness. And he could also inspire oppressed millions to demolish empires.

His eloquence reminds me of the story of ancient Greeks who, when Pericles spoke, said, "How well he speaks." But when Demosthenes spoke, they said, "Let us march."

Among his many virtues was his defense of the powerless unborn. President REAGAN understood that the precious gift of life was not confined to the privileged, the planned, and the perfect. Some have said that the most fearful aspect of dying is the terrible aloneness you must endure at the particular judgment; no advocate, no relative, no spouse, no child, just you, your sins and God. But I am sure President REAGAN is not alone. I believe the silence was broken by the voices of thousands of little children, voices that were never heard in this world but are heard in the next, all pleading, "Dear Lord, spare him, for he loved us very much."

And then I can imagine Mr. REAGAN heard a gentle voice, "Come, beloved of my father, and enter the kingdom which has been prepared for you since the beginning of time."

Mr. President:

> The shadows have lengthened, evening has come, and the busy world is hushed. The fever of life is over, and your work is done. May God in his mercy give you a safe lodging and a holy rest and peace at the last.

Hon. Jim Matheson
OF UTAH

Mr. Speaker, I rise today to honor President RONALD REAGAN. We can all admire the journey of his life. It was a life built on love of family and a profound love of our country.

In this time of mourning, I offer my sincere condolences and prayers to the President's family, especially to his wife Nancy. I hope that the sincere good wishes of all of their fellow countrymen can help to bring them some comfort at this time.

Above all else, the President was a leader who had strong opinions, yet he always respected the institution of government and worked within both parties to provide enduring success to millions of Americans.

Before he was President, RONALD REAGAN was the Governor of a western State and a leader who understood issues important to the West. As a Member of Congress from the Rocky Mountain West, I hold a deep appreciation for President REAGAN's efforts to protect the western way of life.

One issue that stands out is that of the MX missile. In the seventies and eighties, the Department of Defense was working to build the massive MX missile racetrack system in Utah's West Desert, despite Utah's opposition. President REAGAN was a strong advocate for national defense, and the military initially thought he would be a supporter of this proposal. As a fellow westerner, President REAGAN understood Utah's desire to protect its ranching and farming heritage. He understood why the State and its citizens adamantly opposed the project.

My father was Governor of Utah at that time. He found an open door in the Reagan administration, and he worked in a bipartisan manner with the administration to put an end to this plan. Thankfully for my State, President REAGAN came into the situation with an open mind, and he was willing to listen to local stakeholders about their concerns with the MX proposal.

President REAGAN established a process by which affected people could actually make their feelings known, which even now is a testament to the importance of a responsive Federal Government.

That was REAGAN's approach. While he was a man of strong convictions, he was known for his civility and kindness in a business that is often abrasive. Ever the gentleman, his example is a good reminder to all of us in elected office of what it takes to truly serve our constituency.

I honor President REAGAN's service to this great Nation. He will be missed.

Hon. F. James Sensenbrenner, Jr.

OF WISCONSIN

I first met RONALD REAGAN over 40 years ago when I was an undergraduate student at Stanford University in California. He and I and some others were involved in a primary election campaign for a U.S. Senator from California which proved to be very unsuccessful. But in the meetings that I attended that Mr. REAGAN chaired, I recognized him as being a unique person with an uncanny knack to bring out the best in everybody.

He certainly proved that during his subsequent career: two successful terms as Governor of California and two successful terms as President of the United States, leaving office with the highest approval rating of any departing President since Franklin Roosevelt.

Look at the shape America was in when RONALD REAGAN was elected in 1980. We went through a horrible decade of the seventies. There was a Vietnam war, there was Watergate, there was Nixon's resignation, Gerald Ford's unsuccessful "Whip Inflation Now" campaign, Jimmy Carter's malaise, and long lines at the gas pump to buy 5 gallons of gas.

When President REAGAN took office, he got us out of our national funk. His "Morning in America" speech and his philosophy gave us as a Nation and as individual Americans the self-confidence to do what America has always done; that is, to achieve the ultimate dream, to overcome the impossible, and to have each and every one of us reach our highest and best.

Much is said about REAGAN turning around the economy and winning the cold war, and some of the debate on the cold war was about the so-called Strategic Defense Initiative, but there was a decision that RONALD REAGAN made earlier that laid the groundwork for the collapse of communism. He persuaded then-German Chancellor Helmut Schmidt to deploy Pershing II and cruise missiles in West Germany. That was extremely controversial at the time both in Europe and the United States. People said displaying more missiles would encourage an arms race.

Well, Mr. Schmidt agreed to deploy them. He might have lost his job as a result of it, but he was able to see the fall of the Berlin Wall and the unification of Germany during his lifetime, and we have got to give credit to RONALD REAGAN's international skills for doing that.

God bless you President REAGAN, may you rest in peace.

Hon. Baron P. Hill

OF INDIANA

Mr. Speaker, this past weekend Americans learned of President RONALD REAGAN's death. The President was an honorable and decent man whose legacy forever will be linked with the great love and optimism he had for his country. Unfortunately, his long and courageous struggle with Alzheimer's disease took him from us long before his death.

As a fellow midwesterner, I appreciated the traditional American values he brought to Washington: his good humor, his love for his family, and belief in America. At a time when Americans had lost confidence in themselves, President REAGAN reminded us we could achieve any goal, no matter how lofty.

When President REAGAN addressed a grieving Nation after the *Challenger* explosion, he honored the astronauts for the way in which they lived their lives and affirmed that we would never forget them. Eloquently, he quoted the poem "High Flight," declaring the astronauts had "'slipped the surly bonds of earth' to 'touch the face of God.'"

Mr. Speaker, today in this House, we are honoring President REAGAN for the way in which he lived his life and led our Nation. And as he takes his own journey to touch the face of God, I am confident in this statement: That his life and achievements will forever be remembered by this grateful Nation.

As the country and the world mourn his death, we will remember President REAGAN as a great American who was a beacon of freedom for people everywhere. I think I speak for all of the Hoosiers in offering my condolences to his wife Nancy and the children.

Hon. J.D. Hayworth

OF ARIZONA

Mr. Speaker, I rise with the formidable challenge in 2 minutes to convey the thoughts and prayers of Arizonans and Americans as we remember our 40th President. While it is true that RONALD REAGAN was a son of Illinois and a Governor of California before becoming the President of us all, it is also true that Arizona played an important part in his life.

Arizona was the place where RONALD and Nancy REAGAN honeymooned. Arizona was the place where some of their children attended high school. Arizona was the place where Nancy's parents lived; and Arizona was the site of one of President REAGAN's final political appearances. Even as our favorite son, Barry Goldwater, gave birth to then RONALD REAGAN's political career in that epic speech "A Time for Choosing" in 1964, telecast nationally, which really put RONALD REAGAN on the political stage, it was former President REAGAN who arrived in downtown Phoenix 5 days before the 1992 election to offer words of support to candidates of our party.

I had the privilege of emceeing this gathering, and I was offstage with the former President as our now senior Senator offered remarks of introduction, and those remarks included the statement from Margaret Thatcher that the cold war was won by one man, RONALD WILSON REAGAN, and that victory came without a single shot being fired.

Mr. Speaker, I was in a unique position to hear the words of my friend from Arizona and to look at the reaction on the face of our former President.

Mr. Speaker, it is well known that many of us who enter the public arena suffer from no lack of self-esteem.

Mr. Speaker, I can tell you that President REAGAN was incredibly humble, and that humility was expressed on his face as he offered a characteristic shrug of the shoulders before going out to offer his words to the assembly.

In closing, Mr. Speaker, and to my colleagues, let me simply say this. One of my constituents whose daughter-in-law escaped from behind the Iron Curtain said "President Lincoln freed the slaves of America. President REAGAN freed the enslaved millions of Eastern Europe."

God bless America. God bless RONALD REAGAN.

Hon. Gil Gutknecht

OF MINNESOTA

Mr. Speaker, I join my colleagues today in paying tribute to a man who influenced my life personally, and I think I speak for many of my colleagues when I say that we would not be in politics, I indeed would not be in Congress, if it were not for RONALD REAGAN.

President REAGAN embodied the values that made America the "shining city on the hill": faith, family, freedom, and personal responsibility. Born to humble beginnings, he never lost the common touch. Few public officials had more empathy for the common people. He could make us laugh or cry, depending on what the situation called for. Most of all, he made us proud, proud to be Americans.

RONALD REAGAN came into office during a great malaise. He made us believe again in ourselves, in our capacity to achieve great things. He ignored his critics and the cynics. He shouldered on with unstoppable optimism. He consigned communism to the ash heap of history. As Margaret Thatcher said, he won the cold war without firing a shot. He changed our party. He changed the way Americans see themselves; and in the end, he changed the world.

Borrowing from the song, I said to my wife, Mary, when he left office, he was a long time coming. He will be a long time gone. I thank God for giving us such men.

Hon. Edward R. Royce

OF CALIFORNIA

Mr. Speaker, first, both personally and on behalf of my constituents in Orange County, let me offer my condolences to Mrs. Reagan and the Reagan family. I, like so many of my colleagues, probably would not be standing here today if it were not for RONALD REAGAN.

He was an inspiration for a whole generation of young Americans, and his message of limited government and unlimited freedom, as well as his boundless optimism about America's future, motivated me and so many others to get involved in the affairs of our Nation. I first met RONALD REAGAN as a student in California. That experience led me to become involved in the Youth for Reagan movement.

Over the years, I was privileged to meet him many more times. It was one of the most memorable meetings in 1986. I was visiting the White House as a State senator on the day that President REAGAN ordered the bombing of Libya because of their open support for international terrorism. The President told me what a difficult decision it was, but how the future of our Nation and the safety of our citizens depended on firm action.

President REAGAN was never afraid to take a stand, never afraid to do what was right, even if it was not popular at the moment.

In 1964 RONALD REAGAN spoke these words to a generation of Americans:

> You and I have a rendezvous with destiny. We will preserve for our children this, the last best hope of man on Earth, or we will sentence them to take the last step into a thousand years of darkness.

President REAGAN understood the evil of communism. He knew the cold war would end. He knew that there would be winners and there would be losers. Thanks to his resolve, freedom won. Thanks to his resolve, millions of people were set free.

President REAGAN also understood that free markets go hand in hand with individual liberties. In 1981 he said:

> We who live in free market societies believe that growth, prosperity and, ultimately, human fulfillment are created from the bottom up, not the government down. Only when the human spirit is allowed to invent and create, only when individuals are given a personal stake in deciding economic policies and benefiting from their success—only then can societies remain economically alive, dynamic, prosperous, progressive, and free.

At his second inauguration, speaking inside the rotunda of this Capitol building, President REAGAN said:

> [O]ur nation is poised for greatness. We must do what we know is right, and do it with all our might. Let history say of us: "These were golden years—when the American Revolution was reborn, when freedom gained new life, and America reached for her best."

Throughout his career, RONALD REAGAN was always helping America reach for her best. He inspired us with his spirit, with his optimism; and he led us with his commitment to principle and unwavering resolve. America and the rest of the world are better, safer, and freer places today because of RONALD REAGAN. We will miss him dearly.

Hon. Max Sandlin

OF TEXAS

Mr. Speaker, it is with a profound sense of loss and sadness that I rise today to honor the memory of one of our Nation's most influential leaders, former President RONALD REAGAN. Much has been said, and rightfully so, about President REAGAN's infectious love of this great Nation. RONALD WILSON REAGAN firmly believed that the United States of America had a unique role to play in the world and a singular place in history. In his first inaugural address he reflected on this faith in country in attributing the unparalleled prosperity and opportunity of this great land to the fact that:

> Freedom and the dignity of the individual have been more available and assured here than in any other place on earth.

Mr. Speaker, his singular commitment to the inherent worth of the individual is a hallmark of RONALD REAGAN's personal and political legacy. His sincere devotion to that core idea defined his personality, and it defined his Presidency. President REAGAN defied then-conventional wisdom that American heroes were a thing of the past. He said, "Those who say that we are in a time when there are no heroes just don't know where to look. You can see heroes every day going in and out of factory gates. Others, a handful in number, produce enough food to feed all of us and then the world beyond. You meet heroes across a counter, and they are on both sides of that counter." President REAGAN's heroes were, in his words, "the citizens of this blessed land."

Mr. Speaker, President REAGAN has often been called the Great Communicator, but President REAGAN told us himself that he preferred to think of himself as a communicator of great things. However, to reduce RONALD REAGAN to the words he spoke would be a tremendous disservice to his legacy, just as it would be wrong to reduce Abraham Lincoln's legacy to the Gettysburg Address or FDR's to the eloquent power of his fireside chats. President REAGAN truly believed the ideas he communicated, and that faith drove in many ways a shift in the course of American politics.

Mr. Speaker, President REAGAN was a unique figure in our politics. His devotion to principle, his commitment to the American people, his singular faith in the power of one were infectious. Yet despite his unrepentant drive to achieve what has been appropriately called the Reagan revolution, he pushed his agenda with a smile and he relished open and honest debate. Notwithstanding sometimes profound disagreements, President REAGAN understood that at the end of the day, we were not Democrats and Republicans but, rather, Americans and friends. He truly understood that there is a tremendous difference between strong beliefs and bitter partisanship.

Mr. Speaker, President REAGAN was an eternal optimist who changed the world with hope and taught Americans that, even in the face of trials and tragedy, "Nothing ends here; our hopes and our journeys continue." It has been said of President REAGAN that although he was our oldest President, he made America young again.

And so, Mr. Speaker, I rise today to express my deepest sympathies to Mrs. Reagan and to the President's children and their families and to honor the memory of a great American who loved America at least as much as she loved him.

Hon. George Radanovich
OF CALIFORNIA

Mr. Speaker, today I rise in support of the resolution paying tribute to President RONALD REAGAN who once said America is too great for small dreams. Whether through his faith in God's providence, his deep love for his wife, Nancy, his career as an actor, his service as Governor of the State of California and ultimately as our Commander in Chief, President RONALD REAGAN envisioned and achieved big dreams. These dreams included lowering the tax burden on citizens through his advocacy of smaller government and striving for peace in the tenuous times of the cold war.

As a boy in the fourth grade, I had the honor of shaking Mr. REAGAN's hand at the Mariposa Airport when he was on his way to Yosemite after he became the Governor of the great State of California. He is the very reason that I later became a Republican and devoted my life to public service.

President REAGAN died on the very weekend of the commemoration of D-day where just 20 years ago he heralded the heroes that lay before him in Normandy as those who "helped end a war." Fittingly, we now herald this American hero for his unmatched achievements, including ending the cold war. History will forever remember him for removing this threat of nuclear holocaust.

There are good men in the world, and there are great men. Great men employ their power humbly and create peace quietly. President REAGAN embodied these traits and reminded us to believe in ourselves as the greatest country in the world.

Hon. Charlie Norwood

OF GEORGIA

Mr. Speaker, I rise on the floor today to join my colleagues and the legions of Americans and freedom-loving people around the world in honoring the memory and the legacy of President RONALD WILSON REAGAN. In the days that have passed since President REAGAN slipped the surly bonds of this world, much has been said about our Nation's 40th President, of his boundless energy, eternal optimism, strong character, good judgment and, most important of all, his unmatched ability to lead and to deliver hope to America and the world at a time when it was needed most. Despite those who would suggest otherwise, the accomplishments and good fortune that befell this Nation and ultimately those behind the Iron Curtain on President REAGAN's watch did not happen accidentally or through luck or simply being in the right place at the right time.

No, Mr. Speaker. Providing unfailing hope and guidance to a grateful Nation and all the world in a time of much despair is not luck. It is called leadership. And President REAGAN will be remembered as a leader without peer, period.

Winston Churchill once said, "The price of greatness is responsibility." President REAGAN understood and accepted that responsibility like no one else, and he left greatness in his wake.

Mr. Speaker, if the measure of a man is the difference that he makes, then history will record that President RONALD REAGAN was nothing less than a giant. He will be missed, but his legacy of leadership will live on in the history of this Nation.

Hon. Mike Pence

OF INDIANA

Mr. Speaker, I thank the chairman, my favorite Reagan protege in the Congress, for yielding me this time.

Mr. Speaker, RONALD REAGAN will be remembered as a great man and a great American leader, who personified the highest ideals of the American people at home and abroad. After 8 years of his Presidency, the communism of Soviet Russia was collapsing, the American military was rebuilt, the Nation's economy restored, and its moral fabric renewed.

Many remember him as the Great Communicator, but as the President said many times, he was not a great communicator. He communicated great things. Those were the traditional American values of this midwesterner turned national leader. They came from the profound Christian faith inculcated in a young DUTCH REAGAN by his beloved mother Nelle and from his heart. And, as the President said, "they came from the heart of a great nation."

Those ideas were simple, straightforward, and distinctly American. President REAGAN believed that freedom depended on limited government. He fiercely advanced the principles of less government, less taxes, a strong military, and a commitment to traditional moral values.

And President REAGAN changed the course of my life. While youthful ambition led me to politics, it was the voice and the values of RONALD REAGAN that made me a Republican. The Bible says, "If the trumpet does not sound a clear call, who will get ready for battle?" RONALD REAGAN's great gift was to sound a clear call to return our Nation to the ideals of its Founders, and it was said that when he spoke, people did not just agree. From coffee shops to tractor seats to high offices in tall buildings, when the American people heard REAGAN speak, they said, "Darn right."

I had the privilege in 1988 as a candidate for Congress to sit with the President in the Blue Room of the White House and speak to him personally, and on that occasion, that great privilege of my life, I was able to look the President in the eye as he asked me how my campaign was going. I said, "Mr. President, it is going fine, but I just want to thank you for everything you have done for our country and to encourage my generation of Americans to believe in this country again."

I said then, and I say again, thank you, Mr. President. May God bless you, as, through you, God most certainly blessed the United States of America.

Hon. Martin Frost

OF TEXAS

Mr. Speaker, I rise today to honor President REAGAN's legacy to our country. I was elected in 1978, 2 years before RONALD REAGAN assumed the Presidency. I served in Congress the entire 8 years of his Presidency and had the opportunity to observe him at close range. We often disagreed on domestic policy; however, we were largely in agreement on foreign policy, and REAGAN, indeed, left an indelible mark in the field of foreign affairs. He correctly understood the economic vulnerability of the Soviet Union and exploited this to win the cold war without firing a shot. He increased U.S. defense spending, an effort which I supported, and when the Soviet Union tried to keep pace, it fell apart from the economic strain.

The watchword of his administration was "peace through strength." President REAGAN brought hope and optimism to our country at a time when it was sorely needed. Also, he demonstrated through word and deed that one could disagree with their domestic political adversaries and still be friends at the end of the day. This is an element that is sorely missing from today's highly charged partisan atmosphere in Washington.

RONALD REAGAN won his share of battles in Congress, but he did it without lasting rancor. That was perhaps his greatest legacy. We could use a little bit of that spirit today.

Hon. Barbara Cubin

OF WYOMING

Mr. Speaker, I rise today to pay tribute to a great man, a great President, and a true friend to the people of Wyoming.

We all probably have our way of remembering President REAGAN, but for me I will always see him atop his big white horse, pointing out to the distance as if to say, "The future is that way, and we must ride into it." Here is the picture that I remember so well.

Today we are lucky enough to live in that future. The millions once enslaved behind the Iron Curtain are free, and the cold war is over, with freedom the victor.

They say that fortune favors the brave, and fortune favored President REAGAN. He helped us to believe in ourselves again and to believe in common dreams that bind us together as Americans.

When President REAGAN took office, we were gripped with the fear that perhaps America's greatest days were behind us. Eight years later when he walked out of the Oval Office and into the sunset of his life, we knew that in America our best days will always be on the horizon.

Mr. Speaker, the people of Wyoming will be eternally thankful to RONALD REAGAN. We will be eternally thankful that he was there on that white horse to point the way not into the sunset, but instead into a shining new "morning in America."

Hon. Lincoln Davis

OF TENNESSEE

Mr. Speaker, the death of President REAGAN, given his publicly known battle with Alzheimer's, did not come as a surprise to many. Still, those of us in the United States and around the world are greatly saddened by his departure and by our loss.

He was an indelible figure, known not only in American history, but known throughout world history. The man that helped bring about the end of the cold war will always be praised for his eternal optimism, love of country, principle stance on issues, the eloquence in which he communicated with the Nation, and his abundant faith.

It is my firm belief that President REAGAN saw the best in everyone. As with most Americans, REAGAN understood America's greatness lies within its people. It is the character of the American people that has guided us through all the obstacles we have had to overcome. And we recently celebrated the American spirit during the 60th anniversary of D-day.

President REAGAN was perceived as a man guided by principles. No matter what side of the aisle we were on, we always knew where he stood. His legacy will be the challenge that he opened to bring about peace between two superpowers. His work can be best summed up by the English author Richard Adams: "The thinker dies, but his thoughts are beyond the reach of destruction. Men are mortal, but ideas are immortal."

The man of abundant faith in country, family, and God, REAGAN embodied the American spirit. Even in knowing his time on Earth was nearing an end, he wrote: "When the Lord calls me home, whenever that may be, I will leave with the greatest love for this country of ours and eternal optimism for its future."

Our thoughts and prayers are with Mrs. Reagan and their children at this difficult time. May God bless them, and may God bless the United States of America.

Hon. Jeff Miller

OF FLORIDA

Mr. Speaker, most Presidents have been defined by the events of their day. Whether it is war, the economy, or domestic policy, these leaders have all been forced to react to the issues. RONALD WILSON REAGAN, however, did not fit this mold. His Presidency defined the events of his day, which boldly resembles the world that we each live in.

Taking office in a relatively peaceful period in our history, where the cold war was in an assumed perpetual state, rather than a quid pro quo acceptance of an evil empire on the other side of the globe, President REAGAN challenged the conventional wisdom of appeasing the Soviet Union and challenged them directly, helmet to helmet, on the field of ideology.

President REAGAN's administration had an exceptional consistency through his 8 years—life, liberty, and the pursuit of happiness, words we often take for granted while denying ourselves a conscious thought that there are many who are denied these God-given, inalienable unalienable rights.

On June 12, 1987, from what was West Germany's Brandenburg Gate, President REAGAN spoke directly to communist states, telling them what was painfully obvious to the Western world: A totalitarian system just did not work.

{W}e see failure, technological backwardness, declining standards of health, even want of the most basic kind—too little food. ... After ... four decades ... there stands before the entire world one great and inescapable conclusion: Freedom leads to prosperity. Freedom replaces the ancient hatreds among the nations with comity and peace. Freedom is the victor.

This, of course, was the famous speech where President REAGAN asked Mr. Gorbachev to tear down the Berlin Wall and to let men and women be free. President REAGAN pledged cooperation in reducing nuclear weapons, maintaining peace, but doing so in a setting befitting civilized nations. This declaration, while a defining moment in his Presidency, was consistent of a President who believed, truly believed, in a free-market economy and in a world that called on personal responsibility and a hand up rather than a handout; limited government; the right of men and women to live free, and children to grow up in a world that did not require them to know the duck-and-cover routine.

Mr. Speaker, God bless the GIPPER, and may God rest his soul.

Hon. Darlene Hooley

OF OREGON

Mr. Speaker, I rise today to pay tribute to the life of President RONALD WILSON REAGAN, a man whose legacy will be remembered for generations to come.

I remember President REAGAN as an optimistic leader who stood up for what he believed in and who led our Nation with passion, grace, and wit. President REAGAN believed in the resourcefulness of the American people and believed that their ingenuity, courage, and hard work could build a better America and a better world.

President REAGAN envisioned America as a can-do country, and he was devoted and unwavering in his commitment to the American people. His message of optimism provided hope for many Americans during challenging times for our Nation and for the world.

Today we remember his service and his leadership and join the rest of the country in mourning his passing. My thoughts and prayers are with his devoted wife Nancy and his entire family.

Hon. Todd Russell Platts

OF PENNSYLVANIA

Mr. Speaker, I rise to pay tribute to RONALD WILSON REAGAN, our Nation's 40th President, a true statesman and patriot, a husband and father, and a Great American. I offer my sincerest condolences to Mrs. Reagan and the entire Reagan family. My prayers are with them in this time of mourning and remembrance.

When RONALD REAGAN was elected President in 1980, America was facing a crisis. The crisis went deeper than the economic problems of double-digit inflation, rising unemployment, long gas lines, and threatening military actions of the Soviet Union. After Vietnam, Watergate, and the hostage situation in Iran, America actually began to experience a crisis of faith in itself. More than any other person, President REAGAN helped us to overcome our doubts and remind us that America is, in fact, a "shining city on a hill."

RONALD REAGAN was the eternal optimist, a believer in America's abilities, ideals, and innate goodness. His faith in the greatness of our Nation was perhaps best expressed when he said:

> In this land of dreams fulfilled, where greater dreams may be imagined, nothing is impossible, no victory is beyond our reach, no glory will ever be too great.

Through his outlook and conviction, President REAGAN restored America's confidence in itself.

As a result of RONALD REAGAN's inspiring leadership as our President, the world changed dramatically. Economic stagnation was replaced with a dynamic economy. President REAGAN challenged the Soviet Union to "tear down this wall!" and the Berlin Wall came down. He saw a day when Eastern Europe would join the free world, and it did. He stayed firm at Reykjavik and, for the first time, Russia and America stopped building, and started destroying, nuclear weapons.

RONALD REAGAN understood the price of freedom. Forty years after D-day, and 19 years and 364 days before he passed away, President REAGAN commemorated "the boys of Pointe du Hoc" who took the cliffs at Normandy for the Allies during World War II. He said:

> The men of Normandy had faith that what they were doing was right, faith that they fought for all humanity, faith that a just God would grant them mercy on this beachhead or on the next. It was the deep knowledge—and pray God we have not lost it—that there is a profound moral difference between the use of force for liberation and the use of force for conquest. You were here to liberate, not to conquer, and so you and those others did not doubt your cause. And you were right not to doubt.
>
> You all knew that some things are worth dying for. One's country is worth dying for, and democracy is worth dying for, because it's the most deeply honorable form of government ever devised by man. All of you loved liberty. All of you were willing to fight tyranny, and you knew the people of your countries were behind you.

It is this understanding of history, this moral clarity, that helped RONALD REAGAN to lead us to the freer world we have today. It is what helps to make President REAGAN one of the giants of the 20th century, along with his personal hero, Franklin Delano Roosevelt.

Six years ago, in commemoration of RONALD REAGAN's 87th birthday, I had the pleasure of joining First Lady Nancy Reagan and Ambassador Jeane Kirkpatrick at the Reagan Library in California. I was there as an elected member of the Pennsylvania General Assembly. But I was there, most importantly, as an American citizen who was honored to pay tribute to and to express my deep gratitude to President REAGAN for his tremendous service to our Nation. In my conversation with Mrs. Reagan that day, my message was simply one of thanks. Thanks to her and, through her, to President REAGAN for their dedicated, hard-working and outstanding service to our great Nation and its citizens.

RONALD REAGAN's service to others, his statesmanship, his love of country, and his unwavering commitment to the principles of freedom, liberty, and justice for which our Nation stands, were great examples for all of us fellow citizens to emulate. President REAGAN was truly inspiring to countless citizens. His example helped to affirm my own commitment to the ideals of public service, to the ideals of giving back to one's Nation, and certainly helped to affirm my interest in serving the public office, including here in Congress.

I am greatly honored to join with fellow Americans in saying: Mr. President, thank you for a job well done and a life well lived. You will long be missed and never forgotten. God bless you and God bless this great Nation you loved so dearly, the United States of America.

Hon. Jo Ann Emerson

OF MISSOURI

Mr. Speaker, as we mourn the passing of President RONALD REAGAN, I remember one experience in 1985 that to me defines President REAGAN best. It was my daughter Katharine's first visit to the White House with the Emerson family. As we approached the Oval Office, outside of which we were to wait for the President, the door swung open. Katharine had been obediently holding my hand, but at that moment she broke away from me and she ran toward President REAGAN. The Secret Servicemen standing between us and the President moved to stop her. "No, no," President REAGAN calmly said to them. Katharine flew past the Secret Servicemen and jumped into the President's arms, and he lifted her up high.

The genuine joy on both of their faces struck me then. Today the memory reminds me that as strong a man as he was, President REAGAN could easily match the enthusiastic happiness of a 2-year-old.

Even before she met him, RONALD REAGAN was my daughter's hero. It was not the President's rhetoric that won her. It was not his stalwart countenance under the distress of terror in the Middle East, his unwavering courage in the face of communism, or his passionate leadership in the shadow of a nuclear threat. Not even the lure of the jellybean jar on his desk made REAGAN a great man to Katharine.

Plainly put, the quality that won her was the same one that won us all: his sincerity.

He was quintessentially American. He was a midwesterner. He was a success story. He was a visionary. And finally, RONALD REAGAN was not just a leader whom we believed in; he was a leader who believed in us.

But when I remember RONALD REAGAN, I think of him calling off the Secret Service agents and happily sweeping Katharine up into his arms. He swept us all up that same way, and the tide of sincerity on which he carried us is the same one welling up in the eyes of our Nation right now.

A photo of Katharine in President REAGAN's arms, taken seconds after she defied us to pursue a hug from her hero, today hangs in the front room of my Washington office. Every time I walk through that door, I see the photo and think of him as millions of us do: as a member of our family.

Hon. Dennis Moore

OF KANSAS

Mr. Speaker, the United States of America lost one of our giants with the passing last Saturday of our 40th President, RONALD WILSON REAGAN.

We come together today and this week in Congress, Democrats and Republicans, to pay tribute to the man who played a primary role in ending our cold war with the Soviet Union and who, as the Center for American Progress said earlier this week, projected "a never-failing sense of optimism which restored faith in the American Presidency in a Nation still scarred by Vietnam and Watergate."

The *Los Angeles Times* said this week:

His sunny self-assurance, his insistence that there really were simple answers to difficult problems, his knack for actually making things happen, all were soothing changes for a country that had endured Vietnam, Watergate, a Presidential resignation, an energy crisis, double-digit inflation, and the seizing of American hostages in Iran in the course of one tumultuous decade.

In particular, Mr. Speaker, we remember RONALD REAGAN for standing firmly with Federal Reserve Chairman Paul Volcker in the early eighties to drive down inflation and revive the economy, thus setting the stage for the prolonged American economic expansion of the early nineties.

While President REAGAN had deeply held core convictions, as a national leader he was also able to compromise and change directions when policies were not working. After instigating a large tax cut in 1981, for example, he later asked for tax increases to fight an exploding Federal deficit and tight monetary conditions. Without President REAGAN's active support, the Gramm-Rudman-Hollings Act, which ultimately led to deficit reductions through imposition of pay-as-you-go rules, would never have become law.

President REAGAN signed into law bills protecting 1.9 billion acres of wilderness in Washington State and Oregon. Known as a lifelong crusader against communism, President REAGAN combined military and diplomatic strength to develop a relationship with Soviet Leader Mikhail Gorbachev that ultimately led to limits on nuclear weapons and the end of the cold war.

The *Washington Post* recently said that President REAGAN was able to win the respect of Europeans through his "commitment to winning the Cold War and his willingness to work peacefully to bring about the demise of the Soviet Union."

Even in times of failure and disappointment, President REAGAN stood tall, and he won the respect of all. Following the disaster at the Marine barracks in Lebanon and the Iran-Contra scandal, President REAGAN accepted responsibility saying, "This happened on my watch" and "if there is to be blame, it properly rests here in this office and with this President. And I accept responsibility for the bad as well as the good." That was a quote from President REAGAN, and I think that shows the measure of the man that President REAGAN was.

In the twilight of his life, President REAGAN again provided hope and inspiration for millions of Americans with his valiant battle, with the devoted support of his wife, Nancy, against the ravages of Alzheimer's disease. Mr. Speaker, my father is afflicted with this cruel and debilitating condition. I share the hope of Nancy Reagan and millions of others that expanded stem cell research will some day unlock new discoveries needed to successfully treat Alzheimer's disease, diabetes, Parkinson's disease, and cancer.

I greatly respect the religious convictions of those people who are concerned about the expansion of stem cell research, but I hope soon we will find some middle ground between the two extremes and enable us to go forward with this research which one day may save the lives of millions of Americans. One of the legacies of our 40th President will be that we worked together to find a way to join in harnessing this technology and promise. The potential human health and scientific benefits of stem cell research are simply staggering, and I hope that we can join and leave a legacy for President REAGAN and for Nancy Reagan as well.

In conclusion, I reflect back on RONALD REAGAN's last major public address, his speech to the 1992 Republican National Convention. He could have been speaking, though, to all Americans, Mr. Speaker, because he said, he closed with these words:

My fellow citizens, ... I want you to know that I have always had the highest respect for you, for your common sense and intelligence and for your decency. I have always believed in you and in what you could accomplish for yourselves and for others.

And whatever else history may say about me when I am gone, I hope it will record that I appealed to your best hopes, not your worst fears, to your confidence rather than your doubts. My dream is that you will travel the road ahead with liberty's lamp guiding your steps and opportunity's arm steadying your way.

I hope that we in Congress, Mr. Speaker, can come together for the American people for an agenda; and I truly believe that even though we have honest, good-faith differences between the parties, we can put aside some of the rancor, some of the partisanship, and work on the American agenda the way that RONALD REAGAN wanted us all to do.

Mr. Speaker, I could think of no better way to remember the legacy of President RONALD REAGAN than by those words that he gave.

Hon. Mac Thornberry

OF TEXAS

Mr. Speaker, like many Americans, I feel a real and personal sense of loss with the death of President RONALD REAGAN. He was a great man and a great President, ranking in the top tier of all of our Chief Executives. He will be remembered as a pivotal historical figure; but, at the same time, many Americans feel as though they have lost a member of their family. Such was the unique character and legacy of RONALD REAGAN, the President and the man.

My wife Sally and I each had the honor of serving as political appointees during the second term of the Reagan administration. We were down in the bowels of the bureaucracy, but proud to be working for and certainly inspired by President REAGAN. With his optimism and his confidence in America, he inspired at least a generation of conservatives to be involved in public life and to advance the ideals for which he stood.

As important as his accomplishments domestically and internationally were, perhaps his most important success was to help the American people believe in themselves again. After the tumult of assassinations, Vietnam, Watergate, and malaise, RONALD REAGAN came to remind us of the core values of the Founding Fathers and the special place that the United States has in the history of the world, that "shining city on a hill."

President REAGAN was called the Great Communicator, but he said that what was truly great were the ideas he communicated. Those ideas were fundamental in the creation of the United States. As he noted in his farewell address, he communicated "great things ... {that} came from the heart of a ... nation—from our experience, our wisdom, and our belief in principles that have guided us for two centuries." RONALD REAGAN brought out the best in us because he knew the best of us.

Our Nation was blessed to have been given RONALD REAGAN, the President and the man.

Mr. Speaker, I believe that the accomplishments which cause RONALD REAGAN to stand among our greatest Presidents can be traced to a set of fundamental beliefs to which he adhered throughout his political career.

One of them was strong, steadfast confidence in the American people. President REAGAN knew that government must be limited so that the unlimited potential of individual Americans could be unleashed. He knew that when families were able to keep more of the money they earned, not just the family but the whole country would benefit. The result of his tax relief and restraint of government was the longest period of economic growth in the Nation's history.

President REAGAN also believed, with the signers of the Declaration of Independence, that freedom is a gift of God, intended for all peoples. In his speech to the British Parliament in 1982, which he viewed as among his most important, he said:

> We must be staunch in our conviction that freedom is not the sole prerogative of a lucky few, but the inalienable and universal right of all human beings.

President REAGAN was often underestimated, but his clear words required clear thoughts, and those clear thoughts came from a clear vision and clear values, the articulation of which was refined over a lifetime of work. The amount of work and thought RONALD REAGAN put into developing and expressing his views are only now becoming known, with the publication of some of the thousands of articles and letters written with his own hand.

He clearly believed that one must not be afraid to speak the truth, sometimes to the discomfort of his advisors. In the well-known speech in which he called the Soviet Union the "focus of evil in the modern world" he went on to urge his listeners and the country to:

> {S}peak out against those who would place the United States in a position of military and moral inferiority ... I urge you to beware the temptation of pride—the temptation of blithely declaring yourselves above it all and label both sides equally at fault, to ignore the facts of history and the aggressive impulses of an evil empire, to simply call the arms race a giant misunderstanding and thereby remove yourself from the struggle between right and wrong and good and evil.

Throughout his career of public service, RONALD REAGAN did not remove himself from the struggle between right and wrong, good and evil. He engaged in that struggle, and he changed the course of history.

Before the British Parliament, President REAGAN repeated the question asked by Winston Churchill in one of his wartime speeches: "What kind of a people do they think we are?" President REAGAN answered, "Free people, worthy of freedom and determined not only to remain so but to help others gain their freedom as well."

Being a "free people, worthy of freedom" and "help[ing] others gain their freedom as well" remains America's challenge. My hope is that we pursue those aims with the determination and spirit that RONALD REAGAN displayed throughout his career.

A President whose basic political philosophy about the role of government continues to occupy center stage in our domestic debates more than a decade after he left office; a President who changed the course of world history and helped free millions of people from totalitarian bondage; a man who restored a Nation's confidence in itself and continues to inspire defenders of freedom everywhere—quite a record. Quite a life.

Again, our Nation was blessed to have been given RONALD REAGAN.

Hon. Benjamin L. Cardin

OF MARYLAND

Mr. Speaker, I rise on behalf of the people I represent in the Third Congressional District to express my sincere condolences to the Reagan family and to memorialize our 40th President, RONALD WILSON REAGAN.

I had the opportunity to serve for 2 years in the Congress when RONALD REAGAN was President of the United States, and I also had the opportunity when I was speaker of the State legislature to work with President REAGAN on behalf of the National Conference of State Legislators.

Mr. Speaker, RONALD REAGAN was one of the most effective Presidents in the history of our Nation. He brought an agenda of change to Washington, and he developed public support for that change and then congressional support for that change. He did it using the process, to bring about a change of policy and expectation of our country. He also established America as a world leader, proud of our commitment to democracy and willing to get involved in international events to bring about change for the good. He laid the foundation for the end of the cold war.

As I said, Mr. Speaker, he was a remarkable President and will be missed by all.

On January 20, 1981, President REAGAN spoke of his abiding commitment to "a special interest group that has been too long neglected. It knows no sectional boundaries or ethnic and racial divisions, and it crosses political party lines. It is made up of men and women who raise our food, patrol our streets, man our mines and factories, teach our children, keep our homes, and heal us when we're sick—professionals, industrialists, shopkeepers, clerks, cabbies, and truck drivers. They are, in short, "we the people," this breed called Americans."

Mr. Speaker, he will be missed by all.

Hon. Wayne T. Gilchrest

OF MARYLAND

America mourns these past few days the passing of a true American, one who reflects not only the values of the country in the 21st century or the 20th century, but RONALD REAGAN had inherent in his body and his soul and his mind and his heart the idea that each of us has a passion for freedom, that each of us has a sense of urgency for justice.

Jefferson will be remembered for many, many things; but we will all remember those words, "We hold these truths to be self-evident, that all men are created equal."

And Lincoln will be remembered for many, many things, but we will all remember those words after the Civil War: "With malice toward none, with charity for all, let us work together to bind up the Nation's wounds."

And a century later, another American that reflected the true values of our country said that "you will not be judged by the color of your skin, but by the content of your character."

These men through the centuries brought America together. They united America. They had a vision for America.

RONALD REAGAN will be remembered for many, many things, but we will all remember with a sense of seriousness and joy when he said, "Mr. Gorbachev, tear down this wall!"

So what Mr. REAGAN was trying to do was to impart that passion for freedom, that urgency for justice, not only for Americans and the vast array of cultures that we have here but for the rest of the world.

Mrs. Reagan, the Reagan family, America, President RONALD REAGAN will be missed, but always remembered.

Hon. Mark Green

OF WISCONSIN

Mr. Speaker, I entered college in the late seventies, and so I remember well those times and the challenges that we faced: soaring inflation, soaring interest rates, soaring unemployment, gas prices that were sky high, on the world stage hostages in Iran, and the cold war loomed large.

I remember that as President REAGAN took office, some pundits, some experts out there arguing that the Office of the Presidency had become too big for one man. And they said maybe it was time to look at a different institution, co-Presidency or something like that. And then on to the stage came RONALD REAGAN.

Through shear force of character, through his inspirational leadership, I am proud to say that he shaped the modern Republican Party, he shaped the Office of the Presidency, he shaped a new America, indeed he shaped a new world, a new world that offered hope for freedom-loving people all around the world.

Mr. Speaker, not a bad accomplishment for one man.

Hon. Michael C. Burgess

OF TEXAS

Mr. Speaker, it has been said that RONALD REAGAN loved Texas and Texas loved RONALD REAGAN right back. So it was especially poignant that news of his passing occurred during our State Republican Convention this past weekend. Indeed, State Senator Jane Nelson from my district in north Texas was quoted in the newspaper as saying, "We stopped at that point. We had a preacher on hand that gave him a beautiful tribute. We were able to come up with a picture, and we all sang 'Amazing Grace.' There were a lot of tears, mine included."

County judge Mary Horn was quoted in my local paper as saying, "He was the same up close as you perceived him to be on television. He was very sincere and very nice. When he talked to you, he talked to you. He didn't pay attention to things going on around him. You had his full attention."

State Representative Myra Crownover said, "I remember that while REAGAN was the oldest elected President, what sticks in my mind was the way he connected to young people. We had been through a decade of young people being disconnected with taking pride in America, and he lit that spark again." Representative Crownover went on to say, "You have to be appreciative of what his family is living through." Someone described it once as being halfway to Heaven. I am so glad he has been released so he could go the rest of the way.

Hon. Tom Feeney

OF FLORIDA

Mr. Speaker, for all Americans, RONALD REAGAN was a happy warrior who fought all of his life for freedom with a gracefulness and a confidence that inspired all of America. But for American contemporary conservatives like myself, RONALD REAGAN was more than that. He was our Plato, laying the philosophical groundwork for limited government, freedom, and self-responsibility.

He was our Moses. After Lincoln, republicanism had been adrift in fighting our way out of a desert filled with statist tendencies and the march toward bigger government and welfare dependency, something Frederick Hayek described as "The Road to Serfdom." REAGAN reminded conservatives that America had a great rendezvous with destiny ahead.

Reagan was our Washington, the first contemporary President to consistently lay out conservative principles and steadfastly, calmly, and timely lead us during threats to freedom from big government and taxation at home, threats from tyrannical hegemony from abroad, to secure what our first President called the "sacred fire of liberty."

Finally, RONALD REAGAN was a Churchill, warning of external threats not only to our homeland's freedom but of gathering storms building globally which endangered the aspirations of freedom fighters across the globe. And like Churchill, he then led us and led the free world in refusing to appease or co-exist with totalitarian threats but instead insisting, like King Henry at Agincourt, that we wade into the enemy and win.

Finally, to quote Senator Benjamin Hill when he was speaking of the death of Robert E. Lee, I would like to quote him with respect to RONALD REAGAN: "He was a foe without hate; a friend without treachery; a soldier without cruelty; a victor without oppression; and a victim without murmuring. He was a public officer without vices; a private citizen without wrong; a neighbor without reproach; a Christian without hypocrisy; and a man without guile. He was a Caesar, without his ambition; Frederick, without his tyranny; Napoleon, without his selfishness, and Washington, without his reward."

This week America gives President REAGAN his very just reward.

By 1980, America's leaders were presiding over a self-described "national malaise" domestically, 12-percent interest rates, 20-percent mortgage rates, and a rising misery index across the land.

Internationally, America seemed resigned to co-existence with an evil empire that had enslaved and killed tens of millions, and drawn down upon two-thirds of the world's people an "iron curtain" of suffering and hopelessness.

A decade later, it was morning again in America. Tax rates were cut from 70 percent to 25 percent, gross domestic product rising at the fastest rates since World War II, stock markets booming and the American spirit transcending long-forgotten malaise.

Hon. Scott Garrett

OF NEW JERSEY

Mr. Speaker, I rise today as we pay our respects to one of the greatest leaders that this Nation has ever known, a man who will forever be held as a model for what is great about America.

As we take this time to mourn the loss of one of our Nation's greatest leaders, we should also celebrate his heroic and historic life that he lived. RONALD REAGAN exemplified the best qualities that you would ever want in a leader. He was compassionate, he was caring, he was visionary, and he was strong. He took our Nation from a crisis in confidence to a country the entire world would view as a standard bearer of justice and liberty.

Americans put their trust in RONALD REAGAN and, in turn, RONALD REAGAN put his trust in each one of us. He had faith in the American individual, in one's ability to care for one's self. RONALD REAGAN knew that we could do more for ourselves than any oversized bureaucratic burdensome Federal Government could ever do. RONALD REAGAN believed that doing more for ourselves was really the best way that we could regain that long missing self-confidence and our American pride again.

So today, in the wake of the President's death, we must continue to learn from his teachings. And we must long remember after today the contributions that RONALD REAGAN made to this Nation.

So may the legacy of RONALD REAGAN live on as long as we are all proud to raise up the Stars and Stripes and call ourselves the United States of America.

Hon. John Kline
OF MINNESOTA

Mr. Speaker, I just wanted to rise and join my colleagues in expressing my love and admiration and respect for President RONALD REAGAN. I very much appreciate that here on the House floor last night and today colleagues from both sides of the aisle have stepped up to express their respects. I think that is an important thing. It is an indicator of what a truly great man, a great President, a great leader we had in RONALD REAGAN.

Many of us had the privilege and honor of working closely with President REAGAN. I was very fortunate that in his first months in office I had the position of being his Marine Corps aid and carrying the nuclear football, the codes, traveling with him, and having the opportunity to share some thoughts. It usually was him sharing the thoughts and me listening in rapt attention, but what a wonderful man.

When you were with and near RONALD REAGAN, it really was "morning in America." I never knew any one of us who worked with him or anyone who was in his presence who could not feel his love for life, his love for our country, his unstoppable optimism. And on the one hand he was, as we have heard many of our colleagues say, friendly, lovable, affable, ready with the joke; and on the other hand he was truly a man of steel.

He had a wonderful vision for America, a vision as he articulated of a "city on the hill," a beacon of hope and opportunity for the world. And his resolute determination that we would not continue in the impossible impasse of the cold war, the very cold war that necessitated me and my colleagues to carry those nuclear codes; he refused to accept that as inevitable and he set out with the determination that is hard to imagine today, to end that impasse, to win the war, to defeat the evil empire. I was proud to serve with him.

I just want to express my love to him and my love to his family.

Hon. Terry Everett
OF ALABAMA

Mr. Speaker, I insert at this point in the *Record* my celebration of President RONALD REAGAN's life, truly a man that made a great difference in this country and this world.

Mr. Speaker, I join this House and all the American people in mourning the loss of former President RONALD WILSON REAGAN. His passing is not only a sad time for America, but for all nations.

President REAGAN gave hope and optimism to a world fearful of an uncertain future. He stirred forgotten emotions of patriotism at home while evoking courage in millions abroad struggling under the yolk of communism.

He helped to end the cold war, and his legacy is much in evidence today as once again a strong and patriotic America leads the world against the evil of tyranny.

Another legacy of President REAGAN—one for which he was attacked by the shortsighted—was his vision of a strategic missile defense for our Nation and our allies. Thank God RONALD REAGAN did not waiver in his resolve to pursue research into a missile defense for America. His unbridled determination to protect America from nuclear annihilation ultimately brought the Soviet Union to its knees.

Today, 20 years later, President Bush is leading the launch of a long-awaited missile defense system that will make America more secure from the threat of nuclear attack by a rogue nation or terrorist organization. The groundwork research and development of this vital defense program, the Strategic Defense Initiative, was begun under President REAGAN.

I am honored to chair the House Armed Services Subcommittee on Strategic Forces which has a direct role in the funding and oversight of this landmark missile defense system. And, I am proud to know that my subcommittee's efforts are the continuation of the promise made by RONALD REAGAN to bring about a safer future for our families.

On a personal note, the people of the Second District of Alabama have a special love for RONALD REAGAN. On July 10, 1986, Air Force One landed at Dothan Airport and President RONALD REAGAN joined hundreds of our citizens of the Wiregrass for fried chicken and a discussion of his tax cut plan. His charm and conservative message were very warmly received. It was clear to everyone there that he hated to leave, and we hated to give him up.

Now Alabama and America must say a final farewell to our beloved former President. Frankly, I can't imagine an America without RONALD REAGAN. He symbolized more completely than anyone else in modern history what we loved so much about our country. He made America "America" again and for that we will always be grateful.

On behalf of the people of the Second District of Alabama, I send my condolences to Nancy Reagan and her family. We join with the Nation and the world in sharing in your grief.

Hon. Doc Hastings

OF WASHINGTON

Mr. Speaker, RONALD REAGAN is a large part of why I have the honor of standing here today. I am from Washington State but in the midsixties I lived in California. In 1966 I had the privilege of casting my first vote for RONALD REAGAN in the gubernatorial primary and subsequently in the general election when he was elected Governor.

I moved back to Washington in 1976, and I served as a Reagan delegate to the Presidential Convention in Kansas City. He inspired me to get involved in public service, and 2 years later, I was elected to the Washington State Legislature.

Reagan viewed the government as a servant of the people, not their master. Throughout his career, he worked for less government control over our lives. During his first inaugural address he said:

> [I]t's not my intention to do away with government. It is rather to make it work—work with us, not over us; to stand by our side, not ride on our back. Government can and must provide opportunity, not smother it; foster productivity, not stifle it."

While he made no apologies for what he believed, he was a pragmatist, not willing to sacrifice the good for the perfect. He has been quoted as saying: "Die-hard conservatives thought that if I couldn't get everything I asked for, I should jump off the cliff with the flag flying—go down in flames. No," he said, "if I can get 70 or 80 percent of what ... I'm trying to get ... I'll take that and then continue to try to get the rest in the future."

We can all point to a handful of people who shaped us into what we are today. My list certainly includes RONALD REAGAN, who helped shape both my political ideology and the day-to-day manner in which I try to govern—without acrimony, with a touch of humor, and with an unwavering faith in the American people.

Hon. Katherine Harris

OF FLORIDA

Mr. Speaker, tonight we join Americans from all walks of life and every political persuasion in mourning a President whose courage, vision, optimism and resolve renewed the Nation he loved.

As we look back with the clarity and assuredness that history affords, how easily we forget the staggering challenges that RONALD REAGAN inherited on January 20, 1981.

Haunted by the ghost of Vietnam, America seemed in retreat as Soviet aggression either enslaved or threatened significant regions of four continents. Meanwhile, the American people struggled as stagnant economic growth, double-digit inflation, and 20-percent interest rates ate away their life savings and crushed their hopes for the future. Most ominously, our leaders spoke of a crisis in the American spirit, of a pervasive malaise that appeared to have infected our hopes, our dreams and our will to persevere.

These problems seemed so severe and so insoluble that pundits and politicos wondered if the burdens of the Presidency had become too large, too complex and too demanding for any one person to handle, but not RONALD REAGAN.

They also believed that the United States could only hope to become comfortable in its prison of mutually assured destruction with the Soviet Union and that the era of nuclear tyranny was with us forever, but not RONALD REAGAN.

These so-called experts were even convinced that a vibrant economy was impossible without double-digit inflation, but not RONALD REAGAN.

Rising from the humblest of beginnings, RONALD REAGAN taught us once again how to embrace the extraordinary. His historic Presidency restored our spirit, revitalized our economy and transformed yesterday's garrisons of tyranny into today's arsenals of liberty.

Mr. Speaker, RONALD REAGAN brought us together by reminding us of the unique blessings that we enjoy as a Nation, and as we grieve his passing this week, let us celebrate a life that exemplified the strength, the character and the resiliency of the American spirit

Hon. Johnny Isakson
OF GEORGIA

Mr. Speaker, I am honored to stand here today on behalf of myself and the citizens of the 6th District of Georgia and express my deep sympathy to the family of RONALD REAGAN and my grateful appreciation for the life of RONALD REAGAN.

I had the occasion to meet Mr. REAGAN for the first time in 1970 when he began his pursuit on the national political stage, and I watched in amazement as this man transformed a decade of dissent and discord into a decade of hope and prosperity through the power of his positive attitude and to his great patriotism to his country.

As a young man in the fifties, I remember crawling under the bomb shelters and under my desk when we prepared for the cold war and the worst of the tyranny of communism, and I watched 35 years later as, through his powerful persuasiveness, RONALD REAGAN broke down the Berlin Wall, broke down the Soviet Union and brought peace and prosperity to more of the world.

On this day on behalf of all of my constituents, my children and my grandchildren, I give thanks for the life of RONALD REAGAN, and I thank God that RONALD REAGAN came America's way.

Hon. Jim Gibbons
OF NEVADA

Mr. Speaker, I want to add my thanks to the gentleman from California (Mr. Cox) for granting me the time to speak this afternoon.

I rise today to express my most sincere and heartfelt condolences to the family of RONALD WILSON REAGAN and to the millions of Americans, Mr. Speaker, who join me and all of us in mourning the passing of this great leader this week.

I also rise to voice a great sense of loss and bereavement felt by a multitude of my fellow Nevadans who are now reflecting upon and celebrating the tremendous impact that our Nation's 40th and arguably most influential President has had on all of our lives.

REAGAN's political accomplishments alone could fill volumes; yet his political goals would have been far more difficult to come by if not for his eternally honorable character and personality. This week, as Americans mourn this great loss together, we will reflect not only on his political legacy, but also upon REAGAN's personal contributions to America and to our culture.

RONALD REAGAN was more than a President or a Commander in Chief. President REAGAN was a smalltown boy who mastered his own destiny to become an inspiration and great motivating force for the principles and policies that many of us continue to fight for every day in the House of Representatives.

During my tenure in Congress, it has been one of my most distinguished honors and personal joys to lead my colleagues on multiple measures designed to pay homage to Mr. REAGAN. Most notably, in May 2002, legislation I sponsored to grant RONALD and Nancy REAGAN the Congressional Gold Medal became a reality when President Bush presented Nancy Reagan with this award, the highest honor Congress can bestow, in the Capitol rotunda.

Ironically, in light of the tremendous impression his life has left upon the American public, even the Congressional Gold Medal seems a tiny token of appreciation that can only be overshadowed by the monumental outpouring of respect, reverence and appreciation flowing from all corners of our great Nation this week.

So as we contemplate the magnificent life of President RONALD REAGAN and mourn his passing, we are reassured by the fact that this body can and should keep his legacy alive. Congress can best honor President REAGAN by continuing progress along a path of conservative policies that REAGAN himself would be proud of, and with that, I once again send my warmest regards to the Reagan family.

Hon. John R. Carter

OF TEXAS

Mr. Speaker, today our Nation weeps in a very sad week when we recognize that we have lost a President who changed the Nation and acted upon a policy that created positive change not only for this Nation, but for the entire world.

Many of us who went into politics in the eighties, as I did, went in because we were inspired by RONALD REAGAN. I actually ran for office the first time in 1980, and something that I will never forget is that RONALD REAGAN took the time for a young, just-getting-started fellow who was running for State representative in Texas, to drop me a personal note of encouragement. Here was a man who was going to lead the Nation, and yet he took the time for one small elected official. I will never forget that.

RONALD REAGAN believed in America. He knew America to be the most noble Nation on the face of the Earth, and he absolutely trusted the American people, that they would do the right thing, because he knew them to be the noble people who created this Nation. That message, with which he inspired our country, brought us out of malaise and started us on the path of glory to know that we are doing the right thing.

We have missed RONALD REAGAN. We will miss him tremendously because he inspired us to the greatness that we have, and for that reason, he has been a blessing upon this Nation. We will not forget.

Back in Williamson County, where I come from, we celebrate RONALD REAGAN's birthday every year, and that is our big birthday celebration because we know RONALD REAGAN is the modern founder of the Republican Party today, and that inspiration causes us to celebrate his birthday.

Our thoughts and prayers are with his family, and we hope that they get through this with not too much crisis for all the blessings they have bestowed upon our Nation.

Hon. J. Randy Forbes

OF VIRGINIA

Mr. Speaker, I rise today with a heavy heart to honor one of America's greatest statesmen, President RONALD REAGAN.

As RONALD REAGAN makes his final trip to Washington, we remember this truly humble American hero. We remember a man with an ordinary beginning who went on to do extraordinary things, to chart the course for a generation, for a Nation and for the world.

Mr. Speaker, Washington is a town of leaders, and each of us who comes to Washington has a vision for the direction of our Nation. Rarely is there a man like RONALD REAGAN who cannot only lead leaders, but who can do so with such integrity, principle and honesty.

In the midst of a Nation whose spirit had been crushed with war and economic burden, in the midst of people gripped with fear from the spread of communism, RONALD REAGAN picked us up and breathed hope into our hearts. He reminded us of what we were fighting for. He said:

{T}he ultimate determinant in the struggle that's now going on in the world will not be bombs and rockets, but a test of wills and ideas, a trial of spiritual resolve, the values we hold, the beliefs we cherish, the ideals to which we are dedicated.

He reminded us that as Americans we have a responsibility to help those in need: "We cannot turn away from them," he said, "for the struggle here is not right versus left; it is right versus wrong." How true his words still ring today.

RONALD REAGAN reminded us that government is not the answer to our problems, people are. "{G}overnment's view of the economy could be summed up in a few short phrases," he said. "If it moves, tax it. If it keeps moving, regulate it. And if it stops moving, subsidize it."

By exposing and destroying burdensome and oppressive regulation and taxes, he restored the spirit that America is built upon: optimism, opportunity and self-reliance. In doing so, he not only energized the economy, but he rejuvenated the pride and self-worth of Americans.

Finally, RONALD REAGAN reminded us of the importance of faith in our democracy. He said, "Freedom prospers when religion is vibrant and the rule of law under God is acknowledged." He will be missed, but his words and spirit will continue on.

Hon. J. Gresham Barrett

OF SOUTH CAROLINA

Mr. Speaker, President REAGAN changed our hearts with his optimistic outlook on life, the world and our place in it. He came to office at a time in our history when we were a little bruised and battered, and, simply said, he pulled us up by our bootstraps and taught us how to get back on the horse that knocked us off.

He once said that America is too great for small dreams, but to RONALD REAGAN these were not merely words that were used in a 30-second sound bite. These were words that went to the core of the man.

He reminded us that even though we may have our differences, our common bond as Americans sets us apart from the rest of the world. He believed in all that is good in America because he believed there is good in every American.

RONALD REAGAN was a hero to me and a hero to an entire generation. He leaves a legacy of hope and prosperity that will last for generations to come.

I know there is a special place in Heaven for RONALD REAGAN, and I know in my heart he heard the words, "Well done."

Hon. Lincoln Diaz-Balart

OF FLORIDA

Mr. Speaker, I rise today to honor a man who I believe to be the greatest American President of the 20th century. President RONALD REAGAN defeated the most powerful and dangerous military empire in the history of the world without firing a single shot. President REAGAN knew instinctively that America represents good, and he knew that communism represents evil. He never wavered in his conviction that freedom is the birthright of all mankind.

The enemies of the United States never forgave him for his firmness, for his character, for his faith in the people of the United States and his faith in the cause of liberty. Even in his death, they continue to attack him. His hatred is evidenced by the declaration made by the tyrannical regime in Havana a few hours ago: "He, who never should have been born, has died." That monstrous statement illustrates the ultimate evil of the tyrant who has enslaved the Cuban people for over 45 years. President REAGAN knew that the Cuban tyrant and that communist tyrants everywhere have represented and represent the antithesis of liberty, freedom and human dignity.

I think he was an extraordinary leader, Mr. Speaker, someone who inspired us all, changed America for the better and saved the world from tyranny.

May RONALD WILSON REAGAN, apostle of freedom, democracy and human rights, rest in peace.

Hon. Fred Upton

OF MICHIGAN

Mr. Speaker, I am one of those fortunate to have worked and served in the Reagan administration for $4^{1}/_{2}$ years. I started off as a legislative aid, and I ended up being in charge of congressional affairs at OMB under Director Stockman and then under Director Jim Miller. RONALD REAGAN had a vision, an agenda; and he knew how to get things done. He surrounded himself with good people that were smart, who shared his vision, and in fact knew the political process to get things done.

Back then, times were tough. We had the cold war, we had double-digit inflation, double-digit unemployment, double-digit interest rates; and yet he was still able to get his agenda through and move the country forward. The odds were stacked against him. Republicans did not control the Senate; and in this body, in the House, they did not control the House either. In fact, the margin was 70 or 80 votes short in the House. Yet he was still able to get his agenda through.

On the minority side, the Republican side, we had two terrific dynamic leaders, John Rhodes and Bob Michel, two Republicans who were minority leaders, never Speaker. They were both good, decent, honest people; but they never had the votes, or not the Republican votes. So RONALD REAGAN appealed to the American people for his support. Reaganesque is a word today that you will find in the dictionary, a powerful word; and in fact he put policy over politics, and look at the results.

He beat an incumbent President, a good honest, decent guy, Jimmy Carter, who has done wonderful things since his Presidency; but the real test is reelection, and RONALD REAGAN won 49 of the 50 States. If that was not a mandate in terms of his agenda, I do not know what is. That mandate, winning 49 States, I think will serve as the record for any President running for reelection.

Yes, history will judge where he stands, rightfully so. But in large part it already has. RONALD REAGAN was a great American President, a wonderful man who touched tens of millions of lives across this country in every respect of their life. I was proud to serve a wonderful President for those years.

Hon. Christopher Cox
OF CALIFORNIA

The first time I met RONALD REAGAN was the day I began work for him in the White House. We shook hands and exchanged pleasantries in the Oval Office. Of course, it is difficult to forget one's first meeting with the President of the United States, but what I particularly remember is how quickly he put me at ease. Of course, he told a joke.

Learning that I was a Harvard graduate, he told me the story of a friend of his who had graduated from Harvard Law School, had become a partner in a large firm but had lost his position due to a problem with drinking and drugs, and consequentially, in succession, he lost his wife, his family, his income, and even ran afoul of the law, being put in jail for shoplifting. But now he was out of jail. He had cleaned up his life and, most important, he had met a wonderful woman to whom he wished to propose marriage. But, and it was on this point that he asked the President's advice, he had not told this woman about his background for fear of losing her. So he asked the President, should I tell her that I went to Harvard?

I knew immediately where I stood. Two years later, I was with the President in the Oval Office, and I have a picture hanging on my desk of this moment, and I am sitting across from his desk, across from him, just the two of us. He has a big smile on his face, and I am about to burst out laughing because he was, of course, telling another joke.

It was a special privilege to travel with the President on Air Force One, and what I particularly remember is the way the President came back to cheer up the staff, to regale us with stories and jokes. I was particularly fond of his amazingly authentic Irish brogue.

But I will not forget especially the last time I saw him as President. It was here in this Capitol. He had summoned us, the Republican Members, just days before the inauguration to give us a private valediction. No press, no public, just us. And he spoke from the Democratic sides of the aisle, from the rostrum on the left, a mistake I attributed to his lack of familiarity with House procedure. It was a mistake of mine, however. He knew exactly what he was doing. And as he described his political career, he described how he did not leave the Democratic Party, the Democratic Party left him; and he strode purposefully to this other rostrum to the delight of the Republican Members.

But what he told us that day rose far above party and partisanship. Because, of course, he saw a consistent thread throughout his career in his support for FDR, his campaigning for Harry Truman, his support and campaigning for Ike, and of course his own administration. A few moments after he finished here on the floor, we went to Statuary Hall and he mingled with the Members and we had a few private moments there. This was, of course, just a few feet from where in the rotunda later today his body will lie in repose. He did not tell me a joke at that time. Instead, after congratulating me on my recent election to Congress, something we had had the chance more exuberantly to celebrate after I and my new colleague, the gentleman from California (Mr. Rohrabacher), visited with him in the Oval Office in June, he told me, "never forget to trust the people who sent you here" and "always fight for the principles that you and I share."

It was the serious side of him because he was all about ideas. And while his humor, his gregariousness, his avuncularity has been much remarked upon in recent days, that was an important aspect of his leadership; but it does not tell us about the substance of his leadership, where he was taking the country. And it was the ideas that President REAGAN brought to Washington that mattered most of all.

It is well known and much remarked upon that RONALD REAGAN won the cold war without firing a shot. He led the global movement to tear down the Berlin Wall. He led an economic renaissance at home by dramatically reducing the burden of taxes across the board, from a marginal rate of 70 percent down to 28 percent. But it is just as important to recognize the leading role that President REAGAN played in supporting our country, such issues as the civil rights of women and men here at home.

President REAGAN, of course, appointed the first woman to be ambassador of the United Nations. He appointed the first woman to be a Justice of the U.S. Supreme Court. He appointed the first woman to be Secretary of Transportation, the first Latina to be Treasurer of the United States.

On November 2, 1983, he made Martin Luther King's birthday a national holiday. He appointed the first African American chairman of the U.S. Civil Rights Commission, my good friend and great American, the late Clarence Pendleton. He extended the Voting Rights Act for a quarter century. He named the first Hispanic to the Cabinet, Lauro Cavasos, as Secretary of Education.

On August 10, 1988, he provided compensation to Japanese Americans who had been deprived of their civil liberties and their property during the infamous internment of World War II ordered by FDR.

Today, we can see the wisdom of President REAGAN's policies from a distance. He appointed the first-ever Presidential Commission on AIDS and gave national direction to the effort to stop the spread of this terrible disease.

His was the statesmanship of a true leader. While fighting Soviet expansion in Africa, he fought apartheid and imposed sanctions on the racist Government of South Africa by Executive order. He demanded as a condition of lifting those sanctions the release of Nelson Mandela. And yet he refused to declare economic warfare against the civilian population of that country, black, white, and all races as the United Nations had done in imposing its sanctions on Zimbabwe. So today, whereas Zimbabwe has become a living hell, an autocracy that has stripped away all pretense of law or property or personal safety, South Africa has a real democracy where all men and women can vote and where all are equal before the law.

In Central America, he prevented the Soviet Union from establishing a beachhead in our own hemisphere, and likewise in Nicaragua. And throughout Central and South America and the Caribbean, just as in Central Europe and Asia, democracy grew and prospered.

Mr. Speaker, from that day in January 1981, when President REAGAN was sworn in, until last Saturday, the American people always knew where to look for a hero. President REAGAN did great things not only for our country but for our world. Today, more than 1 billion people live in freedom because of his global leadership. In fact, all of the people of the world, those who enjoy the sweet blessings of liberty and those who still yearn for freedom, will always know where to look for a hero.

Hon. Tim Ryan

OF OHIO

Mr. Speaker, when our country was confronted with a terrible menace of dangerous ideology, REAGAN rallied America and united the world to decisively defeat the threat of communism. We are grateful for that leadership.

RONALD REAGAN elevated the Office of the President. When mistakes were made, RONALD REAGAN personally accepted responsibility. It did not matter what focus groups, polls, his advisers, or political consultants said, he understood that the buck stopped with him and him alone.

He was an American icon, forever remembered for his warmth and the respect he afforded to others, and our thoughts and prayers today are with Nancy and his children and his family at this very difficult time.

Even when President REAGAN broke the hearts of the Democrats, he was respected for his honesty, his beliefs, and the dedication he displayed in pursuing them.

As a young elementary school student during the *Challenger* disaster, it was enormous comfort to those of us who were all watching, because there was a teacher on the *Challenger* at that time, to listen to President REAGAN as we began to question why America was sending these astronauts up into space; why there was a teacher on the *Challenger* at that time. And when President REAGAN said to us that the future does not belong to the fainthearted, it belongs to the brave, he was communicating to us what America was all about.

I also remember as a young man the way President REAGAN interacted with then-Speaker Tip O'Neill. They laughed and they talked and they joked. And that was a great example for those of us who were beginning to get acquainted with the political system.

I remember the courage and the humor that President REAGAN showed when he was shot, hoping that the doctors were all Republican and telling his wife, who was terrified, that he forgot to duck.

I also cannot help but remember President REAGAN, during the Washington Redskins ceremony at the Rose Garden after winning the Super Bowl, hitting Gary Sanders on the money as he ran a drag pattern across the Rose Garden.

The differences then, despite our disagreements, were real; but because of the way President REAGAN led, he taught us that there is a big difference between strong beliefs and bitter partisanship. Strong beliefs and a love of country are the only way to bring this country forward as we face the enormous challenges that we have before this body today.

RONALD REAGAN always stressed that we are a can-do country. Democrats and Republicans both believe this. And I believe it is that sense of optimism, as we look back on history, that the Presidents who moved the Nation forward were optimistic and believed the best and the brightest in this country would continue to move us forward.

Mr. Speaker, I believe we can get back on the right track with strong leadership and a real commitment to confronting the problems that face American families today. In the words of RONALD REAGAN, "we can do better." With tolerance and inclusion, uniting rather than dividing, we can continue the legacy of RONALD REAGAN.

So when we return to work next week, I hope this House will be inspired by the leadership of RONALD REAGAN instead of mired in the partisan politics that have too often affected our work as of late. We should be inspired by his patriotism and devotion to our country, and we should remember his faith, his optimism, and his unwavering commitment to his convictions as we do the work of the American people.

In the words of President REAGAN, whose comforting message he gave us some 18 years ago—and we will never forget RONALD REAGAN, nor the last time we saw him—for now he has "'slipped the surly bonds of earth' to 'touch the face of God.'" We will miss him.

Hon. Henry E. Brown, Jr.

OF SOUTH CAROLINA

Mr. Speaker, like so many Americans, President REAGAN was not only my President, but also my inspiration. My own calling to public service in 1981 was in no small part as a result of President REAGAN's example. Without his leadership and passion for our great Nation, I would not be standing in this great Chamber before Members today.

He was a shining light and a beacon of hope not only for our Nation, but also for the world. At a time in history when it was desperately needed, he sought peace in our world and was a champion of democracy and freedom. We are all better as a result of his contributions, and his legacy will live forever.

If I had to describe President REAGAN with just one adjective, it would not be courageous, optimistic or kind, or any number of other fitting adjectives for such a great man, it would be American. Above all things, President REAGAN was an American. He so embodied the spirit, courage and hope of America that he was able to reach out and touch his fellow citizens. He trusted the American people to be able to make decisions for themselves, and in turn they trusted him. He had a dream to make America stronger by putting more responsibility back into the hands of the people. He understood that Americans could manage their hard-earned dollars better than any government agency. He empowered the citizens to work harder and to improve our Nation from the ground up.

I am proud to model my views on government after one of our great Presidents, President REAGAN. Even those who have never met him or who disagree with him politically felt a special connection with President REAGAN. He was a people's President, arguably unlike any others before or after.

He invigorated and inspired those young men for the battle ahead, just as he invigorated and inspired a Nation while he was in office. President REAGAN always celebrated life, and he loved every day of it. I am honored to be celebrating the life of such a great American with Members today. We were blessed and honored as a Nation to have President REAGAN as both our leader and as our friend.

Mr. President, you were not just marking time. You made a tremendous difference in the lives of all Americans. You made the Nation stronger and the world a safer place for democracy. Today we still enjoy the fruits of the Reagan revolution. You fought for freedom, and today it does not waver. You were the inspiration of so many, including myself, and today we remember and say thanks to you. On behalf of the entire First Congressional District of South Carolina, a grateful Nation and myself, thank you, Mr. President, and may God bless you and your family.

Hon. Mike Ross

OF ARKANSAS

Mr. Speaker, the Great Communicator, an all-American patriot, relentless pursuer of freedom, these qualities describe America's 40th President, RONALD REAGAN.

We can all agree that President REAGAN's enduring love for his country and his idealistic outlook renewed faith and hope to a generation of Americans. My fond memories of President REAGAN will include, among others, that defining moment nearly 14 years ago as I watched with pride as he, as a former President, chiseled away at the Berlin Wall. I was truly moved by the immense joy and pride that he radiated and that radiated on the faces around him. You see, it had not been that many years before that in his famous speech he said, "Mr. Gorbachev, tear down this wall!"

President REAGAN's commitment and service to our country and the world will be forever remembered in the hearts and minds of people around the globe. I join millions of others throughout the world who continue to keep Mrs. Reagan and their family in my heart and in my prayers as we pay tribute to the 40th President of the United States of America, former President RONALD REAGAN.

Hon. Tom Cole

OF OKLAHOMA

Mr. Speaker, there are few men in our history whose lives can be said to have changed the world. RONALD REAGAN was one of those men.

RONALD REAGAN was an inspiration to me personally and politically. In 1984, I was honored to head his reelection campaign in Oklahoma. I also served as chairman of the Oklahoma Republican Party during his Presidency. A favorite memory of mine is of a meeting with the President and Republican State Party chairmen from the South at the White House in 1988. A 15-minute meeting turned into an hour-long treasure as he regaled us with one hilarious political story after another. RONALD REAGAN loved politicians, he loved politics, and he loved public service.

I cannot claim to have known RONALD REAGAN well. I was privileged to be with him on more than a few occasions. All the same, he changed my life and the lives of millions of others. He was a voice of faith, faith in America, faith in her people, faith in their future, and, most profoundly, faith in freedom.

RONALD REAGAN inspired us to do great things. With him we accomplished much. It is for us to continue to build that "shining city on a hill" to which he so often referred. There is much yet to do. RONALD REAGAN was my hero; but more important, he was an American hero. We mourn his passing, but we celebrate his life of achievement and patriotism.

Mr. Speaker, there are few men in our history and there will be few men in our future who live their lives in such a way that the world will be changed because of their existence. RONALD REAGAN is one of those men. His dignity, character, strength and convictions will distinguish him in the pages of history and define him as one of the greatest Presidents of the 20th century. President REAGAN was an inspiration to many and his optimism for America's future encouraged those across all party lines. He knew there was a brighter tomorrow through the path of strong values, hard work, tough decisions and perseverance. His leadership pulled America through the end of the cold war, pushed the Soviet Union and the eastern bloc onto the "ash heap of history" and restored the virtues of idealism and optimism to our country. He was a visionary who instigated the rebirth of conservatism and shaped the Republican Party into the governing national majority we see today.

RONALD REAGAN was a source of inspiration to me both personally and politically. I was serving as executive director of the Oklahoma State Party when REAGAN was elected. In 1984, I was honored to head his reelection efforts in Oklahoma. I also served as Oklahoma GOP chairman during his Presidency, so I had opportunities to meet and work with him.

RONALD REAGAN had a magic that really appealed to people. A favorite memory is of a meeting with the President and Republican State Party chairmen from the South in 1988. A 15-minute meeting turned into an hour-long treasure as he regaled us with one hilarious political story after another. His wit and humor are as fresh in my memory today as they were 20 years ago. I was privileged to see up close what so many Americans intuitively felt when watching him on television. He was an extraordinary man who lived life and enjoyed being with people. It is no wonder he was able to move thousands of people and mobilize them to support his efforts. It's a gift few of us have—and he had that magic in abundance.

Not only is RONALD REAGAN a personal hero to me, his influence has shaped a generation of politicians. And by doing that he instilled the values that the Republican Party embraces today. Countless Republican officeholders got into elective politics because he fired their imagination. More profoundly, he showed that the institution of the Presidency does work. We seldom remember that after the trials of Watergate and 20 years of failed or shortened administrations, some thought our country was too big for one man to govern, inspire and shape. No one, particularly those who worked with RONALD REAGAN, question that today.

And let us not forget that he was a very effective politician whose drive to succeed and will to win were intense. He lost primary after primary in 1976 before coming back from the political graveyard in North Carolina, Texas and Oklahoma. Former Republican National Chairman Frank Farenkopf tells the story that on election day in 1984, the President was so far ahead in the polls that he and Ed Rollins cancelled a rally in Minnesota. He did not need to be bothered, they reasoned. After he won 49 States and only lost Minnesota by about 2,500 votes, the President liked to tease both of his advisors about their election day gaffe. It became a joke, but the President wanted Minnesota in his column.

Much has been made in recent days of RONALD REAGAN's courage. We saw his physical courage when an assassin sought to take his life in early 1981. We saw it again when he confronted the ravages of Alzheimer's with grace, candor and sensitivity. But President REAGAN also had the courage of his ideas and an ability to see the right path for his party and his country.

One of RONALD REAGAN's biographers, Edmund Morris, tells of his astonishment when he read the President's diaries from his time in office. He learned how many of the major and complex decisions of the Reagan administration were made by the President, alone and in private. RONALD REAGAN did not care, Morris recounts, who got the credit as long as his decisions were implemented and his goals for America came closer to realization. Recently Kiron K. Skinner and Marty Anderson's fine works detailed the depth and breath of REAGAN's view of the world—a view he implemented in office.

In describing another great man at another time in history, Winston Churchill writes in his "History of the English Speaking Peoples" that Robert Peel was:

> ... the dominating force and personality in English politics ... {who} whether in Opposition or in office ... towered above the scene. He was not a man of broad and ranging modes of thoughts, but he understood better than any of his contemporaries the needs of the country and he had the outstanding courage to change his views in order to meet them.

Robert Peel, Mr. Churchill added,

> ... saw the industrial revolution in Britain that made her the pre-eminent world power in the nineteenth century was driven not by the government but by private enterprise, by capital, by entrepreneurs, by a free people willing to take risks.

There are many differences between Robert Peel and RONALD REAGAN. Mr. Peel split his party and destroyed a governing coalition to support free trade—a decision validated by history. As a Governor and then as a President, RONALD REAGAN united a party badly divided over ideas and led it out of the political wilderness. The Republican ascendancy in national government today is a direct result of his leadership. But in reading Winston Churchill's appraisal of Robert Peel's political biography, he was the dominating personality in American politics for a generation.

From the vantage of the early 21st century, it is hard to recall the mood of the country and its troubles at his election in 1980. Watergate, defeat in Vietnam, unrestrained Soviet adventurism, double-digit inflation and interest rates, massive unemployment, an energy crisis, American hostages in Tehran, the end of the postwar U.S. domination of the global economy—all these combined to give some a sense that America's best days were behind her; that perhaps free enterprise and freedom were not the answer; that we had to accept totalitarian communism as a legitimate and equally plausible alternative to our own way of life. RONALD REAGAN rejected these ideas. He was optimistic about America. He believed the United States was a "shining city on the hill," a beacon of hope and freedom to the world. He understood communism was evil and free peoples must defend themselves against the darkness of tyranny and oppression. He saw a bright and prosperous future for all Americans, one where their work could carry them as far as they dared to dream. Looking back, we take all these things for granted, but RONALD REAGAN was ridiculed by the intellectuals and so-called realists of his day. It took real courage to stand up for his beliefs to put them into practice, and to defend them from the faint of heart while they took root and blossomed. To paraphrase Mr. Churchill's assessment of Mr. Peel, RONALD REAGAN understood his countrymen better than anyone else on the political stage. They needed leadership, he gave it and they loved him for it.

Like Mr. Peel, RONALD REAGAN also had the courage to change his views. A New Deal Democrat, his partisan affiliation and ideological vantage point slowly shifted over time from a liberal Democrat who believed in government intervention to a conservative Republican who trusted Americans and the people of the world to solve their own problems. As anyone who has even a passing understanding of Hollywood and its cultural and political outlook knows, this was not an easy thing to do. RONALD REAGAN learned about communists first-hand when he battled to keep them out of the entertainment industry. Much of his later political success was based on a willingness to stand up to Soviet aggression. Yet, when a glimmer of light came through the darkness behind the Iron Curtain, President REAGAN saw America's chance for victory through negotiation and began to talk to the Soviets and their leader, Mikhail Gorbachev. Many of his longtime supporters decried his decision and they did so with good reason because the Soviets historically did not negotiate in good faith. But the President had the courage and the vision to see the great opening and he took it. And, like so many times in the past, he was right. And we are better for it.

Mr. Speaker, like many Americans I cannot claim to have known RONALD REAGAN well. I was privileged to be with him on more than a few occasions, but more often I watched him on television or read about him in the morning's newspapers with the rest of the country. All the same, he changed my life. And he changed the lives of millions around the world. His was a voice of faith. Faith in America, in her people, and in freedom. He inspired us to do great things. With him we accomplished much. Though he has gone to a better place, it is for us to continue to build that "shining city on the hill." There is much yet to do, but RONALD REAGAN's legacy and memory will inspire us in our task.

Hon. David Wu

OF OREGON

I would like to share a personal story, one little vignette about my experience with President REAGAN. It was during my student days, during my college senior year. Then-Governor REAGAN came to Stanford to speak. The speech was organized. It was sometime between his 1976 Presidential campaign and his 1980 Presidential campaign. He had been Governor of California.

His speech at Stanford was organized by the Young College Republicans or the Young College Conservatives. Whoever organized it, they carefully screened the audience, and a lot of folks were screened out. But for whatever reason, I was screened in.

Then-Governor REAGAN gave a very good speech, after which he took questions. I was one of the ones who rose to ask a question. Of course, it was a challenging question. As I was going into the question, members of the audience started to boo me, and the moderator rose to cut off my question. It was at that point that Mr. REAGAN stepped up and said, "No, no, no, I want to hear the young man out, and I want to answer his question." I had my say, he answered the question, and of course he got a standing ovation.

But I think it is that moment, that image of Mr. REAGAN, that I remember, his graciousness, his openness, his generosity of spirit, the willingness to hear folks out and hear debate. That is a sign of greatness in any individual, and there were lessons for that day almost 30 years ago, and they are perhaps lessons today for the Washington in which we work today.

My best wishes to the family, and God bless RONALD REAGAN.

Hon. Dan Burton

OF INDIANA

Mr. Speaker, I, like all of my colleagues, would like to extol the wonderful accomplishments of President REAGAN, the economy coming back from the doldrums, the destruction of the Berlin Wall, and the communist menace that we faced so much back in the sixties, seventies and eighties. But what I want to talk about today are personal experiences I had with RONALD REAGAN.

When I was running for office over a period of 10 or 12 years, I promised my mother, who was a waitress for many, many years at L.S. Harris & Company, that if I ever got elected to the Congress of the United States, the first thing I would do is take her in the front door of the White House and introduce her to the President of the United States.

I got elected in 1983. I called the White House and they said, yes, we can give you a couple of minutes with the President. I called my mom, and I took her in the front door of the White House expecting a very perfunctory kind of meeting where he would shake hands and take a picture, and that would be it. Unbeknownst to me, he contacted my office and tried to find out everything he could about me. When we walked in, he put his arm around me and said to my mother, "This is one of the finest young Congressmen in the Congress. I want you to know that I really appreciate all of the things he has done," and he reeled off three or four things I had accomplished that I did not think he had any idea about.

I could see my mother's chest expanding, expanding, and expanding. Here is a little lady from the Midwest who had a very tough life, was abused as a wife, and protected me and my sister from abuse from my father. She had nothing but a tough life, and here was the President of the United States telling her what a great guy her son was. I will never forget that as long as I live. She walked out of that office with my stepfather and me, and she was so proud. She carried a picture of the President and us together for the rest of her life. She was so proud to the day she died. He was that kind of a guy.

I remember another time I debated Al Gore when he was in the House and Tom Downey of New York on the Strategic Defense Initiative when the President first started talking about defending this country from an incoming missile attack. I debated Al Gore and Tom Downey on a special order for probably 30 or 40 minutes, and I thought that was the end of it. And 2 days later, I got a personal handwritten letter from the President thanking me for sticking up for him. Who would believe the President of the United States would take the time to write a handwritten note to a new Congressman just because he took a position that paralleled the President's? He was a wonderful, down-to-earth man.

One more little anecdote, and then I will let the rest of my colleagues talk. When I first got elected, they had a dinner for all of the freshmen Congressmen. After the dinner, we were walking around the Green Room, and everybody was patting the President on the back and saying what a great job he had done with the tax cuts. As he walked by me, I thought I better talk about something besides tax cuts because he is just walking past everybody, and I really wanted to talk to the guy.

As he walked by, I said, "President REAGAN, one of my favorite movies was 'King's Row.'" He said, thank you very much, took two steps past me, stopped, turned around and came back, and talked for 10 minutes about that movie. It was one of the greatest thrills of my life to get a real insight into what he did as a movie actor. He really enjoyed it as well. All my colleagues gathered around. It was one of the highlights of the evening.

That is the kind of guy RONALD REAGAN was. He cared about people in addition to being a great President.

I would like to say to his family, God bless you, all of you. Mrs. Reagan, you were great to us when you were First Lady. God bless you and your family. The good Lord, I am sure, has a very high place in Heaven for RONALD REAGAN.

Hon. Rahm Emanuel

OF ILLINOIS

Mr. Speaker, I do not have stories like the gentleman from Indiana (Mr. Burton), personal interaction with former President REAGAN, but as somebody growing up and loving politics, I obviously watched his Presidency as a student of politics.

Here was a guy known as a Great Communicator, an eternal optimist. It makes sense when one thinks about it: A guy who grew up in Dixon, IL, a troubled home, faced a series of disadvantages, and one day wakes up in the White House.

What is there not to be optimistic about? And he had that sense of optimism, and everybody can talk about different skills or techniques or tactics as a communicator; but the truth is he never left Dixon, IL. He had that common touch. He knew about walking-around folk, and he understood their lives, and he could tell a great story that gave people a sense of his ideas. So he spoke of our common wisdom and our common sense.

One of the other things that I very much admired on the policy, although I do have differences obviously, was President REAGAN's commitment to the earned income tax credit. In 1986, he greatly expanded the earned income tax credit; and if I can quote him, "This is the best antipoverty, the best profamily, the best job creation measure to come out of Congress."

That was President REAGAN on the earned income tax credit; and he understood that through a tax credit we can help create jobs, help be profamily, did not have to have a government bureaucrat to do it, but it was something we could do through the Tax Code to reward work, reward responsibility, and fight poverty at the same time.

I think that was a tremendous program. We expanded it in 1993 and again later on in 1997, but RONALD REAGAN in 1986 really put the muscle behind the earned income tax credit, a great program that I think lifted millions of American families and children out of poverty and did it by rewarding work, not dependency.

Last, RONALD REAGAN spoke to our patriotism and our sense of love. He came into office at a time when people did not think you could do the job of the Presidency. It was just so overwhelming. And with his ease, his grace and his confidence, he restored people's confidence in that office.

Mr. Speaker, he has a legacy of patriotism and confidence in America and the American people, and it will endure. Our hearts go out to Mrs. Reagan and his entire family, to a great, great patriot.

Hon. Steve Buyer

OF INDIANA

Mr. Speaker, RONALD REAGAN's belief in the ideals of individual liberty reassured America to believe in itself and inspired people all over the world.

Like a flower perfect in its bud and as it is in its bloom, it spreads its seeds before it dies. So did RONALD REAGAN as he spread the seeds of liberty and its attributes to the people of the world through the pursuits of freedom.

His critics viewed him as a throwback in time, almost antediluvian; but what RONALD REAGAN possessed were principles and ideals that were ageless. They served as guideposts for our country in time.

I will always remember his courage to take a stand in the face of adversity, especially the evils of tyranny. He understood that liberty is protected by the vigilant who must be ready to prepare and defend freedom, thereby preserving peace.

I will always remember his charm and smile. They were infectious. He was always able to stay above the fray, undeterred with his calm demeanor and balanced temperament. I believe his optimism inspired people in more ways than this body could ever articulate. To RONALD REAGAN, one cannot believe impossible things, for it oppresses the soul and thwarts hope.

He dared Americans to dream big and made it fashionable to be a dreamer of dreams. His sentimentality reflected his care and concern for people. I thank the REAGAN family for permitting the state funeral so that people can mourn their President.

On behalf of my constituents in Indiana, I extend their thoughts and prayers of many Hoosiers to the Reagan family.

Hon. Stephanie Herseth

OF SOUTH DAKOTA

Mr. Speaker, many Members of this House worked closely with President REAGAN and were fortunate to call him their friend. Many were inspired to service by his example and point to his Presidency as a turning point in their lives. For many in my generation, he is the first President we really remember from the beginning of his Presidency to the end. He is the first President who inspired us with his confidence and optimism as well as his humility.

He is the first President in our memory to truly embody that graceful strength that we seek from our leaders in times of crisis and uncertainty. We will all remember President RONALD REAGAN in our own way, shaped by our own perspective. What I will always remember most is the respect, the dignity, and the sincerity with which he treated others, as will all America for generations to come. My thoughts and prayers are with his wife, Nancy Reagan, his family, and his many friends.

Hon. Mark R. Kennedy
OF MINNESOTA

Mr. Speaker, our country had suffered its fair share of lumps in the seventies, and in 1980 we were looking for a leader who would draw a line in the sand and say "no more." We found that rare man in RONALD REAGAN. RONALD REAGAN succeeded where others failed because throughout his public life he concerned himself with getting things done, not winning applause. In fact, one of REAGAN's hallmarks was the plaque he kept on his desk that said: "There is no limit to what you can accomplish if you don't care who gets the credit."

As a businessman, I admired RONALD REAGAN's dedication to this seemingly modest goal. Putting success ahead of personal accolades is a difficult lesson for many to learn, but a talent all great men seem to instinctively possess. It is an axiom that turns productive individuals into innovative leaders, and it turned RONALD REAGAN into one of the greatest leaders and greatest Presidents we have had. Ironically, the more REAGAN sought to distance himself from the successes he knew grew from the sweat and tears of the American people, the more it turned out that those people admired him for his principled leadership. That leadership earned RONALD REAGAN widespread respect and helped REAGAN form broad bipartisan coalitions to renew America. The results were immediate, winning historic legislative victories on providing tax relief and strengthening our military. The economy flourished as our national pride returned.

I can recall what a difference RONALD REAGAN made in my own life, from the depressed job market I entered after graduating from college in 1978 to the vastly improved job opportunities I found after graduating from business school in 1983. The world was a wholly different place in those 5 years because the Reagan era had become the Reagan revolution.

The impact that RONALD REAGAN had on our world is immeasurable. When he took office, our collective national spirit had been lulled to sleep in the morass of the sixties and the seventies. REAGAN seized the sleeping giant and shook it wide awake with a jolt of optimism and patriotism and a reminder of our destiny as Americans that our best days lay ahead.

May God bless the spirit and family of RONALD REAGAN, our 40th President, and one of our true national heroes.

Hon. Bob Etheridge
OF NORTH CAROLINA

Mr. Speaker, on behalf of the people of the Second District of North Carolina, I rise to pay my respects to the late RONALD REAGAN, the 40th President of the United States of America. My wife, Faye, and I join all North Carolinians and all Americans in expressing our condolences to former First Lady Nancy Reagan and the entire Reagan family.

RONALD W. REAGAN served two terms in our Nation's highest office after winning overwhelming margins of victory in the Presidential elections of 1980 and 1984. His time in office was marked by renewed pride in America, and he is to be commended for his steadfast devotion to liberalization from the oppression of communism and that vicious rule in nations throughout the world.

Regardless of one's position on President REAGAN's policies and politics, all Americans remember his warmth of spirit and the respectful manner in which he engaged in public debate. This approach kept acrimony to a healthy minimum even when conflicting views on vitally important issues were debated in this House and in this city. That example stands in marked contrast to the divisiveness and bitter partisanship we have too often witnessed since his Presidency.

Finally, Mr. Speaker, all Americans stand in solidarity and salute Nancy Reagan and the whole Reagan family for the dignity and grace that they have displayed through the former President's long and difficult struggle with Alzheimer's disease. Their struggle has been our struggle, for it reminds us of the afflictions millions of Americans face in anonymity every day. The Federal Government must act to ease this needless suffering by increasing research funding and modernizing regulations to allow for potentially lifesaving research using stem cells and other medical techniques. The pain on Mrs. Reagan's face should prod the conscience of this country to end the cruel victimization of stricken patients who require potentially lifesaving research.

In conclusion, the passing of President REAGAN closes an important chapter in American history. As the leaders of the 20th century pass from the scene, we must endeavor to carry on their legacy of progress at home and American leadership in the world. On behalf of the people of North Carolina, I rise today to say, rest in peace, Mr. President.

Hon. Mike Ferguson

OF NEW JERSEY

Mr. Speaker, on behalf of the people of the Seventh District of New Jersey, I rise to pay tribute to the life and legacy of one of the great Presidents in the history of the United States, RONALD REAGAN. In the farewell address at the end of his second term, President REAGAN said that those in his generation:

{W}ere taught, very directly, what it means to be an American. And we absorbed, almost in the air, a love of country and an appreciation of its institutions.

In many ways, President REAGAN was my first President. His presence was the dominant force in America and in politics when I first started thinking about policy issues, the role of government, and America's unique place of leadership in the world. And I believe, for my generation and for so many more, President REAGAN enabled us to do just what he had been taught in his generation: to absorb, almost in the air, a love of country and an appreciation for its institutions.

After the turmoil and tumult of the sixties and the seventies, President REAGAN helped America regain its confidence. He helped us to remember who we were, what being an American meant, and the greatness which would allow America to play a pivotal role on the world stage. RONALD REAGAN believed in "peace through strength," and he won the cold war. He believed in the dignity and the value of every human person, and

he believed in an optimistic vision for the future of America which resulted in one of the golden ages of American patriotism, prosperity, and progress. He was able to be a tough leader and a formidable adversary; and he did it with his own human touch, with a warm sense of humor, and his ever-present humility.

Future generations will teach their children just as we are teaching ours that the life and legacy of President RONALD REAGAN will take its rightful place alongside the greatest leaders in our Nation's history and as one of the pivotal figures of the 20th century who quite literally changed our world for the better. For this, we will forever be in his debt. May he rest in peace.

Hon. Artur Davis

OF ALABAMA

Mr. Speaker, it is probably somewhat appropriate that I follow my friend from New Jersey (Mr. Ferguson) because, like some other Members in this body, I passed from being a child to being a grown man under the Reagan Presidency during those 8 years. And it is appropriate and I am honored to stand here today as part of the great bipartisan tradition in this country to express my condolences to the Reagan family.

This is not a moment for party. It is a moment for solemn reflection about America and about someone who cared very deeply about America. Make no mistake, there are some on my side of the aisle who, including myself, have profound disagreements with the direction of what has been called the Reagan revolution.

All of us in this Chamber do not share the same vision or the same viewpoints on a number of the President's policies during the eighties, but this is a time to give him his due, and this is a time to remember what the best tradition of RONALD REAGAN's conservatism meant.

One of my strongest memories of RONALD REAGAN was one of his last great speeches when he went to the Berlin Wall about 24 years after John F. Kennedy went there, and he said symbolically to Mikhail Gorbachev, then the leader of the Soviet Union, that if he was serious about reform, if he was serious about freedom, he should come to this place, open this gate, and tear down this wall. And somehow 15 months later the wall was gone.

RONALD REAGAN was fortunate that he lived to see successes on his own terms. He lived to see the wall come down in Berlin. And I have to believe this: We can debate as historians what caused the Soviet empire to fall without a shot being fired. We can debate as people who follow history what caused the Soviet Union to implode. But we ought to be generous enough this week to say that RONALD REAGAN's courage was a part of that. His willingness to stand up to the Iron Curtain was no small part in the dismantling.

How do we honor RONALD REAGAN? There are different opinions in this Chamber about how we do that. Let me close my time today by giving just one Member's opinion. President REAGAN spoke very eloquently of a "shining city on a hill." If we are to ever build a "shining city on a hill" that is America, we have to recognize that a shining city has no hollows, a shining city has no walls, and a shining city is one where all of our people somehow have a foundation and a chance for growth.

RONALD REAGAN's conservatism, properly understood, oriented to the needs of our times, ought to mean at least this: It ought to mean that we believe in one community in America. It ought to mean that we believe in a community that is strong enough to raise up all of our people and strong enough to reconcile all of our differences.

So I end today by saying that whatever our differences with our friends on the other side of the aisle, whatever our differences with the direction of the eighties, we ought to be secure in the sense that we are all Americans, and we ought to be secure in the sense of freedom that RONALD REAGAN spoke about that day in Berlin, because there are all kinds of walls that still need to come down, and to truly salute this man's legacy, that ought to be our business today.

Hon. Curt Weldon
OF PENNSYLVANIA

Madam Speaker, I first met RONALD REAGAN through a local leader in our State, Faith Whittlesey, who was one of RONALD REAGAN's earliest supporters in the eastern part of America for the Presidency. And it was a glorious day in 1984 when RONALD REAGAN came to my home county, stood on the steps of the courthouse where I was then the vice chairman, and held my hand up alongside of another famous American, Tug McGraw, and endorsed me for the congressional seat. I did not win that year, Madam Speaker, but I came within 412 votes of unseating a 10-year, very popular incumbent. I won the seat 2 years later and have been here ever since.

I took up two of RONALD REAGAN's key issues: his work with the Soviet Union, now Russia, and his work on missile defense. And over the past 18 years that I have been in Congress, it has been my pleasure to try to live up to the expectations and to the role model that RONALD REAGAN established for all of us.

Madam Speaker, he was someone who understood the Russian people, and he was someone who taught us in America that in the end, if we would simply trust but verify, if we would simply stand up and be candid with them, that in the end they would respect us. On the issue of missile defense, it was RONALD REAGAN who said that we should not leave America unprotected and vulnerable.

How amazing it is 18 years later, Madam Speaker, that one of the most popular officials in Russia today is RONALD REAGAN. In polls that have been conducted in Russia, they look to RONALD REAGAN because he was a leader of stature and because he was someone whom the Russian people respected, because he saw through the communist leadership and held fast with the Russian people for a better time. So it was appropriate that when I last traveled to Russia 3 weeks ago for my 37th trip that we discussed a new initiative with the Russian people, in honor of RONALD REAGAN, taking their radar systems and using them with our radar systems to develop a joint missile defense system. How proud RONALD REAGAN would be.

But for all of his work in helping us defeat communism, in helping us move toward missile defense, and helping to reinvigorate our economy, I will remember RONALD REAGAN, Madam Speaker, most for what he was as an individual person. He was a very humble man. He would take the time to meet with anyone regardless of their stature in life.

As a first-term Republican, I had the honor of being invited to the Oval Office with my family. I took my five kids down to the Oval Office with my wife, and my youngest was then 4 years old, and he was more concerned with the inside furnishings of the Oval Office than he was with the stature of the President. That did not matter to RONALD REAGAN. In fact, I would later find out that in the book of the favorite photographs of RONALD REAGAN, this photograph would appear, which is also on the wall of the Reagan Presidential Library in California. How proud I am that my family had the chance to meet RONALD REAGAN and that my 4-year-old son, who is now 21 years old, who is here making faces at the camera, received a signed personal photograph from RONALD REAGAN and received words of encouragement back then that are still important to each of my five kids today.

I remember RONALD REAGAN most for not just what he did for the world, but what he was as a role model for everyone that met him. He was someone who genuinely cared about people. He was someone who would take the time to reach out to a 4-year-old or a 6-year-old and give them words of encouragement.

RONALD REAGAN is a role model for all of us, and for that we give thanks, and we thank his wife and send our sympathies to the entire Reagan family.

Hon. Michael R. McNulty

OF NEW YORK

Madam Speaker, President REAGAN's long struggle with Alzheimer's disease has ended, but the legacy of his extraordinary life remains.

In 1998, my mother died as a result of the impact of Alzheimer's disease; so I know what families go through during times like that. And I will always be inspired by Nancy Reagan and the other members of the family for their tender caregiving to the former President over that very long period of time.

Many people today have mentioned the occasion of the tearing down of the Berlin Wall by the people, and I recently looked at those pictures of the former President when he participated in chipping away at the wall. I was on the Committee on Armed Services at the time, and I had a chance to do that, too. As I was standing there watching people chipping away at the wall, tearing it down piece by piece, I noticed as the pieces were falling off the wall, some of them would catch the pieces and put them in their pockets. I said to myself, aha, they are taking souvenirs of the Berlin Wall, and I thought I might like to do that.

And already capitalism being in evidence, I looked down, and there were vendors selling pieces of the wall. They were in little cellophane wrappers marked with the date they were taken off the wall. But ever the skeptic, I said to myself, how do I know that those pieces came off the wall?

So I further looked around, and I saw this guy walking back and forth with hammers and chisels, renting them out. So I went over with my translator and made the deal and gave him some money, and I did what President REAGAN did, and I chipped off some pieces of the wall. I brought them back home, and I gave them to veterans as a thank you to them for their dedication through the years and for the fact that they were responsible for what was happening on that particular day and at that particular time in history.

President REAGAN was a proud and patriotic American whose persistent advocacy for democracy led in part to the breakup of the Soviet Union and its devolution into 15 individual democratic republics. And I was in one of those republics as a member of a delegation from Congress on their independence day. In Armenia I watched in awe as 95 percent of all the people in that country went out and voted. I watched them stand in long lines for the privilege of voting in a free election for the first time in their lives. I noticed they brought covered dishes with them, and after they voted, they held little celebrations and banquets in each of the polling places.

And what a thrill it was to be with them the next day in the streets of Yerevan, their capital, as they danced and shouted and sang, "*Ketze asat ankakh Hayastan*," which means "Long live free and independent Armenia." Then they pointed to the United States of America as their example of what they wanted to be as a democracy.

So I thank all of the men and women who served in the uniform of the U.S. military through the years for helping to make that happen, and I also thank the Commander in Chief for 8 years, RONALD REAGAN, for helping to make that happen.

Today I join with all Americans in mourning his passing and in expressing deep gratitude for his tremendous public service as both Governor and as President.

Hon. Jim Ramstad

OF MINNESOTA

Madam Speaker, I rise to proudly pay tribute to the greatest President of the 20th century, RONALD WILSON REAGAN, whose suffering has ended and heavenly life begun.

My fellow Minnesotans join me in mourning the loss of America's 40th President and celebrating the life of a man who personified both the greatness and goodness of America. All Americans and freedom-loving people around the world owe President REAGAN our deepest gratitude for his strong, principled leadership that ended the cold war and brought freedom to millions of people.

As we celebrate President REAGAN's remarkable career and historic legacy, we also celebrate a man of strong character, deep conviction, unforgettable charm, and wonderful wit. No Minnesotan will ever forget President REAGAN braving the below-zero windchill to ride in a convertible in St. Paul's Winter Carnival Parade and proclaim, "I thought my ears would fall off." It was that cold.

Madam Speaker, as America honors our beloved 40th President, we also thank God for a leader who restored pride and made the American people believe in themselves again. Always the eternal optimist, President REAGAN instilled confidence and optimism at a time both were in short supply in our country.

Thanks to President REAGAN's strong leadership and undying belief in free-market capitalism, the great entrepreneurial spirit of the American people was unleashed, and prosperity was restored here at home.

Madam Speaker, our hearts go out to Nancy Reagan and the Reagan family on their great loss. Mrs. Reagan has showed the whole world the true meaning of love and loyalty these past 10 very painful years as her beloved husband suffered from cruel Alzheimer's disease, the same deadly, debilitating disease that took the life of my own mother just months ago.

So today, Madam Speaker, as we celebrate the life and legacy of RONALD REAGAN, let us honor this great President by keeping his legacy alive, a legacy of love for his faith, family, friends, and country; a legacy of freedom, liberty, and opportunity for all people; a legacy of public service deeply rooted in faith, principle, character, and conviction. And let us always remember President REAGAN's warm, infectious, kind smile that lit up every audience, inspired us and gave us hope, just as we remember our "rendezvous with destiny."

Rest in peace, Mr. President, in the loving embrace of our Lord and Savior.

Hon. Adam H. Putnam

OF FLORIDA

Madam Speaker, I was in grade school when President REAGAN was elected, so my thoughts and observations are not based on any particular policy, but on the man, on the spirit itself.

We took great courage as a Nation in watching him as he dealt with an attempt on his life. We watched in awe at his unwavering commitment to freedom everywhere around the world and his commitment to "peace through strength," which allowed him to win the cold war without a shot being fired.

He moved an entire generation of young people to that same cry for freedom, the battle to spread liberty and democracy and freedom and equality around the world, and he did it with a sunny, hopeful, cheerful, optimistic demeanor. He appealed to the very best in us, never preying on our worst fears, but backed up by a steely resolve, backed up by principle, backed up by the notion that it was better to be right than to be popular. In doing so, he succeeded with an understanding, a very clear understanding, of the power of the American spirit when it is unencumbered, when it is let loose to achieve its own potential and carve out its piece of the American dream. He always believed in the goodness of the American spirit and the human spirit around the world. He understood that the strength of America, the resilience of America is in her people. He inspired in us all of those great factors without preying on the worst.

Madam Speaker, may we ever be vigilant gatekeepers of his "shining city on the hill." God bless the Reagan family, God bless America, and God bless this institution to which President REAGAN has given so much.

Hon. John A. Boehner

OF OHIO

I rise today in tribute to a great American, RONALD REAGAN.

We have heard extensive remarks this morning about his two major accomplishments, I believe: the end of the Soviet Union as we know it, and setting in place employer tax rates leading to an economic recovery. If we think about what happened, he was the first to call for the end of the Soviet Union and, frankly, the first to predict the end of the Soviet Union as we knew it. No one in my lifetime has done more to spread freedom around the world than RONALD REAGAN, and we all owe him a great debt not only here in our country, but around the world.

His tax policies of the early eighties led to an economic recovery in the eighties, and I believe the entire expansion of the nineties can be traced back to the lower tax rates set in the early eighties, giving investors a reason to invest in our economy.

But I think RONALD REAGAN's greatest contribution to our country was his optimism, his hope, and his belief in the strength of the American people. One only has to look at what we went through in the sixties and the seventies and what RONALD REAGAN inherited when he took office. America, to say the least, was on its heels. We had gone through the problems of the Vietnam era; we had gone through problems with the Presidency; we had gone through the problems of the energy crisis; and this new animal that came upon our economy called inflation.

America was beginning to wonder about itself, and it was RONALD REAGAN who talked about the "shining city on the hill" and all that America could be. It was RONALD REAGAN that knew and said that our best days lie ahead, not in the past, and he was right. The hope that he brought, the enthusiasm he brought, and the belief in the American people was something that did, in fact, renew the American spirit.

His patriotism and the patriotism he brought to our country was something that we have not seen for some time. I know in my case, my entire family and I grew up in the Democratic Party, and it was RONALD REAGAN who showed me that I was a Republican. It was RONALD REAGAN who encouraged me to take a more active role in my community. I was proud to be a volunteer on his campaign in 1980. And, Mr. President, let me say this: You were my hero then; you continue to be my hero.

It was RONALD REAGAN who inspired me to make a commitment to public service and to do my share on behalf of the American people, and forever I will be grateful.

Mr. President, we still love you.

Hon. Jeff Flake

OF ARIZONA

Madam Speaker, those of us who have had the good fortune to be born and raised in Arizona have always had the words and life of Barry Goldwater to shape our political philosophy. It was during the Goldwater campaign of 1964 that RONALD REAGAN came to national prominence. During that campaign, REAGAN delivered a speech so memorable that it was known thereafter simply as "The Speech." It was, in my opinion, the greatest political speech ever delivered.

In it, REAGAN included the words:

> You and I are told ... that we have to choose between a left or right, but I would ... suggest that there is no such thing as a left or right. There is only an up or down—up to a man's age-old dream, the ultimate in individual freedom consistent with law and order—or down to the ant heap of totalitarianism.

Equally memorable was the phrase:

> This is the issue of this election. Whether we believe in our capacity for self-government or whether we abandon the American revolution and confess that a little intellectual elite in a far-distant capital can plan our lives for us better than we can plan them ourselves.

Madam Speaker, having now spent 4 years in the far distant capital, I can attest that this insight from RONALD REAGAN still bears remembering.

I was never able to meet President REAGAN personally. It is one of my great regrets in life. But like all Americans, I am well acquainted with his goodness. I will always be grateful that he was my President.

Hon. Shelley Moore Capito

OF WEST VIRGINIA

Madam Speaker, America has lost a great patriot with the passing of President RONALD REAGAN. My fellow West Virginians join me in mourning his death.

As our President, he shepherded America through tough times, cutting taxes and invigorating our Nation's economy. President REAGAN's service as a statesman reflected the good freedom could do when waged against tyranny.

In June 1987, President REAGAN stood in front of the Brandenburg Gate in Germany, calling upon Mikhail Gorbachev to "tear down this wall!"

Reagan aimed to replace the instability brought by fear of nuclear war with the firm backing of freedom.

When the wall fell, a wave of sovereignty rolled through Eastern Europe, washing away suppressive governments and leaving in its wake democracies firmly backed by individual liberty.

Americans will always measure their President against the high bar RONALD REAGAN has set for the Presidency. But along with being a statesman, a peacemaker, and a leader, RONALD REAGAN was a kind man who I was very honored to have met, a loving husband and father, and a compassionate human being.

I will always remember RONALD REAGAN for his ability to lift up the American people, inspiring us to rely on ourselves, not on our government, to overcome challenges in our lives. His legacies will be remembered for years to come. Freedom over fear, the individual before its government, and the strength of America overall.

May God bless America, and may God bless our President, RONALD REAGAN.

Hon. Candice S. Miller

OF MICHIGAN

Madam Speaker, as we mourn the loss of President RONALD REAGAN, let us also celebrate the absolutely incredible life that he lived, a life that had such a positive impact certainly on our Nation and, in fact, the entire world.

Madam Speaker, I live in Macomb County, MI. That is the home of the so-called "Reagan Democrats." That term really had its genesis in Macomb County and has become certainly part of our nomenclature. It describes a huge block of citizens, average Americans, principally ethnic, blue collar, who had voted Democratic for literally generations.

And then along came RONALD REAGAN, and he captured their hearts and he captured their minds with the power of his ideas and the vision for America, ideas that were powerful, yet very, very simple: that freedom is a universal right of every human being; ideas about personal responsibility and the fundamental values that built our Nation, and the eternally optimistic idea that America is a great Nation whose best days continually lie in our future.

President REAGAN never wavered, never backed down from his defense of freedom, of his belief that we could achieve "peace through strength." Of course, his strong stand created countless critics, and yet today those critics must recognize the rightness of his cause and his methods. History has certainly proven him to be right.

Because of the leadership of President REAGAN, Soviet communism collapsed and hundreds of millions of people who lived under Soviet domination now live as free people.

Because of the leadership of President REAGAN, our national spirit and the spirit of free enterprise rose up and has spread across the entire globe.

Because of his leadership, the world continues to look to America to export liberty and freedom and democracy.

Our Nation and the world owe a debt to President REAGAN that can really only be repaid in one way: We must continue to fight for democracy, for freedom, and for liberty, and so we shall.

God bless President RONALD WILSON REAGAN. May he rest in peace.

Hon. Ron Kind

OF WISCONSIN

Madam Speaker, I, too, rise today to mark the death of President RONALD REAGAN and to pay tribute to a great American. I extend my deepest sympathies and prayers to Mrs. Reagan and the entire Reagan family. With President REAGAN's death, our country lost yet another member of the greatest generation, a member who typified his generation with his work ethic, his optimism, and his patriotism.

I believe that all of us, regardless of political affiliation, were impressed by how much President REAGAN loved America, how much he believed in its basic goodness and the decency of this great country. He was so proud to represent a country that stood for freedom and equality, and he worked for many years to help spread freedom across the globe.

I was fortunate enough to witness first-hand the effect of freedom spreading across the world. After graduating from college, I had the privilege of traveling to Europe and spending time in the countries that were formerly part of the Soviet Union that were struggling to gain a place in the world as free nations. My travels included a stop in Berlin to celebrate the reunification of Germany. I hammered away with a sledgehammer at the Berlin Wall with thousands of people from all over the world. I still have a piece of that wall, which sits on my desk.

It was inspiring to be a part of history in this way, and I can only imagine how wonderful it must have been for President REAGAN to have played such a seminal role in the transformation of the Soviet Union and the Eastern bloc nations. With the end of the cold war, we face an exciting new world of independent nations throughout Eastern and Central Europe.

As we face current challenges throughout the world, I look back to the patriotism and optimism with which President REAGAN approached international and domestic issues, and I feel grateful that we have his example.

Aside from his leadership on issues of international importance, I also appreciate President REAGAN's willingness to find bipartisan compromise in order to achieve results. To him, politics was not a blood sport; it was the art of the possible. Coming to Congress several years after both President REAGAN and Speaker Tip O'Neill had retired, I always enjoyed listening to my colleagues tell of the two men swapping stories and jokes as they negotiated important pieces of legislation.

President REAGAN's bipartisan spirit and constant optimism are testament to his leadership skills and his love for his country. It is an approach to governing and it is an approach to leadership that we need to restore.

May God bless his soul.

Hon. Philip M. Crane

OF ILLINOIS

Madam Speaker, today I rise to pay tribute to and express my sympathy on the passing of one of Illinois' greatest sons, RONALD REAGAN.

I was inspired by RONALD REAGAN some 40 years ago when he, the Great Communicator, first outlined his vision for America. His vision was one of free enterprise, strong defense, and limited government. I was so drawn to these principles that I worked with fellow conservatives to nominate him for President in 1968 and again in 1976.

The biggest heartbreak in my political career came in 1976 when we were unable to secure REAGAN the nomination. But we stayed at it. RONNIE stayed true to his principles; and, finally, in 1980 we had a man in the White House who I knew would turn this country around. REAGAN did just that. He turned around our economy, he ended the cold war, and he renewed hope for Americans.

Reagan was able to accomplish so much in his years as President because he approached everything as a gentleman. He never allowed politics to become personal. He treated everyone with respect even when he disagreed with you. And always his wit and humor won you over.

I am proud to say that I knew RONALD REAGAN not so much for his accomplishments, and there were many, but I am more proud to have known him for the man he was. As President, REAGAN brought his hometown-Illinois values with him to the White House. And these are the same values we all share in Illinois, the value of hard work, of faith, family, and unlimited opportunity.

Reagan was, as history will bear, one of America's greatest Presidents. And I ask my colleagues to join me in remembering his family and this Nation during our season of mourning. And may God bless us all.

Hon. Robert B. Aderholt

OF ALABAMA

Madam Speaker, what do you say about a man like RONALD REAGAN that has not already been said? RONALD REAGAN took the oath of office here in Washington, DC, in 1981 and, actually, just a short distance from where we are standing here this afternoon. At the time he took office, I was 15 years old. I did not realize at that time the impact that this new President would have on this Nation and the world. I did not realize the moral and strong leadership that he would provide this Nation.

RONALD REAGAN served in the highest office of our land throughout my time in high school, college, and my first couple of years of law school. And with most of America, I listened to the tributes as they started pouring in over this past weekend. During the weekend and since that time, President REAGAN's speeches, his remarks and comments have been played and reviewed time and time again.

However, over the weekend I heard one speech that I had never heard before. It was a speech that President REAGAN delivered at a prayer breakfast in Dallas, TX, on the morning of August 23, 1984. It is so relevant to our situation today that if you did not know better, you would think he delivered the speech just a few days ago.

He discussed religion and its role in the political life of our Nation. He made clear from the beginning of his speech that he was not speaking as a theologian or as a scholar, but rather as someone who had been around for quite a few years.

He talked about the critical role in the political life of this Nation that faith and religion had played and, furthermore, how that had worked to benefit our Nation.

He went on to say that the Founders understood that there was a divine order which transcends the human order. He then eloquently stated that he believed George Washington knew the city of man cannot survive without the city of God, and that the visible city will perish without the invisible city.

While time will not permit me to discuss all of his remarks today, I would like to include his remarks in the *Record* that President REAGAN made at that prayer breakfast in Dallas in 1984. Of course, it would not be appropriate to talk about RONALD REAGAN without talking about how much he loved life and how much he valued life. He was a man of compassion, and people of all ages would do well to emulate RONALD WILSON REAGAN.

REMARKS AT AN ECUMENICAL PRAYER BREAKFAST IN DALLAS, TX
AUGUST 23, 1984

Thank you, ladies and gentlemen, very much. And, Martha Weisend, thank you very much. And I could say that if the morning ended with the music we have just heard from that magnificent choir, it would indeed be a holy day for all of us.

It's wonderful to be here this morning. The past few days have been pretty busy for all of us, but I've wanted to be with you today to share some of my own thoughts.

These past few weeks it seems that we've all been hearing a lot of talk about religion and its role in politics, religion and its place in the political life of the Nation. And I think it's appropriate today, at a prayer breakfast for 17,000 citizens in the State of Texas during a great political convention, that this issue be addressed.

I don't speak as a theologian or a scholar, only as one who's lived a little more than his threescore ten—which has been a source of annoyance to some—{laughter}—and as one who has been active in the political life of the Nation for roughly four decades and now who's served the past 3½ years in our highest office. I speak, I think I can say, as one who has seen much, who has loved his country, and who's seen it change in many ways.

I believe that faith and religion play a critical role in the political life of our nation—and always has—and that the church—and by that I mean all churches, all denominations—has had a strong influence on the state. And this has worked to our benefit as a nation.

Those who created our country—the Founding Fathers and Mothers—understood that there is a divine order which transcends the human order. They saw the state, in fact, as a form of moral order and felt that the bedrock of moral order is religion.

The Mayflower Compact began with the words, "In the name of God ..." The Declaration of Independence appeals to "Nature's God" and the "Creator" and "the Supreme Judge of the world." Congress was given a chaplain, and the oaths of office are oaths before God.

James Madison in the Federalist Papers admitted that in the creation of our Republic he perceived the hand of the Almighty. John Jay, the first Chief Justice of the Supreme Court, warned that we must never forget the God from whom our blessings flowed.

George Washington referred to religion's profound and unsurpassed place in the heart of our nation quite directly in his Farewell Address in 1796. Seven years earlier, France had erected a government that was intended to be purely secular. This new government would be grounded on reason rather than the law of God. By 1796 the French Revolution had known the Reign of Terror.

And Washington voiced reservations about the idea that there could be a wise policy without a firm moral and religious foundation. He said, "Of all the dispositions and habits which lead to political prosperity, Religion and morality are indispensable supports. In vain would that man (call himself a patriot) who (would) labour to subvert these ... finest {firmest}[1] props of the duties of men and citizens. The mere Politician ... (and) the pious man ought to respect and to cherish (religion and morality)." And he added, "... let us with caution indulge the supposition, that morality can be maintained without religion."

I believe that George Washington knew the City of Man cannot survive without the City of God, that the Visible City will perish without the Invisible City.

Religion played not only a strong role in our national life; it played a positive role. The abolitionist movement was at heart a moral and religious movement; so was the modern civil rights struggle. And throughout this time, the state was tolerant of religious belief, expression, and practice. Society, too, was tolerant.

But in the 1960's this began to change. We began to make great steps toward secularizing our nation and removing religion from its honored place.

In 1962 the Supreme Court in the New York prayer case banned the compulsory saying of prayers. In 1963 the Court banned the reading of the Bible in our public schools. From that point on, the courts pushed the meaning of the ruling ever outward, so that now our children are not allowed voluntary prayer. We even had to pass a law—we passed a special law in the Congress just a few weeks ago to allow student prayer groups the same access to schoolrooms after classes that a young Marxist society, for example, would already enjoy with no opposition.

The 1962 decision opened the way to a flood of similar suits. Once religion had been made vulnerable, a series of assaults were made in one court after another, on one issue after another. Cases were started to argue against tax-exempt status for churches. Suits were brought to abolish the words "under God" from the Pledge of Allegiance and to remove "In God We Trust" from public documents and from our currency.

Today there are those who are fighting to make sure voluntary prayer is not returned to the classrooms. And the frustrating thing for the great majority of Americans who support and understand the special importance of religion in the national life—the frustrating thing is that those who are attacking religion claim they are doing it in the name of tolerance, freedom, and openmindedness. Question: Isn't the real truth that they are intolerant of religion? {Applause} They refuse to tolerate its importance in our lives.

If all the children of our country studied together all of the many religions in our country, wouldn't they learn greater tolerance of each other's beliefs? If children prayed together, would they not understand what they have in common, and would this not, indeed, bring them closer, and is this not to be desired? So, I submit to you that those who claim to be fighting for tolerance on this issue may not be tolerant at all.

When John Kennedy was running for President in 1960, he said that his church would not dictate his Presidency any more than he would speak for his church. Just so, and proper. But John Kennedy was speaking in an America in which the role of religion—and by that I mean the role of all churches—was secure. Abortion was not a political issue. Prayer was not a political issue. The right of church schools to operate was not a political issue. And it was broadly acknowledged that religious leaders had a right and a duty to speak out on the issues of the day. They held a place of respect, and a politician who spoke to or of them with a lack of respect would not long survive in the political arena.

---
[1] White House correction.

It was acknowledged then that religion held a special place, occupied a special territory in the hearts of the citizenry. The climate has changed greatly since then. And since it has, it logically follows that religion needs defenders against those who care only for the interests of the state.

There are, these days, many questions on which religious leaders are obliged to offer their moral and theological guidance, and such guidance is a good and necessary thing. To know how a church and its members feel on a public issue expands the parameters of debate. It does not narrow the debate; it expands it.

The truth is, politics and morality are inseparable. And as morality's foundation is religion, religion and politics are necessarily related. We need religion as a guide. We need it because we are imperfect, and our government needs the church, because only those humble enough to admit they're sinners can bring to democracy the tolerance it requires in order to survive.

A state is nothing more than a reflection of its citizens; the more decent the citizens, the more decent the state. If you practice a religion, whether you're Catholic, Protestant, Jewish, or guided by some other faith, then your private life will be influenced by a sense of moral obligation, and so, too, will your public life. One affects the other. The churches of America do not exist by the grace of the state; the churches of America are not mere citizens of the state. The churches of America exist apart; they have their own vantage point, their own authority. Religion is its own realm; it makes its own claims.

We establish no religion in this country, nor will we ever. We command no worship. We mandate no belief. But we poison our society when we remove its theological underpinnings. We court corruption when we leave it bereft of belief. All are free to believe or not believe; all are free to practice a faith or not. But those who believe must be free to speak of and act on their belief, to apply moral teaching to public questions.

I submit to you that the tolerant society is open to and encouraging of all religions. And this does not weaken us; it strengthens us, it makes us strong. You know, if we look back through history to all those great civilizations, those great nations that rose up to even world dominance and then deteriorated, declined, and fell, we find they all had one thing in common. One of the significant forerunners of their fall was their turning away from their God or gods.

Without God, there is no virtue, because there's no prompting of the conscience. Without God, we're mired in the material, that flat world that tells us only what the senses perceive. Without God, there is a coarsening of the society. And without God, democracy will not and cannot long endure. If we ever forget that we're one nation under God, then we will be a nation gone under.

If I could just make a personal statement of my own—in these 3½ years I have understood and known better than ever before the words of Lincoln, when he said that he would be the greatest fool on this footstool called Earth if he ever thought that for one moment he could perform the duties of that office without help from One who is stronger than all.

I thank you, thank you for inviting us here today. Thank you for your kindness and your patience. May God keep you, and may we, all of us, keep God.

Thank you.

Hon. Tim Murphy

OF PENNSYLVANIA

Madam Speaker, the people of Pennsylvania join me in offering their sympathies and prayers to Nancy Reagan and all the members of the Reagan family. But more so, we offer our gratitude for sharing this great man.

In his memory, I humbly offer these words:

While flags fly low we gather here to offer words of praise.
With tributes to our leader gone, reflect, remember, pray.
Our Nation's forests, oceans, plains, majestic mountain skies where some saw only clouds above, he saw hopes spirit rise.
While enemies in shadows crept where evil's hatred stood, some brooded and in weakness slept.
He saw strength in our good.
America, your song shall soar over this Nation blessed, though some will turn to doubt and fear, his hope shall never rest.
The Sun shall set and darkness fall, yet stars their beacons give.
Do not ye grieve that he is gone, rejoice that he has lived.

Hon. Thaddeus G. McCotter

OF MICHIGAN

Madam Speaker, I rise to offer a long delayed thank you to President REAGAN for his help with a personal matter of mine. By the time I turned 15 in 1980, I had grown acutely aware of a quadrennial rift between my parents. My father was a Truman Democrat, my mother was an Eisenhower Republican, and my brother and myself were, of course, KISS fans.

Then one cold November night, there was a thaw. My father walked in the door, sat my mother down and, in a hushed, tremulous tone, as if every fellow Irish Catholic Democrat he had known from his days in the St. Francis Home for Boys Orphanage, every worker in a Detroit Labor Day parade, and everybody on every St. Patrick's Day pub crawl might somehow overhear him, Dennis Vincent Patrick Mullen

McCotter admitted to his wife, "I cannot believe I went and did it, Joan, I voted for him." He voted for RONALD WILSON REAGAN.

This vignette of American democracy's unifying force occurred in millions of homes across our Nation in 1980. The resulting national unity, which was brought about through the thawing of so many families' political cold wars, ultimately led to the end of the global cold war.

Madam Speaker, today the words of Albert Camus ring true: "A man does not show his greatness by being at one extremity or the other, but rather by touching both at once." Truly, President REAGAN was a unifying force for moral good in our Nation and our world. And thus his great humility would have precluded him from ever agreeing, RONALD REAGAN was a great man. He will be mourned and missed and forever remembered.

I offer my perpetual gratitude to the man, and my profound condolences to his family.

Hon. Deborah Pryce

OF OHIO

Madam Speaker, the citizens of Ohio join me in my sincere condolences to Mrs. Reagan and her family during these very difficult times and to express my humble thoughts on the legacy of RONALD REAGAN. While we have all heard him called the Great Communicator, he was so much more. He had a commanding presence. He captivated all who listened by his simple and eloquent demeanor, but he was so much more. He was great at communicating, yes, but, more important, he communicated great things.

His ideas resonated with the American people because they were the people's ideas. His vision for America made sense to us all because we had those same dreams in our very own hearts. His principles were clear because they were the very values we all held so dearly then as we do now: freedom, responsibility, "peace through strength."

The irony is that RONALD REAGAN did not speak to the people; we somehow spoke through him. We saw ourselves and we heard our own hearts in the words that he spoke. He was one of us, and that is why this Nation truly mourns his loss this week.

May we all seek to promote the principles that RONALD REAGAN embodied, lived and enunciated so courageously over the course of his magnificent life.

Hon. Richard Burr

OF NORTH CAROLINA

Madam Speaker, I rise today to join my colleagues and the rest of the Nation to mourn the passing of one of our Nation's greatest Presidents, but also to celebrate his legacy. While RONALD REAGAN is considered by almost everyone as an extraordinary leader and one of the greatest Americans, it was not RONALD REAGAN's vision, his confidence, his charm or his strength that truly set him apart.

It was his boundless optimism and his overflowing love and concern for his fellow men that made REAGAN who he was; these were his underlying sources of everything he accomplished. REAGAN saw himself as an ordinary man, called to serve his country to the best of his ability, and serve he did.

He inspired a Nation to rediscover the principles of freedom that have made our country great. We remember RONALD REAGAN as a man who maximized his gifts from an unknown to an actor to a Governor to the leader of the free world. Our President was one who never stopped growing and giving.

President REAGAN's life provides a witness to how we should all live, stirring up whatever gifts and potentials we have so that the world is a better place when we leave, more so than when we arrived. We remember President REAGAN as one who named bad leadership for what it was, and turned his people toward a nobler path. He said the only places communism would work are in Heaven because they do not need it and in Hell because they already have it.

Today, we are enjoying a world where communism is defanged and former communist nations rank among our closest allies, much of which is due to President REAGAN's unflinching commitment and resolve to seeing peace and freedom flourish throughout the world.

President REAGAN was a true man of the people. What REAGAN did more than anything else, and it will be his lasting legacy, is replace despair with hope. Most people, even his detractors, admired and respected his integrity. He never thought that he had all the answers or that he was put on Earth to reveal and implement God's plan for the rest of us.

Madam Speaker, he has now, and as he noted in the eulogy of the crew of the *Challenger* shuttle, "slipped the surly bonds of earth" and put out his hand and "touched the face of God."

The days of this week will be remembered for many, many years. Let them be remembered well. Let them be the passing of the torch. A new day is dawning. Leadership, vision, optimism, and faith most of all are needed at every level in our great country and in our homes. REAGAN used to say that America's greatest days are ahead of it. Now it can be said so are his.

Hon. Rob Portman

OF OHIO

Madam Speaker, I rise today to join my colleagues in expressing condolences to the family of President RONALD REAGAN but also, of course, to celebrate the life of one of America's true heroes.

President REAGAN once announced America is too great for small dreams. It was this optimism about America and his confidence in the American people that I remember most vividly when I first met him in 1981. He had an infectious optimism that, like so many, I was infected with. It had a lasting impression on me.

Shortly after taking office, President REAGAN acted on his optimism and his certain beliefs launching the boldest economic plan since Franklin Roosevelt's New Deal.

His program for economic recovery called for the largest tax cuts in American history. Think about this. Over his tenure, our Federal tax system went from 14 income tax brackets with a top rate of 70 percent to a much simpler 2 brackets with a top rate of 28 percent. This unleashed growth and brought America's economy roaring back.

He also acted on his strong beliefs in dramatically strengthening our Armed Forces. He chose to go toe to toe with the Soviet Union in the cold war and confront the failure of communism, leading to the freedom of millions of citizens in Eastern Europe and what was to become the former Soviet Union.

I see that legacy of RONALD REAGAN today. I see it in our approach to the economy that this body has undertaken to try to strengthen the economy and grow jobs, and I see it in our effort to win another global war, this one against terrorism.

For all of his accomplishments, one of RONALD REAGAN's traits I most admired was his humility. He was a regular guy. His midwestern modesty and intuitive understanding of the role of leadership in an America founded on equality and democracy made him a natural leader and a beloved figure.

One also had to appreciate President REAGAN's humor. He once said, "Politics is a very rewarding profession. If you succeed, there are many rewards. If you disgrace yourself, you can always write a book." Well, fortunately for our country and the world, he was a very successful politician, and we all, all of us, continue to share in the rewards.

In his 8 years as President, so much of his ambitious vision for American and the world was accomplished. And for his optimism, his ideas, his humility, his humor and public service, our Nation and the world are better off today. May God bless him and his family and continue to bless the country he so loved.

Hon. George R. Nethercutt, Jr.

OF WASHINGTON

Madam Speaker, last Saturday our Nation lost one of its greatest leaders. As we mourn RONALD REAGAN's passing, we celebrate his life of service as a lifeguard, an entertainer, a union leader, a spokesman, a Governor and a President.

As leader of the free world, he not only defended liberty, he expanded the realm of freedom. He liberated millions with the power of his ideas.

As President, he revitalized the American political system. The bipartisan celebration of his life here is a tribute to his greatness. Let us remember Mr. REAGAN's example and work to improve civility and public discourse in American politics.

President RONALD REAGAN was an American hero and a personal hero of mine. I met him 18 years ago, but it feels like yesterday. We all feel we knew RONALD REAGAN. When he stepped off Air Force One in Spokane, we realized that he was a big man. He was larger than life. He was very personal. He was gracious. He wowed the crowd, and he touched each individual.

Having met Mr. REAGAN, I know first-hand how his unwavering vision for our shining city willed the Nation to new heights. Even after his passing, his vision must and will continue to guide us.

God bless RONALD REAGAN and his family and his lasting legacy of freedom.

Hon. W. Todd Akin

OF MISSOURI

Madam Speaker, I rise, as my colleagues before me, to recognize this great President, RONALD REAGAN. He was a visionary leader who challenged the entire political order of his day. He had the courage to call evil evil; the Soviet empire the evil empire. For that, and for his conviction that freedom would prevail, he was bitterly criticized by his detractors.

Along the same lines, he pioneered a concept of economics that said if we have lower taxes, that it would energize the economy and ultimately that the government would raise more revenue. That was also bitterly criticized. It was called Reaganomics, and yet it worked, and it has worked again to bring us out of the last recession, the same principles.

He believed in the concept of defending America. It was the idea of a missile defense. They called it star wars, his detractors, and yet we are building those very things.

He was a man who challenged the political order of his day and redefined an entire political movement and advanced the cause of freedom around the entire world, and for that we all need to say to God, thank you for this great President.

Hon. Eric Cantor

OF VIRGINIA

I rise today to proudly stand with my friends and colleagues to pay tribute to President RONALD REAGAN. President REAGAN had the courage to lead America to greatness again after so many others had written us off as a country whose best days had passed. He was a lone voice who dared to believe that the cold war could be won and communism could be conquered peacefully through strength.

He led the United States from double-digit inflation, skyrocketing interest rates and recession to unprecedented economic growth and prosperity. His commonsense ideas of lower taxes and limited government brought us out of those troubling times. His ability to inspire and effect change was truly unique.

I remember fondly my parents' pride in being delegates to the 1980 Republican Convention and casting votes to nominate RONALD REAGAN to be President. While in high school and college during his Presidential term, I was dramatically affected by his moral clarity and courage.

President RONALD REAGAN had the positive spirit and courage of his convictions that inspired our generation and future generations to enter public service and make a difference in our country.

My family and I send our condolences to Mrs. Reagan and the Reagan family. Nancy Reagan deserves our steadfast support at this time and has earned our respect alongside her husband for her faithful service to our country.

Religion played a crucial role in his life. RONALD REAGAN knew he could set out and accomplish his goals because of his strong faith in God. His mother Nelle taught her son to believe in a loving and merciful God. Her teaching helped guide her son throughout his life as actor, Governor, and President.

Having spent several decades battling the evils of communism as president of the Screen Actors

Guild and as Governor of California for two terms, REAGAN held strong convictions that were based on his faith in God and led him to run for President in 1980. He would win in a landslide and become our Nation's 40th President.

REAGAN's religious convictions would immediately be put to the test. After surviving an assassin's bullet in the third month of his Presidency, REAGAN believed God saved his life. He said:

> I've always believed that we were, each of us, put here for a reason, that there is a ... divine plan for all of us. I know now that whatever days are left me belong to Him {God}.

He believed God saved his life for a reason, and he set out to ensure that he fulfilled God's plan for him in the White House. In an era when people tried to diminish the role that faith and religion play in the political life of the United States, REAGAN knew that the United States was "richly blessed with His {God's} love and generosity." REAGAN also knew that if we failed to remember that the United States is a Nation under God, then the United States would be a "nation gone under."

During the eighties, REAGAN's religious convictions allowed him to set an agenda that was new and optimistic. His strong faith enabled him to preserve and never waiver when opponents called his economic and foreign policy plans radical and dangerous. As a result, REAGAN played an integral role in winning the cold war, in restoring economic prosperity to the United States, and in helping liberate millions of people from the evils of communism. He entered the White House with a goal to change the country—he ended up changing the world. He led his life with a mission to fulfill God's plan and, in turn, accomplished so much for all of us.

My family and I send our condolences to Nancy Reagan and her family. Nancy Reagan deserves our steadfast support at this time and has earned our respect alongside her husband for her faithful service to our country.

Hon. Jerry Weller
OF ILLINOIS

Madam Speaker, today we come before this House in a saddened state. A man of unquestioned integrity and strong character has passed from our Nation's midst into the hands of God. RONALD REAGAN was a man with a good heart, and he had more of an impact on the world than any living American today.

We express our condolences to Mrs. Reagan and the Reagan family.

Many of us are very grateful because of how RONALD REAGAN inspired us, encouraged our activity in public service, and I know he encouraged my involvement in public service. I cast my first vote in 1976 for RONALD REAGAN in the Republican primary, and I had the privilege just 5 years later to serve in the Reagan administration. I have many fond memories of RONALD REAGAN.

Man is not measured by what we say, but by what we do. President REAGAN believed in the right of freedom for individuals and nations. He spoke honestly of the need for government reform in the United States and publicly hoped for a brighter future for the citizens of the Soviet empire.

Yet his words were not empty and did not ring hollow. President REAGAN backed up these beliefs by reducing the government's burden of taxes on individuals. He committed himself to rebuilding our American military. He inspired Americans to believe in themselves and their country, and, through almost sheer will, defeated communism without firing a single shot. As he spoke, the world listened because the force of America was behind his voice.

When President REAGAN uttered those fateful words, "Mr. Gorbachev, tear down this wall!" a collective shiver shot down the spine of the Soviet Union, as if communism's death knell was being rung for all the world to hear. Even President REAGAN's opponents concede that he defeated the Soviet empire.

Under President REAGAN's leadership, America experienced an unmatched period of economic growth. Under President REAGAN's legacy, hundreds of millions of people around the world now live safe from the fear of the threat of communism, free from the threat of Marxism-Leninism, and eager to extend an open hand to our former enemy and now our friend, Russia and the former Soviet states.

The spirit RONALD REAGAN embodied was of a special sort. Whether it was reinvigorating the American economy or comforting the loved ones of those lost on the *Challenger* space shuttle, President REAGAN never forgot who he worked for and what cause he was dedicated to. RONALD REAGAN was committed to the American citizen, the American dream and the American spirit.

Madam Speaker, as a man, a patriot, a fellow Illinoisan and U.S. President, RONALD REAGAN will be greatly missed, and I deeply mourn his passing, but I cannot help but think that long after the pain and sorrow of his departure has diminished, the legacy that President REAGAN left with us of commitment to one's country, of faith in one's resolve, of hope for a better tomorrow will be remembered and live on in the hearts and minds of Americans for generations to come.

Hon. James P. McGovern

OF MASSACHUSETTS

Madam Speaker, I rise today to join with my colleagues in marking with sadness the passing of President RONALD REAGAN. I send my deepest condolences to Mrs. Reagan and the entire Reagan family and to those friends who knew the President best.

RONALD REAGAN was a man of principle, deep patriotism and great humor. He loved his country, and he loved the American people. His was, in many ways, the quintessential American life: moving from a small town to chase the American dream in California, achieving success through hard work and determination, and finally giving back through public service.

One of the things I most admired about President REAGAN was his ability to disagree without being disagreeable. During the eighties, I was a staff member for the late Congressman Joe Moakley from Massachusetts. We had a front row seat to the great political battles between the Reagan White House and the House of Representatives under Speaker Tip O'Neill. While President REAGAN and Tip O'Neill had sharp political differences, they never had sharp words. Their arguments were never nasty. They were never personal. At the end of the day, their battles shifted from policy to who could tell the most outlandish story or the funniest Irish joke. It is an example that I believe all of us should try to do a better job of following.

Madam Speaker, I would also like to take a moment to say just how much respect and admiration I have for Nancy Reagan. These last several years have been extremely difficult for her as President REAGAN battled Alzheimer's disease. Mrs. Reagan has faced this tremendous adversity with strength, dignity and class, and she serves as an inspiration to us all.

Again, my wife Lisa and I send our sympathy and our prayers to the Reagan family during this sad time, and I thank the gentleman for yielding me the time.

Hon. Ron Lewis

OF KENTUCKY

Madam Speaker, I rise today to mourn the death of President RONALD REAGAN and to pass along the thoughts and prayers of the people of the Second District of Kentucky to the Reagan family.

So much of President REAGAN's life was dedicated to public service. From the summer shores of his Illinois hometown to the silver screens of Hollywood, to Sacramento, Washington, DC, and his final heroic battle with Alzheimer's disease, President REAGAN's vision and confident leadership continues to inspire national spirit, improving quality of life in the United States and extending freedom and democracy across the globe.

During his inaugural address in 1981, President REAGAN remarked, "we're too great a nation to limit ourselves to small dreams." His dream, family, work, neighborhood, peace, and freedom embodied the hopes of millions of Americans, shepherding the Nation into economic recovery and renewed national pride while demonstrating an uncompromising moral leadership abroad that brought communism to its knees.

He was a man whose love for his country stirred the spirit of his countrymen to a new age of patriotism and pride in America. His keen understanding of right and wrong, good and evil provided the leadership needed to defeat an evil empire.

His was an exemplary life, uniquely American, and worthy of the love and admiration of so many men and women across the world. May he rest in peace.

Hon. Sam Graves
OF MISSOURI

Mr. Speaker, I proudly rise with my friends and colleagues today to pay tribute to a man who inspired a Nation and a generation. His America was a strong Nation, where opportunities were limitless.

His list of accomplishments is long and distinguished. He won the cold war, he brought back our confidence, he cut taxes and grew the economy. He was an outstanding leader throughout the world.

I did not have the pleasure of knowing President REAGAN personally; but like millions of Americans, I marveled at his abilities. He comforted us after the *Challenger* disaster, he stood tall against communism, and he made it morning again in America.

RONALD REAGAN's enduring legacy, though, will be that he was a people's President. His concern for every American was genuine. He spoke with a twinkle in his eye and always had a story that illustrated his point perfectly. He was for us, because he was one of us.

America will soon say goodbye to one of our greatest Presidents. Mr. Speaker, his courage, humor, and grace will be missed by all of America. The "shining city on the hill" will continue, but for now with a heavy heart.

Hon. Max Burns
OF GEORGIA

Mr. Speaker, once or twice a century we are given a President who stands above the rest. President REAGAN was such a leader. He united this country in a way that we have not been united since. He did so by simply speaking out for what the vast majority of the people of this country knew to be the truth: President REAGAN declared that there is a God and that we, as a Nation, are under his authority.

Like President Washington before him, he made no apology to anyone's sensibilities. He called the evil empire of communism exactly what it was and committed this Nation to defeating it. He was the first President to begin the battle to reverse the overreach of Federal bureaucracy in the lives of our citizens.

Let us truly honor the memory of RONALD REAGAN by never ending the fight he so nobly waged for God and for country.

Hon. John N. Hostettler
OF INDIANA

Mr. Speaker, on behalf of the citizens of Indiana's Eighth Congressional District, I rise not only to pay tribute to RONALD WILSON REAGAN but to also thank him for being a Commander in Chief of which we could always be proud.

The most important role of any American President is that of Commander in Chief of our Armed Forces; and I, for one, do not need to wait for history to conclude that he was one of the greatest Commanders in Chief this Nation has ever had.

Last year, my son Matthew and I were honored to attend the commissioning of the newest U.S. supercarrier, *CVN–76*. I could not think of a better namesake for *CVN–76* than RONALD WILSON REAGAN. The ship's motto is appropriately, "Peace Through Strength." While he is rejoicing in Heaven, the American people should feel comforted in knowing that his legacy lives on in a mighty U.S. warship that bears his name and will provide firepower for freedom for another 50 years.

So communists and terrorists and other enemies of freedom, you have been forewarned. You have not heard the last from RONALD REAGAN. And as he used to say when he was President, "You can run, but you cannot hide."

In conclusion, Mr. Speaker, may the prayers and thoughts of a loving free world comfort his wife, Nancy, and their children during their time of supreme sorrow and unimaginable loss.

Hon. Dennis Moore

OF KANSAS

Mr. Speaker, I think it is truly unfortunate that it takes a time of crisis or tragedy to bring our Nation together. This week, for example, we have seen and heard from Members of both sides of the aisle a tribute to a great President, RONALD REAGAN. He was a humble man; he was a gracious man and kind. We may have had differences of opinion on policy, but I think we all concede he was a good, decent man.

I never presume to speak for my friends on the other side of the aisle, but I think all of us would agree that we have the greatest Nation in the whole world, and one of the things that makes us so great as a Nation are the personal liberties and individual freedoms that we all share here in this country. The Bill of Rights of our Constitution gives us more economic and personal freedoms than people almost anywhere in the world, and we are a better Nation for that. And I think that is something RONALD REAGAN would say if he were here right now.

I think we can learn a lot of important things, and a lot of speakers on both sides of the aisle have enunciated some of those things this morning. We should try harder to disagree without being disagreeable. We should always treat one another with respect. And we should understand that we are all Americans and we are all in this together. We all want basically the same thing for our country and for our people.

If we can do that, I think we are going to be better as a Nation and stronger as a people. We need to find ways to bring us together and not to divide us. I think 85 to 90 percent of the people in this body are good, decent, honorable people who want to do the right thing for our country, Republicans and Democrats.

We need to understand that even when we have honest good-faith differences on policy issues, such as the $7 trillion debt we have right now, and the $500-plus billion deficit, this should not be about Republicans and Democrats; this should be about what is right for our country, and this should be about what is right for our children and our grandchildren and future generations in this country.

I hope that we will take this occasion, the passing of a great President, RONALD REAGAN, to come together and again dedicate ourselves to doing what is right for our country and putting aside partisan politics.

Hon. Ginny Brown-Waite

OF FLORIDA

Mr. Speaker, I rise today to add my voice to the chorus extolling the life of President RONALD REAGAN. On a similar occasion, over a century ago, Lincoln said of Washington, "How do you add glory to the Sun?"

I was at President REAGAN's inauguration, and when he said, "It is time for us to realize that we're too great a nation to limit ourselves to small dreams," my spine stiffened, and so did that of so many people in the crowd. I got goosebumps when he called out that "peace is the highest aspiration of the American people. We will negotiate for it, sacrifice for it; we will not surrender for it, now or ever."

From that day on, I knew America was back. You see, many people speak of the Reagan revolution. I like to think of it as the Reagan restoration. REAGAN restored our optimism, our belief in our ability to create, and the belief that God put man on this Earth to be free and that he made America to prove it.

President RONALD REAGAN changed the paradigm. He changed America's foreign policy from one of benign containment to active confrontation. And for the first time since communism began extending its sinister reach, we saw its hand pushed back.

Our sympathies certainly go to the entire Reagan family.

Hon. Stevan Pearce

OF NEW MEXICO

Mr. Speaker, as we consider world history, we know that each generation will be faced with its own challenges. And though I am certain that the human race will survive; for a Nation to survive these challenges, each generation must continually produce men and women who are sufficient to the moment and equal to the task. It needs to generate men and women who see without limits, who work without tiring, and who sacrifice without restraint. A nation must find within itself in these times of trouble those who will forgo comfort and give up the beaten paths of certainty to find new courses of action and overcome all obstacles in pursuing the truth. Mr. REAGAN was sufficient for the moment and equal to the task.

Mr. Speaker, we are here to mourn the passing of a President, but we are here to celebrate the life of leadership and sufficiency that Mr. REAGAN represented.

Hon. Rush D. Holt

OF NEW JERSEY

I am pleased to join with my colleagues in recognizing the lessons of the life of RONALD REAGAN and his legacy. Among those lessons would be a sense of civility in debate. Among those lessons would be disagreeing without being disagreeable. Among those lessons would be the ability to recognize the humanity of our opponents, and they are lessons that we should all take to heart.

Another part of the legacy, and I think the lasting legacy of President REAGAN, will derive from the painful period as we watched Alzheimer's take this vibrant and warm and really great person into, as Mrs. Reagan said, a different place, a different world. And I hope we will use this to rededicate ourselves to research in Alzheimer's and stem cell research so that others will not follow the former President in this path that was really painful for all of us to watch.

Hon. Jack Kingston

OF GEORGIA

I first heard about RONALD REAGAN in probably 1970, when Joan Baez, on my Woodstock album, referred to the Governor of California as Ron Ray Gun. And this was a young person, so I thought if Joan Baez is against him, it is probably a good thing. Yet as I went through my years and got in college, I had an opportunity to hear Mr. REAGAN speak at the Kansas City Republican Convention in 1976. And in his concession speech on the nomination going to Gerald Ford, he gave a great speech and he talked about what we have to do as Americans to preserve the great lifestyle that we live. I was very impressed with that speech. So in 1980, when he ran for President and was the nominee, certainly I was very enthusiastically in support of him.

He was elected in a year when we had hostages in Iran, the economy was in the tank, and the spirit of America was in the doldrums. He won by a landslide, with great expectations, though, and a great mandate. He needed to cut taxes, and he did. He moved along and created an economy that gave 19 million new jobs over the next 8 years. Inflation was reduced, as well as interest rates. He built defense to the extent that we got over, finally, Vietnam. He talked about things like the evil empire of the Soviet Union and "peace through strength." And he said things that were politically incorrect at the time, like "Mr. Gorbachev, tear down this wall!," even though people in our own party did not like him saying those things.

He was very basic. Nancy Reagan led the Just Say No to Drugs campaigns, and I think it was very effective in getting young people to think twice about it.

He had that Irish twinkle in his eye. And when he got shot, even though it was a very serious wound, he said to the hospital staff, gee, I hope you are all Republicans.

He had that kind of calmness and happiness about him as he went through things. And I, along with so many young people, was inspired by him. So when I ran for the State legislature in 1984, I pulled out a photograph that Libby, my wife, and I had taken with RONALD REAGAN in 1980, and I ran an ad that said, "REAGAN-Kingston: Face it, we need conservatives at all levels of government."

But I believe that was a key factor in helping me. He had those kinds of coattails. He believed in family, America. He loved Nancy. He showed us a husband and wife relationship at its finest. He was kind. The Carter-Reagan, Mondale-Reagan campaigns were not nasty, mean or vicious. In fact, he would say to Jimmy Carter if he disagreed with some of Mr. Carter's facts, "There you go again."

He liked joke-telling and told the jokes about the Soviet Union and got his point across, but when he was in the Oval Office, he always wore his coat out of respect for the Oval Office and the Office of the Presidency.

In his final speech as he left Washington, DC, he said:

{A}s I walk off into the city streets, a final word to the men and women of the Reagan revolution ... My friends: We did it. We weren't just marking time. We made a difference. ... We made the city freer, and we left her in good hands.

The lights of this city shine, but the future will burn brightly because of man and the leadership of RONALD REAGAN.

Hon. Christopher Shays

OF CONNECTICUT

Mr. Speaker, I count my blessings for President RONALD REAGAN. I count my blessings for this man because he spoke from his heart and he spoke the truth. Obviously he was an exceptional communicator, but he was also extraordinarily honest. You did not have to wonder where RONALD REAGAN was coming from. He had core principles: confronting tyranny, expressing strength to the world, believing in our market economy, reducing the size of government.

The bottom line is, he had extraordinary faith in our country, in the promise of America that the best of America is yet to come. And the best generations of Americans are yet to come. He trusted Americans to spend their own money and lead their own lives. In the process he knew our country and the world would benefit.

I am absolutely convinced President REAGAN totally changed the debate. He helped our country recognize that people have their own sense of self-worth and that we trust them to do the right thing.

Hon. Christopher Cox

OF CALIFORNIA

Mr. Speaker, when President REAGAN took office on that cold day in 1981, the world needed a hero, and on that day President REAGAN sent a message to every American and to every human being enslaved by the Soviet empire. Confronting not the armies of Saddam Hussein or Slobodan Milosevic, but the largest military machine in the history of the world, President REAGAN simply said, "no weapon in the arsenals of the world is so formidable as the will and moral courage of free men and women."

Then he led a worldwide movement for individual liberty and the human rights of all people. Today the Soviet Union sits on the ash heap of history, and the Reagan legacy can be measured in lives liberated and dreams fulfilled.

Before RONALD REAGAN became President in 1981, there were 56 electoral democracies on Earth. Today there are 117. Today more than a billion more people are living in freedom than on the day that he took office.

President REAGAN also liberated America, the land that he called the last best hope of mankind. Many Washington pundits at the time believed that the United States was suffering from an inevitable decline. President REAGAN had a different view. He believed that America's greatest days were ahead, if only we could free our people from the shackles of big government. He knew that people, not governments, create prosperity, and that markets are the dynamic expression of individual freedom reinforced by property rights and the rule of law.

He believed that the government management of an economy, whether in the form of wage controls, price controls, or regulation of production, produced growth and misery in direct proportion to the loss of freedom. Upon assuming the Presidency, he immediately ended price controls on oil, and within 4 months the price of oil fell over 60 cents per gallon.

When a government union broke the law and mounted an illegal strike against the taxpayers, President REAGAN upheld the rule of law, and even the Soviet Union noticed. Secretary of State George Schultz said this may have been the best foreign policy decision RONALD REAGAN ever made.

RONALD REAGAN and a Democratic Congress cut marginal income tax rates from 70 percent to 28 percent and ushered in the longest peacetime economic expansion in American history. Inflation fell from over 12 percent to 1 percent, and interest rates dropped dramatically. People were free to work and keep most of what they earned and to save for their family's future instead of relying on the state.

In 1981, RONALD REAGAN was the first President to take the oath of office on the west front of the Capitol. He said he wanted to be looking west to symbolize the pioneer vision and spirit that he knew still lived in America. Later today his body will be carried up those same western steps of the Capitol. In just a few hours, President REAGAN will lie in state a few feet from where we are now gathered.

As we imagine him looking up at the monumental artwork in the dome, at the Apotheosis of George Washington, perhaps we will hear him again speaking to us in the words he once used in this very place:

> Now we're standing inside this symbol of our democracy, and we ... hear again the echoes of our past: a general falls to his knees in the hard snow of Valley Forge; a lonely President paces the darkened halls and ponders his struggle to preserve the Union; the men of the Alamo call out encouragement to each other; a settler pushes west and sings a song, and the song echoes out forever and fills the unknowing air.

As we gather in the rotunda and gaze upon the flag-draped vault that holds the mortal remains of our 40th President, I know that if we listen, we will hear those echoes of the past. We will hear that pioneer song because it is the American sound. Like RONALD REAGAN, it is hopeful, big-hearted, idealistic, daring, decent and fair.

Mr. President, we loved you in life because you helped us love America, and you so nobly represented the country we love. As we lay you to rest, we will always respect and honor your leadership, your humility, your strength, your humor and your character. You told us that those who say we are in a time when there are no heroes just do not know where to look. Mr. President, all of America now knows where to look. You and our beloved First Lady, Nancy Reagan, will be our heroes for as long as there is an America and as long as love of freedom is carried in human hearts.

Hon. Dennis Moore

OF KANSAS

Mr. Speaker, I thank the gentleman from California (Mr. Cox) for his very cogent remarks, and I really appreciate the civility with which this has been conducted today.

The gentleman from California mentioned the fact that President REAGAN and a Democratic Congress presided over large tax cuts back during President REAGAN's term, and I grant that. But at the same time, President REAGAN was not a strict ideologue and he understood that when large deficits appeared, that we as a Nation needed to do something to deal with those large deficits and not put our country deeper and deeper in debt.

He agreed to actions to correct that course, and I think we as Democrats and Republicans hopefully can come together here and recognize that a $7 trillion debt and deficits of over half a trillion dollars cannot go on, and our kids and grandkids and the future generations of this Nation cannot sustain that kind of problem if it continues.

I hope we will come together with an attitude of civility that was characterized by President REAGAN and work on these problems together because we have a lot more in common than we have differences. We are all Americans. We all love our country, and we want to do what is right by our country.

Mr. Speaker, I want to conclude by saying that I think if we work together and understand that we are all in this together, we will do the very best we can for the Nation we love, the United States of America.

May God bless Mrs. Reagan and the Reagan family, and may God hold RONALD WILSON REAGAN in His loving arms.

Hon. Kevin Brady

OF TEXAS

Mr. Speaker, Heaven is a little sunnier and a little more optimistic with the arrival of one of the greatest American patriots and Presidents of the 20th century, President RONALD REAGAN.

He inspired me, as he did many others. Across the country and around the world, millions are mourning the death and remembering the life of this man, patriot, and President. There is a sense of profound loss, and rightly so, in the hearts of all Americans. This week we will all search for a way to pay our respects to a man who made it "morning in America" again.

President REAGAN's message of hope restored America's faith in what we could become. He loved this country, and he believed in the people that called it home. His optimism was infectious and at the end of his term as President Americans had caught his vision and understood their place in the world.

REAGAN's stewardship ushered in an era of peace and economic prosperity. Reaganomics—reducing the size of government, allowing Americans to keep more of their own hard-earned money instead of having it taxed away—brought about an economic revival in our Nation.

REAGAN's leadership ended the cold war, brought down the Berlin Wall, and charted a new course for both America's and the world's future. A future that was secure—made possible by "peace through strength." We would do well to bear this wisdom in mind as we continue to defend America against the threats posed by adversaries.

It is very difficult for one person or a single nation to pay tribute to a life as big, as bold, and as heroic as RONALD REAGAN's. His own words are perhaps the best testament of his convictions. His actions are the most sincere depictions of the character that defined his life. His humility and grace endeared him to all American's hearts.

In announcing to the world that he had been diagnosed with Alzheimer's disease, Mr. REAGAN wrote:

{L}et me thank you, the American people, for giving me the great honor of allowing me to serve as your President. When the Lord calls me home, whenever that may be, I will leave with the greatest love for this country of ours and eternal optimism for its future.

I now begin this journey that will lead me into the sunset of my life. I know that for America there will always be a bright dawn ahead.

President REAGAN's legacy will live on in the hearts and memories of all Americans. His integrity, dignity and wisdom are immortal and will challenge us each day to "act worthy of ourselves"—worthy of America.

Thanks to RONALD REAGAN there are bright days ahead for America.

Hon. Mark E. Souder

OF INDIANA

Mr. Speaker, I rise today to honor RONALD WILSON REAGAN, the 40th President of the United States, great American patriot, and conservative stalwart.

This past weekend, I joined a delegation of Members from this body in honoring the veterans—both living and fallen—who brought freedom to Europe by storming the beaches of Normandy. Unfortunately, transportation problems have prevented me from participating more fully in commemorating the passing of a truly great President. Had I been able, I would have certainly joined my colleagues in unanimously voting to mourn the passing of RONALD REAGAN.

RONALD REAGAN was born in Tampico, IL, a small town in the heart of America. His Midwest Christian upbringing helped to mold REAGAN into the conservative icon that he has become. When I was 14 years old, living in a small rural Midwest town, I heard RONALD

REAGAN's "A Time for Choosing" speech for Barry Goldwater. That speech and many of his other speeches, which I would listen to on records, inspired me to get involved in politics and to fight for conservative values. I know REAGAN did not inspire me alone.

RONALD REAGAN did not just speak about conservative ideals. He lived them and led with them. At a time when conservatives and conservatism were derided and ridiculed, he showed young politicians a new way to be a conservative.

In 1981, President REAGAN became the President of the United States. A boy from a small town had proven the American dream was still alive. At a time when a belief in America and freedom seemed to be at an alltime low, REAGAN's optimism renewed the confidence of a Nation. REAGAN's plans for economic revitalization, smaller government, and a strong military moved the United States toward a brighter future.

Over the course of two terms, he turned the United States and the world around. He was not content with the status quo domestically or internationally. Today, the world and the country are better for it. Our current prosperity is based on the course he charted. The freedom that millions of people enjoy can be attributed in part to him.

This past weekend was the 20th anniversary of REAGAN's moving "D-day" speech. This Saturday marks the 17th anniversary of his "Berlin Wall" speech. Both of these speeches were devoted to freedom. As one of the 20th century's greatest advocates of freedom—both political and economic—RONALD REAGAN has few equals.

As RONALD REAGAN ends his journey, I mourn his passing, but I am overwhelmed with gratitude that he was able to accomplish so many things for the United States of America.

Hon. John B. Shadegg

OF ARIZONA

Mr. Speaker, RONALD REAGAN ran for President to change America. In the end, he had changed the world. As Arizonans, we can be proud that our State played a vital role in the Reagan revolution.

Barry Goldwater started what became the Reagan revolution with his own run for the Presidency. For the first time since Calvin Coolidge, conservatives had a champion. Some dismissed Goldwater's loss as the end of the nascent conservative movement, but they were wrong: it was just the beginning.

Reagan took to the national political stage during the Goldwater campaign 40 years ago with his seminal speech "A Time for Choosing."

In losing the battle for the White House, Goldwater passed the conservative torch to RONALD REAGAN to continue the war of ideas. Together they nurtured the conservative movement and helped it grow. In 1966, REAGAN's campaign for Governor of California struck the same themes as Goldwater's Presidential campaign. He won in a landslide. It was the biggest political victory of the conservative movement since Goldwater had defeated the sitting U.S. Senate majority leader in 1952.

My father, Stephen Shadegg, was Goldwater's campaign manager, speechwriter and a close friend. Growing up in Goldwater's shadow and being a part of the conservative movement from birth gave me a special appreciation for who REAGAN was. As with Goldwater, REAGAN's greatest tool was the truth. When RONALD REAGAN said something, you knew it came from the heart.

Reagan was one of the few politicians who had deeply held beliefs and never strayed from fundamental principles. The rarest commodity in Washington, DC, is courage, yet REAGAN was nothing if not courageous.

He also touched people's lives. Just look at the hundreds of thousands of people who stood in line for hours this week to pay their last respects. A telling tribute to a man who had done so much for his country and whose citizens admired and loved him in return.

President REAGAN is rightly remembered for numerous accomplishments. We are all better off today thanks to the economic revolution that brought double-digit interest rates and inflation to its knees. His tax policy proved that "a rising tide" of economic recovery "lifts all boats."

Reagan is best known as the aggressive opponent of communism, the strong cold warrior that stood up to the Soviets and their allies across the globe. Less known is that this doctrine of "peace through strength" allowed President REAGAN to sign the largest arms reduction treaty at the time.

RONALD REAGAN was a normal citizen who used his charm and steadfast beliefs to shape the United States into the country it is today. He provided great optimism, sparked economic growth, gained military superiority, and bridged international relations.

We all have a special memory of REAGAN. Obviously for me, the 1964 speech was a formative part of my political life. In the speech he outlined his dedication to limited government and personal responsibility, ideals that guide me as I serve the people of my district and Arizona:

> This idea? that government was beholden to the people, that it had no other source of power is still the newest, most unique idea in all the long history of man's relation to man. This is the issue of this election: Whether we believe in our capacity for self-government or whether we abandon the American Revolution and confess that a little intellectual elite in a far-distant capital can plan our lives for us better than we can plan them ourselves.

He had a simple vision. He knew that individual choice and freedom were essential for people to feel pride in themselves, instead of dependence on the government. REAGAN knew that the true American dream was to be free to live your life and achieve your goals without government interference or regulation.

President REAGAN was one of the towering figures of the 20th century and one of the greatest defenders of freedom that America and the world has ever known. RONALD REAGAN was an heir to Barry Goldwater's vision that the greatness of America lies not in its government but in its people. His faith in the individual, belief in free enterprise, and unending conviction in providing freedom of choice in everyday decisions, helped to restore "the great, confident roar of American progress, growth, and optimism."

Rather than mourn our loss following the passing of President RONALD REAGAN, we should instead celebrate his life and his countless contributions to our country. And we should renew the promise to keep America that "shining city upon the hill."

Hon. Mary Bono
OF CALIFORNIA

Mr. Speaker, I rise today to pay tribute to one of our Nation's greatest Presidents and a fellow Californian, President RONALD WILSON REAGAN.

A child of America's heartland, he became a man of the West. A towering presence, he gained fame as a movie star and entertainer before turning his considerable gifts to public service. A man of great wit, faith, optimism, conviction and conscience, he believed fervently in the good of all men but especially the American people.

It was from his unwavering faith and from the people, first in his adopted State of California and later throughout the Nation, that he drew his great strength. A natural leader, he commanded respect and loyalty from all who had the honor of serving with him. President REAGAN brought grace and dignity to the high office he held, always treating those around him with respect and kindness. He never lost his connection to the working people and spoke to all Americans with such clarity and honesty that he will be forever known as the Great Communicator.

Along with his beloved wife, Nancy, President REAGAN was a frequent visitor to the Palm Springs area which I have the honor of representing in Congress. The Reagans frequently spent New Year's Eve with their dear friends, Ambassador and Mrs. Walter Annenberg, enjoying the relaxing desert environment and a friendly round of golf. A playground for movie stars and Presidents, the Palm Springs community was a welcome haven from the hectic world of celebrity and politics. The Reagans had many local friends and contacts, and the Palm Springs area was and still remains Reagan country.

As someone who has always said that it is perhaps harder to be the spouse than the individual holding elected office, First Lady Nancy Reagan was a reservoir of strength for the President throughout their remarkable life together. His most fervent supporter and staunchest defender, Nancy deserves our recognition and thanks for her role in this most American story.

President REAGAN's many achievements are now part of our Nation's proud history, and the contributions he made ensured a safer world and a brighter future for the American people. History will recall that his words helped bring down the walls that kept the people of the Soviet Union oppressed and isolated from the freedom of the West. His economic policies and the strength of his convictions laid the foundation for the greatest economic boom in America in the "American century." But, the history lessons will never be able to convey the sense of purpose and pride he instilled in our Nation through the sheer strength of his spirit and the optimism of his words.

We owe this remarkable American a tremendous debt of gratitude. His leadership redefined the political landscape in our country and energized our people with purpose and hope. To paraphrase the poet, "we shall not soon see his like again."

Mr. Speaker, on behalf of the people of California's 45th District, I extend my deepest sympathy and condolences to First Lady Nancy Reagan, their children and the entire Reagan family. I have no doubt that President REAGAN has seen his faith rewarded as he goes to his rest. May God bless President RONALD REAGAN.

Hon. Charles H. Taylor

OF NORTH CAROLINA

Mr. Speaker, today I rise to join my colleagues and remember the vision and achievements of our 40th President, RONALD WILSON REAGAN. RONALD REAGAN came to Washington with a core set of values that guided him through his two terms as our Nation's leader. President REAGAN fought to reduce taxes, diminish the role of an intrusive Federal bureaucracy, and to end forever the oppressive communist regime in the Soviet Union and Eastern Europe.

The times during which REAGAN sought to achieve these goals could not have been more daunting. America in 1981 was a land of broken spirit. Many citizens could not live the American dream due to interest rates in the double digits. The Soviet Union had surpassed the United States in military capability. But RONALD REAGAN achieved what he set out to do through a combination of ideology, pragmatism, charm, self-effacing humor, and, yes, hard work.

When the President left office in 1989, the Nation was in the midst of an economic renaissance. The Reagan tax cuts led to 96 straight months of economic growth. Record numbers of Americans were experiencing the pride that goes along with home ownership and economic self-sufficiency. The communist bloc would soon be a memory due to REAGAN's determination. Ending communism was a stand upon which REAGAN absolutely would not compromise. To him, the Soviet Union was truly an evil empire which was morally at odds with the United States and the principles of human dignity. REAGAN battled head to head with Gorbachev at five peace summits and at home secured more money for our Nation's defense. Thanks to this combination, millions upon millions now live in freedom and Russia is a valued ally in America's quest for global freedom.

Perhaps the most enduring legacy of RONALD REAGAN was his ability to make us proud to be Americans. REAGAN gently lifted our spirits with his cheery optimism and geniality. He soothed our fears with a good joke or a funny story. He could have been our friendly neighbor or our favorite uncle. A reporter once asked REAGAN what Americans saw in him, to which he replied "Would you laugh if I told you that I think, maybe, they see themselves, and that I'm one of them? I've never been able to detach myself or think that I, somehow, am apart from them."

On a personal note, I cannot forget the warmth and kindness that I was shown by this great man. I first met REAGAN in 1976 and later visited him at the Oval Office. He provided me with invaluable advice during my first run for Congress. During this meeting, he spoke of the beauty of our mountains and the kindness of the people of North Carolina. He remembered fondly his visits to western North Carolina before he was a candidate and afterward. During every meeting with RONALD REAGAN I was treated with kindness, grace, and great humility.

Few political leaders have had the vision and integrity of RONALD REAGAN. He had the guts and the courage to tackle the toughest problems of America in the eighties. He left his office with a stronger and prouder Nation than he inherited. He made us want to believe in ourselves and he made us a better people. Mr. Speaker, I and my constituents in western North Carolina will always be grateful for RONALD REAGAN's service to our Nation.

Hon. Ander Crenshaw

OF FLORIDA

Mr. Speaker, this week our Nation lost an individual who had an enormous impact on our country and the world. RONALD WILSON REAGAN, our Nation's 40th President, had a great and positive impact on our economy, our security, and our national pride. I believe that just as his achievements will remain with us for many decades, so too will his legacy of exercising sincerity and consistency in all actions, both inconsequential and monumental.

President REAGAN was an ordinary man who became an extraordinary leader. I will remember him most for his sense of optimism and hope. In the most difficult of times, it was President REAGAN who had the power to allay our worries, raise our spirits, and guide this Nation to prosperity.

Working on RONALD REAGAN's first campaign in Jacksonville in 1980, I saw first-hand his strength of character and his sense of optimism and hope. RONALD REAGAN lifted this Nation up at the time when we needed it the most. He made us feel good about being American. RONALD WILSON REAGAN knew who he was and he knew what he believed. These are the qualities of a great leader.

President REAGAN's strength of character and firm beliefs led to revolutionary policies in dealing with the economy, national security, and Federal taxation.

Under the Presidency of RONALD WILSON REAGAN, our Nation experienced a lengthy period of economic revival where inflation was brought under control, employment grew, and a stifling Federal tax burden was lifted from millions of hard-working Americans.

President REAGAN's defense policies were pivotal in the collapse of the Soviet Union and the end of the cold war. His commitment to a strong national defense and a safe and secure world is personified through the phrases, "Trust but verify," "Peace through strength," and most of all, "Mr. Gorbachev, tear down this wall!"

At the end of his two terms in office, the Reagan revolution had succeeded in giving the Nation its longest recorded period of peacetime prosperity without recession or depression. President REAGAN succeeded in keeping his campaign promise of restoring the great, confident roar of American progress and growth and optimism.

Mr. Speaker, I am so very pleased to have known this man. I am even more pleased that RONALD REAGAN answered the call to public service and contributed all that he did. His leadership blessed our great Nation. Our country will never forget his awesome contributions. For now and years to come, may the people of the United States examine the life of our 40th President, and reflect upon his great achievements. RONALD WILSON REAGAN lifted this Nation, and changed the world.

Hon. Ernest J. Istook, Jr.

OF OKLAHOMA

Mr. Speaker, like millions of Americans, I want to pay tribute to President RONALD REAGAN, the 40th President of the United States. I have shed many tears this week, because I loved RONALD REAGAN, and I know how much he loved this country and the American people.

President REAGAN inherited a country disillusioned and with serious economic problems, yet when he left office 8 years later, it was truly "morning in America." This was more than an economic boom. President REAGAN restored pride and dignity to the United States and to the Office of the Presidency. He advocated personal responsibility and limited government—government that gives a hand up, not a hand out.

He deserves more credit than anyone else for the collapse of communism and the fall of the Iron Curtain, bringing freedom to many millions of people. He spoke proudly and freely of morals and principles, of right and wrong, of good and evil. He believed in the goodness of the American people, and he helped us believe in ourselves.

Recently, my wife and I made a special trip to visit the Reagan ranch near Santa Barbara, CA. The humble and simple nature of his beloved ranch home reflects the genuine basic values that he cherished and lived by. America is a better place because of RONALD WILSON REAGAN, who greatly loved our country and who championed our ideals.

Hon. Lamar S. Smith

OF TEXAS

Mr. Speaker, I was honored to have served in Congress for the last 2 years of President REAGAN's second term.

President REAGAN devoted his life to the preservation of freedom. He believed that "no weapon in the arsenals of the world is so formidable as the will and moral courage of free men and women."

His global fight against communism is one of the most significant events in world history. Many said this enemy of freedom could not be conquered. But the Berlin Wall fell because President REAGAN made it fall.

Since the President's death last Saturday we have heard all or parts of the speeches that inspired so many for so long. They earned him the nickname the "Great Communicator."

Mr. Speaker, President REAGAN will always be the Great Communicator because of what he said and did. But his public remarks were also notable for what he did not say and what he did not do.

He did not pound the podium. He did not flail his arms, or yell. He did not substitute manufactured emotion for reason. He did not exploit human suffering.

The style and manner of his speech combined with the power of his ideas made verbal and physical gimmicks completely unnecessary.

Mr. Speaker, there are many ways to judge a President's place in history. I believe a question we must ask is: What kind of impact on world and national events does a President have after he leaves office? By that standard President REAGAN is a historical giant. Consider two examples:

First, President REAGAN initiated the largest peacetime expansion of our military ever. It gave him the strength to win the cold war without firing a shot.

But would our soldiers, sailors and airmen have achieved such rapid success in the first Gulf war if we sent our 1980 forces and weapons to fight? Would we have won the ground war in 100 hours without President REAGAN's military buildup? Of course not. I believe we would have prevailed, but not with such stunning success.

And our modern, 21st century military that is fighting the war on terror in Iraq today would be years, if not decades away, without President REAGAN's peace-through-strength doctrine.

Second, President REAGAN launched the boldest economic growth plan since the New Deal. When he came to office there were 14 income tax brackets, with the top rate a suffocating 70 percent. After he left office only two income tax brackets existed, with a top rate of 28 percent. Yes, we know this created the longest economic boom in history throughout the eighties. But what about the nineties?

Mr. Speaker, without President REAGAN's 3-year across-the-board tax reduction plan in 1981, and without the fundamental restructuring of the Nation's Income Tax Code in 1986, we would not have experienced the job creation machine of the nineties. We would not have created a new class in America—the investor class. And our economy certainly would not have survived and rebounded as it did after the 9 11 terrorist attacks and corporate scandals.

President REAGAN left office with a united America, a strong America, and a prosperous America. His America is the country every President—every American—aspires to live in.

Hon. Kendrick B. Meek

OF FLORIDA

Mr. Speaker, RONALD REAGAN forever changed the landscape of American politics. He will be remembered as a President who loved his country and inspired us all to be better Americans.

President REAGAN was a principled leader, and many times his beliefs put him at odds with Democrats. Despite these disagreements, he taught us that there is a big difference between bitter partisanship and strong beliefs.

My thoughts and prayers are with Mrs. Reagan and her children at this difficult time.

Hon. John Sullivan
OF OKLAHOMA

Mr. Speaker, on the passing of President REAGAN it is right and good that our Nation gathers for mourning, prayer, and remembrance.

As I inventory my memories of RONALD REAGAN, I can't help but smile at the recollection of such a good and sensible man. The first time I voted for a President, I voted for RONALD REAGAN. Each time since I cast my first ballot, I have compared every candidate to President REAGAN.

That's because RONALD REAGAN set the standard, he personified leadership. He was America. He was our greatness, our promise, our free will, and our character.

RONALD REAGAN showed us love of family, even in the midst of challenges to our values and barbs to tradition.

He and Nancy were unafraid to show their affection, to put their pure love for each other on display. When you saw the Reagans together, you couldn't help but feel part of their family. Their mutual fondness and love brought true meaning to the term "first family."

Not only a defender of traditional values, RONALD REAGAN brought common sense to bear on government. He reigned in the scope of the Federal Government, while spurring growth in the private sector.

RONALD REAGAN changed the world. He spread democracy to places where freedom was a term without meaning. President REAGAN stood up to the rising tide of communism, instead presenting the future that liberty ensures.

He changed the world by example, showing the power of a free people. He ended the cold war with fearless resolve, lifting our fears of imminent attack by Soviet missiles and giving a future to nations ravaged by the ills of communism.

Not only did RONALD REAGAN change the world, he changed America. He led us back to prosperity. He made us proud to be Americans again. RONALD REAGAN brought us closer to his image of a "shining city on a hill," and showed us that we could be great again. Under REAGAN's guidance the rest of the world came to look to us for our leadership again.

And although we are saddened by his death, we are comforted by the promise he restored in America. President REAGAN said "For while I take inspiration from the past . . . . I live for the future." So must we.

Hon. Dennis R. Rehberg
OF MONTANA

Mr. Speaker, I remember working in Washington during RONALD REAGAN's transition in 1980. It was heartening to see the change in attitude and renewed patriotism among the public and in Washington. You see, in those days so many Americans felt discouraged about their government and their future.

And then the sheriff rode into town. He brought with him a wholesome, western perspective. His optimism was contagious, and he had a love for this country and its people as big and as colorful as the Montana sky. His was a kind of hope that people hadn't seen in our Nation since well before Vietnam, Watergate, and the tough economic times that he came to vanquish.

"Sheriff" REAGAN's determination and infectious charm disarmed this town of its grip on the American taxpayer, in favor of limited government, free enterprise, and a renewed faith in the power of the American dream. Abroad, our President's unwavering stand for liberty brought down the Iron Curtain, ended the cold war, and helped restore freedom to millions of people around the world. He made us—made me—proud to be an American.

Several years ago, that sense of pride motivated me to successfully lead the effort in Montana to change the name of our annual Republican Lincoln Day Dinners to Lincoln-Reagan Day Dinners, in honor of the two greatest Republicans, Abraham Lincoln and, of course, RONALD REAGAN.

Hon. Silvestre Reyes

OF TEXAS

Mr. Speaker, I rise to express my sorrow on the passing of President RONALD REAGAN.

I had the privilege of meeting President REAGAN twice—once when I participated in a G.I. Forum event in El Paso, TX, honoring veterans, and the other time while I was in the Border Patrol providing security as the President visited Brownsville, TX.

It was easy to see that President REAGAN was blessed with a good nature and positive spirit. All Americans remember his abiding love of country and strong defense of freedom.

President REAGAN has left a lasting legacy in the way he confronted communism and helped to end the cold war. He was the kind of leader we needed during those difficult years. For that, our Nation, and the world, will be forever grateful.

On behalf of my constituents in El Paso, I extend heartfelt condolences to the Reagan family during this very sad time.

Hon. Tom Latham

OF IOWA

Mr. Speaker, former President REAGAN's influence on the world was tremendous. He was bigger than life. Whether it was on the Silver Screen or before thousands of cheering Americans—he was, in so many ways, the American dream. His messages of hope and possibility touched so many people around the world.

Many Iowans have a special place in their heart for RONALD REAGAN or "DUTCH" as he was known to those who used to listen to him on the radio during the thirties.

In 1932, after graduating from college, REAGAN began working as a temporary staff announcer for radio station WOC in Davenport, IA. In 1933, WOC merged with radio station WHO in Des Moines, and REAGAN was hired as chief sports announcer for the new station. Here, REAGAN announced Chicago Cubs baseball games—reading them from teletype reports. I remember him recounting how he was forced to improvise games for as long as 15 minutes when the teletype machine would unexpectedly stop.

At the time, radio personalities were treated as big stars and what a great place to start a career in entertainment—in Iowa. As we all know, Mr. REAGAN went on to a career in movies but many Iowans remembered listening to his sportscasts and helped him in pursuit of higher office in the seventies and eighties.

I can remember "Dutch's Dollies"—a group of ladies who were longtime fans cheering wildly at his campaign events. They were loyal supporters with very long memories of their man DUTCH.

There are many great stories about RONALD REAGAN and his ties to Iowa, but I want to express my admiration for the entire Reagan family.

RONALD REAGAN touched me in a manner I could not anticipate—through Alzheimer's disease.

For the better part of the last decade I shared the sadness of this disease with the Reagan family. Like all Americans, we read about the Reagan family's long goodbye to the President. During their painful days, the entire Latham family was saying their own long goodbye to my father Willard Latham, who succumbed to the disease in 2001.

RONALD REAGAN will be remembered for many things but for millions this week we are reminded of the ravages Alzheimer's disease has on its victims and their families. Let us all pray for those who are devastated by this affliction and let us keep the Reagan family in our thoughts and prayers.

Hon. Jon C. Porter
OF NEVADA

Mr. Speaker, today is a day of reflection. We reflect on the life and leadership of former President RONALD WILSON REAGAN. We remember all that is good in our country, and all our Nation has to offer its people. RONALD REAGAN made a significant and lasting contribution to the strength of our economy, our military, and restored America's self-confidence.

President REAGAN was an inspiration to me as I embarked upon a political career in Boulder City, NV, more than 20 years ago. He instilled in me that America was indeed a place everyone can rise as high and as far as his ability will take him. His own humble beginnings are proof of that. He taught me the meaning of civility, and to respect your political adversaries despite your disagreements.

President REAGAN changed the course of history, for both the United States and the world. He implemented foreign policy that would later end the cold war and free many nations from the Iron Curtain.

President REAGAN strengthened our economy. His leadership taught us that the Federal Government is not the solution for our problems and set us on a course that would lessen taxes and decrease inflation, helping many Americans achieve the American dream.

On behalf of the people of the Third Congressional District from the great State of Nevada, I offer my deepest sympathy to Mrs. Reagan and the entire Reagan family.

To conclude, let me recap the final words of President REAGAN's farewell address to the American people from the Oval Office:

> My friends: We did it. We weren't just marking time. We made a difference. We made the city stronger. We made the city freer, and we left her in good hands. All in all, not bad, not bad at all.

Mr. President, thank you for all you've done for the Nation and the world. Americans will miss you.

Hon. Todd Tiahrt
OF KANSAS

Mr. Speaker, we have lost a giant in American politics and world history. RONALD WILSON REAGAN was not only a great President, he was a good man. He will be remembered fondly for his character and with great appreciation for his tremendous triumphs in spreading peace and freedom throughout the world.

In addition to tearing down the iron curtain of communism, rebuilding America's military, presiding over the Nation's longest period of growth and prosperity, it was the little things that made him great. He cared about people, including the smallest among us. His heart of kindness reflected that of his Creator's in its compassion toward "the least of these."

RONALD REAGAN comforted us when we grieved. Whether to the families of the 101st Airborne Division or to a Nation in shock after losing the space shuttle *Challenger*, President REAGAN knew what to say and how to say it. He also knew when to be silent and simply offer a reassuring embrace. He was the most powerful man in the world, yet he exuded the warmth and kindness of a gentle grandfather. We respected not just the office he held, but the man who held it.

President REAGAN earned his respect. He knew what he believed, established his goals upon those beliefs and committed to achieve his dreams. The world is a much improved place because he lived by his deeply held convictions.

RONALD REAGAN knew you shouldn't penalize people for working hard, so he fought to enact sweeping tax relief that spurred unparalleled economic growth. He knew there was a difference between good and evil, so he called out the evil empire, and it ultimately crumbled. RONALD REAGAN knew people wanted to feel good about this country again, so he told us it was "morning in America"—and we saw that it was.

He touched numerous lives in the Fourth Congressional District of Kansas. Every year I attend the Lincoln Day Celebration in Independence, KS, I am reminded by local residents of RONALD

REAGAN's visit there in 1966. They remember it as if it were yesterday. And they still love him.

We love RONALD REAGAN. We have named our national airport, Washington's largest government building and more than 50 other sites across this country in tribute to our Nation's 40th President. He captured our hearts with his next-door-neighbor kindness, rekindled our patriotism with his effusive and infectious love for this country, and he inspired us with his principled leadership.

In his personal and moving letter disclosing his bout with Alzheimer's disease, the President conveyed the essence of his entire being. In that letter, he was optimistic about America, and he asked us to take care of his beloved Nancy because he was concerned about the burden she would bear. There was not a word of self-pity or dread. RONALD REAGAN wrote about the sunset of his life, but proclaimed for America, "a bright dawn ahead."

Mr. Speaker, we too believe that America's future is bright, but it pales in comparison to the place where RONALD REAGAN now lives.

President REAGAN had a strong faith in God and spoke of his reliance on prayer in both good and difficult times. During his address at the National Prayer Breakfast in 1982, President REAGAN said he believed the United States was a blessed land that had been set apart in a special way. But, he also had the following warning:

> Sometimes, it seems we've strayed from that noble beginning, from our conviction that standards of right and wrong do exist and must be lived up to. God, the source of our knowledge, has been expelled from the classroom. He gives us His greatest blessing, life, and yet many would condone the taking of innocent life. We expect Him to protect us in a crisis, but turn away from Him too often in our day-to-day living. I wonder if He isn't waiting for us to wake up.

President REAGAN went on to urge Americans of faith to get involved and "to restore our spirit of neighbor caring for neighbor." In his conclusion he added:

> We are told in II Timothy that when our work is done, we can say, "We have fought the good fight. We have finished the race. We have kept the faith."

RONALD REAGAN's struggles on this Earth are finished, but his work carries on. He indeed fought the good fight, and we are all better off because of it.

May God bless RONALD WILSON REAGAN, and may God provide strength, peace and encouragement to Mrs. Reagan and the Reagan family in the days ahead.

Hon. Michael Bilirakis
OF FLORIDA

Mr. Speaker, I rise today to honor America's 40th President, RONALD WILSON REAGAN.

President REAGAN was an ordinary man who led an extraordinary life. He came from a middle-American family of modest means to become the leader of the most powerful Nation in the world, inspiring its people along the way.

President REAGAN was a decisive leader. He was a strong Commander in Chief. He was a statesman. He was a gifted communicator. He was a skilled political adversary. He was an eternal optimist. He was a patriot. He was, above all, an American. He used these skills, and his love for our country, to change the course of history for the better.

President REAGAN accomplished much during his Presidency. He helped defeat communism and end the cold war. He rebuilt our national defenses. He advanced freedom throughout the world. He led the longest economic recovery in our Nation's history. He lowered taxes. He fundamentally changed the way we think about government. "We meant to change a nation," he said in his farewell address to the American people, but instead, "we changed a world."

President REAGAN literally helped save a world that needed saving.

President REAGAN convinced us to believe in ourselves again. He took charge of a wounded Nation that doubted itself and helped us rediscover our pride and patriotism. He reminded us that America and its people are fundamentally good, decent and deserving of God's blessings. He restored America's greatness and instilled in us his eternal optimism that our best is always yet to come.

President REAGAN left America better, stronger, freer and more prosperous than we ever had been. Looking back on his accomplishments in the White House, he said that he was proud that

"We weren't just marking time. We made a difference," adding with his usual humility "All in all, not bad, not bad at all."

Not bad at all, Mr. President.

President REAGAN battled Alzheimer's disease with the same dignity and courage with which he lived his life. He asked us, in his last letter to America, to remember that he had "the greatest love for this country of ours and eternal optimism for its future." We know he loved America. I think it is clear America loved him.

Mr. Speaker, I am proud to have known President REAGAN and am honored to have, in some small measure, done my part to ensure that his vision for America and the world came to pass. We all owe him a debt of gratitude for dedicating his life to improving ours.

In this time of great sadness for the Reagan family and the American people, let us take comfort in the knowledge that the leader we so loved has fulfilled his earthly mission and has finally reached the place of peace in which we all may one day rejoice. May God eternally bless RONALD REAGAN and continue to watch over the "shining city on a hill" he so loved.

Hon. Mac Collins

OF GEORGIA

Mr. Speaker, today, I pay tribute to a great American, our 40th President, RONALD REAGAN.

Under RONALD REAGAN's Presidency and leadership, America stood tall again in the world as a "shining city on the hill." Americans were proud once again to be Americans.

RONALD REAGAN assumed the Presidency when America was facing an Iranian hostage crisis, a rising inflation rate, increasing unemployment, and an energy crisis that saw Americans waiting in lines to purchase gasoline.

Upon assuming the Presidency, RONALD REAGAN proposed a bold economic and defense program. His economic policy created the longest peacetime job expansion in history. Under his leadership, our defenses were rebuilt to handle any adversary. It was his leadership that saw America triumph as the communist evil empire that scarred Europe fell.

President REAGAN fought for his convictions and followed up his campaign promises with successful action. Under his leadership, government bureaucracy and regulations were reduced. Taxes were lowered and a strong national defense was rebuilt to fight against the spread of communism. These moves won him a landslide reelection victory.

I agree with the words of this great President when he said, "government is not the solution . . . government is the problem."

I also agree with President REAGAN's words at the 1992 Republican National Convention in Houston, TX, when he said:

{A} lot of liberal democrats are saying it's time for a change; and they're right; the only trouble is they're pointing to the wrong end of Pennsylvania Avenue. What we should change is a Democratic Congress that wastes precious time on partisan matters of absolutely no relevance to the needs of the average American. . . .

It's time to clean house. Clean out the privileges and perks. Clean out the arrogance and the big egos. Clean out the scandals, the corner-cutting and the foot-dragging.

RONALD REAGAN was a President who, in a time of politicians, proved himself a statesman. He was a leader who, when others demanded compromise, preached conviction; a gentleman who, in time of average men, stood taller than anyone else.

He ranks as one of the finest men ever to hold the office. He was successful as a radio broadcaster, actor, union leader, Governor and President. But, above all else, he was a successful American whose legacy lives on in these halls and across this land. May God bless this great man, his family and this land that he so dearly loved.

Hon. Edward L. Schrock

OF VIRGINIA

Mr. Speaker, today I rise to honor and remember a great man, a great leader and a great President.

RONALD WILSON REAGAN is a man none of us will soon forget. In the annals of American and world history, RONALD REAGAN will be recognized and remembered with the great leaders of our past like Winston Churchill, George Washington and Abraham Lincoln.

As a principled leader, he challenged political leaders in our Nation, in both parties, to go beyond the status quo, to think beyond the realms of the possible, to reach new heights in public discourse by doing more than debate the problems ailing the American people, and to actually find a solution.

He actively worked to enact new policies that brought our Nation out of the malaise of the seventies.

He fought communism and tyranny, bringing freedom to more people in the world than has ever been achieved in history.

His principle of "peace through strength," not only led our Nation to become the preeminent superpower in the world, but it also brought the Soviet empire down to its knees, ending the cold war once and for all.

When was the last time we have seen a world leader stand boldly on the doorsteps of an enemy and challenge him to "Tear down this wall"? President REAGAN knew what had to be done and he did it. Why? Because it was the right thing to do.

I think most Americans will remember RONALD REAGAN for the inspiration he gave us all. He helped us to believe in ourselves again. After our failed efforts in Vietnam and the protests and marches against our actions there, after Watergate, after economic malaise, and after the Iran hostage crisis, America was in a state of despair with very little hope in the future.

But President REAGAN helped us to believe we could be better, and we became better. He showed us America could be strong and win the cold war, and we became strong and won it. He promised us he would invest in the American people to turn the economy around. He made that investment and dividends are still paying off today.

President REAGAN optimistically led the way. The Nation followed and we are better off because of it.

In spite of all that President REAGAN did for our Nation, the one thing that speaks volumes about his character and the man that he was, was the way he loved Nancy. He was not embarrassed about his love for her, rather he demonstrated it at every opportunity.

President REAGAN was committed to his family, to his Nation and to the world. He was dedicated to his integrity, principles and the belief that America could become that "shining city on a hill."

Today, we say goodbye to this great man, leader, President and husband. We miss President REAGAN. May God bless him and his family.

Hon. Solomon P. Ortiz

OF TEXAS

Mr. Speaker, my memories of RONALD REAGAN are much like the memories of so many of those who met President REAGAN and who were absolutely charmed by him.

RONALD REAGAN wasn't just called the Great Communicator because he could give good speeches; he was a brilliant communicator on all levels. He understood how the everyday person on the street understood issues, and he framed things in such a way that people believed him. He presented his ideas simply and eloquently.

He was also excellent one on one. His Irish charm was all-encompassing. That charm made him an agreeable opponent when we disagreed on issues. He welcomed opposition on a matter; he understood that democratic societies only flourish when both sides of an issue are clearly heard. He relished debate.

President REAGAN's acting career was helpful to him in his political career, although his detractors often denigrated him for it. But he was a good actor; his performance in "Kings Row" was widely hailed. But World War II intervened and his advancing career was diverted to military service, making movies for the troops.

My personal memories of the President were times we saw each other in the White House or the Capitol. The first time we met, my 10-year-old daughter, Yvette, accompanied me to the White House party for new Members of Congress. After being rebuffed by a security guard when she asked if she could get REAGAN's autograph, the President found out and obliged her with his autograph.

I remember another meeting with him that was rather high stakes on the international stage. I'd just returned from El Salvador in the mideighties with a CODEL of House Members where we'd sought to bring back good information about the rebel uprisings in Central America, particularly there in El Salvador.

Talking about—and debating at points during the conversation—international policy with the President of the United States in the Oval Office was a heady moment. We marveled that a migrant worker from Robstown and a lifeguard from Illinois would wind up in this room, talking about such important things.

He loved this Nation and felt a great responsibility to it. When his tax cuts and economic policies produced mountains of massive deficit, he stepped up and reversed his policy, raising taxes higher than any President before him—or since—has ever done. His insistence that the Soviets tear down the Berlin Wall rang truer than anyone would have believed at the time.

He had a sweet soul. This was one of the central tenets of the man. He loved his wife deeply, and the entire Nation has come to love her even more after they left the White House. Nancy Reagan's monumental strength in the face of facing her dear husband's illness, without him entirely with her, might have broken lesser people.

One of the President's greatest contributions to humanity, and to this Nation, may have come after he left office to begin the long dark walk away from us, and his beloved family. That this strong, vigorous man was so removed, so empty, was chilling for all of us. The eyes that danced with Irish charm began to narrow with confusion.

The Nation was deeply moved watching this much-loved President face the indignities of Alzheimer's so bravely and with such conviction. We have been moved to seek new science and new treatments for the cruel disease that claims the last decades of many Americans, and drains their families.

For all we have said here today, RONALD REAGAN will be remembered most profoundly as an eternal optimist, embodying the quintessential American spirit. At our core, we are all optimists, thinking about tomorrow. Former House Speaker Tip O'Neill once illustrated President REAGAN's indomitable optimism with a story the President told him. President REAGAN compared himself to the kid who walks into a room full of horse dung, and asks excitedly, "Where's the pony?"

I join the House of Representatives today in honoring the life and service of RONALD WILSON REAGAN and offer my condolences, those of my family, and those of my south Texas constituents, to Mrs. Reagan and the rest of their family.

May the Lord bless President REAGAN's soul, and comfort Mrs. Reagan and their family in this time of loss.

Hon. Dale E. Kildee

OF MICHIGAN

Mr. Speaker, I remember RONALD REAGAN as an enthusiastic American patriot. He truly enjoyed being President. He was just like everyone's uncle or grandfather. He always had a kind word to say. He could disagree without being disagreeable.

I have served with six Presidents, and I liked him personally.

Even one of his principal opponents, House Speaker Tip O'Neill, liked him.

President REAGAN was well known for his great sense of humor. On St. Patrick's Day, Tip O'Neill invited President REAGAN to the Speaker's dining room to have lunch with the Irish Members of Congress. In his remarks, President REAGAN said, with great humor, "I am told that on St. Patrick's Day, one should spend time with saints and scholars, so you know that when I leave here I will have to go to two other places."

We all loved it.

On the international level, President REAGAN made it difficult for the Soviet Union to compete with us, either economically or militarily.

May he rest in peace.

Hon. Karen McCarthy

OF MISSOURI

Mr. Speaker, I rise today to honor former President RONALD WILSON REAGAN and to extend my deepest sympathies to former First Lady Nancy Reagan and the Reagan family. I join with the millions of Americans who mourn the death of our 40th President. President REAGAN demonstrated an unwavering commitment to freedom, justice and democracy and left an indelible mark upon our Nation and the world.

On this occasion of remembrance, we are reminded of the pain and devastation wrought by Alzheimer's disease, a neurological illness which President REAGAN endured during the last decade of his life. From this challenge, Mrs. Reagan has led a valiant effort to enable ongoing embryonic stem cell research, in the hope for a cure for this debilitating disease, as well as Parkinson's, diabetes, cancer and multiple sclerosis.

On April 28, I joined more than 200 of my colleagues in the House of Representatives in sending a letter to President George W. Bush in support of Mrs. Reagan's efforts on behalf of scientific research on stem cells. In February 2003, Senators Hatch, Feinstein, Kennedy, Specter and Harkin introduced legislation to ban human reproductive cloning but allow nuclear transplantation research to continue under strict Federal guidelines. I commend them for their leadership on this important issue and know that with the continued support of Mrs. Reagan, progress toward a cure for Alzheimer's and other diseases will be possible, ensuring a brighter future for millions of Americans.

As we honor the life and legacy of President REAGAN and extend our condolences to his family and friends, let us remember the dignity and grace with which he lived his life and provide a fitting tribute to his memory by renewing the commitment to this noble cause.

Hon. David L. Hobson

OF OHIO

Mr. Speaker, I rise today to join my colleagues, indeed all Americans, in paying tribute to a great man, the 40th President of the United States—RONALD WILSON REAGAN.

President REAGAN was an extraordinary and visionary leader, who saw our great Nation as having a unique role, purpose, and destiny in the world. He saw it as a beacon of freedom, a land of unlimited opportunity, and in his words, a "shining city on the hill."

Mr. REAGAN took office during a time of great pessimism. There was Watergate; Vietnam; the hostage crisis in Iran; and gas lines, runaway inflation, and double-digit interest rates here at home. There were those who told us that we had to lower our expectations, that we could no longer shape our destiny, and that our best days were behind us.

RONALD REAGAN saw a different future. It was a future in which we were limited only by the size of our dreams; where the spirit of our pioneer ancestors was still alive, it just needed to be rekindled. It was a vision where hard work, imagination, creativity, and a little luck would allow ordinary men and women to accomplish extraordinary things.

Taxes were cut, inflation and interest rates were reduced, and gas lines disappeared. Americans went back to work; the economy roared forward; and in the process, Mr. REAGAN restored our confidence, uplifted our spirits, and made us proud to be Americans again.

The rebirth here at home was accompanied by equally dramatic changes abroad. The march of totalitarianism that seemed inevitable a few years earlier, was halted as Mr. REAGAN rebuilt our defenses. The creaky Soviet system disappeared quietly, without a shot being fired. And the Berlin Wall, the greatest symbol of oppression, fell, and millions of people around the world tasted freedom for the first time.

We Americans, and indeed all freedom-loving people around the world, owe President REAGAN an enormous debt. We will miss him, but history will never forget what he accomplished in 8 short years. As a grateful Nation comes together to say goodbye, our collective thoughts and prayers go to Mrs. Reagan and her family.

Hon. Jim Nussle

OF IOWA

Mr. Speaker, I rise to honor President RONALD REAGAN. RONALD REAGAN once said, "We in government should learn to look at our country with the eyes of an entrepreneur, seeing possibilities where others see only problems." It is that spirit that brought me and many others into the public service profession. I am proud to have cast my first Presidential vote for RONALD REAGAN in 1980. Fortunately for this country and the world, a majority of my fellow citizens agreed.

RONALD REAGAN served as a beacon of hope and inspiration. His vision of a stronger, optimistic America inspired me to action. In 1980 I was a young student at Luther College in Decorah, IA, and I jumped right into grassroots politics on my campus. I was selected to attend the Republican National Convention that summer and was one of the youngest delegates there.

Iowans are proud of our connection to President REAGAN. WOC, a Davenport radio station in my district, gave RONALD REAGAN his first job out of college and he lived in Iowa for several years.

RONALD REAGAN made the future something to charge toward rather than fear. His philosophy was based on a brilliant truth: He knew without a doubt that having faith in Americans would create the best America.

The Reagan revolution is still the foundation for my core beliefs: The American people make better decisions about their daily life than the government can for them. Keeping America secure is job one. Peace is best achieved when you negotiate from a position of strength.

I keep a plaque on my desk with a quote from RONALD REAGAN. It reads "There's no limit to what a man can do or where he can go if he doesn't mind who gets the credit."

Today I join my colleagues, thousands of Iowans and millions of Americans in giving credit to RONALD REAGAN for renewing our Nation and for changing the world forever with his leadership and ideals.

Thank you Mr. President, for reminding us why we should be proud to be Americans and for making us feel safe when nothing in the world seemed safe. Above all, thank you for your humor, optimism and for believing the best in us. We will never forget you.

Hon. Christopher H. Smith

OF NEW JERSEY

Mr. Speaker, RONALD REAGAN was a great world leader with a fierce devotion to freedom, democracy, and the sacredness of human life—including the unborn.

He advocated "peace through strength" and played a major role in dismantling Soviet communism which he rightly called the evil empire and stopped its extension into Latin America and elsewhere. I remember some of his critics laughing when he challenged Gorbachev in Berlin to "tear down this wall!" They're not laughing any more.

RONALD REAGAN championed the 1981 tax cut—the largest tax cut in history—totaling $750 billion by 1986. All wage earners—low, moderate and upper-income levels—got a 25 percent across-the-board cut in personal income taxes. Long term capital gains were also cut and the results were stunning—19 million new jobs created as Americans began to believe and hope again.

RONALD REAGAN was strongly prolife and fervently believed that women deserved better than abortion and that unborn children are precious and deserve respect.

Having been elected to Congress in 1980 along with President REAGAN, I saw first-hand and often how genuine he was. He was a man of abiding principle who inspired our Nation to greatness, always believing America's best years lay ahead.

He endured personal hardship—including an assassination attempt—with incredible poise, dignity, and even humor.

Who can forget President REAGAN telling Nancy after he was shot, "I forgot to duck."

President REAGAN will be missed, but his legend will endure.

Hon. Jeb Bradley

OF NEW HAMPSHIRE

Mr. Speaker, I rise today to pay tribute to one of the greatest leaders of the past century, a man who committed himself to making our Nation more powerful, united, secure, prosperous, and proud.

By definition, a leader is one who guides, and as President of this great country, RONALD WILSON REAGAN guided us with grace and dignity through one of the most critical periods in our country's history. His optimism led our county into a new era and brought hope and freedom to millions of people in the world.

When the cold war pitted the United States and the Soviet Union against each other in an ideological struggle of the highest stakes, President REAGAN steered the Nation and led the free world with steady resolve and confidence.

Throughout his time in office, President REAGAN stood for the principles and ideals of the American people. His steadfast moral clarity was not expressed in political rhetoric but implemented by action. His style was clear and bold. He redefined and transformed his political party with a new image and momentum. He set a new standard of political cooperation in American Government. He created a new economic policy. Finally, he reestablished American leadership through the force of his vision and the power of his personality. Most poignantly, it was with that vision that he spoke boldly before the Brandenburg Gate in Berlin in 1987 to demand Soviet President Mikhail Gorbachev to "open this gate! ... tear down this wall!" The rest is history. Within months the wall came down, Eastern Europe was free, and the Soviet Union collapsed.

RONALD REAGAN spent 8 years turning American hopes and dreams into reality and affirming our status as the greatest nation on Earth, and for that, America is forever indebted to him.

God bless RONALD REAGAN.

Hon. William L. Jenkins

OF TENNESSEE

Mr. Speaker, steadfast leadership, eternal optimism, profound faith, inspirational articulation, fierce patriotism: when America needed these qualities in a leader, President RONALD REAGAN stepped in to fill the void. We come here to the Congress today to celebrate and honor the life of a man who will forever be etched in history as one of the greatest leaders of the 20th century.

The stories have been told so often by those of us who supported President REAGAN over the years that they seem mundane, almost like a fictional novel or a movie script. High taxes, a struggling economy, a need for international stature and respect, and low morale affected the Nation. At that time, a man who had come from the most humble beginnings stepped up to offer his vision for America. Washington politics tend to bring a variety of characters to the Capital City, and RONALD REAGAN was the unlikeliest of candidates: a child of a transient family with little income. He dreamed of being a writer or an artist, became a sports broadcaster, then a Hollywood actor, later a union leader, even later a Governor, and finally a President.

His political affiliation would change over the course of a lifetime, but his core belief system remained essentially unchanged. Throughout his life, RONALD REAGAN believed America was capable of great things and its people could and would lead the way if left unburdened by taxation and regulation. President REAGAN also had an insatiable thirst to let the rest of the world enjoy the gifts of freedom and liberty. The "shining city on a hill" would be the beacon for the rest of the world.

Often dismissed or underestimated by political opponents, President REAGAN had the most valuable weapon in the political arsenal: a bond with the people. Even in the face of his political defeats, it was the support of the American public that sustained and invigorated him.

In 1980, a Nation in need of change selected RONALD REAGAN to restore the shine to a tarnished America. Over the course of two terms, President REAGAN revolutionized the Republican Party and changed the political atmosphere in a way still being felt today. He did what he said he would do. He lowered taxes, igniting an economic boom that reverberates to this day. A more streamlined Tax Code was authored. Regulatory burdens were challenged. Our Armed Forces were restored and then strengthened. The threatening scourge of communism was confronted in a way that America's enemies had not anticipated. Not only did President REAGAN turn to face this menace, he outargued his opponents and used the tools of freedom and democracy to win a war few thought could be won without the use of massive weaponry.

After achieving these monumental victories, one would think that perhaps President REAGAN's ego would match the size of his victories. Nothing, however, was further from the truth. President REAGAN always gave the credit to the American people and American ideals. He treated his job as a valuable temporary loan from the American people, a loan that should be respected and returned with dutiful appreciation. He left the Office of the Presidency with a poignant farewell from the Oval Office:

> We've done our part. And as I walk off into the city streets, a final word to the men and women of the Reagan revolution, the men and women across America who for eight years did the work that brought America back. My friends: We did it. We weren't just marking time. We made a difference. We made the city stronger. We made the city freer, and we left her in good hands. All in all, not bad, not bad at all.

Truer words have never been spoken, as President REAGAN left Washington having achieved the triad of goals he was elected to accomplish in 8 short years: improving the economy, restoring American prestige internationally, and reestablishing the confidence of the American psyche.

Just a few years later, his quiet exit from public life was as graceful as his exit from the White House. RONALD REAGAN's well-documented final battles with Alzheimer's disease were fought with the same conviction and courage that his many public battles were fought. We all knew the "long goodbye" would eventually knock at the door. And, while we sadly mourn our loss today and send our deepest sympathy to Nancy and the rest of the Reagan family, we can also take solace in and celebrate one last Reagan victory: the Great Communicator now has been welcomed to a place where his faculties are restored, his great skills have been returned to him, and he probably smiles down on us as a grateful America says "Thank you, Mr. President" once again.

Hon. Jerry Moran
OF KANSAS

Mr. Speaker, we are blessed to live in a country filled with so many men and women willing to go beyond the call of duty, to accomplish great things for the benefit of their fellow citizens. Each day, ordinary souls are called upon to perform extraordinary tasks. I rise to pay tribute to one of the greatest individuals of our time—President RONALD REAGAN.

Like the World War II veterans honored last week during the dedication of the National World War II Memorial in Washington, DC, and those honored this past Sunday on the 60th anniversary of D-day in Normandy, President REAGAN was a great American, steadfast in his appointed duty, thorough in thought, long on compassion and short on vanity.

His love of freedom and embrace of optimism were virtues of many in the greatest generation. Let us pray that our generation, and the generations to come, remember that freedom is a worthy cause.

I traveled to the beaches of Normandy this week, joining President Bush, Speaker Hastert, and others, to commemorate the 60th anniversary of D-day. During the ceremonies, I could not help but feel REAGAN's presence.

In his own speech on that shore 20 years ago, President REAGAN said:

> The men of Normandy had faith that what they were doing was right, faith that they fought for all humanity, faith that a just God would grant them mercy on this beachhead or on the next. It was the deep knowledge—and pray God we have not lost it—that there is a profound moral difference between the use of force for liberation and the use of force for conquest.

President REAGAN understood, like our World War II soldiers, that what they were doing was not to harm, but to help. That even though sacrifices would be made—the greater good was at stake and no price was too high.

In announcing that he had Alzheimer's disease, RONALD REAGAN said that he was beginning the journey that would lead him "into the sunset of {his} life." He said, "I know that for America there will always be a bright dawn ahead." Since 1994, REAGAN had suffered the cruelty of Alzheimer's, so our sorrow today is tempered by the knowledge that the President has indeed gone to a better place—a place where he has a front row seat to watch all the bright dawns that lie ahead for America.

President REAGAN is responsible for so many of those bright dawns that we have to look forward to. He changed the world by living his convictions. Not "clinging to" them or "sticking to" them, but living them. REAGAN's core beliefs were exactly that. They were at his core and were therefore part of his every action.

REAGAN's convictions gave him confidence. He was a man of the people. He listened. And when he heard what the people needed, he took action in accordance with his convictions. On the domestic front, the people said they were tired of their economy spiraling downward, so REAGAN worked to reverse that trend.

To accomplish these feats, President REAGAN was not afraid to take hard stances. But he also knew that these changes would take bipartisan efforts. We should all remember, respect, and try to live up to REAGAN's model of bipartisanship. His efforts to change America were based upon his philosophy and beliefs—not upon any partisan gamesmanship.

On foreign policy, Americans said they were tired of living in fear, so REAGAN worked to bring security. President REAGAN engineered the end of the decades-long cold war. Because of his policies, and his faith that freedom would prevail, our children and grandchildren are not growing up with the constant fear of mutual destruction. We all are able now to live in a world that, though still imperfect, strives toward peace, works for justice and rejects tyranny.

I call upon my colleagues to remember REAGAN's strength. Remember him as he was while in office. In his final radio address as President, on January 14, 1989, REAGAN said, "The hope of human freedom, the quest for it, the achievement of it, is the American saga." REAGAN's hope, his quest, and all his achievements—those are what we all honor and remember.

Now, too, the Great Communicator has gone the way of so many of our greatest generation. I rise not only in sadness for his passing, but more important, in celebration of his life, his accomplishments and his deeds. I rise to pay tribute to President REAGAN in the words he used to honor the crew of the *Challenger* space shuttle in 1986:

> We will never forget {him}, nor the last time we saw {him} ... as {he} prepared for {the} journey and waved good-bye and "slipped the surly bonds of earth" to "touch the face of God."

Hon. Devin Nunes

OF CALIFORNIA

Mr. Speaker, I rise today to extend my condolences to First Lady Nancy Reagan, as well as the children, family and close friends of former President RONALD REAGAN.

Mr. REAGAN was a visionary leader who guided our great country through difficult and dangerous times. He faced adversity with a smile and quick wit. He solved problems with sober determination. He gave us hope for the future of freedom and prosperity. He reminded us what it meant to be proud Americans.

We mourn his loss but remember that he left us with a rich heritage of memories, ideals, and a trail of lives changed at home and abroad because of his efforts. For that, we will be eternally grateful.

Hon. Timothy V. Johnson

OF ILLINOIS

Mr. Speaker, I rise today in honor of our 40th President and Illinois native, RONALD REAGAN, and in strong support of H. Res. 664. Many words come to mind when President REAGAN's name is invoked; principled, loyal, patriotic, compassionate, caring, and humble, to name a few.

His philosophy in life was the same philosophy that he employed in his approach to politics and government; believe in the good of people, believe that what is right will eventually triumph, believe in the value of each and every human life, and believe in the strength and the power of freedom and individual liberty. He once said that America is too great for small dreams.

He truly saw our great Nation as the "shining city on the hill" and as the beacon of freedom for oppressed people throughout the world. Nowhere else in the world and at no other time or place in history has one nation been so prepared and had the means to promote freedom, peace, and stability than the United States does right now. Ours is a heavy burden but one that must be borne. REAGAN understood that.

He also once said that "you can tell a lot about a fellow's character by his way of eating jellybeans." In this simple way, he told us that, in the end, character is what matters and that life is really a series of simple choices between what is right and what is wrong. No one person is responsible for another person's destiny. It is the choices that we make everyday that we must account for. REAGAN believed, as I do, that an individual's personal initiative and the willingness to accept the consequences and rewards for their actions and, most importantly, the freedom to do so, is what make our Nation great.

He believed in people. He believed in America. He traveled to towns in what is now my congressional district, like Charleston, IL, in 1976 and Mattoon, IL, in 1980, because every person was important to him. The people in rural Illinois and similar places across the country believed in him, because he believed in them. He often asked, "Did we forget that government is the people's business and every man, woman, and child becomes a shareholder with the first penny of tax paid?" REAGAN constantly promoted this philosophy of government. The government of the United States belongs to all of us and public servants have an obligation to the people to be good stewards of their dollars, uphold the Constitution, and protect them from all enemies both foreign and domestic.

He believed in peace. When naysayers told him that building our military and our nuclear arsenal would finally push us into a war with the former Soviet Union, he knew that principled diplomacy, firm, yet reasonable rhetoric, the economic power of our Nation, and the promotion of freedom would bring communism to its knees. And when it did, he called on "the scientific community ... who gave us nuclear weapons, to turn their ... talents ... to the cause of mankind and world peace, to give us the means of rendering these nuclear weapons impotent and obsolete." He believed in "peace through strength" and he proved that it works.

I will miss President REAGAN and I send my deepest sympathies and condolences to his family with the thanks for sharing him with me and the rest of the Nation. He inspired many. He lived by example. Rest in peace, Mr. President.

Hon. Michael G. Oxley

OF OHIO

Mr. Speaker, the leadership that RONALD REAGAN provided changed the country and the world.

I had the privilege to be elected to Congress during the heady days of the Reagan revolution. I had barely won a special election in June 1981 to keep the Fourth Ohio District in Republican hands, and as a young freshman Congressman was quickly invited to the White House to meet the President and his aides.

It was more than a welcome to Washington because the President's tax cut package was pending on the floor the next week, and I think they were there to take my temperature as well as to make sure that I was going to vote for the tax cut.

I was proud to support the tax cut, the military buildup that helped win the cold war, and the President's policies up and down the line.

President REAGAN's economic program lifted us out of the malaise of the late seventies, when America was doubting its greatness, and set the stage for a historic period of prosperity that benefited all segments of our society.

Still, I believe that RONALD REAGAN is most likely to be celebrated as the President who led the way in winning the cold war. People in the past had always talked about the containment of Soviet communism and yet REAGAN's theory behind the cold war was essentially we win and they lose. He was able to lead the country and Congress into modernizing our military and ultimately brought about the end of what he called the evil empire.

For those of us who grew up in the shadow of nuclear annihilation, what could be more important than the victory that was won without firing a shot? It was won with ideas, and was something that I honestly thought I would never see in my lifetime.

I had the thrill of traveling with President REAGAN on the Heartland Express during a whistlestop campaign tour through Ohio in 1984. Everytime there would be a crowd gathered in a crossroads in a small town, the President would stand in the back of the train and wave. He was obviously in a buoyant mood. Large crowds cheered him during stops in Sidney and Lima, and people still remember that today.

We remember President REAGAN for his vision, leadership, and infectious optimism.

I don't think I ever met anybody in politics or anywhere else who didn't like RONALD REAGAN as a person. They may have disagreed with him on a number of issues but they never disliked him personally. I think President REAGAN's legacy in politics is this ability to disagree without being disagreeable, to see politics as a noble calling and that you have your debates and arguments and have a beer afterward. That is missed very much today in Washington and I don't think we're the better for it.

Our country will accord its highest honors to RONALD REAGAN as we pay our heartfelt respects to him this week. But he will be remembered each day that men and women live in freedom, because what RONALD REAGAN ultimately believed in was dignity and liberty for each individual.

Hon. Paul Ryan

OF WISCONSIN

Mr. Speaker, first, I would like to share my heartfelt condolences with Nancy Reagan and the Reagan children. Our Nation owes them a special debt of gratitude for their strength in caring for their husband and father over the past decade as he battled Alzheimer's disease and for everything they've done to uphold his dignity and legacy for our country.

As we prepare to lay former U.S. President RONALD REAGAN to rest, it's important that we reflect on his brave and principled leadership—and the hope he gave to countless individuals in our country and around the world.

Looking back at the footage of REAGAN's speeches and other public appearances, one of his most striking qualities was his enduring optimism. At the time that he entered the White House, self-doubt and pessimism had practically paralyzed our Nation and most Americans saw no end in sight to soaring inflation, economic stagnation and the cold war.

Though he had a realistic view of the challenges that faced the United States, REAGAN believed in us. He knew that free individuals have immense potential for good, and he knew the strength of our American system of free enterprise and self-government. His can-do spirit infused our country and brought a renewed sense of hope and opportunity to those who had nearly forgotten what America stands for.

Fundamentally, RONALD REAGAN trusted us. He trusted that Americans knew how to spend the money they earn better than the Federal Government does. He trusted that, once barriers to private enterprise and economic growth were lifted, American creativity and drive would bring our economy and jobs back. He trusted American resolve in defense of liberty. And he trusted people enough to speak plainly with them about his beliefs and intentions.

President REAGAN's words carried weight because we knew he meant what he said—and the Soviets and the rest of the world knew it too. He was not a poll watcher. He was a man of conviction—a man with a clear philosophy that guided his actions. This philosophy was rooted in a love of freedom and a deep faith in God.

Speaking to students at Moscow State University on May 31, 1988, RONALD REAGAN said:

> Democracy is less a system of government than it is a system to keep government limited, unintrusive: A system of constraints on power to keep politics and government secondary to the important things in life, the true sources of value found only in family and faith.

Imagine what it must have been like for him to bring this message to the heart of an empire where government had for decades superceded individual rights. RONALD REAGAN's commitment to actually winning the cold war, his determination to secure "peace through strength," and his recognition that communism is a bankrupt, immoral ideology were essential to ending the Soviet threat and liberating the Eastern bloc nations and their people.

When you consider the countless individuals who owe their freedom in part to RONALD REAGAN's leadership and the many Americans who today have close friends or family with whom they have reunited in areas formerly off-limits—who had been shut away behind the Iron Curtain—you get a sense of why so many across the world feel a personal connection with RONALD REAGAN.

On top of all his achievements, beyond all that RONALD REAGAN did to rejuvenate our economy, win the cold war, and renew our country's sense of purpose and optimism, there was the man himself. He had great confidence in America's founding values as well as an excellent sense of humor. And he succeeded in raising the level of discourse in our political arena. People might have disagreed with him on policy decisions, and his opponents in Congress argued fiercely with him, but at the end of the day they respected one another. It was a time of greater civility in politics, and we should strive to recapture that.

We look to RONALD REAGAN's example as an inspiration today and express once more the thanks of a very grateful Nation.

Hon. Martin T. Meehan

OF MASSACHUSETTS

Mr. Speaker, this week America is united in mourning for President RONALD REAGAN.

President REAGAN will be remembered as a great optimist who helped convince America to believe in itself again.

He believed that the cold war would end and the Berlin Wall would fall during his lifetime. And he was right. His words inspired people living behind the Iron Curtain to believe that freedom was attainable.

RONALD REAGAN was a loyal Republican but an American first. With his profound personal decency and disarming sense of humor, he rose above the kind of bitter partisanship that infects American politics today.

Personal attacks were below him. He was a patriot and a man of integrity—and he never questioned the patriotism or integrity of others.

Our politics were polarized then as they are now. But President REAGAN knew how to compromise and get things done for the American people.

The Speaker of the House during the first 6 years of his Presidency was Tip O'Neill of Massachusetts. Speaker O'Neill was a staunch Democrat with a very different vision for government, and a great leader in his own right.

Working across party lines, President REAGAN and Speaker O'Neill passed reforms to preserve and strengthen Social Security. They enacted sweeping tax reform to close tax loopholes and lower marginal rates.

As we mourn and honor President REAGAN, this Congress should pledge to follow in his example.

Hold firm in your beliefs, but respect those who differ. Compete vigorously at election time, but then go to work for the American people. Stand united in times of sorrow and adversity.

RONALD REAGAN's final accomplishment will endure as one of his most important—bringing attention to the tragedy of Alzheimer's with his eloquent letter to the American people.

One of the best ways to honor him is to rededicate our efforts to find a cure for this terrible disease.

I join my colleagues in honoring the memory of President RONALD REAGAN.

Hon. Chris Cannon

OF UTAH

Mr. Speaker, I rise today to celebrate the life of President RONALD REAGAN.

First, let me extend my condolences to Nancy Reagan and the entire Reagan family for this tremendous loss. But let me also thank Nancy and her family for taking care of the President for all these years. Rest assured the Nation mourns with you today.

When I think of President REAGAN the feeling that stirs within me is hard to put in words. In reflecting on what to say I realized the best way for me to explain my feelings is to explain who I am. Simply, I am a Reaganite!

Being a Reaganite provided me the wonderful opportunity to come to Washington and work in the Reagan administration. I did not come to Washington for a job but I came to Washington to be a foot solider in the Reagan revolution. I had the opportunity to trade in the walking of precincts to walking the halls of his administration. And for this I am forever grateful.

This opportunity allowed me to play a small part in President REAGAN's goal of giving America back to America. As a result of his leadership, we did not hang our heads any longer but rather we raised them up and remembered our moral standing in the world. Through his leadership, a Nation was motivated.

At the time President REAGAN was elected to office, the country was losing faith and confidence in its being. In 1980, the Soviets had invaded Afghanistan, inflation was in double digits, home ownership was near impossible and optimism was nonexistent. By the time his administration ended, the Soviet empire crumbled, inflation's back was broken, home ownership soared and morning dawned in America. With a set of principles, one man who wanted to make a difference set out and changed the world.

But to see President REAGAN's legacy, as George Will stated, one has to see what no longer exists. We no longer see Soviet expansion and aggression, we no longer see the Berlin Wall and we no longer see devastating economic plight. These are testaments to his courage and his ability to communicate his resolve to the Nation.

President REAGAN realized another decade of detente would not protect America and another decade of stagnant economic policies would not free the individual. Through his force of personality and conviction he set about changing our future. And he relegated our worries to the ash heap of history.

President REAGAN pursued policies that resulted in derision and loathing from some. But he had no hesitation in pursuing his goals because he knew what was right. His beliefs were steadfast and unwavering. He set his course and plowed through the skeptics. He was not Teflon. He was Iron.

Being a Reaganite is not solely relegated to a certain place and time or a certain individual. Instead, it is set a set of beliefs. A set of beliefs imbued in many Members of Congress, their staffs and individuals throughout this country. It is a longing to assert and maintain America's rightful place in the world, as the "shining city on the hill."

President REAGAN, thank you for restoring hope in America. It has been "morning in America" since your Presidency.

Hon. Nick J. Rahall II

OF WEST VIRGINIA

Mr. Speaker, President RONALD REAGAN wrote an indelible chapter in America's and in the world's history. As our Country mourns his loss, our prayers go out to Mrs. Reagan and his family, and our future will long hold to the lessons of his public service.

Hon. Jerry F. Costello

OF ILLINOIS

Mr. Speaker, I rise today to pay tribute to President RONALD REAGAN, an Illinois native, as the Nation celebrates his many contributions to the United States and the world. While I did not always agree with him, he always had my admiration and respect for his strong leadership and his dedication to the American people. His relationship with the citizens of this great country may be his ultimate legacy. President REAGAN spoke directly to their hopes and fears and was embraced for his role as the Great Communicator. Above all else, he made us feel good about America again.

From humble beginnings, President REAGAN went on to play a pivotal role in some of the great events of the 20th century, most notably the cold war and eventual fall of the Soviet Union. While never afraid to take a hard line, he was a pragmatic leader who acted without malice, which was evident in the support he received from Democrats. It was this aspect of his leadership that we should all try to replicate.

President REAGAN's impact on American politics was profound, inspiring legions of young people to public service, not unlike what President Kennedy accomplished years before.

Mr. Speaker, RONALD REAGAN loved the United States of America, and he was a stalwart leader in the pursuit of freedom and democracy. President REAGAN had a personal vision for the country that was undeniable and unshakable, and the lines of people waiting to view his casket are a testimony to the fact that he had a tremendous emotional impact on this Nation. I would like to extend my condolences to his wife Nancy and the rest of their family, and I join the rest of America in honoring his dedicated service.

Hon. James A. Leach
OF IOWA

Mr. Speaker, Americans often measure history in Presidential cycles. When we look at the individuals who have served in the White House it is the conjunction of character and circumstance that defines and demarcates administrations.

It would be misguided to suggest that any individual "won" the cold war, but it was RONALD REAGAN's inspiration—"Mr. Gorbachev, tear down this wall!"—that symbolized American resolve. He gave hope to those oppressed and he gave voice to those who stood tall. Communism imploded, largely on his watch.

Domestically, President REAGAN articulated the values of the frontier. "Government is not the solution ... {it} is the problem," he said in his first inaugural address. But he was not a "no government" ideologue. While his administration contrasted in many ways with the social activism of Franklin Roosevelt, he did not favor undoing the New Deal. "How can we love our country and not love our countrymen?" he asked, "and loving them, {not} reach out a hand when they fall ...?"

Reared on the sweeping plains of the Midwest and, later, an adopted westerner, he loved open spaces—of the land and of the mind. He put his faith in freedom.

RONALD REAGAN understood the American character. With the most authentic voice in the history of democratic politics, he spoke to a world hungry for values. He succeeded because his was the voice of American optimism.

Hon. W.J. (Billy) Tauzin
OF LOUISIANA

Mr. Speaker, I share your grief at the passing of former President RONALD REAGAN and join you in remembering his remarkable service to our country.

I was fortunate to have served as a Member of Congress during President REAGAN's 8-year tenure. At the time, I was a member of the democratic Boll Weevils, a group frequently called upon to help President REAGAN with his legislative agenda. I can attest to what some of you know and what others have read or heard about him—he was among the greatest of our Nation's Presidents. He was permanently grounded in principle, so much that no one who worked for him had any doubt about what was expected of him.

President REAGAN is rooted in the essence of our Nation's character. He appealed to our better instincts and was unyielding in his devotion to our country. I was always amazed at the way he appealed to young people. I think it was because they could see the truth in him. Like a grandfather who had seen it all and abandoned the notion of judging us, he preferred to see the goodness in us all. We, in turn, could imagine that goodness leading us to that shining "city on the hill." Those who came later missed the opportunity to encounter true greatness. Those who experienced him will never forget it.

Thank you for your compassionate support in honoring the legacy of our former President RONALD REAGAN.

Hon. William O. Lipinski
OF ILLINOIS

Mr. Speaker, I rise today to pay tribute to the life of the 40th President of the United States, RONALD WILSON REAGAN. President REAGAN was the most courageous, daring and fearless

President that I have had the pleasure of serving with in my 22 years in the U.S. House of Representatives. RONALD WILSON REAGAN was one of the two greatest Presidents of the 20th century. RONALD WILSON REAGAN was one of the most outstanding Presidents in the history of the American Republic. I was a great fan of and on many occasions, a very strong supporter with my vote of President REAGAN.

I will always remember the day when my wife, Rose Marie, and I, met with President REAGAN in the Oval Office. He was as friendly and down-to-earth as the man next door. We had our picture taken with him and asked him to autograph cards with the Presidential seal for each of our children, Laura and Dan, which he did. President REAGAN first wrote the cards out differently for each my daughter and son, but said he should have known better and so he wrote the same greeting for both of them.

It was a great honor to meet President REAGAN and serve with him in the U.S. Government for many, many reasons. But, I believe mainly because he gave back to America its optimism, its pride, its enthusiasm, and its belief in itself. There can be no greater service than that of a President who can render to America these qualities; and for that, President REAGAN truly was one of the greatest Presidents of the United States.

Hon. Ron Paul
OF TEXAS

Mr. Speaker, all Americans mourn the death of President RONALD REAGAN, but those of us who had the opportunity to know President REAGAN are especially saddened. I got to know President REAGAN in 1976 when, as a freshman Congressman, I was one of only four Members of this body to endorse then-Governor REAGAN's primary challenge to President Gerald Ford. I had the privilege of serving as the leader of President REAGAN's Texas delegation at the Republican Convention of 1976, where RONALD REAGAN almost defeated an incumbent President for his party's nomination.

I was one of the millions attracted to RONALD REAGAN by his strong support for limited government and the free market. I felt affinity for a politician who based his conservative philosophy on "... a desire for less government interference or less centralized authority or more individual freedom ..." I wish more of today's conservative leaders based their philosophy on a desire for less government and more freedom.

RONALD REAGAN was one of the most eloquent exponents of the freedom philosophy in modern American politics. One of his greatest achievements is the millions of Americans he helped convert to the freedom philosophy and the many he inspired to become active in the freedom movement. One of the best examples of President REAGAN's rhetorical powers is his first major national political address, "A Time for Choosing." Delivered in 1964 in support of the Presidential campaign of Barry Goldwater, this speech launched RONALD REAGAN's career as both a politician and a leader of the conservative movement. The following excerpt from that speech illustrates the power of RONALD REAGAN's words and message. Unfortunately, these words are as relevant to our current situation as they were when he delivered them in 1964:

It's time we asked ourselves if we still know the freedoms intended for us by the Founding Fathers. James Madison said, "We base all our experiments on the capacity of mankind for self-government."

This idea? that government was beholden to the people, that it had no other source of power is still the newest, most unique idea in all the long history of man's relation to man. This is the issue of this election: Whether we believe in our capacity for self-government or whether we abandon the American Revolution and confess that a little intellectual elite in a far-distant capital can plan our lives for us better than we can plan them ourselves.

You and I are told we must choose between a left or right, but I suggest there is no such thing as a left or right. There is only an up or down. Up to man's age-old dream—the maximum of individual freedom consistent with order or down to the ant heap of totalitarianism. Regardless of their sincerity, their humanitarian motives, those who would sacrifice freedom for security have embarked on this downward path. Plutarch warned, "The real destroyer of the liberties of the people is he who spreads among them bounties, donations and benefits."

The Founding Fathers knew a government can't control the economy without controlling people. And they knew when a government set out to do that, it must use force and coercion to achieve its purpose. So we have come to a time for choosing.

One of the most direct expressions of RONALD REAGAN's disdain for big government came during a private conversation when we where flying from the White House to Andrews Air Force Base. As the helicopter passed over the monuments, we looked down and he said, "Isn't that beautiful? It's amazing how much terrible stuff comes out of this city when it's that beautiful."

While many associate RONALD REAGAN with unbridled militarism, he was a lifelong opponent of the draft. It is hardly surprising that many of the most persuasive and powerful arguments against conscription came from President REAGAN. One of my favorite REAGAN quotes comes from a 1979 article he wrote for the conservative publication *Human Events* regarding the draft and related "national service" proposals:

> ... it {conscription} rests on the assumption that your kids belong to the state. If we buy that assumption then it is for the state—not for parents, the community, the religious institutions or teachers—to decide who shall have what values and who shall do what work, when, where and how in our society. That assumption isn't a new one. The Nazis thought it was a great idea.

I extend my deepest sympathies to RONALD REAGAN's family and friends, especially his beloved wife Nancy and his children. I also urge my colleagues and all Americans to honor RONALD REAGAN by dedicating themselves to the principles of limited government and individual liberty.

Hon. Xavier Becerra

OF CALIFORNIA

Mr. Speaker, I rise today in solemn remembrance of President RONALD REAGAN. I do not stand alone. All across the country, and the world, we mourn. We remember a strong Governor, President, husband, and father. Let us stand firmly by Mrs. Nancy Reagan and her family, offer our prayers and show our support and appreciation—let us through our actions bring comfort to the Reagan family to help them cope during this difficult time. Little can be said to make this difficult time easier. Given the outpouring of support that this country and his family have received from the world, words are not necessary.

Words are not necessary to honor a man whose popularity stemmed from his ability to communicate. No words I can say today can erase the sorrow and feelings of loss shared by so many communities that he touched throughout his tenure as Governor of my State of California and as the President of our Nation. Even the Great Communicator often relied on actions—not words—to help those who needed it. At a time when the immigrants of our Nation had nowhere to turn, President REAGAN signed the historic Immigration Reform and Control Act, granting hard-working and deserving families legal permanent residence, paving the way for new American citizens, and thus uniting our Nation.

Today, as a united Nation, we stand together as fellow Americans and with the world to mourn the loss of RONALD WILSON REAGAN, 40th President of the United States—the picture of unity communicating our sorrow, remembrance and honor for a leader.

Hon. Michael C. Burgess

OF TEXAS

Mr. Speaker, as we pause to remember the life and service of the late President RONALD REAGAN, no greater testament to his achievements as leader of this Nation exists than the sentiments of gratitude being offered by millions of Americans. It is my great honor to lift up just a handful of the reflections on the passing of President REAGAN made by residents of my congressional district:

> He was a great American; his message was one that still resonates today.
> —The Honorable Jane Nelson,
> Texas Senate.

> I had a chance to tell him how much I wanted him to run for President and that if he did, I promised to work really hard for him. He was just the same up close as you perceived him to be on television. He was very sincere, very nice. When he talked to you, he talked to you. He didn't pay attention to things going on around him; you had his attention. The world is certainly a better place because of RONALD REAGAN being here and serving as the President of the United States.

I'm sad we lost him, but it's wonderful he's now receiving his just rewards.

—The Honorable Mary Horn,
Denton County, Texas.

President REAGAN made us feel good again about being Americans, and not just being proud of our country, but really invoking that patriotic spirit again. We've lost a great, great man.

—Dianne Edmondson,
Chair, Denton County GOP.

I remember that while REAGAN was the oldest elected President, what sticks in my mind was the way he connected to young people. We had been through a decade of young people being disconnected with taking pride in America, and he lit that spark again.

—The Honorable Myra Crownover,
Texas House of Representatives.

He will always be remembered as the architect of the policies that ended the cold war—"peace through strength." He, more than anyone else, was directly responsible for giving us the possibility of the world living in peace: He ended the cold war, ended the unspoken hostilities between the United States and Russia, and brought an end to the Soviet domination in Eastern Europe. He unleashed the power of the American economy. Yes, it cost money to defeat the Soviet Union; it cost money to defeat Soviet tyranny. Was it worth it in the long run? You bet it was.

Hon. Rodney P. Frelinghuysen

OF NEW JERSEY

Mr. Speaker, I rise to remember the life and legacy of RONALD REAGAN.

This past weekend, it was fitting, and in some ways almost proper, that we paid tribute to the brave young soldiers of D-day and simultaneously remembered the life and service of President RONALD REAGAN. Like those soldiers who sacrificed on Normandy Beach, REAGAN inspired a country at a critical time in our Nation's history through his optimism and advocacy for the ideals of democracy, freedom and love of liberty.

He helped end the cold war, confronted the curse of communism, rebuilt American self-confidence and our Armed Forces, and above all, made America a standard bearer for freedom and justice.

Many of our children are not old enough to remember the dangers that stood before us at the height of the cold war or how President REAGAN's resolve helped end it.

Still, over the next few days, maybe even weeks, and certainly in the history books to be written, they will learn, as will our children's children, about who REAGAN was and what he did for America.

Like so many of us, I continue to read with interest about the life and times of our former President. One recent newspaper column touched me and I would like to share just a few lines of that with my colleagues.

The columnist wrote:

> What an era his was. What a life he lived. He changed history for the better and was modest about it. He didn't bray about his accomplishments but saw them as the work of the American people.

Mr. Speaker, this is the sign of a leader. We are a grateful Nation for his good humor and inspiration.

Thank you Mr. President—for your service; for your optimism; and for your belief and commitment to doing what was right for America.

Our thoughts and prayers remain with the Reagan family during this time of mourning.

Hon. Harold E. Ford, Jr.

OF TENNESSEE

Mr. Speaker, President REAGAN led the Nation with resolve and courage. He showed these same qualities in his battle against Alzheimer's disease.

President REAGAN will be remembered for many things—being a great communicator, a devoted husband and an unflinching patriot.

But I will remember him most for reminding America that when we are at our best, very little can deter or defeat us. God bless you Mr. President and thank you for your service to our country.

Hon. Bart Stupak

OF MICHIGAN

Mr. Speaker, President RONALD REAGAN was an American icon. He's the President who won the cold war. And he'll always be remembered for his eternal optimism, his strength, great wit and charm.

Even when he disagreed with Democrats, he was respected for the honesty of his beliefs and the dedication he displayed in pursuing them. He taught us the difference between strong beliefs and bitter partisanship. He lived by the noble idea that at the end of the day Democrats and Republicans were simply Americans and friends. I wish we had more of that today.

We should be inspired by this 40th American President's patriotism and devotion to our country. And we should remember his faith, his optimism and his unwavering commitment to his convictions as we do the work of the American people.

Hon. Tom Udall

OF NEW MEXICO

Mr. Speaker, this week our Nation mourns the death of RONALD WILSON REAGAN, the 40th President of the United States. It has been stated in many of the newspaper and television commentaries that he was one of the more complex figures of the 20th century. As with all our major political leaders, he had his share of triumphs and failures.

RONALD REAGAN's irrepressible spirit and his conception of America as a "shining city on the hill" engendered a sense of renewal in America. Indeed, his optimism in our Nation and her people was as genuine as the man himself. Simply put, RONALD REAGAN was a great American and a President who honored the office and considered it a privilege to serve.

Without question, President REAGAN represented the best of civility in American politics and the finest traditions of standing up for what you believe in. Even during the most intense political showdowns, he and former House Speaker Tip O'Neill could always sit down together after the day was done, as friends and fellow Americans. It was an era of bipartisan cooperation that seems, unfortunately, to have waned in recent years.

President REAGAN's legacy will forever be his vision which played a role in bringing about an ultimate end to the cold war, as well as his drive to foster liberty and democracy where previously only tyranny had thrived. Former Soviet President Mikhail Gorbachev says he believes his dialog with President REAGAN "kick-started the process which ultimately put an end to the cold war."

President REAGAN also understood the art of political compromise. He followed his 1981 tax cut with two large tax increases. In fact, no peacetime President raised taxes so much on so many people. This is not a criticism: The lesson of those increases tells you a lot about what was just with President REAGAN's leadership. President REAGAN, confronted with evidence that his tax cuts were fiscally irresponsible, changed course. His actions in this area contrast dramatically with today's Washington.

Mr. Speaker, in my opinion, one of RONALD REAGAN's greatest legacies is focusing attention on the disease that took his life—Alzheimer's. People are now receiving earlier diagnoses and better treatments for the incurable brain-wasting disease partly because he supported Alzheimer's research as President, and more importantly, because he went public with his diagnosis in 1994, increasing awareness of the need for more research.

As her husband's health declined, former First Lady Nancy Reagan spearheaded public awareness campaigns and described what it was like to be a caretaker for an Alzheimer's patient, which she referred to as "the long goodbye." She continued to publicly advocate for stem cell research as a way to help others with the disease.

Doctors now are better able to diagnose the disease early, and provide patients with drugs and other measures to delay its progression. I pledge to do everything possible to help fight the plight of Alzheimer's disease. I challenge every Member of this body to respond to Mrs. Reagan's plea to do more for life-saving research.

RONALD REAGAN was of a kind and gracious mind, and at the same time, a man of grit, determination and leadership. He served his country the way he lived his life.

My thoughts and prayers go out to his extraordinary wife Nancy and his children, Patti Davis, Ron Prescott Reagan, and Michael Reagan. I hope it is a consolation to the entire Reagan family that so many people grieve their loss and are thinking of them during this difficult time.

Hon. Gary G. Miller

OF CALIFORNIA

Mr. Speaker, President RONALD REAGAN will be remembered in the annals of history as one of the greatest leaders of the United States. His deeds and words will echo in time as the foundation for a smaller, more efficient government, a fairer tax system and the liberation of millions of oppressed people throughout the world.

RONALD REAGAN was known as the Great Communicator. His words brought hope to those in need, comfort to those who suffered and optimism to an entire Nation trampled by economic and governmental insecurity. Yet President REAGAN's ability to communicate went beyond the words that he spoke. He reached out to the Nation and the world using not only his voice, but his strength of spirit and supreme character.

President REAGAN's passing is mourned by each of us. But his legacy will continue through the ideals he aspired for America. A grateful Nation thanks RONALD REAGAN, a true American hero.

Hon. C.W. Bill Young

OF FLORIDA

Mr. Speaker, on behalf of myself and the people of the 10th Congressional District of Florida whom I have the privilege to represent here in the U.S. Congress, I rise in support of this resolution to pay tribute to the life of President RONALD REAGAN and to express condolences to his family.

President REAGAN was a true American patriot who always kept life's priorities—God, country, and family—in order. He assumed the Presidency at a time when Americans were being held hostage in Iran, our fighting forces were fraying around the edges, and raging inflation and interest rates were stifling our economy, sending our Nation into the turmoil of recession, and driving our government deeper and deeper into debt.

Beginning with his swearing in as the 40th President of the United States, President REAGAN restored in the American people a feeling of pride and patriotism that had been lost in the late seventies. The hostages were brought home, the morale of our fighting forces rose, and the economy began to rebound.

People flew the American flag with pride again. The United States resumed its leadership role in protecting freedom and peace around the world and at the pinnacle of the world economy. He stared down communist leaders throughout the world and set the stage for its fall in the Soviet Union and throughout Eastern Europe. He reduced the world's supply of nuclear weapons and allowed democracy to flourish again in our hemisphere and eventually in the former Soviet states.

He battled Congress to reduce taxes to allow the American people to keep more of their hard-earned money and to reduce the size and scope of the government programs and bureaucracy. He also ensured the long-term security of the Social Security Trust Fund by leading a bipartisan legislative effort to preserve and protect the retirement benefits of workers long into the 21st century.

President REAGAN was our Nation's leading cheerleader and consoler. He used his wit and humor to entertain and to drive home an important point. He led a Nation in mourning when we lost the *Challenger* crew and our Marines in Lebanon. Throughout his 8 years in office we laughed together and we cried together. In the end though, we all gained a renewed sense of pride in being Americans.

He taught us the value of the simple phrases of "peace through strength" and "trust but verify" and he shared with all of us his simple vision of a Nation where we would be the "shining city on a hill."

The United States and the world are better places today because of RONALD REAGAN's service not only as President of our great country, but as a true patriot. He was a good man whose love and commitment to his wife Nancy was an inspiration to us all.

Perhaps the greatest testament to his strength of personality, of character, and of leadership is the fact that even in death he can make us feel good about ourselves as individuals and as a Nation. You can feel the pride of our Nation surge yet again as we reflect on his life and times.

Mr. Speaker, we all will recall that President REAGAN would end his conversations with America by saying "God bless America." This week, Mr. Speaker, our Nation and the world say "God bless RONALD REAGAN." Thank you for your lifetime of reminding us to always take pride in living in the greatest Nation in the world.

Hon. Betty McCollum

OF MINNESOTA

Mr. Speaker, today as this House honors the life of the 40th President of the United States, RONALD REAGAN, we remember both the man and the public servant. As President REAGAN lies in state under the dome of this Capitol, the American people reflect on a man of optimism, a leader committed to freedom and a citizen who personified the American spirit of boundless ambition and achievement.

President REAGAN lived a life unlike any other American President. A sports broadcaster, a movie star and a television personality, President REAGAN entertained Americans with his charm, smile and warmth. He combined the skills of an actor with the determination of a pioneer to transform public life as he entered the political realm in California and finally was elected by the American people to the White House.

As President of the United States, RONALD REAGAN won two large election victories in 1980 and 1984 to set this Nation on a course to transform our economy and confront communism.

The outcomes and consequences of his policies will be interpreted by historians for years to come, but there is no doubt President REAGAN motivated a new generation of conservatives to join his crusade as well as a generation of progressives to unite in pursuit of an alternative path of action.

Our State of Minnesota had a unique relationship with President REAGAN. Minnesota was the only State in the Union to never give President REAGAN an electoral victory. Minnesotans stood twice with our homegrown son, but we respected the President, his skills as a communicator and his determination to elevate the American spirit.

President REAGAN lived a truly American life and, in his final years, stood hand in hand with Mrs. Reagan to encounter Alzheimer's with dignity and grace. The life of President REAGAN the leader and RONALD REAGAN the man will be remembered, honored and celebrated this week by Congress, the American people and people in nations around the world.

On behalf of the families of Minnesota's Fourth Congressional District, we extend our prayers and sincerest condolences to Mrs. Nancy Reagan, her children and all of the family and friends of President REAGAN.

Hon. Pete Sessions

OF TEXAS

Mr. Speaker, RONALD WILSON REAGAN first entered into our national consciousness in 1964, asking Americans to make a choice in the face of the growing threat of socialism both at home and abroad. We know him as the eternal optimist, the Great Communicator, and the man who maintained that communism would surely fall aside onto the "ash heap of history."

I had the personal privilege of knowing President REAGAN when my father, Judge William S. Sessions, served as Director of the FBI during his administration. Like many of my generation, I was inspired by the optimism of RONALD REAGAN, a leader who never lacked the courage and the principle to do what he felt was right even in the face of great obstacles. President REAGAN saw the world in black and white, whether it was confronting the programs of the "Great Society" as the beginnings of a new "undemocratic socialism" or chiding the actions of the evil empire in Eastern Europe.

This moral clarity was the hallmark of his Presidency. RONALD REAGAN came in to office with three core principles and an agenda by which to implement them. He believed that the government was too big, that it taxed too much, and that the Soviet Union was an evil empire, getting away with atrocities across the world. From the first day of his Presidency, REAGAN began to move systematically toward enacting his campaign promises, and, in so doing, he rejuvenated the American spirit.

America is forever indebted to this President whose resolve and determination to pursue "peace through strength" helped to end the cold war and ensured that, as the President himself said, "America's best days are yet to come. Our proudest moments are yet to be. Our most glorious achievements are just ahead." Thank you, President REAGAN. May God bless you as you enter your rest in that shining city.

Hon. Lois Capps

OF CALIFORNIA

Mr. Speaker, I rise today in support of H. Res. 664 honoring the late Honorable RONALD WILSON REAGAN. I was proud to add my name as an original co-sponsor of this resolution.

The former President was devoted to his country and will long be remembered for his service to America. My heart goes out to his family during this time of loss.

President REAGAN was also a longtime member of our Santa Barbara community. Santa Barbara County was home to the spectacular mountaintop ranch the former President and First Lady affectionately referred to as the "Western White House."

President REAGAN carried with him traits characteristic of California's Central Coast—a sunny disposition and optimistic outlook—to Washington and to the world. His "morning in America" slogan changed the tone of politics in our Nation's Capital and enabled him to work in a constructive bipartisan manner on a number of important issues.

The Reagans should also be commended for the strength and honesty they demonstrated during their long struggle with Alzheimer's. Their example brought much needed attention to the challenges facing millions of American families that deal with this affliction every day.

And their ongoing commitment to this disease is demonstrated at the various Alzheimer's research, awareness, and prevention efforts around the country. On the Central Coast, for example, the Ronald and Nancy Reagan Family Fund provides grants for respite care services for Alzheimer's patients in Santa Barbara County.

Today I join my colleagues in celebrating the service of the late President RONALD REAGAN. The best honor we can bestow upon him is to carry on his optimistic spirit and faith in the American people for generations to come. That is what RONALD REAGAN—a great American and great Californian—would have wanted.

Hon. Michael H. Michaud

OF MAINE

Mr. Speaker, I rise to honor the life of President RONALD WILSON REAGAN and to extend my condolences to the entire Reagan family.

Regardless of political affiliation, I think we can all agree that President REAGAN was a tireless public servant who cared a great deal about this country. Leading our country during a difficult period, President REAGAN earned the respect of many throughout the world—a respect that has become all the more evident since his passing on Saturday.

As this body and our Nation remembers the late President throughout the week, we would be remiss not to reflect upon the disease with which he was afflicted—Alzheimer's.

President REAGAN's leadership extended to the fight against Alzheimer's beginning in 1983, when he designated November as National Alzheimer's Disease Month, and continuing in 1994 when he announced that he was affected by the disease. In 1995 he and his wife Nancy lent their name to create the Alzheimer's Association's Ronald and Nancy Reagan Research Institute.

As was evident in President REAGAN's battle with the disease, Alzheimer's does not discriminate: It afflicts the rich and the poor, the famous and the regular hard-working citizen alike. Four and a half million Americans live with Alzheimer's, and it is the fourth leading killer of older Americans. It is a progressive disease that robs many of precious memories and beautiful relationships.

With an aging baby boom generation, our country will soon see a sharp increase in those affected by Alzheimer's. The time to act is now. As a member of the Congressional Task Force on Alzheimer's Disease, I urge my colleagues to renew our efforts to battle this disease. I can think of no better tribute to President REAGAN than to join together to fight the disease that afflicted him in his later years.

Hon. Henry Bonilla

OF TEXAS

Mr. Speaker, I rise to honor the life and legacy of President RONALD WILSON REAGAN. As we mourn this great loss we reflect on the many ways our country is stronger, freer and more prosperous as a result of President REAGAN's fearless leadership.

A firm believer in lower taxes, sound fiscal policies and reduced regulation, President REAGAN launched the boldest economic plan since Franklin Roosevelt's New Deal. As a result of his leadership and tenacity, the Federal Tax Code was greatly simplified and taxes were reduced, ushering in the restoration of prosperity. He encouraged people to have confidence in their Nation and trust that things really were getting better—a sentiment that economic and social indicators would eventually confirm. In fact, President REAGAN's reforms led to the longest period of peacetime growth in U.S. history.

President REAGAN's leadership also sparked a movement against drugs which resulted in dramatic declines in illicit drug use in America and around the world. President REAGAN was committed to reversing the permissive attitudes of the sixties and seventies that illegal drug use was glamorous, harmless and victimless. President REAGAN inspired and convinced the Nation that the drug problem was not hopeless and could be solved. As a result of his leadership, the Nation spoke with one voice in denouncing drug use. Largely due to his efforts, illicit drug use was cut in half and crime, drug-related hospital admissions and highway deaths declined.

President REAGAN restored America's sense of optimism and patriotism. A true believer in the American dream, he proclaimed America as a place where everyone can rise as high and as far as his ability will take him, and referred to his own humble beginnings as proof. He taught all Americans and newly liberated people across the globe that hard work and faith in God could result in prosperity and a better outlook for tomorrow.

President REAGAN will perhaps be most remembered for his efforts to stomp out communism worldwide and end the cold war. President REAGAN simply refused to accept communism's claim to moral superiority. From the beginning of his Presidency, REAGAN realized that America could not afford passiveness or weakness in the face of Soviet defiance and escalating nuclear threats. President REAGAN recognized that peace could only be achieved through strength and diligently worked to restore faith in our military and a sense of American pride in the efforts of our servicemen and women. Efforts to restore our military superiority were coupled with a willingness to dialog and a sincere desire to negotiate an end to the nuclear arms race. President REAGAN was able to negotiate a treaty with the Soviet Union to launch the process of real arms reduction. His efforts eventually led to the destruction of the Berlin Wall, the fall of communism and the end of the cold war. President REAGAN's leadership ushered in a new era of freedom and democracy, not only in the Soviet Union, but throughout the world.

President REAGAN planted democracy in regions of the world that have never tasted the joys of freedom. He swept up a downtrodden America with little response to or respect for leadership and reenergized their faith in freedom, the Presidency, and our military. President REAGAN's vision and convictions brought all Americans together, raised our morale and once again made us the proudest citizens in the world. He will be remembered not only in the minds of Americans, but in our hearts as well.

Hon. Ralph Regula
OF OHIO

Mr. Speaker, President RONALD REAGAN was a warm thoughtful leader who governed by the golden rule of caring for others. Many speakers have paid eloquent tribute to his role as both a world leader and a best friend of the American people. Because of our shared love of land I developed a personal relationship with President REAGAN that I will always cherish.

Hon. Jo Bonner
OF ALABAMA

Mr. Speaker, I rise today to honor the memory of a great leader, a great man, and a great American. When President RONALD WILSON REAGAN passed away on June 5, 2004, his death brought more than an end to his valiant 10-year struggle against Alzheimer's disease. It brought an end to one of the brightest and most optimistic periods in American history.

While President REAGAN had been out of the public eye and under the loving care of his beloved wife, Nancy, for over a decade, he was never far from our minds or our hearts. During these past 10 years, while he was traveling down the road into the sunset of his life, we have all had the opportunity to consider his true greatness and his many achievements. We have all come to understand that he was more than just our President and the most powerful man in the world; he was, instead, the personification of—and the symbol for—the boundless potential possible in this country.

From Dixon, IL, to Detroit, MI, from Washington, DC, to Los Angeles, CA, and at all points in between, men and women everywhere recognize President REAGAN for what he truly was: a gifted leader and a compassionate American with a vision for our future and an unwavering belief in the spirit and goodness of mankind.

To say that RONALD REAGAN was an example of the American dream would be an understatement. RONALD REAGAN was the American dream, the product of a poor middle class family who, as the result of his own intelligence, determination and strong personality, was able to attend college, enjoy a successful career in broadcasting and motion pictures, and eventually rise to the position of Governor of California.

For most, that in and of itself would be a remarkable career. But President REAGAN did not stop there. Rather, he continued to focus on what he saw as a need for a strong leader in the White House, someone who could work with a divided Congress and an American public still reeling from the political and economic crises of the seventies to restore this Nation to its position as the "shining city on the hill."

During his 8 years in office, he did just that. The Reagan revolution, as it came to be known, provided the impetus for significant changes here at home and around the world. The economy in this country which had been in steep decline for a number of years righted itself and enjoyed a strong period of growth for the next 9 years. The cold war was brought to an end, communism in many countries ultimately collapsed, and a whole new generation of men, women, and children around the world were able to enjoy a new life free from the fear of oppression.

Perhaps his greatest accomplishment, however, was in giving Americans a new sense of hope and pride. President REAGAN restored a strong sense of optimism and hopefulness to this country, and made everyone feel proud that they could once again say with assurance and determination, "I am an American."

Mr. Speaker, just as our Nation paused last week to remember and reflect on this good man and great leader, let us, as a Nation, remember President RONALD REAGAN in the same way that he is remembered by his family: a man full of love, laughter, and life, someone full of boundless optimism and faith, and someone who always believed that America's best days are indeed ahead.

Our country—indeed, our world—has been blessed that we were able to share in a small way in the tremendous life he led. May we never forget the lessons he taught us or the leadership he displayed, and may we continue to keep Mrs. Reagan and the entire Reagan family foremost in our thoughts and prayers.

Hon. Michael N. Castle

OF DELAWARE

Mr. Speaker, I rise today to pay tribute to President RONALD REAGAN. We all join together this week to mourn his passage, but more important to celebrate his life. President REAGAN meant many things to many people in the United States and throughout the world. Put simply, the world is a better place because RONALD REAGAN lived. From his days as an actor and motivational speaker to his time as Governor and President to his final days on his California ranch, RONALD REAGAN was a true gentleman who impacted the lives of those around him.

RONALD REAGAN was sworn in as the 40th President of the United States the day American hostages were released from Iran—a poignant beginning to the challenges which would lie ahead. As President, he survived an attack on his life and a battle with colon cancer; he fought communism; he guided the American people through rough economic times and uncertain international struggles; he made history in nominating the first woman to serve on the U.S. Supreme Court; and led Americans through the tragedy of the space shuttle *Challenger*.

But to limit our descriptions of President REAGAN to the milestones in his Presidency would be incomplete. His most impressive qualities are the intangibles that are felt but hard to describe.

So many Americans connected with President REAGAN on a personal level. His ability to communicate was unparalleled. "Larger than life" was never a phrase used to describe RONALD REAGAN—not because he couldn't have been, but because he didn't want to be. He truly operated as a man of the people.

My first term as Governor of Delaware overlapped with his second term as President of the United States. I had the honor and privilege of working with President REAGAN on what I see as one of his greatest landmark accomplishments—welfare reform. The empathy he felt for the American people and the challenges they faced in trying to make ends meet were represented in this landmark legislation. He epitomized a leader who didn't give hand-outs—but a hand up.

The optimism he felt for every American, our Nation and the world was evident to all. His "glass half full" mentality guided us through times of peace and times of uncertainty; through the end of the cold war and rough economic times. No matter what our Nation faced, President REAGAN's sense of patriotism, togetherness and hope for the future was infectious.

His love of country made us believe that America was blessed to do great things for many people. Sadly, this was probably best communicated in what has come to be known as his "Letter to the American People" when he told the world he was diagnosed with Alzheimer's disease, when he wrote:

> I now begin this journey that will lead me into the sunset of my life. I know that for America there will always be a bright dawn ahead.

Everything he did, he did with grace. He will be remembered—even by those who may have disagreed with him—with respect for his willingness to work together and negotiate, with humor. He and Democratic Speaker Tip O'Neill used to joke that we are "all friends after 6 p.m." meaning that at the end of the day, politics was put aside and friendships could grow.

I like to think of President REAGAN as a flexible conservative, one who was willing to listen to all sides of an argument, even if he didn't agree, for the chance that he might learn something new or understand a different angle. He didn't pretend to be an expert on all issues, and that is why so many politicians and the American people respected him. He wanted to turn the issue on all sides to see if there were any new approaches that could be taken. Yet at the same time, he was deeply rooted in his beliefs of smaller government, lower taxes and personal responsibility—which continue to guide the Republican Party today.

President REAGAN is considered the modern day father of the Republican Party and his long legacy and sunny optimistic spirit will live on in all Americans. And as we all gather today to celebrate the man who meant so much to our country, I would like to invoke the words he used in bidding goodbye to the passengers on the space shuttle *Challenger*:

> We will never forget them, nor the last time we saw them, this morning, as they prepared for their journey and waved good-bye and "slipped the surly bonds of earth" to "touch the face of God."

The GIPPER, the Great Communicator, the flexible conservative and the great conciliator has gone home. But his legacy will never be forgotten.

Hon. Earl Pomeroy

OF NORTH DAKOTA

Mr. Speaker, my thoughts and prayers go out to Mrs. Reagan and her family as our Nation mourns the loss of President REAGAN.

Our Nation has lost a leader. President REAGAN inspired Americans to a higher purpose. He believed, and led all Americans to believe, that our country could be the "shining city on the hill." It was his spirit and faith in American values that helped reinforce America's faith in itself.

I was serving in the North Dakota Legislature on the day President REAGAN was shot. I remember the somber atmosphere and deep concern from Republicans and Democrats alike as legislators gathered around a television anxiously awaiting word on the President's condition. With characteristic optimism, President REAGAN went on to recover from his wounds and continue to lead the Nation as our President.

President REAGAN's passing brings us sadness at the loss of an American leader, but reminds all of us of his lasting legacy of service to our Nation.

ADJOURNING AS FURTHER MARK OF RESPECT TO THE MEMORY OF THE LATE HONORABLE RONALD WILSON REAGAN, FORMER PRESIDENT OF THE UNITED STATES

Mr. DeLAY. Mr. Speaker, I ask unanimous consent that when the House adjourns pursuant to Senate Concurrent Resolution 116, it do so as a further mark of respect to the memory of the late Honorable RONALD WILSON REAGAN, the former President of the United States.

The SPEAKER pro tempore. Is there objection to the request of the gentleman from Texas?

There was no objection.

ADJOURNMENT

Mr. DeLAY. Mr. Speaker, I move that the House do now adjourn.

The motion was agreed to.

THE SPEAKER pro tempore. Accordingly, pursuant to Senate Concurrent Resolution 116, the 108th Congress, the House stands adjourned until 12:30 p.m. on Monday, June 14, 2004, for morning hour debates; and pursuant to the order of the House of today, it does so as a further mark of respect to the memory of the late Honorable RONALD WILSON REAGAN, the former President of the United States.

Thereupon (at 3 o'clock and 6 minutes p.m.), pursuant to Senate Concurrent Resolution 116, the House adjourned until Monday, June 14, 2004, at 12:30 p.m., for morning hour debates, and pursuant to the order of the House of today as a further mark of respect to the memory of the late Honorable RONALD WILSON REAGAN, former President of the United States.

Memorial Tributes in the House of Representatives 159

Monday, June 14, 2004

APPOINTMENT OF MEMBERS TO ATTEND THE FUNERAL OF THE LATE HONORABLE RONALD WILSON REAGAN, FORMER PRESIDENT OF THE UNITED STATES

The SPEAKER pro tempore. Pursuant to House Resolution 663, and the order of the House of December 8, 2003, the Speaker appointed himself and the entire membership of the House to attend the funeral services for former President RONALD WILSON REAGAN held Wednesday, June 9, 2004, in the rotunda of the Capitol and Friday, June 11, 2004, at the Washington National Cathedral.

Wednesday, June 16, 2004

Hon. Robert Menendez

OF NEW JERSEY

Mr. Speaker, today I am proud to be joining Senators Bond and Mikulski, and my House colleagues, Representatives Chris Smith and Ed Markey, in introducing the RONALD REAGAN Alzheimer's Breakthrough Act of 2004. This legislation will significantly increase our government's investment in Alzheimer's disease research and patient and caregiver support initiatives.

As a son whose mother suffers from Alzheimer's, I know personally the sacrifice—both financially and emotionally—of families caring for a parent with this horrific disease. It is the story of so many Hispanics in this Nation—a story of so many Americans. My family fled Cuba to come to find freedom in the United States. My mother worked her entire life as a seamstress in the factories of New Jersey. She spends half of her Social Security check on prescription drugs. If it was not for my sister and me, she would not live with the dignity she deserves.

Because of my personal experience with Alzheimer's, I have always admired Nancy and RONALD REAGAN's strength and perseverance throughout the President's battle with this heart-wrenching and devastating illness. By having gone public, RONALD REAGAN increased awareness of this debilitating disease, providing hope, comfort, and companionship to 4.5 million Americans living with Alzheimer's today. We feel there is no more fitting tribute to honor President REAGAN's memory than to join together in a bipartisan manner and support the RONALD REAGAN Alzheimer's Breakthrough Act.

Today, Alzheimer's disease is the most common cause of dementia in older people. One in 10 people over 65 and nearly half those over 85, suffer from Alzheimer's disease. And with the aging of our population, we can expect those numbers to increase. In fact, unless scientific research finds a way to prevent or cure the disease, it is estimated that between 11.3 and 16 million people in the United States will have Alzheimer's disease by the middle of the 21st century.

Just a few weeks ago, I, along with the Alzheimer's Association, released a report that focuses on the impact of Alzheimer's on Hispanics. The report predicts that, because Hispanics are the fastest growing population in the country and have the greatest life expectancy of any ethnic group, the community will experience a sixfold increase in the disease by 2050. In numbers, this means that 1.3 million Hispanics will have Alzheimer's disease by 2050, compared to fewer than 200,000 currently living with the disease.

The legislation introduced today will increase the National Institutes of Health funding to $1.4 billion a year so we can continue to advance our ability to one day prevent, treat, and ultimately cure this disease. This increase is necessary if we are going to be serious about reducing both the physical and economic costs of Alzheimer's. According to experts, delaying the onset and progression of Alzheimer's for even 5 years could save as much as $50 billion in annual health care costs. Alzheimer's costs American businesses more than $36.5 billion annually due to lost productivity of employees who are caregivers and the health care costs associated with the disease.

Alzheimer's is a far-reaching disease and a serious strain on families because it not only affects families' lives, jobs, and finances, but also their mental and physical well-being. In response, this legislation provides a tax credit of up to $3,000 to help pay the expenses of families who care for loved ones with long-term care needs.

In addition, this bill increases authorization levels for a series of programs to help families care for their loved ones; increases funding levels for research initiatives focused on prevention and care; and authorizes funding for a public education campaign to inform the public about prevention techniques.

Congress needs to make wise investments on behalf of the American people. Alzheimer's research is one of those important and critical investments we must make now, so that future generations of Americans will have the medical resources and knowledge to cope with the challenge of caring for a parent, family member, or friend living with this disease. By making this investment today, it is my hope that one day soon a cure will be found so Alzheimer's will be a part of medical history instead of a family's reality.

Thursday, June 17, 2004

Hon. Henry Bonilla

OF TEXAS

Mr. Speaker, I ask to enter the following tribute recognizing President and Mrs. Reagan's involvement in the war on drugs into the *Congressional Record*.

A TRIBUTE: PRESIDENT & MRS. RONALD REAGAN'S LEADERSHIP IN THE WAR ON DRUGS

We, representing countless parents. community volunteers, civic leaders, business leaders, physicians, teachers, church leaders, policy makers, law enforcement officers, media representatives, and youth from across America, want to express our deepest gratitude to President and Mrs. REAGAN for their extraordinary leadership in the battle against drugs and for saving the lives of so many children through drug prevention. Together they encouraged and supported a nationwide effort to reduce the demand for drugs by increasing Americans' knowledge and changing their attitudes and behavior. They inspired us with hope, knowledge, and conviction. The result was a dramatic turn around in illicit drug use in America, and thus lives were saved, health care costs were reduced, crime was reduced, and innovative strategies and scientific research were developed to enhance drug abuse treatment, prevent AIDS, and other drug-related social problems. Our nation and the world owe them a tremendous debt. We recommit ourselves to continuing in this noble fight to protect our children from the nightmare of drugs and to carry forward the message of prevention with hope and optimism.

Milestones of the Reagan legacy include: Raising the drinking age throughout the country from 18 to 21. The workplace drug prevention program including federal drug testing and standards. Nancy Reagan's Just Say No campaign that ratified and promoted the Parents' Movement. These programs brought about a dramatic fall in illegal drug abuse throughout the nation after two decades of rising levels with the peak coming in 1978 and the bottom in 1991. President REAGAN's leadership was a key in this element in this historic progress.

Robert L. DuPont, MD, First Director of National Institute on Drug Abuse, President of the Institute for Behavior and Health, Inc., Maryland.
Joyce Nalepka, Drug Free Kids: America's Challenge, former President of Nancy Reagan's National Federation of Parents for Drug Free Youth, Silver Spring, Maryland.
Edward Jacobs, MD, FAAP, Everett Clinic, Everett, Washington.
Theresa Costello, Philadelphia, Pennsylvania.
Daniel Bent, Fair Mediation, Honolulu, Hawaii.
Sue Rusche, National Families in Action, Atlanta, Georgia.
Eric Voth, MD, FACP, Chairman, Institute on Global Drug Policy, Topeka, Kansas.
Michelle Voth, Kansas Family Partnership, Topeka, Kansas.
David Evans, Esq., Drug Free Schools Coalition, Flemington, New Jersey.
Calvina Fay, Executive Director, Drug Free America Foundation, Inc., St. Petersburg, Florida.
Peggy Sapp, National Family Partnership, Miami, Florida.
Steven Steiner, DAMMAD, Tioga Center, New York.
Steven Steiner, Barton, New York.
Rebecca Hobson, Richton, Mississippi.
Brenda Truelove, Gainesville, Georgia.

Karen Dewease, Petal, Mississippi.
Julie Steiner, Barton, New York.
Mikki Howard, Austin, Indiana.
Martha McWhirter, Lawrence, Mississippi.
Susie Dugan, PRIDE Omaha, Omaha, Nebraska.
Judy Dinerstein, Naperville, Illinois.
Betty Sembler, Chairman, S.O.S.—Save Our Society From Drugs, St. Petersburg, Florida.
Grainne Kenny, International President, EURAD (Europe Against Drugs).
John English, Springfield, Oregon.
Susan Baum, Loyalhanna, Pennsylvania.
Frank Richardson, Binghamton, New York.
Patsy Parker, Moss Point, Mississippi.
Sharon L. Smith, President—MOMSTELL, Mechanicsburg, Pennsylvania.
Connie Moulton, Committees of Correspondence, Danvers, Massachusetts.
Robert Peterson, Esq., Vice President of International Affairs, PRIDE Youth Programs, Fremont, Michigan.
Jay DeWispleare, Executive Director, PRIDE Youth Programs, Fremont, Michigan.
Lea Cox, Concerned Citizens for Drug Prevention, Norwell, Massachusetts.
Jack Gilligan, Global Drug Prevention Network, Peoria, Illinois.
Malcolm K. Beyer, Jr., Student Drug-Testing Coalition, Jupiter, Florida.
Peter Stoker, Director, National Drug Prevention Alliance, Great Britain.
Carla Lowe, Legal Foundation Against Drugs, Sacramento, California.
Jim Kester, Austin, Texas.

Beverly Barron, Former Executive Director of Texans War on Drugs, Odessa, Texas.
Peggy Goble, Great Meadows, New Jersey.
Karin Kyles, New Canaan, Connecticut.
DeForest Rathbone, Chairman, National Institute of Citizen Anti-drug Policy, Great Falls, Virginia.
Mr. & Mrs. Robert Dey (DEA Retired), Georgetown, Texas.
Ginger Katz, President of the Courage to Speak Foundation, Connecticut.
State Representative Toni Boucher, Assistant Minority Leader District 143, Connecticut.
Geraldine Silverman, New Jersey Federation for Drug Free Communities, Short Hills, New Jersey.
Wevley William Shea, Anchorage, Alaska.
Beverly J. Kinard, President, Christian Drug Education Center, Canon City, Colorado.
Judy Kreamer, Educating Voices, Inc., Naperville, Illinois.
Becky Vance, Executive Director, Drug Free Business Houston—A division of the Council on Alcohol and Drug Abuse, Houston, Texas.
Cathey Brown, Rainbow Days, Inc., Dallas, Texas.
Lynda Adams, Alaskans For Drug Free Youth, Ketchikan, Alaska.
June M. Milam, Former CEO, DREAM, Inc., Madison, Mississippi.
Joyce Tobias, Parents' Association to Neutralize Drug & Alcohol Abuse (PANDAA), Annandale, Virginia.
Judy Cushing, President-C.E.O., Oregon Partnership, Portland, Oregon.
Judy Arendsee, Rancho Sante Fe, California.
Stephanie Hayes, Former Board Chairman, Texans War on Drugs, Alpine, Texas.

Thursday, June 24, 2004

Hon. Michael K. Simpson

OF IDAHO

Mr. Speaker, every visitor who comes to my office is greeted by a plaque that bears the inscription of RONALD REAGAN's signature and this quote, "There's no limit to what a man can do or where he can go if he doesn't mind who gets the credit." These words are characteristic of the great man that served as the 40th President of the United States of America. I am involved with politics today because of the inspiration I received from RONALD REAGAN. I believe he was the true example of what a statesman can be, and I hold that example close to my heart as I carry out my own duties.

President REAGAN will always be remembered as an unabashed patriot. He was convinced of the ability of the United States to provide the hope of freedom to those enslaved by totalitarianism and communism. President REAGAN's vision of the world and the future of this country would not be dimmed or daunted by ideological threat, and he was not afraid to stand up to tyranny and aggression. From the beginning of his Presidency, President REAGAN realized the potential cost of inaction and weakness in the face of Soviet defiance and nuclear threat, and he took action. Through a series of defense budgets, he increased defense spending 35 percent during his two terms, ensuring the country the resources necessary for security. Additionally, President REAGAN managed to negotiate the first U.S.-Soviet treaty to reduce the number of nuclear weapons through a series of four summits with Mikhail Gorbachev. President REAGAN was always clear about what he expected and never more so than when he pleaded at the Brandenburg Gate, "Mr. Gorbachev, tear down this wall!"

President REAGAN planted democracy in regions of the world that have never tasted the joys of freedom. He taught newly liberated people across the globe that hard work and faith in God could result in prosperity, a sense of satisfaction in one's own legacy, and a better outlook for tomorrow. He wanted the American dream to be a reality throughout the world.

President REAGAN will also be remembered as a man of humble beginnings. He proclaimed America as a place where everyone can rise as high and as far as his ability will take him. Born in Tampico, IL, President REAGAN used his abilities to establish a career in Hollywood. He continued to work and learn as he rose through California politics and went on to serve two successful terms as the leader of our Nation. He wanted all Americans to have the same freedom and opportunity to pursue success, and he consistently promoted that ideal through policies of limited government. He said, "Government can and must provide opportunity, not smother it; foster productivity, not stifle it."

What makes RONALD REAGAN most unforgettable was his unfailing optimism. Even as our Nation mourns, we cannot help but smile at the thought of his cheerful and radiant personality. President REAGAN possessed a sense of humor strong enough to withstand even the pain of an assassin's bullet. Demonstrating his trademark good nature, he said to the doctors about to operate on his bullet wounds, "I hope you're all Republicans." It was this characteristic sanguinity that swept up a downtrodden America and re-energized its faith in freedom, the Presidency, and our military.

RONALD REAGAN was many things. He was a man of reason, a man of sincerity, a man willing to listen. And he is a man whose character, grace, and wisdom will be deeply missed by this Nation.

Tuesday, July 6, 2004

Hon. Duncan Hunter

OF CALIFORNIA

... this cold war was won by American service personnel. I look at Korea and Vietnam as two of the important battles in that war—battles which helped to bring that war to a successful conclusion.

The gentleman {Mr. Wilson of South Carolina} makes a great point about people who used to be behind the Iron Curtain now serving side by side with Americans. And I am reminded also that troops from Nicaragua and El Salvador, which were the centers of the so-called Contra wars during the eighties, when America's liberals said RONALD REAGAN should stay out of Central America; that if the Soviets want to have an influence in Central America, which they were having with the communist Sandinista and the FMLN in Salvador, let them have it, said the liberals, and let us stay out of Central America; we cannot possibly win that war. And of course they brought back the old Vietnam thing, they said you are going to get bogged down in another Vietnam. Today we have fragile democracies in each of those countries, and they have sent troops to stand side by side with Americans in Iraq to try to bring freedom to yet another country.

I was told, incidentally, that the Salvadorans in particular have fought fiercely in the Iraq theater; that they are excellent fighters and they very much support the coalition, and that they have brought a measure of strong support to our operation there. So I thank the gentleman for bringing that up because I think that is important.

When RONALD REAGAN was bringing down the Wall, and when he met that first move of force by the Russians during his administration, when the Soviet Union started to ring Western Europe with SS-20 missiles and RONALD REAGAN started to push in ground launch cruise missiles and Pershing missiles into Europe, the liberal commentators across the world said, essentially, now you have gone and done it; we will never have peace with the Soviet Union, and we have to get this RONALD REAGAN out of there.

Yet, by meeting the strength of the Soviet Union with American strength, the President produced a situation where at one point the Russians picked up the phone and said, Can we talk? And when they started talking, they talked not about a negotiated settlement but they talked really about the disassembly of the Soviet empire brought about by American strength.

I think this operation in Iraq, while it is tough and hard and very dangerous, is going to produce a good result in that very difficult part of the world.

Hon. Joe Wilson

OF SOUTH CAROLINA

Mr. Speaker, I want to also join in thanking the gentleman from Hawaii {Mr. Abercrombie} for his constructive suggestion.

But I want to reiterate again too that the war we are into, this global war on terrorism, is not something the United States sought. It is my humble opinion that the first attack was really in 1979, with the attack on our Embassy in Tehran. We can all remember the signs that were carried at that time were "death to America." It does not need a discussion. That is what the intent is. And the reason for this feeling is because the United States represents freedom of association, of speech, as we just saw, freedom of women to participate in society, and freedom of media. All of this is being opposed by people who want to construct a 14th-century lifestyle.

This is not a religious war. To me, it is a group of extremists who, as we saw last week, there was a heinous suicide bomber who attacked a Shiite mosque in Pakistan. Imagine just going straight into a mosque and killing 20 people. This is just something that has to be faced, and we either face the enemy overseas or we will again see them here in the United States, as we did on September 11.

September 11 was the culmination of a direct attack on the United States in 1993 on the World Trade Center, a direct attack on our Embassies in 1998, at Embassies all throughout Africa, and then, of course, the infamous attack on the USS *Cole* in Yemen in the year 2000, and finally the attack of September 11, 2001. America is responding.

And I am very grateful that just as after World War II we helped rebuild Germany so it would not be a breeding ground for communism, we are helping to rebuild Iraq. I am sorry that it does not get the attention it should. It is probably just dull to hear that there is freedom of the press and media in Iraq. It is dull to hear the schools have been reopened. It is dull to hear the hospitals have all been reopened and the health clinics are available. But it is not dull. It is creating a civil society that protects the American people. We were able to protect the American people and defeat communism, and I am confident we can do the same thing in defeating terrorism.

I am so happy the gentleman brought up RONALD REAGAN. It was 20 years ago virtually this minute that he was attempting to win the cold war by putting Pershing missiles in Western Europe. Millions of people demonstrated against that in the United States and Western Europe. It ultimately led, again, to our victory.

I had the extraordinary opportunity Sunday to meet with people at our church who are from Russia, and I was telling them how incredible it was for me to be there with them, because 15 years ago we were told that they like living under communism; that due to their serf background, they liked being slaves; that they really did not want to have to make decisions of who to elect and how to elect, what jobs to take, how much money to earn, whether they could buy a car or not; that they really enjoyed living in oppression.

We know that is not true. The dear Russians that I met with on Sunday said how much they appreciated what President REAGAN and the American people have done to provide for their liberation. The same analogy applies to the people of Iraq and Afghanistan. It is such a positive time to see what our troops are doing.

Hon. Robin Hayes

OF NORTH CAROLINA

Mr. Speaker, President Bush stood up for freedom, as well he should.

Just a couple of weeks ago at President REAGAN's funeral here in Washington, I had the unique privilege of standing in line waiting to walk by the casket of former President REAGAN with Mikhail Gorbachev.

They called REAGAN a cowboy; but Mikhail Gorbachev, his adversary at that time, was at his funeral saying that that man stood up for freedom, and he won the cold war, just like President Bush is standing up and winning the war on terrorism and our troops are making that happen.

Hon. Duncan Hunter

OF CALIFORNIA

Mr. Speaker, I thank the gentleman from North Carolina (Mr. Hayes). It must have taken a lot of grit for Mikhail Gorbachev to have all of the previous speakers or the speakers at that ceremony talk about how RONALD REAGAN equipped him; but, you know, he put up with that and then paid his respects to President REAGAN. And I think there is a message there, and that is that the goodness of America comes through, and ultimately it persuades others to follow the path of freedom. I thank the gentleman for his comments.

Wednesday, July 7, 2004

Hon. J.D. Hayworth

OF ARIZONA

Mr. Speaker, yesterday was the official end of the period of national mourning for former President RONALD REAGAN. During this month there have been many tributes to this great President, all of which were deserving.

Recently, I was given a copy of a book review by the well-respected administrative law judge John C. Holmes, who is now retired. In August 1998, Judge Holmes reviewed Dinesh D'Souza's book, "RONALD REAGAN: How an Ordinary Man Became an Extraordinary Leader." It was an excellent review that summed up how so many of us view RONALD REAGAN and his life. I would like to submit the review for the *Record* and I commend it to my colleagues.

{From the *Free Press*, 1997}
RONALD REAGAN: HOW AN ORDINARY MAN BECAME AN EXTRAORDINARY LEADER

(By John C. Holmes)

Dinesh D'Souza, who served briefly as a low-level advisor to President REAGAN in 1987–88, is an open admirer of REAGAN's accomplishments. Yet not even REAGAN's harshest critics are more revealing of his character flaws and human weaknesses. Rather than expressing scorn and derision, however, the author is in turn bemused, delighted, curious, and intrigued in candidly reporting the former president's character and personality idiosyncrasies. After careful examination, he concludes that REAGAN's very real limitations in fact assisted as much as deterred this seemingly ordinary man in becoming an extraordinary leader. Beneath his apparent simplicity was a complex and sometimes contradictory person.

For example, REAGAN's sunny personality and near continuous optimism masked a psychological curtain that could descend on even his most intimate friends and family, keeping them at a distance. There was also the contradiction that, while constantly extolling the virtue of the family and its values, REAGAN exhibited a disjointed personal one, having been divorced from his first wife, Jane Wyman, and distant from his son, daughter, and stepdaughter. REAGAN's acknowledged short attention span masked a tenacious adherence to those principles and policies that concerned him most. His good-natured jokes and story-telling, sometimes criticized as irreverent and irrelevant, served to disarm and win over adversaries from Tip O'Neill to Mikhail Gorbachev. His famous line in the presidential debate with Walter Mondale that he "would not use Mondale's youth and inexperience against him" caused an involuntary grin and chuckle from his surprised opponent, totally diffusing the increasingly serious campaign issue of REAGAN's age, and propelling REAGAN into one of the largest presidential victories ever. He loved pomp and cavorted with the wealthy, but had a singular capacity to connect with, and was beloved by, the common man.

The author dispels or modifies some public misconceptions. While REAGAN himself self-deprecatingly joked about his nap times, he worked sometimes grueling hours, particularly for a man of his age, exhibiting strong discipline in doing homework on those issues he needed to know. His discipline in keeping physically fit probably saved his life early in his presidency when he was the recipient of a would-be assassin's bullet that lodged less than an inch from his heart. His character was revealed during this frightening time when despite the seriousness of the situation he could extemporaneously joke to his wife Nancy: "Honey, I forgot to duck!" and to his treating physicians: "I hope you're all good Republicans." Such good humor in the face of adversity won him a reservoir of good will by an appreciative public.

TAKING ON THE "EVIL EMPIRE"

REAGAN was a naive, rosy optimist, thinking that, if he could only show Gorbachev how ordinary Americans lived, Gorbachev would recognize the differences between the two systems and make big changes for the better. REAGAN was a foolhardy, almost comical belligerent, standing at the Berlin Wall and challenging Gorbachev to "tear down this wall!" He was an embarrassment, a blind, unsophisticated patriot who had the gall, bad manners, and political incorrectness to call the free world's adversary an "Evil Empire." He was an actor who knew nothing of foreign policy, a genial dummy who straddled between reckless action and somnolent inattention. Or so he was portrayed and so many believed.

But D'Souza recognizes REAGAN's historic accomplishment in fostering the dissolution of the Communist empire, which emanated at least in substantial part from the man's own willful, steadfast purpose. This dissolution was not foreordained, as has become the fashionable view. The author demonstrates the transparency of REAGAN's critics, quoting extensively from their pronouncements on the growth, stability, and power of the Soviet economy and the folly of attempting directly to challenge Russia itself. Liberal historian Arthur Schlesinger Jr. observed in 1982 that "those in the United States who think the Soviet Union is on the verge of economic and social collapse are wishful thinkers." John Kenneth Galbraith, Harvard economist and guru during the Kennedy-Johnson years, pronounced that "the Russian system succeeds, because, in contrast with the Western industrial economies, it makes full use of its manpower." Such assessment was concurred in by even "neutral" economists such as Paul Samuelson and Lester Thurow, who as late as 1989 marveled at the Russian growth process.

As for confronting Russian expansion, Sovietologist Stephen Cohen of Princeton University thought that REAGAN was pathologically wrongheaded in apparently abandoning the comforting previous policies of containment and detente for the objective of "destroying the Soviet Union as a world power and possibly even its Communist system." Strobe Talbot, then a senior correspondent at Time magazine and later deputy secretary of state in the Clinton administration, indignantly scoffed at REAGAN's unrealistic and misguided attempts to return to the '50s goal of rolling back Soviet domination in Europe.

Though criticized as too ideological, REAGAN appointed skilled pragmatists to implement his aggressive foreign policy. They included the maligned but effective Bill Casey at the CIA, Cap Weinberger at Defense, and George Schultz at State. REAGAN's overarching plan was relatively simple: he would outspend the Russians on defense, thereby showing the vulnerability of the Russian economic system which REAGAN, almost alone, was convinced would not keep pace. This culminated in the proposed future deployment of defense missiles and lasers dubbed "Star Wars," a concept ridiculed by many, and not fully understood even by REAGAN, but greatly feared by the Russian leadership. D'Souza presents the still-minority viewpoint, which I believe history will eventually confirm, that the elevation by the Russian leadership of Gorbachev was largely stimulated as an antidote for the very presence of REAGAN, who by then had emerged as a popular and effective world leader who articulately advocated challenge of Russian aspirations for world dominance. REAGAN took an immediate liking to Gorbachev and instinctively felt they could do business. His subsequent perseverance in challenging Gorbachev to reform the system, combined with U.S. military buildup, precipitated the eventual dismembering of the formerly impenetrable Russian political hegemony and military might.

For this accomplishment alone REAGAN should be recognized as the single most important person in the second half of this century in pointing our world in the direction of freedom and democracy. However, to the surprise and even anguish of liberal opponents, and the consternation of some conservative friends, his challenge was not limited to the communist totalitarian system, but to dictators everywhere, whether in the Philippines, South America, or Africa. The resulting extensive conversion from socialist and totalitarian states to democracies and free economies was truly remarkable, never before seen in the history of the world.

TAKING ON BIG GOVERNMENT

As REAGAN ran against the political wisdom and apparent majority public opinion in advocating defeat of, rather than detente with, communism, so too he opposed the belief that a powerful central government was essential to ensure freedom, justice, and the general welfare. REAGAN presented the then-heretical view that central government was the problem, not the solution. While REAGAN accepted much of Roosevelt's New Deal as a necessary reaction to the economic emergency following the Great Depression, he felt the Great Society agenda fostered by President Johnson took the country too far along the path toward a suffocating central government that would eventually stifle individual initiative and freedom. His conversion from Democrat to Republican resulted.

REAGAN carried his message forward in speech after speech, initially while traveling the country for General Electric. Although the 1964 Republican Convention produced the spectacularly losing campaign of Barry Goldwater, REAGAN's nominating speech—which has been since dubbed merely "The Speech"—launched him into the national scene as the future messenger and leader of the conservative cause. It also brought him to the attention of king-makers in California, who lured him into a successful run against the incumbent, the firmly entrenched Governor Pat Brown, who, like every candidate REAGAN has run against, underestimated his talents, personality, and character.

As Governor, REAGAN preached austerity, but in his first term did little in practice to put California's economic house in order. His main contribution, perhaps, was in standing up to the most radical of the free speakers, thereby keeping the universities open and restoring a modicum of stability during those turbulent times. The author labels REAGAN's governorship as only moderately successful. REAGAN, however, gained a stage that eventually catapulted him into the presidency.

While running for and entering the presidency, his economic message remained the same: limited government. On the one hand, as his critics are quick to point out, REAGAN never directly achieved his economic goals, as the high cost of defense build-up and his insistence on a tax cut made a balanced budget impossible. Moreover, this imbalance was exacerbated by the Democratic-controlled Congress, whose "compromise" meant more spending on cherished domestic programs rather than cuts that would have helped pay for the defense build-up. On the other hand, his intense lobbying efforts on his first budget, while not reaching all the results he envisioned, provided the mechanism for a future more limited domestic spending program, and provided more funds for the private sector through tax cuts. Through a numbing recession in 1982, with critics contending his "voodoo" supply-side economics were a proven failure, REAGAN elected to "stay the course," retreating to his California ranch for resuscitation and refusing the siren song to "do something." He was assisted by a supportive Federal Reserve, which tightened credit to reduce the fever of double digit inflation prevalent during the preceding Carter administration. With recover came increasing public and business confidence. A growing economy meant more dollars to pay for the defense build-up.

The author points to the "outrageous" act of firing the air traffic controllers as a further plank in economic recovery. Though their union, the Professional Air Traffic Controllers (PATCO), was one of the few to support REAGAN's presidential bid, REAGAN had no compunction in firing them and replacing them by non-union workers. Considering them "untouchables," no previous president had so directly taken on unions and government workers. To REAGAN, the moral basis was simple: government workers were servants of the people and not their masters. The law supported his viewpoint. Condemned, ridiculed, and pressured even by allies, and temporarily losing popular support, particularly from new-found "Joe Six-Pack" converts to the Republican party, REAGAN stuck to his guns. This action, and his subsequent refusal to compromise, so shocked and silenced union leaders and government workers that corporations and government agencies were afforded for years to come the opportunity to downsize and "reorganize." The seemingly forgotten principal that jobs were a privilege and not a right was at least partially restored and the economy further stimulated.

REAGAN's goals were not all achieved while in office. Nevertheless, he left an agenda that is still in many respects being followed today. Free international trade through agreements such as NAFTA, and the outline for fiscal savings as drawn up in the "Contract for America," were REAGAN initiatives. Even the line-item veto, scorned and laughed at as a campaign throw-away, and impossible to enact, has become law, ironically co-opted by President Clinton and touted as his own accomplishment. While temporarily contributing to a huge unbalanced budget and an unfavorable foreign trade deficit, the successful war against communism eventually allowed a resulting "peace dividend," a prosperous economy, and a curtailed federal government. A balanced budget would be achieved 10 years after he left office.

REAGAN again knew instinctively what the most sophisticated economists were oblivious to. Reduction of tax rates during times when government has become too large and costly can actually increase total revenues by freeing the private sector from stifling governmental costs and regulations, thereby enabling sales and profits (as well as taxes paid) to rise. What was to become known worldwide as "privatization" resulted from these policies. Where previous Republican administrations had merely attempted to cut around the edges to make governments a little more efficient and accountable, REAGAN attacked it head on, by word and deed freeing the private sector to accomplish its goals with minimal intervention.

TAKING ON "MALAISE"

A third area that REAGAN sought to change flowed naturally from and was dependent upon success in his attack on communism and big government: restoration of the prestige and respect of the presidency, and the confidence, optimism, and patriotism of the American people. Following the "Peace and Prosperity" and "Return to Normalcy" of the 1950s under Eisenhower, we had experienced the assassinations of President Kennedy, Martin Luther King, and Robert Kennedy; the quagmire of Vietnam, causing President Johnson's decision not to run; Nixon's seemingly moderately successful presidency brought down by Watergate; and the failed Carter presidency, ending in American hostages being ignominiously held in Iran, communism seemingly on the march in international expansion, and Carter himself describing a "malaise" in the American psyche. Onto the stage strode the unlikely candidate the conservatives lusted for, but mainstream Republicans merely tolerated, and Democrats welcomed as "easy pickings"—seemingly too old, too ideological, and too inexperienced to be elected or to accomplish the job.

The reigns of government had barely been grasped when a sickening feeling of deja vu returned as an attempt was made on REAGAN's life. REAGAN's humorous reaction and relatively quick recovery boded well, allowing him to initiate his foreign and domestic programs. The sputtering of the economy in late 1981, leading to recession, however, dispelled this good will and left the nation in a sullen mood. As recovery finally came and REAGAN's "stay the course" was more or less vindicated, his personality and talents as a "Great Communicator" began to sharpen and shape the American and world landscape. He entreated the people of the United States, the country he felt destined to be "a shining city on the hill," to support and further his program and policies. He restored a sometimes teary-eyed patriotism, encouraging Americans to take pride in and celebrate our country, its meaning, and its history. Using his powers as a former actor and the sincerity of his own belief in the goodness of America, whose "morning had just begun," he sought to enlist the people to assist the world along a better path to a brighter future. He returned a pride in military service, severely wounded since the Vietnam war. His own dedication to duty and pride of office restored dignity and world leadership to the presidency.

History may record REAGAN as having been extraordinarily lucky to have accomplished his successes at such an advanced age, barely before senility and the eventual ravages of Alzheimer's disease fully took over. D'Souza does not think so. He credits—too much, some will argue—REAGAN's ability to cut through the thicket of unimportant matters and take the correct action at nearly every important juncture. Far from being a mere bystander, REAGAN led on matters that mattered, even when his decisions were unpopular.

D'Souza notes a nearly mystical aura that President REAGAN himself privately acknowledged as governing some of his actions. While many presidents donned the mantra of churchgoing for public consumption, and REAGAN himself supported, mainly as a sop to the religious right, a constitutional amendment to allow public school prayer, his own religious beliefs were more complex. Not an active churchgoer before or during his presidency, he apparently firmly believed in an intervening and active higher authority from whom he privately sought solace and guidance. When asked what person he most admired, REAGAN invariably answered, "The man from Galilee." Though public ridicule was made of his wife Nancy's seeking guidance from astrologers, without serious objection and perhaps active support from the President, REAGAN's truer belief would have been the personally delivered opinion of Mother Theresa that he had been put on this earth for a divine purpose.

This book will not find favor with liberal economists, with those Jeanne Kirkpatrick labeled "Blame America Firsters," or with apologists for the former Soviet communist system who then had advocated accommodation and appeasement, but many of whom now find its demise historically inevitable and REAGAN irrelevant. One of D'Souza's obvious purposes in the book is to attack this attempted instant historical revisionism. In so doing, he can fairly be accused of straying too often from a "pure" chronicle of REAGAN to a strident attack on his critics. No doubt in anticipated rebuttal, D'Souza points to a "stacked deck" committee chaired by Arthur Schlesinger Jr. and commissioned by the editors of the New York Times in December 1996 to render a collective verdict on how history will rank the U.S. presidents. Not surprisingly these "history experts," which included Doris Kearns Goodwin, James MacGregor Burns, ex-Governor Mario Cuomo, and ex-Senator Paul Simon, liberals all, ranked REAGAN in the lower half, below George Bush and in the undistinguished company of Jimmy Carter, Chester Arthur, and Benjamin Harrison. In contrast, D'Souza believes REAGAN should be ranked with the Roosevelts, Wilson, Lincoln, and Washington.

Interestingly, however, the ideologically conservative "true believers" who allege that REAGAN was merely a popular messenger for an irresistible movement will not be overjoyed with the book. D'Souza paints REAGAN as a unique individual, the likes of which are unlikely to return. Though REAGAN articulated the principals of the ascending conservative movement, he was flexible rather than rigid, and his sunny personality lent itself to compromise on everything except his hardcore principals. This enabled REAGAN to overcome popular reluctance to accept his conservative agenda.

D'Souza describes an apparently simple, but actually a flawed, complex, and contradictory man who accomplished his aims by concentrating on a few specifics that were fundamental to his beliefs. To this reviewer, who was initially extremely skeptical of REAGAN's governing capability, let alone his electability to the presidency, but who has come to the happy realization that there really was something in the stars that brought forth this unlikely man to lead our country at such an important time in history, RONALD REAGAN gets it exactly right.

Tuesday, July 13, 2004

Hon. Nick Smith

OF MICHIGAN

Mr. Speaker, after listening to the previous speakers, I think of RONALD REAGAN's words, "There you go again."

Every 4 years we sort of experience the spinning and the demagoguery that takes place in this Chamber using these podiums and C–SPAN to criticize the sitting President. Of course, Republicans did it 4 years ago and 8 years ago.

When I first came into office and was elected in 1992, the Democrats in this Chamber were using this forum to criticize the first President Bush, all the things that went wrong. But I think of what the criticisms were of President REAGAN when he came into office. When President REAGAN came to office America was demoralized. President Carter had spoken about our malaise in Watergate, and our defeat in Vietnam had all shaken our self-confidence.

We had given up the Panama Canal. The Shah of Iran and supporters of the Ayatollah Khomeini held 52 of our Americans hostage for more than a year at our Embassy in Tehran. The military rescue mission, of course, failed in the desert, and we lost eight of our servicemen in that venture.

Communism was on the march, and after South Vietnam fell, Cambodia followed. The Sandinistas took control of Nicaragua and communist insurgencies were under way in Ethiopia, Angola, and certainly the Soviets invaded Afghanistan in 1979 and were suppressing the solidarity movement in Poland.

Our economic situation was very dire in 1980, and President REAGAN came in and actually renewed our faith. America, in most American's minds, no longer seemed to be special, and we needed that kind of determined leadership.

The point I want to make, in reacting to some of the Democrats' criticism of this administration, was the criticism that President REAGAN received when he believed we should stand up to the Soviet Union and we ended up doing that.

It was President REAGAN's resolve that repulsed communism in the Caribbean and Central America and repulsed it also in Afghanistan. It was REAGAN's resolve that nurtured solidarity in Poland and gave heart to the dissidents of the Soviet bloc, and it was REAGAN's faith in American ideals that toppled the Berlin Wall. All of this time he was being criticized as being a trigger-happy President that might push the red button for a world war III with the Soviet Union.

When he went to Berlin, and he was writing a speech for Berlin, he started out writing in that he wanted to include "Mr. Gorbachev, tear down this wall!," and all of his advisers and his speechwriters said, No, do not do that; it will anger the American people and the world. They will think you are too bold; they will think you are too challenging. That might end up in war. You should just try to get along and make peace. But he insisted it go in despite that criticism, and that leads me to what historians are going to say 30 years from now in analyzing the decision and the determination of this President to go into Iraq.

Most everybody in this Chamber and the Senate had the same kind of intelligence information that the President and the administration had. Some of that intelligence information, we have now discovered, was very inaccurate in some regards.

Hon. Jim McDermott
OF WASHINGTON

Mr. Speaker, in London yesterday Prime Minister Tony Blair did something that leaders do. Speaking to the House of Commons, Mr. Blair said, "I accept full responsibility for the way the issue was presented and, therefore, for any errors made."

Leaders lead, and leaders know the buck stops with them. Leaders lead, and leaders accept responsibility when things go wrong.

An independent report in England blamed its intelligence community for massive intelligence failures before the Iraq war. What did Tony Blair do? The Prime Minister got up in front of his nation and the world and accepted personal responsibility.

That did not happen when a similar report was released to the United States. The President did not accept responsibility. The President assigned blame.

In 1961, President John F. Kennedy accepted full responsibility for the Bay of Pigs fiasco. It did not matter that the planning for the Bay of Pigs had started in the Eisenhower administration. It did not matter that the intelligence failures directly led to the foreign policy disaster that was the Bay of Pigs. President Kennedy stood before the Nation and the world and accepted personal responsibility.

At one news conference not long afterward, President Kennedy used his legendary wit and intelligence to sum it up. "There is an old saying," Kennedy said, "that victory has a hundred fathers and defeat is an orphan."

The buck stops at the President's desk, except in this administration. Since the release of the U.S. report on pre-Iraqi intelligence failures, this President has done everything possible to pass the buck.

During the administration of President RONALD REAGAN, the Iran-Contra scandal was a crisis that shook the Nation to its core and the White House to its foundation. President REAGAN was given ample opportunity to assign the blame to Oliver North. What did RONALD REAGAN do? When asked directly about Mr. North, RONALD REAGAN said, "I do not feel betrayed. He has a fine record."

Leaders lead. Whatever your politics, you have to acknowledge that President REAGAN was a leader. When our country faces a crisis, people look to the President for leadership.

Not long ago, America faced a moral crisis. America faced an ethical crisis. America faced a military and political crisis. When pictures of prison abuse stunned the world, the world looked to America, to our President, for a response. The President did not stand up and accept responsibility.

Outside the White House and then in an interview broadcast throughout the Middle East, the President did not or could not or would not tell the world he accepts responsibilities for the failures of the Americans under his command. He could not utter the words that the world needed to hear and that Americans needed to say.

Over the last half century, Presidents from both political parties have braved grave crises. They did what leaders do. They did not pass the buck. They stood and accepted responsibility, until now.

In little over 110 days, the American people will elect a new President, and leadership is fundamental to that choice.

The British historian Arnold Toynbee once said, "As human beings, we are endowed with freedom of choice, and we cannot shuffle off our responsibility upon the shoulders of God or nature. We must shoulder it ourselves. It is up to us."

Martin Luther King Junior once said, "The ultimate measure of a man is not where he stands in moments of comfort and convenience but where he stands at times of challenge and controversy."

In just over 110 days, this Nation will make the most important political decision of the next 4 years. Democrats and Republicans will argue issues, and that is expected, but fundamental to the selection of the person who leads the free world for the next 4 years is the quality of leadership. Leadership is more than a commercial or a campaign brochure. Leadership is one of the most important qualities the President must have. There is a record of what America expects and what Americans demand of their President. Leadership is at the top of the list.

The President had to be taken out twice from the White House to finally say that he was sorry for what had happened to the Arab prisoners that were held in Iraq. You have to ask yourself, does this President believe that the requirement of his job is to accept the responsibility, Mr. Speaker? Because he has not shown it yet. He never has said, "I accept responsibility."

One hundred and ten more days, Mr. Speaker.

Monday, July 19, 2004

Hon. Christopher Shays

OF CONNECTICUT

Mr. Speaker, on June 5, 2004, our Nation lost a distinguished statesman, a world leader and a fine President in RONALD REAGAN. President REAGAN was a man of his word, and his principles were unquestionable. He had extraordinary faith in the promise of America and the belief that the best of America is yet to come.

On July 2, 2004, Ambassador Joseph Verner Reed, Under-Secretary-General of the United Nations, paid homage to Mr. REAGAN at Kyung Hee University in Seoul, Korea. I submit the text of Mr. Reed's address to be entered into the *Record*.

STATEMENT OF AMBASSADOR JOSEPH VERNER REED AT THE GRADUATE SCHOOL FOR PAN PACIFIC INTERNATIONAL STUDIES OF KYUNG HEE UNIVERSITY, SEOUL, REPUBLIC OF KOREA

An event in the United States eclipsed matters in the media recently, and that was the passing of President RONALD REAGAN.

I was privileged to have been appointed to three posts by President REAGAN. First as Ambassador to the Kingdom of Morocco, then as Deputy Permanent Representative to the United Nations as Ambassador to the Economic and Social Council and lastly as the Under-Secretary-General for Political and General Assembly Affairs of the United Nations.

Several years ago I was privileged to accept on behalf of President REAGAN, here at Kyung Hee University, the Great World Peace Award. It was an honor and a privilege.

RONALD WILSON REAGAN—father, husband, actor and dedicated public servant—restored the pride, optimism and strength of the United States and earned deep respect and affection of his fellow citizens. When he passed away, we witnessed an outpouring of solemnity, sorrow and reflection in our country. In the view of many people, President REAGAN remains the most significant United States President since Franklin Delano Roosevelt. He was a man who changed the course of American politics, culture and world history. He was right on the most important questions of his era: the role of government and the defeat of the Soviet Union. The structure of the American economy was altered profoundly by his term. Top tax rates have never returned to their previously punitive levels. America's current standing in world affairs is also a direct result of President REAGAN's calling the Soviet Union's bluff in the 1980s and restoring US military power and self-confidence. This was not evident at the time. Everything President REAGAN did was challenged. He was a polarizing figure—more disdained in Europe than President George W. Bush is today. For at least half his presidency he was unpopular at home as well, as most effective Presidents are.

With his Californian optimism, President REAGAN transformed conservatism into a progressive force, into a political philosophy that took risks and changed things. President REAGAN took conservatism into a reformist, unapologetic governing philosophy. That achievement endures in the United States.

I feel blessed to have been appointed to posts in public service by President REAGAN. He inspired; he amused; he gave conviction a sunny disposition. Because of him, millions live in freedom where they once labored under tyranny. Because of RONALD WILSON REAGAN, America was recharged and freedom reborn. In life it is rare to live under a political leader who evokes love as well as respect.

President REAGAN's extraordinary political gifts carried him through—his talents as a communicator, his intuitive understanding of the average American, his unfailing geniality even after being hit by an assassin's bullet, his ability to build and sustain friendships across partisan lines. Those gifts—and his conviction that words counted for far more in politics that mere deeds—enabled him to convince large majorities that as long as he was in charge, it would remain "Morning in America". I believe the cool eye of history will place RONALD REAGAN in the list of the great Presidents.

President REAGAN believed that America was not just a place in the world, but the hope of the world. He came to office with great hopes for America. He was optimistic that a strong America could advance peace, and he acted to build the strength that this mission required. He was optimistic that liberty would thrive wherever it was planted, and he acted to defend liberty wherever it was threatened. And RONALD REAGAN believed in the power of truth in the conduct of world affairs. When he saw evil camped across the horizon, he called that evil by its name. Who can ever forget President REAGAN in Berlin calling "Mr. Gorbachev, tear down this wall"?

RONALD WILSON REAGAN belongs to the ages; a great American story has closed.

Tuesday, July 20, 2004

Hon. Randy "Duke" Cunningham
OF CALIFORNIA

Mr. Speaker, I rise today to pay tribute to the USS *Ronald Reagan* and its crew on their arrival this week at their new home port of San Diego, CA.

I am pleased that one of President REAGAN's many legacies is the Navy's newest nuclear carrier, the USS *Ronald Reagan*. The ship recently set sail from Norfolk for its rightful home in San Diego. Throughout his political career, President REAGAN always concluded his campaign in San Diego. He called it his lucky city. It is only fitting that our "shining city on the hill," San Diego, will be home to the USS *Ronald Reagan*.

This ship is perhaps the most fitting tribute to RONALD REAGAN's legacy of strength and security, to the imprint he had on our past, and the promise that we hold for the future. The ship's motto, "Peace Through Strength," was borrowed from one of President REAGAN's radio addresses and embodies the essence of his vision of national security.

The USS *Ronald Reagan* is the most advanced aircraft carrier in the world. It has the newest hull design, 2 nuclear reactors, a length of 1,092 feet, a top speed over 30 knots, over 6,000 highly-trained service members, and more than 80 of the world's top aircraft. Finally, its 4.5 acres of flight deck are American territory that can be used to project our presence anywhere in the world.

A U.S. ship is a powerful symbol and the USS *Ronald Reagan* stands to be the most powerful of all. It will be a welcome sight to many around the world who see it as an example of America's strength and protection of freedom. It will also bring caution to people and nations who would deny that freedom.

Mr. Speaker, I ask that you urge our colleagues to join me in recognizing the outstanding service of the USS *Ronald Reagan* and its crew and wish them the best in all their future endeavors. San Diego anxiously awaits the arrival of the USS *Ronald Reagan* and our opportunity to welcome it home to its lucky city.

Thursday, July 22, 2004

PUBLIC BILLS AND RESOLUTIONS

Under clause 2 of rule XII, public bills and resolutions were introduced and severally referred, as follows:

By Mr. Ose (for himself, Mr. DeLay, Mr. Doolittle, Mr. Gallegly, Mr. Gary G. Miller of California, Mr. Sessions, Mr. Hobson, Mr. Rohrabacher, Mr. Gibbons, Mr. Neugebauer, Mr. Baker, Mr. Smith of Texas, Mr. Duncan, Mr. McKeon, Mr. Hyde, Mr. Souder, Mr. Osborne, Mr. Cannon, and Mr. Radanovich):

H.R. 4980. A bill to direct the Secretary of the Interior to arrange for the carving of the figure of former President RONALD REAGAN on Mount Rushmore National Memorial, and for other purposes; to the Committee on Resources.

Hon. Darrell E. Issa
OF CALIFORNIA

Mr. Speaker, I rise today, on the eve of the home porting ceremony of the USS *Ronald Reagan*, to welcome America's newest aircraft carrier and its crew to San Diego.

The USS *Ronald Reagan CVN–76*, our Nation's ninth Nimitz class carrier, is the world's most advanced and most capable carrier ever built. The USS *Reagan*, along with its crew of 6,000 and its commanding officer Captain James A. Symonds, will give America greater capabilities to address threats to the safety of Americans and international peace and stability than ever before.

For most of the world's history, the oceans have been a dangerous and lawless place. For over 60 years, however, America's Navy has reigned supreme over the world's oceans. Today, our Navy ensures freedom of the seas for all nations who seek to use the world's shipping lanes for peaceful purposes. The USS *Ronald Reagan* enhances our Navy's ability to do its job.

For California, the USS *Ronald Reagan* will serve as a proud reminder of the legacy left behind by our former Governor and President. President REAGAN understood the importance of maintaining a strong and effective military. Throughout his administration, which brought about a successful end to the cold war, President REAGAN rebuilt America's armed forces with a steadfast belief in the pursuit of "peace through strength." Because of this legacy, it is entirely fitting that the most powerful and diplomatically visible symbol of the American Navy now shares both the name and home State of President RONALD REAGAN.

The crew of the USS *Reagan* will find the San Diego community to be warm and welcoming. San Diego has a mix of many cultures and, as someone who moved my family here 20 years ago, I can assure the entire crew that San Diego is a great place to live, work, and raise a family.

Mr. Speaker, in closing, I would like to recognize Mrs. Reagan who will participate in tomorrow's home porting ceremony. The USS *Ronald Reagan* is a testament to the many great things RONALD and Nancy REAGAN accomplished together. RONALD REAGAN gave our Nation hope and reminded us that with hard work and determination we could do great things. President REAGAN may have moved on, but his legacy is as strong and steady as the ship that now bears his name.

Tuesday, September 7, 2004

MESSAGE FROM THE SENATE

A message from the Senate by Mr. Monahan, one of its clerks, announced that the Senate has passed a concurrent resolution of the following title in which the concurrence of the House is requested:

S. Con. Res. 135. Concurrent resolution authorizing the printing of a commemorative document in memory of the late President of the United States, RONALD WILSON REAGAN.

SENATE BILLS REFERRED

A concurrent resolution of the Senate of the following title was taken from the Speaker's table and, under the rule, referred as follows:

S. Con. Res. 135. Concurrent Resolution authorizing the printing of a commemorative document in memory of the late President of the United States, RONALD WILSON REAGAN; referred to the Committee on Administration.

Tuesday, September 28, 2004

AUTHORIZING PRINTING OF COMMEMORATIVE DOCUMENT IN MEMORY OF PRESIDENT RONALD WILSON REAGAN

Mr. DOOLITTLE. Mr. Speaker, I ask unanimous consent that the Committee on House Administration be discharged from further consideration of the Senate concurrent resolution (S. Con. Res. 135) authorizing the printing of a commemorative document in memory of the late President of the United States, RONALD WILSON REAGAN, and ask for its immediate consideration in the House.

The Clerk read the title of the Senate concurrent resolution.

The SPEAKER pro tempore. Is there objection to the request of the gentleman from California?

Mr. LARSON of Connecticut. Mr. Speaker, I reserve the right to object, although it is not my intention to object; and I turn to the gentleman from California for an explanation of his request.

Mr. DOOLITTLE. Mr. Speaker, will the gentleman yield?

Mr. LARSON of Connecticut. I yield to the gentleman from California.

Mr. DOOLITTLE. Mr. Speaker, I rise today to support this resolution which authorizes the printing of a commemorative document in memory of the late President of the United States, RONALD WILSON REAGAN. I will be offering an amendment that will require the document to be printed under the direction of the Joint Committee on Printing, to be compiled by both bodies of Congress for the use of the full Congress.

Mr. LARSON of Connecticut. Mr. Speaker, I thank the gentleman for that explanation. Clearly, Congress most recently published tributes to President Nixon and in the past President Johnson and President Truman, and I am in concurrence with our distinguished gentleman from California.

Mr. Speaker, I withdraw my reservation of objection.

The SPEAKER pro tempore. Is there objection to the request of the gentleman from California?

There was no objection.

The Clerk read the Senate concurrent resolution, as follows:

S. CON. RES. 135

Resolved by the Senate (the House of Representatives concurring),

SECTION 1. COMMEMORATIVE DOCUMENT AUTHORIZED.

A commemorative document in memory of the late President of the United States, RONALD WILSON REAGAN, consisting of the eulogies and encomiums for RONALD WILSON REAGAN, as expressed in the Senate and the House of Representatives, together with the texts of the state funeral ceremony at the United States Capitol Rotunda, the national funeral service held at the Washington National Cathedral, Washington, District of Columbia, and the interment ceremony at the Ronald Reagan Presidential Library, Simi Valley, California, shall be printed as a Senate document, with illustrations and suitable binding.

SEC. 2. PRINTING OF DOCUMENT.

In addition to the usual number of copies printed, there shall be printed the lesser of—

(1) 32,500 copies of the commemorative document, of which 22,150 copies shall be for the use of the House of Representatives and 10,350 copies shall be for the use of the Senate; or

(2) such number of copies of the commemorative document that does not exceed a production and printing cost of $1,000,000, with distribution of the copies to be allocated in the same proportion as described in paragraph (1).

AMENDMENT OFFERED BY MR. DOOLITTLE

Mr. DOOLITTLE. Mr. Speaker, I offer an amendment.

The Clerk read as follows:

AMENDMENT OFFERED BY MR. DOOLITTLE:

In section 1, strike "Senate document, with illustrations and suitable binding" and insert "House document, with illustrations and suitable binding, under the direction of the Joint Committee on Printing".

The amendment was agreed to.

The Senate concurrent resolution was concurred in.

A motion to reconsider was laid on the table.

Tuesday, October 5, 2004

Hon. Ron Paul
OF TEXAS

Mr. Speaker, I rise to oppose H.R. 163 {Universal National Service Act of 2003} in the strongest possible terms. The draft, whether for military purposes or for some form of "national service," violates the basic moral principles of individual liberty upon which this country was founded. Furthermore, the military neither wants nor needs a draft.

The Department of Defense, in response to calls to reinstate the draft has confirmed that conscription serves no military need. Defense officials from both parties have repudiated the need to reinstate the draft. For example, Secretary of Defense Donald Rumsfeld has said that, "The disadvantages of using compulsion to bring into the armed forces the men and women needed are notable," while President William Clinton's Secretary of the Army Louis Caldera, in a speech before the National Press Club, admitted that, "Today, with our smaller, post Cold War armed forces, our stronger volunteer tradition and our need for longer terms of service to get a good return on the high, up-front training costs, it would be even harder to fashion a fair draft."

However, the most important reason to oppose H.R. 163 is that a draft violates the very principals of individual liberty upon which our Nation was founded. Former President RONALD REAGAN eloquently expressed the moral case against the draft in the publication *Human Events* in 1979: "... {conscription} rests on the assumption that your kids belong to the State. If we buy that assumption then it is for the State—not for parents, the community, the religious institutions or teachers—to decide who shall have what values and who shall do what work, when, where and how in our society. That assumption isn't a new one. The Nazis thought it was a great idea."

Some say the 18-year-old draftee "owes it" to his (or her, since H.R. 163 makes women eligible for the draft) country. Hogwash! It just as easily could be argued that a 50-year-old chicken-hawk, who promotes war and places the danger on innocent young people, owes more to the country than the 18-year-old being denied his (or her) liberty.

All drafts are unfair. All 18- and 19-year-olds are never drafted. By its very nature a draft must be discriminatory. All drafts hit the most vulnerable young people, as the elites learn quickly how to avoid the risks of combat.

Economic hardship is great in all wars and cannot be minimized. War is never economically beneficial except for those in position to profit from war expenditure. The great tragedy of war is that it enables the careless disregard for civil liberties of our own people. Abuses of German and Japanese Americans in World War I and World War II are well known.

But the real sacrifice comes with conscription—forcing a small number of young vulnerable citizens to fight the wars that older men and women, who seek glory in military victory without themselves being exposed to danger, promote. The draft encourages wars with neither purpose nor moral justification and that are too often not even declared by the Congress.

Without conscription, unpopular wars are difficult to fight. Once the draft was undermined in the sixties and early seventies, the Vietnam war came to an end. But most important, liberty cannot be preserved by tyranny. A free society must always resort to volunteers. Tyrants think nothing of forcing men to fight and serve in wrongheaded wars. A true fight for survival and defense of America would elicit, I am sure, the assistance of every able-bodied man and woman. This is not the case for wars of mischief far away from home which we have experienced often in the past century.

A government that is willing to enslave some of its people can never be trusted to protect the liberties of its own citizens. I hope all my colleagues join me in standing up for individual liberty and to shut down this un-American relic of a bygone era and help realize the financial savings and the gains to individual liberties that can be achieved by ending Selective Service registration.

Hon. John A. Boehner

OF OHIO

Mr. Speaker, I rise today to commend my neighbors in Butler County, OH, for renaming a park at the former site of the Voice of America's Bethany station "Ronald Reagan's Voice of Freedom Park." This park is enjoyed by Butler County families each and every day, and it has been made all the more special by the fact that it is located on the same spot from where Voice of America broadcasts originated from 1944 to 1994.

In many ways, this name change isn't much of a name change at all. RONALD REAGAN was and in many ways still is the Voice of America.

It's that voice which brought us back from the Vietnam era and the malaise of the seventies. It's that voice that urged Mr. Gorbachev to "tear down this wall!" And it's that voice that ended the cold war through his policy of "peace through strength."

So we're not marking the end of one name for this park and the beginning of a new one. Instead, we're celebrating the passage of title from one cold war messenger of freedom to another. RONALD REAGAN recognized what an effective and influential tool the Voice of America was in our battle to end the cold war. In fact, in 1983 he delivered an address via Voice of America, in which he outlined his vision for long-term negotiations with the Soviet Union. He recognized the vital role Voice of America played in our struggle against the Soviets, and he used it to the advantage of our Nation and our fight for freedom.

Last week, another American President—George W. Bush—spoke in that park. He spoke of a different battle—this time against the evils of terrorism—in which we are currently engaged. Just like the cold war, it will be a long struggle—but one which we know we will win. Why? Because we have the same message of freedom on our side that we did when REAGAN and the Voice of America led us to victory against communism. And so that message of freedom and the Voice of America continues, in that park and across the globe.

Mr. Speaker, I thank my friends back home in Butler County who were involved in the effort to place President REAGAN's name on the park. In this year of tributes to a man I know as a hero, I can think of very few higher than this one.

Wednesday, October 6, 2004

Hon. Trent Franks

OF ARIZONA

Mr. Speaker, one of the core principles on which our Nation is founded is the belief in an individual's God-given right to pursue happiness without government interference. Traditionally this has been understood as an endorsement of the quintessential entrepreneurial spirit and of free-market economics. The great, late President RONALD REAGAN liked to talk about America as a "city on a hill," a light that offers guidance to the nations of the world.

I rise today to pay tribute to a small island nation that has been a shining example in a sometimes troubled region of the world. Under the capable leadership of Prime Minister Nelson Oduber, the Government of Aruba has led the way in exemplifying stable and democratic good governance and in creating an ownership society with a growing, prospering private sector. Most of us understand the vital role a lively private sector plays in a nation's success.

During Mr. Oduber's terms in office, a long list of government-owned companies were either fully or partially privatized. Among them were water production facilities and power plants, the public transportation company, the seaport and the airport, the national telecommunications company and the postal services. Many of these former government agencies today are 100 per cent privately owned. The government has demonstrated that its belief in a free market with a plethora of empowered stakeholders is much more than lip service.

The companies on their part showed that they were well able to get the capital from the financial markets without help from the government. Today, not one of these companies' employees is on the taxpayer-funded government payroll. In addition, the companies can quickly and proactively respond to market forces without any government interference.

While it sometimes seems easier to criticize countries that are doing things wrong, I thank you, Mr. Speaker, for the opportunity to pay tribute to a small nation, a stable ally of the United States, that has put into practice the principles we believe are essential in creating a better, freer, more prosperous and more secure world.

Memorial Tributes

IN THE

Senate of the United States

IN EULOGY OF

Ronald Reagan

In the Senate of the United States

Monday, June 7, 2004

PRAYER

The Chaplain, Dr. Barry C. Black, offered the following prayer:

Let us pray.

Almighty God, generous giver of wonderful gifts, thank You for the life of former President RONALD WILSON REAGAN and for the gift of talented leaders. We praise You for people with vision who see things that are not and ask why not. Thank You for visionaries who call us out of the night of selfish living to the sunrise of sacrifice and service. Help us to celebrate the lives of faithful leaders while they can still hear our appreciation.

Thank You for the Members of Congress who provide stellar leadership. Keep them from evil and infuse them with a spirit of kindness.

As death reminds us of life's brevity, we turn our eyes toward You, O God. You are our refuge and strength and not even death can separate us from Your love. We pray in Your changeless Name. Amen.

Hon. William H. Frist

OF TENNESSEE

Mr. President, this week we mourn the passing of RONALD WILSON REAGAN, the 40th President of the United States. My wife Karyn and I, and indeed the entire Senate family, extend our deepest sympathies to his beloved Nancy and the entire Reagan family. More than 15 years have passed since RONALD REAGAN gave his final cheerful salute as President of the United States. He left the Oval Office with the highest approval rating since Franklin Delano Roosevelt.

RONALD REAGAN had restored our confidence and our optimism in what it meant to be an American. The countless tributes and recollections of the past few days have brought forth a flood of memories, not only of his extraordinary leadership but of his truly exceptional character. We remember RONALD REAGAN and love him as we did the day he left the highest post in the land. We feel a strong personal and unbreakable connection with our 40th President.

Some attribute RONALD REAGAN's ability to connect with the American people to his abilities as an actor. No politician was better or more comfortable around the camera. When he looked into the lens, he was looking directly into the eyes of the American people. His timing was flawless, and he had a soft touch that could disarm even his most stubborn political opponents.

After being wounded by an assassin's bullet as he lay on a hospital gurney drifting toward unconsciousness, RONALD REAGAN quipped to his beloved Nancy, "Honey, I forgot to duck."

So many stories like this remind us that RONALD REAGAN was a man of remarkable courage, coupled with boundless good humor. There was more to him than what he said and how he said it, as there was more to Abraham Lincoln than his stirring speeches, and more to Franklin Roosevelt than his fireside chats. RONALD REAGAN believed in what he said, and that conviction came through. He believed there is good and evil in the world and that America stands for the good. He believed we must protect freedom wherever it may be threatened and plant its seeds wherever freedom may take root. He believed democracy to be not the privilege of a fortunate few but the rightful and ordained destiny for all mankind.

At the 1992 Republican Convention in Houston, TX, he expounded on these beliefs, telling the American people:

> Whether we come from poverty or wealth; whether we are Afro-American or Irish-American; Christian or Jewish, from big cities or small towns, we are all equal in the eyes of God. But as Americans that is not enough. We must be equal in the eyes of each other.

There was one thing—second only to the Almighty—in which he had more faith than all else, and that was the American people. We trusted RONALD REAGAN, we respected RONALD REAGAN, we loved RONALD REAGAN, because he trusted, respected, and loved each and every one of us.

This week we will bear witness to a rare and extraordinary tribute to one of our greatest leaders. Half-masted flags will snap in the wind. Cannons will pound the air with salutes. And a horse-drawn caisson will solemnly pull the flag-draped casket of RONALD WILSON REAGAN up to the Hill of our Capital City.

Americans will line up by the thousands to pause at his side, bow their heads, and pay their final respects. Hundreds of leaders will gather at the National Cathedral to show their deep appreciation of a grateful Nation and a grateful world, and on Friday, when President REAGAN is laid to rest, each of us will give a moment of our day to remember a man who gave us his very best.

All of this is right and fitting. This is how we honor the lives of great leaders whom we love. But our tribute to RONALD REAGAN must be more than a passing historical moment. Although we say goodbye to the man, we must never say goodbye to his values. Let this week reaffirm the goodness of our Nation. Let it reaffirm our faith in freedom. Let it reaffirm democracy as the destiny of all mankind. And let our fond memories, our deep affection and regard for RONALD WILSON REAGAN reaffirm that we believe, above all, in ourselves as Americans.

Hon. Elizabeth Dole

OF NORTH CAROLINA

Mr. President, this past weekend we lost one of America's greatest leaders, RONALD REAGAN. I had the privilege of serving under President REAGAN's strong, principled leadership for 7 years—2 years in his White House as assistant to the President, or public liaison, and almost 5 years as his Secretary of Transportation.

Greatness in a President is marked by the ability to chart and implement a new course, a better course, and by his level of decency and integrity. RONALD REAGAN knew why he wanted to be President. He came to office with the clearest of vision, a passion for achieving his goals and in conveying them with an eloquence almost unsurpassed.

RONALD REAGAN made all of us, the American people, believe in ourselves again. He literally changed the world. Despite conventional wisdom, he determined that communism had to be defeated, not tolerated. He rejected the Iron Curtain, rejected the status quo, and his legacy to the world is freedom. His strength of character and bedrock belief in right and wrong ended the cold war, and his leadership unshackled the yoke of tyranny for millions upon millions of people who had known only oppression.

I will always remember his remarkable rapport with the American people and what a true gentleman he was. During my time on his White House staff, I brought scores and scores of people, organizations, and groups into the Oval Office, the Cabinet Room, the Roosevelt Room, and he treated every person with courtesy and respect. Occasionally, there would be some who had a difference of opinion with him on some issue or another, and they were going to give him a piece of their mind. Well, they came into his presence and you could almost see that anger just fading away. He would express his views, he would address their concerns, and then he might sit back and tell them a story or two—perhaps a humorous one—and maybe pass jellybeans around. They would be ready to climb any hill for RONALD REAGAN. When the President explained his position, obviously, he did it in a very eloquent manner.

What a remarkable person his wife Nancy is. What a tremendous partner. She was his best friend, his confidant, his trusted, beloved spouse. She deserves great credit for his accomplishments and hers.

When I left the Cabinet, a farewell function was planned, and we talked about the fact that it would be nice to invite to that farewell party people who would not otherwise be able to meet the President of the United States. He readily agreed.

I can remember one young woman from Arkansas. She was a part of the Make a Wish group. She had a terminal illness and her great desire was to meet President RONALD REAGAN. I can still see her there in the White House and the compassionate way in which he greeted her and talked with her.

There was a young man named Tommy, from my hometown of Salisbury, NC, who was in a wheelchair; he had to wear a helmet most of the time because if he were to fall, it would be very severe. His mother and his uncle very tenderly brought him to Washington to carry out his wish to meet the great RONALD REAGAN, President of the United States. Once again, to watch the President and his compassion as he talked with Tommy is something I will remember forever.

One of the things that will really be an inspiration to me for the rest of my life is a conversation I had with the President when the two of us were alone. We were waiting in the holding room for him to give a speech. You don't often find yourself alone with the President of the United States. On this particular day, as we waited for the speech I said:

> Mr. President, I just cannot resist. I have to ask you how in the world, when you have the weight of the world on your shoulders, are you able to be so gracious, so thoughtful, and so kind? I never see you flustered or frustrated. How do you do it with such weight on your shoulders?

He kind of leaned back, and he loved to tell a story and to reminisce. He said:

> Well, Elizabeth, when I was Governor of California, it seemed like every day yet another disaster would be placed on my desk, and I had the urge to hand it to someone behind me to help me. One day I realized I was looking in the wrong direction; I looked up instead of back. I am still looking up. I don't think I could go 1 more day in this office if I didn't know that I could ask God's help and it would be given.

There is no doubt in my mind that President REAGAN was welcomed into the gates of Heaven with open arms and with the words "Well done, good and faithful servant." Well done, indeed.

God bless President RONALD REAGAN and his family, and God bless this great land of the free, America.

Hon. Lamar Alexander
OF TENNESSEE

Mr. President, a few years ago when RONALD REAGAN was President of the United States, he attended one of the many press dinners which are held. I think it was the gridiron dinner. I think it is well known that maybe 90 percent of the press corps in Washington had a different point of view on issues than President REAGAN did, but they liked him anyway, and they respected him and he had fun with them, just as they did with him.

I remember on that evening he strode into the gridiron dinner looking like a million dollars, smiling big. The press rose, smiling back, applauding. He stood in front of them until it subsided, and then he said to his adversaries in the media, "Thank you very much. I know how hard it is to clap with your fingers crossed." And they laughed, and they had a wonderful time with President REAGAN.

The first thing we think about, those of us who had any opportunity to get to know him— a great many of us—was that RONALD REAGAN was a very friendly man. He was a congenial person, an easy person to know, the kind of person you want to spend a lot of time with, if you had the opportunity, and that what you saw in private was what everyone else saw in public.

Howard Baker, the former majority leader of the Senate when RONALD REAGAN was President, got to know him especially well, and then in 1987, President REAGAN invited former Senator Baker to come to be his Chief of Staff, which he was for nearly 2 years.

I remember Senator Baker telling me that, to his surprise, when his 9 a.m. meetings came every morning with President REAGAN, he discovered that Mr. REAGAN had a funny little story to tell to Senator Baker, his Chief of Staff. What surprised Senator Baker even more was President REAGAN expected Senator Baker to have a funny little story to tell back. So for that whole 2 years, virtually every morning at 9 a.m. when the President of the United States and the Chief of Staff of the White House met, they swapped funny little stories. It is very reassuring to me that two men who have maybe the two biggest jobs in the world were comfortable enough with themselves, each other, and their responsibilities to begin the day in that sort of easy way. That is the part of RONALD REAGAN we think more about.

Another part of RONALD REAGAN which I think is often overlooked is that he was a man of big ideas. I would say intellectual, although I guess there is a little difference between being devoted to ideals and being intellectual but not much difference.

Unlike most people who are candidates for President of the United States, RONALD REAGAN wrote many of his own speeches. When he had a few minutes, he would sit in the back of a campaign airplane and make notes on cards in the shorthand that he had. His former aide, Marty Anderson, has written a book about that and told that, to a great extent, RONALD REAGAN's words were his own words, ideas he expressed or ideas he gathered himself and ideas he had thought through and wanted to promulgate.

Maybe that is partly why he seemed so comfortable with himself when he finally entered public life. He came to it late in life. He was 55 when he became Governor of California, so by then he knew what he thought, and he had a sense of purpose, and he knew what he wanted to do.

I got an idea of that kind of big thinking when I went to see President REAGAN in my second year as Governor—third year, I guess it was, his first year as President in 1981. I talked to him about a big swap which I thought would help our country.

I suggested, "Mr. President, why doesn't the Federal Government take over all of Medicaid and let the State and local governments take over all responsibility for kindergarten through 12th grade?" "That would make it clear," I said, "where the responsibility lies. You cannot fix schools from Washington, and it would make our health care system more efficient if we did things that way." He liked the idea. It fit his unconventional brand of thinking. He advocated it. It was a little too revolutionary for most people in Washington in the early eighties.

He had the same sort of unconventional attitude toward national defense policy. Many people overlooked the fact that RONALD REAGAN did not just want us to have as many nuclear weapons as the Soviet empire did, he wanted to get rid of nuclear weapons. He saw them as wrong, as bad, and he wanted a world without nuclear weapons. Instead of mutual assured destruction, which was the doctrine at the time, he built up our strength so we could begin to reduce nuclear weapons and then unilaterally begin to do it before the Soviets did, hoping they would then follow. We can see the results.

At the time, some people said RONALD REAGAN was naive to think we could transfer power from Washington, from an arrogant empire at home, or naive to think we could face down an evil empire abroad, and especially naive to think our policy should be based upon getting rid of nuclear weapons. It turned out RONALD REAGAN saw farther than most of those critics did.

Perhaps his most famous speech, not my favorite speech—my favorite speech is the one we heard a lot about this weekend, 20 years ago at Normandy, which moved the whole world to tears and reminded Americans why we are Americans and what we fought for—but his most famous speech may be the one in 1987 at the Brandenburg Gate in Berlin where he said, "Mr. Gorbachev, tear down this wall!"

Earlier this year, I visited Berlin with John Kornblum who at the time was U.S. minister and deputy commandant in the American sector of West Berlin where tanks challenged tanks and white crosses marked gravesites of those who were killed trying to escape over the wall from East Berlin. Mr. Kornblum talked about the development of that speech that RONALD REAGAN gave that day. Those words, or the thought, "tear down this wall," went into the speech at an early stage. Some fought to keep it in. Many fought to take it out. Those who had thought RONALD REAGAN was wrong to say the Soviet Union was an evil empire were not anxious for him to say, "Mr. Gorbachev, tear down this wall!"

Some suggested that President REAGAN try his hand at German as President Kennedy had in a memorable speech at the Berlin Wall in the early sixties. Some suggested that the speech should not be made at the Brandenburg Gate. That was too provocative, Mr. Kornblum remembers. But the speech was made at the Brandenburg Gate, and Mr. REAGAN did keep his words in that speech. He did make his point, and his point was clear: "Mr. Gorbachev, tear down this wall!"

For those of us who had a chance to see the new countries of Eastern Europe and their enthusiasm for freedom and for a free market system, we can see the legacy of RONALD REAGAN and his unconventional thinking. I think it is important for us to remember that this genial President was a man of ideas.

RONALD REAGAN also taught us something about leadership. I recall in 1980 when he and Mrs. Reagan visited the Tennessee Governor's mansion during the Presidential campaign. I had not known him very well. He had served as Governor. He was several years older. He was from the West. It was really my first chance to meet him.

After an hour or an hour and a half of breakfast with him the next morning, I remember going away thinking this man has a better concept of the Presidency than anyone I have ever been privileged to meet.

RONALD REAGAN understood what George Reedy said in his book, "The Twilight of the Presidency," is the definition of Presidential leadership: First, see an urgent need; second, develop a strategy to meet the need; and, third, persuade at least half the people that you are right.

RONALD REAGAN was as good as anyone at persuading at least half the people that he was right. He taught that and he also taught us the importance of proceeding from principles.

Sometimes we are described in Washington these days as being too ideological, too uncompromising, too partisan. President REAGAN was a principled man. He operated from principles in all of his decisions, insofar as I knew. He advocated his principles as far as he could take them, but he recognized that the great decisions that we make here are often conflicts between principles on which all of us agree. It might be equal opportunity versus the rule of law. And once we have argued our principle and the solution, and strategy has been taken as far as it could go, if we get, as he said 75, 80, or 85 percent of what we advocated, well, then that is a pretty good job.

So he was very successful because he argued from principles. He argued strenuously. He was good at persuading at least half the people he was right. Then he was willing to accept a conclusion because most of our politics is about the conflict of principles.

There is another lesson that he taught us, and that was to respect the military. Now, that seems unnecessary to say in the year 2004 where we have a volunteer military that is better than any military we have ever had in our history; when we have witnessed the thousands of acts of courage, charity, kindness, and ingenuity in Iraq and Afghanistan recently; when the men and women of our National Guard and Reserves are also being called up. We have a lot of respect for our military.

In 1980, we were showing a lot less respect for the men and women of our military. I remember riding with President REAGAN in a car in Knoxville during the 1980 campaign. As we pulled out of the airport by the National Guard unit, there were a number of the soldiers waving at him, understanding and sensing that he respected them. He turned to me and said something like this: I wish we could think of some way to honor these men and women more. He said, We used to do that in the movies in the thirties and forties. We would make movies honoring men and women in the military and that is how we showed our respect for them.

Well, he did find a way to honor them during his Presidency in the eighties, and by the time he left at the end of that decade there was no question but that the American people remembered to honor the men and women in the military.

There is one other aspect of President REAGAN's leadership that I would like to mention, which is probably the most important aspect of the American character, and that is the belief that anything is possible. The idea that we uniquely believe in this country, and people all around the world think we are a little odd for believing it, is that no matter where you come from, no matter what race you are, no matter what color your skin, if you come here and work hard, anything is possible.

That is why we subscribe to ideals such as all men are created equal, even though we know achieving that goal will always be a work in progress and we may never reach it. That is why we say we will pay any price, bear any burden, as President Kennedy said, to defend peace, even though we know that is a work in progress and we may never reach it.

That is why we say more recently we want to leave no child behind when it comes to learning to read. We know that is a work in progress and we may not reach it, but that is our goal.

We Americans say that anything is possible, and nothing symbolizes that more than the American Presidency. And no President has symbolized that more in the last century than RONALD REAGAN. He has reminded us of what it means to be an American. He lifted our spirits, he made us proud, he strengthened our character, and he taught us a great many lessons.

Hon. Thad Cochran

OF MISSISSIPPI

Mr. President, with the death of President RONALD REAGAN, our Nation has lost a very successful and inspirational leader. He led us to believe in ourselves and our system of government, our market economy, and our ability to defend freedom and liberty against all threats.

President REAGAN had a contagious sense of optimism. He believed deeply America was capable of solving our problems through our democratic process of self-government, and that other nations could do the same.

His greatest success was improving our economy and establishing a more peaceful and cooperative relationship with the former Soviet Union, in particular with the former communist countries of Eastern Europe.

The Berlin Wall was a symbol of intransigent tyranny. He called for it to be torn down and it was, giving the people of Eastern Europe the opportunity for freedom and hope for a brighter future. We will always remember President REAGAN's great smile, his good humor, his sincerity, and his love of country. We are a better Nation and the world is a safer place because of RONALD REAGAN.

Hon. John Cornyn

OF TEXAS

Mr. President, as the whole world knows by now, America and the world lost a great man, RONALD REAGAN, last Saturday. After battling Alzheimer's disease for the last 10 years, he finally succumbed and left this life for the next.

This week, in this Senate, on television, in the newspapers, and all around the world we will hear people talking of their memories of this great man and what a difference he made in this country and to freedom-loving people all around the world. I offer a few of my own comments in that regard out of respect for him and his family and the great example he was for all who believe in freedom, hope, and opportunity.

RONALD REAGAN, perhaps during his entire political career, was underestimated. He was written off by some as an actor or by some as a nice man but maybe not particularly effective. Because he was a man of good humor who loved a good joke, some thought he could not and should not be taken seriously.

The fact is, RONALD REAGAN demonstrated for everyone how a serious person—that is, someone who believes deeply in their principles, indeed in the principles upon which this country was founded, and who is willing to put themselves out in the public domain and to argue and fight, sometimes to lose but sometimes to win, in advocacy of those principles—RONALD REAGAN reminded us that a good man, indeed a kind human being, a gentle person, a loving husband and father, can also survive in this sometimes difficult, some might even say ugly, world of electoral politics.

In many ways, his death gives another reason to remember that politics today seems in many ways to become personal, so adversarial. Indeed, it need not be. There is no reason why individuals cannot disagree about public policy and differing points of view. There is no reason they cannot do that without becoming personal and hurtful.

I believe it was Margaret Thatcher who once said that a person who reverts to name-calling simply has run out of anything else to say. Indeed, what we ought to be focused on is the policies we believe are in the best interests of the American people and avoid the sort of personal acrimony and hurt which too often seems a characteristic of our modern politics.

RONALD REAGAN taught us you can be a successful politician, you can rise to the greatest heights in our system—indeed, to be the leader of the free world—and still keep your good humor, still treat every person with dignity and respect, and still show the milk of human kindness to others.

The one thing that made RONALD REAGAN such an attractive person in public life was his basic principles. Indeed, there are some who underestimated him his entire political career. What they failed to appreciate was the power of his convictions and the ideals for which he stood. One of those convictions was putting people first. RONALD REAGAN said putting people first has always been America's secret weapon. It is the way we have kept the spirit of our revolution alive, a spirit that drives us to dream and dare, and to take great risks for a greater good.

I know RONALD REAGAN has been touted as a great man. I believe he was a great man. But he never considered himself to be a great man, merely a man committed to great ideas.

He also was sometimes criticized for being too much of a dreamer, but he made no apologies about that. He said, "There's no question I am an idealist, which is another way of saying I am an American."

But when I think of the policies of the Reagan administration and the successes of what some have called the Reagan revolution, but which I think in many ways was not revolutionary as much as it was a restoration of our basic principles upon which this country was founded, I think of the fall of communism and the subsequent liberation of tens of millions of people who had known nothing other than oppression and tyranny and dictatorship, and, also, the resurgence of the American economy.

First, so far as his role in the fall of communism, although he was a genial, friendly, humor-loving optimist, he was a hardnosed realist when it came to the terrible impact and consequences of communism on people across this globe. Indeed, he knew it was important for us to maintain a strong military and made no apologies when it came to the importance of "peace through strength," not going hat in hand to our allies or our enemies asking them to do us a favor but recognizing that America has a unique role in the world as the one remaining superpower, after the fall of the Soviet Union, and recognizing the failure of communism as an alternative to freedom and democracy.

But it was, in large part, his commitment to rebuilding our military and "peace through strength" and hardnosed negotiating across the conference table with various opponents of our country and leaders of other countries that caused freedom to reign for tens of millions of people who had never known freedom.

The other thing he believed in was the freedom here at home. He believed that big government was the enemy of individual freedom, and that if, in fact, we were going to be able to continue to enjoy the kind of prosperity and opportunity that has been synonymous with America, we needed to get a handle on big government. Indeed, when RONALD REAGAN became President, it is hard to believe now, but the highest marginal income tax rate was 70 percent. By the time he left office, it was 28 percent. Today it stands at 35 percent.

But RONALD REAGAN understood, as all Americans understand—all folks outside of Washington especially understand—that in order to grow the economy you do not tax it more, you cut taxes, because only then can you provide the incentive for the individual American worker to work hard, save their money, invest their money, perhaps in their small business, and then create jobs and opportunity for others who may not have those jobs or that opportunity. It was by growing the economy, by providing that incentive for work and investment and savings and risk taking that we have all been the beneficiaries in modern times of the new economic freedom that was brought in by RONALD REAGAN's leadership.

Most of all, I think my memories of RONALD REAGAN center around his call for us to believe in ourselves once again, to believe in America again, and believe in the ideals we all identify with this great country of ours. America is different from virtually every other country in the world in that it was founded on ideals, on an ideal of liberty and justice for all, something not shared by any other country in the world that was formed or based on history or collective experience. But, of course, our country was formed on the basis of these ideals, and RONALD REAGAN believed in them fervently and, more importantly, he fought for them, even against those who suggested that perhaps it was not possible for America to be great again.

There were those who suggested that somehow America's greatest days were behind us. RONALD REAGAN never believed that. He always believed America's greatest days lay ahead of us. And indeed they do, even today.

He understood and preached, perhaps better than anyone, that big government and high taxes are the enemy of individual freedom, that smaller government and lower taxes would be an incentive to work and savings.

I mentioned a moment ago his belief in the individual initiative of risk takers, of entrepreneurs, of those who would take the risks, make the investment, and create jobs for the American people. At one point he said:

> Too often, entrepreneurs are forgotten heroes. We rarely hear about them. But look into the heart of America, and you'll see them. They're the owners of that store down the street, the faithfuls who support our churches, schools, and communities, the brave people everywhere who produce our goods, feed a hungry world, and keep our homes and families warm while they invest in the future to build a better America.

Now, those who only saw the genial, friendly, humor-loving side of RONALD REAGAN did not know the entire man. As I mentioned, behind that genial countenance was a man of strong principle and a man as tough as they come. For example, when the air traffic controllers defied a back-to-work order, he fired them, emphasizing the fact that the greater good is always paramount and more important than special interests.

Of course, he survived an assassin's bullets with great humor, telling his wife, "Honey, I forgot to duck," and expressing to his physicians, the ones who saved his life in the emergency room, "I hope you're all Republicans."

With every fearsome challenge he encountered in life, he met it with good humor, humanity, kindness, and optimism in a way that inspired and continues to inspire the American people, which, to me, will be one of his greatest legacies.

He also taught us that politics can be a noble calling. Unfortunately, today, it seems that is forgotten too often and people ask: How in the world can you be involved in politics and be a good person? How can you believe in doing the right thing and be involved in politics since it is all about getting reelected and raising money and a fight for power? But, indeed, RONALD REAGAN exemplified the fact that a good person, with strong convictions, committed to great ideals and the principles upon which this country was founded, can be successful in life and in politics. Indeed, he was as the leader of the free world.

Mr. President, as the Nation grieves with his family, we also celebrate the life of this great man, a quintessential American whose hopes and dreams knew no bounds.

RONALD REAGAN loved America, and America loved him back.

Hon. Conrad Burns

OF MONTANA

Madam President, I come to the floor today after receiving the news over the weekend of the passing of President REAGAN. I see today these young folks called pages who work for us on the floor of the U.S. Senate. They will be here this week during a very historic period. Here are young people who never met President REAGAN. They have never seen him give a speech live, nor have had conversations with him, and never really will be able to hold the man in their hearts like some of us who were inspired to go into political life by his words and by the example that he set for political life. It is too bad they didn't get to do that. But that is not their fault.

This week, we will be celebrating his life. He will come to this town, and there will be a lot of recollections from those who knew him. I did not get to serve with him because he left the Presidency the same year that I was elected to the Senate. I came here under the Presidency of President George Herbert Walker Bush.

One of the photographs of which I am most fond, of the President and me, one I shall cherish to the end of my life, was taken in 1982 when he came to Billings, MT. We had a little bit to do with that meeting. I think it was the first personal meeting I ever had with the President. You could tell from the way he carried himself, the way he walked, the way he spoke, the way he treated people, the handshake, that he was not only the Commander in Chief and President of the United States, but he was also a man of the people. He had midwestern roots—Illinois, the great prairies. He was successful in Hollywood. He was a successful broadcaster. He was of an age, at the time he was called to political life, that basically everyone said he was too old. Yet he went on to serve two terms.

You may not have agreed with everything he stood for, but you didn't ever have any problem figuring out where he stood. He never wavered. He was the same the day he left office as the day he came into office. That example probably put into public life a lot of us who never thought of it.

I can remember something that happened in 1988, when I ran. In this political life, they said you have to come back to Washington, DC, and you have to have your picture taken with President REAGAN. They gave me the date to be here. I said, "I am sorry, I can't be there that date."

They reminded me and said, "This is the White House calling. This is the date."

I said that I wasn't concerned about what color their house was, but on that date I happened to have an auction. I am an auctioneer. I had to make a living first, in 1988.

So that conversation closed. Then all at once, the political director called up. I explained the same thing to him. I said, "It is not that important, no big deal. I am busy, he is busy, we have a date, they didn't jibe, so we will move on."

Well, as it turned out, even the President called. He said, "I understand about auctions, once you have one advertised. You go ahead and have the auction."

That surprised me a lot. He was something. He was one of those who really won the cold war without firing a shot. And the chemistry between him and Prime Minister Thatcher of England was one of an unbelievable partnership. They stood alone against the world on the deployment of tactical nuclear weapons as a deterrent to the aggression of a country that he called evil. You see, he had come to the Presidency knowing that about communism. He knew it for what it was—degrading, dehumanizing. There was no upward mobility, no chance of any individual ever attaining any kind of freedom—either economically or politically. There was no opportunity to take their own talents and go into the field of their endeavor. He understood communism for what it was and he said, "This cancer has to go."

As a result, through his steadfast leadership—and I know there were lonely times with decisions that he made—he brought down the Berlin Wall without a shot being fired.

We honor him. This should be a week of celebration of a life—a life in the history of this country that will live as long as the country lives, as long as free men want to breathe. His name will be remembered. He has made his mark.

At that first meeting in Billings, I was sitting on a horse, and we were getting ready to take him into a building. There were two others who were supposed to escort the stagecoach. I can remember him saying, "You know, the rowels on those spurs aren't very big." And I said, "You don't need a big rowel if you have a spirited horse." He said, "I understand that."

We will celebrate this man's life this week. We named a post office in Billings, MT, 59105, after RONALD REAGAN this year. I am proud of that.

But what a gifted man he was, the way he could communicate, the way he could touch people, the time he gave to this country for which we should be very thankful. He wasn't a perfect man. I haven't seen one yet who didn't have a few bruises, scars, marks, bumps, warts, and such. But he was an American, and he was an American who took those principles to heart. He lived them every day he drew breath—while he was in the White House and after he left the White House.

Mr. President, we welcome you back to Washington this week to celebrate your life and your contribution to this great country. We say, Thank you.

SUBMITTED RESOLUTIONS

Mr. FRIST (for himself, Mr. Daschle, Mr. Lott, and Mr. Dodd) submitted the following concurrent resolution; which was considered and agreed to:

S. CON. RES. 115

Resolved by the Senate (the House of Representatives concurring), That in recognition of the long and distinguished service rendered to the Nation and to the world, by the late RONALD WILSON REAGAN, the 40th President of the United States, his remains be permitted to lie in state in the rotunda of the Capitol from June 9 until June 11, 2004, and the Architect of the Capitol, under the direction of the President pro tempore of the Senate and the Speaker of the House of Representatives, shall take all necessary steps for the accomplishment of that purpose.

IN MEMORY OF RONALD WILSON REAGAN, 40TH PRESIDENT OF THE UNITED STATES

Mr. FRIST. Mr. President, I ask unanimous consent that the Senate proceed to the immediate consideration of S. Res. 371, which was submitted earlier today.

Mr. President, I ask unanimous consent that the resolution be agreed to and the motion to reconsider be laid upon the table.

The PRESIDING OFFICER. Without objection, it is so ordered.

The resolution (S. Res. 371) was agreed to, as follows:

S. RES. 371

Resolved, That in recognition of the long and distinguished service rendered to the Nation by the late RONALD WILSON REAGAN, the 40th President of the United States, when the Senate recesses or adjourns on each of the days during the period from June 7 through June 11, 2004, it do so as a further mark of respect to the memory of RONALD WILSON REAGAN.

Tuesday, June 8, 2004

PRAYER

The guest Chaplain, Dr. Prentice Meador, of Prestoncrest Church of Christ, Dallas, TX, offered the following prayer:

Shall we pray.

Holy Father, we affirm You as Lord of our lives and our Nation. We are comfortable to come into Your presence on this special moment because You have invited us before Your throne. Gratitude and praise flows from our hearts for giving our Nation blessings that would have astonished our ancestors.

Lord, in this historic week, our Nation mourns the death of President RONALD REAGAN. Father, we celebrate his patriotism, optimism, and courage. Bless Mrs. Reagan, her family, and our Nation with peace from Your heart.

And, Father, may we never forget our heritage. Sovereign Lord, we are keenly aware that 60 years ago today, heroic men were fighting their way off the beaches of Normandy. Lord, we shall never forget places like "Bloody Omaha," Carentan, Sainte-Mère-Eglise, Caen, Bastogne. Keep in our memory those who fought together and now lie together in death that we might be free. Father, may their voices of valor be heard in this Chamber in clear, crisp tones.

Merciful Father, in a world that sometimes drowns out such voices, empower the women and men of this great body to hear again words from our past: integrity, faith, bravery, sacrifice, and godliness. At this special time, I pray that each Senator might recommit to the clarity of Your truth, the depth of Your wisdom, and the power of Your love.

Father, help the Senators to know that many in this Nation pray for them and their faithfulness to their most solemn obligations. May they bow their knees before You so they may know what is right for our country. Lord, sanctify this assembly by dwelling in the hearts of each of these respected leaders. May glory, honor, and dominion be Yours forever and ever.

In Your most holy Name. Amen.

Hon. Judd Gregg

OF NEW HAMPSHIRE

I rise today, as many Americans, to pay my respect and thanks, and also to celebrate the life of Ronald Reagan, an extraordinary man who has had such a huge impact on our generation and the generations to come in the world—especially Americans' place in the world.

I have a lot of fond and personal memories about Governor and President Reagan. First, I had the opportunity to meet him with my wife Kathy when he and Nancy Reagan came to New Hampshire to campaign in 1976. He was running against a sitting Republican President, Gerald Ford, appointed, of course, coming out of the Watergate era. Some in our party thought maybe it was time to move on, put a new face on our party, and put someone forward who had a certain charisma and attitude which was a little different. Certainly Reagan met that test.

As we traveled around New Hampshire, he was not the national figure he is today, although he was a significant figure. In fact, he was a movie star. People were flocking to meet him and see him. They wanted to hear what he had to say. But as we traveled around, a fairly small contingent in a bus and a few cars, we had a chance to get to know him a little bit. What came through most apparently to myself and Kathy was he was a genuine person who had a real sense of self and who had a way of making people feel at ease around him. He had a charisma, to say the least.

Then I had the great fortune of being elected to Congress in 1980. Prior to that, ironically I had been at the famous national debate in January 1980 where President Reagan actually set the course for getting the nomination and moving on to become the President with the famous comment, "I am paying for this microphone, Mr. Green." Ironically, I was at the site and in charge of the site in advance of the nomination. So I had a chance to see a bit of history there.

But in 1990, along with 54 other Republicans, I was elected to the House of Representatives, and we came here with President Reagan. We had a purpose. We had a definite purpose. People will recall at that time coming out of the seventies the inflation rate was 12 percent, interest rates were 22 percent, and we had American citizens being held captive in Iran. The President—then-President Jimmy Carter—said we were in a period of national malaise. We didn't feel that way. We felt America was a great and wonderful Nation. Ronald Reagan epitomized that view of the future being bright rather than dark—the future being one of unlimited opportunities rather than one of a decreasing pie. So 54 of us arrived in the House of Representatives.

It was a unique situation because the House of Representatives was being controlled at that time—and people do not appreciate it today, but it had been controlled by the Democratic Party for 26 years; continuously controlled by the same party, and it produced a lot of very interesting and very aggressive and strong individuals to manage the House. The strongest, of course, was Tip O'Neill, who was then the Speaker. He was not going to tolerate those 54 new Republican Members who arrived in the House of Representatives and were carrying the water for President Reagan. We were treated with an experience in education on how politics really works by Tip O'Neill, as we were exposed to what real power can do and how it can be managed in a congressional body.

We continued to charge the Hill, however, for the President, because President Reagan had a clear and defined agenda. He intended to fundamentally shift this country. The shift was going to be toward strengthening our national defense capabilities, toward reducing the burden of government, toward reducing the burden of taxation, and toward reestablishing our confidence as a Nation. There was a lot of legislation brought forward, with very difficult battles over the budget, very difficult battles over issues of making our defense capability stronger once again.

We became known as Reagan's robots. That was a derisive term used by some of our friends in the media and it was thrown at us. As Reagan's economics were called Reaganomics, a derisive term put out in the intelligentsia community by our friends who saw it as inappropriate economics and saw it as waterbearers for a President whom they considered to be superficial, and in some cases a caricature, but we took that as sort of a red badge of courage, those who came in that class. We enjoyed the fact we were tweaking the institution of the House at the time led by Speaker O'Neill, whom I happened, over the years, to come to like as an individual very much. He obviously had a very strong personality and led the House very aggressively in a very partisan way. It was a unique and special time to have a chance to serve under a President such as President REAGAN.

Going to the White House with Kathy and our two oldest children, I remember a lot of fond personal memories of how kind he was. Our daughters were then quite young. I think they were 4 and 5 or maybe 5 and 6. He took them aside and got hotdogs for them; he got popcorn for them.

He was just a wonderful, inclusive individual and had a naturalness about him that was extraordinary and made everybody who was around him, when they had the chance, feel good. It was that personality that I think caused him to be able to be President during a time when there was a fair amount of strident partisanship. At the same time, there was less of a personal vindictiveness in the atmosphere, which was nice at that time, to have at least that sort of atmosphere where people were not into the personal assassination level that we sometimes see occur in politics, although it did happen to some degree.

The fond memories are there from an individual standpoint, but the real memory, the real force of President REAGAN goes beyond the personal contact. It goes to what his mission was, what he accomplished for our Nation, which was so extraordinary, and what he accomplished for the world. It has been discussed. There is nothing unique about the discussion because it is so broadly accepted now what he did accomplish.

That was, essentially, this: He took a Nation which was, as I said by its own definition, by its then-leader, Jimmy Carter, in a period of national malaise and he turned us and reawakened our natural optimism. We are a Nation of optimists. We are a Nation that believes we can accomplish whatever we seek to pursue, whatever goal we set. He made us believe in that again. His "city on the hill" belief in our Nation was deep in him, but, more important, he was able to project it across our country and give people a sense of self and a sense of purpose that was optimistic and upbeat, that was essential to our country at that time.

Probably equally important to the world, he set America back on a course of leading us in what was then the true great confrontation of the 20th century, which was the question of whether communist, socialist economics, and a totalitarian state would dominate or whether democracy and market-oriented economies would dominate.

There were three major trends of the 20th century that were tested. The first, of course, was the issue of the philosophy of communist versus market-oriented economies. The second, of course, was totalitarianism, first presented in fascism and second presented in the communist states of Stalin, by Stalin and Mao, versus democracy. The third was the issue of relativism. On those first two issues, he led the world and delivered the results which said unequivocally that democracy and market-oriented economies were the future for mankind and that individual rights meant something.

In accomplishing that, he passed on to our generation and all the generations to come a gift of freedom and a gift of possibility in the area of economic well-being that was not necessarily a given. It would not necessarily have occurred without him. It is possible the Soviet Union and certainly the mutations of the Soviet Union could have proceeded for a considerable amount of time. We could still be dealing with that issue today had he not been willing to stand up, because he had unequivocal confidence in our Nation and in the values that drive our Nation, had he not been willing to stand up and say essentially that we were going to compete in that race at a level that would essentially make it impossible for the Soviet Union and communist-style regimes to compete with us. That is what he did.

He did it first in the military where he essentially said to the Soviet Union, we are just simply going to outbuild you and we are going to exceed your ability to compete, so they crumbled from within. Second, he did it by establishing, once again, that the basic values of democracy far exceeded any values that were being put forward, and clearly our much better lifestyle than anything being put forward by a Soviet communist state.

So we owe him a great debt of thanks and we certainly owe his family a great debt of thanks. We thank Nancy Reagan for her wonderful service to this Nation. We thank his family for the gift of this great man to our country.

Hon. Olympia J. Snowe
OF MAINE

Our Nation mourns the passage of a man who called Americans to their common purpose and renewed our age-old faith in the limitless possibilities of freedom.

With heavy but immensely grateful hearts, our country grieves the passing of President RONALD REAGAN and extends our collective thoughts and prayers to his extraordinary wife Nancy and his children, Michael, Patti, and Ron.

Reflecting today on the hope that President REAGAN inspired in America, I am reminded of the story of Benjamin Franklin near the close of the Constitutional Convention. Franklin pointed to the painting behind Washington's chair, a landscape of the Sun just on the horizon and remarked:

> I have often looked at that sun behind the President without being able to tell whether it was rising or setting. But now I have the happiness to know it is a rising and not a setting sun.

Let the record forever show that in a time of great consequence, President REAGAN assured an uncertain Nation that ours remains always a rising Sun. He brought a passionate belief in American ideas to bear in advancing freedom as a force for good in the world and heralded a new dawn of confidence at home.

Like so many Americans, I remember well the steep challenges facing the Nation in 1980. At that time, having already served 2 years in the House of Representatives, we could look back to the late seventies as an incubator of change that foreshadowed the transformation to come.

Before President REAGAN, we had become conditioned to accept limitations on what we might aspire to as individuals and as a Nation. But out of those days of national disillusionment and political drift came a bold leader to inspire confidence.

The year 1980 was the culmination of a period of self-doubt for America. Internationally, our country was mired in the cold war and reeling from the Iranian hostage crisis. On the domestic front, our economy had been sapped by double-digit inflation, double-digit prime interest rates, and stifled by massive tax burdens, including a top tax rate of 70 percent. We also had been undercut by a serious energy crisis. In fact, we had gasoline lines here in Washington and all through the country. So suffice it to say, these were not bright days in Washington or America. As I said at the time, whoever won the White House would bear the responsibility for making America productive once again, and President REAGAN did. With his conviction that the greatest untapped potential lies in the American people themselves—by embracing hope, not resignation, and by projecting an optimism in our Nation and her people that was as genuine as the man himself—he charted a course for America for greater prosperity and security.

As President, as we know, he confronted the world's only other superpower, laying the foundation for victory in the cold war. He campaigned to reduce the size of the Federal bureaucracy, to return tax dollars to the families that had earned them, and to devolve out of Washington and back to local governments—all ideas whose time had come, just as President REAGAN's had. Not only that, but he reinvigorated America with his unabashed faith in her essential goodness.

The other night, I had the opportunity to recount the Reagan era with my husband, former Governor Jock McKernan, who also served 4 years in Congress under the Reagan Presidency representing the other congressional district in the State of Maine. We were recalling a time in which we visited the White House, regarding the shaping of defense policy. As Senator Gregg has mentioned, we were building up our national defense.

We remembered the statement the President made at the time, which I think summed up his belief in trying to make a distinction between the United States of America and the Soviet Union. He said, "You know, it tells something about a country when more people want to leave the country than want to come in." His simple logic was indeed compelling.

President REAGAN was a conservative Republican from California, and I, of course, was a moderate Republican from New England. Obviously, there were times—and many times, in fact—when we differed on policy. Yet I can also recall meeting with him and other members of the Republican Caucus, as well as Democrats. We had numerous meetings at the White House either in the Cabinet room or within the Oval Office itself. We were able to negotiate our differences, whether it was within our party or across party lines. The issues ranged from defense policy, to the MX missile, to Central America, to the budget. Indeed, we had numerous budget discussions where we negotiated the actual budget resolutions and the budget numbers themselves.

Thinking back this week, I also recall how the President was willing to hear disparate views on trade policy. In fact, Jock and I met with the President in the Oval Office to discuss the potential negative impact of trade proposals on Maine's industries such as potatoes, shoes and lumber in advance of the President meeting with Canadian Prime Minister Brian Mulroney. Indeed, coincidentally, I saw the former Prime Minister in the Capitol prior to the viewing in the rotunda on Wednesday night, and I recounted that meeting with the President.

Moreover, I spearheaded an effort for Republican women in the House and Senate to meet with President REAGAN to discuss matters critical to America's women. In the end, these initiatives led to ultimately passing landmark child support enforcement legislation and pension reform for widows that previously had not even been part of the Federal lexicon, let alone part of Federal policy. And in speaking of women's issues, I fondly reflect on my cherished friendship with the President's daughter, the late Maureen Reagan who died in 2001, and how we also worked together on behalf of issues of concern for women in this country.

And on an entirely different issue once again, to this day I have on my wall a letter of appreciation from President REAGAN for my efforts to help develop and pass the 1986 Omnibus Diplomatic Security and Antiterrorism Act, which he signed and which contained a provision I authored to create an accountability review board within the State Department to investigate all incidents involving serious security failures.

He was always respectful of divergent views and willing to keep his Oval Office door open, even as he always knew what he believed. In terms of his principles, his compass was steady. At the same time, he was certainly committed to the fine and, in Washington, all too rare art of listening. He was also willing to seek consensus, even though we surely had a partisan environment at that time.

We had a divided government, and obviously a Republican Presidency. But again, he was willing to forge a consensus because he believed that was the only way you could get things done. Rather than by controversy and division, in the end he recognized you had to reach your goals with persuasion and openness. So he was willing to develop pragmatic approaches in the final analysis because he was a problem-solver. Actually, he gave life to what he once said, "if I can get 70 or 80 percent of what it is I'm trying to get . . . I'll take that and then continue to try to get the rest in the future."

He certainly did live by that axiom throughout his tenure of 8 years, regardless of the differences. Ultimately, he wanted to achieve the great things he set out to do when he became President and also to ensure he could be resolute in implementing his vision for this country.

He was entirely comfortable with stepping outside of others' conventional perception of himself and his politics. He was extremely credible as Commander in Chief, as leader of this country when he set about to build up our military and to defy the Soviet Union and to ultimately bring down the Wall. The fact is, he also, on the other side of the coin, ultimately negotiated the first pact to reduce the United States and Soviet nuclear arsenals—he negotiated that with Mikhail Gorbachev—because, again, he understood what needed to be accomplished in the end.

His legacy will forever be his vision that brought about the end of the cold war because, again, he saw the difference between dictatorships and democracy and our ability to foster liberty in the dark corners of the world. Indeed, I will never forget the meeting I participated in with members of Solidarity in January 1988 in Poland. There was no question that, for them, knowing of our resolutions in Congress in support of freedom for the people of Poland, Vice President Bush's 1987 visit to Warsaw, and certainly President REAGAN's relentless pursuit of the ideal of freedom for people everywhere, gave them a hope they translated into strength and persistence in finally prevailing. How extraordinary that Solidarity's leader would become Poland's President—and how fitting that Lech Walesa would attend President REAGAN's funeral to express his profound appreciation and deepest respect.

And who would have predicted two decades ago that Mikhail Gorbachev—leader of the former Soviet Union—would be attending the funeral of President RONALD REAGAN, who brought about the collapse of the Soviet Union and urged Gorbachev to tear down the Berlin Wall? But that is yet another testament to President REAGAN's legacy.

Some thought President REAGAN's bold descriptions of the wide chasm that separated democracy from despotism were ill considered. Yet he viewed the world through that crystal clear prism of, in the words of Shakespeare, "simple truth miscalled simplicity." I believe that says it all because President REAGAN understood that in order to be an effective leader, to be a strong President, to be the leader of this country who was a force for good and to project that force for good, you ultimately had to move the process, and you had to work within the system and with the other branch of government to make that happen.

Another great of the 20th century refused praise for having lent his lionhearted strength to an entire nation. Instead, Winston Churchill remarked, it was his nation that had the "lion's heart" all along, and it fell to him only to "give the roar."

So it was with President RONALD REAGAN. His words summoned our resolve and our goodness, and his steady hand guided America to a triumph for all free people. As providence would have it, President REAGAN gave America's roar during what would become—in no small part, thanks to him—the last decade of the cold war. With "peace through strength," RONALD REAGAN called America to a purpose he described in his own hand in 1980 when he wrote:

> I believe it is our pre-ordained destiny to show all mankind that they too can be free without having to leave their native shore.

For this legacy, the American people and free people everywhere are in his debt, just as he is in our hearts and his family, as well, in our prayers.

Hon. Barbara Boxer

OF CALIFORNIA

Mr. President, I rise today to pay my respects to one of California's own, President RONALD REAGAN.

I first met President REAGAN right after I was elected to Congress in 1982. We were a large Democratic freshman class, and when I was invited to the White House, I wondered how President REAGAN would greet us. After all, he had campaigned hard for a Republican Congress, and having lost an election myself I knew the feeling of disappointment. When we arrived at the White House, President REAGAN could not have been more gracious to us; the same for Mrs. Reagan. I still have the photo from that evening hanging in my home office.

Twenty-two years ago, RONALD REAGAN taught me that you can disagree without being disagreeable, that you could set aside those disagreements even though they were deep.

President REAGAN once said, "A lot of trouble in the world would disappear if we were talking to each other instead of about each other."

He believed if we were all respectful and pleasant to one another, we could find those areas of common ground. We can reach across the aisle. We can get things done. Believe me, that was a good lesson for me and for all of us that evening because clearly, in the Senate, with the rules of the Senate, the only way to get things done is by working together. I look at the occupant of the chair, and I know that with our disagreements on many issues, we have come together on a few occasions, and we have won for our constituents and for this country.

When I look back to President REAGAN's record, I realize that not only did he bring this kind of an attitude of working together to Washington, but that had been his hallmark in California as well. As a Republican Governor, he was working with a Democratic State legislature. So it seems President REAGAN had to learn how to do this both in the State and in the Nation's Capital.

In those years as Governor, in keeping with the values and wishes of most Californians, he helped to establish the Redwood National Park. He regulated auto emissions to reduce pollution. He signed a bill that liberalized a woman's right to choose. He opposed the State proposition that discriminated against teachers based on sexual orientation. You can see Governor REAGAN was willing to reach across and find consensus.

RONALD REAGAN, of course, did continue to reach across the aisle when he became President. Although there were serious disagreements, he worked closely with a Democratic House to ratify and sign important arms control agreements, increasing funds for math and science education, reauthorizing the Superfund hazardous waste cleanup program, which is so important. The basis of the program is that the polluter should pay. Interestingly, we don't seem to have that kind of support today.

President REAGAN once said, "There is no limit to what a man can do or where he can go, if he doesn't mind who gets the credit." And how important that quote is when it comes to politics. President REAGAN was a conservative. He was not an ideologue. He fulfilled a campaign promise to appoint the first woman to the Supreme Court. He chose Sandra Day O'Connor as the first woman Justice of the U.S. Supreme Court, even though she was considered too moderate by many conservatives. He tried to abolish the National Endowment for the Arts but, after losing that fight, he moved on. I remember that. He moved on without trying to force the issue through the backdoor. I respect that.

I remember the fight to keep the National Endowment for the Arts. Many Republicans in my State didn't agree with President REAGAN. They mobilized with the Democrats. President REAGAN said, Well, this is what I think. He went forward, and when he lost, that was it.

Of course, there are other issues of disagreement—from offshore oil drilling to the role of the National Government, to the fight against AIDS, to policies in Central America. Those disagreements were deep, but they were never taken personally by President REAGAN. He and House Speaker Tip O'Neill were genuinely fond of each other. They often shared a drink after work, and they laughed after a day of locking horns. Their good nature was infectious. It raised the level of comity throughout the Nation's Capital. How I long for those days. It is time that in the spirit of RONALD REAGAN and Tip O'Neill, we see more bipartisan spirit in our work.

In California, there are tributes to RONALD REAGAN running around the clock. I know it is true nationally, but because he was our Governor and we are so proud he is part of our legacy, we are seeing and listening to RONALD REAGAN's stories and RONALD REAGAN quotes. I found one of these very interesting.

There was a question asked to President REAGAN after he had completed his 8 years in office. The question was: What do you most want to be remembered for? His answer was this: The millions of jobs that were created while he was President and America regaining respect in the world. Millions of jobs created and America regaining respect in the world. You think about how universal those two achievements are because right now that is a lot of the focus of attention—job creation and respect in the world. It is interesting how prophetic those words are.

I personally believe that 50 years from now, if not now, President REAGAN will be remembered for his focus on freedom for the people behind the Iron Curtain. He saw in Soviet President Mikhail Gorbachev a man he could successfully challenge to step to the plate. And when President REAGAN said, "tear down this wall!" he said it directly to Mr. Gorbachev. He touched Mr. Gorbachev, and he touched America. He touched people around the world.

In a moving eulogy in yesterday's *New York Times* Mr. Gorbachev wrote:

> REAGAN was a man of the right but while adhering to his convictions, with which one could agree or disagree, he

was not dogmatic. He was looking for negotiations and for cooperation.

In that, you have to understand that respect for other people and their ideas, the ability to step into their shoes is very important.

We name buildings and rooms and public places after leaders, and we have named many public places after RONALD REAGAN. But I truly believe that now the greatest thing we can do in RONALD REAGAN's memory is to find a cure for the disease that took his life and took him away from his loved ones and the world stage long before his physical life ended.

Alzheimer's disease is a plague that ravages millions of Americans and those who love them. Caused by abnormal plaques and tangled nerve fibers in the brain, the disease attacks the cells that control thought, memory, and language. The brain, if you look at it, becomes more and more like a child's brain. It kills nerve cells that are vital to memory. If you think about it, when you lose your memory, you lose who you are. And to see someone like RONALD REAGAN, who held all the power for 8 years that anyone could ever dream to hold, and to have him not be able to remember that is a tragedy.

Alzheimer's lowers the level of chemicals that carry messages between nerve cells and the brain. The progress of Alzheimer's is usually slow, but it is inexorable. Beginning with mild symptoms, such as forgetfulness, Alzheimer's gradually robs its victims of the ability to think clearly, speak clearly, understand others, or care for themselves in any way.

Ten years ago RONALD REAGAN knew he was battling Alzheimer's. He knew he was losing the battle. In an act of tremendous courage and in a handwritten open letter, he told the American people he was suffering from the illness. He wrote, "I now begin this journey that will lead me into the sunset of my life."

And he movingly wrote, "I know that for America there will always be a bright dawn ahead."

So even in his darkest hour, President REAGAN's eternal optimism shone through.

Nancy Reagan stood by her husband throughout this long ordeal, protecting him in his most vulnerable time. In recent years, she has become a leading advocate of increased funding for medical research to fight Alzheimer's and other diseases. She has been brave and courageous in her advocacy.

Ironically, just a few weeks ago, I wrote an open letter to her praising her for her strength and moving forward to use her considerable influence to push forward stem cell research.

To honor RONALD REAGAN and relieve the suffering of millions of American families, we must pursue every avenue of research and treatment for Alzheimer's and other diseases.

In memory of RONALD REAGAN and all of the families who have lost loved ones to Alzheimer's, let us seek a brighter dawn for Alzheimer's victims and their families.

So, Mr. President, Californians are speaking across party lines for a man who was able to set aside ideology to make progress, to work with those who might not have agreed with him on every point. I think it is a terrific lesson to all of us in this time and in this place in our Nation's history.

Hon. Harry Reid

OF NEVADA

Mr. President, RONALD REAGAN is seen by the State of Illinois as being his birthplace, as well it should. They feel very strongly about the legacy of RONALD REAGAN in Illinois. California, of course, is where RONALD REAGAN became famous. They have tremendous ties to RONALD REAGAN. The State of Nevada has lots and lots of ties to RONALD REAGAN. Not only are we a neighbor to the State of California, but the history of RONALD REAGAN and the State of Nevada are intertwined. I come to the Senate today to join a procession to praise RONALD REAGAN as a great leader and a fine man.

My first trip to the Oval Office was to meet with RONALD REAGAN. I was a young Congressman and I was called to the Oval Office to discuss with the President the situation in Nicaragua, aid to the Contras. I was joined there by three other Members of Congress. Vice President Bush, at the time, was there. It is the first time I had the opportunity to visit with, in any depth,

RONALD REAGAN as President of the United States.

There was a time when I was Lieutenant Governor of Nevada, and Governor O'Callaghan was unable to go to an event at Lake Tahoe. I represented the State. Governor REAGAN at the time, and I spent time together, but it was in a public setting and really not a time where you got to know anyone well.

My first trip to the Oval Office was one that I will always remember. Not only was it my first trip to the Oval Office, it was my first experience in sitting down and talking with RONALD REAGAN, President of the United States. His personality came through in that meeting. I have often repeated the story of my visit there.

A Congressman said to RONALD REAGAN at the time, "Mr. President, I'm afraid you're going to invade Nicaragua." President REAGAN did not wait a second. He came back so quickly, with that smile on his face, and said, "I'm not going to invade Nicaragua, but I want those SOBs going to bed every night thinking I'm going to."

That was RONALD REAGAN. His views of the world were views that all of us could understand. He made it very clear to us that he was not going to invade Nicaragua but he was not about to show any weakness to the Nicaraguans. That is exactly how he said it. From where I come, that was talk that I understood.

I have fond memories of RONALD REAGAN. RONALD REAGAN, of course, is someone we all watched on TV, "Death Valley Days." But those in Nevada remember him also, and the papers in Nevada have been full the last few days about his entertainment qualities in Las Vegas.

He came to Las Vegas as an entertainer. He appeared on the Las Vegas strip as an entertainer. We were discussing what he did. I don't know what he did, but he came all the time. He was a headliner. I don't know if he sang or danced. I don't know what he did. He made money and they kept bringing him back.

He was born in the Midwest but he was really a son of the West. He stood for a lot of what we now identify with RONALD REAGAN. He believed in freedom, independence, and opportunity. These are the values that all Americans share. We probably understand them a little better in the West.

He handled the Soviet Union much as he handled the situation in my first meeting in the Oval Office. He was direct and to the point with us about how he felt about Nicaragua. In the situation with the Soviet Union, he was direct and to the point.

The first breakthrough in peace for Israel in the Middle East came as a result of a hawk by the name of Menachem Begin. Menachem Begin was the leader of the underground against the British. He was someone who fought the British as no one else did. He did it in secret. But he was the leader. And Menachem Begin's own family did not know that he was the leader of the underground until after the British announced that he was. It took Menachem Begin, somebody who was very hawkish, to make a deal with Egypt. None of the other Israeli leaders could have done it because they would have been seen as capitulating to the Egyptians.

The same with President REAGAN. No one could take away his communist-fighting credentials. He had them from the time he was an actor, with the Screen Actors Guild, Governor, and President.

I watched a TV program, and the same speech that RONALD REAGAN gave as head of the Screen Actors Guild, he gave as Governor, he gave as President. He was a certified anticommunist. So who could better make a deal with the communists than RONALD REAGAN?

No one could question his credentials, no more than they could question the credentials of Menachem Begin. Had it been Jimmy Carter or Bill Clinton, it would not have happened. But no one could question his communist-fighting credentials, and, therefore, people accepted the deal we made with the Soviet Union, which was good for the world and good for our country.

RONALD REAGAN has been a good neighbor to the State of Nevada. The State of Nevada shares a national treasure. It is called Lake Tahoe. There is only one other lake like it in the whole world, and that is Lake Baikal in Russia. I acknowledge that Lake Tahoe is smaller than Lake Baikal, but so is every other lake in the world. But it is an alpine glacial lake that is a wonder of beauty. RONALD REAGAN identified that something needed to be done about this beautiful lake.

I spoke yesterday to Paul Laxalt. Paul Laxalt and I have been political adversaries all of my adult life and a lot of his life. But I do not have a better friend than Paul Laxalt. We are friends. We call each other all the time. We have done that for many years. Even though we have been political adversaries, we are friends.

Anyway, I called Paul Laxalt yesterday and asked him to talk to me about his relationship with RONALD REAGAN. Everyone in Nevada knows and most everyone knows in Washington—my distinguished friend from New Mexico is in the Chamber who served with Senator Laxalt in the Senate—RONALD REAGAN's No. 1 guy in the Senate was Paul Laxalt, period. I do not say that saying, oh, somebody may question that. That is a fact of life. RONALD REAGAN said it. That is the way it was.

Paul Laxalt said RONALD REAGAN should be remembered for two things by Nevadans. First is the bi-State compact to which the two Republican Governors, Laxalt and REAGAN, agreed. They sent it to the California and Nevada State legislatures, and it was ratified eventually by both legislatures. They recognized that something had to be done to preserve Lake Tahoe.

Second is what he did to stop the MX missile from coming to the State of Nevada. The MX missile—most people don't know what that means—but it was a missile, the MX, with 10 warheads on each missile. It was to cover hundreds and hundreds of square miles through Nevada and parts of Utah. That would have been a blight to the environment there, but it was also deemed to be wasteful moneywise. So RONALD REAGAN personally intervened, and that never came to be.

That is what Paul Laxalt wanted the people of Nevada to remember about his best friend, RONALD REAGAN—what he did for the State of Nevada. Of course, there were many other things.

Paul told a story that they were campaigning together. Paul Laxalt gave every one of his nominating speeches, the time he did not win and the two times he won. He said RONALD REAGAN was such a forgiving man that he never held a grudge. They were campaigning in some northeastern State, and somebody had given a speech—somebody RONALD REAGAN had helped a lot—and he gave a speech blasting RONALD REAGAN's economic program. He was a Republican, and everybody around REAGAN was mad at him. So he was getting ready to give this speech, and he said to Paul, "I can't remember, why am I mad at this guy?" It was because he did not hold grudges. It was not in his nature.

So it is wonderful we had someone like Paul Laxalt who had such close contact with the President of the United States. But not only did he have contact with Paul Laxalt, President REAGAN did many other things for the people in Nevada.

Sig Rogich was a special assistant to the President. Because of RONALD REAGAN, Sig Rogich developed a great personal friendship with the first President Bush. They are friends. People wonder why President Bush always comes back to Nevada. It is to see his friend Sig Rogich. He, of course, made Sig Rogich an Ambassador to Iceland, where Sig Rogich was born.

Sig Rogich is an extremely successful businessman. But people should also understand Sig Rogich was head of the Tuesday Team that developed that great campaign slogan for President REAGAN: "It's morning in America."

Rogich wrote and directed most of those pieces. He was heavily involved in the life of President REAGAN. He came and moved back here. But, as a result, not only do we have Rogich back here, but Frank Fahrenkopf became chairman of the National Republican Committee. I talked to Frank Fahrenkopf today. He said REAGAN did this in typical fashion. He had been offered the job in 1980. He had a great law practice in Nevada and did not want to come to Washington.

Jim Baker called him and said, The President wants you to give a report about what happened in the 1982 elections—where the Democrats did very well; the Republicans did very poorly. He was asked to come back and give a report.

Frank said, "Well, I have to fly all night because I'm going with 10 State chairs. We are going to China."

And Baker said, "I think it would be a good idea if you came. The President wants you to come back here."

So he got back here. And Senator Laxalt said to Frank Fahrenkopf, "Would you reconsider being the national chairman of the Republican Party?"

And Frank said, "Well, Paul, I have a problem. I have this law practice."

He said, "Well, think about it." He said he knew he was in trouble when he went to breakfast at the White House and they seated him right across from the President, and the President said, "Dick Richards is retiring as chairman of the National Republican Party." He said, "We have here Frank Fahrenkopf who has said he is going to think about it."

So he knew right then he was going to be the national chairman because the President asked him to do it. So Frank Fahrenkopf became the national chairman of the Republican Party.

But my favorite RONALD REAGAN memento—I have always been opposed to term limits. I have opposed term limits for the House and Senate. I have always spoken forcefully against that. I think it is wrong. It is wrong that we have the 22d amendment to limit the Presidents to 2 terms.

RONALD REAGAN agreed with me. He did not like term limits. He thought the 22d amendment was bad. I offered a resolution to do away with the 22d amendment. I spoke out against term limits. President REAGAN, after he had retired as President of the United States, wrote me a handwritten note. Here is what he said, "Dear Harry, I'm glad ..."—it is in RONALD REAGAN's handwriting, and I have that in my scrapbook. I love my scrapbook and have this in it. I had announced that I supported repeal of the 22d amendment. Here is what he wrote:

> I'm glad you are moving on repeal of the 22nd Amendment. I've made a number of speeches to national business groups... In every speech I've announced my support for repeal and have received an ovation from every audience. I charge that the 22nd is a violation of the people's right to vote for whomever they want.
>
> RONALD REAGAN

Here is the guy. He believed in States rights. He believed in people being able to make their determination, not some arbitrary law that we passed saying: You can't serve in the Senate because you have been there two terms. He believed the people have the right to choose their representatives.

I have a number of pictures with RONALD REAGAN. I liked him as a person. I did not agree with everything he did politically, as we all know, but I liked him as a person.

So I stand here today honored that I had a chance to work with President RONALD REAGAN, someone with whom I knew and felt comfortable. He surrounded himself with good people. They were not mean spirited. They were good people. They were pragmatists. I liked the people with whom he surrounded himself.

He is going to be remembered in history, of course, as one of our great Presidents. This is a time to mourn his death, but it is more important to appreciate his life.

I can remember a person with whom I practiced law when RONALD REAGAN was President. He said, "He has no chance of winning. He is an actor. Look how old he is."

Well, people liked him for who he was, not how old he was or what he had done before he was elected Governor of the State of California. His amazing journey was the American dream come true. He helped bring the dream a little closer to all of us.

Hon. Pete V. Domenici

OF NEW MEXICO

Mr. President, I was privileged to become chairman of the Senate Budget Committee at the same time RONALD REAGAN was sworn in as President. I never thought I was going to have that job, but with his victory, we took over the Senate. I recall Senator Howard Baker called me at home, and his greeting was "Mr. Chairman." I kind of wondered what he was talking about, and then he told me. That was quite startling because I knew I was going to be chairman when RONALD REAGAN would be asking that we carry out his program.

From January 1981 until President REAGAN left office in January 1989, it was my privilege to work closely with him and his senior advisers, as with any President before or since. I suspect I saw President REAGAN exhibit all his legendary traits: the man of principle, the man of strength, the man of strong convictions, the man of humor, and, in one famous case, a man with an Irish temper.

Even before he was sworn in, Mr. REAGAN asked Cap Weinberger to head up his transition team for the Reagan budget and fiscal policy. I worked closely with Cap and then Dave Stockman, whom I knew when he was a Member of the House. He was announced to be the incoming OMB Director.

I was impressed by the three principles that RONALD REAGAN insisted on in the budget that I would prepare: Restraint of domestic spending, long overdue increases in defense spending, and tax cuts to stimulate the economy. The economy was a dormant economy. Those three principles guided every decision that I had with the President and his senior staff. He was not going to compromise on these three principles.

I saw his strength on many occasions, most notably, of course, after the assassination attempt. But I also saw his strength when he insisted that the air traffic controllers either go to work or lose their jobs. That signal, clear and strong, persuaded me this man was, in fact, a man who would risk political standing in order to stand for the good of the public.

I saw his humor time and time again. Once when I showed up late for a meeting with him, there were other Senators present. It was very embarrassing. He was amused. And when my good friend, Senator Howard Baker, became Chief of Staff to the President, he told me one of his jobs was to try to come up with a good joke to tell the President, that REAGAN's humor came from the same sense of perspective that produced his strength and commitment to the American people.

I learned first-hand that the Irish in President REAGAN also included a bit of an Irish temper. In 1993, I had the delicate task of telling the President that I would not put off my budget for the upcoming fiscal year, and that I would not be able to supply him with the entire increase in defense spending for the upcoming fiscal year. Cap Weinberger had made that request on behalf of the President. Cap and I discussed this for weeks, and we put off this action over the Easter holiday and for weeks to give them a chance to work on their defense budget.

The Senate Armed Services Committee chairman, Senator John Tower, and I discussed it, and Senator Tower knew we couldn't get the entire request. Finally, just as the markup of the budget was to occur, at about 10 minutes until 10 in the morning, the President called me on the telephone in the back room of the Budget Committee's hearing.

"Hello," I said to the President.

"Hello, Pete," he said pleasantly. "You know, I really need you to put off the markup of the budget until we can get an agreement on the defense spending."

"Mr. President, I really appreciate and am honored by your call, but I have delayed this for too long and just cannot get the full number that you have requested for defense."

"Well, will you postpone the markup?" he asked with little amiability in his voice.

"No, sir; I cannot do that," I replied.

At that point, the President said goodbye. At least I think that is what he said. I was told later by someone who was present in his office during the call that the President turned a little red in his face and threw the phone on the floor. Yet he was absolutely wonderful to me after that. He campaigned for me. He turned his budget over to me for implementation. And I had a great relationship not only with him but with those who served him, in particular Dave Stockman.

Let me note something about the first budget exercise. The President and his staff had some thoughts about the proper legislative approach. I disagreed and argued for something we now know and have learned to use, and we understand it well. But it was truly historic, the use of a process called reconciliation. That was the first time we ever did it. Nobody understood it. The President, with the guidance of Leader Howard Baker, went along with our recommendation. Senator Fritz Hollings joined me in this historic reconciliation effort. We had all the President's budget restraints in it. We had his tax cuts in that extraordinary document. And in the budget resolution for fiscal year 1992, we had room for all the President's defense spending increases to which he ended up agreeing.

Some Members of the Senate expressed dismay and even anger over the use of this process called reconciliation. Even some Republicans were perplexed by its complications and wondered how it would really work. I know the President and his staff relied on us in the Senate and on the committee to carry out what we promised.

It is to President REAGAN's credit that he supported us every step of the way. Perhaps that was one of the things I admired most about this man. He made a decision, entrusted it to those on whom he relied, and used all of his power to make a plan succeed.

I cannot tell you how complimented I felt when Howard Baker came to me and said, "The President says if you and I think we can do this, then he will back us all the way." And he did.

What a great President. What a great American. What a great man. It was truly my privilege to work with him. I think history will record that our work was of historic importance as the President moved toward making this economy stronger than ever, this Nation more secure than ever, and the world safer than ever.

In closing, let me say I honestly wish I had occasion to know him even better. I didn't have the opportunity to get to know him on a personal basis. Most of what I learned of him is expressed and explained in the remarks I have made. But the wonderful stories I have heard about him are clearly believable, because what I saw of him was remarkable. What I saw of him in the numerous meetings was truly incredible.

Some spoke ill of him during those days. It is wonderful to note that most of those have forgotten those days and are now part of this great chorus in our country that is praising him as one of our greatest.

I knew most about the economic situation because of the Budget Committee, but it is easy for me to see how he succeeded in foreign affairs. It is clear no one could have accomplished what he did with the Soviet Union, because most Presidents would not be believed, and most Presidents would not be permitted to propose and make the kinds of agreements with the Soviet Union that he did.

To sum it up, he made a stronger America. Our economy grew somewhere between 18 and 20 million jobs. Think of that. We are now talking about 2.2 million jobs. He took an economy that was in terrible shape. Does anybody remember 21-percent interest? We have grown so accustomed to low inflation and low interest rates in the last few years that most of us don't understand inflation was so rampant and interest rates so high that, in our grocery stores, those who filled the shelves would also bring along a stamp and they would change the price as they walked down the aisles, because the foodstuff had to go up day by day, week by week. Can you imagine what Americans would think about that today? But we had to take it back then and we had to wait for something else to work. That something else was RONALD REAGAN's policy, his approach to lower taxes, which stimulated this economy.

So it is with deep regret that I join with many others and many in the Senate who will have words to say about him. Again, my best to his wife Nancy and his family. I understand their great grief. But they had him for a very long time, and I am sure with the passage of time they will begin to understand that. I hope they can and I hope they will.

Hon. Arlen Specter

OF PENNSYLVANIA

Mr. President, I have sought recognition to comment about the passing of President RONALD REAGAN, and to comment about the great legacy he has left and the occasions when I had an opportunity to meet and deal personally with President REAGAN.

While I had met him prior to the 1980 election cycle, I had an opportunity to work with him during that Presidential election year when he was elected President of the United States and I was first elected to the Senate. I recollect his presence in Philadelphia on one August day, when the timing for his presentation was to coincide with the beginning of the 6 o'clock news cycle, so he would be carried live over the broadcast stations. I recollect standing behind the curtains at the Bellevue-Stratford Hotel, where he was later to be the guest of honor at a fundraiser on my behalf.

What a sense of expectation there was by then-Governor REAGAN and Mrs. Nancy Reagan, with Mrs. Reagan expressing the question: Do you really think it is possible we will be successful in this Presidential bid? I commented that I thought the chances were excellent. Precisely at 6 o'clock, the curtain was pulled back, and the President-to-be stepped forward and made an eloquent speech.

He traveled to Pittsburgh where again he was the guest of honor at a fundraiser. I recollect attending that event, and at one appropriate moment he demonstrated his insight into the drama and to the field by grabbing my hand by the wrist and lifting it high in a traditional victory celebration. Watching him as a campaigner was a very instructive opportunity.

The day after the election, when he was victorious, I, along with the other 15 Republican Senators who were elected on that same day, was called by President REAGAN to hear words of congratulations. The Republicans took control of the Senate in that 1980 election with a 53 Senate majority. President REAGAN's sense of cheer and sense of optimism was with him at all times. I was to learn as I got to know him better that he really liked to make congratulatory phone calls when there was good news in the offing. As President, he had the practice of calling every nominee to the Federal bench to personally tell the nominee that he, the President, had nominated the individual to be a Federal judge, and, of course, that is great news, but that was the sort of moment that President REAGAN relished.

When we were sworn in, in January 1981, Senator Howard Baker, the majority leader, designated me as spokesman for the group. He did that because I was last in seniority. Seniority at that time among Republican Senators was decided on the basis of alphabetical listing, after the preference was given to former Members of the House and former Governors.

As the spokesman for the class, I had the honor of sitting next to the President during our frequent luncheon meetings. At one of the meetings, Senator Mack Mattingly was seated across the table. This was after the President had been reelected in 1984. Senator Mattingly said to the President, "Why is it, Mr. President, that you don't age at all?"

President REAGAN was fast with one of his famous stories. He said:

Well, Mack, it is like the two psychiatrists who came to work the same time every day. Both were immaculately dressed. When they left in the afternoon at the same time, one psychiatrist was totally disheveled, and the other continued to be immaculately dressed. After day after day, week after week, month after month of this happening, finally one day when they left, the disheveled psychiatrist said, "How is it that we come to the office the same time every day to see our patients, and day after day, week after week, month after month, you leave immaculately dressed and I am disheveled?" The immaculately dressed psychiatrist looked at his colleague and said, "Who listens?"

This was President REAGAN's way of saying he can take all of the tough spots of the Presidency and still retain his composure and still retain his vigor and his freshness.

I was very much impressed with President REAGAN when he was near the end of his first term and he was asked a question about whether he was going to run for reelection. His answer was, "The people will tell me whether I should run for reelection." I have been asked the same question from time to time. I have used President REAGAN's answer because I believe it is a really terrific answer.

The first legislation which I proposed after being elected to the Senate involved the armed career criminal bill. I sought a meeting with the President. That was a bill, which has been enacted into law, that provides for mandatory sentences of 15 years to life for career criminals who have three or more major felonies on their record.

When I described it and discussed it with President REAGAN, he immediately related that to his own experience, and referred to a James Cagney movie in which there was a three-time loser. He became a supporter and ultimately signed that bill into law.

President REAGAN traveled frequently to Pennsylvania and on those occasions would invite Senator Heinz and me to join him. One such occasion was extraordinarily memorable. It was on the 200th anniversary of the signing of the U.S. Constitution. It was a real experience to ride with the President in Air Force One and in a limousine and to have a chance to talk with him and discuss with him some of the major issues.

He had made a comment that when we develop the strategic defense initiative, we would share it with other nations. I asked him about those plans and how he could carry that forward since the strategic defense initiative was not likely to be accomplished for many years and it would require an act of Congress to share one of our national assets. The President's reply was that this was a matter of leadership, and that in moving toward the strategic defense initiative, we wanted to assure other countries we would not use it only for ourselves but would make it available to others.

At that time, the mutual assured destruction doctrine was operative with the stalemate between the United States and the Soviet Union, each knowing that if there were to be an aggressive act, it would be responded to. So the mutual assured destruction doctrine was in effect, and to move to a strategic defense initiative required assurances that this kind of defense would be shared.

President REAGAN leaves a phenomenal legacy. Perhaps his greatest achievement was presiding over the end of the cold war, in which the United States defeated the Soviet Union. When the United States was rearmed, the Soviet Union could not keep up and ultimately was bankrupt.

President REAGAN led the arms control talks with Soviet President Gorbachev. With his famous words at the Berlin Wall to tear the wall down, and ultimately with the demise of the Soviet Union, all of Eastern Europe was free, and liberty and democracy has come to so much of Eastern Europe and to so many people in the world because of President REAGAN's leadership.

His optimism and sense of buoyancy were just what the United States needed when he came to office in 1981. His emphasis on less government, his determination to lower taxes, and his spirit of determination to defeat communism were trademarks and legacies which will last forever.

One final note. When President REAGAN came to Independence Hall on the 200th anniversary of the signing of the Constitution on September 17, 1987, we arrived at the hall and there was an enormous wheel with George Washington and then sequenced, John Adams, Thomas Jefferson, and the wheel came all the way around and RONALD REAGAN was situated right next to President George Washington. I asked President REAGAN how it felt to be on that wheel right next to President Washington. He said, "Arlen, it is a humbling experience."

I think the humility of President REAGAN in the context of his great achievements is another addition to a really great legacy.

Hon. Tom Daschle

OF SOUTH DAKOTA

Mr. President, we have heard many remembrances of President REAGAN these last few days. One of my own favorite stories about President REAGAN appeared in the *Boston Globe* on St. Patrick's Day, 1983. It begins:

> In his corner office, House Speaker Thomas P. O'Neill Jr. has proudly hung a photograph of President REAGAN. It shows the two men, their faces agitated in the heat of a argument over jobs and the economy, each jabbing a finger at each other.
>
> Underneath, a puckish inscription from 'RON REAGAN' to 'Tip' reads, 'From one Irishman to another—Top o' the morning to you.' That photograph conveys the flavor of perhaps the most important political relationship in Washington, for it juxtaposes the sharp partisan confrontations between the two men with the personal cordiality that suits the current mood of bipartisanship.

The headline on that article read: "REAGAN and O'Neill: Each One Needs the Other."

RONALD REAGAN was many things in life: An actor, a Governor, the President.

For countless millions throughout the world, he was the voice and the image of American confidence and optimism.

Even those who disagreed strongly with many of his policies admired his sunny disposition, his easy grace and charm, his quick wit, and his unshakable conviction, as he said so often, that America's best days are just ahead of us.

He was a self-made son of small-town, middle America who loved this Nation because of the chance it gave him—and generations of Americans before and after him—to go as far in life as their talents and ambitions could take them.

Historians will still be taking the measure of RONALD REAGAN and his Presidency for decades to come. But even now, it is clear that President REAGAN presided over, and helped bring about, enormous changes in America, and in the world.

His unflinching opposition to communism helped bring down the wall and bring about the end of the Soviet Union. For that, the world owes RONALD REAGAN a great debt of gratitude.

Americans, and friends of America throughout the world, are saddened by President REAGAN's death.

Our hearts go out to the Reagan family, especially Mrs. Reagan and the Reagan children and grandchildren, as well as to President and Mrs. REAGAN's friends. Even when someone has been slipping away for a long time, as President REAGAN did, the final goodbye is still heartbreaking. We wish them comfort in this time of great sorrow.

In his 1987 autobiography, "Man of the House," Tip O'Neill recalled the time President-elect REAGAN visited him in his office in early 1981. The Speaker told the man who was soon to be President that in the House, Democrats and Republicans "are always friends after 6 o'clock and on weekends."

For the next 6 years, until he retired, Tip O'Neill recalled, President REAGAN always began their phone conversations by asking, "Tip, is it after 6 o'clock?"

It has been nearly 10 years since President REAGAN wrote his courageous letter to America telling us that he had Alzheimer's disease.

In the decade since President REAGAN began his quiet withdrawal from public life, the civility and personal decency that we associate with him seems, at times, to have all but disappeared from much of our public discourse. The elbows in politics have become sharper, the words have become meaner—and the accomplishments have become scarcer.

Sadly, there is a tendency today to assume ill will and bad motives of those who belong to the other party—or even another wing of one's own party.

This decline of civility in politics and public discourse is not good for America. It does not make us safer, or stronger.

President REAGAN spoke to all that was good and decent in America. We would honor him by restoring decency to our politics.

RONALD REAGAN was a man who believed deeply in his core principles. He would not want any of us to compromise our own core principles in his memory. But there is such a thing as principled compromise. President REAGAN understood that. He knew that accommodation was needed to make the system work.

Like many conservatives, President REAGAN had some basic philosophical qualms about Social Security. But he appointed a bipartisan commission to find ways to save Social Security from imminent insolvency—and he backed the commission's plan. That was principled compromise at work.

Twenty-four years ago this week, RONALD REAGAN had just clinched the delegates needed to win his party's 1980 Presidential nomination. It was a nomination he had worked for for 12 years.

A newspaper reporter asked him what he thought he needed to do next.

He replied that he wanted to dispel the notion that he was a hardnosed radical who would oppose compromise on principle. As he put it: You know, there are some people so imbued with their ideology that if they can't get everything they want, they'll jump off the cliff with the flag flying. As Governor, I found out that if I could get half a loaf, instead of stalking off angrily, I'd take it.

Perhaps because he himself was a Democrat early in his life, President REAGAN never demonized his political opponents—even when he disagreed profoundly with them.

When Tip O'Neill turned 70, President REAGAN hosted a reception for him at the White House. There they were: the opposing champions of laissez-faire economics and New Deal liberalism. President REAGAN toasted Tip O'Neill by saying, "Tip, if I had a ticket to Heaven and you didn't have one too, I would give mine away and go to Hell with you."

President REAGAN and Tip O'Neill, I am convinced, are reunited in Heaven now.

As we prepare here in the Capitol to say our final goodbye to President REAGAN, let us remember his capacity to see the best in everyone, including those whose political views differed starkly from his own. Let us remember that there is no dishonor in accepting a half a loaf.

In the months ahead and for as long as we are given the honor of serving in Congress, let us search and work for principled compromises that serve the interests of the vast majority of Americans. In that way, we can help to preserve President REAGAN's great belief and hope that America's best days are, indeed, just ahead.

Hon. Richard C. Shelby

OF ALABAMA

Mr. President, I rise today to pay tribute to the life and the legacy of former President RONALD REAGAN. President REAGAN served our country with honor and distinction, and I feel privileged to have the opportunity to reflect on the contributions he made to our country and to the world.

Upon hearing the news of his death, I thought back to the footprints he left on my memory. He was, indeed, one of the greatest leaders, I believe, of our time, and I was honored to know him.

President REAGAN provided our country with an enormous amount of hope following a period of national remorse and confusion about the direction of our country and about its place in the world. Let us not forget the context into which he emerged to seize his place in history and to move the United States forward with a determination and an optimism about the future that was so recently lacking.

The ghost of Vietnam haunted our foreign policy and the specter of Watergate informed our politics.

The election of RONALD REAGAN, however, truly changed America. He instilled hope that every American could be optimistic about his or her future; hope that communism would not endure and that freedom and democracy could ultimately vanquish the forces that sought to pull our country, and many others, into the abyss of despair and hostility that permeated much of the world; hope that personal freedom without the encumbrances of big government would revitalize the economy; hope that the rejuvenated Armed Forces he would lead as Commander in Chief could make the United States once again truly the leader of the free world in a struggle for survival against the Soviet Union.

President REAGAN's eternal optimism gave our country a renewed sense of self, a belief that the American dream was possible and that every individual had the opportunity to create his or her own success. RONALD REAGAN believed that each new day was filled with high purpose and opportunity for accomplishment. He gave America back the hope we had lost for many years.

President REAGAN's leadership and courage were central to ending the cold war. He was certain that freedom and democracy could prevail in all corners of the globe if only the one country with the capacity to do so would step in and show the way.

Many Americans who were not yet born or were too young to understand could not appreciate what this man accomplished. The first half of the 20th century was marked by warfare on a global scale. The First World War—the war to end all wars—had decimated much of Europe. A generation was lost to the trenches and newly introduced technologies of destruction such as the machine gun and the tank.

The war that followed, World War II, managed to go well beyond its predecessor, as the failure of European diplomacy once again dragged the continent into the continued horrors and devastation that man wrought. The epic struggle against the forces of fascism, a struggle we remembered this past weekend with the anniversary of the Normandy landings, was a fight against evil in every sense of the word. Its ending, however, set the stage for a new type of conflict—a conflict that would take the second half of the century to resolve, mercifully without the nuclear war that existed as the logical culmination of the standoff that came to be known as the cold war.

The skills, strengths and enormous fortune that kept the cold war from turning hot transcended, of course, multiple Presidential administrations. It was brought to its successful resolution, however, through the vision and strength of exactly one man: President REAGAN. Decades of conflict management, in which experienced diplomats and elected officials sought primarily to prevent nuclear war and to contain the Soviet threat, had succeeded in preventing nuclear war. That was an incredible feat, to be sure.

What set RONALD REAGAN apart, however, was his vision of a world without the nuclear standoff that had become an indelible image in the public psyche of virtually the entire world. What set RONALD REAGAN apart was his visceral belief that the United States, and the freedom and prosperity it represented, had to, and could, not just contain the threat but eliminate it without the awful specter of nuclear war coming to fruition.

Derided by his opponents both here and abroad as a dangerous cowboy, President REAGAN stood firm in his beliefs and led the country to victory. He believed, correctly, and at variance with the views of many a university professor and politician, that the United States could force the Soviet Union over the cliff on which it rested, buttressed on the backs of the millions it held in its tyrannical grip.

This was a truly great man.

Limited government, lower taxes, and individual responsibility will also be part of President REAGAN's legacy. He believed that each American and each community were the best problem-solvers. Rather than making government bigger to address the challenges our country faced, REAGAN stood firm in his commitment to the contributions that could be made through personal empowerment and a renewed sense of political and social responsibility.

I was just a second-term Congressman when President REAGAN came into office. Although a Democrat at the time, I closely identified with his commitment to lower taxes, limit government and rebuild the military. I shared President REAGAN's conservative philosophies, and he helped me, and millions of other Americans have a restored faith in the purpose of our government.

I also recall a time when President REAGAN asked me to breakfast at the White House. I, a second-term Congressman at the time, was certainly impressed. I had always been a conservative Democrat, and he had hoped that I would change parties, as he had done when the Democratic Party ceased to represent the values he held dear. I declined his offer to do so at the time, explaining my strong desire to work to fix the Democratic Party from within. The President knew better, telling me that the party was in the midst of a transformation that would not be reversed any time soon. It took me more years to fully appreciate the President's wisdom. But appreciate it, I did, and I followed his lead in abandoning the party of my youth in deference to another. While I took a little longer to change than he would have liked, he did provide me with much of the foundation as to why I needed to leave the Democratic Party. I have always appreciated his guidance, humility and humor.

I believe history will treat RONALD REAGAN well. He uplifted a frustrated country through his optimism and hope. He changed a troubled world with his devotion to the spread of freedom. RONALD REAGAN embodied the American spirit, and our country and the world are forever grateful for his service.

I offer my condolences to Mrs. Reagan and the entire family. They have endured much heartache with his illness, much grief with his passing, and much joy with his life. My thoughts and prayers are with them in this difficult time.

May God bless RONALD REAGAN and his memory.

Hon. George Allen
OF VIRGINIA

Mr. President, my colleagues, and Americans, President RONALD REAGAN will be returning to Washington tomorrow for the very last time. I rise to honor the memory and life of the greatest leader of the 20th century and to express my sympathy to his wonderful and loyal family—in particular, his loving wife and partner Nancy.

Nancy Reagan has always been an outstanding and inspirational role model for our entire Nation. And that has never been more clearly displayed than through her wonderful courage and love during the difficult journey she and President REAGAN traveled during the past decade.

Like so many, I was inspired to actually answer the call of public service because of then-Governor RONALD REAGAN's positive, principled message. In 1976, I began as a young lieutenant in the Reagan revolution when I was asked to chair Young Virginians for REAGAN. Today, I am still motivated to work to advance his individual empowering philosophy in government.

RONALD REAGAN entered the political stage in 1964 with a speech which summed up a philosophy that would guide him through his Presidency two decades hence, and which turned the tide of world history.

Mr. REAGAN said in 1964:

> You and I have a rendezvous with destiny. We will preserve for our children this, the last best hope of man on earth, or we will sentence them to take the first step into a thousand years of darkness. If we fail, at least let our children ... say of us we justified our brief moment here. We did all that could be done.

Indeed, RONALD WILSON REAGAN did have a rendezvous with destiny. President REAGAN rejuvenated the spirit of America. His determined, optimistic leadership lit the torch of liberty and allowed it to shine in the dark recesses of oppressed countries around the world.

RONALD REAGAN believed in the innate goodness of mankind. He believed and advocated the wisdom of our country's foundational principles. He believed that given the opportunity, all men and women would seek freedom and liberty and with it unleash creativity, ingenuity, hard work, and economic growth.

He touched deeply the hearts and minds of Americans through his genuinely believed, commonsense conservative words of encouragement—from his first inaugural speech in 1981, to his inspirational State of the Union Addresses, to his moving memorial tribute to our lost *Challenger* explorer, to his strong demand to tear down the wall of oppression, to his passionate tribute to the defenders of liberty at Normandy 20 years ago this week. Those were the words he delivered. Those words which he delivered are now as much a part of the fabric of America as the threads of our flag, Old Glory. Lee Greenwood's song, "God Bless the U.S.A.," was an anthem to RONALD REAGAN's renewed America.

Historians will surely discuss and debate the impact of RONALD REAGAN's 8 years as President for generations to come. But there is no doubt his legacy has already been revealed. In fact, he foresaw his legacy. He was there at the bicentennial in 1981 of the Battle of Yorktown. He gave a wonderful speech at Yorktown, VA.

He said as follows:

> We have come to this field to celebrate the triumph of an idea—that freedom will eventually triumph over tyranny. It is and always will be a warning to those who would usurp the rights of others: Time will find them beaten. The beacon of freedom shines here for all who will see, inspiring free men and captives alike, and no wall, no curtain, nor totalitarian state can shut it out.

To put this in context, when RONALD REAGAN became our 40th President, Americans had lost their faith in our leaders and in the role of America in the world. Government at home was restraining its citizens with oppressive taxation and burdensome regulations. Our national malaise led to historically high unemployment, high interest rates and inflation, low productivity, and a stagnant stock market.

Our moral authority around the world had been eroding, and confidence in the ideals of liberty and democracy were replaced by the fear of expanding tyranny, communism, and repression.

America yearned for a leader who could change the direction of our Nation and make them proud of our heritage once again. RONALD REAGAN answered that call.

Many tributes this week rightfully point to President REAGAN's unwavering optimism and belief in the inner strength of Americans, and indeed all human beings. He understood that they could be motivated and inspired to higher ideals with our competitive nature. No more handwringing. He wanted action. Indeed, he challenged us to look no further than his administration and ourselves for solutions. He said, "If not us, who? And if not now, when?"

Beyond his unshakable faith in mankind was his consistent adherence to principles which were unfashionable and often scorned when he came to office but today which are solidly embraced and winning the minds of people across our country and throughout the world. He acted on his beliefs that government interference should be restrained and that free people should be unrestrained, without limits. We prospered and we thrived with the creation of jobs and opportunities.

One of my very favorite principles of President REAGAN was declared in his 1985 State of the Union Address when he said, "Every dollar the ... Government does not take from us, every decision it does not make for us will make our economy stronger, our lives more abundant, and our future more free."

And so it is. Through tax cuts that return tax dollars to those whose hard work and ingenuity earned them, to reducing burdensome regulations, President REAGAN presided over the beginning of the most robust peace expansion of our economy in the history of our Nation.

But President REAGAN believed the blessings of liberty must not be bestowed only on a few nations and only to those blessed to be born on free soil; RONALD REAGAN, with the strength of his convictions, exported and advanced democracy to continents, countries, and people yearning to taste the sweet nectar of liberty.

He knew the evil communistic empire could not be sustained and would collapse under the weight of a determined effort to challenge the Soviets on their failed policies, both foreign and domestic. He reversed decades of policy calling for containment of that oppressive tyrannical system, and he boldly asserted that the advancement of freedom and liberty must be America's No. 1 foreign policy objective. Indeed, he believed that it is our solemn moral obligation to do so.

Now we are seeing his greatest legacy. Hundreds of millions of free people, from the Baltics in Lithuania, Estonia, Latvia through Poland, Hungary, Slovenia, Slovakia, the Czech Republic, Bulgaria and Romania, all people once repressed behind the Iron Curtain are now joining NATO. They are true friends and allies. Yes, they are breathing that invigorating wind of freedom.

One of the last public statements RONALD REAGAN made was in 1983. He provided us with a vision which will guide us now and in the future. RONALD REAGAN said:

> History comes and history goes, but principles endure and ensure future generations to defend liberty—not as a gift from the government, but a blessing from our Creator. Here in America the lamp of individual conscience burns bright. By that I know we will all be guided to that dreamed of day when no one wields a sword and no one drags a chain.

It is RONALD REAGAN's inspiring character, courage, unflinching adherence to principles, policies, and eloquence that brought forth a renaissance for the United States of America, a rebirth of freedom, and the world also experienced that renaissance at a crucial juncture in history. He fanned the flames of freedom and that torch of liberty will continue to burn brightly by his inspiration and example. We all thank God for blessing the United States and the world with RONALD REAGAN.

President REAGAN, as you finally enter the gates of that "shining city on the hill" you always talked about, rest peacefully, knowing you left the world a much better place than it was when you arrived. For that, the free people of your Nation are eternally grateful.

Hon. Ted Stevens

OF ALASKA

Mr. President, I come to the Senate today to join others to remember a good friend and a great American leader.

In 1977, I was elected to the Senate leadership and served as assistant minority leader until the 1980 election. I don't think anyone at that time could have predicted the sweeping changes that were about to take place. When RONALD REAGAN was elected, he ushered in a new era of government so profound it became known as the Reagan revolution. That was an exciting time in Washington.

I became assistant majority leader and began a new life—Howard Baker was the majority leader. The day before I was to marry my wife Catherine, Howard called and asked me to replace him on a trip to China because Deng Xiaoping wanted to understand what Reaganism meant. My wife Catherine and I were married on December 30, and we left for China on December 31. To prepare for those talks, I reviewed all of President REAGAN's actions as Governor of California and his promises made during the election. I was honored to be offered the opportunity to explain and defend his record.

When Congress convened in 1981, those of us in the Senate leadership went down almost weekly for meetings at the White House. Occasionally, President REAGAN came up to Howard Baker's office as majority leader to meet with us. I don't think any other President has done that as often as RONALD REAGAN. President REAGAN always tackled very serious subjects in these meetings, but he kept us relaxed. He usually began our discussions in the Cabinet room with a joke or a story. His leadership brought out the best in all of us.

During his administration we were able to accomplish a lot for the American people and set the Nation and the world on a new course. Much has been said already about the mark President REAGAN left on our national defense and foreign policy. Those were his greatest contributions as President, and I viewed those decisions from a unique advantage point.

I was sworn in as chairman of the Senate Appropriations Defense Subcommittee just days before President REAGAN took the oath of office. He immediately began to move toward a 600-ship Navy, new aircraft development, and space-based missile defense systems. President REAGAN understood that the first thing we had to do was restore our military capability. The Soviets were outspending us at that time and stealing our secrets. The President took control of that situation, and in the years since President REAGAN left office, either Senator Inouye or I have been chairman of the Appropriations Defense Subcommittee. Each of us has carried forth the vision President REAGAN had for our military.

History has overlooked President REAGAN's personal commitment to arms control, however. In 1985, the President supported the creation of the Arms Control Observer Group in the Senate, a group of Senators that served as official observers at any arms control negotiations involving the United States. I co-chaired that group along with Senators Lugar, Nunn, and Pell. Our goal was to avoid the problems we faced in the seventies when three successive arms control treaties were unable to achieve ratification in the Senate. Our group went to Geneva three or four times a year and came back and briefed the President, Secretary Shultz, and the Senators who were involved in arms control matters.

The President encouraged the Soviets to decrease the size of their arsenals and to reduce the size of our nuclear forces. This was one of the most significant parts of the Reagan agenda, the overall concern with arms control.

The President also created a revolutionary new approach to defense space research. He brought down the walls between isolated research projects and advocated a more comprehensive approach. A lot of the aspects of the missile defense system, which he called star wars, were based upon the research he put into effect then.

When President REAGAN passed away on Saturday, I noted that his death coincided with another sad day in American history: On June 5, 36 years ago, another great American leader, Senator and Presidential candidate Robert Kennedy, was struck down by an assassin's bullet in Los Angeles. Although they were from different generations and different political parties, Robert Kennedy and RONALD REAGAN had a lot in common. Both men were leaders who did more than just point the country in the right direction. In the words of Bobby Kennedy, they inspired Americans to envision a "world that never was and ask 'Why not?'"

On June 12, 1987, President REAGAN inspired all of us to envision a new world when he gave his famous speech at the Brandenburg Gate. I will never forget the image of President REAGAN standing before that gate demanding that Gorbachev "Tear down this wall!"

Weeks before he gave that speech, the President learned that his remarks would be carried in East Germany over the radio, and in one part of the speech he spoke directly to the people of East Germany. One can only imagine the hope the people on the other side of that wall must have felt when they heard the President of the United States declare in their native tongue: "There is only one Berlin."

Here at home, President REAGAN built, as he called it, a "shining city upon a hill." He borrowed that phrase from John Winthrop, an early Pilgrim who used it to describe the kind of America he envisioned.

For REAGAN, the idea of a shining city was:

> A tall proud city built on rocks stronger than oceans, wind-swept, God-blessed, and teeming with people of all kinds living in harmony and peace, a city with free ports that hummed with commerce and creativity, and if there had to be city walls, the walls had doors and the doors were open to anyone with the will and the heart to get there.

I will always be grateful to President REAGAN for teaching us to believe in that shining city and for opening its doors so Alaska could finally enjoy full citizenship.

Under President RONALD REAGAN, the freeze on the transfer of Alaskan lands to our new State and to the Alaskan Native people was finally lifted, and we began to receive the land that rightfully belonged to us under the Statehood Act that admitted Alaska into our Union. President REAGAN instructed the Department of the Interior to move as quickly as possible on that. I do not believe it would have happened that fast had he not been elected.

Under President REAGAN, the Village Built Clinic Program began, and we set out to establish Indian health service clinics in every Native village in Alaska.

Under President REAGAN, we finally addressed the injustice of Aleut internment during World War II by awarding reparations to Aleuts who had been taken from their homes and sent to what were called "duration villages" in southeastern Alaska for the duration of the war.

President REAGAN understood Alaska's military and geopolitical significance better than any other President. The modernization of Alaska's military bases accelerated during his administration.

What most Alaskans probably remember best about President REAGAN is how well he understood our State and our way of life. When he came to Fairbanks to meet Pope John Paul II, he told the crowd that every time he came to Alaska he thought of the poet Robert Service and threatened to recite "The Shooting of Dan McGrew." In fact, he did that just that one night when Catherine and I were attending a dinner in Chicago. We had just flown in from Fairbanks, and I told the crowd that was present that the 20-degree weather in Chicago could not compete with the harsh weather back home, where the temperature was 50 below. RONALD REAGAN got up to give his remarks, and he recited Robert Service's poem "The Shooting of Dan McGrew" from memory.

I distinctly remember him saying this phrase from Service's poem:

When out of the night, which was fifty below, and into the din and the glare,
There stumbled a miner fresh from the creeks, dog-dirty, and loaded for bear.

On the plane ride home, the President told my wife Catherine that his mother had kept a first edition of Robert Service's poetry by his bedside and read those poems to him as a child. Catherine later sent him a first edition of Robert Service that she found in a bookstore in New York, and he wrote her a nice letter back telling her he planned to memorize "The Cremation of Sam McGee" once more.

I tried many times to get the President to come back to Alaska, but, unfortunately, he decided, as the years went by, that he wanted to go back to California to ride horses.

We understood that, and honored him for it. Alaskans took comfort in knowing that even if his heart belonged to California, he was raised on the words of Robert Service, our favorite poet.

One of my fondest memories of President REAGAN is, strangely enough, a phone call I received from him as chairman of the Appropriations Subcommittee on Defense. The President called to ask me if I had placed funding in the Defense bill that year to procure a new pair of Air Force I airplanes. I told him that I had. President REAGAN told me that he had not requested that funding and would veto the bill.

He said, "Ted, I'm the President."

I said, "Sir, I understand that, but you won't be President by the time the new planes arrive."

There was silence on the other end of the line, and when he finally spoke, the President said, "Ted, do you have a design for these planes?"

I will never forget that because the first time a President flew in those new planes was when one of them took the retired President and Nancy back to California in 1989.

This week, President REAGAN will fly back to Washington for the last time. Thousands of Americans will pay tribute to him in the Capitol rotunda and millions more will reflect on his life. Catherine and I extend our deepest sympathies to Nancy and the Reagan family, as all of us will mourn the loss of a true American hero.

Hon. Jon Kyl

OF ARIZONA

Mr. President, America mourns the loss of an epoch-making leader, RONALD WILSON REAGAN.

As the biographer Lou Cannon has said, REAGAN "possessed a special 'something' that transcended the appeal of ordinary politicians," and he knew it. Even so—and this is an important point—he was neither a vain man nor in love with power. In not misusing that special appeal that he had, he showed such character and goodness. He could have been, but was not, a demagog. He was trying to accomplish his exalted vision of this country, only that. And in large measure, he succeeded.

Militarily, he rebuilt America's capacity to defend itself and its allies. REAGAN's defense buildup led to U.S. victories in the cold war, the Persian Gulf war, and beyond. In fact, dealing skillfully with a Congress controlled during most of his Presidency by the other party, he secured funding for weapons systems that are still being used.

Diplomatically, he achieved with the Soviet Union, our adversary during most of the last century, an accord that eliminated whole classes of nuclear weapons from the stockpiles of both countries.

Politically, he enabled us to regain confidence in America. His confidence in his country and its goodness was utterly unshakable, so he was just the right leader to rise to the fore when the national spirit had been battered by our withdrawal from Vietnam, the scandal of Watergate, and the malaise that his predecessor identified but could not seem to counteract.

Economically, he slew the dragon of double-digit inflation. He braved unpopularity to stay the course with Paul Volcker, Chairman of the Federal Reserve, in tightening the money supply. This steadfastness saw the United States through its worst economic crisis in 50 years. The economy slid deep into a recession before recovering in late 1982.

Along with tightening the money supply to kill inflation, REAGAN was convinced that marginal tax rates must be cut to stimulate growth. These anti-inflation and tax policies defied the conventional wisdom of that time. But they worked. They gave us what the late, great journalist Robert Bartley called "the seven fat years," a time of unprecedented job creation and economic expansion in America.

Even as RONALD REAGAN won through in domestic policy, he was a statesman who left his mark on the world.

During his two terms in office, early 1981 to the end of 1988, he championed the cause of human rights in the Soviet Union and Central and Eastern Europe, standing up for freedom, democracy, and civil society. He spoke passionately of God-given rights and said self-government and free markets were the only way to vindicate those rights. He wanted the people who were living under oppression to regain their dignity, and his words gave hope to millions.

In his 1982 "Evil Empire" speech before the British House of Commons, President REAGAN said:

> While we must be cautious about forcing the pace of change, we must not hesitate to declare our ultimate objectives and to take concrete actions to move toward them. We must be staunch in our conviction that freedom is not the sole prerogative of a lucky few, but the inalienable and universal right of all human beings.

The Reagan administration fostered democracy around the world in the eighties, in Central America, South America, Asia. The Philippines, Taiwan, and South Korea all liberalized their societies in ways that may not have been possible without the Reagan administration's support.

President REAGAN will go down in history for his doctrine of "peace through strength." It turned this country around militarily and diplomatically and turned the course of the cold war dramatically in our favor. It was also a negotiating strategy—just not the right one, it turned out—for dealing with a communist power that was ailing economically but still aggressive. The Soviet Union had last invaded a country the year before he was elected, Afghanistan in 1979. The U.S.S.R. was engaged in the seventies in a rapid military buildup. I remember also that the prevailing nuclear standoff between the two superpowers when REAGAN came into office was frightening. They were locked in a decades-old equilibrium under which neither attacked the other because each could, at the push of a button, destroy the other's populations with nuclear weapons. President REAGAN once said this nuclear standoff, which was called mutual assured destruction, was "a sad commentary on the human condition."

He had the courage and the imagination to think of a way out of it: erecting a defense against nuclear arms. This would end the practice of holding civilian populations hostage to the atomic bomb. It was, he believed, both militarily and morally necessary to strike off in this new direction. As he pointed the way, he endured heavy criticism and even ridicule, but it didn't faze him.

His idea was brilliant, for even if embarking on this high-tech shield against missiles did not lead to a deployable U.S. system right away, he knew the Soviets would pour their resources into matching our progress toward missile defense. It was a competition they could ill afford. The extra burden—economically, and even psychologically, of keeping up with missile defense and the entire REAGAN military buildup—hastened the collapse of the Soviet economy and the communist system itself.

People who didn't agree with President REAGAN called him a saber rattler and worse. Opponents wrung their hands at this peace-through-strength approach, insisting a buildup of U.S. military capabilities couldn't possibly help us if the goal was a safer and more peaceful world. Yet the critics were wrong. President REAGAN, the so-called saber rattler, sat down with Soviet leader Mikhail Gorbachev in Washington in December 1987 and the two men signed the Intermediate Nuclear Forces Treaty which abolished the use of all intermediate and shorter range missiles by the United States and the Soviet Union.

The following year the Reagan administration created the On-Site Inspection Agency to conduct U.S. inspections of Soviet military facilities and to aid Soviet inspections at our facilities. The REAGAN-Gorbachev diplomacy set the stage for the 1990 signing between NATO and the Warsaw Pact of the Conventional Forces in Europe Treaty.

One of the well-known personal traits of RONALD REAGAN was that he didn't care who got credit for successful policies. Goodness knows, his detractors, then and even now, will deny him any credit he might deserve for making the world safer. He did make the world safer, though. That is the truth of it. And history will remember him that way.

We can say of RONALD REAGAN what Lincoln said in praise of his, Lincoln's, personal role model Henry Clay:

> He loved his country partly because it was his own country, but mostly because it was a free country.

The role model of our time is RONALD REAGAN. His principles are the principles we now embrace. They will help us to keep this a free country and to help others who want to be free.

As we continue in the wake of September 11 to fight the war on terror, we all take comfort and inspiration from the jaunty optimism and the seriousness of purpose of RONALD REAGAN. And President George W. Bush practices REAGAN's doctrine of "peace through strength." He has done so by confronting and defeating tyranny in Afghanistan and Iraq; by pursuing deployment of missile defenses; by leading the international community to stop the spread of weapons of mass destruction; and by demonstrating to the world that the United States is willing to rally free peoples in defense of our civilization and our democratic way of life.

Thank you, RONALD REAGAN, for showing the way.

Hon. Sam Brownback

OF KANSAS

Mr. President, I rise to pay tribute to RONALD REAGAN, my political guiding light. I came to Congress on the second REAGAN wave in the 1994 election, when Republicans took over the House of Representatives. Many of us were raised on RONALD REAGAN. His was my first Presidential campaign in 1976, when I was still a student at Kansas State University. I was riding in a tractor in Kansas when I heard the "Evil Empire" speech. I started pounding on the dashboard, saying, That is right, that is right. Then all the pundits came on afterward and said how terrible it was. I was a bit confused but decided REAGAN was right and the pundits were wrong. He went on to prove that.

He was a great contributor to our time and our legacy. I only had the pleasure of meeting RONALD REAGAN once. I was a White House fellow in the Bush 1 White House. We met him in southern California. People had always given examples of his legendary humor. This meeting was no exception. We were having a meeting for a period of time, and then one of the people with whom I was traveling asked him a question, "What one thing didn't you get done as President that you wish you had gotten done." I think he had heard this question before and he had given this line before, but he tilted his head back, and you could see the glint in his eye and the smile comes across the face, and he said, "I wished I had brought back the cavalry." That was a line people enjoyed at the time, and it was the sort of humorous thing he was so known for in his policies. It was part of his greatness.

While he was a great President, he didn't consider greatness to be inherent to him. He considered this country great. He considered the position of President to be great. But he wasn't full of the feeling of greatness for himself, and he always had self-deprecating humor. That was part of him.

Following on the previous speaker, Senator Kyl, I had a chance several years back to talk with Eduard Shevardnadze, Foreign Secretary under Mikhail Gorbachev, about when REAGAN and Gorbachev were negotiating on missile reduction and nuclear weapons reduction. This was a meeting that took place within the last 3 or 4 years with Mr. Shevardnadze. I asked him to reflect on that time period when we were having a military defense buildup here under RONALD REAGAN and what took place in the Soviet Union in that time period. I wanted to get a measure from him on that.

He said of REAGAN:

REAGAN saw the central weakness of the Soviet Union. That was its inability to produce goods and services. They were spending somewhere between 60 to 80 percent of the GDP of the Soviet Union on the military. Along comes REAGAN and says: I am moving more chips on the table. You will have to match me if you want to stay in this race.

The Soviet Union then was looking around saying, how do we stay in the race when we are putting virtually every chip we have right now into this military buildup for the cold war. And it was a long way from secure at that point in time that the Soviet Union was going to fall any time soon. This was a very well-established, militarily strong country. What it forced in the Soviet Union was for them to restructure their economy and move to openness to try to get more chips on the table to grow their economy.

They introduced the likes of glasnost and perestroika, openness and restructuring of the economy. But when you looked at the totalitarian communist system, glasnost and perestroika were inherent inconsistencies and led to the demise of the Soviet Union, that along with RONALD REAGAN's words. These words are from Eduard Shevardnadze. Many talked about star wars and how the Soviet Union, at that time when REAGAN announced star wars—the Soviet Union's leadership sent its best scientists to come back and appraise it and tell the political leadership if the Americans could do this. The Soviet scientists came back after a few months of studying the American proposal—the Reagan proposal—for star wars and said we could not. They spent another few months looking at it and then returned to the Soviet leadership and said if the Americans are willing to stay on this path and put the money into doing it, they can do it.

It sent a shock wave through the leadership in the Soviet system that the United States could get this accomplished. Clearly, the deciding factor of opening that system led to the demise of the Soviet Union and the end of the cold war. There was this wave of freedom for people who had been in oppressed societies for their entire existence, and that was RONALD REAGAN. He understood the source of our national greatness was not our wealth or our military power but, rather our belief in the dignity of the individual and in the God-given freedom of ordinary people to order their lives as they wished. That was the source of his view of the United States being a "shining city on a hill" and a model to people the world over, and an inspiring example of a political system that put power in the hands of the people, not bureaucrats or judges. That was RONALD REAGAN.

We remember President REAGAN for restoring our national confidence at a time when our country was on the heels of the Vietnam war and the impeachment of a President, uncertain about the way forward. We remember him for his staunch defense of innocent, unborn human life—an issue on which he never wavered—and for the extraordinary step he took in authoring a book as President, entitled "Abortion and the Conscience of the Nation," because he felt so strongly about the prolife cause. We remember his brave challenge to a new Soviet leader to "tear down this wall," because it was an affront to human dignity. We remember his vital role in bringing the cold war to an end—an end hastened by both President REAGAN's military buildup and his revitalization of the American economy.

In all of RONALD REAGAN's political life was his passionate belief in two core principles: human freedom and human dignity, both inalienable because they were given by God. He believed in the unbounded inventiveness and ingenuity of the individual freed from the tyranny of government but firmly rooted in our recognition of a higher moral authority. He understood that, in his words, "The City of Man cannot survive without the City of God, that the Visible City will perish without the Invisible City."

President REAGAN recognized that the vitality of our society and culture has always been dependent on the religious faith and practice of the people. As he said:

> Those who created our country ... understood that there is a divine order which transcends the human order. They saw the state, in fact, as a form of moral order and felt that the bedrock of moral order is religion.

RONALD REAGAN was never reticent in speaking about his own faith and the primary place it held in his life. In all of these things, President REAGAN was, and continues to be, an inspiration to millions, and certainly to me. He transformed the world for the better, and we are thankful he graced this Nation with his life, his example, and his divine calling.

Our thoughts and prayers go out to him and to his family. And for all of us who mourn his passing, may we continue to be inspired and elevated by all he was, all he achieved, and all he sought for us to be.

God bless you, RONALD REAGAN.

Hon. Byron L. Dorgan

OF NORTH DAKOTA

Mr. President, I would like to extend my deepest sympathy to the Reagan family, and to send a thank you from a grateful Nation to someone who served this country so well. And I know that the citizens I represent in North Dakota feel the same way.

President REAGAN had a profound impact on the demise of the Soviet Union and the end of the cold war. I recall in the eighties, in the middle of the cold war, when the lives of two men intersected—RONALD REAGAN and Mikhail Gorbachev. These two men were very different in many ways, but they changed the course of history. Together, President REAGAN and Mikhail Gorbachev sat down together to reduce the threat of nuclear weapons, to reduce the stockpile of nuclear weapons in both countries.

The Soviet Union no longer exists. Eastern Europe and the Warsaw Pact no longer exist. The communist threat and cold war that stemmed from them is gone. And much of the credit, in my judgment, belongs to President RONALD REAGAN.

We all recall the historic occasion when he stood at the wall in Berlin and said, "Mr. Gorbachev, tear down this wall!" It was a moment I will never forget.

But President REAGAN was defined by more than this moment.

When hundreds of American troops were killed in Lebanon, it was RONALD REAGAN who went to the press room and said he was accountable. You don't see many in politics do that, but he did.

In 1986, I served on the House Ways and Means Committee, in which we provided the most significant tax reform that had been done in many decades in this country—under the leadership of a President who said let's reduce tax rates for all Americans and get rid of some of the tax loopholes. This President led and the Congress followed. I was proud to be a part of that.

His Presidency was not without substantial controversy and difficulty. I felt his fiscal policy would produce very large budget deficits, and it did. And the Iran-Contra scandal was a serious problem for the administration. Yet, despite those problems and setbacks and controversies, I think President REAGAN provided leadership in some very important areas.

The charm of President REAGAN was considerable. He had that cowboy hat kind of cocked back on his head. He had movie-star good looks. He had that famous smile. He was a great storyteller with a gleam in his eye. He told the story often about the pile of manure and the child who insisted that if there is a pile of manure, there must be a pony somewhere. The President loved to regale people with stories.

I don't pretend to have known him well, but I sat behind him on the west front of the Capitol in 1981, when he gave his inaugural address. I recall that he announced to the country that planes had just left the tarmac in Iran with the American hostages now freed. It was a gray, cold day and the first inaugural of President REAGAN. As he began to speak, the clouds began to part and rays of sunshine began to come through. It was a remarkable moment.

And I was a freshman Member of the House when, one day, I was called to the bank of telephones in the Democratic Cloakroom. They told me it was President REAGAN calling.

The President wanted my vote for a policy he was proposing to the Congress. I listened to him, but in the end, I felt he was not right on that particular issue, and I said I could not support him on it. He said, "Well, you are a good man, and thanks for taking my call." It was just like him to frame it that way.

I had the opportunity to have breakfast with him, along with a handful of my colleagues, one morning in the White House. Once again, he regaled all of us with wonderful, charming stories.

I have always said that if you could have dinner with anyone, you could not do better than RONALD REAGAN or Tip O'Neill, both Irish, both wonderful people with a wit and a charm, and both great storytellers.

I believe that for President REAGAN, politics was not bitter or rancid. In fact, he used to talk about the "11th commandment" for his party: Thou shalt not speak ill of someone in his own political party. It is a commandment that has been long forgotten, regrettably. I am afraid that today's politics have taken a turn for the worse.

President REAGAN was aggressive in debate but always respectful. I believe he personified the notion that you can disagree without being disagreeable.

He was a man of great strength. After he was shot during an assassination attempt—seriously wounded—he was wheeled into the hospital emergency room, and he was ready with a quip for the doctors.

He was a remarkable person. When the *Challenger* accident occurred and this country was horrified by seeing the explosion of the *Challenger* and the death of those astronauts, it was RONALD REAGAN who came on television and talked about that ill-fated flight. But he did it in such an inspiring way, and finished with the refrain from that poem: "{They have} slipped the surly bonds of earth" and "touch{ed} the face of God."

Later in life, as President REAGAN lived in retirement in California, he began a long journey into the darkness of a devastating illness called Alzheimer's. His last statement to the American people was a poignant statement, in which he described his illness and its consequences.

This is a man who served his country with great distinction, someone with whom I had disagreements from time to time, but someone whom I believe is owed the admiration of an entire Nation.

I am reminded of a book that David McCullough wrote about another President, John Adams. In the book, you learn that John Adams wrote to his wife Abigail, as our Founding Fathers tried to put this country of ours together—and he asked these questions: From where will the leadership come? Who will be the leaders? How will the leadership emerge to create this new country of ours? And then he would plaintively say to his wife: There is only us. There is me. There is Ben Franklin. There is George Washington. There is Thomas Jefferson and James Madison. There is George Mason.

Of course, in the rearview mirror of history, we recognize that these men were some of the greatest human talent ever assembled on Earth. But every generation has asked that same question for this great democracy. From where will the leadership come? Who will be the leaders? And this country has been fortunate that, in generation after generation, men and women of virtually all political persuasions have stepped forward to say: Let me serve this great country.

RONALD REAGAN was one of those leaders. He served in California as Governor and then served two terms as President of the United States. He had, in my judgment, a kind of a peculiar quality, a quality that gave him an almost quenchless hope, boundless optimism, an indestructible belief that something good was going to happen, and he communicated that to a grateful Nation.

So today we say thank you. Thank you for your service. God bless your memory, and God bless your family.

Hon. Wayne Allard

OF COLORADO

Mr. President, some people have the capacity to change your life. For me, RONALD REAGAN was one of those people. RONALD REAGAN's message of strengthening individual liberties, maintaining a strong national defense, cutting through the thicket of government regulations and lowering taxes inspired me to run for public office in the eighties. He made me believe it is possible to bring about change for the better.

I first ran for the Colorado State Senate in 1982, the second year of REAGAN's Presidency, and fought to pass resolutions there supporting the policies that the President advocated, such as the balanced budget amendment.

I was a small businessman. I operated a private veterinary practice. So RONALD REAGAN's vision of strengthening America's small businesses, because they are the backbone of our economy and way of life, had a great deal of appeal. His belief in small government and cutting taxes to allow people to decide how best to spend their own money have been two of my guiding principles since I was first elected to public office. I believe him to be the father of the modern Republican Party.

My wife Joan and I never had the opportunity to meet RONALD REAGAN until he came to Colorado in 1988. Talking to him one on one was an emotional high point of my life. We smiled all the way back home to Loveland, CO. I have kept his picture hanging in my office, first in the U.S. House of Representatives and now in the Senate, ever since.

It is hard to describe to the young people who live in our vibrant economy and confident culture just how unsure and discouraged Americans were in the late seventies. Everything that could go wrong had. America seemed to be shrinking before our eyes. Those in charge of our government had apparently given up on winning the cold war. The Soviet Union loomed dangerous and, we were told, invincible. We were being admonished to get used to a dysfunctional economy that combined high inflation with low growth, a demoralized military, an ever more intrusive and intruding government, a depressed and depressing spiritual malaise that left many in doubt about our fundamental values. No one offered a way out.

RONALD REAGAN's fresh voice of optimism was like manna to our hungry spirits. He talked about how our idling economy could regain its formidable power. He talked about how great our country was and how much greater it could be. He talked about facing down our foes and our fears. He talked about restoring American pride and patriotism. He, more than any other individual in the second half of the 20th century, brought America back from the brink of self-imposed defeat and despair. He made us proud once again.

RONALD REAGAN was a monumentally gifted man, and a man of many gifts.

To those in doubt, he brought the gift of optimism.

To his supporters and allies, he brought the gift of confidence and assurance.

To an audience, he brought a magnificent gift of humor.

To his opponents, he brought the gift of disagreeing without being disagreeable.

His gift to the world was even more significant. He brought about the end of a cold war that had cast a 50-year shadow of fear over all the people on the planet.

RONALD REAGAN never doubted his country's need to defend itself from all foes. "Of the four wars in my lifetime," President REAGAN said, "none came about because the United States was too strong."

It is of paramount importance for us to remember, during this period of threat and conflict, the wisdom of one of his favorite phrases: "Peace through strength." Among his greatest achievements was to rearm us, to reinvigorate the American military, and to let our adversaries know, beyond any doubt, that they were in a race they were not going to win.

In the past 15 years or so, the United States has decisively fought and won two significant wars. The keys to those victories were highly motivated and skilled combat personnel fighting with unmatched military equipment and employing unprecedented tactics.

How did this renewed and reinvigorated American military might come about?

Let's look back to RONALD REAGAN's acceptance speech at the 1980 Republican Nominating Convention. As only the Great Communicator could, he laid out his vision for us with not only clarity, but with a conviction that rings true and is still good counsel today.

He said:

> We are awed—and rightly so—by the forces of destruction at loose in the world in this nuclear era. But neither can we be naive or foolish. ... We know only too well that war comes not when the forces of freedom are strong, but when they are weak. It is then that tyrants are tempted.

He added:

> Let our friends and those who may wish us ill take note: the United States has an obligation to its citizens and to the people of the world never to let those who would destroy freedom dictate the future course of human life on this planet. ... This nation will once again be strong enough to do that.

He was, of course, as good as his word. Once assuming office, President REAGAN launched a military renaissance that not only led to the demise of the Soviet Union, Soviet communism, and the cold war, but also set the course for our military leadership that continues to this day ensuring our safety.

President REAGAN's initiative was threefold: upgrade our military equipment; improve the training and morale of our service men and women to improve recruitment and retention; and restore national pride in—and global respect of—the U.S. military.

A major accomplishment of President REAGAN's was the development of a credible, modern strategic deterrent. He reinvested in our strategic ballistic missile weapons inventories, modernized a complement of land, sea, and aircraft-based platforms to project our strategic force.

This display of offensive force proved to be an effective deterrent, but President REAGAN envisioned a world with far fewer of these destructive weapons, and pressed throughout his Presidency for significant reductions of nuclear weapons. In 1983, President REAGAN launched the Strategic Defense Initiative in the hopes of one day rendering all such ballistic missiles impotent and obsolete.

Today we are building on his legacy by deploying strategic missile defenses and aggressively eliminating excessive nuclear stockpiles. President REAGAN's legacy to us, of a safer world, is one we must constantly guard and honor.

There is no doubt that President REAGAN was one of the greatest Presidents of the modern era. A man of huge confidence and unwavering principle, he revived the American spirit, revitalized our economy and engineered the fall of communism. He changed the world for the better. We share his family's grief, and keep them in our prayers.

In his memory, let us recommit ourselves to President REAGAN's goal of ensuring that America always remains the bright, "shining city on the hill."

Hon. Chuck Hagel

OF NEBRASKA

Mr. President, on January 20, 1981, RONALD REAGAN, after being sworn in as the 40th President of the United States, looked out over The Mall and addressed the Nation. He told us that the challenges of our day required:

> Our best effort and our willingness to believe in ourselves and to believe in our capacity to perform great deeds, to believe that together with God's help we can and will resolve the problems which now confront us. And after all, why shouldn't we believe that? We are Americans.

I remember the celebrations that evening as if they happened yesterday. It was a bitterly cold evening. As our Nation celebrated a new beginning, it was as if the cold January winds swept away a Nation's doubts and fears and replaced them with a renewed American spirit.

RONALD REAGAN was a unique American leader who understood the greatness and the goodness of America. He knew who he was and what he believed. Over the last century, no American President was as well grounded as RONALD REAGAN. He had faith and confidence in the people of America, and that trust was reciprocated.

As much as anyone who came before or after him, RONALD REAGAN possessed an innate understanding of the significance of the American Presidency. RONALD and Nancy REAGAN set the gold standard for grace, dignity and class in the White House. REAGAN understood the weight and consequences of his office beyond the borders of the United States. The world looked to him as a standard bearer of freedom. REAGAN also understood the importance of the Presidency to young people. The responsibility of being a role model to a nation's youth rested easily on his shoulders.

RONALD REAGAN is known as the Great Communicator. While he certainly was one of the best communicators ever to hold the Presidency, he was far more than just a talented communicator. REAGAN was a thinker and a writer. He was constantly writing beautiful letters and his speeches in longhand. Today, these speeches and letters are national treasures. REAGAN thought deeply about the great issues of his time without getting dragged down into the underbrush of detail and trivia. He was not a superfluous man. Our Nation was guided by his clarity of purpose, understanding of the purpose of power and the limitations of government.

Since President REAGAN left the American political stage, we have missed his imagination and creativity. Since his days of sitting in a radio studio doing play-by-play broadcasts for baseball games from news wire service copy, he had a genuineness that served him well. He was a masterful storyteller. In today's age of processed politics and politicians, President REAGAN's candor and humor are sorely lacking.

RONALD REAGAN was a child of humble beginnings who never forgot the little guy. He believed every American had something special to contribute. REAGAN let people know that each thread of the American fabric mattered. In late September 1980, I was working as an adviser on the REAGAN-Bush campaign.

One evening, I was part of a group invited to an estate near Middleburg, VA, where then-Governor and Nancy REAGAN were staying. They wanted to thank us for the work we had done for the campaign with a wonderful dinner. As the evening was ending, an aide to Governor REAGAN asked me to remain after the dinner because Governor REAGAN wanted to speak with me. I was taken into the house where Governor REAGAN was staying. He sat down next to me and told me he wanted to talk about Vietnam. He wanted to know about my experience and what I thought about the war. That was the kind of man he was. He wanted to understand things. He wanted to know things and he wanted to make the world better than it was.

Though his individual accomplishments are great, RONALD REAGAN will be remembered for something far greater than the sum of his individual accomplishments; he will be remembered for renewing the American spirit. He was a true American original. We will never see one like him again.

Over the last decade as we struggled to meet the challenges of our time, RONALD REAGAN slipped away from us. He now belongs to the warmth of eternity and the pages of history. However, he has not left us to meet our challenges alone. The lessons of his leadership and the strength of his spirit that swept across our country on a cold day in January 24 years ago, guide us still today.

Hon. Don Nickles

OF OKLAHOMA

Mr. President, I rise today to pay tribute to a man who meant a great deal to me and a great deal to my State and to our country. That, of course, is President RONALD REAGAN. It is with sadness I learned that he recently passed away. But I have great confidence he has moved on to a better home. I express my condolences and sympathies to his family and also thank them for their generosity in sharing RONALD REAGAN with us in the public life, both as Governor of the great State of California, and also as President of the United States for 8 wonderful years.

I had the privilege, in the same year as RONALD REAGAN was elected President, to be elected to the Senate. I have many fond memories of RONALD REAGAN. I remember very well during his inaugural address when the rumors were coming out, and then later confirmed, that the American citizens who were held hostage in Iran for 444 days were released. I remember the euphoria that came across the stage. I remember the euphoria that came across America. It was such an exciting, positive change. Americans really felt great. This was suppressing our country, the very fact that we had American citizens held hostage for over a year, in many cases being beaten or tortured or abused, with American flags burning in Tehran continually. It was such a great day when they were released.

I happen to think it was because, in many respects, the leadership of Iran decided they did not want to worry about this new President, RONALD REAGAN, and what actions he might take. I think they made a very good decision. I was very pleased they did so. I was very euphoric at the time and probably could not have been much more excited at that time.

When we were sworn in, there were 18 new Senators elected in 1980 and sworn in early in 1981. Of the 18, 16 were Republicans. The leadership of the Senate changed for the first time, I believe, since 1954. So we had new committee chairmen; we had new leadership. Howard Baker assumed the responsibility and role as majority leader and did an outstanding job. The Senate was a great place to work and to serve, and to work with a President as generous, as humorous, and with such strong leadership as RONALD REAGAN.

I look at the economy that RONALD REAGAN inherited, and I see great accomplishments. A lot of people do not remember that in 1980 the inflation rate was 13.5 percent and it fell to 4.8 percent by 1989. The interest rate in 1980 was 15.27 percent and fell to 10.87 percent by 1989. Actually, the interest rate had risen to 18.87 percent in 1981. I remember that now. Interest rates were at 18 and 19 percent. The unemployment rate in 1980 was over 7 percent. In 1981 it reached 7.6 percent but by 1989 it was down to 5.3 percent.

So we had record high inflation rates, record high interest rates, and maybe not record high but very high unemployment rates. We inherited an economy that was going nowhere fast. It was going in the wrong direction. You could not afford to build a home. You could not afford to expand your business. It was a very difficult time.

RONALD REAGAN came in with such great enthusiasm, such an optimist. He did not say, "let's moan about it," but "let's do something about it." He had an economic game plan for which we fought, and we passed in the House and the Senate. These were remarkable accomplishments when I think about it.

He actually was responsible for pushing Congress, Democrats and Republicans, to pass enormous changes in the Tax Code. I happened to enjoy working on taxes, and during his 8 years he actually moved the maximum tax rate from 70 percent to 28 percent. That is a phenomenal accomplishment. Phenomenal. And he was able to do it with a bipartisan majority. It was not a strictly partisan House and Senate. As a matter of fact, the House was always controlled by the Democrats. Tip O'Neill, who was the Democrat leader, the House Speaker at the time, was opposed. So we had big confrontations, political confrontations, big battles over the tax cuts, and over the budgets. Yet they passed them.

Even though we had big battles, we had a certain dignity and respect in large part because of RONALD REAGAN. And because of his affection for individuals, Democrats and Republicans, even political adversaries who would have political battles still had a collegial, working relationship. They respected each other and respected individuals regardless of their political philosophy. As a result, he was able to enact enormous changes in the Tax Code and budgets, and increase defense.

RONALD REAGAN came in with an agenda, and he largely accomplished those objectives. The result has been economic freedom in this country.

He was not satisfied, frankly, with just expanding and improving the economic lot of Americans. He wanted to improve the economic lot and the freedom of people throughout the world. RONALD REAGAN was the leader of the free world, and he spoke eloquently and often and encouraged freedom through the world and countless countries that have been oppressed or suppressed through communist leadership. RONALD REAGAN was speaking to them. He would go right over the leaders of Congress. If he wanted to get something done budgetwise, taxwise, or defensewise, and if Congress was not listening, he would go to the American people. And when he would travel internationally he would go over the leadership of those countries and speak to their people with great success.

We all remember his speech when he was in Berlin, the speech that says: "Mr. Gorbachev, tear down this wall!"

The favorite picture of all my memorabilia that I have in my home is a picture of me standing before the Berlin Wall, and behind it somebody spray-painted on the wall: "When this wall falls, the rest will, too." And they did. The Berlin Wall did fall, and I think it was in large part because of RONALD REAGAN's leadership.

When that wall fell, other countries that had been suppressed and under the reins of the Iron Curtain of communism began speaking up, exercising their rights, and demanding freedom and obtaining it.

RONALD REAGAN was the leader in winning the fight in the cold war. As Mr. Gorbachev said, probably no one else in the world could have done it, but RONALD REAGAN did it. And he was able to do it with Mr. Gorbachev. Many times they were political adversaries in negotiating arms control treaties and so on. Yet they still became friends as only RONALD REAGAN could do. He could become friends with his adversaries and eventually that kind of friendship and bond would lead to arms control reduction, would lead to a significant reduction in nuclear weapons, would lead to agreements with our NATO allies and other countries to expand freedom.

RONALD REAGAN, probably more than any individual since Churchill or Roosevelt, was responsible for expanding freedom throughout the world. I compliment him for his great contributions in doing so.

He became somewhat of a role model for many of us. I was elected with this group in 1980. Many of us called ourselves Reaganites and considered ourselves part of the soldiers in the field trying to get an agenda done to expand freedom. I am proud to have been part of that. I am proud to have had the opportunity to serve with such a great individual.

I remember many times going down to the White House, talking issues. I remember RONALD REAGAN almost always having humor, almost always not caring who got the credit as long as we accomplished our objective.

I remember many times he let other people wrestle with the details, but he knew where he wanted to go. He knew the course he was trying to direct our ship of state, and he managed it very well.

I have a lot of fond memories. I remember RONALD REAGAN coming in to campaign for me in 1986. We had him visit Norman, OK, the University of Oklahoma, Lloyd Noble Arena. We packed the place. It was more than packed. The fire marshal had to turn down people who could not get in. We had thousands and thousands of people. I told President REAGAN: This is Reagan country. They love you here. You don't need to make a prepared speech. You can say whatever you want. They will applaud. They love you here.

There was a nice, big sign: "This is Reagan country." Very positive. The entire rally speech could not have gone better from my standpoint. It was great.

RONALD REAGAN concluded his speech. He said, "That is why we need Don Rickles in the Senate." And I thought: Did he really say that? I told him to wing it, and he did. I have had that honor of being able to call myself Don Rickles for a long time.

But RONALD REAGAN leaves a legacy. He leaves a legacy of decency. He leaves a legacy of integrity. I think he helped restore so much pride in America. He was a true patriot, a patriot who loved this country from the very inner core of his being. And it was contagious. It was contagious through the fact that not only did he love America, but he made Americans feel better about our country.

He made other people envy us to some extent. They wanted to be like us. They wanted to be free. What does America have that we don't have? They have freedom, optimism. And that freedom would be economic freedom, personal freedom, and political freedom.

RONALD REAGAN wanted to expand it all for all people. He believed everybody—even if they lived in China or Russia or North Korea or El Salvador—if people were trying to take that freedom away, he was freedom's friend. He carried that banner very well.

He helped people learn to love and respect the United States. I can honestly say I have the greatest admiration and respect for RONALD REAGAN. I loved RONALD REAGAN. He has moved this country forward in a way that I think all of us can be very proud.

Again, I express my condolences and sympathy to Nancy Reagan and to the family. Nancy Reagan was one great First Lady. The love and affection she showed toward her husband throughout not only his Presidency and governorship but, frankly, throughout the last 10 years is more than commendable, and it is the kind of role model that we expect from Nancy Reagan. She is a first-class First Lady, a first-class lady for all of us.

Again, my condolences and sympathy to her. And I thank her and her family for allowing us to share RONALD REAGAN for many years as the leader of our country. He has made this country and this world a much better place to live.

Hon. Barbara A. Mikulski

OF MARYLAND

Mr. President, I, too, rise in memory of President RONALD REAGAN. President REAGAN will be remembered for his strong convictions, his unfailing optimism, and his deep and abiding patriotism.

My heartfelt condolences go out to the Reagan family. They have been through so much in the last 10 years.

Our former First Lady, Nancy Reagan, has met one of the greatest challenges that one can face with grace, dignity, and dedication. Her courage is a model for the Nation. I know how tremendously difficult it is for a family when a loved one has Alzheimer's. My own dear father suffered from this disease. And, my family and I know what the long goodbye meant. So, I speak for my family, and I think all families who have endured this disease when we salute Nancy Reagan as we pay our respects to our President.

Mr. President, as our country reflects on President REAGAN's life, many will ask, how should we honor him? I believe the greatest tribute we could give to President REAGAN and the Reagan family is a living memorial, something that he would want to see us do, not something we would like to do, and something that would have lasting value. Therefore, I would like to issue a bipartisan call to support legislation that Senator Kit Bond and I will be introducing next week, legislation to create breakthroughs for Alzheimer's disease.

Let's honor President REAGAN's life with new research and new initiatives on how to prevent Alzheimer's, how to care for those who have it, how to support the gallant caregivers, and how, ultimately, to find a cure.

President REAGAN was a man of vigor. Let's attack Alzheimer's with the same type of vigor that President REAGAN demonstrated during his life.

The time to act for real breakthroughs is now. Just last month, Senator Bond and I held a hearing on Alzheimer's research. Expert after expert told us: We are on the verge of amazing breakthroughs; we will lose opportunities if we don't move quickly; we are at a crucial point where National Institutes of Health (NIH) funding can make a real difference.

Researchers, families, and advocates all said the same thing, we need to do more, we need to do better.

Let's answer that call by introducing and passing the RONALD REAGAN Alzheimer's Breakthrough Act of 2004.

Friends, we are on the brink of something that could make a huge difference in the lives of American families. We know that families face great difficulties when a loved one has Alzheimer's. There is great emotional cost as well as financial cost. We know that for our public investment we could get new treatments that would prolong a patient's cognitive abilities.

Each month we delay admission to a long-term care facility is important to the family and to the taxpayer. Everybody wants a cure; that is our ultimate goal. But even if we keep people at home for 1 or 2 more years, to help them with their memory, their activities of daily living, it would be an incredible breakthrough, and what a great tribute it would be to President REAGAN.

It is amazing how far we have come. From the time President REAGAN took office in 1981 until the time he wrote that incredibly moving goodbye letter to the Nation—and I note it with great emotion because, again, I know how my own father felt. Back in the early eighties, when President REAGAN first came to office, Alzheimer's was a catch-all term. Today, doctors diagnose Alzheimer's with 90-percent accuracy. Every day NIH is making progress to identify risks, looking at new kinds of brain scans for appropriate detection, and understanding what this disease does to the brain.

How did we get this far, this fast? With a bipartisan commitment like the one represented by Senator Bond, Senators Specter and Harkin, the Alzheimer's Task Force that is led by Senators Collins and Clinton, and all of us who are working on this issue. With a bipartisan commitment of the authorizers and appropriators, we have been working to increase the funding for the National Institute on Aging. Remember, there are 19 institutes at the NIH. One of them is the National Institute of Aging.

In 1998 the National Institute on Aging was funded at approximately $500 million. Thanks to our bipartisan effort, it is at $1 billion. Now is the time to do more.

That is why I want to join with my esteemed colleague, Senator Kit Bond, who himself has been a very strong advocate for research and breakthroughs, to introduce the RONALD REAGAN Alzheimer's Breakthrough Act of 2004.

We want to strengthen our national commitment to Alzheimer's research, to increase and double the funding of research at NIA, to give them the resources they need to make those breakthroughs they say they are on the horizon of doing. This will mean more clinical trials to test the best way to detect, prevent, and treat Alzheimer's.

NIH is looking at a range of behaviors and therapies that can make an incredible difference.

In our legislation, we also call for a national summit on Alzheimer's to bring together the best minds to examine current research, to look at priorities, and also to look at how we can help families.

While we are looking at research to find the cure or the cognitive stretch out, we have to support the caregivers. God bless the caregivers. These are family members, often spouses, who take care of someone with Alzheimer's. The first caregiver is always the family. We saw that with Nancy Reagan who went from being First Lady to first caregiver.

We need to support families. We need to give help to those families practicing self-help. We now have legislation on the books to do that. But, we need to add more to the Federal checkbook. Most families don't know where to turn to get what services are available. I have a family caregiver tax credit that would reimburse families for prescription drugs, home health care, and specialized daycare. Too often, for families with Alzheimer's, family responsibility brings them to the brink of family bankruptcy.

There are other things we want to be able to do with this legislation, such as providing news people can use. The legislation would establish a network so information can get out people about the advances, and things that could be done right now to slow the onset of symptoms. We need to get the word out, such as the wonderful program developed by the Alzheimer's Association called "Maintain Your Brain." But private philanthropy cannot be a substitute for public policy and public funding. We have to fund these initiatives.

I believe very strongly in this. There are 4.5 million people with Alzheimer's. They live in every State, in cities and suburbs and on farms. They are from every walk of life, like my father, who owned a small grocery store, or a man who was the President of the United States. Alzheimer's is an all-American disease. It affected an all-American President. Now we need an all-American effort to find the breakthroughs.

I encourage everyone to consider this when Senator Bond and I introduce this legislation. This research and treatment is very important. I do not want to be so bold as to speak for Mrs. Reagan, but based on what I know she has gone through and what other families have gone through, I believe the legacy she would approve of is an all-American effort—an effort to speed up the day when no family ever has to have that very long goodbye.

Hon. Christopher S. Bond

OF MISSOURI

Mr. President, I thank and commend my colleague from Maryland who has been a great champion of the effort to deal with the terribly distressing and fatal disease of Alzheimer's in proposing—and I am happy to join her—a measure to honor RONALD REAGAN, his memory, his life, his work, and his family with a living tribute, a redoubled effort on behalf of this Nation to deal with Alzheimer's.

Senator Mikulski and others who have lived with and lost a loved one from Alzheimer's can say very clearly how difficult it must have been for Mrs. Reagan and the Reagan family as this true leader went through the final stages of his life, crippled and debilitated by Alzheimer's, to see this man who was so vigorous, who had contributed so much be reduced to the indignities of Alzheimer's.

His life and legacy can be honored in many ways. People will remember him for many reasons. I will speak of those in a moment. But by increasing research for Alzheimer's disease, helping to limit the number and maybe even eliminate Alzheimer's, providing assistance to families who must deal with patients with Alzheimer's, and providing assistance in identifying and preventing Alzheimer's is vitally important.

One of the facts that struck me as we listened to the experts was that as we get older more and more of us are going to suffer from Alzheimer's disease. We were told in our hearing about a month ago that if you reach 85, you have a 50-percent chance of getting Alzheimer's disease. What a tragic figure. There is something we must do, and we believe this legislation is one way of making a major effort, showing a commitment, reaching out a hand of hope to the families of those who have Alzheimer's, providing information to all of us on what we might be able to do to lessen the likelihood we will be struck with Alzheimer's.

As Senator Mikulski said, this bill will serve as a tribute to President REAGAN by doubling the funding for Alzheimer's research at the National Institutes of Health. It would increase funding for the National Family Caregiver Support Program to $250 million. It would reauthorize the Alzheimer's demonstration grant program that provides grants to States to fill in gaps in Alzheimer's services, such as respite care, home health care, and daycare.

I have done a fair amount of work in home care and daycare. I can tell you that a family living with a patient with Alzheimer's needs a break. They need someone to care for that loved one so they can get out and renew their batteries, refresh their view on life. This can help.

We would authorize $1 million for a safe return program to assist in the identification and safe, timely return of individuals with Alzheimer's disease and related dementias who too frequently wander off from their caregivers. We hear the tragedies where they can't find their way home and fall victim to natural or even automobile accidents while they are gone. We would establish a public education program to educate members of the public about prevention techniques, how you can maintain your brain, as you age, based on the current research being undertaken by NIH.

We would establish a $5,000 tax credit to help with the high health costs of caring for a loved one at home.

Today, as Senator Mikulski said, about 4.5 million Americans have Alzheimer's, costing about $100 billion a year. But if current trends continue, and as more of us age, by 2050, 11 to 16 million individuals could have this disease.

Over the past 20 years tremendous progress has been made in the prevention, diagnosis, and treatment of Alzheimer's. It is now possible to diagnose Alzheimer's with more than 90-percent accuracy. There are new drugs, new treatments introduced each year, and investments in research have set the stage for scientific and medical advances to prevent or slow down the progression of Alzheimer's. Quite frankly, most of the successful research to date has been in slowing the impact, not preventing it. But this research offers hope for the 4.5 million people and their families who suffer from the disease today.

These are some of what we can do as an honor to the President. It is my great pleasure to speak in this Chamber about the life and leadership and the truly remarkable legacy of the 40th President of the United States, RONALD REAGAN.

We mourn his loss. We pray for comfort for his family. But most of all, we give thanks for his life, his leadership, and his contributions. Truly, he is a man who changed the mood of the country. He changed the economy of the country. And in many ways, he changed the mood and the attitude of the world.

People talk about President REAGAN as the Great Communicator. Nobody could deliver a line better than he could. But do you know something about communication? Communication is only as good as the message you have to communicate. The power of RONALD REAGAN was that he delivered with enthusiasm, with optimism, with cheer, with love, a message of hope, freedom, and opportunity, not just for Americans but for the world.

I had the pleasure of getting to know RONALD REAGAN. He was a genuinely optimistic person who brought the spirit of optimism and hope to us as Americans and to enslaved peoples around the world. RONALD REAGAN was a man who took disappointment and moved on. He was a man of unfailing good humor, care, and thoughtfulness. Even people who disagreed with his policies across the board could not help but like him.

And those of us who may have disappointed him found it did not interfere with his friendship. He campaigned for me in 1972 when I was a 33-year-old kid running for Governor of the State of Missouri. I had never seen anything like it. When he came into town, we had all of the security and escorts. But it wasn't until he went up on stage and started making his presentation that I saw what it was that had brought so many people from southwest Missouri in to hear this leader. He had a message then—the same message—of optimism, growth, and hope for the future.

I was fortunate enough to be elected and to serve with him for 2 years. Two years after that, I hosted the Republican National Convention, and I had made a commitment to our President at the time, who selected our State for the national convention. So I supported him and not President REAGAN. But about 10 years later, when I was running for the Senate, he came to Missouri three times and he put on the most amazing campaign rallies I ever had. We still talk about it, because people came to hear his message. I stood there, side by side with Jack Danforth, and we smiled and glowed in the wonderful feeling he generated. He helped me a great deal.

President REAGAN helped the United States. He came to the Presidency at a time when a lot of people were saying maybe the Presidency cannot work, maybe nobody can govern this country, maybe it is too much to expect somebody to lead. Well, he led very boldly. Quite simply, he thought that if you returned tax dollars to the average American and took off the fetters on small business, you would create jobs and build the economy. By the significant lowering of the tax rates, as my friend from Oklahoma, Senator Nickles, said, he put money back into the pockets of small businesses, and small business became the engine of economic growth, creating three-quarters of the new jobs. He built an economy, and that economy allowed us to put money into defense.

He tried to negotiate with the Soviets. He asked Mr. Gorbachev if he would sit down and talk with him about how we could end the competition between Soviet communism and the United States. Mr. Gorbachev didn't respond. So he built up our defenses and showed the Russians, the Soviets, that they could not defeat us. He went boldly to Berlin and called on Mr. Gorbachev—much to the distress of the State Department, I might add, and some of his own team—"Mr. Gorbachev, tear down this wall!"

Well, that wall came down literally and figuratively. He had a message that went far beyond Mr. Gorbachev. That message went to the enslaved peoples behind the Iron Curtain. I had the pleasure of visiting some of those countries right before and right after they fell, a few years after President REAGAN had set in motion the inexorable machine of freedom. His message of hope, freedom, and opportunity continues to reverberate around the world. I have had the pleasure of meeting with people and traveling to other countries and seeing how this message—the American dream—he championed is taking hold. He wasn't the only one responsible for it, but we never had a better proponent of it. I believe this message of the American hopes and the American ideals, for which RONALD REAGAN spoke so eloquently, is winning the battle.

Finally, in his last and boldest move, when RONALD REAGAN learned he had Alzheimer's—a disease which was not spoken about often because people hated to think of what would happen to their loved ones, so they didn't talk about it—he said, "I have ... Alzheimer's disease," and Americans woke up and they thought, this is a world leader who is suffering from this disease; let's do something about it. Let's get serious about Alzheimer's disease. That public announcement gave us a push that I believe we can continue by carrying on with his work with a living memorial.

So as we say goodbye to this remarkable American, we join in our prayers and thoughts with Mrs. Nancy Reagan and her family, and we celebrate the life of a great American who made a real difference for people throughout the world. Let us honor his memory by helping millions more whom we might be able to save from the scourge of Alzheimer's disease and the burdens and the sorrow that imposes on their families.

Hon. Gordon Smith

OF OREGON

Mr. President, in the elections of 1980 and 1984, the State of Oregon sent its electors to the electoral college to vote for RONALD REAGAN. He was the last Republican to win the State of Oregon in a Presidential election, and he did so at a time of great peril both for my State and our country.

When that occurred, America was in economic malaise, communism seemed to be in its ascendancy, and America was struggling for leadership. Winston Churchill once said of a predecessor as British Prime Minister, "He had had the misfortune to live in a time of great men and small events." When you think of where America was and where it ended after 8 years of the administration of RONALD REAGAN, truly it can be said that all free men and women are better and freer, more prosperous and more at peace because RONALD REAGAN was a great man called to a great time.

As I contemplated what I could do in my small way to add some measure of tribute to the life of RONALD REAGAN and to express to Nancy Reagan and her family my heartfelt condolences, I thought I should keep my words to a minimum and focus, instead, on the warm and wise words of President REAGAN in his farewell address. It has been the practice of the Senate for the last 140 years that on or around the birthday of George Washington, a Senator is selected to read Washington's farewell address. I thought I would begin that tradition this day, with President REAGAN's great speech, to come to the floor on or around President REAGAN's birthday, and share his speech—or if one of my colleagues would like to do so, I would offer them the opportunity. I believe that this new tradition would be a fitting tribute to RONALD REAGAN, to let RONALD REAGAN's words speak again to the American people, far more eloquently than I could on an occasion when we all struggle to find the right superlatives to say thank you to him.

So with the Chair's indulgence, I will read the farewell address of President RONALD REAGAN, given shortly before he left the Oval Office and George Herbert Walker Bush became the President.

The words of President REAGAN:

FAREWELL ADDRESS

This is the 34th time I'll speak to you from the Oval Office and the last. We've been together eight years now, and soon it'll be time for me to go. But before I do, I wanted to share some thoughts, some of which I've been saving for a long time.

It's been the honor of my life to be your president. So many of you have written the past few weeks to say thanks, but I could say as much to you. Nancy and I are grateful for the opportunity you gave us to serve.

One of the things about the presidency is that you're always somewhat apart. You spend a lot of time going by too fast in a car someone else is driving, and seeing the people through tinted glass—the parents holding up a child, and the wave you saw too late and couldn't return. And so many times I wanted to stop and reach out from behind the glass, and connect. Well, maybe I can do a little of that tonight.

People ask how I feel about leaving. And the fact is, "parting is such sweet sorrow." The sweet part is California, and the ranch and freedom. The sorrow—the goodbyes, of course, and leaving this beautiful place.

You know, down the hall and up the stairs from this office is the part of the White House where the president and his family live. There are a few favorite windows I have up there that I like to stand and look out of early in the morning. The view is over the grounds here to the Washington Monument, and then the Mall and the Jefferson Memorial. But on mornings when the humidity is low, you can see past the Jefferson to the river, the Potomac, and the Virginia shore. Someone said that's the view Lincoln had when he saw the smoke rising from the Battle of Bull Run. I see more prosaic things: the grass on the banks, the morning traffic as people make their way to work, now and then a sailboat on the river.

I've been thinking a bit at that window. I've been reflecting on what the past eight years have meant and mean. And the image that comes to mind like a refrain is a nautical one—a small story about a big ship, and a refugee and a sailor. It was back in the early eighties, at the height of the boat people. And the sailor was hard at work on the carrier Midway, which was patrolling the South China Sea. The sailor, like most American servicemen, was young, smart, and fiercely observant. The crew spied on the horizon a leaky little boat. And crammed inside were refugees from Indochina hoping to get to America. The Midway sent a small launch to bring them to the ship and safety. As the refugees made their way through the choppy seas, one spied the sailor on deck, and stood up, and called out to him. He yelled, "Hello, American sailor. Hello, freedom man."

A small moment with a big meaning, a moment the sailor, who wrote it in a letter, couldn't get out of his mind. And, when I saw it, neither could I. Because that's what it was to be an American in the eighties. We stood, again, for freedom. I know we always have, but in the past few years the world again, and in a way, we ourselves rediscovered it.

It's been quite a journey this decade, and we held together through some stormy seas. And at the end, together, we are reaching our destination.

The fact is, from Grenada to the Washington and Moscow summits, from the recession of 1981 to 1982, to the expansion that began in late 1982 and continues to this day, we've made a difference. The way I see it, there were two great triumphs, two things that I'm proudest of. One is the economic recovery, in which the people of America created—and filled—19 million new jobs. The other is the recovery of our morale. America is respected again in the world and looked to for leadership.

Something that happened to me a few years ago reflects some of this. It was back in 1981, and I was attending my first big economic summit, which was held that year in Canada. The meeting place rotates among the member countries. The opening meeting was a formal dinner for the heads of government of the seven industrialized nations. Now, I sat there like the new kid in school and listened, and it was all François this and Helmut that. They dropped titles and spoke to one another on a first-name basis. Well, at one point I sort of leaned in and said, "My name's RON." Well, in that same year, we began the actions we felt would ignite an economic comeback—cut taxes and regulation, started to cut spending. And soon the recovery began.

Two years later, another economic summit with pretty much the same cast. At the big opening meeting we all got together, and all of a sudden, just for a moment, I saw that everyone was just sitting there looking at me. And one of them broke the silence. "Tell us about the American miracle," he said.

Well, back in 1980, when I was running for president, it was all so different. Some pundits said our programs would result in catastrophe. Our views on foreign affairs would cause war. Our plans for the economy would cause inflation to soar and bring about economic collapse. I even remember one highly respected economist saying, back in 1982, that "the engines of economic growth have shut down here, and they're likely to stay that way for years to come." Well, he and the other opinion leaders were wrong. The fact is, what they called "radical" was really "right." What they called "dangerous" was just "desperately needed."

And in all of that time I won a nickname, "The Great Communicator." But I never thought it was my style or the words I used that made a difference: It was the content. I wasn't a great communicator, but I communicated great things, and they didn't spring full bloom from my brow, they came from the heart of a great nation—from our experience, our wisdom, and our belief in principles that have guided us for two centuries. They called it the Reagan revolution. Well, I'll accept that, but for me it always seemed more like the great rediscovery, a rediscovery of our values and our common sense.

Common sense told us that when you put a big tax on something, the people will produce less of it. So, we cut the people's tax rates, and the people produced more than ever before. The economy bloomed like a plant that had been cut back and could now grow quicker and stronger. Our economic program brought about the longest peacetime expansion in our history: real family income up, the poverty rate down, entrepreneurship booming, and an explosion in research and new technology. We're exporting more than ever because American industry became more competitive and at the same time, we summoned the national will to knock down protectionist walls abroad instead of erecting them at home. Common sense also told us that to preserve the peace, we'd have to become strong again after years of weakness and confusion. So, we rebuilt our defenses, and this New Year we toasted the new peacefulness around the globe. Not only have the superpowers actually begun to reduce their stockpiles of nuclear weapons—and hope for even more progress is bright—but the regional conflicts that rack the globe are also beginning to cease. The Persian Gulf is no longer a war zone. The Soviets are leaving Afghanistan. The Vietnamese are preparing to pull out of Cambodia, and an American-mediated accord will soon send 50,000 Cuban troops home from Angola.

The lesson of all this was, of course, that because we're a great nation, our challenges seem complex. It will always be this way. But as long as we remember our first principles and believe in ourselves, the future will always be ours. And something else we learned: Once you begin a great movement, there's no telling where it will end. We meant to change a nation, and instead, we changed a world.

Countries across the globe are turning to free markets and free speech and turning away from ideologies of the past. For them, the great rediscovery of the 1980s has been that, lo and behold, the moral way of government is the practical way of government: Democracy, the profoundly good, is also the profoundly productive.

When you've got to the point when you can celebrate the anniversaries of your 39th birthday, you can sit back sometimes, review your life, and see it flowing before you. For me there was a fork in the river, and it was right in the middle of my life. I never meant to go into politics. It wasn't my intention when I was young. But I was raised to believe you had to pay your way for the blessings bestowed on you. I was happy with my career in the entertainment world, but I ultimately went into politics because I wanted to protect something precious.

Ours was the first revolution in the history of mankind that truly reversed the course of government, and with three little words: "We the people." "We the people" tell the government what to do; it doesn't tell us. "We the people" are the driver, the government is the car. And we decide where it should go, and by what route, and how fast. Almost all the world's constitutions are documents in which governments tell the people what their privileges are. Our Constitution is a document in which "We the people" tell the government what it is allowed to do. "We the people" are free. This belief has been the underyling basis for everything I've tried to do these past eight years.

But back in the 1960s, when I began, it seemed to me that we'd begun reversing the order of things—that through more and more rules and regulations and confiscatory taxes, the government was taking more of our money, more of our options, and more of our freedom. I went into politics in part to put up my hand and say, "Stop." I was a citizen politician, and it seemed the right thing for a citizen to do.

I think we have stopped a lot of what needed stopping. And I hope we have once again reminded people that man is not free unless government is limited. There's a clear cause and effect here that is as neat and predictable as a law of physics: As government expands, liberty contracts.

Nothing is less free than pure communism—and yet we have, the past few years, forged a satisfying new closeness with the Soviet Union. I've been asked if this isn't a gamble, and my answer is no because we're basing our actions not on words but deeds. The detente of the 1970s was based not on actions but promises. They'd promise to treat their own people and the people of the world better. But the gulag was still the gulag, and the state was still expansionist, and they still waged proxy wars in Africa, Asia, and Latin America.

Well, this time, so far, it's different. President Gorbachev has brought about some internal democratic reforms and begun the withdrawal from Afghanistan. He has also freed prisoners whose names I've given him every time we've met.

But life has a way of reminding you of big things through small incidents. Once, during the heady days of the Moscow summit, Nancy and I decided to break off from the entourage one afternoon to visit the shops on Arbat Street—that's a little street just off Moscow's main shopping area. Even though our visit was a surprise, every Russian there immediately recognized us and called out our names and reached for our hands. We were just about swept away by the warmth. You could almost feel the possibilities in all that joy. But within seconds, a KGB detail pushed their way toward us and began pushing and shoving the people in the crowd. It was an interesting moment. It reminded me that while the man on the street in the Soviet Union yearns for peace, the government is Communist. And those who run it are Communists, and that means we and they view such issues as freedom and human rights very differently.

We must keep up our guard, but we must also continue to work together to lessen and eliminate tension and mistrust. My view is that President Gorbachev is different from previous Soviet leaders. I think he knows some of the things wrong with his society and is trying to fix them. We wish him well. And we'll continue to work to make sure that the Soviet Union that eventually emerges from this process is a less threatening one. What it all boils down to is this: I want the new closeness to continue. And it will, as long as we make it clear that we will continue to act in a certain way as long as they continue to act in a helpful manner. If and when they don't, at first pull your punches. If they persist, pull the plug. It's still trust but verify. It's still play, but cut the cards. It's still watch closely. And don't be afraid to see what you see.

I've been asked if I have any regrets. Well, I do. The deficit is one. I've been talking a great deal about that lately, but tonight isn't for arguments. And I'm going to hold my tongue. But an observation: I've had my share of victories in the Congress, but what few people noticed is that I never won anything you didn't win for me. They never saw my troops, they never saw Reagan's regiments, the American people. You won every battle with every call you made and letter you wrote demanding action. Well, action is still needed. If we're to finish the job, Reagan's regiments will have to become the Bush brigades. Soon he'll be the chief, and he'll need you every bit as much as I did. Finally, there is a great tradition of warnings in Presidential farewells, and I've got one that's been on my mind for some time. But oddly enough it starts with one of the things I'm proudest of in the past eight years: the resurgence of national pride that I called the new patriotism. This national feeling is good, but it won't count for much, and it won't last unless it's grounded in thoughtfulness and knowledge.

An informed patriotism is what we want. And are we doing a good enough job teaching our children what America is and what she represents in the long history of the world? Those of us who are over 35 or so years of age grew up in a different America. We were taught, very directly, what it means to be an American. And we absorbed, almost in the air, a love of country and an appreciation of its institutions. If you didn't get these things from your family, you got them from the neighborhood, from the father down the street who fought in Korea or the family who lost someone at Anzio. Or you could get a sense of patriotism from school. And if all else failed, you could get a sense of patriotism from popular culture. The movies celebrated democratic values and implicitly reinforced the idea that America was special. TV was like that, too, through the mid-sixties.

But now, we're about to enter the nineties, and some things have changed. Younger parents aren't sure that an unambivalent appreciation of America is the right thing to teach modern children. And as for those who create the popular culture, well-grounded patriotism is no longer the style. Our spirit is back, but we haven't reinstitutionalized it. We've got to do a better job of getting across that America is freedom—freedom of speech, freedom of religion, freedom of enterprise. And freedom is special and rare. It's fragile; it needs protection.

So, we've got to teach history based not on what's in fashion but what's important: Why the Pilgrims came here, who Jimmy Doolittle was, and what those 30 seconds over Tokyo meant. You know, four years ago on the 40th anniversary of D-Day, I read a letter from a young woman writing of her late father, who'd fought on Omaha Beach. Her name was Lisa Zanatta Henn, and she said, "We will always remember, we will never forget what the boys of Normandy did." Well, let's help her keep her word. If we forget what we did, we won't know who we are. I'm warning of an eradication of the American memory that could result, ultimately, in an erosion of the American spirit. Let's start with some basics: more attention to American history and a greater emphasis on civic ritual. And let me offer lesson No. 1 about America: All great change in America begins at the dinner table. So, tomorrow night in the kitchen I hope the talking begins. And children, if your parents haven't been teaching you what it means to be an American, let 'em know and nail 'em on it. That would be a very American thing to do.

And that's about all I have to say tonight. Except for one thing. The past few days when I've been at that window upstairs, I've thought a bit of the "shining city upon a hill." The phrase comes from John Winthrop, who wrote it to describe the America he imagined. What he imagined was important because he was an early Pilgrim, an early freedom man. He journeyed here on what today we'd call a little wooden boat; and like the other Pilgrims, he was looking for a home that would be free.

I've spoken of the shining city all my political life, but I don't know if I ever quite communicated what I saw when I said it. But in my mind it was a tall proud city built on rocks stronger than oceans, wind-swept, God-blessed, and teeming with people of all kinds living in harmony and peace, a city with free ports that hummed with commerce and creativity, and if there had to be city walls, the walls had doors and the doors were open to anyone with the will and the heart to get here. That's how I saw it and see it still.

And how stands the city on this winter night? More prosperous, more secure, and happier than it was eight years ago. But more than that; after 200 years, two centuries, she still stands strong and true on the granite ridge, and her glow has held steady no matter what storm. And she's still a beacon, still a magnet for all who must have freedom, for all the pilgrims from all the lost places who are hurtling through the darkness, toward home.

We've done our part. And as I walk off into the city streets, a final word to the men and women of the Reagan revolution, the men and women across America who for eight years did the work that brought America back. My friends: We did it. We weren't just marking time. We made a difference. We made the city stronger. We made the city freer, and we left her in good hands. All in all, not bad, not bad at all.

And so, good-bye, God bless you, and God bless the United States of America.

I would only add, God bless RONALD and Nancy REAGAN, and God bless the United States of America.

Hon. Mike Enzi

OF WYOMING

Mr. President, this past weekend, the news quickly made its way across the country and around the world. RONALD REAGAN, our 40th President, had died. For many of us, we received the news with a mixture of sadness together with a sense of relief that his long battle with illness was now over and he had now found peace at the end of his life.

I first met RONALD REAGAN when I was president of the Wyoming Jaycees at the National Convention which was held in California, and he was the Governor. I next met the President when I was mayor of Gillette, WY, and the National League of Cities held its national meeting and the President flew to California and addressed it.

Now the greatest thinkers and writers will take up their pens in an attempt to determine his place in history and his significance as one of our greatest Presidents. For those of us who observed his service as our President and admired his leadership, those questions had been long since answered. For us, his place in history was long ago determined by his place in our hearts.

Many of those who will examine his life in detail will tell a story about a man who was born without the great privileges and trappings you might expect of such a successful life. That is true, but there is so much more to the story.

RONALD REAGAN was born in Illinois, the son of a traveling shoe salesman. Growing up he was strongly influenced by his mother who taught him how to read at an early age. She urged him to read good books that would encourage him to dream and set goals in his life. She knew that he could be anything he wanted to be if he was willing to work hard and expect more of himself than anyone else had any reason to expect. That, more than anything else, really determined his character and ultimately mapped his destiny.

His natural confidence and determination began to show itself during his school years and again, later, when he began his career as an actor. He was a natural leader and he took a leadership role at virtually every stage of his life. In his college days he served as student body president. In his acting days he served as the president of the Screen Actors Guild. In between he worked hard and built a career as a successful actor in film and on television.

If that had been all he had done, it would have been a remarkable life. He would have earned the rags to riches label and inspired others to follow his path just by his success in Hollywood and on television. That would have been enough for just about everyone. It was not, however, enough for RONALD REAGAN.

With his beloved wife, Nancy, by his side, RONALD REAGAN began to pursue his dream. He wanted to make a greater impact on the world than he could by being a television and movie star, so he began to take a more active role in politics. He discovered he had a talent for that, too. After a great deal of thought and deliberation, he decided to put his vision for America to the test. He took his case to the people and began a run for Governor of California.

People thought it was an impossible dream and he could never win a State like California. RONALD REAGAN proved them wrong. He put together a coalition of both Republican and Democratic voters and, when all the votes were counted, he had made it happen and he was elected Governor by almost 1 million votes.

REAGAN then set his sights on the Presidency of the United States and, after a narrow loss to Gerald Ford, he spent the next few years traveling around the country, sharing his dream for a better United States with the people who came to hear him speak. Many doubted he could do it, but once again, he found the support he needed to win the Republican nomination. The contest for the Presidency put him up against an incumbent who talked about the serious problems facing the Nation. RONALD REAGAN, on the other hand, spoke with passionate certainty that working together the Nation could overcome them. When the votes were counted, RONALD REAGAN had won the Presidency in a landslide.

As President, RONALD REAGAN proved himself to be a man of principle, someone who said what he believed and believed what he said. He had excellent communication skills, and his speeches on television were extremely effective.

When he took the oath of office as our 40th President, he took over the reins of a country that had great problems. He had often referred to our economic woes as the "misery index." There was high inflation, high interest rates, and high unemployment. Perhaps worst of all, the Nation seemed to have lost its confidence in its ability to dare to do great things—and succeed.

There was a lot of doubt and cynicism that any one individual could do much to change things and reenergize the Nation. Again, RONALD REAGAN proved the doubters wrong. As President, his spirit of optimism, patriotism and personal pride in his country proved to be infectious. Before long, there was a new spirit in the United States, a renewed sense of pride and excitement about our flag and our Nation that hadn't been around for a while. RONALD REAGAN was just what we needed. He inspired a generation to look toward the future with hope and a renewed commitment to the principles upon which our Nation was founded. It is still alive today. It is his legacy that he left with us, his gift to the younger generations of the Nation.

During his two terms in the White House, RONALD REAGAN spoke the truth, regardless of the sensitivities of those who might not want to hear it. It was over the objections of much of his staff that he challenged Soviet leader Mikhail Gorbachev to "tear down this wall!" when he was in Berlin. It was against the advice of much of his staff to refer to the Soviet Union as an evil empire. For RONALD REAGAN, it was simple. If it was the truth, it must be said. For him, there were good guys and bad guys in the world. If the good guys worked hard and were determined to succeed, they won. In RONALD REAGAN's world, we were the good guys. And, during RONALD REAGAN's Presidency, more often than not, we won.

For historians and the history books, RONALD REAGAN will be remembered as the President who brought a successful end to the cold war; had a great deal to do with the collapse of communism in the Soviet Union and the destruction of the Berlin Wall; and, dramatically turned the Nation's economy around. For those of us who observed his style as our President, he will also be remembered for his spirit, and his attitude of patriotic optimism, which rejuvenated the Nation when our spirit was low. He was a great leader and a great American. His words and his actions will long be remembered.

RONALD REAGAN dared to do the impossible, not because it was easy but because it had to be done. The challenges he encountered in his life brought out the best in him, and the challenges we faced as a Nation under him brought out the best in all of us. His is a legacy that we will always cherish. We will miss him.

Hon. Bill Nelson

OF FLORIDA

Mr. President, on this occasion, when the Nation is mourning the loss of President REAGAN, I wish to bring to the attention of the Senate a couple of stories which are fresh in my memory about President REAGAN.

I had the privilege during his two terms as President of serving in the House of Representatives, representing a district from the State of Florida.

The first story I wish to share is of a time of great loss to this country, the loss of the space shuttle *Challenger*. The American people could hardly believe it. The entire technological prowess of our country was symbolized by America having a very successful space program. We were the first to the Moon. This new contraption called a space transportation system was reusable, with new technologies that had been developed. America was quite proud.

I had the privilege of flying on the 24th flight of the space shuttle, 6 days in orbit, returning on January 18, 1986. Only 10 days later, the crew that we had stayed with in quarantine—we had been one of the most delayed flights in the history of the space program—was the crew of the *Challenger*.

We all know the story. Ten miles high in the Florida sky, the *Challenger*'s solid rocket booster had hot gases escaping from a field joint in that rocket. The gases happened to come out at a place where the strut was burned. That caused the solid rocket motor to then cantilever and it punctured the big apricot-colored fuel tank that held all of the liquid hydrogen and liquid oxygen. The whole space shuttle then disintegrated.

Naturally, the feelings I had were very raw and very emotional on that day, having trained with that crew and having just returned from space 10 days earlier.

America's feelings were as raw and as emotional because our whole symbol of technological and scientific prowess had suddenly disintegrated in front of our eyes on our television screens.

At a time of a grieving Nation, there can be only one person who can speak for the country. That is the President. President REAGAN rose to the occasion. That speech on television that night, delivered from the Oval Office, was a masterpiece, in which he ends up quoting a Canadian pilot from World War II—a pilot who had experienced the joys of flying—and those immortal words that ended the poem that he had reached out and touched the face of God.

President REAGAN applied that poem to the feelings of the country at the time about what the seven astronauts had experienced. That is political genius. That is a leader. That is a leader who has the ability through communication to connect, to inspire, and in this particular case, on January 28, 1986, to help the Nation through the process of grieving, to accept what had happened and then pick up and move on, which we have.

And of course, 17 years later, we had another very similar kind of experience when we lost seven astronauts.

That speech, in my mind, was only exceeded by the speech that occurred 3 days later by President REAGAN at the Johnson Space Center in Houston in a memorial service for the astronauts, the astronauts whose bodies at that point still had not been recovered from the floor of the Atlantic Ocean where, hopefully, they had perished before they ever hit the water. Somehow that crew compartment had been punctured at that altitude and therefore there would have been instant decompression and there would have been instant loss of consciousness.

But with all of that swirling in all of our minds, with all of that swirling in the minds of that NASA community—NASA really is a family—again, the leader of the Nation had to rise to the occasion to summarize and to continue the process of healing in the time of grief.

I saw rough, tough test pilots who were some of the best of the best of our astronaut pilots grabbing each other and hugging in that time of grief. And President REAGAN, in the moment, gave comfort to all of those, especially to the families of that crew who were lost, led by the commander of that mission, Dick Scobee.

Another story I wish to tell about President REAGAN is very personal to me as well. It was just about the middle of the decade of the eighties. I was a Member of the House of Representatives. There was a particular vote coming up that was critically close. I had already made up my mind that the way I was going to vote in this particular case was the way President REAGAN had wanted the vote to go but had not telegraphed that to the leadership of either side because there was something I wanted to tell the President.

There was a 6-month-old infant in my hometown of Melbourne, FL, who was dying because he needed a liver transplant. Mind you, this is 20 years ago. Twenty years ago we did not have the very sophisticated system we have set up today which allowed people to exchange information about organ donors. Twenty years ago it was catch as catch can. Twenty years ago, if a donor became available, it was just almost accidental that you found out if there was a donor of a particular organ. And when it involved an infant, like a 6-month-old infant, you not only had to match the blood type for a liver transplant, but the liver had to be the exact size in order to successfully transplant. You can see the difficulty. You can see this child lie dying, with only hours to live.

The preparation had been made for the jet airplane to fly the child to the University of Pittsburgh Medical Center where all the surgeons were standing by. They kept waiting and waiting for a donor. No donor was produced because we did not know when any became available. There was not an exchange of information.

So at my home in Melbourne, on a weekend, the call from the President of the United States came. He said, "Bill, this is President REAGAN. We are going to have a close vote and I need your vote." I said, "Mr. President, I have already decided that I am voting with you. Now there is something that I would like to ask you—to help in the saving of the life of a child." I told him the story, and he said he would have Margaret Heckler, the Secretary of HHS, call me the next day and get the particulars, which he did.

Margaret Heckler immediately held a press conference, and because of that press conference, within 3 days, a tragic death of a child on the west coast of the United States that we would have never known about was known, and the parents donated the child's liver, which was of the same blood type and the same size. That liver was packaged and cooled and flown to Pittsburgh, arriving at the same time Ryan Osterblom arrived, as they wheeled him into surgery.

Mr. President, as you can see, I have a catch in my voice because that little boy is going to college this year. He wants to be a surgeon. After that successful transplant, the President had called the mother, Karen Osterblom, and for years he continued to correspond with them.

It is going to be my pleasure to have the family come up here on Thursday as the President is lying in state and have them walk through the line in the rotunda of the U.S. Capitol to show their respects to President REAGAN.

Hon. James M. Inhofe
OF OKLAHOMA

Mr. President, we have heard so many stories about a great man, the GIPPER, and none of them are surprising because he was always such a gentle person. I have to share with you that I had the honor, about a month ago, of giving the commencement address at Oral Roberts University. When I did, I used a lot of the 1964 speech "A Rendezvous with Destiny." I said it should be required reading for anyone to graduate at any level in America to read "A Rendezvous with Destiny." It is a speech that changed my life.

Ronald Reagan gave it in 1964. I remember I almost memorized that speech. In fact, I still have most of it memorized. As a result of that, the next year I decided, well, if he did it, if he really feels this concerned, I should, too, and I went and filed for office and ran for the State legislature. So that is how I happened to get started.

But that is not as far back as we go. I believe I have had the honor of knowing Ronald Reagan longer than any other Member of this U.S. Senate. In fact, I am sure that is true. Even though I represent the State of Oklahoma, I moved to the State of Oklahoma when I was 8 years old. I moved from Des Moines, IA. We were enduring the poverty of the Depression at that time. Everyone was poor, not just us.

My dad was an insurance adjuster. Ronald Reagan was a sports announcer for WHO Radio in Des Moines, IA, and they shared the same office. They became very close friends, and they used to play the pinball machine at that time. You guys would not know what that is. I guess they don't have those anymore. On Saturdays they would play cards for a couple hours. All I know is, it was a room above the drugstore.

But the man I had seen occasionally at that time I thought of as a giant. He was a very large person. We were not all that large. I remember that when I was growing up.

Well, we moved to Tulsa, OK, shortly after that. But we did not lose contact. As the years went by, Ronald Reagan, who my dad affectionately referred to as "Dutch," "Dutch Reagan"—every time there was a Dutch Reagan movie we would see it. You see, we never went to movies. In those days, we just didn't go to movies except when there was a Dutch Reagan movie. It did not matter what it was conflicting with.

One time we went to Durant, OK, in the southern part of Oklahoma. My home was in the northern part. I remember driving on those roads at that time. I say to my good friend from Minnesota, the roads were—if you could average 30 miles an hour, you were doing well. So we drove 5 hours down, watched a Dutch Reagan movie, and drove 5 hours back. We never would consider missing a Dutch Reagan movie.

Then, of course, the famous speech took place in 1964. That is when he expressed his interest in politics. But at that time my father was much better off and so was our family. So when Dutch Reagan was going to run for Governor of California, my father became one of his first large contributors. Again, the friendship had never stopped at any point. So he won.

At the time, after he served in that capacity and ran for President—I know that the presiding officer right now knows what I am talking about because he and I were both mayors of major cities back at the same time in 1980 when Ronald Reagan was elected President. I was the mayor of Tulsa, OK, for 4 years. Ronald Reagan and I were closer together than we had ever been before—I was out in Oklahoma—because he had me do his domestic policy stuff. He would have me on TV. At that time, they did not have CNN and Fox, but they had "Good Morning America" and the "Today" show. So I was debating all these liberal Democrat mayors on the Reagan policy—the dynamics of the free enterprise system as opposed to the government doing everything, and my arguments worked beautifully. So I am sure I spent 10 times as much time with him at that time than I do with George W. today, and I am here in Washington. But it was a real pleasure.

Those of us present—and right now I see in the Chamber the Senator from Minnesota, Mr. Norm Coleman, and the Senator who is presiding, Mr. Voinovich—all three of us were mayors. We understand what a hard job it is. When I was mayor, I was able to build a low-water dam, and President Reagan referred to it in his speeches as the largest totally privately funded public project in America. Those were the dynamics of Ronald Reagan. That is what he thought, that government should be doing less, people doing more. And it worked.

What a visionary the guy was. When I see things that are going on today and I remember things that he said many, many years ago. Right now we have a serious problem in America. Probably one of our most serious problems is we do not have an energy policy. So we make speeches. All of us make speeches on a regular basis about why we do not have an energy policy and why we should have one. I would like to read to you what RONALD REAGAN said. This was in 1979. Listen carefully because this applies to today, but it was 1979:

> Solving the energy crisis will not be easy, but it can be done. First we must decide that "less" is not enough. Next, we must remove government obstacles to energy production. And, we must make use of those technological advantages we still possess.
>
> It is no program simply to say "use less energy."

Sound familiar?

> Of course waste must be eliminated and efficiency promoted, but for the government simply to tell people to conserve is not an energy policy. At best it means we will run out of energy a little more slowly. But a day will come when the lights will dim and the wheels of industry will turn more slowly and finally stop....
>
> The answer, obvious to anyone except those in the administration it seems, is more domestic production of oil and gas. We must also have wider use of nuclear power within strict safety rules, of course. There must be more spending by the energy industries on research and development of substitutes for fossil fuels.

And on and on and on. That speech very well could have been made today because the problem still exists today. And he knew it was coming.

When he talked about the SDI, the Strategic Defense Initiative, that was something no one seemed to care about, and no one believed there was any great risk facing the American people. Yet he saw that risk. The risk was there. We all know now the risk is very real, even today. So he looked back at the ABM Treaty that was put in place in 1972.

He said, "This is senseless now. It may have made sense in 1972 when Henry Kissinger and Richard Nixon put this in, but the policy of mutual assured destruction is not a good policy." So he said, "What we will have to do is have a very strong country." And he was quite scriptural. He quoted from Luke, "If a strong man shall keep his court well guarded, he shall live in peace." And that is exactly what he was doing in his rebuilding of the defense system of America. We are so thankful he did that in those days. But he was saying we must do away with the ABM Treaty. Finally, after all this time, we recognized 2 years ago he was right, and we got rid of the ABM Treaty—how prophetic.

As for tax cuts, he gave credit to his predecessors. He said, "We do need more money. The best way to get more revenue for government is to reduce tax rates." He said, "That is what President Kennedy did 25 years ago. He reduced tax rates." And keep in mind, that was a Democratic President. And by reducing tax rates, he almost doubled the revenue coming in at the end of his term. It gave people the freedom and money to invest and to breathe and to reinvest in the country. So that is the problem. That is what President George W. Bush has been trying to do. That is the reason we are out of the recession he inherited, and we are now coming out because we have reduced some of those marginal rates. We know we need to do more. This is what the President did.

If you remember, in 1980, the total amount of revenue that was generated from marginal rates, taxes paid by people, was $244 billion. In 1990, it was $446 billion. It almost doubled in that 10-year period. Yet that 10-year period was the period where we had the largest reduction in taxes, thanks to RONALD REAGAN, of any 10-year period or 8-year period in our Nation's history: marginal rates going down from 70 percent to 28 percent. Yet it had the effect of doubling the revenues. This guy knew it, and he did it. That is good advice for us today.

I have mentioned quite often that it should have been required for all of our graduates to read "A Rendezvous with Destiny." Let me read a couple things to remind us on this very solemn occasion how grateful we are now to have had a President who was so prophetic.

In talking about the freedom of our country, he told a story about Castro and how a Cuban had escaped Cuba in a small craft and had floated over to the south shores of Florida. As his small craft came up there was a refugee there, and he told the refugee about the atrocities of Castro's communist Cuba. After he was through, the refugee said, I guess we don't know how lucky we are in the United States.

He said, How lucky you are? We are the ones who are lucky. We had a place to escape to.

That is what RONALD REAGAN said, that we would be the beacon of freedom, the last place in the world to escape to. If we lose it here, there is nowhere else to escape to.

On the recognition of the dynamics of the free enterprise system, he said,

They also knew, those Founding Fathers, that outside of its legitimate functions, government does nothing as well or as economically as the private sector of the economy.

He practiced that. It worked. His domestic policies worked.

He was prophetic. He accurately described such things as:

> We have so many people who can't see a fat man standing beside a thin one without coming to the conclusion that the fat man got that way by taking advantage of the thin one.

RONALD REAGAN talked about bureaucracy, how difficult it would be for him to cut down the size of government. He is the one who said, in that very famous speech in 1964, there is nothing closer to life eternal on the face of this Earth than a government agency once formed. And he went on to explain the reason for it. The reason for it is very simple. Once a government agency is formed to respond to a problem, the problem goes away, and the bureaucracy stays there. The longer they stay there with nothing to do, the stronger they become. So that happens. He was able to cut that down by reminding people that that problem did exist.

He said in 1964:

> Let's set the record straight. There is no argument over the choice between peace and war, but there is only one guaranteed way you can have peace—and you can have it in the next second—surrender.

That was the message he had. You had to be strong. You had to have a Nation that believes in God, and you had to stand up for those things and not lie down and surrender. That is what people were trying to do at that time.

He said in that speech:

> There is a price we will not pay. There is a point beyond which they must not advance.

That was his rendezvous with destiny.

I look at American heroes like the senior Senator from Hawaii who fought so valiantly and is very familiar with what this President did for our U.S. military.

I will say this: The rendezvous with destiny was a very real one. Military historians have looked at us and said there is no way we could have won the Revolutionary War. Here we were, a handful of farmers and trappers with crude weapons and the greatest army on the face of the Earth was marching toward Lexington and Concord, and they fired the shot heard round the world.

As RONALD REAGAN would reflect on that great speech by Patrick Henry, he said there are three sentences in that speech that answer the questions of military historians, but people have forgotten about it. We are not weak when we make the proper use of those means which the God of nature has placed in our power. Armed in the holy cause of liberty in such a country as that which we possess, we are invincible by any force our enemy will send against us. And besides, we will not fight our battles alone. There is a just God who reigns over the destiny of nations who will raise up friends to fight our battles with us.

Those are the favorite three sentences out of the "Give Me Liberty or Give Me Death" speech Patrick Henry made.

For me, I think about the honor to be able to stand here in the Senate and, on behalf of the American people and on behalf of my wife and myself and our family of 20 children and grandchildren, to say we thank RONALD REAGAN for his sacrifices. We thank God for RONALD REAGAN. We thank God for his life. We thank God for allowing us to share that rendezvous with destiny with RONALD REAGAN.

Hon. Norm Coleman

OF MINNESOTA

Mr. President, I share that sense of humility that has been so eloquently expressed by my friend from Oklahoma, to be able to stand on this Senate floor and to thank God for RONALD REAGAN, for what he gave us and what we learned from him. I must admit to being a bit envious to be in the Chamber with my friend from Oklahoma who knew RONALD REAGAN when he was a young man.

My friend, the presiding officer, on the way to the Chamber—again, we were all fellow mayors—talked about when he was mayor of Cleveland. There were some difficult times, and he talked to the President. He talked about what a good man the President was. What a good man, that he really cared, that he listened, and that he wanted to do things, wanted to make a difference. Sometimes when those around him were not making a difference, he took care of it and got it done. I think my colleagues were part of history being made.

I was able to watch history during that time. But I am honored and humbled to be here today. To those of us who grew up in the Midwest and for those like myself who made it our home, RONALD REAGAN has a very special significance. Places like Dixon, IL, have been dubbed flyover zones by sophisticated, powerful people who live on the coast. But we know places like that are the heartland, strong, simple, and true. That was RONALD REAGAN.

What we love about the Midwest is what America and the world came to know and understand and love about RONALD REAGAN.

To go on and on in flowery rhetoric about RONALD REAGAN would not fit the subject matter. Like he did so well, his life deserves a few well-chosen words.

Oscar Wilde once said, "Life is not complex. We are complex. Life is simple and the simple thing is the right thing."

RONALD REAGAN could have said that because, surely, he lived it.

Democracy is superior to communism. America is the world's best hope. Liberty requires limited government. The best is yet to come. Those were RONALD REAGAN's moral anchors from the start of his public life to the end. Without deviation, they shaped his outlook and actions for half a century.

He certainly didn't originate any of them, but we all know they are far more prominent in the fabric of American life today because of the power of his witness, as he lived his life, the power of what he did with those moral anchors as part of him.

In the last few days, we are hearing a lot about REAGAN as the Great Communicator. I think we put too much emphasis on the craft. As far as RONALD REAGAN was concerned, the key to being a good communicator was having something to say. He was the message he delivered, and so he touched hearts and changed minds.

He understood the key to American progress was our spirit. Resources, wealth, and past accomplishments have ruined more people and nations than they have made. He knew we needed a sense of the heroic, a stirring of our souls to rise above selfishness, division, and fear. He inspired us.

He restored our confidence in the idea of leadership. Vietnam, Watergate, inflation, gas lines, and the hostage crisis were causing many to wonder if the American hour had passed. Not RONALD REAGAN. He stubbornly held onto a wonderful vision of the future rather than focus on temporary negative circumstances. He led us.

And perhaps of greatest importance, by his own choice, RONALD REAGAN was not the star of our dramatic national resurgence. Neither was government. In REAGAN's mind and words, the heroes who restored the American economy and won the cold war were ordinary Americans doing simple things, doing their duty—kind of like a national bond raising. He united us.

Mr. President, I also grew up as a Democrat. President REAGAN deeply inspired me, and he had a lot to do with the fact that I am standing on this side of the aisle today. He inspired me with ideas, such as if you want to grow an economy, you cut taxes and put money in people's pockets; they will spend it on a product or service, and there is a job connected to that. He understood that. He showed the power of it. I understood that. It wasn't just about policy, it was about optimism.

When I ran for mayor in St. Paul in 1993, my slogan was "St. Paul's best days are yet to come." When I switched parties in 1996, Jack Kemp came over to my house, and I made the announcement. It was that spirit of hope, optimism, entrepreneurship, and opportunity that he showed worked. That was the key, by the way. For him, it was not about politics; it was about results.

My friend from Oklahoma quoted President REAGAN saying that solving the energy crisis will not be easy, but {that} it can be done. He understood the importance of getting it done.

I think RONALD REAGAN would be honored to know we are shutting down the Federal Government on Friday. His only concern might be that we are starting it again on Monday. He changed us and transformed the world, without a doubt. Some days, Mr. President, I get concerned that we are changing back.

As we remember his life, I hope we all remember that the simple things are the right things: Freedom, hope, liberty, and optimism.

I thank God that he gave us RONALD REAGAN when we needed him most. Now, this is our time. I pray that we will courageously follow his example and embrace America's destiny in this challenging hour.

Hon. John McCain
OF ARIZONA

Mr. President, the strength of Abraham Lincoln's resolve to restore the Union, whatever the terrible cost to do so, was his unshakable faith that in America any father's child could come to occupy the same place that his father's child had attained. That uniquely American conviction also inspired RONALD REAGAN to reach his great place in our country's history and in the hearts of his countrymen. I doubt RONALD REAGAN was much surprised to become President, despite his humble origins. And I know for certain he never took for granted a single day he occupied the office. He believed such an honored privilege was within the reach of any American with principles, industry and talent, and that once attained, it was to be held with great care to preserve for succeeding generations the blessings of liberty that had so enriched his own life. His patriotism, which he expressed eloquently and often in his public remarks, was never affected. He believed every word. Nor was his unfailing good humor and optimism an actor's performance. He lived in a "shining city on a hill," and he never forgot it.

I first met President REAGAN and his lovely wife, Nancy, not long after I returned from Vietnam. But I knew of him in the years before I regained my liberty, when my fellow prisoners-of-war and I would discuss in tap codes and whispered conversations the Governor of California who was giving such eloquent voice to the convictions we believed we had been sent to war to advance. In the more than 30 years that have passed since I first met him, I have never lived a day that I wasn't grateful for the privilege of the REAGANs' friendship, and the strength of his faith in America that inspired my own, and so many others.

His accomplishments in office were historic, and will be long remembered as will the humility, grace and decency with which he achieved them. It was an honor to have known him, and Cindy and I shall miss him very much. We offer our sincerest condolences to Nancy, and to Michael, Patti and Ron, and pray that God grants this good man eternal life, reunites him with his daughter, Maureen, and with all his loved ones who have preceded him.

Hon. Ernest F. Hollings
OF SOUTH CAROLINA

Mr. President, at a luncheon with Bernard Baruch, Mr. Baruch commented that Harry Truman "had a good memory" and "he also had a good bad memory." We are hearing both at the passing of former President RONALD REAGAN. There is no question that if a President is to be credited for the end of the cold war that credit should go to RONALD REAGAN. We were anxious about the depletion of our defenses in the U.S. Senate in the year preceding President REAGAN's administration so we passed a 5 percent across-the-board increase in the defense budget. But President REAGAN came on board and really moved to strengthen our defenses, building a 600-ship Navy and not hesitating to deploy intermediate missiles in Europe. He also moved to formalize our ballistic missile defense system, calling it the Strategic Defense Initiative and increasing its support. President REAGAN can also be credited with a competitive trade policy. Though he had the power to rescind the antidumping order on the importation of motorcycles, he let the order stand; reviving as we all know the Harley Davidson industry. Moreover, he imposed voluntary restraint agreements in steel, semiconductors, machine tools and automobiles. There is no question, for example, that Intel would have had a hard time surviving had it not been for Sematech and REAGAN's VRA (voluntary restraint agreement) on semiconductors.

But at this time of praise, those with "good bad memory" forget it was RONALD REAGAN who started supply side economics. Former Senator Bob Dole led the opposition to its forerunner, Kemp-Roth, and former President George Herbert Walker Bush characterized this cutting revenues to increase them as "voodoo." With REAGAN looking for an issue at a low point in his administration, he locked onto supply side, ignoring his campaign pledge to "balance the budget within one year." It is good to note that in this country after 200 years existence, with the cost of all the wars from the Revolution up to the war in Vietnam, the national debt stood at less than $1 trillion. REAGAN's supply side or "voodoo" gave us the first trillion dollar debt and he left office having increased the national debt $1.7 trillion. Under Bush 41, in 4 years the debt increased $1.4 trillion. President Clinton over 8 years slowed the increase of the debt to $1.6 trillion with spending cuts and tax increases, leaving a projected surplus. President George W. Bush, with three tax cuts or Reagan "voodoos," has eliminated the surplus and increased the debt over $2 trillion in 4 years. As his chief counselor Vice President Cheney said, "Deficits don't matter." Since the beginning days, this country has shown sacrifice at a time of war by adopting a tax measure to pay for the war. But not for the war on terrorism. We in the Congress need a fourth tax cut, voodoo, to get reelected. Today the GI fighting the war is also going to have to pay for the war. At this time of remembrance, let's not forget that REAGAN dignified "voodoo."

Hon. Dianne Feinstein

OF CALIFORNIA

Mr. President, on Saturday, our Nation lost a strong leader and the State of California lost an adopted son.

As a citizen, RONALD WILSON REAGAN embodied the American dream. He personified the image of California—can-do, risk-taking, cutting-edge. RONALD REAGAN was all of those things.

As a President, he unified a country and helped bring an end to the cold war, the premier struggle of his time in public life.

My fondest memory of President REAGAN took place while I was mayor of San Francisco at a March 1983 dinner the President and First Lady hosted for Queen Elizabeth II in San Francisco. The Queen was thrilled to visit California for the first time and especially pleased to be welcomed by a President from California.

During that trip the Queen quipped at one point that she knew England had exported many traditions to the United States, but she hadn't realized the weather was one of them.

San Francisco's London-like weather aside, as mayor I was enormously proud of the wonderful welcome we had provided for the Queen of England.

Growing up in small-town central Illinois in the years leading up to the Great Depression, President REAGAN was instilled with the values that would guide him as a person and as a leader. There he learned the importance of hard work and optimism as the key ingredients for success.

It was this optimism combined with his ever-present sense of humor that characterized him best, enabling him to both "fill the screen" and make a stellar entrance wherever he went.

After 4 years at Eureka College, where he was known as a gritty, though undersized tackle on the football team, he began searching for a job in broadcasting. In 1932, at the height of the Depression, he headed into the job market confident that a job would be his soon.

After several years as a broadcaster covering University of Iowa football games and later recreating Chicago Cubs' games based on telegraph reports, a young RONALD REAGAN traveled to California to cover the Cubs' spring training.

It was his first trip west of Kansas City and it nurtured his fascination with Hollywood. While he was there, he used his considerable charm to convince a movie agent to arrange a screen test for him at Warner Brothers Studios.

Before long, he returned to the Midwest, packed his bags and started the quintessential American journey westward in search of opportunity. Of course, he found it as a movie star.

He won many fans through his on-screen charisma. The optimism he inspired was exemplified by his role as Notre Dame football player George Gipp in the film "Knute Rockne—All-American." Years after Gipp's death, Coach Rockne gave a pep talk to his team urging them to "win one for the Gipper" one of the more memorable lines in American sports history.

But President REAGAN's greatest impact on the world was as a politician. As a labor leader with the Screen Actors Guild, his roots as an activist were shaped significantly by a deep concern about communism.

Yet despite his strongly anticommunist views, he condemned the unfair smearing of many liberals by Senator Joseph McCarthy and the House Un-American Activities Committee. He refused to reveal names publicly, but exposed some people to the FBI privately.

As Governor of California he had a strong record of environmental protection: adding 145,000 acres to the State's park system, protecting Lake Tahoe from rampant development, blocking the construction of dams on the Dos Rios and Eel Rivers, and stopping the paving of a Federal highway through the Sierra Nevada Mountains that would have cut through the John Muir Trail.

He also signed legislation to protect rivers on California's north coast and approved strict car emissions standards that forced the Nation's automakers to manufacture cleaner-burning cars. But he lobbied against the Coastal Protection Act approved by voters in 1972 and resisted air pollution controls imposed by the Federal Government.

Despite his personal opposition to abortion, Governor REAGAN loosened an 1872 statute to allow abortion in cases of rape, incest, when a mother's health was at stake, or when there was a high risk that a baby would be born with birth defects. Many States followed Governor REAGAN's lead on this important issue.

However, his move to close down mental health facilities in California resulted in widespread homelessness in urban areas. Though he sought to steer the mentally ill into community-based mental health facilities the end result was a spike in homelessness, a problem that we continue to deal with to this day.

While in Sacramento, he generally approached fiscal policy as a moderate, first presiding over a $1 billion tax increase to balance the State budget and another subsequent increase. He eventually lowered taxes, but in his two terms as Governor, State spending doubled overall and the State's work force grew by 34,000.

As President, he was a unifier and an optimist. His infectious, upbeat attitude rallied people to his goals. He was extremely successful in passing legislation by joining that optimism with a willingness to compromise with a Democratic Congress.

In his dealings, he was tough, but ready to negotiate. There is no better example of this than his relationship with former Soviet leader Mikhail Gorbachev. He often used harsh rhetoric in challenging the actions of our cold war adversary, but it was always backed by his core beliefs.

Once, as he prepared for his first summit with the Soviet leader, he met with a room full of foreign policy advisors, each offering their suggestions about what he should say. After a half-hour of discussion, President REAGAN turned to his advisors and said, "Gentlemen, I've been thinking about what I'm going to say to this man my whole life. And I know exactly what I'm going to say."

Gorbachev described REAGAN as "a great President, with whom the Soviet leadership was able to launch a very difficult but important dialogue."

His tough negotiating stance yielded some important accomplishments including signing treaties reducing intermediate-range nuclear missiles and limiting strategic arms. These acts of diplomacy combined with his relentless advocacy for freedom played a major role in bringing about an end to the cold war.

At the same time, REAGAN had a tendency to overreach in the area of foreign policy. The invasion of Grenada, the intervention in Lebanon that left American soldiers uncertain of their role and vulnerable to attack, and, above all, the Iran-Contra scandal—were all cases in which the Reagan administration went too far in seeking to reshape the world.

At home, President REAGAN sought to limit the size of government and tap the entrepreneurial spirit of the American people. And though he was famous for cutting taxes, he approved two tax increases during his first term in the White House.

Unfortunately, the tax cuts were coupled with sharp increases in defense spending that resulted in massive deficits. The Federal budget finally recovered from those years of deficit spending during the late nineties, but the surpluses that were generated disappeared in the blink of an eye under the current administration's fiscal policies.

President REAGAN's cuts to public housing, job training, and the broader social safety net were another serious blow domestically. And, as cities and mayors across the country were reeling from the advent of AIDS—no place suffered more than San Francisco—President REAGAN failed to act. He would not even publicly comment on the AIDS crisis.

Though people did not always agree with his policies, it cannot be denied that President REAGAN redefined politics through his tremendous skills as a communicator. In particular, his ability to define clear goals and persuade others to support those goals earned him the admiration of many Americans.

As we all know, President REAGAN suffered from Alzheimer's Disease during the last decade of his life.

As we honor his memory in the days and weeks to come, it is my hope that we will consider what we can do here in Congress to battle this terrible disease.

A good first step would be to approve legislation that supports embryonic stem cell research. This research offers tremendous hope, not only to those who suffer from Alzheimer's, but also the millions of people with cancer, diabetes, Parkinson's, multiple sclerosis and spinal cord injuries. What a fitting tribute passage of this bill would be to President REAGAN.

In closing, there probably is no American who has more fully lived the American dream from actor to Governor to President than RONALD REAGAN. Today, we mourn his loss, but recognize that his was a full life.

Thank you for your service to this country, President REAGAN.

Hon. Russell D. Feingold

OF WISCONSIN

Mr. President, today I pay my respects to a beloved leader who, with grace, wit, and charisma, led our country through some of the great challenges of the 20th century. President RONALD WILSON REAGAN was a dedicated public servant whose confidence and optimism reinvigorated the American people and made him one of the most honored and respected Presidents in our Nation's history.

Although he lived most of his life in California, President REAGAN was a fellow midwesterner. Born in 1911 in Tampico, IL, RONALD WILSON REAGAN attended high school in nearby Dixon and worked his way through Eureka College. There he earned his B.A., played on the football team, and participated in school plays. He eventually won a contract in Hollywood and appeared in 53 films over 2 decades.

The father of four children became increasingly involved in politics and in 1966 was elected the Governor of California, and was reelected in 1970. His optimistic message, at a time when the country was beset by inflation and by the taking of American hostages in Iran, helped him to win the Presidency in 1980. Four years later, he was reelected in a 49-State sweep.

In foreign affairs, it is impossible to separate President REAGAN's legacy from the astounding change in world affairs that began while he was in office: the collapse of the U.S.S.R. and the end of the cold war. President REAGAN spoke frankly and frequently about the bankruptcy—both moral and economic—of the Soviet regime. His words and actions energized dissidents and activists struggling for change and for justice in the face of communist repression and tyranny. His optimism helped to give them confidence that they were, indeed, on the right side of history.

President REAGAN not only recognized the monstrous nature of communist totalitarianism, but he also understood the horror of a geopolitical reality that made the entire world hostage to the threat of nuclear annihilation. He had the courage to act, to reach out to the Soviet leadership and to craft landmark arms control agreements, including one that, for the first time, eliminated a class of nuclear weapons.

On the domestic front, it was under the leadership of President REAGAN that the solvency of the Social Security Program was extended through reforms to the existing program. Although modest in their overall scope, those reforms were seen by many as politically risky, and President REAGAN provided critical leadership that helped assure both a reluctant Congress and an uncertain public. Today, we should build on the REAGAN reforms, and strengthen the existing program, as he did.

Another significant domestic policy challenge that President REAGAN tackled was the simplification of our Tax Code. In the face of special interest pressures, and under the leadership of his Secretary of Treasury, Donald Regan, as well as a bipartisan group of Members of the House and Senate, President REAGAN was able to push through the last significant reforms to our increasingly complex Tax Code in 1986.

At the time, I was the chairman of the Taxation Committee in the Wisconsin State Senate and we were holding a variety of hearings around the State, addressing parallel reforms. These hearings and reforms were driven by President REAGAN's proposal. Though far from perfect, that reform effort is another model for action we need to undertake again. And policymakers in Congress and the executive branch would do well to follow President REAGAN's example in this matter.

Of course, no review of President REAGAN's legacy would be complete without acknowledging his Alzheimer's disease which, sadly, defined the last 10 years of his life as well as the lives of his family. As the author of Wisconsin's Alzheimer's program, I have become all too aware of the heartbreaking tragedy that this dread disease brings to a family.

President REAGAN's brave, public acknowledgment of the disease, and the wonderful efforts of his wife Nancy, have done a great deal to educate the country about this horrible affliction. They have also helped to spur government investment in the research needed to find a cure, and to raise awareness of the need for long-term care services for those suffering from Alzheimer's.

President RONALD WILSON REAGAN helped to transform America and the world. He and his achievements will forever be honored and remembered.

Hon. Mark Pryor
OF ARKANSAS

Mr. President, the Capitol today is overflowing with visitors, flags stand at half-staff, and the Nation has collectively stopped this week—all to honor a remarkable man who accomplished remarkable things during a remarkable time.

President RONALD REAGAN gave his life to public service and has left a legacy of leadership that will always be remembered.

We remember President REAGAN's strong vision for political and economic freedom which was instrumental in the fall of communism and the spread of democracy in Eastern Europe. The world held its breath as America stared communism in the face, but in the end we peacefully won over the respect and cooperation of our enemy. Less than a year after REAGAN left office, Mr. Gorbachev stepped down, the Berlin Wall fell and the cold war ended.

I will never forget President REAGAN's historic speech on June 12, 1987, in front of the Brandenburg Gate near the Berlin Wall when he called on Mikhail Gorbachev to "Open this gate! Mr. Gorbachev, tear down this wall!"

Today, the United States is working with Russia to replace tyranny and fear in Iraq with peace and stability.

Of President REAGAN, Gorbachev said:

A true leader, a man of his word and an optimist, he traveled the journey of his life with dignity and faced courageously the cruel disease that darkened his final years. He has earned a place in history and in people's hearts.

We also remember DUTCH, the Great Communicator, the GIPPER, as a man of great optimism and humor. My kids' history books recall the dates and facts of this time, but they do not convey this Hollywood actor turned President's good-natured spirit or genuine optimism for a better tomorrow. Nor can they express his unyielding dedication and love for our country. However, I believe the outpouring of respect and affection shown by the American public this week says we will forever remember his character and personality.

Finally, we remember a man who never stopped believing, never stopped advocating

America's ability to succeed and prosper. He stuck to his convictions and his visions for America, whether popular or not.

RONALD REAGAN's initiatives didn't please all Americans and Democrats and Republicans did not always agree on President REAGAN's foreign policy or domestic agenda, but he never encouraged or played the biting partisan games that exist today. Even with those people whom he had genuine ideological differences, President REAGAN always showed a level of respect and acknowledged that we are all Americans and we are in this together.

Years ago, President REAGAN and Speaker of the House Tip O'Neill used to joke that, "between 9 and 6 we are enemies, but at 6 o'clock let's go have a cocktail together." To truly honor and remember President REAGAN—this man of great accomplishment, optimism, and oratory—perhaps we could find ways to work better together for a better tomorrow.

I extend my deepest sympathies to the Reagan family in their time of sorrow, and I hope it is of some comfort that Americans and many others throughout the world mourn by their side.

A COMMUNICATION FROM THE PRESIDENT OF THE UNITED STATES OFFICIALLY NOTIFYING THE CONGRESS OF THE UNITED STATES OF THE DEATH OF FORMER PRESIDENT RONALD REAGAN—PM 84

The PRESIDING OFFICER laid before the Senate the following message from the President of the United States, together with an accompanying report; which was ordered to lie on the table:

To the Congress of the United States:

By this message, I officially inform you of the death of RONALD REAGAN, the fortieth President of the United States.

RONALD REAGAN was a great leader and a good man. He had the confidence that comes with conviction, the strength that comes with character, the grace that comes with humility, and the humor that comes with wisdom.

Through his leadership, spirit, and abiding faith in the American people, President REAGAN gave our Nation a renewed optimism. With his courage and moral clarity, he enhanced America's security and advanced the spread of peace, liberty, and democracy to millions of people who had lived in darkness and oppression. As America's President, he helped change the world.

The sun has now set on RONALD REAGAN's extraordinary American life. Just as he told us that our Nation's best days are yet to come, we know that the same is true for him.

GEORGE W. BUSH.
THE WHITE HOUSE, *June 8, 2004.*

ADJOURNMENT UNTIL 9:30 A.M. TOMORROW

Mr. COLEMAN. Mr. President, if there is no further business to come before the Senate, I ask unanimous consent that the Senate stand in adjournment under the provisions of S. Res. 371 as a mark of further respect for President RONALD WILSON REAGAN.

There being no objection, the Senate, at 6:10 p.m., adjourned until Wednesday, June 9, 2004, at 9:30 a.m.

Wednesday, June 9, 2004

PRAYER

The Chaplain, Dr. Barry C. Black, offered the following prayer:

Let us pray.

Eternal God, author of true freedom and shelter from life's storms, as our Nation pays its final respects to former President Ronald REAGAN, we look again to You, the source of our hope for years to come.

In a world of change and decay, You remain the same yesterday, today, and forever. Undergird this land with a foundation of right living that exalts a nation. Deliver us from the evils that bring national decline. Surround our military with the shield of Your presence and give wisdom to all warriors for freedom. Guide our lawmakers as they seek to keep America strong. Strengthen them with Your spirit and inspire them with Your precepts.

In these challenging days, we place our confidence in You, for Your steadfast love and faithfulness sustains us.

We pray in Your strong Name. Amen.

Hon. William H. Frist

OF TENNESSEE

Mr. President, I wish to make a few remarks regarding President RONALD REAGAN. It was in January 1977, as Jimmy Carter prepared to take the oath of office as President, that RONALD REAGAN met with the man who would become his chief foreign policy adviser for the next several years, Richard Allen.

The two spent several hours together discussing in detail the vast array of issues. As Allen recalls—and some people have heard this on the news—Mr. REAGAN said a whole range of memorable things, but none was more profound than this:

> My idea of American policy toward the Soviet Union is simple and some would say simplistic. It is this: We win and they lose. What do you think of that?

RONALD REAGAN's words would have been shocking to the trained ears of any foreign policy expert of that day. The consensus was the cold war simply could not be won. We could not defeat communism. That is what people thought. That is what they felt. All we could do was to hope to contain the Soviet Union and chip away at the fringes of its influence.

After his meeting with RONALD REAGAN, Richard Allen never looked at the world in the same way. When RONALD REAGAN entered the White House and laid out his vision for winning the cold war, America never looked at the world the same way. And when RONALD REAGAN left the White House and events he helped put in motion came to pass, the world, indeed, would never be the same.

What were the reasons for RONALD REAGAN's historic foreign policy success? How did he come to leave a more indelible mark on the world than any American President since Franklin Delano Roosevelt?

First, RONALD REAGAN believed in a strong military to defend our Nation and to protect peace. He marshaled the resources from this body for a remarkable 35-percent increase in defense spending during his Presidency. Critics accused REAGAN of unnecessarily provoking the Soviet Union and putting America on a path to nuclear war. But for RONALD REAGAN, a strong national defense was an instrument for peace. It was government's first and foremost duty to its people. He knew the Soviet Union could not match our capacity to fund our national defense, and should the Soviets attempt to keep pace, as they did, the communist state would be unable to sustain itself.

Second, RONALD REAGAN believed that America, our allies, and our common values were on that winning side of history. The destiny of mankind was not to live in the shadow of tyranny, dictatorship, but to be guided by the light of liberty, by the light of democracy. That was the destiny.

As REAGAN said in his watershed "Westminster" speech:

> {T}he march of freedom and democracy ... will leave Marxism-Leninism on the ash-heap of history as it has left other tyrannies which stifle the freedom and muzzle the self-expression of the people.

Third, RONALD REAGAN viewed the world through a lens of moral clarity. He believed there was right and wrong and good and evil, strength and weakness, but, most importantly, he was not afraid to talk about the world as he saw it or use his words to help shape the world in that vision.

He called the Soviet Union the evil empire. Why? Because the Soviet regime was repressive and godless and imperialist.

In 1987, he stood before the Brandenburg Gate in Berlin and challenged the Soviet leadership:

> {Mr.} Gorbachev, if you seek peace, if you seek prosperity for the Soviet Union and Eastern Europe, if you seek liberalization: Come here to this gate! Mr. Gorbachev, open this gate! Mr. Gorbachev, tear down this wall!

Within months, the wall was torn down. The cold war was won, and the new and lengthy era of peace for America and among the major powers of the world was born.

In this week of tribute to the life of RONALD REAGAN, let us remember the simple ideas upon which his foreign policy was based: a strong military as an instrument of peace; liberty and democracy as the destiny of mankind; and the moral clarity to see the world as it was and what it should be.

Let us also remember that without the courage and the character of RONALD REAGAN, his ideas would have remained just ideas, and the world would have remained the same.

As Mr. REAGAN once wrote of his determination to stand up for what he believed:

> But bearing what we cannot change and going on with what God has given us, confident there is a destiny, somehow seems to bring a reward we wouldn't exchange for any other. It takes a lot of fire and heat to make a piece of steel.

Hon. Edward M. Kennedy

OF MASSACHUSETTS

Mr. President, I join my colleagues on both sides of the aisle in paying tribute to RONALD REAGAN. As all of us who had the privilege of working with him know, he brought a special grace to the White House and the country in everything he did. We often disagreed on specific issues, but he had an undeniably unique capacity to inspire and move the Nation.

The warmth of his personality always shone through, and his infectious optimism made us all feel that it really was "morning in America." It was impossible not to respect and admire the way he revived the spirit of the Nation in that era, restored the power and vitality of the Presidency, and made it a vigorous and purposeful place of effective national and international leadership.

It was no coincidence that he opened his 1984 reelection campaign year by citing two Democratic Presidents, John F. Kennedy and Franklin D. Roosevelt, in his State of the Union Address. Nor was it a coincidence that at the Republican Convention that year, not the Democratic Convention, the band played "Happy Days Are Here Again."

He governed as a conservative Republican, often very conservative. But he had a special genius for reaching out to all Americans. Somehow, the hard edges of his policies always seemed smoother when he discussed and defended them. He was willing to step back from them when necessary, such as when it proved impossible to cut taxes, increase spending for defense, and balance the budget at the same time.

He was an intense competitor who wanted to win, not just for himself but for his beliefs. But his goal was to defeat his opponents, not destroy them. He taught us that even though the battle would inevitably resume the next morning, at the end of each day we could put aside the divisions and debates. We could sit down together and laugh together, especially at his endless stream of stories. He took issues seriously, but he had a sense of perspective that never let him or us take ourselves too seriously. As a leader, he was a President of large principles, not small details. Some criticized him for that, but it was often the source of his strength.

On foreign policy, he will be honored as the President who won the cold war, and his famous words "Mr. Gorbachev, tear down this wall!" will be linked in history with President Kennedy's "Ich bin ein Berliner." He came to office convinced that we could not trust the communists, or perhaps even negotiate with them, and his commitment to a strong national defense was never doubted by Soviet leaders.

But he also understood the importance of working with our allies to protect our security, and he also understood the madness of "mutually assured destruction." He had an instinct that Mikhail Gorbachev might be different, and was quick to respond when I learned on a visit to Moscow in 1986 that President Gorbachev was prepared to negotiate a separate arms control treaty on the critical issue of nuclear missiles, in Europe. The Intermediate-Range Nuclear-Force Treaty they negotiated the following year eased tensions in Europe, and became the needed breakthrough in U.S.-Soviet relations that made it possible to see light at the end of the long dangerous tunnel of the cold war.

President REAGAN was never afraid to be controversial, to confront when he had to, and lead where he believed. There were intense disagreements with many of his policies, then and now. But beyond all that was a defining reality. He came to power at a time of self-fulfilling pessimism, a pervasive belief that public policy could barely move molehills, let alone mountains. The true achievement of the Reagan revolution was the renewal of America's faith in itself.

It was more than the fact that he was a superb communicator. Some attributed at least part of his success to the fact that he had been an actor. But his deepest convictions were matters of heart and mind and spirit, and on them, he was no actor at all.

He was very generous to the Kennedy family on many public and private occasions. Caroline and John went to see him in the White House early in 1985 to ask if he might be willing to participate in some way in a dinner we were planning at my home in support of my brother's Presidential library. He was delighted to attend. "Of course I'll help you," he said. "You don't have a father to help."

At the dinner a few weeks later, he stood with us in the receiving line and shook the hand of every guest. He was quick to mention that he had not supported President Kennedy in 1960. "I was for the other fellow," he told us. "But you know, it's true, when the battle's over and the ground cooled, well, it's then that you see the opposing general's valor."

He proceeded to give one of the finest tributes that my brother ever received. As he said of Jack, "He seemed to grasp from the beginning that life is one fast-moving train, and you have to jump aboard and hold on to your hat and relish the sweep of the winds as it rushes by."

He summed it up by saying of my brother, "You have to enjoy the journey. . . . I think that's how his country remembers him, in his joy, and it was a joy he knew how to communicate." That's how America remembers RONALD REAGAN, too.

Hon. Jim Bunning

OF KENTUCKY

Mr. President, I rise to pay tribute to the memory of our 40th President, RONALD WILSON REAGAN.

Mary and I have deep sadness today and we send out our heartfelt condolences to Nancy and the rest of the Reagan family.

I didn't personally meet RONALD REAGAN until 1983, but I wish I had known him before.

I will never forget how even though we hardly knew each other, he was there when I needed him.

This first happened when I was running for Governor of Kentucky in 1983. To be honest, not many people were helping me. I entered the race late to try to help the Republican Party because we didn't have a candidate. Most people either weren't very interested or weren't giving me much of a chance. But I called President REAGAN and he helped me and even came out to campaign for me. I'm sure some of his advisers told him not to, and told him there was nothing in it for him. But he came anyway.

At a time when not many other people believed in me, RONALD REAGAN did. That was very special to me personally.

I didn't win that race, but President REAGAN's faith in me and his support transformed me from someone who had merely watched him from afar to an appreciative admirer.

He had no reason to come and assist me other than to help because of the goodness in his heart.

I asked, and that was enough for him.

Later I was at the 1984 Republican Convention in Dallas when he gave the great speech about believing in America and how our Nation symbolized hope to the world as a "shining city on the hill."

It was spellbinding and uplifting. Even though it was a political convention, I think his message of optimism and his belief in the goodness of America touched all Americans.

President REAGAN believed in me again when I ran for Congress in 1986. To be honest, I wasn't really interested at first in coming to Washington. But when RONALD REAGAN and his White House turned on the power of persuasion, it was almost impossible to say "no." And with RONALD REAGAN's support, I was fortunate enough to win and to come join him as a Member of Congress for his last 2 years in office. Again, he believed in me and I've never forgotten it.

I attended his last two State of the Union speeches as a Member of the House and they were spectacular performances.

I remember during his last State of the Union when he dropped a copy of the enormous continuing resolution spending bill Congress had passed in late 1987 and warned us that we'd better get our work done on time because he wouldn't sign another bill like that.

We knew he meant it and Congress listened and the next year we did get our work done on time.

I believe the secret to RONALD REAGAN's appeal was that he had such strong and profound fundamental beliefs about the role of government and he was so confident in his ability to communicate those beliefs in simple, but powerful ways that average Americans could understand.

People sensed that he was sincere in his own beliefs. They knew he was comfortable in his own skin and had a clear idea of the direction where he wanted to lead the country. Because he was confident in himself and believed in America and its people, the American people returned that faith. They believed in him and they listened to him. When he led, they followed.

They followed RONALD REAGAN when it came to his staunch opposition to taxes.

They listened to him when he warned us about the evils of communism and asserted our moral superiority in the struggle between the East and the West.

Many in Washington criticized him when he warned that the old Soviet Union was an evil empire.

But RONALD REAGAN understood that the Soviets were a moral threat to our way of life, and that we were engaged in a struggle that we had to win.

The naysayers said RONALD REAGAN was dangerous, but the American people knew he was fundamentally right, and history will show him to be a visionary who probably saved our Nation and the world.

Like every other President, RONALD REAGAN had his critics. And he made mistakes. But there is no doubt that the strong consensus among the American people is that RONALD REAGAN was a great President.

He was an unusually strong and optimistic leader that we all want to emulate. That's why his passing has hit so many of us so hard.

Even his strongest critics will tell you that they liked RONALD REAGAN the man and human being. They knew that even though he might disagree with their policies that he still liked them as people and that he would treat them with respect.

That was a hallmark of REAGAN and another strength of his administration—he was always a gentleman and treated others with respect. He might not have won every policy and political argument, but he fought cleanly and conducted himself with civility and grace.

In the end, I believe that few of us will see another leader the likes of RONALD REAGAN during our lifetime.

I believe that when he took office he set out to change not only the Nation but the face of the world. That is exactly what he did.

Hon. Robert F. Bennett

OF UTAH

Mr. President, on the passing of former President REAGAN, my mind, like everyone else's, goes back to a personal experience—not one that I had with RONALD REAGAN himself because I did not know him that well, but in 1976, I was being interviewed for a job in the REAGAN campaign for President. The individual, the former President's campaign manager at the time, who was conducting the interview, went through all of the specifics of the job he wanted me to take. The interview went very well. I seemed to have the credentials they wanted, and it was clear that a job offer was sitting there on the table. But I was a little troubled, even though things were going well, because I wanted to make something very clear.

I did not know RONALD REAGAN. I had met him, but I did not know him. I only knew the caricature of REAGAN which was out there in the media, which was that he was a rigid, ideological, hardline conservative who would never, ever budge from an ideological position. So I said, in the spirit of full disclosure in this job interview, I want to make one thing clear. I said, "I am not a true believer."

The individual conducting the interview smiled a little and he said, "That's all right, neither is the Governor."

That was my first glimpse into what made RONALD REAGAN a truly successful politician. He was a politician of absolutely firm resolve, there is no question about that. There were things he believed and he believed with such passion that he would never, ever deviate from them. But there were also some things he realized could be compromised that did not require an absolute, hardline ideological stance, and the great genius of the man is that he had the wisdom to be able to discern which issue fell into which category, which issue was one in which there must be no compromise, and which issue was one where he could, in the words of former Senator Dole, take 80 percent of the deal and be happy with it. That requires a degree of wisdom and sensitivity that very few of us possess. RONALD REAGAN possessed it, and that was the core of his genius.

In the words of the country music song, he knew when to hold them and when to fold them.

On the issue of the evil empire, that was a time when he would hold them. On the issue of the evil empire, he would give no quarter, and he was criticized firmly for that, even within his own administration. The story is told of a meeting where members of the administration were discussing how they would deal with the Soviet Union in a certain situation, and after one point of view was presented President REAGAN turned to the individual and said, "If you believe that, what are you doing in this administration?" He was that firm in his determination that the Soviet Union was, indeed, an evil empire and had to be confronted as such.

But when the confrontation truly came and the Soviet Union found they were up against an immovable object in RONALD REAGAN and they began to maneuver, then he could see the areas in which 80 percent was good enough. He could discern the difference between where he had to stand absolutely firm and where he had to negotiate. He skillfully exploited all of those differences in such a way that the evil empire first ceased to be evil and then ultimately ceased to be an empire.

I find one of the great ironies of history the fact that upon his passing, on the pages of the *New York Times*, Mikhail Gorbachev is quoted in praise of RONALD REAGAN. The man whom REAGAN outmaneuvered, outnegotiated, and ultimately forced from office was singing his praises at his passing. That is an indication of how good RONALD REAGAN was at the job of being President of the United States.

We have all talked about how optimistic he was, how filled with hope he was, what a congenial fellow he was, what a great communicator he was. And all of that is true and all of that is right and proper in this eulogy. But we should not allow ourselves to forget in these discussions of his wonderful qualities how effective a President he was. We live in RONALD REAGAN's America. Indeed, we live in RONALD REAGAN's world. He is more responsible for the kind of America we have today than any other man. He is more responsible for the kind of world in which we live than any other man.

That does not mean he is solely responsible, by any means, because there are many people who have affected America and have affected the world for good and ill, and no one man can be solely responsible for what happened. But he is more responsible than any other individual for the kind of country we have and for the kind of world in which we live—and both are substantially better than that which he found when he became President.

Let us look back for a minute at what America was like when RONALD REAGAN became President.

We think of the Great Depression and how devastating that was as an economic event in our lives. When RONALD REAGAN came to the Presidency, we were in the midst of the great inflation. I remember it very clearly. I was delighted in that period—absolutely delighted—to be able to get a bank loan, so I could meet payroll in the business I was running, at an interest rate of $21\frac{1}{5}$ percent. I remember talking to my banker who told me, Today the Treasury auction has sold 30-year government securities at 15 percent. It was absolutely stunning. The great inflation was destroying value, destroying confidence, and created what is the most serious recession we have had since the Great Depression—the double digits of the eighties which occurred in REAGAN's Presidency but were the consequence of the great inflation that went before. This President stood absolutely firm on his economic policy that was being ridiculed, that was being castigated, that was being sneered at; and his message to the country was stay the course. We did stay the course. His party lost a lot of seats in that next election, but he stood firm. Along with Paul Volcker at the Federal Reserve, they squeezed inflation out of the economy, created an economic situation where today as the heirs of that enormously difficult but significant effort we find the time when interest rates are at their lowest in 20, 30, or 40 years.

I remind people who derided RONALD REAGAN as the playboy, lifeguard, football player with no intellectual base that he was the only President of the United States who had a degree in economics—classic economics, Keynesian economics—and he viewed the world in Keynesian terms and set an economic course that produced the base of prosperity we live in today. Yes, he was an optimist. Yes, he was a politician of joy. Yes, he was a pleasant fellow. But he was an enormously successful President in his domestic policies.

During his Presidency, the American economy grew as measured in terms of gross domestic product as much as if it had acquired the entire economy of Germany. We added as much gross domestic product—that is as much output in the American economy—during the time he was President as the entire economy of Germany.

Let us not forget that contribution as we remember and properly celebrate his sterling personal qualities.

Internationally, of course, we have talked about that. Other Senators have talked about that. But let us remember once again at the time his policies were very controversial, at the time his policies were derided by the wise men, at the time they said he was a cowboy who was going to set off all kinds of danger internationally, and at the end of his Presidency, as I say, the evil empire was no longer evil and very quickly it was no longer an empire. And instead of setting off dangerous international consequences, what he did by standing firm on his resolve was transform the world by ridding it of its greatest threat. That was not bad for a B actor who presumably didn't know anything beyond what was on those 3 × 5 cards.

The best summary comes from one of his staffers who wrote a book. The staffer was named Dinesh D'Souza. He wrote a book called "REAGAN," and the first chapter of that book is entitled, "The Wise Men and The Dummy."

In that chapter, D'Souza said when REAGAN came to the Presidency, it was widely assumed among all the liberal wise men in the country that he was a dummy. The untold secret is the conservative wise men felt the same way. The conservative wise men thought he won the Presidency because he was a great actor: He looks good on television, but we can't allow him to make any of the decisions. He is a front, and we will put together the conservative agenda. Then we will have him as our puppet to go out and sell it to the American people, and we will have the best of all possible worlds.

Well, as D'Souza records, at the end of the day, on every major issue that came before the REAGAN Presidency, it turned out the wise men were wrong and the dummy was right. And the dummy, because he was President of the United States and because he understood the proper use of power and he exercised it with tremendous skill, had views that prevailed, and we are the beneficiaries of his wisdom.

At this time of his passing, I do not mourn because RONALD REAGAN has been released by death from a tremendously debilitating, frustrating, and ultimately tragic situation. RONALD REAGAN is now in a better place that does not require us to mourn but to rejoice. This time is a time to celebrate, a time to be grateful, and a time to thank providence for giving America at this time in its history this particular statesman, the one who knew when to stand with absolute resolve, when to be willing to make the deal, and possess the innate wisdom to know the difference.

We live in RONALD REAGAN's America. Indeed, we live in RONALD REAGAN's world, and we are all better for that.

Hon. Jeff Sessions

OF ALABAMA

Mr. President, it is a great honor for me to be a Member of this body at this point in history and to be able to have the privilege of making a few comments on the life and career of RONALD REAGAN.

My words are inadequate to the task. Many have spoken more eloquently than me. Many have written beautifully about his life and the meaning of his Presidency.

I will just say that I do remember being personally inspired by him. As a young high school student, I came to believe Barry Goldwater would be a good President. I believed that from the values he was articulating. I did what I could. I put a bumper sticker on my daddy's pickup truck. Although he had never been involved in politics in any way, he allowed me to do that.

Of course, things did not go well in that election. Things were going poorly. But on the eve of that election, the Nation and many of the people who shared those basic values about classical America, what we as a Nation represent—limited government, individual responsibility, personal freedom, a strong national defense—were electrified by a speech by RONALD REAGAN. I think they call it "A Rendezvous with Destiny." Some just call it "The Speech." I remember it to this day.

After the Goldwater campaign ended—and it certainly was a major defeat for him—RONALD REAGAN sort of inherited the flame of classical American values and made them the basis of his personal beliefs and his campaign for the Presidency.

I was also later honored to be President REAGAN's U.S. Attorney for the Southern District of Alabama. It was a Presidential appointment, confirmed by the Senate. I was a U.S. attorney, and I served in that job as one of his lieutenants in the war on crime for the entire two terms of his Presidency, and, indeed, for 4 more years under former President Bush. That was a great honor for me.

As we talk about what President REAGAN accomplished, I do want to take a moment to talk about crime and drugs. Crime and drugs had been surging for 20 years when President REAGAN took office. The elites in this country actually believed that prison was ineffective, that it did not work, that it was counterproductive, that you should not put people in prison, that we ought to ask how they committed the crime, what the root causes of criminal behavior were, and what we could do to help the criminal.

We lost sight of the victim. We lost sight of accountability. We lost sight of righting wrong. And it resulted in crime rates that doubled and tripled in the 20 years prior to President REAGAN taking office.

Drug use had surged during the sixties and seventies. By the time President REAGAN took office, half of the high school seniors in America admitted to having used an illegal drug in their life. That is a stunning number. That is according to a University of Michigan study.

Nancy Reagan began her "Just Say No" program. President REAGAN passed mandatory sentencing policies. He passed through the Congress the Federal sentencing guidelines that eliminated parole and had guaranteed sentences for incarceration, with many substantial sentences for serious violations of the law. I believe the sentencing guidelines were probably the biggest change in law enforcement in the history of this country since its founding.

The result was that drug use went down. It went down every year President REAGAN was President. For 12 years it declined steadfastly. We now have less than half of high school seniors who say they have used an illegal drug in their life. The crime rate began to fall. We are still seeing declines in crime. That is because we went back to the fundamental precepts of crime and punishment, and how you do it. Some people are just dangerous. They need to be incarcerated. They need to be removed from society for the protection of society.

States picked up on this. Most crimes are prosecuted in the States, but that leadership of the bully pulpit by the President led to State reforms and crackdowns and improved capacity in prisons to deal with repeat offenders. It has been a key element in the reduction of crime and why Americans are safer today than they were in 1980. It is something that I think we have not heard much about in the discussion of the accomplishments of President REAGAN.

I was also honored to have been his nominee for a Federal judgeship. It turned into a very unpleasant experience for me and my nomination did not clear the Senate Judiciary Committee, of which I am now a member and on which I am honored to serve. But he stood steadfastly for me. The fact he believed in my ability to be a Federal judge was something I cherish. And I cherish the letter he wrote me when I asked that my name be withdrawn from that appointment. It is something I will always cherish. It was personal and meaningful to me.

RONALD REAGAN had a deep and fully formed philosophy about America and American ideals when he came to office at age 69. This is something that did not come to him lightly. It was over a lifetime of evaluation. Even in the face of the most fierce opposition, he never wavered in those beliefs. Indeed, his very life seemed to embody the highest and best of American values. His very life, the way he carried himself, embodied American values. His courage to remain true to the highest of these ideals was his greatest strength, I believe.

His goal was to free the greatness of individual Americans, assured that their goodness and industry would lift the Nation and inspire the world to freedom and progress. He believed in the individual American citizen. He believed that government should allow their creativity and industry to flourish, and as they flourished, and as they worked hard, and as they were creative, the world and America would benefit from it.

His courage to be true to those ideals, I believe, was his secret strength. He understood that intuitively, and he remained true to it. He called us, in his very special way, to the natural optimistic spirit of America.

His record of achievement was extraordinary. He led us with courage and steadfastness to defeat the evil empire. He cut our taxes. He called on us to renew our spiritual, moral, and family values. He said criminals should be punished. He not only communicated these values with words, but his actions and policies and life were dedicated to that.

As a result of his constancy and courage to fight for these values, a serious period of pessimism abounding in our land at that time ended. The Soviet Union collapsed. The economy began its 20 years of remarkable growth. Matters of faith, morality, and family were lifted up. The crime rate fell, and drug use fell.

The success of the REAGAN Presidency was stunning in its scope, and it could not have come at a better time for the country. Like President Washington, President REAGAN's life was given over to the country. He loved his country and he was selfless in his commitment to it. His selflessness and the purity of his principles inspired those who worked for him.

I remember—and I will close; I know there are others who would like to speak—but I do remember how, as a U.S. attorney, we did not need to be told in detail what the President wanted. We heard his philosophy. We heard his campaign. We knew he wanted us to be more productive. We knew he wanted us to take charge of our governmental office and make it work for the people and produce as high an output as it could possibly achieve. We also knew he expected us to crack down on criminals and crime.

I think that was good leadership because all the departments of the government understood where REAGAN came from, what administration they were a part of. They did not have to be instructed in detail on how to accomplish the goals of his administration. That was one of his great strengths. The impact of it was incalculable in many ways around the world.

I will just close with this story. In 1993, several years after President REAGAN left office, I had the opportunity to go with a church group to Russia. It was a Methodist group. We stayed in a town 5 hours from Moscow, about 40,000 people, many of whom had not seen Americans before. We had a very nice time there. I stayed for a number of days with a Russian family.

The first day we got there, the Russian host's daughter was to be baptized. Father Gannati was the Russian Orthodox priest. He came and he did a nice service, and it took some time. Then we had dinner after the baptism. Father Gannati explained that just 2 years before, he was not able to wear his robes in public. The state caused him to be moved from town to town every year so that he could not build bonds and roots in a given community. He could not meet the governmental leaders. They would not meet with him because they were atheists and they would not meet with believers. So it was a very interesting time.

He described how since then he could wear his robe, the mayor had him down to meet with him the day before this event, and that he was able to stay and rebuild the church there that had been damaged ever since the Russian revolution had occurred.

At the conclusion of those remarks, our host jumped up and said, "I propose a toast to RONALD REAGAN, who allowed us to believe in God again." Right in the center of the evil empire, the impact RONALD REAGAN had to change the nature of the world in which we lived was felt in a very real way.

Hon. Craig Thomas

OF WYOMING

Mr. President, I rise to join other colleagues in talking about President RONALD REAGAN, the Great Communicator, the great humanitarian.

"I will lie down and bleed awhile, and then I will rise and fight again". RONALD REAGAN quoted Sir Andrew Barton's words after returning home from campaigning against Gerald Ford. Poignant words for a man who just 4 years later was elected the 40th President of the United States.

The Nation and the world have lost a great treasure. RONALD REAGAN was a master wordsmith, an international diplomat, a man whose genuine humanity gave Americans and people around the world a new sense of self-worth. He loved America first and foremost, so we stood behind our leader, our captain, our coach—to win one for the GIPPER.

RONALD REAGAN held a deep devotion to principle, sought "peace through strength," and encouraged everyone to believe in their convictions. He had a keen intellect, but he was underestimated by his critics. He disarmed many naysayers with his quick wit, crooked smile, thoughtful words, and a jar of jelly beans.

He will forever be remembered by ending the cold war. His words "Mr. Gorbachev, tear down this wall!" echo in our mind's eye. Known as the Great Communicator, his philosophies changed the political direction this country was taking. His domestic policies gave us a smaller government rather than a larger one. These are just a handful of changes that will be the legacy left by RONALD REAGAN. Certainly, we can all be very proud of the leadership he has given and follow the example he left behind.

Beneath the steely smile, RONALD REAGAN was a cowboy. Westerners remember REAGAN for his love of horses, his Wrangler jeans, his cowboy hats, something we all appreciated out West. In fact, in 1968, RONALD REAGAN came to Wyoming to speak to the Wyoming Republican State Convention in Cheyenne. Clarence Brimmer, now a U.S. district judge in Cheyenne, remembered the cowpoke from California who delivered a motivating speech. He said recently, "He was really outstanding, not just as a speaker, but in a cowboy suit he was really sharp. He wowed all the ladies."

The passing of RONALD REAGAN has brought about a great deal of grief for all of us in the country and throughout the world. But through his dignified leadership, universal diplomatic skills, and his energetic persona, RONALD REAGAN established a legacy that will live for generations to come. We should take pride in his life, in his accomplishments, and recognize what he left us—the great dawning of a new America.

Hon. Lisa Murkowski

OF ALASKA

Mr. President, I, too, rise to join my colleagues in honoring our Nation's 40th President, RONALD REAGAN. It is most fitting and I know that I have watched, as have Americans across the country, as we see the stories of RONALD REAGAN and his life and his contributions to this country, stories coming from not only those of us standing on the Senate floor but from other countries, from small communities. People are focusing on the man that was RONALD REAGAN, a great leader for this country. The stories that have been told have been wide-ranging, covering President REAGAN's role in the cold war, his truly undying sense of optimism for the country, the discussions about Reaganomics, and, of course, all those personal stories that make President REAGAN so unforgettable.

Alaska certainly has its stories to add and to share as well. President REAGAN's impact on Alaska began before he even entered the Office of the Presidency. In 1980, the Alaska National Interest Lands Conservation Act, putting over 100 million acres of land under Federal control, was pending before the Congress. With REAGAN's election that year, leaders in the House and Senate—at the time, both were under Democratic control—knew that if they were going to get a bill signed into law, it would have to be then, before President REAGAN was sworn in, and the act, for better or for worse, was signed into law on December 2, 1980. But President REAGAN understood Alaska and Alaskans.

In his book entitled "REAGAN, In His Own Hand," the President asked this very important question, "Will Alaska wind up as our biggest State, or will it be our smallest State surrounded by our biggest national park?"

He tried to ease the impact these land withdrawals had on Alaskans living in and around the new parks and refuges. He fought for access to these lands to provide for economic development, and it was his administration that determined that oil drilling should be allowed in a small section of the Arctic National Wildlife Refuge, a debate that continues today.

Alaskans remembered all that President REAGAN did for us in both Presidential elections by giving him wide and broad-based support throughout the State.

President REAGAN had the opportunity to visit Alaska several times. He liked to talk about his ties to the State. He was a big fan of Robert Service, and one of his favorites was a poem entitled "The Shooting of Dan McGrew." It is a poem about a particular barroom brawl, and most people may remember the beginning of it: "A bunch of the boys were whooping it up at the Malamute saloon."

It is a wonderful, kind of down-and-dirty, rough-and-tumble poem that personified what many wanted to believe about Alaska and the Last Frontier.

But President REAGAN was quite fond of that. I had an opportunity last night to pull out "The Shooting of Dan McGrew" and read it yet one more time, and it brought good smiles to my face.

I ask unanimous consent to have printed in the *Record* the full contents of "The Shooting of Dan McGrew."

There being no objection, the material was ordered to be printed in the *Record*, as follows:

THE SHOOTING OF DAN MCGREW

(By Robert Service)

A bunch of the boys were whooping it up in the Malamute saloon;
The kid that handles the music-box was hitting a jag-time tune;
Back of the bar, in a solo game, sat Dangerous Dan McGrew,
And watching his luck was his light-o'-love, the lady that's known as Lou.

When out of the night, which was fifty below, and into the din and glare,
There stumbled a miner fresh from the creeks, dog-dirty, and loaded for bear.
He looked like a man with a foot in the grave and scarcely the strength of a louse,
Yet he tilted a poke of dust on the bar, and he called for drinks for the house.
There was none could place the stranger's face, though we searched ourselves for a clue;
But we drank his health, and the last to drink was Dangerous Dan McGrew.

There's men that somehow just grip your eyes, and hold them hard like a spell;
And such was he, and he looked to me like a man who had lived in hell;
With a face most hair, and the dreary stare of a dog whose day is done,
As he watered the green stuff in his glass, and the drops fell one by one.
Then I got to figgering who he was, and wondering what he'd do,
And I turned my head—and there watching him was the lady that's known as Lou.

His eyes went rubbering round the room, and he seemed in a kind of daze,
Till at last that old piano fell in the way of his wandering gaze.
The rag-time kid was having a drink; there was no one else on the stool,
So the stranger stumbles across the room, and flops down there like a fool.
In a buckskin shirt that was glazed with dirt he sat, and I saw him sway;
Then he clutched the keys with his talon hands—my God! but that man could play.

Were you ever out in the Great Alone, when the moon was awful clear,
And the icy mountains hemmed you in with a silence you most could *hear;*
With only the howl of a timber wolf, and you camped there in the cold,
A half-dead thing in a stark, dead world, clean mad for the muck called gold;
While high overhead, green, yellow and red, the North Lights swept in bars?—
Then you've a haunch what the music meant . . . hunger and night and the stars.

And hunger not of the belly kind, that's banished with bacon and beans,
But the gnawing hunger of lonely men for a home and all that it means;
For a fireside far from the cares that are, four walls and a roof above;
But oh! so cramful of cosy joy, and crowned with a woman's love—
A woman dearer than all the world, and true as Heaven is true—
(God! how ghastly she looks through her rouge,—the lady that's known as Lou.)

Then on a sudden the music changed, so soft that you scarce could hear;
But you felt that your life had been looted clean of all that it once held dear;
That someone had stolen the woman you loved; that her love was a devil's lie;
That your guts were gone, and the best for you was to crawl away and die.
'Twas the crowning cry of a heart's despair, and it thrilled you through and through—
"I guess I'll make it a spread misere," said Dangerous Dan McGrew.

The music almost died away . . . then it burst like a pent-up flood;
And it seemed to say, "Repay, repay," and my eyes were blind with blood.
The thought came back of an ancient wrong, and it stung like a frozen lash,
And the lust awoke to kill, to kill . . . then the music stopped with a crash,
And the stranger turned, and his eyes they burned in a most peculiar way;
In a buckskin shirt that was glazed with dirt he sat, and I saw him sway;
Then his lips went in in a kind of grin, and he spoke, and his voice was calm,
And "Boys," says he, "you don't know me, and none of you care a damn;
But I want to state, and my words are straight, and I'll bet my poke they're true,
That one of you is a hound of hell . . . and that one is Dan McGrew."

Then I ducked my head, and the lights went out, and two guns blazed in the dark,
And a woman screamed, and the lights went up, and two men lay stiff and stark.
Pitched on his head, and pumped full of lead, was Dangerous Dan McGrew.
While the man from the creeks lay clutched to the breast of the lady that's known as Lou.

These are the simple facts of the case, and I guess I ought to know.
They say that the stranger was crazed with "hooch," and I'm not denying it's so.
I'm not so wise as the lawyer guys, but strictly between us two—
The woman that kissed him and—pinched his poke—was the lady that's known as Lou.

I have a wonderful personal anecdote about President REAGAN. He visited Fairbanks, AK, in 1984. It was a monumental visit because he joined Pope John Paul II in Fairbanks for a summit there. The President and Nancy Reagan arrived in Fairbanks on their way back from China. The following day, the Pope was arriving on his way to Korea. As we do in Alaska, we can facilitate great unions because of our strategic location at the top of the globe. So they were able to meet at the Fairbanks International Airport.

During his stopover in Fairbanks, the President spent his time at my parent's home out on the Chena River. They were there for a couple of days. It would not be much of a story except that the home was brand spanking new. It had not yet been furnished. So in an effort to make sure the President and Mrs. Reagan were comfortable, the community literally furnished the home, complete with very fine Alaskan artwork. It was perhaps a showcase home for a couple of days. Everything from the city's artwork to the china ultimately had to be returned to wherever it came from. The community went all out for the President and Mrs. Reagan.

Because this was a new house, there were some kinks that still needed to be worked out, specifically the water. It didn't have hot water. Apparently, after a long flight, it is quite nice to stop and take a shower, or perhaps Mrs. Reagan needed a warm bath. But there was no hot water. A call was made to then-Senator Murkowski at about 3 a.m. asking how come there was no hot water. As the story goes, the President and my father were wandering around outside trying to figure out how to make the hot water come on. They learned you had to keep the water running for awhile. That was the way President REAGAN was. He was willing to go out and try to be helpful and fix the problem. He was a man who wanted to make things work, to cut through the redtape and bureaucracy, reduce the size of government, and a man who was not afraid to stand up and promote his vision for America, but also knowing when it was time to compromise on issues. He was an individual who truly made America feel good about itself again.

I will close by reading a quote from RONALD REAGAN during his speech at the 1992 National Republican Convention. I feel it is truly a fitting reminder of this great man's legacy. I read as follows:

> My fellow citizens—those of you here in this hall and those of you at home—I want you to know that I have always had the highest respect for you, for your common sense and intelligence, and for your decency. I have always believed in you and in what you could accomplish for yourselves and for others.
>
> And whatever else history may say about me when I'm gone, I hope it will record that I appealed to your best hopes, not your worst fears, to your confidence rather than your doubts. My dream is that you will travel the road ahead with liberty's lamp guiding your steps and opportunity's arm steadying your way.
>
> My fondest hope for each one of you—and especially for the young people here—is that you will love your country, not for her power or wealth, but for her selflessness and her idealism. May each of you have the heart to conceive, the understanding to direct, and the hand to execute works that will make the world a little better for your having been here.
>
> May all of you as Americans never forget your heroic origins, never fail to seek divine guidance, and never lose your natural, God-given optimism.
>
> And finally, my fellow Americans, may every dawn be a great new beginning for America and every evening bring us closer to that "shining city upon a hill."

Hon. James M. Talent

OF MISSOURI

Mr. President, it is an honor for me to join the Senate in honoring the memory and celebrating the life of RONALD REAGAN. I want to say, first of all, how much I have appreciated the eloquence and the personal memories that have been offered on the Senate floor and in public by those who knew and remembered President REAGAN. I, of course, remember him. I didn't know him personally.

I also want to say how much especially I have appreciated the grace and the charity shown to the former President by those here who were, when he was in office, his political opponents. I think it is a great testimony to their charity of spirit that they have done so and also a comment on how our system operates in times such as this. We can remember and appreciate a person for his good qualities without necessarily having to retreat from any disagreements we may have had with that person over political issues.

I am reminded of what Winston Churchill said on a similar occasion when he was offering remembrances of a colleague who had died, with whom he had had many differences. He said:

> The fierce and bitter controversies which hung around him in recent times were hushed by the news of his illness and are silenced by his death. In paying a tribute of respect and of regard to an eminent man who has been taken from us, no one is obliged to alter the opinions which he has formed or expressed upon issues which have become a part of history; but at the Lychgate, we may all pass our own conduct and our own judgments under a searching review. It's not given to human beings, happily for them for otherwise life would be intolerable, to foresee or to predict to any large extent the unfolding course of events. In one phase men seem to have been right, in another they seem to have been wrong. Then again, a few years later, when the perspective of time has lengthened, all stands in a different setting. There is a new proportion. There is another scale of values. History with its flickering lamp stumbles along the trail of the past, trying to reconstruct its scenes, to revive its echoes, and kindle with pale gleams the passion of former days. What is the worth of all this? The only guide to a man is his conscience; the only shield to his memory is the rectitude and sincerity of his actions. It is very imprudent to walk through life without this shield, because we are so often mocked by the failure of our hopes and the upsetting of our calculations; but with this shield, however the fates may play, we march always in the ranks of honour.

I stand here for a few minutes to remember a man who always marched in the ranks of honor and whose shield was the sincerity and rectitude of his actions at all times. He was not a mentor, because I did not know him personally, but he was a hero of mine.

Much has been said in the last few days about his humor and amiability. I agree that was a very important part of RONALD REAGAN, of who he was and of his success. When I think of him, when I visualize him, I visualize him smiling, telling a joke, or offering some witticism or some piece of humor. I think that was a big part of his success.

It is important not to take yourself too seriously. That is a quality that often is lacking in this town. I think I can say that without being deemed uncharitable. But it was not a quality that was lacking in RONALD REAGAN. He thought deeply about issues. He thought deeply about the country. I think people underestimated, to some extent, how deeply he thought and understood what was going on. He never pretended to know everything. I think that helped him a lot in his Presidency.

We should also remember President REAGAN, however, not just for his qualities and his personality, but also for what he believed. He thought ideas were important, and he was right. I remember George Will said a few years ago—and I am paraphrasing him; he probably said it more eloquently than this—but the gist of his remarks was, the collapse of the Soviet Union proves that ideas not only have consequences, but that maybe only ideas have consequences.

President REAGAN's friends and opponents have sometimes characterized his political philosophy as being an antigovernment philosophy or a simplistic belief in making government smaller whatever the circumstances the country was confronting. I do not think that is correct. I think at best it is oversimplistic.

President REAGAN understood that the issue of our time during his Presidency and the issue of our time now, I suggest, is not whether government is going to be big or small, certainly in an absolute sense and often in a relative sense as well, but whether the government, in doing whatever functions we believe it ought to do, will consistently respect the values and institutions of private life.

It is not a question of whether government is important, because it is; it is a question of whether the government believes it is more important than the private society and culture and people it is governing. That is where President REAGAN drew the consistent line of his philosophy in his public life. His faith was in what the American people had built and have built and are continuing to build on their own, and in the associations and networks of private life that give life meaning, that give people a chance for happiness and opportunity. He believed in what people build in their families, in their small businesses, in their local schools, in their voluntary associations and organizations, in their churches, synagogues, and temples. He believed in the great traditions of American culture. He knew those traditions and the institutions that represent them grow and evolve organically over time and that they represent the wisdom of many generations of people about how we ought to live in our society so that we can have the maximum amount of justice and freedom and opportunity for all of our people.

What he wanted was for the government to be vigorous in the areas it was supposed to operate but to respect those institutions rather than trying to overthrow them.

He said once in 1970:

> It's not my intention to do away with government. It is rather to make it work—work with us, not over us; to stand by our side, not ride on our back. Government can and must provide opportunity, not smother it; foster productivity, not stifle it.

I remember a few years ago when we were debating welfare reform in the Congress—and I was in the House at the time—a key point in that debate was when the Congress decided collectively that we were not talking about whether we were going to try in some sense to get rid of the welfare system. We were not going to retreat from the impulse of the sixties to help people who were in poverty get out of poverty.

What we wanted, however, was a system that tried to do that in a way that respected and upheld the values that generations and generations of Americans have relied on to move up the economic ladder. We wanted a system that instead of punishing work, encouraged and required it. We wanted a system that instead of providing incentives against marriage, encouraged marriage and talked about its importance. We wanted a system that did not uproot neighborhoods and neighborhood institutions, that did not sweep them aside in the name of an all powerful and prescriptive government, but rather a system that helped build up again the vital parts of neighborhoods.

The reason that bill has been so successful, the reason it was supported by a vast majority in both Houses, and why it has been successful all over the country is not because it represented, I submit, a retreat by the government from its commitment to helping people achieve the American dream, but rather because it represented a conscious commitment by the government to work with the values of Americans, to respect those values and not to uproot them.

There is no question where President REAGAN would have been in that fight, where he was in that fight, because the seeds of welfare reform were planted during his administration.

I am not going to go on. There are others who wish to speak. I thank the Senator from Florida for allowing me to go out of order because we try to go back and forth on both sides of the aisle.

Let me close with one of my favorite quotes from President REAGAN. We are all doing that. It is from his second inaugural address in January 1985, and many have commented on President REAGAN's optimism about America, how he was optimistic about America because he not only believed in those values and the institutions that represented them, but he had a tremendous faith in their power. I think he knew we were going to triumph over the Soviet Union in the cold war because he knew what we believed in was right, was powerful, and was good, and he was not afraid to state it in those terms.

Here is an example of his optimism from his second inaugural address:

> [Now] we ... hear again the echoes of our past: a general falls to his knees in the hard snow of Valley Forge; a lonely President paces the darkened halls and ponders his struggle to preserve the Union; the men of the Alamo call out encouragement to each other; a settler pushes west and sings a song, and the song echoes out forever and fills the unknowing air. It is the American sound. It is hopeful, big-hearted, idealistic, daring, decent, and fair. That's our heritage; that's our song. We sing it still. For all our problems, our differences, we are together as of old. We raise our voices to the God who is the author of this most tender music. And may He continue to hold us close as we fill the world with our sound—in unity, affection, and love—one people under God, dedicated to the dream of freedom that He has placed in the human heart, called upon now to pass that dream on to a waiting and hopeful world.

Hon. Bob Graham

OF FLORIDA

Mr. President, later today, the body of President RONALD REAGAN will be brought into this Capitol so that all Americans can pay their final respects.

Much has been said, much has been written about our 40th President and the impact he had on our Nation and the world. In at least one respect, I believe part of his legacy has been mischaracterized, and I rise today, as has my friend and colleague from Missouri, to set the record straight.

The issue that I would like to address is RONALD REAGAN's view of the size of government. It is true that President REAGAN believed the Federal Government was too large and too costly, but he did not believe that was true of all governments.

As a former Governor of California, he believed governments closer to the people, governments at the State and local level, had the primary responsibility for essential public service and, thus, they should have the resources to respond to public needs.

The people would serve as the control of whether the State and local officials had fulfilled the voters' expectation of the role of their State, their county, or their city. I know this first-hand.

My tenure as Governor of Florida overlapped with President REAGAN's administration for 6 years. During that time, President REAGAN and key members of his administration, even as they attempted to eliminate the U.S. Department of Education and shrink Federal spending on education, helped me pass a tax increase in Florida that led to great improvements in our State education system.

An education reform movement swept the country in 1983 and 1984 with the issuance in April 1983 by the National Commission on Excellence in Education of a landmark report entitled "Nation at Risk: The Imperative for Educational Reform."

At the time that report was issued, President REAGAN made this statement:

> Parental authority is not a right conveyed by the state; rather, parents delegate to their elected school board rep-

resentatives and State legislators the responsibility for their children's schooling.

During a meeting of the National Governors Association in 1983 President REAGAN told the Governors they would be responsible for implementing reforms, including how to cover the costs of those reforms. He was not interested in having the Federal Government play a larger role; in fact, he was intent on cutting the Federal role in education.

I recalled those words when back in Tallahassee I began to push a major educational reform package through the legislature. I was not alone. For instance, our colleague, the then-Governor of Tennessee, Lamar Alexander, was instrumental in the development and adoption of a similar reform package in Tennessee, and we had the opportunity to work together during that process with then-Governor Alexander talking to Republican members of the Florida legislature as I reciprocated in conversations with Democratic members of the Tennessee legislature.

The Florida package had a goal. The goal was we would raise the level of education in Florida as judged by student performance on standardized tests and other measurements and also per-student funding of education to among the top 25 percent of the States in America. We increased student performance standards at all levels and had the most challenging standards for graduation from high school of any State in the Nation.

The package included basic things such as smaller class sizes, more class and curriculum opportunities for students, and a career ladder with pay increases which recognized our best teachers. But all of those reforms depended upon additional State financing. I proposed several steps to raise the necessary revenue, including a revision of our corporate profits tax. I advocated the plan with the assurance that better schools would improve our State's economic climate. We even printed up buttons which read: "Education Means Business."

I was therefore very disturbed that the success of the educational reform program was threatened by the lack of support by Republicans in the State senate and the State house of representatives. I called President REAGAN's Education Secretary, Dr. Terrell Bell from Utah. I reported that I was attempting to do exactly what the President had said States should be doing, but could not get any Republican support.

After consulting with the White House and gaining the President's personal permission, Secretary Bell called me back and asked what he could do to help.

I gave him the names of a half dozen or more Republican legislators. Secretary Bell called them on behalf of the President to ask them to support the reform package. I am pleased to say that with strong bipartisan support, the education reform program in Florida passed in 1983, and then by 1986 Florida had moved to 13th in the Nation in our per-pupil spending, and our test scores had the greatest rate of increase in 1986 of any State in the Nation.

This program showed that greater gains in student performance can be achieved through the right set of educational reform. This would not have happened without the support of President RONALD REAGAN.

My point is RONALD REAGAN was a more nuanced political leader in terms of his view of the role of government than he is generally given credit for by both his critics and his fans. On behalf of all Floridians, I express my appreciation for his support of improved education in Florida, and on behalf of all Floridians I express my condolences to President REAGAN's family, especially his beloved Nancy.

Hon. Orrin G. Hatch

OF UTAH

Mr. President, I would feel really bad if I didn't take a few moments to speak about my friend, Ron REAGAN. I, as much as anybody in this body, revered him, respected him, and loved him.

When I was running back in 1976, I filed literally on the last day, May 10. I had zero name recognition except among the legal community and among my initial church community. But it was zero in the public polls. I ran through the preconvention, the convention, and came out second in the convention, which enabled me to force a primary, and through the primary on $35,000, $18,000 of which was my own, which was a lot of money then back in 1976. I was about 9 points ahead and pulling away at that time against the favored in the race—the Republican Party favorite and the favorite of most of the delegates of the State convention. But he had spent about $150,000, and he was starting to slip. I was starting to pull ahead by about 9 points, according to the polls.

Since I was the first to come out for RONALD REAGAN in that race at that particular time in Utah as a candidate, we decided to ask RONALD REAGAN if he would preprimary endorse me in my race for the U.S. Senate.

I have to say when I called it didn't take them long, recognizing my friendship and my support for the first time in his political career, as far as I know—at least that is what I was told by those who were running his campaign, that he was going to preprimary endorse me, and he did. By that time I was probably known by about 60 to 65 percent of the people in Utah.

After the endorsement, I won the primary. I probably would have won the primary by 10 or 15 percentage points. But after his endorsement, I won the primary 2 to 1, and I was known by, I believe, well over 95 percent of my fellow constituents in Utah.

I went to 36 States for RONALD REAGAN as one of his major surrogates. I went to New Hampshire, and I was Nancy Reagan's date that night as I spoke for RONALD REAGAN in the cattle call. That is what it was called in New Hampshire.

In 1980, I gave the keynote address at Plains High School, Jimmy Carter's own high school in Plains, GA, before 2,000 people.

I did everything in my power to elect RONALD REAGAN. We had a friendship that transcended the usual friendships that are lovely and wonderful around here but nevertheless usually don't rise to the level that his friendship for me and mine for him really rose to.

I truly love RONALD REAGAN. I know what a great President he was. I know he did bring down the Iron Curtain, that he was the primary mover and articulator of the themes that actually ended the cold war.

Most scholars will now say there are four reasons why REAGAN was able to win the cold war: first, his military buildup; he put too much pressure on the Soviets; second, the placing of the Pershing II missiles in Europe, which was a very gutsy thing to do at the time, and highly criticized; third was the threat to build SDI, the Strategic Defense Initiative, and the Soviets knew we could do it; and fourth was a placing of the Stinger missiles in Afghanistan. I was here through all of those times.

I honor this great President, and I honor his dear wife who has been a wonderful wife and supporter, who I know deeply, who has been an advocate for so many things that are right, and especially in later times. Embryonic stem cell research—she is right on that issue, and I support her. I honor both of them this day.

I join my colleagues, millions of Americans, and indeed countless more around the world in mourning the loss of the greatest American President of the 20th century, President RONALD WILSON REAGAN.

After suffering nearly a decade, our beloved President died this weekend. I join those in this body here today in sending our condolences to Mrs. Reagan and their entire family.

It is hard to imagine any American alive who has not been touched by the legacy of RONALD REAGAN. Even those born after he left office in 1989 have benefited from his selfless service, as they grew up in an era of unprecedented global freedom, a result of the end of the cold war brought on by President REAGAN's bold vision of this country and our faithful mission in the world.

Certainly, I was touched by the life of President REAGAN.

Perhaps I might not be here today were it not for the invigorating support of this great leader, whose endorsement of my candidacy in my first Senate run was certainly instrumental in my service to the people of Utah.

I was pleased and honored to return the favor at every opportunity—and, in 1980 and 1984, I campaigned for RONALD REAGAN in almost every State of the Union.

Let no one believe that this repaid my debt, political or personal, to this great man—because I believe I will remain in his debt as long as I live, and so will our country.

President REAGAN was both political mentor and inspiration to me as a young Senator.

We both started as Democrats.

We were inspired by our country's bold international leadership and sacrifice during World War II, under a Democratic President.

Yet we both saw the political landscape shift early in our adult lives.

We both grew dismayed at our country's direction, as citizens lost faith, lost optimism and lost the dynamism that once made this land great.

At the same time, we both grew to appreciate the principles of the Republican Party, where individual initiative and personal freedom are enshrined, and where the fight against international communism took a backseat to no other foreign policy.

When I came to the Senate in 1977, our country was still fresh from the defeat symbolized by communist tanks crashing into Saigon in 1975.

By the time RONALD REAGAN became President, the defeat in 1975 had been interpreted by our global nemesis, the Soviet Union, as a weakness in American resolve; it inspired the Soviets to proxy adventures in Latin America, Africa and Asia.

As the liberal elites of the seventies denounced and disparaged our international sacrifices of the past decade, as it became commonplace to equate the use of American force with the encroachments of communist tyranny, America became uncertain of itself and turned inward.

It was not our finest moment.

Our late colleague, Senator Moynihan, once remarked,

{T}he central conservative truth is that it is culture, not politics, that determines the success of a society. The central liberal truth is that politics can change a culture and save it from itself.

In the seventies, liberal culture had brought this country to a period of social decline and international withdrawal.

As communist tyranny gained around the world, drug use here reached an all-time high.

The economy of the most productive nation in the world was unraveling with high taxes and higher inflation.

Our sense of mission was gone; our belief in our natural strengths and goodness receded.

One of the things I loved the most about RONALD REAGAN was that he recognized his duty to lead a conservative movement back into the political majority; by so doing he declared that we would never concede to cultural decline.

REAGAN's victory in 1980 put an end to this malaise and changed our country forever.

Originally from the Midwest, REAGAN moved to California and found his talent in the industry of American dreams, showing our country that an American everyman could be a star.

Many scorned REAGAN the actor for seeking political office.

But, once again, he showed them wrong. He won our hearts as a President—as he had as an actor—showing us all that a man well-practiced in the arts of both heart and mind could be a perfect leader for a nation which had lost its sense of imagination.

Only in America could a man from the middle class, from the middle of the country, rise to become the greatest American leader of the 20th century.

RONALD WILSON REAGAN achieved this by appealing to the essential American values in all of us—the values of individualism and enterprise, initiative and optimism, charity and sacrifice. And he restored those values in our country's policies.

Many misjudged REAGAN. Many underestimated him. Many confused a man of simple beliefs with a simple man.

Those of us who knew him well recognized REAGAN as a man of deep convictions. Deft of wit, he always deflected a tough moment with humor. But, under it all, a gravity of purpose shone through.

What I came to admire in RONALD REAGAN was his core belief that government could lead society, but not build society. He recognized that government's most important economic role was to foster American innovation and industry. And his policies followed that principle.

In foreign policy, he knew that communism was an abominable scourge on the face of the planet. He eagerly tackled that challenge as he had most obstacles in his life, and in so doing left a legacy unparalleled by any American leader.

Who can forget his momentous call, "Mr. Gorbachev, tear down this wall!"?

And who can forget watching as the wall fell just 2 years later?

In the most fundamental way, President RONALD REAGAN inspired us all to believe in our great Nation, and what it could do to help its people lead better lives.

As a junior Senator, I watched President REAGAN take office, facing his first challenge: an economy misfiring on all cylinders, mired in the mud of inflation, high taxes and bureaucracy.

With a strong voice of optimism, President REAGAN unfurled an ambitious plan to rejuvenate the economy and lead the Nation to economic recovery.

I remember how excited we were to see his bold plan, the change in direction that our new President charted.

He led us to pass the landmark Economic Recovery and Tax Act, including the Kemp-Roth personal income tax cuts of 25 percent over 3 years.

This major initiative stimulated the economy by providing for accelerated depreciation deductions and an investment credit.

It also enhanced the retirement of millions of Americans by introducing individual retirement accounts.

And perhaps most significantly, it indexed income tax brackets to inflation, limiting this punishing form of spending growth.

The result? The economic boom in the eighties.

Inflation dropped from 13.5 percent in 1980 to 3.2 percent in 1983.

By 1986, the 4th year of the tax cuts, economic growth had increased a cumulative 18 percent.

And, when RONALD REAGAN left office in January 1989, more than 18 million jobs had been created.

Some have criticized the REAGAN era as years of profligate spending and an irresponsible increase in the Federal deficit.

However, only in 1 year, 1983, did either personal income tax collections or total receipts go down from the previous year. It is true that the budget deficit did increase during the REAGAN Presidency, but this was clearly due to large increases in spending, not because of the REAGAN tax cuts, without which we would not likely have had the increase in prosperity most Americans enjoyed.

President REAGAN also led the way for Congress to approve the landmark 1986 Tax Reform Act.

Despite the naysaying of critics, President REAGAN did it again. The 1986 act lowered the top marginal income tax rate from 50 percent to just 28 percent. Also, it reduced the number of tax brackets from 14 to just 2.

While I did not support some of the provisions in the final product of the 1986 act, particularly some of the drastic changes in depreciation, which I believed would help contribute to a crisis in real estate and the savings and loan industry, the act itself with its simplification and lower tax rates was a major accomplishment.

The fact that subsequent Presidents and Congresses have reversed the gains made in terms of simplicity does not take away from the monumental victory that President REAGAN scored by his leadership of the Tax Reform Act of 1986.

Throughout the REAGAN era, I had the privilege of serving on the Labor and Human Resources Committee, much of it as chairman. I worked closely with the President and his staff on issues related to public health and welfare issues showcasing the President' compassion and dedication to improving the quality of life of all Americans.

The country was still in a major recession, and we worked to pass the Job Training Partnership Act. This legislation changed the emphasis of job assistance from providing government jobs to unemployed workers to providing them job training which would help unemployed find jobs in the private sector.

The President's initiatives often focused on releasing decisionmaking initiatives from an old Federal bureaucracy, as with the innovative health block grants that returned decisionmaking to the States, providing them with the resources and flexibility to deliver preventive services, maternal and child health care, and mental health services in a totally new model.

As chairman of the committee, I was criticized for putting this legislation through. But we were vindicated when the General Accounting Office reviewed these initiatives several years after their creation. It concluded that they were successful, and provided a more efficient way to address the health needs of America's diverse population.

I also remember how strongly the Reagan administration supported biomedical research, a love for and appreciation of the power of scientific inquiry Mrs. Reagan carries forward to this day.

Other key accomplishments under President REAGAN's tenure were significant Food and Drug Administration legislation, such as the Orphan Drug Act, the Drug Price Competition and Patent Term Resolution Act, the National Organ Transplantation Act, pediatric emergency medical services, vaccine compensation, tobacco warning labels, and the national practitioner data bank.

How well I remember the battle President REAGAN waged to seat C. Everett Koop as the Surgeon General.

Again recognizing that the country needed inspired leadership more than bureaucracy, President REAGAN informed us that he wanted to nominate C. Everett Koop to be the Surgeon General.

Many balked, citing Dr. Koop's age—65—as a barrier. The Public Health Service Act limited the age of PHS Commission Corps officers to 64$^{1}/_{2}$.

But our President, himself past that age, recognized the superior leadership skills of Dr. Koop.

It was a long battle, but one which had to be fought. Dr. Koop defined the modern-day role of Surgeon General, and today is revered by all, Democrats and Republicans alike, for his independent-minded advocacy of public health, from AIDS awareness and prevention to antitobacco initiatives.

I would be remiss if I didn't highlight President REAGAN's other significant health care accomplishment.

As we know, the use of illegal drugs had hit a historic high in the late seventies.

Again, President REAGAN recognized that government needed to find new ways to address this social blight. He proposed and we legislated the creation of the Office of National Drug Control Policy, which has taken the leadership role in anti-drug policy ever since.

Once again, however, the President recognized that leadership was as much in the message as in the bureaucracy.

His beloved First Lady introduced the "Just Say No" campaign, a flat rebuttal to an ingrown acceptance of drug use in our society.

Derided by some elites, this program of declaring unequivocally the unacceptable use of illegal drugs has become a foundation of all subsequent drug use.

No one suggests—then or now—that the problem of drug use is simple, and that prevention and treatment policies can be cauterized from interdiction policies.

But no one suggests, after years of confirming studies, that a drug policy can be effective absent a strong component of social rhetoric.

I loved President REAGAN, and I loved his personal style of leadership.

But I loved even more his undying love and affection for one of the classiest First Ladies this country has come to know.

Nancy Reagan's quiet support of her husband, so evident in all his successes, is often overlooked, as is her courage in leading the "Just Say No" campaign.

I remember as if it were today when President REAGAN signed the 1986 drug law, the one that created the Office of the Drug Czar and gave added resources to prevention and treatment.

I was standing behind the President when he signed the bill. He said with that special twinkle in his eye, "I am going to give this pen to the woman who has crusaded to end drug use in this country."

With that, he walked past expectant advocates and lawmakers straight to his wife Nancy, and presented her with the pen.

Some focus on President REAGAN's talents as an actor and imagemaker. Yet I have never known a more authentic man.

And when he concluded that AIDS was a challenge to the public health that was reaching emergency proportions, he declared this as national policy.

At the time, some criticized his administration. They wanted him to act sooner. They wanted more money. They wanted more research.

But what I remember was a compassionate man who recognized that we needed to build the research infrastructure to make effective use of new funding.

While the HIV virus was not identified until 1983, the Reagan administration invested close to $6 billion in fighting the disease by the end of his term in 1989. Once the President recognized the challenge, he radically increased the response of the government, and the breakthroughs with retroviral medicines in the nineties would simply have not occurred were it not for those investments.

We all know that one of a President's greatest legacies is his nominations to the third branch of government.

In appointing more judges than any President in American history, President REAGAN's judicial legacy can be seen on two levels.

First, he described, in both principled and practical terms, the kind of judge America needs.

We had seen decades of judicial activism, through which judges took more and more control over the policies governing the country and the culture in which Americans lived.

President REAGAN came into office not just saying judges were going too far, but explaining why. He refocused Americans on the principles America's Founders laid down at the dawn of the Republic: the people, through their elected representatives, decide how they wish to be governed and make the law to do so. Judges can only interpret and apply that law, they cannot make or change it.

Implementing those basic principles, President REAGAN shaped the judiciary by the individuals he nominated and appointed. He appointed some of the legal academy's best minds to the U.S. Court of Appeals—such as Ralph Winter to the Second Circuit, Frank Easterbrook and Richard Posner to the Seventh Circuit, and of course Robert Bork to the District of Columbia Circuit.

I served on the Judiciary Committee during those years, seeing first-hand the depth and breadth and quality of President REAGAN's nominees.

America's Founders insisted that this separation of powers, this restriction on judicial power, was absolutely critical for the freedom that self-government under a written constitution makes possible.

For some whose agenda the people do not favor, however, a judiciary that won't make law means their preferred law just won't get made. And they fought President REAGAN's nominees with increasingly intensity.

The first cloture vote ever taken on an appeals court nominee, for example, occurred during President REAGAN's first term, and the confirmation process changed entirely in his second.

The seeds sown then have borne fruit today in the filibusters being used against President Bush's nominees. But the issue remains the same, whether unelected Federal judges may take over from the people the business of making law and defining the culture.

President REAGAN's record of judicial appointments is certainly a profound legacy. He truly blazed a trail on this issue and, through his leadership, Americans now know more about how appointing the right kind of judge is so important to protect their freedom.

Many believe that President REAGAN's lasting legacy will be his successful leadership during the last stage of the cold war.

RONALD REAGAN's tenure began at what was our lowest point in the cold war. The loss in Vietnam and the Watergate debacle led to a withdrawal from our global policy of containment. The Soviets filled the gap, and their proxies gained around the globe.

Emboldened, the Soviet Union engaged in its most extensive military expansion in that dictatorship's history; during the seventies, the Soviets expanded their nuclear missile arsenals as well as their conventional arsenals in virtually every armament category. At the end of the seventies, the previous President was left shamefaced, following the invasion of Afghanistan, declaring his "surprise" at Soviet behavior.

President REAGAN came to office dedicated to redressing the military balance and engaging the cold war.

His administration saw the largest peace-time growth of military spending in modern American history. That escalation combined American resolve with American ingenuity, and this was no more evident than in President REAGAN's Strategic Defense Initiative.

The President rejected conventional deterrence doctrine when he stated, "[We] must seek another means of deterring war. It is both militarily and morally necessary ... I propose to channel our technological prowess toward building a more secure and stable world ... Our only purpose is to search for ways to reduce the danger of nuclear war."

What President REAGAN imagined, when he stated this back in 1984, is slowly coming to be, 20 years later. We have moved too slowly, but not because we lacked in vision.

President REAGAN was willing to challenge the Soviets diplomatically, militarily and by proxy. He was unabashed in declaring that regime an evil empire. Who today denies the inherent evil of the gulag?

He was bold in responding to the emplacement of Soviet SS–20s in occupied Europe with Pershing's in Germany. Who today denies that this didn't signal to the Soviets our new-found resolution to combat them geopolitically?

RONALD REAGAN rejected the so-called "Vietnam syndrome" long before our victory in the first Gulf war allowed Americans to believe in the justice of our use of force. He knew that the United States had a role in the world, that the use of American force was not immoral and that the United States could do good for the world.

This military escalation challenged the Soviet leadership and ultimately bankrupted its coffers. The decision to roll back directly challenged and refuted the fundamental ideological tenet of communism, that it would prevail as an inexorable law of history.

This perverted notion was based, of course, on the acceptance that the highest stage of history would rest on imprisoning nations and extinguishing history.

REAGAN knew in his heart that this was the greatest falsehood perpetrated on modern history and he built his foreign policy—the Reagan doctrine—on the idea of rolling back this ideology, this tyrannical power, and tearing down the walls that kept its citizens imprisoned.

RONALD REAGAN did not accept the status quo.

He did not accept a static geopolitical division of the world between the free nations and the captive nations of the evil empire.

He and his allies—and I will be proud to my dying day to have considered myself one of his allies—believed that we could roll back communism, on the ground, and in the minds of people.

RONALD REAGAN went to England in 1983, before the leftist Oxford Union, and announced the creation of what would become the National Endowment for Democracy, which would support programs around the world fostering democratic principles and practices.

Last year, on the 20th anniversary of this bold initiative, President Bush announced a major push by the NED into the Arab world.

Democracy remains relevant after it has triumphed over communist tyranny.

But for democracy to succeed, people striving to break the yoke of tyranny had to have a friend in the United States. RONALD REAGAN did not limit his friendship to diplomacy and military posturing.

A key aspect of the Reagan legacy was the Reagan doctrine's policy of support for anticommunist movements around the world. We supported Solidarity in Poland, using the International Labor Organization.

We supported the resistance in Nicaragua—and the wars over that policy were sometimes almost as intense here on Capitol Hill.

And we supported the Afghan resistance.

We've had democracy in Poland for over a decade, and Poland is the shining example of the New Europe, a country whose government and soldiers have bravely and proudly served besides ours in Iraq.

Nicaragua has also had democratic elections over the past decade.

And while the Iran-Contra episode was a policy debacle, I remain proud of my service in this Senate during that investigation, as I remain unflinching in my belief that it was right to help Nicaraguans resist the tyranny and thuggery of the Sandinistas.

And our support for the Afghan resistance led to the withdrawal of Soviet forces from Afghanistan, dealing the Soviet Union a military, financial and psychological blow from which it would never recuperate. This blow created a major fissure in the notion of communist inevitability that, many of us believe, would lead to the crumbling of the Soviet empire.

Many are quick to disparage that policy, because of what arose from the tumult of the Afghan resistance and the rise of the Taliban. We made mistakes in implementing the policy, we now see, primarily having to do with recruiting Saudi participation and relying on Pakistani management of arms flows.

But our biggest mistake was abandoning Afghanistan after the collapse of the Soviet puppet regime, leaving that poor country an orphan child of the cold war. But we made no mistake in contributing to a devastating Soviet defeat, a defeat that brought about the end of the cold war.

When RONALD REAGAN left office, this country had been transformed.

Malaise was not associated with the American economy, nor the American spirit.

Optimism, that personal trait of RONALD REAGAN, was what characterized our standing in the world, our economy, and our belief in ourselves.

REAGAN, a child of the Midwest who understood mythically the role of the western frontier in the American psyche, left us looking to the horizon, to the future.

RONALD REAGAN was a humble man, who left office gladly, having served his term, but who never stopped loving the American people.

It was such love that led to one of the most moving letters to the American public ever written in our history, the letter he wrote on November 5, 1994, announcing that he was slowly succumbing to Alzheimer's Disease.

This is a horrible disease, as so many American families know.

My colleagues in the Senate know that, after much soul searching and study, I have become a strong proponent of embryonic stem cell research, because of the promise it offers for treatment of some of the most wrenching illnesses Americans face today, such as Alzheimer's, Parkinson's and juvenile diabetes.

President REAGAN's widow, my dear friend Nancy, knows that I will remain dedicated to supporting this research through all my days in the Senate.

Even though retired and enjoying the privacy that was always important for him and his family, President REAGAN wrote on November 5, 1994 one of the bravest and most moving letters in American history.

He said:

Upon learning this news, Nancy and I had to decide whether as private citizens we would keep this a private matter or whether we would make this news known in a public way....

So now, we feel it is important to share it with you. In opening our hearts, we hope this might promote greater awareness of this condition. Perhaps it will encourage a clearer understanding of the individuals and families who are affected by it.

After speaking of the burdens he knew his long illness had in store—not for him, but for his beloved Nancy, he thanked his fellow Americans. He said:

{L}et me thank you, the American people for giving me the great honor of allowing me to serve as your President. When the Lord calls me home, whenever that may be, I will leave with the greatest love for this country of ours and eternal optimism for its future.

I now begin this journey that will lead me into the sunset of my life. I know that for America there will always be a bright dawn ahead.

These are the virtuous and loving words of a patriot, of a brave and humble man, of a man who lived every day in the belief that our best days lie ahead. It is America that pauses this week, and I thank God for the gift of the greatest American President of the 20th century, RONALD REAGAN.

We have lost a great American.

I think it is fitting to quote another great American, Daniel Webster who spoke so eloquently about the passing of two other Presidents, Thomas Jefferson and John Adams. Webster's words were never more true than today:

A superior and commanding human intellect, a truly great man, when Heaven vouchsafes so rare a gift, is not a temporary flame, burning brightly for a while, and then giving place to returning darkness. It is rather a spark of fervent heat, as well as radiant light, with power to enkindle the common mass of human kind; so that when it glimmers in its own decay, and finally goes out in death, no night follows, but it leaves the world all light, all on fire from the potent contact of its own spirit.

I pray that America will always be alight with the spirit of RONALD REAGAN.

Hon. Trent Lott

OF MISSISSIPPI

Mr. President, I ask unanimous consent the remarks of our former colleague, Senator Connie Mack, be printed in the *Record*.

There being no objection, the material was ordered to be printed in the *Record*, as follows:

RONALD W. REAGAN
1911–2004

(A tribute by former U.S. Senator Connie Mack (R–FL))

RONALD REAGAN was more than the President, he was an inspiration, he was my friend.

As America mourns the passing of former President RONALD REAGAN, one of the most loved American Presidents in history, it is appropriate that our Nation take a moment to reflect on the life of this remarkable man. He will not only be remembered for his vision and leadership, but also for his conviction to principles, his sense of pride and love of country.

President REAGAN made a difference in my life both personally and politically. When he was elected in 1980, I remember vividly saying to my wife Priscilla "this is such an important election for our Nation that I have to become involved. I had no idea his election would one day lead me to seek elective office and eventually to represent Florida in the U.S. Senate.

Knowing RONALD REAGAN and serving in the U.S. Congress when he was President of the United States has been one of the greatest honors of my life. I remember when he came to Florida in 1988 to campaign for me in my race for the U.S. Senate. I introduced him saying: "Mr. President, we will never forget that you gave us back a belief in ourselves and our Nation. You restarted our economy giving people hope and opportunity. You rebuilt America's military and led the fight for freedom around the world." RONALD REAGAN was more than the President, he was an inspiration ... he was a friend.

Each year, the magnitude of President REAGAN's accomplishments at home and abroad become increasing apparent. As recognition of his achievements and their impacts on our lives today grows so does the Nation's gratitude toward him. He embodied the American spirit that helped lift the morale of our country.

American Presidents affect history in their own way, but fewer have made more of an impact or shaped the history of their times than RONALD REAGAN.

In the election of 1980, Americans were faced with one of the most simple, yet defining questions in American politics: "Are you better off now than you were 4 years ago?" Were we as Americans willing to accept that the once proud land of the free and the home of the brave was now worn and tired and lacked direction? America said "No!"

RONALD REAGAN reaffirmed my philosophy as well as that of a whole generation which believed that wealth and prosperity emerge from the spirit of creativity that resides in individuals not government, and to the belief in the principles of less taxing, less spending, less government and more freedom. Freedom deeply mattered to RONALD REAGAN, and freedom deeply matters to me.

With RONALD REAGAN's election came a renewed vitality in America. He brought a belief that freedom must ring from the bells of this great Nation and that opportunity should not be limited. He reminded us of the America that was there all along. A freedom-loving country waiting to be unshackled from a government that had grown too big and cost too much which dictated what was best for us. No, we wanted better and RONALD REAGAN led us there.

Under President REAGAN's leadership, the spirit of America was rekindled and the flame of freedom burned bright—free markets, free ideas, free trade and freedom as the centerpiece of our foreign policy. The Reagan revolution had no boundaries. The winds of freedom swept across America and gained momentum throughout the world. Freedom's ring was heard in Latin America, where nations turned back communism and accepted the free will of the people. In Eastern Europe, freedom broke the rusted chains of totalitarianism and caused the Berlin Wall to fall.

RONALD REAGAN never lost faith in the freedom, dignity and liberty of mankind. He understood that freedom is never more than one generation away from extinction. He never doubted that freedom was more than a virtue. It was a right given to each of us by a sovereign God.

RONALD REAGAN did not invent freedom. He defined it. For through his wit and humility, he carried his role in history as the man who gave freedom a face. And through his undying faith in those who entrusted in him the role as their leader, RONALD REAGAN achieved greatness.

Even though President REAGAN has now completed the journey he began so many years ago, our Nation has not yet completed the path we began under his leadership. RONALD REAGAN made America stronger, more prosperous and more confident. We still need to do more to make our country and the world a better and safer place to live, work and raise a family. We must continue his legacy so as to ensure that America remains that shining city on the hill that President REAGAN described to us.

To Nancy and the Reagan family, our Nation is forever in your debt for sharing this unique and special individual with us, the American people.

President REAGAN, we say goodbye for now. You have touched our lives deeply. You have indeed lived the words of Sacred Scripture: "You have fought the good fight, you have finished the race, you have kept the faith."

Godspeed Mr. President.

Hon. William H. Frist

TENNESSEE

Mr. President, these past few days we have seen an extraordinary outpouring of affection for our 40th President, RONALD WILSON REAGAN.

In a few short hours, he will lie in state under the Capitol dome where dignitaries from around the world and citizens from across the country will pay their respects to the man from Dixon.

In his 1982 State of the Union Address, President REAGAN told the Nation, "We don't have to turn to our history books for heroes. They're all around us." In life, RONALD REAGAN was a hero to millions. To the freedom fighters in the Soviet Union, to his fellow citizens striving toward that American dream, RONALD REAGAN told the world that we are meant to be free.

He was a man of faith and deeply held convictions. Like James Madison, RONALD REAGAN believed that in the creation of our Republic was the hand of God. He believed our freedoms flow not from the State but from the Almighty. Our task was and remains to awaken in the people this essential truth.

I close with a story I believe captures RONALD REAGAN's remarkable character, his courage, and his vision. It was 1997. From a news report was a story of an emigre.

> Walking in Arm and Hammer Park near his home, REAGAN was approached by an elderly tourist and his 12-year-old grandson, Ukranian emigres now living near Toledo, OH. They spoke with him for a moment and the grandfather snapped a picture of the boy sitting with the former President. An article about the encounter and the picture appeared first in the *Toledo Blade* and then in newspapers around the country. The other day, the grandfather recalled their meeting. We went to the park for a picnic with our friends, he said, and then he saw President REAGAN. And we began to cheer him and said, Mr. President, thank you for everything you did for the Jewish people, for Soviet people, to destroy the Communist empire. And he said, yes, that is my job.

RONALD WILSON REAGAN was raised in a small town. Part of him remained a small town citizen all of his life. Not in the self-conscious way one thinks of a politician stumping on the campaign trail. RONALD REAGAN's small town roots informed the way he viewed the body politic—what he believed people wanted from life, from each other and from government.

As he explained, when a person grows up in a small town:

> You get to know people as individuals, not as blocs or members of special interest groups. You discover that, despite their differences, most people have a lot in common ... {W}e all want freedom and liberty, peace, love and security, a good home, and a chance to worship God in our own way; we all want the chance to get ahead and make our children's lives better than our own. We all want the chance to work at a job of our own choosing and to be fairly rewarded for it.

RONALD REAGAN believed that the government should serve the people. He believed that the strength of our economy came from the creativity, ingenuity and productivity of the individual, not from the plans and schemes of government bureaucrats or intellectual elites.

This view of America's economic success guided his economic policies here at home, and, in no small way, shaped his political policies abroad.

When RONALD REAGAN became President, the American economy was in a shambles. Inflation was in the double digits. Interest rates were soaring. Americans had to wait in endless lines to pump overpriced gas. Real incomes had stagnated and the American worker was demoralized. In his 1989 "Speaking My Mind" collection of essays and speeches, RONALD REAGAN reflected that:

> Here we were, a country bursting with economic promise, and yet our political leadership had gone out of its way to frustrate America's natural economic strength. It made no sense. My attitude had always been—let the people flourish.

So, he set about slashing Federal income taxes and cutting burdensome regulations. It was his mission to free the American worker and unleash the American entrepreneur. When he came to office, the top marginal tax rate was 70 percent. By the time he left, it was a mere 28 percent. His sweeping tax reforms overhauled the Tax Code and removed 6 million taxpayers from the tax rolls.

At the same time, President REAGAN gave Federal Reserve Chairman Paul Volcker free reign to tighten the money supply and bring down inflation.

Together, these policies worked.

True to the President's forecast, as the economy grew, so, too, did tax revenues. Tax revenues increased faster than GDP. By 1990, the economy had grown by a third—or as the *Wall Street Journal* put it, "roughly the size of Germany." Over the course of his Presidency, the economy created 19 million jobs and the stock market hit a record high. America enjoyed the longest economic expansion up to that time.

Throughout, President REAGAN was assailed for the growing deficit. In typical Washington fashion, he got the blame for adverse economic numbers, but never the credit for economic success. Contrary to his critics, however, the Federal deficit fell from 6.3 percent of GNP in fiscal year 1983 to 2.3 percent in 1988. The deficit actually shrank as a percentage of gross national product.

At the time, his policies were dubbed Reaganomics. Now, they're considered common sense. President REAGAN's guiding principle was simple, yet profound: government policies should grow the economy, not manage it. The impact of this idea was so great that, now, even the other side of the aisle speaks of targeted tax cuts and tax credits, and no longer openly campaigns to raise our taxes.

Indeed, President Clinton crystallized the Reagan revolution when he declared, "The era of big government is over."

President REAGAN believed in the dreams and dignity of the individual. As he said in his second inaugural address, "There are no limits to growth and human progress when men and women are free to follow their dreams."

RONALD REAGAN reminded the American people that economic liberty and human freedom are two sides of the same coin.

Some call it the Reagan revolution. Others call it the Reagan restoration. I prefer the latter term. The man from Dixon—lifeguard, radio announcer, actor, Governor, father, adoring husband, and President of the United States—restored not only our confidence, but our fundamental understanding of the source of America's greatness: the American people.

Indeed, America was blessed to have such a President. Now he will enter the history books as one of our greatest. God bless RONALD WILSON REAGAN. God bless America.

Hon. Mitch McConnell

OF KENTUCKY

Mr. President, I rise today because a mighty oak has fallen. RONALD REAGAN has left his life here on Earth, but oh what a life it was. Born in the middle of our great Republic in the beginning of the last century, his was an American tale from start to finish.

Jack and Nelle Reagan brought a son into the world in Tampico, IL, in 1911. Jack was a shoe salesman with an Irishman's flare for storytelling. Nelle was a devout Christian who made ends meet by doing other people's sewing out of their home. When Jack first saw their healthy baby in his crib, he looked at this little baby and said he looked like a "little fat Dutchman." And the nickname stuck, "DUTCH."

Times were hard for the Reagans. RONALD REAGAN commented years later that:

Our family didn't exactly come from the wrong side of the tracks, but we were certainly within sound of the train whistles.

Even then, it was in RONALD REAGAN's character to look for the Sun behind the clouds. Growing up, he lived a typical American boy's life. He was a lifeguard in the summer and a football player in the fall. In the fading years, when Alzheimer's robbed him of most of his memory, he could still summon up his youth in Illinois, proudly recalling the 77 lives he saved as a lifeguard from the teeming Rock River, notching each one on a log on the shore.

In Illinois, he discovered there was more to life than just football and lifeguarding. There was also acting. Connecting with an audience plugged him into a broader world. As he later said, "For a kid suffering childhood pangs of insecurity, the applause was music."

Ambition led him westward out of Illinois; Hollywood, to be exact. There, as we all know, he started his successful acting career and, more important, met a young actress from Chicago named Nancy Davis. She became the love of his life. Nancy was focused, smart, and loved her RONNIE. Jimmy Stewart once remarked, "If RONNIE had married Nancy the first time, he would have won an Academy Award."

But gradually his time in front of an audience changed from the stage and screen to the assembly hall. Time constraints prevent me from following his ascent to the highest office in the land. Let me simply comment that for most of us being a successful actor and pitchman, union president, two-term Governor of our Nation's largest State, and a national figure to boot would have been enough of a career, especially at the age of 69. But RONALD REAGAN had other thoughts, and so began his run against President Jimmy Carter for the Presidency in 1980.

Neck and neck until the debate a week before the election, REAGAN broke it wide open when he closed by asking Americans a simple question: Are you better off than you were 4 years ago?

On election day, REAGAN won a smashing victory, winning 44 of 50 States. He would top that mark in 1984, winning 49 out of 50 States.

I have listened to and read countless people reflecting on what President REAGAN meant to them and to America. Were there enough time, I would fill up the rest of the afternoon with my thoughts about this great man. But I will limit my observations to what I think will be, in addition to restoring America's faith in itself, the way history will remember RONALD REAGAN, the peacemaker.

I want to address the question, What does it mean to have won the cold war? Revisionists suggest that RONALD REAGAN had little to do with the Soviet Union's fall which they now claim was just inevitable. I can tell you no one thought that in 1979. Communism was on the rise and freedom was in retreat. The United States was the toothless tiger with the uncertain future. Energy shortages crippled us, and rampant crime hunted us down. Interest rates for homes, cars, and businesses were sky high. Our economy was wrenched back and forth between bouts of recession and inflation, both at the same time. America's decline was marked by new, unfamiliar words. We learned "stagflation," "taxflation," and, of course, we learned malaise.

America's economy was not the only thing in decline. So, too, was our foreign policy. Still suffering from a Vietnam syndrome, we watched and did nothing as Afghanistan was invaded by the Soviets, as hostages in Iran were seized, and as Cuban puppets invaded Africa and Central America. Our Navy was weak. Our planes couldn't fly. Our Army lacked volunteers and morale. The nuclear balance was tipping, and our intelligence services were ravaged by firings and mismanagement.

We were declining and the Soviet Union was rising. Some people were ready to give up. Others suggested the Presidency was too big and complicated a job for any single person. It seemed as if we had lost our nerve. But not RONALD REAGAN. You see, he had a vision.

In 1982, he explained his "sick bear" theory:

> The Soviet empire is faltering because it is rigid—centralized control has destroyed ... innovation, efficiency, and individual achievement ... the Soviet dictatorship has forged the largest armed force in the world ... by preempting the human needs of its people and, in the end, this course will undermine the foundations of the Soviet system.

With his customary humor, he had a memorable way of explaining this. He talked of a Soviet citizen who went to a Soviet bureau of transportation to buy a car. After paying and filling out all the forms, he is told by the seller of the car to come back in 10 years to get his car.

The man asks, "In the morning or the afternoon?"

The official responds, "Well, we are talking about 10 years from now; what difference does it make whether it is the morning or afternoon?"

The man replies, "Well, the plumber is coming in the morning."

Beneath the humor, President REAGAN knew the serious truth. The Soviet Union was as inherently weak as the U.S. economy was inherently strong, a fact too few recognized. So when President REAGAN's policies began to revitalize our economy, the confidence restored here was matched by new uncertainty over in the Soviet Union.

Others have and will talk about the Reagan revolution here at home, but in terms of our victory in the cold war, the Reagan economic recovery was the first body blow that eventually exorcised the demon of communism from the Soviet Union.

The real trouble for the Soviet Union was not REAGAN's policies, but REAGAN's values, his courage, and his willpower. Before he was ever elected, President REAGAN recognized that the Soviet Union was an "arsenal of anarchy" throughout the world. It was a "sickness of the human condition," he said. And President REAGAN was never afraid to do that which so many leaders lack the courage to do: look at evil and call it by its name. In this regard, REAGAN was like Churchill. REAGAN was the nemesis of communism, just as Churchill was of nazism. He understood the evil that communism represented and what it would do if unchecked.

Interestingly, REAGAN's understanding of this evil did not begin with the fate of millions, but of just one. In May 1975, a 5-year-old boy fell into the Spree River, which divided then-communist East Berlin from free West Berlin. As firemen from West Berlin—firemen, not soldiers—started to go to the boy's rescue, an East German patrol boat barred their entry into East German waters. The boy drowned.

The mayor of West Berlin described that refused rescue as "an incomprehensible and frightful act, placing political considerations before the saving of a human life." But for REAGAN, it was the sad personification of a harsh and enduring reality: Communism is a system where every human life is sublimated to the ruthless needs of the state.

Focused on the value of a single human life, RONALD REAGAN looked across the globe and saw 600 million people living like slaves under the communist lash. He did not mince words or deeds. He dubbed the Soviet Union the evil empire, a description brutally accurate, yet offensive to the tender sensibilities of most of the media and intelligentsia here at home. He called for a massive defense increase—"peace through strength," he called it—and some even in his own Cabinet opposed it.

In the face of criticism, REAGAN strengthened our defense. He quoted Demosthenes in dismissing the Soviets' empty assurances of their good intentions on arms control, "What sane man would let another man's word rather than his deeds tell him who is at war and who is at peace with him?"

He then translated that demand into a Russian saying of no uncertain words—*doveryai, no proveryai*. In Russian, that means "trust but verify."

RONALD REAGAN did not have timid dreams. He wasn't interested in slowing the decline of freedom or just holding its position steady; he wanted freedom to ring across the globe and communism to be relegated to the ash heap of history. So he went to the Berlin Wall to call out in front of that colossal affront to freedom, "Mr. Gorbachev, tear down this wall!"

He left Reykjavik when it was clear that Mr. Gorbachev was only bargaining for the end of the Strategic Defense Initiative, which matching, the Soviets knew, would spend them into oblivion. Margaret Thatcher notes that Reykjavik, deplored as a loss by REAGAN's critics, particularly by the European and American intelligentsia, marked the beginning of the end of the Soviet Union.

Of course, all the significant arms control reductions came after REAGAN walked away from Reykjavik. But today, President REAGAN is vindicated by some 600 million people who breathe freely because of the collapse of the Soviet empire.

So what does it mean to liberate almost 600 million from fear and terror? It means 49 million Ukrainians will never again worry about a class purge.

It means 17 million former East Germans will never be grabbed in the night by the STASI, the secret police of Eric Honneker.

It means 38 million Poles will never fear General Jaruzelski attempting to crush the Solidarity free labor movement.

It means 22 million Romanians will never know the torture, madness and human experimentation of Nicolae Ceausescu.

It means 16 million in the Czech Republic and Slovakia will never hear tanks rumbling through their city streets to crush self-rule.

It means tens of millions of former West Germans lead lives oblivious to the cosmic nervousness that gripped their mother's and father's generation.

It means that 5 million in Finland no longer look across the Gulf of Finland with dread at 7.2 million people in Latvia, Estonia, and Lithuania, who lived in slavery as a warning to any neighbors who would dare dissent from the Soviet world view.

In all, 600 million lives were emancipated by the victory in the cold war—the greatest liberation in the history of mankind, and hopefully for all time.

Now, having said all of that, let me just mention how much I miss that sweethearted man, especially his sense of humor. I have been reminded from all the replayed speeches just how wonderful he was. For example, during an exchange with the press one day, he said:

I have given my aides instructions that if trouble breaks out in any of the world's hot spots, they should wake me up immediately—even if I am in a cabinet meeting.

It makes you wonder what President REAGAN said to Saint Peter. Something witty, no doubt, and delivered with a warm smile.

So now the long goodbye that Mrs. Reagan, his rock and strength and the love of his life, has spoken of so movingly is nearly complete. So I will close with President REAGAN's own words in his courageous letter to the American people upon discovery of the disease that would ultimately bring about his fall. President REAGAN said 10 years ago:

> When the Lord calls me home, whenever that may be, I will leave with the greatest love for this country of ours and eternal optimism for its future.
>
> I now begin this journey that will lead me into the sunset of my life. I know that for America there will always be a bright dawn ahead.

God bless RONALD REAGAN, an American hero.

Hon. Tom Harkin

OF IOWA

Madam President, our Nation has come together this week to mourn the passing of former President RONALD REAGAN. However anticipated his death may have been, it is still a profound loss for the Reagan family. Our thoughts and prayers are with them all and especially with former First Lady Nancy Reagan.

However, knowing the kind of man RONALD REAGAN was, knowing his relentless optimism and his sunny disposition, something tells me he would prefer that Americans spend this week remembering and celebrating his unique character and quality. "America in mourning" just does not seem Reaganesque because RONALD REAGAN was always about "morning in America." He always looked at the bright side of every situation or circumstance. I remember the story he told about the little boy who walked into a barn and encountered a huge pile of manure. The boy, who was not the least bit disappointed, broke into a big smile and said: I just know there is a pony in here somewhere. That was the RONALD REAGAN we remember and admire.

Iowans relate strongly to RONALD REAGAN because his roots were our roots. He grew up next door in smalltown Illinois and spent 5 formative years in Iowa. In fact, this was where the young RONALD REAGAN found his voice as the Great Communicator—first as a radio announcer at WOC Radio in Davenport and later at WHO Radio in Des Moines where he became one of the most popular sports broadcasters in the region. That was at the height of the Great Depression.

He remembered this period with obvious fondness. In his autobiography, "An American Life," he wrote:

> I spent four years at station WHO in Des Moines and they were among the most pleasant of my life. At 22, I'd achieved my dream; I was a sports announcer. If I had stopped there, I believe I would have been happy the rest of my life.

During his two terms in the White House, I met President REAGAN on many occasions, and just about every time he would eagerly tell me he had been an announcer at WHO Radio. He regaled me with stories of how, sitting in his studio in Des Moines, he faked the play by play of the Chicago Cubs baseball game based upon wire reports as they came through. He seemed to have this fixed in his mind, that when he would see me, it was Tom Harkin and WHO. If this is Harkin, I am going to tell him about my time at WHO. It sort of became a thing that every time we met, he, again, would tell me some story about his time at WHO Radio. So that was my experience with the REAGAN charm.

We disagreed on many important issues, but you could not come into contact with this man and not feel his personal warmth and charm. In fact, I have been struck this week by the bipartisan affection for this former President. He was the genuine article, a man who embodied so many of the traits we hold dear as Americans. We remember his conviction, his courage, his lack of pretentiousness, and, yes, his optimism.

On a personal note, I will always be grateful to President REAGAN for signing into law my bill to establish the National Institute on Deafness and Communication Disorders at the National Institutes of Health in 1988. Quite frankly, his advisers urged him to veto the bill, but the President, who himself suffered from hearing loss, vetoed his advisers. He signed the bill into law. As a result, we have had a series of medical breakthroughs that are helping millions of Americans cope with hearing loss and communication disorders.

Last, he and Nancy fought a heroic battle with Alzheimer's disease, and they did a great deal to raise the level of awareness and understanding of this terrible disease. I am especially proud of the courageous leadership Nancy Reagan has displayed in our efforts to find a cure for this deadly disease by her advocating a more expanded stem cell research program in America.

As I said, the most fitting way to pay tribute to President REAGAN is not so much to mourn his death as to celebrate his life and to honor his service to our country. As he lies in state at the Capitol this week, a thankful American Nation will say farewell to a truly unique American.

Hon. Kay Bailey Hutchison

OF TEXAS

Madam President, I rise today to pay tribute to an American legend, President RONALD REAGAN. Like all Americans, I was saddened to learn of his passing over the weekend. I had left our Republican State Convention at a time when it was moving across the floor that he might be in his final hours. Of course, all of us started reminiscing. It was a moment of great loss, but yet a recollection of his humor, his contagious optimism, and the historic accomplishments he made for our country really were comforting and engendered so many wonderful moments.

Although I was not a Member of this body while he was in office, I have lived and served under his conservative principles and ideologies. He was in his political prime when I was just beginning in politics. During his first campaign, my husband Ray was chairman of the Texas Republican Party and spent many hours traveling with him across Texas. In 1992, I was honored to be temporary chair of the Republican National Convention in Houston, TX, when he delivered his very important message that turned out to be his goodbye to America. It was there that he left us with these final thoughts:

{W}hatever else history may say about me when I'm gone, I hope it will record that I appealed to your best hopes, not your worst fears, to your confidence rather than your doubts. My dream is that you will travel the road ahead with liberty's lamp guiding your steps and opportunity's arm steadying your way. . . . May each of you have the heart to conceive, the understanding to direct, and the hand to execute works that will make the world a little better for your having been here. . . . my fellow Americans, may every dawn be a great new beginning for America and every evening bring us closer to that shining city upon a hill.

At a time of great despair in our Nation, RONALD REAGAN came into office and restored hope. He was an unequaled champion of freedom, smaller government, and market-oriented principles. His philosophies guided our Nation to become the economic and military superpower it is today. Of course, he was often called the Great Communicator for his ability to give a rousing speech that could both rally the troops and yet make an individual in the crowd of thousands feel as if they were having a heart-to-heart talk.

Beyond his optimism, his confidence, and graceful charm was a man of action who implemented great change in the United States of America. Under his leadership, our Nation sowed seeds of prosperity and reduced regulatory burdens on small business. He lowered taxes for all Americans, including reducing the top marginal rate from an oppressive 70 percent to approximately half that, offering new incentives to create wealth and jobs and rebuild America.

He encouraged Americans to embrace their own destiny and realized that government was not the answer to social ills; people were. Good people working in concert to better their communities and their fellow man could accomplish far more than bureaucracy, from his vantage point.

Perhaps most important, President REAGAN took the steps to ultimately win the cold war. He pursued "peace through strength" and achieved an overwhelming victory that was inconceivable to a generation that was raised with fallout drills and backyard bunkers.

Who can forget the famous challenge he laid down when he cried, "Mr. Gorbachev, tear down this wall!"? They were indeed great, dramatic words but more important, words of action. Two and a half years later, what once seemed a permanent divider through the heart of Berlin was torn down piece by piece, section by section, until it was reduced to a pile of rubble.

Visitors to the Ronald Reagan Building and International Trade Center in Washington, DC, can view a section of that wall donated by the people of Berlin in honor of the President and in recognition of his leadership. The segment, which is over 9 feet high and weighs almost 3 tons, is from a section of the wall near the Brandenburg Gate where President REAGAN issued that challenge. It stands as a stark reminder of the great shift in global politics that spread freedom in Europe and encouraged new generations to pursue democracy.

Today, we again find ourselves in a fight for freedom. This generation, like their World War II grandparents and cold war parents, has been called to stand and fight for freedom. Today, we are grappling with a new threat: global terrorism, an enemy with no borders, no uniforms, no respect for traditional rules of war, and more important, no respect for human life.

World War II took bitter years of fighting and sacrifice. The cold war took decades of dedication and patience. This battle against terrorism requires all that and more. The question is: Will our generation meet the test? Will we have what it takes to win the peace? I believe we do. I believe the strength, perseverance, and patriotism that RONALD REAGAN embodied will help see us through.

In 1987, he addressed a joint session of Congress saying:

> Let it never be said of this generation of Americans that we became so obsessed with failure that we refused to take risks that could further the cause of peace and freedom in the world.

Since learning of his passing last weekend, elected officials, former Cabinet members, and newspapers across the world have been penning eulogies, remembrances, and tributes to the beloved President.

James Baker, his former Chief of Staff and Treasury Secretary:

> President REAGAN restored America's source of pride and confidence in itself. He was a wonderful person to work for and a truly great President. His willingness to stick to his principles changed the world.

Former Prime Minister Margaret Thatcher:

> He will be missed not only by those who knew him, and not only by the nation that he served so proudly and loved so deeply, but also by the millions of men and women who live in freedom today because of the policies he pursued. To have achieved so much against so many odds and with such humor and humanity made RONALD REAGAN a truly great American hero.

Secretary of State Colin Powell, who served as his National Security Adviser, said:

> President REAGAN fueled the spirit of America. His smile, his optimism, his total belief in the ultimate triumph of democracy and freedom, and his willingness to act on that belief, helped end the cold war and usher in a new and brighter phase of history.

Mikhail Gorbachev, once REAGAN's adversary, called him:

> A true leader, a man of his word and an optimist ... He has earned a place in history and in people's hearts.

Finally, his Vice President, later our President, George H.W. Bush, has been giving interviews about how much fun he was and how they had lunch every week together and sometimes they would talk substance, sometimes they would talk policy, and sometimes they would just have a good time. They were very close, and yet he never lost that laser beam focus on the big issues, the things that really mattered that would move us one step toward the "peace through strength" that was his guiding principle.

Indeed, his lasting place in the hearts of all Americans has been evidenced by the outpouring of love and admiration that we have seen across the Nation and around the world. RONALD REAGAN was a leader who touched people with his words, inspired them with his actions, and led by his example.

On November 5, 1994, nearly a decade ago, President REAGAN announced to the world that he had been diagnosed with Alzheimer's disease, the illness that would ultimately take his life. His poise and hopeful spirit, even in the face of the heartbreaking years ahead, were remarkable. He said:

> [L]et me thank you, the American people for giving me the great honor of allowing me to serve as your President. When the Lord calls me home, whenever that may be, I will leave with the greatest love for this country of ours and eternal optimism for its future.
>
> I now begin this journey that will lead me into the sunset of my life. I know that for America there will always be a bright dawn ahead.

Thank you my friends. May God always bless you.

Standing by his side through good times and bad, was his beloved wife Nancy, a beautiful woman, very slight in stature but strong as steel. Theirs was a partnership in every respect and one of the great love stories of our time. RONALD WILSON REAGAN was a great President. He left an indelible impression on our country. As we say farewell, our thoughts and prayers are with Nancy and his family. We thank them and we thank the Lord that he gave us RONALD REAGAN at a time when our country needed him the most.

Hon. John E. Sununu

OF NEW HAMPSHIRE

Madam President, as Americans gather in our Capitol and across the country to remember and pay tribute to President RONALD REAGAN, we have been provided a very special opportunity to reflect on his great achievements as our Commander in Chief, as well as the tremendous personal strength which he brought to the Oval Office.

But as we salute President REAGAN for his leadership, his integrity, and his vision, I am struck by the very personal nature of so many of these memories and stories. Whether here in Washington or out across the country, whether it is a U.S. Senator or a teacher in a small school, it seems that so many of these recollections begin with phrases such as, "I remember seeing him during his first visit to our State," or "I shook his hand when he visited our factory," or "I recall a story that President REAGAN loved to tell," or even "because of RONALD REAGAN, I chose to run for office."

These recollections are enormously personal, but I think they are a testament to the way he touched people in a very deep and unique way. He affected the lives of millions of people in America and around the world in countless encounters. Many of these encounters may have been for only a moment or two in a life that spanned decades, but his gift was in his ability to make a strong connection that had real power, the power to bridge generations, the power to last a lifetime, and the power to change a life as well.

We remember his touch, his smile, and his encouragement, not simply because when he walked into a room RONALD REAGAN conveyed a great personal warmth. That was certainly special in and of itself, and something that anyone who had the chance to meet him or see him in person would always remember, but it was because this personal connection conveyed a sense of purpose, a sense of kindness, and an enormous love for public service. That was the power of the Great Communicator, the power of the personal connection that he made.

I consider this the greatest tribute of all. Despite the myriad and extraordinary legislative and foreign policy victories of President REAGAN such as cutting taxes and reforming the Code, rebuilding our Nation's defenses, turning back the Soviets in Afghanistan, or leading the West to a lasting victory in the cold war—despite the enormous substance of these achievements, RONALD REAGAN, in the end, is not remembered first and foremost as a clever politician with great machinations of political strategy or hardball political tactics. Instead, the descriptive words that we heard here and across the country over and over again are integrity, character, courage, and leadership. These are qualities that transcend politics and qualities that transcend time. They are qualities that inspire the young and comfort the aged. They are the qualities of heroes.

RONALD REAGAN was fond of describing the heroes he saw in audiences at every speech he made or heroes he would see as he traveled across the country in every corner of America and coming from every walk of life. He saw in these men and women the very strength of character, courage, integrity, and leadership that he knew made our country unique and which kept our country prosperous and free. But by bringing these very same qualities to the Oval Office and drawing on them time and time again to guide our Nation through demanding and even dark times, he left a legacy that shined like the "city on a hill" which he knew America could be and would again become. It is a heroic legacy, and it is the legacy of a great American.

Hon. John W. Warner

OF VIRGINIA

Mr. President, I join with my colleagues in paying profound respects to our late President RONALD REAGAN, and I do so with a deep, deep sense of humility.

It is interesting, I walked into my reception room just the other day. No matter how long one is around here, I think you sort of have to go back and refresh your recollection as to what you put up in your reception room, and I found six different photographs of myself with the good fortune to be in the presence of our former great President.

I think back over my 26 years in the Senate, having had the privilege of working with all the Presidents in that period of time and, prior thereto, those Presidents when I was in the Department of Defense. Again, I say with a deep sense of respect and humility, I believe it is clear in my mind that I had the greatest opportunity to work with President REAGAN, and probably had more opportunities to be with him in a professional capacity than any other President.

I was ranking for a period of time on the Armed Services Committee and in every way supported him in his remarkable vision to build and restore the Armed Forces of the United States, which buildup, in my judgment, was a major contributor, if not the major contributor, to the eventual demise of the Soviet Union.

There are several pictures of when he visited my home, which was a farm in Virginia, a farm in an area where I grew up in the summers as a very young man. He loved coming down to the farm. My farm was adjacent to the home of former President Kennedy, and the owner at that time was Bill Clements, who was a former Deputy Secretary of Defense. I served under him as Secretary of the Navy. He and I were very close friends. I introduced him to that countryside, and he bought the Kennedy home, which is a very small, modest home, reconstructed, so to speak, and enlarged by President Kennedy and Jacqueline Kennedy, his lovely, dear wife.

President RONALD REAGAN and Bill Clements set it up so he could come down there and spend some quiet downtime. And he loved to ride horses. In those days, I had a pretty good collection of horses, and I was happy to share them with him on occasion. He rode around on my farm. I certainly enjoyed being with him on several occasions. I have one of the pictures of the two of us riding together.

I mention that because in that informal setting when there was just the two of us riding horses—I remember one time Mrs. Reagan was with us—this particular time I remember very well. We rode high up on the hill on the back of the farm. The hill has a vista down into the valley of Virginia. We checked the horses and began to talk about his great admiration for Stonewall Jackson and the various campaigns Jackson had up and down that valley during the Civil War.

I was so impressed with his remarkable knowledge of the facts of that period of history, and in later years, in other discussions with him, again he would frequently make reference to the history of the United States. His knowledge was really second to none. He had a magnificent command of American history.

But on this particular day, he reflected on a little self-deprecating humor, which he was very good at. He told me when Pearl Harbor occurred, he was a lieutenant in the Army Reserve Cavalry, again because he loved horses, he loved to ride. He promptly went down, Pearl Harbor Day or the day after, whatever the case may be, and said, "I want to be activated." And sure enough, he was eventually activated. He wanted to take, as we say in the horse world, the bit in his teeth and charge—"Send me right away out to the front."

I remember he gestured with his hand. But, no, they sent him to an old cavalry post, which was down in one of the Indian territories, and he laughed and joked and said:

When we put those posts out there, the primary thing was to secure the settlers and to hopefully strike a peaceful balance with the Indians and make life such that those territories could be developed.

But he said, "I did a little homework"—as he always did—"before I went to this cavalry post and studied who the commanding officer and the other officers were."

Well, in those days, the custom in the military, particularly the Army, was that when a soldier reported, perhaps with his wife, whatever the case may be, the commanding officer would have them over to pay their respects, to get to know each other as soon as they arrived on the post. In the old days with the covered wagons, it was a long journey. By the time they reached their destination, they were pretty well exhausted—food and otherwise. So this was a chance to introduce them.

REAGAN described the evening with great humor. He said, "I walked in and there was the little colonel. He was a rather short fellow. He was all dressed in his uniform, with his riding boots, his Sam Browne belt. I was there in my lieutenant's uniform. He greeted me very warmly. He looked at me."

And President REAGAN had a remarkable way of cocking his head. His body language was extraordinary. His walk, his mannerism, it was a great part of his character that I admired, how he conveyed so much feeling with just the way he would use his hands and his head, his stride. It emulated such tremendous confidence he had in himself.

But anyway, the colonel said, "Now, REAGAN, where have I seen you? Do I know you?"

Lieutenant REAGAN said, "No, sir, we have never met."

The colonel failed to guess. He circled back again and said, "Look here, young man, I know somehow I have seen you. Let's figure out where that was. What do you do?"

And Lieutenant REAGAN said, "Well, sir, I am involved in making movies."

Suddenly this colonel became silent. Then he said, "That is where I have seen you. You were in that movie called 'Brother Rat,' which was about the Virginia Military Institute, and that movie didn't exactly, in my judgment, properly characterize the magnificence of that institute. As a matter of fact, I think it reflected dishonor upon that institute. And I remember you were in that movie. Lieutenant, your duty on this post is over. I will transfer you."

In due course the President said he was transferred off the post, but I mention that because those of us who had the opportunity to be with him, particularly in informal settings, remember so well the magnificence of this man, the lessons he taught each of us.

Again, going back to those days in the buildup of the Soviet Union, he was very conscious of the fact that the Soviet Union was on pretty shaky financial status at that stage and that the cold war posed a threat to the United States—intercontinental missiles, the threat to the standard forces of NATO, the Warsaw Pact nations, all of which are now, save one, members of NATO.

Those of us who worked in the Senate—I remember John Stennis and Barry Goldwater, Scoop Jackson, John Tower, to name but a few—formed a group to work with the President in a bipartisan way on trying to strengthen America such that we could send a strong signal to the world, particularly the Soviet Union, that we mean business. Don't ever entertain the idea of striking out against the free world, be it the United States or our NATO allies.

And the rest is history. "Tear down that wall, Mr. Gorbachev." And that wall did come down. Those were extraordinary days I was able to share with him, and I say that with the deepest sense of humility. But I don't want to prolong my remarks.

I do want to tell one other chapter. Just a few days ago I was a part of a delegation that went over to the Normandy 60th anniversary. Senator Akaka was with me and the distinguished Senator from New Jersey and his lovely new bride were with me. So there were three of us who had some experience in World War II, of the six here in the Senate. We spent a wonderful day at the ceremonies. But the next day we took time to go out to Pointe du Hoc. It was fascinating.

There on June 6, 2004, I had been on that same spot of land 20 years before with RONALD REAGAN. I remember the delegation. Strom Thurmond led it. Three of us went with him. Of course, Senator Thurmond had made a landing on the beaches on D-day. Other Senators, the Senator from Nevada, and Howard Cannon had likewise participated in the D-day landings. Of course, I was at that time the youngster, 17 years old, in that group back in the United States getting prepared to take our training and become replacements someday. That is all history. There I stood on that ground, and he had passed away within that 24-hour period.

So I thought today I would read some of the remarks he made.

I ask unanimous consent to print the entire speech, a very short speech, in the *Record*.

There being no objection, the material was ordered to be printed in the *Record*, as follows:

PRESIDENT REAGAN'S SPEECH AT THE U.S. RANGER MONUMENT, POINTE DU HOC, NORMANDY, FRANCE, ON THE 40TH ANNIVERSARY OF D-DAY
JUNE 6, 1984

We're here to mark that day in history when the Allied peoples joined in battle to reclaim this continent to liberty. For four long years, much of Europe had been under a terrible shadow. Free nations had fallen, Jews cried out in the camps, millions cried out for liberation. Europe was enslaved, and the world prayed for its rescue. Here in Normandy the rescue began. Here the Allies stood and fought against tyranny in a giant undertaking unparalleled in human history.

We stand on a lonely, windswept point on the northern shore of France. The air is soft, but forty years ago at this moment, the air was dense with smoke and the cries of men, and the air was filled with the crack of rifle fire and the roar of cannon. At dawn, on the morning of the 6th of June 1944, 225 Rangers jumped off the British landing craft and ran to the bottom of these cliffs. Their mission was one of the most difficult and daring of the invasion: to climb these sheer and desolate cliffs and take out the enemy guns. The Allies had been told that some of the mightiest of these guns were here and they would be trained on the beaches to stop the Allied advance.

The Rangers looked up and saw the enemy soldiers—at the edge of the cliffs shooting down at them with machineguns and throwing grenades. And the American Rangers began to climb. They shot rope ladders over the face of these cliffs and began to pull themselves up. When one Ranger fell, another would take his place. When one rope was cut, a Ranger would grab another and begin his climb again. They climbed, shot back, and held their footing. Soon, one by one, the Rangers pulled themselves over the top, and in seizing the firm land at the top of these cliffs, they began to seize back the continent of Europe. Two hundred and twenty-five came here. After two days of fighting only ninety could still bear arms.

I thought I would read part of this very moving speech. It starts midway in the speech and lays out the history of the brave men who participated in D-day landings, and in particular the Rangers.

Behind me is a memorial that symbolizes the Ranger daggers that were thrust into the top of these cliffs. And before me are the men who put them there.

These are the boys of Pointe du Hoc. These are the men who took the cliffs. These are the champions who helped free a continent. These are the heroes who helped end a war.

Gentlemen, I look at you and I think of the words of Stephen Spender's poem. You are men who in your "lives fought for life ... and left the vivid air signed with your honor."

Forty summers have passed since the battle that you fought here. You were young the day you took these cliffs; some of you were hardly more than boys, with the deepest joys of life before you. Yet you risked everything here. Why? Why did you do it? What impelled you to put aside the instinct for self-preservation and risk your lives to take these cliffs? What inspired all the men of the armies that met here? We look at you, and somehow we know the answer. It was faith, and belief; it was loyalty and love.

The men of Normandy had faith that what they were doing was right, faith that they fought for all humanity, faith that a just God would grant them mercy on this beachhead or on the next. It was the deep knowledge—and pray God we have not lost it—that there is a profound moral difference between the use of force for liberation and the use of force for conquest. You were here to liberate, not to conquer, and so you and those others did not doubt your cause. And you were right not to doubt.

You all knew that some things are worth dying for. One's country is worth dying for, and democracy is worth dying for, because it's the most deeply honorable form of government ever devised by man. All of you loved liberty. All of you were willing to fight tyranny, and you knew the people of your countries were behind you.

The presiding officer, with his distinguished military service, understands, as do I, those words. The vision that he had not only for America but the free world, the strength of his convictions, the strength of his actions—it reestablished the strength of the Armed Forces which today have carried on, since that speech, with missions in the Balkans, Afghanistan, Iraq, and other areas of the world.

It takes time to restructure and build up a military. I find this President is doing just that, President Bush. I am happy and privileged to be a part of the team that is working in the Senate to achieve that. As a matter of fact, the bill for the Armed Forces in 2005 is the current business before the Senate.

Before I leave the speech, I was privileged, because of Senator Thurmond and the other Senators with me, we were not more than 15, 20 yards from the President when he gave the speech, right on this little spit of land that I visited 2 days ago.

And suddenly you saw the Secret Service men sort of break and go off and quickly perform the duties they have to protect the President. There was this figure which came up the cliff unexpectedly, unannounced, because there had been a reenactment with men of the Armed Forces currently on duty to scale the cliffs for all to see. So that part was over. Yet suddenly there appeared another individual who had scaled the cliffs and the Secret Service tackled him. I remember the President, always composed, stood there and looked at this scene. Suddenly, an aide went over and whispered in his ear and the President went over and grasped this man and gave him a hug. He was one of the original rangers who scaled that cliff. He wanted to show the President and the world that he was still able to do it. He had bits and pieces of his own uniform on.

Last, what are the ways in which we can honor this great President? Our hearts are so filled with gratitude and a sense of deep remorse at his loss. But it was his wisdom and foresight that strengthened America's military, and I think that requires some special recognition. I don't have all the answers now. I will be happy to work with others.

I am not trying to be the sole author of anything, but some thought has been given to the Department of Defense—and I went back last night and did a little research, and this morning I called the former Secretary of Defense Melvin Laird, a very dear and valued friend, under whom I served as Secretary of the Navy, and we reminisced about our days and some of the initiatives he took. He mentioned one specifically. There was some thought about naming the Department of Defense Building for President Eisenhower. After some very considerable thought, the decision was made not to do that. One of the main reasons—and I remember this very well—is that that building stands as a symbol of the bipartisanship that must be present as we work with the men and women in the Armed Forces. I strive to achieve that, as does the presiding officer and many others.

I am proud of the committee on which I have served—Armed Services—for 26 years, under a series of chairmen and ranking members. We have always tried to put partisanship aside and we have been successful. But it is important that the building be viewed as bipartisan.

Therefore, I remember Secretary Laird saying the naming of the building was not, in his judgment, what we should do. He confirmed that this morning, and I shared that feeling. He said he conceived the idea of naming a corridor for General Eisenhower. There is a technical thing there. The corridor is named after him as a general of the Armed Forces, a five-star general. His picture in uniform and many other pieces of memorabilia are along the corridor by the Office of the Secretary of Defense. Previous Secretaries of Defense have honored the commanders in chief, the Presidents. So there is a corridor set aside for the commanders in chief, with portraits of every President since George Washington. Five living Presidents are there. You have Ford, Carter, George Herbert Walker Bush, President Clinton, and our current President Bush. All of their portraits are there. The way the Department of Defense has handled this in the past is to treat with equality the Presidents and their portraits, the recognition being bipartisan in nature in that building.

We will have to put our minds together to see how best to do it. There is no question that RONALD REAGAN gave a tremendous impetus to the concept of defending this Nation against missiles—missiles fired in anger or accidentally. Those things happen. He had the star wars concept. I was on the committee and we looked at this program. We began to do the initial work in the Congress to give support to the President's program. But eventually, from the standpoint of technology and costs, we looked at different ways to achieve our defense against missiles. It started way back under President REAGAN when we put emphasis on this situation. Some of the thinking preceded President REAGAN on how to defend this country against missiles. Today, we don't have a thing to interdict an intercontinental ballistic missile that would be fired in the direction of our 50 States. That is a separate matter.

Therefore, I think we have to give a lot of careful thought and be ever mindful of how we recognize our commanders, with five still living, in terms of their contributions to the defense of this country. We will come up with an idea. I hope we can, in some way, appropriately recognize this great President for his extraordinary accomplishments in strengthening America.

I conclude my remarks with the deepest sense of humility and gratitude toward the recollection, modest friendship, and the teachings I received from this great President.

Hon. Thomas R. Carper
OF DELAWARE

Mr. President, today and this week, as we pause to reflect on the life of RONALD REAGAN and his role in leading our Nation and the State in which I lived when I was in the Navy, I was thinking back and talking with my children about my first recollection of RONALD REAGAN.

My first recollection was when I was about their age, early in my teenage years, seeing him on television. I may have seen him earlier than that as a kid in the movies, but I do not remember. I remember fully—and the presiding officer is probably too young to remember this—a television show called "Death Valley Days" and watched later, I remember, a television show called "General Electric Theater." He was the host and introduced each week's segment. My family would watch those shows, not religiously, but regularly. I enjoyed them as a kid growing up in Danville, VA.

At the time, RONALD REAGAN, who, I guess, was maybe in his fifties at that time, or maybe forties, had a reasonably successful career in motion pictures, certainly a lot more successful than any of us, except for former Senator Fred Thompson. But he had a reasonably successful career. We were in this in-between place where television was coming of age and playing a role with respect to "Death Valley Days" and "General Electric Theater."

I remember my first thoughts of him were that he was a nice-looking guy, a handsome kind of rugged fellow. He seemed to be amiable. He came across as amiable and exuded a certain warmth and also a sense of sincerity that came across clearly on that small television screen that we owned back in those days.

I remember being surprised in 1964. I think I was 17 years old. I was about to enroll in Ohio State University. I was going to be a Navy ROTC midshipman. I was at the age of 17 a young Republican for Barry Goldwater. I do not know how I ended up on this side of the aisle. Churchill said, "If you are young and not liberal, you don't have a heart; if you are old and not conservative, you don't have a brain." Somehow I ended up as a 17-year-old supporting Barry Goldwater.

I remember watching the convention which was in San Francisco at the Cow Palace. Ironically, another one of our colleagues was there as a Goldwater supporter, too. She was there as a "golden girl." Her seat is right behind me. It is ironic we both ended up where we are in the U.S. Senate. I remember watching on television the 1964 Republican Convention and actually watching the Democratic Convention that year.

I remember being surprised to see RONALD REAGAN speak and address the convention. I knew he had been a film star. I knew he played a role on these two television shows I watched as a kid growing up, but I had no idea. I heard he had been involved in the Actors Guild, sort of a labor union for actors, but I had no idea he was involved in politics to any extent and that he would end up with a major role at that convention speaking on behalf of Barry Goldwater.

He came across in this speech a bit differently than he did in his other roles on television, but he did project a great deal of sincerity, a lot of conviction.

He also suggested a good-naturedness and a certain warmth I have always found refreshing and endearing about him.

We learned that evening, as we watched that speech, that this was a man who had some strong convictions and gave a powerful speech and one who got a lot of people to think about him as a future leader. Not long after that, he was elected Governor of California, served there for the most part with distinction and then ran against Gerald Ford for President, lost and came back a couple of years later, ran against Jimmy Carter and won.

It is interesting, conventions were different then. The first convention I ever remember paying much attention to was in 1964. It was a convention with serious questions about who was going to be the President.

We had the Republicans. Conservatives were supporting Barry Goldwater and we had the Rockefeller Republicans. There was a lot of give and take, and real primaries. It was hard fought right up until the convention.

I remember in 1968 I was a supporter for Eugene McCarthy who was running for President. I respected both McCarthy and Goldwater because they were standup guys. They were willing to take tough positions and not mince their words. I respected them both for that. Conventions were different than they are today.

Although I was impressed by the speech that then-citizen RONALD REAGAN gave, I never imagined he would be Governor of California, and I certainly never imagined he would be President of the United States. I never imagined I would be a Congressman, Governor, or Senator, either. I am probably more surprised by that than I am about him ending up as Governor and President.

As luck would have it, he ended up as President of the United States and I ended up here serving with our presiding officer, and that is something I enjoy very much.

Before I was Governor, I served in the House of Representatives for 10 years. RONALD REAGAN was elected President in 1980; I was elected to the House in 1982. I had a chance to interact with him from time to time during limited opportunities as a Democratic Congressman. He had qualities I admired all those years ago when he was hosting those television shows. His warmth, his sincerity, his good humor, those were qualities he possessed in the real world off the TV screen.

Sometimes the folks we see or admire on television and film or other venues do not turn out to be quite the same when we meet them in person. He was very much the same.

While I did not always see eye to eye with him on environmental issues, for example, and I had concerns about the budget deficits we were starting to rack up, and questions about deploying space weapons, star wars, and the way we conducted our business in Central America, there was a lot he wanted to do and sought to do with which I did agree. He was an early proponent of welfare reform. He was a guy who believed work should pay more than welfare. We have all heard of the earned income tax credit. He was a major proponent of the earned income tax credit because he felt people who worked ought to be better off than folks who were on welfare.

He presided over big tax cuts in the early eighties, 1981, and later on, faced with ever-growing tax deficits, he presided over some of the largest tax increases that were adopted in our Nation's history.

He was a staunch opponent of communism, but a fellow who could reach out not just across the aisle but across the world to Gorbachev to become friends, and they embraced one another at the end of their tenures as they together helped to change the world in a better way.

I find in RONALD REAGAN that he was someone who would stake out a position; he would adhere to that position with his convictions for as long as he could, and at the end, if he had to change, he would. He was willing to do that, but he did not back off easily or readily. He was willing in the end to compromise.

In reacting to folks in my own State in Delaware this week who asked me for my reaction to what he was like, I said, well, whether or not you liked the man's policies, it was hard not to like the man.

Since his death, there has been a fair amount of conjecture about what we should do to pay tribute to him and his memory. Some people have suggested we ought to rework Mount Rushmore and find a way to put his image on Mount Rushmore. We have had a few people suggest maybe RONALD REAGAN's picture should be on the $10 bill instead of Alexander Hamilton. I heard our Republican leader suggest yesterday that maybe we should rename the Pentagon in honor of RONALD REAGAN. I do not know that those are good or bad ideas. I have not given those a lot of thought.

I ask we consider a couple of other legacies that might even be more important and more enduring. One of those deals with the disease that dogged him for the last years of his life, Alzheimer's disease, a disease my mom also suffers from. She lives in Kentucky. I visited her over the weekend. She does not remember much. Actually, she remembers a few things that happened a long time ago, but she does not have any recollection of RONALD REAGAN and all of those years we watched him on television when I was a kid growing up.

My mom is going to be 82 years old this August and my hope is she will live to be as old as RONALD REAGAN. I do not think that is likely, but that would be wonderful if it happened. My mom is 1 of 4 million people in the world today who suffers from Alzheimer's disease. It was something we saw the first signs of 5, 6, 7 years ago, and we knew where it was leading. Her mom suffered the same fate. Her grandmother had suffered the same fate as well.

While there are roughly 4 million Americans today who suffer from Alzheimer's disease, by the year 2020 we are told there could be as many as 14 million Americans who suffer from Alzheimer's disease. It is a tough disease not so much for the person who suffers from it but certainly for their families and those who love them and who are unable to have the kind of relationship we once did.

I know Senator Mikulski is going to be leading the effort, I think with Senator Bond, for us to focus anew as a Congress, as a Senate, on providing meaningful increases in funding to find a cure for Alzheimer's disease; not simply a way to treat the symptoms, but a way to stop it dead in its tracks. I commend them for their actions and I stand fully ready to support them. I hope others will as well.

The other legacy I suggest that may be as important or we may be inspired to address and do something about other than dealing with Alzheimer's disease is civility. I am not the first person who has noticed this of late, but there has been a huge loss of civility not only in Washington, DC, but shortly after I heard of President REAGAN's death I was flipping through the radio channels in my car and I came across one of these right-wing talk shows. There was pure vitriol coming out of the speaker on my radio. I find it hard to listen to that stuff so I turned it off. I find it hard to watch the television shows anymore because it seems there is no meaningful discourse; they are really shouting matches.

RONALD REAGAN, for whatever faults he may have had, was a civil person, he was a gentleman, and at a time when that kind of behavior characterizes too little of what not only goes on here but what takes place in politics throughout our country, he is a good role model in that the way he treated people was the way he would like to have been treated. It is a lesson that was good and meaningful then and it is one we can certainly take again today.

I have heard our own leader, Tom Daschle, begin to speak of late of a new civility, and we need a new civility. We need some civility, not going through the formalities, but treating one another the way we would want to be treated; not just in this Chamber, not just in this Capitol, but throughout this country, even in a Presidential election year.

Hon. Peter G. Fitzgerald
OF ILLINOIS

Mr. President, as one of the two Senators from Illinois, I am very proud of RONALD REAGAN and his contributions to this country. RONALD REAGAN is the only American President who was, in fact, born in Illinois. Many people think of Abraham Lincoln as having been born in Illinois, but he was actually born in Kentucky and later moved there. Of course, I think there is no question that RONALD REAGAN will join Abraham Lincoln as one of our Nation's greatest Presidents. I only want to say a few words about him.

I didn't actually serve in the Senate when he was President. I didn't ever have the opportunity to get to know him. I did, however, get the opportunity to meet him once as a very young man, when I was about 20 years old or so and he was campaigning for President in 1980.

But my first real recollection of him came from watching his address on television in 1976 at the Republican National Convention. He had lost the primaries to incumbent President Gerald Ford but had nonetheless had a very strong showing. He gave a speech at that 1976 convention that literally brought down the house and fired up the delegates. I remember watching that at home and thinking, What an outstanding leader. You could see that this man certainly still had a great contribution to make.

He won against all the odds. All the pundits and many of the commentators dismissed RONALD REAGAN. They thought he was too old. They thought he was too conservative to run and be elected President in 1980. But he proved them all wrong.

I think a pivotal moment came in 1980 during his primary elections. At that time he lost the Iowa caucuses and he had a lot of pressure on him to win the New Hampshire primary. Many of us will recall that New Hampshire primary debate where he grabbed the microphone as others tried to shut it off. He grabbed the microphone and said, "I am paying for this microphone, Mr. Green." He wanted his other opponents to be allowed the opportunity to speak at that debate, as opposed to just having a one-on-one debate with George Bush, who later became his Vice President and succeeded him as President.

I remember watching that Nashua, NH, debate in 1980 from the basement television room of my fraternity house in Hanover, NH, at Dartmouth College. I was very much paying attention to that primary because it was happening in New Hampshire where I was attending college. I will never forget seeing RONALD REAGAN in that debate and his remarkable performance.

Later, in 1980, I had the opportunity to meet him when he came to Illinois to campaign for a U.S. Senate candidate in October, about a month before REAGAN was elected President. I was an intern on the campaign of a fellow by the name of Dave O'Neal who was running for the Senate in Illinois. He actually lost. But as an intern on that campaign, I had the opportunity to meet RONALD REAGAN and to welcome him into the back room before we had the dinner in honor of Dave O'Neal.

I will never forget RONALD REAGAN. Everybody called him Governor at that time. That was the most recent office he had. They didn't call him President REAGAN yet. But when he walked into the holding room, the bartender immediately told him, "Governor REAGAN, we have squeezed some fresh oranges for you. We have some freshly squeezed orange juice for you. Would you like some of this?"

Governor REAGAN looked at him and said, "I'll take it if you put a little vodka in that."

I was struck immediately at the time by his charm and his sense of humor and his relaxed nature, even though he was just a few weeks out from the election day in what everyone thought would be a very close election with President Carter. But, of course, as we know, RONALD REAGAN went on to win in a landslide.

He had a remarkable career. He was an enormous source of inspiration to me as I was finishing college and going on to law school. I was very proud at the time to be a Republican and to have him as the leader of our party, but also to be an American and have him lead our country and represent us in the world. I thought he handled himself with incredible poise and dignity.

His achievements are monumental. You will recall that he had few allies in Congress. The other party controlled both Houses of Congress while he was President. Yet he was able to work his will through Congress by calling upon the American people to lobby Congress for some of his important initiatives, such as lowering taxes. President REAGAN succeeded in lowering the highest tax rates, which at that time were up to 70 percent. He dramatically lowered the tax rates and unleashed a flurry of economic activity that is still with us today.

He went on to achieve major arms control agreements, and also, with the threat of his willingness to spend whatever it took to defend our country—his will in that regard, his sheer will to succeed in defeating what he saw as an evil ideology, communism—in ending the cold war with the Soviet Union, he ultimately succeeded in doing that. No one has a greater claim on ending the cold war than RONALD REAGAN and, as Margaret Thatcher has said, he did so without firing a single shot.

I think one of his greatest accomplishments occurred in his second term, and that was the simplifying of the Tax Code. If you recall, we went for a time where we got rid of a lot of the Swiss cheese loopholes and deductions that are in our Tax Code. We dramatically simplified the Tax Code, collapsed the rates, and it held for a few years. We have gone back now and allowed all the special interests to fill up the Tax Code with all sorts of special interest loopholes and giveaways to politically connected interests. Sometimes I wish we were rereading what RONALD REAGAN said at the time about the necessity of cleaning up that Tax Code.

One of the most cherished treasures in the State of Illinois is the boyhood home in which

Ronald Reagan grew up in the twenties, in Dixon, IL. That home has been purchased and lovingly restored by a foundation and by members of the Dixon, IL, community. It is a wonderful place for Americans who want to pay their respects to Ronald Reagan and his legacy, to go by and visit on Interstate 88 in Dixon, IL, just off Interstate 88. I certainly hope a lot more Americans who are interested in the history of Ronald Reagan will visit that home.

Ronald Reagan himself went back to visit it, I believe, after he left the White House even. He has recounted many tales of his growing up there.

He was actually born in Tampico, IL, in an apartment above a commercial building in downtown Tampico, and later moved to Dixon, IL. Some of his fondest memories are of growing up in Dixon, along the Rock River.

Of course, many people will remember Ronald Reagan talking about one of his proudest accomplishments in life, saving 77 people from drowning over the 7 years that he was a lifeguard along the Rock River in Dixon, IL.

If you go to Dixon, IL, you can see this wonderful small town that shaped Ronald Reagan, his character, his values, his common sense, his midwestern way of thinking, of looking at the world. I don't think that ever left him.

There is also an interesting story not many people are aware of, but President Reagan wrote about this in his biography. He graduated from Eureka College, about 130 miles south of Dixon, in Illinois. After graduating from college, he went back to Dixon and he applied for a job in the sporting goods department, I believe, at a Montgomery Ward store in Dixon, IL.

Guess what happened. Montgomery Ward turned down Ronald Reagan for that job. That set him off in different pursuits, and he ultimately went to Iowa and became an announcer, did Cubs games from a regional radio station there. But he wrote in his biography he wonders what would have happened had he actually gotten that job at the Montgomery Ward store in Dixon, IL. He suspected he might never have left Dixon, IL.

We need to thank somebody who failed to hire Ronald Reagan at Montgomery Ward in 1932, I think, because it was that little twist, that little turn in his life that turned out for the better, not only for him but certainly for our entire Nation and the world.

I ask that we not forget the example of Ronald Reagan and his cheerful optimism about our country and our future. No one could communicate their thoughts as well as Ronald Reagan, in my judgment. I know of no equal he had in public service in terms of communicating with people. He was an inspiring leader.

Ronald Reagan came to the Presidency of a self-doubting nation, a nation more suspicious of its power than inspired by its possibilities. And he understood—as magnificently as any American leader—the restorative force of faith, of conviction, of pride. He was the Great Communicator, not because he mastered the sound bite, but because this midwestern man of 10,000 handwritten letters knew that words matter—words with simple, self-evident integrity, words that reach into the vagueness of a volatile democracy and perfectly describe the essential goodness of our character.

Ronald Reagan returned us to ourselves. He did not work miracles. But he emboldened us to see the grace of God in the destiny of our great Nation. He enabled us to hear the still, small voice in the clamor of great historical conflicts. He reminded us to treasure the simple miracles of life, laughter and love.

This man, who survived into the 21st century, embodied as perhaps none other the panoramic sweep of America's 20th century. Reagan was born in the small town of Tampico, IL. It was 1911, the year of the first coast-to-coast airplane flight, a 49-day ordeal with 69 stops and 16 crash landings. It was also the year of the first aircraft landing—crude though it was—on a ship anchored in San Francisco Bay. A series of ropes stopped the aircraft. Ninety years later, on March 4, 2001, the United States christened the Navy's newest Nimitz-class aircraft carrier, the USS *Ronald Reagan*, a 90,000-ton nuclear-powered fighting ship, and the pride of the most powerful navy in the world.

Ronald Reagan fundamentally changed the face of American politics—and profusely contributed his name to the new political lexicon. What American before or since Ronald Reagan has become the popular namesake for a theory of economics, a political and electoral sea change, and a decisive partisan crossover? I speak of Reaganomics, the Reagan revolution, and Reagan Democrats.

The man was that large. He had strong and distinct views which he was able to communicate with remarkable effectiveness. He had an irresistibly winning personality and was irrepressibly optimistic. Though the establishment of both political parties often ridiculed his beliefs, the people somehow always seemed to have faith and confidence in him. In fact, they loved as perhaps they have loved no other President in modern history.

Conventional intellects and comfortable pundits were aghast when President REAGAN spoke so freely of evil in the world. In a world where evil is neatly banished because it is too judgmental, the moral declarations of RONALD REAGAN were inevitably revolutionary. The Great Communicator understood perfectly well that communication without a moral compass becomes all talk. And so we are the heirs of a more civilized and less menacing world because RONALD REAGAN had the courage to maintain firm beliefs and to stand up for those beliefs.

As a Senator from Illinois, I am proud to remark briefly and comparatively about another great son of Illinois, the only President to be elected from Illinois, Kentucky-born but Illinois-settled Abraham Lincoln, whom our history honors as few others. Lincoln and REAGAN both grew up humbly and gained a natural comfort with people from all walks of life. They were both frequently underestimated by opponents who imagined themselves intellectually, culturally or socially superior. They both possessed an equanimity and fortitude that kept them serene while navigating treacherous waters. They both loved the United States of America. And they both cherished American freedom and staked their public lives on the resolute promotion of it—for Lincoln, against the forces of disunity and enslavement at home, and for REAGAN, against a godless imperial tyranny abroad. I am proud to hail from the State of Illinois.

When we finally measure the worth of a statesman, the words of political or ideological adversaries can speak volumes. And here RONALD REAGAN—a statesman with many more converts than implacable enemies—is a shining beacon in his own shining city. When President Clinton announced in 1996 that "the era of big government is over," it was homage to the durable influence—across the political landscape—of RONALD REAGAN's faith in the American people. When Mikhail Gorbachev recently said of RONALD REAGAN, "he was sincere," he captured with fitting simplicity the worldwide power of the American dream in the hands of America's finest dreamer.

RONALD REAGAN stayed the course, throughout and after his Presidency, until a progressive illness consumed him. Indeed, sliding irretrievably into forgetfulness a decade ago, RONALD REAGAN remembered to say goodbye to his beloved American people.

> When the Lord calls me home, whenever that may be, I will leave with the greatest love for this country of ours and eternal optimism for its future.
>
> I now begin this journey that will lead me into the sunset of my life. I know that for America there will always be a bright dawn ahead.
>
> Thank you my friends. May God always bless you.

May God rest his soul, and may God bless Nancy Reagan, who is also from Illinois, and all the Reagan children and their families.

Hon. Richard J. Durbin

OF ILLINOIS

Mr. President, I join my colleague from Illinois in paying tribute to the late President RONALD REAGAN.

Today the Senate passed by an overwhelming vote a resolution commemorating RONALD REAGAN for his service to America and recalling his legacy.

There has been a lot said on the floor about President REAGAN. I come to this task with a little different perspective than some. Were it not for RONALD REAGAN, I wouldn't be in the Senate today. I say that because I made three vain and futile attempts to be elected to public office. In 1982, I ran for the House of Representatives against an incumbent Republican Congressman. Were it not for the sorry state of the economy in Illinois after the first 2 years of President

REAGAN's Presidency, I would have lost. But because of the economy and the troubles faced at that moment in time, I was successful in my campaign against a long-time Republican incumbent Congressman.

I will not mislead anyone before making these remarks. I will tell you that while a Member of the House of Representatives during the 6 remaining years of President REAGAN's Presidency, there were very few things I agreed with in reference to him. In fact, over 90 percent of the time we didn't see eye to eye. I had some very strong philosophical differences with President REAGAN on economic policy, foreign policy, and many other things. But I will tell you this: He was an extraordinary person, and I think even those of us who disagreed with him politically respected him very much.

I recall when I was elected in one of the largest new classes of Congressmen since Watergate, in 1982, that President REAGAN and Mrs. Reagan invited all of the new Members of the House of Representatives and their spouses to come for a dinner at the White House. It was an amazingly heady experience to walk in as Congressmen-elect with our wives and shake hands with the President and Mrs. Reagan, realizing full well that most of the people in the room were new Democratic Congressmen who had been running against President REAGAN and his policies. But he was gracious to a fault and could not have been more cordial to all of us who gathered that evening. One of my great memories of that period of time between the election and being sworn in was sitting there in the White House at this dinner hosted by President REAGAN and Mrs. Reagan. At the same table was my Senate colleague, then-Congressman Mike DeWine, and his wife Fran, who had made the trip from Ohio for that special dinner with the REAGANs and new Members of Congress days after she had given birth to a little baby girl, whom she brought to the same dinner in a basket which she had right next to the table. We have laughed about it all the time, because obviously after 23 years that little girl has grown up to be a remarkable young woman.

But those are some of the memories I have of President REAGAN opening the door and welcoming in some new Congressmen who had spent months running against him and his policies.

The same thing held true when it came to his State of the Union Addresses. I can remember so many different times when I marched to the House of Representatives Chamber for the State of the Union Address by President REAGAN. After a while I came to understand what the rules were. The rules were these: You didn't have a chance as a Democrat to say anything critical and be successful the night of President REAGAN's speech. He had such a magical style and was so affable and friendly and approachable that after he concluded his State of the Union Address, the best for the loyal opposition was to wave and leave the stage because he was so good. He was one of the best. We did learn that after 24 or 48 hours had passed, perhaps a closer look at what he said could lead to some constructive criticism. But we knew right off the bat when President REAGAN took to the floor of the House of Representatives for the State of the Union Address and walked up those stairs, the best thing the loyal opposition could do was to be quiet.

There was another aspect of RONALD REAGAN which I miss so much. It is part of the political life which unfortunately we don't have enough of. He was President in an era of some great people—Tip O'Neill, Speaker of the House of Representatives, and Bob Michel, Republican minority leader from Illinois. They brought to this business of politics a certain humanity and civility which we have lost almost completely.

I can recall the bitter battles we had on the floor of the House of Representatives with President REAGAN over very contentious issues and the debates going on for days. Ultimately, someone would prevail, and many times it would be President REAGAN and his position. Without fail, when it came to those critical votes, Tip O'Neill, then-Speaker of the House, the leading Democrat, would pick up the phone, call the President and congratulate him. It was a gesture, but it was an important gesture to say that, frankly, we have both given it a good fight; the decision has been made; now let us move on to the people's business.

President RONALD REAGAN understood that, Tip O'Neill understood that, and Bob Michel understood that. I wish our generation of leaders could understand that more, that even though we disagree, and disagree with a great deal of conviction, we should try to look for that human side we can all share. I think time and again President REAGAN did that. I commend him for it.

Even though you have disagreed with him during the course of the debate, when it was all over, you knew you would be treated with respect.

Time and again, my wife Loretta and I would go down to the White House for the Christmas party, the barbeques and picnics. It was always a warm welcome and greeting, even though the President was of a different party where there were very serious differences.

I would like to reflect, too, for a moment on the former First Lady, Nancy Reagan. She has been a pillar of strength since it was announced that the late President was suffering from Alzheimer's; 10 years watching the man she loved the most of any in the world slip into darkness. She said in a few interviews since President REAGAN passed away, the worst part was the advancing years and not being able to share memories anymore because President REAGAN was inflicted with Alzheimer's disease. That takes a toll.

We have had friends who have gone through it. It takes a special commitment and sacrifice to make it through that terrible illness. My heart goes out to Nancy Reagan and her family, all of them, for what they have endured for 10 years, standing by the former President while he was afflicted with this disease.

My colleague Senator Carper mentioned earlier that many people are now talking about tributes to President REAGAN, and he is deserving. Despite my differences with him politically, I voted for the renaming of the Washington National Airport in his memory. I thought that was appropriate for someone who had served our Nation as President of the United States. Now people are trying to think of other things they can do. They are kind of upping the ante: Well, you know, not the 50-cent piece, maybe the $10 bill; no, maybe Mount Rushmore. I would like to suggest to them the most enduring legacy for this President would be to help others in his name. I can't think of anything more important to ask for when the time comes for those to consider what to do in his memory than the contribution suggested by our colleagues Senators Mikulski and Bond, one which I think is worthy of our immediate consideration. They called for the establishment of the RONALD REAGAN Alzheimer's Breakthrough Act of 2004. They believe we are near a breakthrough in treating Alzheimer's and they want us to put special attention and special resources and special efforts in that regard. That not only will serve the memory of President REAGAN and his courageous family who stood by him, but it will also serve to help 4.5 million Americans inflicted with Alzheimer's disease today, and their husbands, wives, children, and their loved ones who stand by helplessly at their side as they drift into the darkness of this dreaded disease. That would be such a great tribute to President REAGAN. I hope we can do it on a bipartisan basis with the civility and humanity which President REAGAN demonstrated during the course of his life.

I might also add that the First Lady's commitment to stem cell research is an exceptional statement on her part. She has broken with some members of the Republican Party on this issue. I know her position is controversial, even within this administration, but she understands, as many do, that unless we are committed to medical research, including stem cell research, the chances that we can successfully deal with Alzheimer's, diabetes, spinal cord injuries, and other terrible afflictions will be diminished. I salute the First Lady and I hope we will, in recognition of her commitment and in memory of President REAGAN, also decide we will step forward in this critical area of medical research involving stem cells.

I am honored that President REAGAN was a friend, at least in passing, on a political basis. I am happy he came from Illinois and happened to believe that perhaps his midwestern roots might have helped him in his various careers. It certainly helped him serving this country as President.

He had an amazing record of victories. I know because I was on the losing end of a lot of those campaigns. I campaigned for his opponents with little or no success. He carried 44 States in the first election and 49 States in the second. Probably few Presidents in history have had a mandate that substantial when they were reelected. It is a tribute to the fact that America loved that President, America wanted RONALD REAGAN to serve, and he served our Nation so well.

Hon. Susan M. Collins

OF MAINE

Mr. President, over the past few days, more than 100,000 Americans have stood in line in California for 12 hours or even more to pay their respects to President RONALD REAGAN. This great show of respect and affection will be repeated during the coming days in Washington.

This overwhelming outpouring cannot be explained by merely citing the traits for which he was so well-known—his likability, his wit and optimism, his courage when attacked by a would-be assassin's bullet or, at the end of his life, by a devastating disease, or even his skills as the Great Communicator. Americans are standing in line because of President REAGAN's ideas and the principles and convictions that gave those ideas their power: The God-given right to freedom, responsibility for one's own actions, and charity toward others. The very ideas that are the foundation of this great Nation were the foundation of President REAGAN's character.

President REAGAN became President at a time when the world had begun to question the strength of that foundation. It was a time when freedom, balanced by personal responsibility and justified by charity, was in danger of becoming just one of the many ways in which human society could be organized. Rather than appease or accommodate communism, he confronted it and exposed its moral bankruptcy.

President REAGAN emboldened freedom-loving people everywhere—those behind the Iron Curtain and those in danger of being enveloped by it—and gave them faith and strength. He believed, as he said in his first inaugural address, that no weapon in the arsenals of the world is so formidable as the will and moral courage of free men and women. He was right.

President REAGAN became President at a time when America had begun to question its place in the world and the values upon which this great Nation was built. He opened the gate of the American spirit. He tore down the wall of doubt.

RONALD REAGAN was a great communicator because he had something great to communicate. He was the right man for his time; and now he belongs to all time.

He will be missed, but President REAGAN's ideas will always be part of the American experience.

Hon. Larry E. Craig

OF IDAHO

Mr. President, I have, for the last day, listened to a good number of my colleagues reminisce about the late President RONALD REAGAN, many of them quoting from his speeches, many of them quoting from books written about him, about his phenomenal life, and his phenomenal presence in this city as one of our Presidents. So I would guess that by this moment nearly everything that can be said about RONALD REAGAN has been said but, then again, not everyone has said it.

I find myself in that situation in these moments just prior to the adjournment of the Senate and hours before a coffin bearing President RONALD REAGAN will arrive at the rotunda of our great Capitol.

What I might do for just a moment is reminisce about a couple of personal experiences I had the privilege of having with the late President that, to me, speaks volumes about the gentleman's personality, his style of Presidency, and what he meant to my State of Idaho.

Idaho, by its conservative character and its independence, was always a strong REAGAN State. It spoke out loudly for the President. It voted in large numbers for the President. There was never a question where Idahoans would be when it came to supporting RONALD REAGAN for his Presidency.

My relationship with him began at the very time he came to Washington. I was a freshman in the House of Representatives in the winter of 1981. Both President REAGAN and I were elected at the same time. I was one of those of the large class of 54 Republican freshmen who entered the U.S. House, many of them because of the strength of RONALD REAGAN, and we all became known as Reagan babies. I suspect that is a title that at the age of 58 I still bear with some pride. Because we came at a time when we had a President who was speaking of change; and the American people were wanting it, demanding it, and his Presidency embodied it.

The situation I want to relate for the *Record* this afternoon occurred during the first budget process of the Reagan administration. David Stockman, a Congressman, had just been appointed Director of OMB. Of course, the major tax cut that our President was so well known for—that began to stimulate the economy and turn the American people back into entrepreneurialism—was all at hand. But there were deficits. So David Stockman came up with the idea that we should sell off our strategic minerals stockpile.

Well, that is something you do not hear talked about hardly at all today, but following World War II, Congress had passed legislation saying that we should stockpile silver and magnesium and titanium and zinc and a variety of other metals in case we got in another war, so we would have these supplies of metals available for industrial purposes.

By 1981, it was largely determined on the part of the Reagan administration and David Stockman that they were just not necessary any longer. It was probably true that some Members of Congress believed the same thing. So when the announcement of the sale of these stockpiles became public—and the money then from their sale was to return to the Treasury, and that money would offset some of the deficits that might occur as a result of the tax cuts—the silver market plummeted. The price of silver on the world market dropped because the large supply of silver being held by our government was going to enter the market at some point. So the market out there was beginning to adjust and prices fell.

Because Idaho at that time was a primary silver producer, not only did prices fall in Idaho, but when they fell, many of our mines closed. There were 400 or 500 miners—men and women—out of work in the Silver Valley of Idaho, known as the Coeur d'Alene mining district, that was in part a direct result of this announcement.

That was my congressional district. I had people out of work. This was largely still an old line labor Democrat stronghold in north Idaho, and the hue and cry was very loud. These men and women were out of work because of President RONALD REAGAN.

I had thought that if RONALD REAGAN really understood the impact of what he was doing, he might change his approach. But because it was a directive from OMB, because it was a part of the budgetary policy of this administration, my small voice simply was not getting heard.

I appealed one evening in a conversation to the then-Secretary of the Interior, Jim Watt. I said: Secretary Watt, how do I get to the President? How do I tell my story, our story, Idaho's story, about this particular problem?

He said: Well, Larry, you have to get to the President directly. Obviously, David Stockman is not interested in hearing your story. The sale of the strategic metals, the sale of the stockpiles, is his idea. He's not going to be your champion. So if you're ever down at the White House, see if you can get the President's ear.

Well, freshmen Congressmen do not often go to the White House. But because of the key tax votes that were coming up, I got invited to the White House to visit with RONALD REAGAN. I had presented on one, small sheet of paper, on one side, a very brief, clear explanation of the impact of the sale of the silver stockpile out of the strategic metals stockpile on the people of Idaho. I put it in an envelope, and wrote across it "To President RONALD REAGAN," and stuck it in my pocket.

Now when I was down at the White House conversations went forward. At the end of the conversation, I said: Mr. President, here is a note I would like to have you read. It's important to my people in Idaho. By your actions, you have put 500 Idahoans out of work.

He said: Really?

I said: Yes, selling off the strategic metals.

He smiled and said: We are?

Well, that did not surprise me. The longer I am here in Washington, I know not everybody knows every detail about everything. That is why you hire and have around you competent people, and Presidents are certainly no different than many of us.

He kept the note. I saw it go into the breast pocket of his suit coat. A day and a half or two later, I got a call from the White House saying: Congressman Craig, can you come down and visit with the President about your problem in north Idaho and the sale of the silver stockpile?

My, I was impressed. I went to the White House. There in the Oval Office was the President and David Stockman, the Director of OMB, the man who had established the policy of selling off the stockpiles to bring money to the Treasury. We discussed it at length. In fact, David Stockman and I had a small debate in front of the President about the pros and cons of doing so.

What I said at that time was: Mr. President, I am not opposed to you selling off the stockpile of silver, but it's how you are approaching it, and how you are approaching it has had a dramatic impact on the market. As a result of that, it has dropped the price of silver worldwide, and men and women in Idaho are now out of work.

He said: Well—in his inevitable way—let me think about that.

A week later, there was a very small but very important announcement that no longer would there be any more sale of the silver stockpile, and, of course, the prices came back and the men and women in north Idaho went to work.

What is the message? The message is that when this President, RONALD REAGAN, understood the impact of an action—if it were hurting people or impacting them adversely, or if it were doing something that was against his market ideas and his philosophical belief in limited government and that government should not be the arbiter nor should government infringe upon the well-being of citizens—he would make changes. And he did. And of course, I have told that story many times in Idaho. It was very clear to Idahoans that the market changed because RONALD REAGAN saw what he was doing or saw what his administration was doing and was willing to make a very important change to impact people's lives.

Last, I remember coming to the U.S. Senate in 1990, certainly after President REAGAN had left this city. The first office I took in the Hart Building had on a conference wall a very large map of the world. It filled the whole wall, and it still had the Socialist Republics of the Soviet Union written across that map. That will tell you how old it was in 1990. I remember at the time looking at that map and saying: Thank you, RONALD REAGAN. You have made that map of the world obsolete. You as the President—not singlehandedly but certainly by the force of your beliefs and by the force of your efforts—have made the Soviet Union obsolete in such a way that it simply withered and died, almost without a whimper. And that, of course, is one of the great legacies of our President, and many of our colleagues have spoken about that.

We are not going to let revisionist historians suggest that the Soviet Union would have crumbled anyway. There was a reality they had to face. The reality was RONALD REAGAN and the national resolve of this country in the cold war, built on the strength and the beliefs of a great President by the name of RONALD REAGAN, that we not only could overcome communism but we would, in essence, arm ourselves and build a military ready and capable of defeating the Soviet Union. That combination of efforts, put together with his willingness to deal with Gorbachev and others, obviously changed the dynamics of world politics and the environment I grew up in as a child, known as the cold war.

I will attend the ceremony in the Chamber tonight, and I will mourn the loss of RONALD REAGAN. But more important, I will celebrate. I will celebrate a great President, a President who came to our country's call at the right time in our history, to lead us with optimism and enthusiasm and vision in a way few Presidents have. So while I will certainly miss the presence of the man, I celebrate his record and the history that will be written about him.

I send my prayers and the prayers of my wife Suzanne to Nancy Reagan and all of the Reagans. They stand with a great legacy they are obviously very proud of, as we all are as Americans.

To RONALD REAGAN I say: Thank you, you built a place in history that is well deserving of the actions you took as President of the United States.

Hon. Frank Lautenberg
OF NEW JERSEY

Mr. President, I wanted to be sure to have an opportunity to make some comments about President REAGAN before we went out of session tonight. I will take the opportunity to do so right now.

I join with my colleagues, so many of whom have already spoken, in tribute to our Nation's 40th President, RONALD REAGAN. My first term in the Senate coincided with the last 6 years of his Presidency. I had the opportunity to work with him on several occasions. As someone who came from modest beginnings and a working-class family, I understood the fact that he rose from his humble beginnings to become one of the crucial world leaders. He was respected greatly. I had a chance to work with him on several occasions, not the least of which was something as simple as raising the drinking age to 21 across the country, thereby saving thousands of families a year from having to mourn the loss of a young person in their household. The bill was signed in the morning at the White House, and I was pleased I was able to return from a convention in San Francisco in time to be there and share those good moments with President REAGAN and then-Secretary of Transportation Elizabeth Dole.

We did a lot of good for families across America with that legislation, and also offered support to say to those who would pollute our environment, "If you pollute, you must pay to clean it up," and that was Superfund. It had a very important beginning in those days.

President REAGAN is appropriately being remembered for his overpowering sense of optimism and rock-solid faith in the fundamental goodness of America. Many of his actions stand as examples of ideas that we ought to consider as we carry out our responsibilities in government. There was no doubt that he was the Great Communicator, and his ideas and his words will long be remembered.

I just returned yesterday from the D-day celebration and commemoration in Normandy. No one will ever forget President REAGAN's speech 20 years ago at Normandy commemorating the 40th anniversary of the D-day invasion; it will be permanently etched in our memories. Or his poignant remarks when the space shuttle *Challenger* exploded, and how he helped America recover from that terrible national tragedy. Or who can forget his insistence that helped break the iron grip of the Soviet Union on millions of people around the globe?

President REAGAN was known for his ideological zeal. But the interesting thing about him at the same time was that he ultimately was a pragmatist. Perhaps the clearest example of his pragmatic side is what happened after he pushed through a massive tax cut in Congress in 1981. One thing that President REAGAN disliked enormously was Federal budget deficits. He thought the idea of borrowing from future generations was truly repugnant.

On the campaign trail in 1980, he promised he would work to balance the budget. When he took office, he argued that a tax cut was necessary to stimulate the economy. He believed the Federal Government would end up with more, not fewer, revenues. But when the revenues didn't materialize as predicted, and the Federal Government began running huge annual budget deficits, his pragmatism took over and he followed his 1981 tax cuts with tax increases that were necessary in 1982 and 1984, determined to reduce the burgeoning budget deficits. His tax increases were a tacit admission that the plan wasn't working as expected. He was pragmatic enough to change the course.

His personality was so unique for someone in that high office. As Mikhail Gorbachev wrote in a *New York Times* op-ed page, President REAGAN was ultimately someone with whom you could negotiate. His suggestion was that he was human enough, he was collegial, funny, and gracious, and you could discuss serious issues with him and accomplish goals.

One of President REAGAN's last great acts of public service was to acknowledge 10 years ago to the American people and to the people of the world that he was suffering from Alzheimer's disease.

He handled his affliction with his customary grace, saying that he was sharing the news with the public in the hope that it might "promote greater awareness of this condition." That was a courageous thing to do. He went on further to say that he hoped it might encourage a clearer understanding of the individuals and families who are affected by it. He really brought a focus on the disease that ultimately consumed his remaining years.

One truly meaningful way that we can honor President REAGAN is to pursue the kind of research that might produce a treatment, or even a cure, for Alzheimer's disease and a host of other illnesses, something his beloved wife Nancy has called for. Since we witnessed the pain of the deterioration of this great individual, we have to be mindful of that for the future.

His life yielded so many more things, besides those obvious ones, during his service as President of the United States.

Hon. Lincoln D. Chafee

OF RHODE ISLAND

Mr. President, I pay tribute to President RONALD REAGAN, a man for whom I had the utmost respect.

A strong, principled leader, President REAGAN used his optimism and humor to help the Nation feel better in a post-Vietnam, post-Watergate country coping with an energy crisis and high inflation.

He brought strong leadership and could relate to people from all walks of life very, very easily. Democrats controlled the House during both of his terms, and the Senate during his last 2 years in office. In order to advance his priorities, he had to bridge the partisan divide and work with members of the other party. He was also very proud of his good personal relations with Tip O'Neill and other Democratic leaders. The proof of his appeal was his ability to carry a Democrat stronghold like my State of Rhode Island in the 1984 election. He was the last Republican Presidential candidate to do so.

With tremendous vision and dignity, President REAGAN will ultimately be remembered for ending the cold war and promoting freedom and democracy throughout the world in a peaceful way.

In closing, I recall a large color photograph on my father's office wall. It is a picture of merriment, Senator Robert Dole having just cracked a joke, with President REAGAN, Alan Simpson and John Chafee standing by, smiling from ear to ear.

Later, my father obtained a copy of the photo and at a later meeting with the President, slid it down the table toward him and asked if he would sign it. Without hesitation, REAGAN penned a line and slid it back.

It read simply, "John—some times it is fun, isn't it?"

RONALD REAGAN, with unfailing good humor and optimism, made Americans feel good about their country again. I believe that is his lasting legacy.

The Chafee family offers our sincere condolences to Nancy, and the Reagan family.

Hon. Christopher J. Dodd

OF CONNECTICUT

Mr. President, I rise today to offer words in memory of America's 40th President, RONALD WILSON REAGAN.

RONALD REAGAN was elected President on the same day that I was first elected to the U.S. Senate. I was somewhat of an anomaly that year, being one of only two freshman Democrats elected to the Senate, compared with 16 Republicans.

Over the years, there is no question that when it came to matters of policy, RONALD REAGAN and I disagreed, in a very fundamental way, on a great many occasions.

But in today's very partisan atmosphere, it is easy to forget that personality can be much more important than agreements and disagreements. Many of the qualities that distinguished RONALD REAGAN—as a President, as a leader, as an individual—went beyond policies and politics.

RONALD REAGAN was one of our Nation's most personable Presidents. His congeniality, wit and trademark sense of humor could bring a smile to the face of even the most ardent political opponent. And he had the uncanny ability to communicate his thoughts to the American people.

As a member of the opposite side of the political aisle, I had a particular appreciation for RONALD REAGAN's openness. As we all know, President REAGAN was a man of great conviction. It wasn't easy to change his mind. But he was willing to sit down and talk. He was open to listening to views that were different from his own, even if he ultimately chose to disagree with them. RONALD REAGAN was able, as the saying goes, to disagree without being disagreeable.

Though we had our differences on many issues, I would never doubt for a minute RONALD REAGAN's commitment to this Nation, just as I don't believe he doubted the patriotism of his political adversaries. RONALD REAGAN believed deeply in our country and in its values, and in its place in the history of humankind. He correctly saw the former Soviet Union, with its regime of repression, imprisonment, and stifling of the individual spirit, as antithetical to everything in which we believe. He presided over a historic time period during which we witnessed the beginnings of a dramatic, global political sea change.

RONALD REAGAN was a leader who reflected the optimism and spirit of this great Nation. At the time he was elected President, our country was experiencing a crisis of confidence. Many wondered if America's best days were behind it. RONALD REAGAN had an unflagging belief in America, and he helped restore a sense of possibility in our land.

As a society, we often elevate our public figures to practically mythological proportions, and our Presidents are no exception. Toward the end of RONALD REAGAN's life, though, we were reminded of his humanity. All of us, particularly those of us who have watched a loved one struggle late in life, were inspired by the dignity, grace, and courage with which he and his family battled a terrible and devastating disease—a disease that ultimately took RONALD REAGAN, in the words of his wife Nancy, to a place where she could no longer reach him.

Many tributes have been and will be paid to President REAGAN's memory. But I can't think of a greater tribute than to commit our Nation to fully researching the causes of, and cures for, diseases like Alzheimer's that cause such great suffering for such great numbers of people.

At this difficult time, my heart goes out to Nancy and the entire Reagan family. America celebrated with you on so many happy occasions. This week, we all join you in your sorrow.

Hon. James M. Jeffords

OF VERMONT

Mr. President, I join my colleagues in remembering our Nation's 40th President, RONALD REAGAN, who passed away last weekend at his home in Bel-Air, CA.

Of course, much has already been said, both in this Chamber and in the media, about the legend of his large life. His career in movies, his entry into politics and, of course, his two terms as President during a most tumultuous time have been well documented in the past several days.

By all of these accounts, RONALD REAGAN was a most admired politician, and while he and I had our policy differences, I have always shared in that admiration.

RONALD REAGAN held true to a strong conservative philosophy, which often made it hard for the two of us to find common ground. I was a Member of the House of Representatives during his 8 years as President, and you might say I was often a thorn in his side. We were on opposing sides when it came to many issues, most notably tax cuts and funding for the arts.

But through all of our sometimes heated discussions and debates, it was so evident to me that President REAGAN held a deep and abiding passion for his country, and an equally deep conviction for what he believed was right.

As Americans take time this week to honor the life of President REAGAN, it is that passion and conviction that they will remember and reflect upon. I believe, that those memories of our Nation's 40th President will inspire our future leaders.

I extend my condolences to his wife Nancy, and to the entire Reagan family on the passing of President RONALD REAGAN. May the memories of his life's accomplishments sustain them in their time of grief, and may the Nation's prayers bring them comfort.

Hon. Blanche L. Lincoln
OF ARKANSAS

Mr. President, I rise today to pay tribute to former President RONALD WILSON REAGAN, our Nation's 40th President.

Like many Americans, I admired President REAGAN's eternal optimism and his belief in America and her people.

I am struck by the numbers of mourners who have paid their respects to our former President. The outpouring of respect and grief is a testament to the great impact that he had on so many Americans. I am sure that one of the reasons so many have taken time to honor President REAGAN is because of the great optimism and purpose that he showed. His trust in the fundamental decency and goodness of the American people is a guide and inspiration to us all.

I admired his sense of civility and his ability to disagree with his opponents without being disagreeable. He fought hard for the policies in which he believed, but after the fight, he shook hands and moved on. We need more of that kind of statesmanship in Washington today. And I hope my colleagues will join me in trying to follow his example.

During one of our Nation's greatest challenges—the cold war—President REAGAN was a strong voice against the enemies of freedom. His leadership and vision helped us to overcome our enemies.

In the final years of his life, he and Mrs. Reagan were an example of the kind of sacrifice and love that we should all seek to emulate. Mrs. Reagan's quiet dignity and support for her husband during the most difficult of times should be an inspiration to us all.

My thoughts and prayers go out to his wife, Nancy, his sons, Michael and Ronald, Jr., and his daughter, Patti.

RONALD REAGAN lived a full life and was a great American. His contributions to the American political system and to our way of life will not soon be forgotten.

Hon. Debbie Stabenow
OF MICHIGAN

Mr. President, I rise today to pay tribute to RONALD REAGAN, our Nation's 40th President. First, my condolences and prayers go out to Nancy Reagan, the Reagan family, and all of those who are mourning his passing.

RONALD REAGAN was an optimist. He was the best kind of optimist—a living example of the fulfillment of the American dream. From a small midwestern town, he rose to become leader of the free world and was respected around the world by both our allies and our Soviet bloc opponents alike.

President REAGAN was called the Great Communicator for a reason. Many of his speeches touched the heartstrings of all Americans. Whether it was his speech at the Berlin Wall or his 1984 tribute to those who died on D-day, President REAGAN always conveyed a positive, optimistic sense of our shared destiny. His words will long be remembered.

President REAGAN loved America, and this love for our country shaded every word he spoke to the Nation as President. He always wanted our country to be the "shining city on a hill."

I also pay tribute and convey my genuine respect to our former First Lady Nancy Reagan, a woman whose unwavering commitment to her husband not only provided a testament to their love but also extended hope and empathy to countless Americans who share in the role of caregiver.

As we begin now to consider ways to pay proper tribute to our admired former President, let us go beyond the erecting of a monument or the etching of a portrait. Instead let us act to help the many Americans who needlessly suffer from the debilitating effects of Alzheimer's disease.

We should increase research funding for Alzheimer's and expand stem cell research, which Nancy Reagan supports.

I am pleased to be a co-sponsor of a Mikulski-Bond bill that will double our investment in Alzheimer's research and refocus our efforts to find a cure. This bipartisan measure, if passed, would leave a lasting legacy to President REAGAN.

Earlier this month, I joined with 57 other Members of this body, both Republican and Democrat alike, to urge President Bush to broaden the current Federal policy regarding stem cell research. By expanding stem cell research beyond those stem cells derived by August 9, 2001, we will take the necessary first step of helping millions of Americans who are plagued by Alzheimer's—Americans, who like President REAGAN, live out their daily lives traveling an unknowable journey of solitude.

If we allow the medical experts to do stem cell research, we can begin the work Mrs. Reagan so steadfastly promotes: finding a cure to this devastating disease.

To find a cure of Alzheimer's would indeed be the greatest tribute we could ever give to President REAGAN.

In this time of grief, let us evoke President REAGAN's gentlemanly service, swift wit, jovial candor, and unconditional patriotism. With differences in philosophy and politics aside, let's all praise a man whose decorum and distinguished character exemplified the office for which he held.

Hon. Kent Conrad

OF NORTH DAKOTA

Mr. President, I want to take a few moments today to join my colleagues in celebrating the life of our 40th President, RONALD WILSON REAGAN.

In many ways, RONALD REAGAN embodied the American dream. He was born in the small town of Tampico, IL, and grew up 30 miles down the road in Dixon, another small town. His was a normal, middle class American family, and he was the all-American boy-next-door: Good looking, popular, an actor, and an athlete. And from that modest background he fulfilled the American democratic ideal that anybody can grow up to become President of the United States.

That ideal—that anyone can grow up to become President—captures America's optimism, so it is fitting that the word that comes most to mind when remembering President REAGAN is exactly that: optimism. President REAGAN was an incurable and infectious optimist when it came to America. By insisting that, as he said, it was morning again in America, he connected with Americans, lifted their spirits, and restored their confidence in our future.

This power to communicate and connect with Americans from all walks of life was central to his success as President. He could sway skeptics and charm supporters with his simple eloquence and self-deprecating wit. People came to know him and feel comfortable with him; and they were moved by his simple, clear messages. President REAGAN perfected the art of selling his policies to the American people and using that ability to pressure Congress to work his will. Not surprisingly, the Great Communicator, as he came to be known, left office with the highest approval rating of any recent President.

President REAGAN was one of the truly larger than life figures of the post-World War II era. He brought a new conservative philosophy to the White House, and he championed freedom at home and abroad. One of the reasons for his success, I believe, was his willingness to compromise, to put aside partisan politics and ideological purity to do what was right for the country. When his 1981 tax cuts caused deficits to skyrocket, President REAGAN supported tax increases in 1982 and 1983 to contain the damage. After tagging the Soviet Union as the evil empire, he negotiated historic arms control treaties with the Soviets, coining the famous phrase "trust but verify" in the process. He had, as his chief of staff Howard Baker once put it, "a capacity to surprise."

And throughout it all, he was a wonderful man, someone who you couldn't help but enjoy being with. I met with President REAGAN several times during the last years of his Presidency. The last time I was with him, President REAGAN was telling two or three of us in the White House an Irish story full of warmth and wit. I believe that best describes President REAGAN himself—a man of endearing wit and great personal warmth.

As America mourns his passing, my thoughts and prayers are with Nancy and the rest of President REAGAN's family and many, many friends.

It is my hope that their memories of his life, laughter, and legacy will be of some small comfort in these days and weeks ahead.

Hon. Jon S. Corzine

OF NEW JERSEY

Mr. President, on Saturday, June 5, 2004, President RONALD WILSON REAGAN, the 40th President of the United States, passed away after a decade-long battle with Alzheimer's disease. I extend my deepest sympathies to the members of his family, who have suffered a terrible loss, and I want them to know that Americans throughout our Nation, regardless of their political party or ideology, share in their loss and mourn with them.

RONALD REAGAN was an exceptional national leader who loved this country and its people. He will long be remembered for his infectious optimism and his faith in America's future. To President REAGAN, America was always a "shining city on a hill"—a beacon of hope for all mankind. He understood just what a great country America is, and always remained a committed advocate for the ideal of freedom that helps define us as Americans.

President REAGAN was known as the Great Communicator, and he richly deserved the accolade. Few politicians, if any, have had his ability not just to connect with the American people but to inspire them. His speeches didn't just make a point, they touched a chord. He talked to Americans in a powerful and personal way.

As is widely understood, RONALD REAGAN had strongly held views about public policy, from his support for lower taxes to his strong anticommunism. But as is less widely appreciated, President REAGAN was not inflexible or dogmatic. He actually was a practical and pragmatic leader who was willing to adjust his approach, sometimes dramatically, when circumstances called for change.

For example, after pushing through a large tax cut at the start of his Presidency, he reversed course and increased taxes when the deficit started to explode. Perhaps most important, after denouncing the Soviets as an evil empire, he was willing to work closely and cooperatively with Mikhail Gorbachev, helping not only to end the cold war but to liberate millions of people and change the course of world history. In doing so, he was not following his party. He was not following the polls. He was following his conscience. And the entire world community owes him a deep debt of gratitude for his vision and his leadership.

There were many issues about which I strongly disagreed with President REAGAN. But I always had great respect for him personally and for the way he conducted himself while in office. President REAGAN knew how to disagree without being disagreeable. He knew that those in the other party were not enemies. He knew that, at the end of the day, we are all Americans and, though we may disagree about particular policies, we all share a love of our country and a commitment to its future.

President REAGAN's life was marked by his fundamental personal decency and his sense of dignity. That was never more evident than when he announced to the world his struggle with Alzheimer's disease in 1994. His and Nancy Reagan's courageous fight against this debilitating disease brought a new awareness to the devastation that accompanies this illness. I hope it also will bring a new commitment to do what it takes to find a cure for this horrible affliction.

In conclusion, Americans throughout our Nation are saddened at the passing of President REAGAN, and our hearts go out to his family. RONALD REAGAN was an extraordinary man whose impact on our Nation, and our world, will be felt for generations to come. Today, we join together to honor his memory and to give thanks for his historic service on behalf of the country he loved so deeply.

Hon. Jon Kyl

OF ARIZONA

Mr. President, Robert Robb is one of the great columnists in American journalism today, and his tribute to RONALD REAGAN is among his best work. I ask unanimous consent to have the following article printed in the *Record*.

There being no objection, the article was ordered to be printed in the Record, as follows:

[From the *Arizona Republic*, June 9, 2004]
MY FIRST FAN LETTER WAS SIGNED "REAGAN"

(By Robert Robb)

RONALD REAGAN wrote my first fan letter.

When he announced for president in 1976, I was editor of the student newspaper at Occidental College in Los Angeles.

The Los Angeles Times had developed an obsessive dislike for REAGAN. And it pounded on his announcement speech, denouncing it and him for superficiality and a lack of specifics.

Of course, it's standard fare for announcement speeches to enunciate broad themes. And the only thing that would have unhinged the Times more than a lack of specifics from REAGAN would have been if he had been specific.

And so I wrote a column for the student newspaper having a bit of sport with the Times' hypocrisy and disequilibrium.

Not much later, I was astonished to receive a letter from REAGAN. Apparently being defended in a student newspaper was an unusual enough event to catch the attention of his campaign.

REAGAN thanked me for my "generous words," and allowed that "a great part of my pleasure was your masterful handling of the Times."

That purposeful understatement was characteristic of REAGAN in political combat. He was far more inclined to give his opponents a gentle and humorous poke in the ribs, rather than a rhetorical knife in the stomach—a restraint he maintained even as the invective and bile against him mounted.

Bill Buckley invented modern American conservatism—a sometimes uneasy blend of anti-communism, free-market economics and traditional cultural values inspired and informed by religious faith. Barry Goldwater launched it as a political movement.

But RONALD REAGAN embodied the conservative movement. He was the glue that held its factions and strands together long enough, for a time, to be politically triumphant.

This was no small feat. American conservatism is more naturally a dissenting movement than a governing one.

Yet REAGAN not only governed, he transformed the country, indeed the world.

What began as REAGAN Democrats are now simply Republicans, and the Republican Party now competes with the Democratic Party for majority status, rather than the semi-permanent minority role the party seemed consigned to before REAGAN.

To compete with Reaganism, Democrats had to overcome their legacy from the 1960s and 1970s, a belief that there was as much wrong as right about America. Democrats reconciled themselves to America's essential goodness, as well as its defining institutions and values: free markets, enterprise, faith and family.

Bill Clinton was a reaction to Reaganism, and today's Republican Party, unfortunately, is as much a reaction to Clintonism as it is a legitimate heir to Reaganism.

Winston Churchill believed that history was the story of great men altering its course. In his History of the English Speaking Peoples, writing about Alfred the Great, who united much of modern-day England in the ninth century, Churchill described his "sublime power to rise above the whole force of circumstances."

As much as REAGAN dominated and transformed the domestic political landscape, his greatness—his sublime power to rise above the whole force of circumstances—was in the way he managed the Soviet Union and communism.

Early in his presidency, REAGAN described the Soviet Union as an evil empire and said it and Marxism-Leninism would be deposited on the "ash heap of history."

This was denounced by foreign policy sophisticates at the time as naive and dangerously provocative.

Yet he quickly embraced Mikhail Gorbachev, who gained power in 1985, and his perestroika reforms. This made conservatives highly nervous, and they openly wondered whether REAGAN was being had.

But REAGAN, having lived through the Hungarian and Polish rebellions, intuited that the Soviet Union could not both liberalize and remain intact.

REAGAN also knew the moment to apply pressure, as in 1987, when he stood before the Berlin Wall and, against the advice of his entire foreign policy team, famously called upon Gorbachev to tear it down.

A few years later, I was in Berlin, after the wall had been torn down figuratively, but not yet physically. You could travel freely in eastern Berlin, but it was like Dorothy stepping from black-and-white into the colorful land of Oz, only in reverse—from the vibrant feel of a free people into the still-stale desolation of the repression of the human soul.

You could visit the wall and even take a blow against it yourself. So, I clawed loose a few chunks and brought them home.

They're mounted now, pieces of history's sadness and joy. I can never look at those chunks of concrete without thinking about RONALD REAGAN, a champion of freedom for our time.

Hon. John Edwards

OF NORTH CAROLINA

Mr. President, I rise today to pay tribute to the late President RONALD REAGAN.

We were of different parties and very different political philosophies but I respected him as a strong leader—a man of principle and dignity. He was also good-natured and affable, never letting political differences drag him down into bitter partisanship.

I was always impressed with President REAGAN's ability to communicate and persuade and his talent for soothing our Nation in difficult times. In good times and bad, he sought to appeal to the best in all of us, to our hopes and better instincts, not our doubts and fears. And while he enjoyed a good political fight, he never demonized his opponents or accused those who differed with him of being unpatriotic. RONALD REAGAN seemed to understand that we could disagree without being disagreeable and that we all love our country, even as we debate the best way to move toward a more perfect union. All of us can learn from his example.

As we pay tribute to our 40th President, this man who rose from humble beginnings to the greatest heights, I offer my condolences to Nancy Reagan and the Reagan family. I join my colleagues in saying farewell to RONALD REAGAN, a modest man who was larger than life.

Thank you, President REAGAN, for your service to our Nation and for the important example you set for us all.

Hon. Robert C. Byrd

OF WEST VIRGINIA

Mr. President, on Saturday, our Nation lost a good man and a great American, the 40th President of the United States, RONALD WILSON REAGAN.

A former sports announcer, actor, television performer, and Governor, this man from a small midwestern town was eventually elected to our Nation's highest office, not once, but twice, in landslide victories. His was a success story, an American success story. He demonstrated that the key to the American dream is still determination, hard work, and perseverance. He did it by appealing to our "best hopes," not our "worst fears."

Historians will study and evaluate the impact of the Reagan administration—his role in ending the cold war and the results of his domestic policies.

What is beyond debate was his uncanny ability to connect with the American people. He knew where he wanted to take the country and attempted to do it with remarkable determination and charm. He restored a much needed sense of optimism in America, and he did it with a cheerfulness that was absolutely contagious.

His optimism was prevalent and penetrating and inspiring even during the darkest moments of his administration. With the *Challenger* explosion, we grieved and despaired, but when President REAGAN spoke of how those courageous astronauts reached out and "touch{ed} the face of God," suddenly all of us realized that we, as a country, would make it through this grievous hour, and the American adventure into space would go on. He was truly the Great Communicator.

I came to know and work with Mr. REAGAN from a unique and important perspective. I was the leader of the opposition party in the U.S. Senate during both of President REAGAN's terms.

From this position, I came to understand and appreciate, probably even more than his strongest supporters, his hold on the American people, and the importance of the leadership that he provided.

In fact, I found him to be as charming in person as he was when speaking to an audience or appearing on television.

Never once did I hear him engage in personal attacks on his challengers.

When we disagreed, which was more often than not, it was always in civil tones. He was always smiling, patting you on the back, asking you about your family, and wishing you the best. You simply could not help but like him. He seemed not to confuse differences of opinion with differences of ideals or values. After all, he liked to point out, "we are all Americans."

That is the way American politics is supposed to be. That was the decency of RONALD WILSON REAGAN. He might consider me a political opponent, but never a personal enemy. Just as I understood his difficulties as the leader of the free world during 8 years of trial and turmoil, he understood my role as the loyal opposition.

As much as I admired and respected him when he was President, never was my appreciation for him and his wife Nancy stronger than in their dealing with his last and greatest struggle—the struggle he eloquently and heartbreakingly called the "journey that {would} lead {him} into the sunset of {his} life"—his battle with Alzheimer's disease. He and Nancy confronted this cruel, crippling disease with an openness and dignity that inspired a Nation.

Mr. President, my wife Erma and I extend our most heartfelt condolences to Mrs. Reagan. She has been an inspiration to America, gracefully fulfilling the role of loyal, loving spouse even as she has watched her greatest love drift away into the fog of Alzheimer's. In the years when they should have been able to enjoy the warm memories of their storybook life together, she endured personal emotional tortures that are difficult to imagine. In these last years, the vigilance and caring she displayed throughout their marriage led her to become an outspoken advocate for medical research, a role for which she has earned the immense respect and gratitude of the Nation.

A Sunset Fancy

(A poem by an unknown author)

I saw the sun sink in the golden west
No angry cloud obscured its latest ray;
Around the couch on which it sank to rest
Shone all the splendors of a summer day,
And long—though lost of view—its radiant light
Reflected from the skies, delayed the night.

Thus when a good man's life comes to a close,
No doubts arise to cloud his soul with gloom;
But faith triumphant on each feature glows
And benedictions fill the sacred room;
And long do men his virtues wide proclaim,
And generations rise to bless his name.

MESSAGE FROM THE HOUSE DURING ADJOURNMENT

At 3:26 p.m., a message from the House of Representatives, delivered by Ms. Niland, one of its reading clerks, announced that the House has agreed to the following concurrent resolution:

S. Con. Res. 115. Concurrent resolution authorizing the use of the rotunda of the Capitol for the lying in state of the remains of the late RONALD WILSON REAGAN, 40th President of the United States.

SUBMISSION OF CONCURRENT AND SENATE RESOLUTIONS

The following concurrent resolutions and Senate resolutions were read, and referred (or acted upon), as indicated:

By Mr. FRIST (for himself and Mr. Daschle):

S. Res. 373. A resolution relative to the death of RONALD WILSON REAGAN, a former President of the United States; considered and agreed to.

By Mr. FRIST:

S. Res. 374. A resolution honoring President RONALD WILSON REAGAN; considered and agreed to.

By Mr. ALLARD:

S. Con. Res. 118. A concurrent resolution expressing the sense of Congress that an artistic tribute to commemorate the speech given by President RONALD REAGAN at the Brandenburg Gate on June 12, 1987, should be placed within the United States Capitol; to the Committee on Rules and Administration.

SUBMITTED RESOLUTIONS
SENATE RESOLUTION 373—RELATIVE TO THE DEATH OF RONALD WILSON REAGAN A FORMER PRESIDENT OF THE UNITED STATES

Mr. FRIST (for himself and Mr. Daschle) submitted the following resolution; which was considered and agreed to:

S. RES. 373

Resolved, That the Senate has heard with profound sorrow and deep regret the announcement of the death of the Honorable RONALD WILSON REAGAN, a former President of the United States, and a former Governor of the State of California.

Resolved, That in recognition of his illustrious statesmanship, his leadership in national and world affairs, his distinguished public service to his State and his Nation, and as a mark of respect to one who has held such eminent public station in life, the Presiding Officer of the Senate appoint a committee to consist of all the Members of the Senate to attend the funeral of the former President.

Resolved, That the Senate hereby tender its deep sympathy to the members of the family of the former President in their sad bereavement.

Resolved, That the Secretary communicate these resolutions to the House of Representatives and transmit a copy thereof to the family of the former President.

SENATE RESOLUTION 374—HONORING PRESIDENT RONALD WILSON REAGAN

Mr. FRIST submitted the following resolution; which was considered and agreed to:

Whereas RONALD WILSON REAGAN, the 40th President of the United States, was born on February 6, 1911, in Tampico, Illinois, to Nelle and John Reagan and raised in Dixon, Illinois;

Whereas as a lifeguard at Rock River in Lowell, Illinois, a young RONALD REAGAN saved the lives of 77 swimmers;

Whereas RONALD REAGAN enrolled in Eureka College where he played football, acted in amateur theater, and graduated with a bachelor's degree in economics and sociology;

Whereas RONALD REAGAN landed his first job as a radio announcer for WOC in Davenport, Iowa, and went on to become a popular sports announcer;

Whereas RONALD REAGAN launched a movie career that spanned 50 movies, including his most famous role as the football legend, "The GIPPER";

Whereas RONALD REAGAN, who received more fan mail than any other actor at Warner Brothers Studios except Errol Flynn, served as president of the Screen Actors Guild from 1947 to 1960;

Whereas on March 4, 1952, RONALD REAGAN married his great love, Nancy Davis, who was to become his lifelong confidante and companion;

Whereas RONALD REAGAN was the father of 4 children: Maureen, Michael, Patti, and Ronald Prescott;

Whereas RONALD REAGAN hosted the popular television series "GE Theater" from 1954 to 1962;

Whereas in 1962, RONALD REAGAN switched his party affiliation from Democrat to Republican and 2 years later delivered a major televised speech in support of Presidential candidate Barry Goldwater;

Whereas in 1966, RONALD REAGAN won the governorship of California and in 1970 was reelected to a second term;

Whereas Governor REAGAN campaigned for the Republican nomination in 1968, and again in 1976;

Whereas on July 16, 1980, the former Governor won the Republican nomination and on November 4, 1980, won the United States Presidency in a landslide vote;

Whereas President REAGAN appointed the first woman to the United States Supreme Court, Justice Sandra Day O'Connor;

Whereas on March 30, 1981, only 2 months into his Presidency, RONALD REAGAN survived an assassination attempt and upon meeting Nancy in the hospital, quipped with characteristic good humor, "Honey, I forgot to duck";

Whereas President REAGAN delivered on his promise to cut taxes for American workers in 1981, and achieved the historic tax cuts of 1986 which overhauled the Federal tax code and reduced tax rates for almost all taxpayers, including removing 6,000,000 Americans from the tax rolls;

Whereas under President REAGAN's leadership, inflation fell, interest rates declined, and by the seventh year of his Presidency, the stock market hit an all-time high;

Whereas President REAGAN presided over the longest economic expansion in the history of the United States until that time and rebuilt the national defenses of the United States;

Whereas President REAGAN won reelection in 1984 carrying 49 out of 50 States—one of the biggest electoral victories in the political history of the United States;

Whereas during summit meetings with Soviet Union President Mikhail Gorbachev in December 1987, President REAGAN signed a treaty to eliminate intermediate-range nuclear forces;

Whereas President REAGAN's steadfast opposition to communism, his unshakeable resolve to defeat the "Evil Empire", and his secure belief in government for and by the people, led to the collapse of the Berlin Wall and victory in the Cold War;

Whereas President REAGAN's belief in freedom as a God-given right of all peoples led to a democratic revolution across Central America; and

Whereas RONALD WILSON REAGAN, father, husband, actor, and dedicated public servant, restored the pride, optimism and strength of the United States and earned the deep respect and affection of his fellow citizens: Now, therefore, be it:

Resolved, That the Senate notes with deep sorrow and solemn mourning the death of RONALD WILSON REAGAN.

Resolved, That the Senate extends its heartfelt sympathy to the wife and family of President REAGAN.

Resolved, That the Senate commends the former President for his Presidency and its many accomplishments.

Resolved, That the Senate calls on all the people of the United States to reflect on the record of the 40th President of the United States during this national period of remembrance.

Resolved, That the Secretary communicate these resolutions to the House of Representatives and transmit a copy thereof to the family of the former President.

SENATE CONCURRENT RESOLUTION 118—EXPRESSING THE SENSE OF CONGRESS THAT AN ARTISTIC TRIBUTE TO COMMEMORATE THE SPEECH GIVEN BY PRESIDENT RONALD REAGAN AT THE BRANDENBURG GATE ON JUNE 12, 1987, SHOULD BE PLACED WITHIN THE UNITED STATES CAPITOL

Mr. ALLARD submitted the following concurrent resolution; which was referred to the Committee on Rules and Administration:

S. CON. RES. 118

Whereas the people of the United States successfully defended freedom and democracy for over 40 years in a global Cold War against an aggressive Communist tyranny;

Whereas President RONALD WILSON REAGAN's demonstration of unwavering personal conviction during this conflict served to inspire millions of people throughout the United States and around the world to seek democracy, freedom, and greater individual liberty; and

Whereas RONALD WILSON REAGAN's determined stand against the Soviet empire during his eight years as President served as the catalyst for the end of that regime: Now, therefore, be it

Resolved by the Senate (the House of Representatives concurring), That it is the sense of Congress that an artistic tribute to commemorate the speech given by President RONALD REAGAN at the Brandenburg Gate on June 12, 1987, during which he uttered the immortal lines "Mr. Gorbachev, tear down this wall!", should be placed within the United States Capitol.

Hon. Joseph I. Lieberman

OF CONNECTICUT

Mr. President, I am honored to have the opportunity to rise today to join my colleagues and, indeed, my countrymen and -women in paying tribute to our departed and, I would say, sincerely beloved former President RONALD REAGAN. We mourn his loss and we give our condolences, of course, to Mrs. Reagan and their family.

I cannot claim, as some can in this Chamber, to have known President REAGAN personally and well. In fact, we met a few times while he was serving in the White House. I was attorney general of Connecticut and visited with attorneys general. We did have one remarkable rendezvous.

Our paths crossed, figuratively speaking, as President REAGAN was departing Washington, having completed his second term as President. I was arriving as a freshman Senator from Connecticut. It was January 14, 1989, and the outgoing President was set to give his final weekly radio address Saturday morning.

As always, he gave a masterful and moving performance, engaging the Nation with his wisdom and his wit. Senate Majority Leader George Mitchell, the new Senate majority leader, asked me to give the Democratic response to President REAGAN that Saturday morning in January. It was a high honor, of course, for me as a freshman Senator to be asked to give the weekly radio address but it was, needless to say, a tough act to follow.

I looked back to my remarks and in them I see I praised President REAGAN for his love of country, his fervent devotion to freedom, and his commitment to the values of faith, flag, and family. I said I was "inspired and encouraged by his sense of patriotism," and I urged all Americans to work together on our unfinished business with "the spirit of purpose and confidence that is the legacy of the REAGAN years."

Today, 15 years later, I am very proud I was able to speak those words, and proud of their truthfulness. My admiration and respect for President REAGAN has only grown with time. The optimism, the idealism, the patriotism, and confidence he radiated infected us all and are exactly what we need today.

President REAGAN won the trust of the American people and used that trust to lead. I believe he won the trust of the American people because he reflected their values and they knew he was the real thing, that he stuck to what he believed was right, whether it was popular or not. His leadership was classic democratic leadership, with a small "d." His moral conviction, combined with his pragmatism, enabled him to do an awful lot for our country and the world. He understood what America was about, which was freedom and opportunity, and extended both in America and throughout the world.

After all, he led our country and the free world to victory in the final battle of the cold war against communism.

RONALD REAGAN's message of optimism and purpose was carried by one of the most effective messengers ever to occupy the Oval Office. His rhetoric, after all, made us swell with pride, sometimes harden with indignation, often resonate with emotion. He also made us laugh.

I loved President REAGAN's jokes and borrowed them often, sometimes with attribution, sometimes not. One of my favorites was the one that said a lot about him and about what he believed, what he was for, and what he was against. It was about the commissar who visited the communist collective farm in Russia. He greeted the farmer, who was the head of the farm, on an inspection tour and asked the farmer how the potato crop had been that year.

The farmer said: Oh, commissar, the potato crop has been excellent. As a matter of fact, if we took all the potatoes we grew on this farm this year and put them one on top of the other, they would reach all the way up to the feet of God.

Troubled, the commissar from Moscow said: Comrade farmer, I am glad to hear you did so well raising potatoes, but what do you mean about reaching up to the feet of God? This is a Soviet communist collective farm. There is no God.

The comrade said, that is OK, because there are no potatoes, either. So it was.

I heard someone in the last few days since President REAGAN's death repeat a one-liner of his where the press was getting on him because they said he was not working hard enough as President. At some public gathering, President REAGAN said he was aware of these criticisms and he was also aware of the old line that hard work never killed anybody, but, President REAGAN said, "I figure why should I run the risk?" And so it was.

His sense of humor and exuberance served him and the country well. Yes, he was a cold warrior, our leader in the final battle of the cold war, but he was also a happy warrior. In this and in so many other ways, RONALD REAGAN reflected the personality and values of the American people. You could disagree with his policies, but you could never find his personality or his sincerity disagreeable.

He treated Democrats and Republicans alike, which is to say with respect. That attitude was contagious and even infected both Chambers of Congress. President REAGAN once urged an audience of young people to live lives "that were a statement, not an apology."

This week we remember a true American giant, whose life was a statement, not an apology—a statement of America's values and its transcendent spirit of our faith in God and our love of country, of our national purpose, which is to uphold and extend the reality of freedom and opportunity in the world.

Hon. William H. Frist

OF TENNESSEE

It has been a different week, a very solemn week, and a week that has required all of us to work together from an organizational standpoint and to pull together what has been almost a celebration of this legacy of RONALD REAGAN.

This evening Members will gather in the Senate Chamber and right around that period of time a number of people will be proceeding to the arrival ceremony. It will indeed be a historic moment for the Senate, for this body, but indeed for the American people. Over 150,000 wellwishers are expected to line the streets as President REAGAN's flag-draped caisson is drawn up to this building, the Capitol, by a single riderless horse.

In the past 5 days, we have witnessed a remarkable unity in the country, a fraternity of spirit in many ways. Partisanship has fallen away, and old political foes have set aside disagreements. Americans have come together to celebrate the remarkable achievements of a truly remarkable man. Lifeguard—the pictures are imprinted in everybody's mind—radio announcer, actor, Governor, father, husband, and finally President of the United States. RONALD WILSON REAGAN achieved extraordinary heights.

But he would tell you, I suspect—and it was reflected in so many of the comments among his friends and colleagues over the last several days—that he was simply being an American, fulfilling the American dream. He described the American dream once as "a song of hope that rings through night winter air; vivid, tender music that warms our heart when the least among us aspire to the greatest things."

RONALD REAGAN brought that song back to our hearts. He believed we could achieve great things, that America could achieve great things, and because of his unshakable belief in freedom and liberty and democracy and his ironclad faith in progress, his love and respect for his fellow citizen, we did. We triumphed over the Soviet empire. We created one of the longest economic expansions in American history. We regained our strength and our optimism. We remembered the special privilege it is to be an American.

But we also remembered that freedom is not for us alone. It is the right of every man and woman across the globe, in every age, in every civilization.

In 1964, two decades before he would be reelected in a landslide victory carrying 49 of the 50 United States, RONALD REAGAN told the Nation, "You and I have the ability and the dignity and the right to make our own decisions and determine our own destiny."

As we would learn later, it was our destiny to choose RONALD REAGAN to be our leader, our standard bearer, and our hero. The history books will record RONALD REAGAN as one of our greatest Presidents. Of this I have no doubt. And the American people will remember him with love and with affection for generations to come.

ADJOURNMENT UNTIL MONDAY, JUNE 14, 2004, AT 1 P.M.

Mr. FRIST. If there is no further business to come before the Senate, I ask unanimous consent the Senate stand in adjournment under the provisions of S. Res. 371 as a mark of further respect for President RONALD WILSON REAGAN.

There being no objection, the Senate, at 3:15 p.m., adjourned until Monday, June 14, 2004, at 1 p.m.

Memorial Tributes in the Senate

Monday, June 14, 2004

Hon. William H. Frist

OF TENNESSEE

Mr. President, today the Senate returns to regular business. Last week the Nation and the world bid a final farewell to President RONALD WILSON REAGAN. The services and ceremony were fitting tributes to our 40th President. I remind my colleagues that we will be printing a memorial book that will include all of the floor tributes and services related to the passing of our former President. For those Members who were unable to speak on the floor, we will allow Senators to submit statements on RONALD REAGAN until June 25 in order to have those tributes printed in the memorial book.

Hon. Jon Kyl

OF ARIZONA

Mr. President, I, too, would like to comment on one of the legacies of our late President RONALD REAGAN, the legacy of ensuring that the free world would prevail over the Soviet Union in the cold war.

I thought it was interesting that in one of the comments about REAGAN very recently made on National Public Radio, June 8 of this year, Mr. Gennady Gerasimov, spokesman for Mikhail Gorbachev, said this:

> I see President REAGAN as a gravedigger of the Soviet Union and the spade that he used to prepare this grave was SDI, the Strategic Defense Initiative, so-called "star wars." The trick was that the Soviet leadership believed that this SDI defense is possible and then, because it's possible, then also we must catch up with the Americans. And this was an invitation to the arms race, and the Soviet economy could not really afford it. In this way REAGAN really contributed to the demise of the Soviet Union.

Who better to know that than the spokesmen for Mikhail Gorbachev who have said similar things? Twenty-one years ago, President REAGAN posed a very important question to the American people. He asked us to consider whether the free people of the world should continue to have to rely upon the threat of a massive retaliation of nuclear weapons to prevent an attack by the opposition. He asked: What would it take to free the world from this threat? He answered as follows:

> I know this is a formidable, technical task, one that may not be accomplished before the end of this century. Yet, current technology has attained a level of sophistication where it's reasonable for us to begin this effort. It will take years, probably decades of effort on many fronts. There will be failures and setbacks, just as there will be successes and breakthroughs. ... But isn't it worth every investment necessary to free the world from the threat of nuclear war? We know it is.

We began making that investment. It was one of the reasons we had a deficit during the Reagan years. It was part of the so-called defense build-up, to invest billions of dollars in the research—yes, there were failures, but there were many successes—to develop a Strategic Defense Initiative, an ability to defend ourselves against a ballistic missile attack from an enemy. A lot of Americans probably think we developed that strategic defense, that we have that capability today. They might remember that during the first Persian Gulf war Patriot missiles shot down some of the Scuds that were fired by Saddam Hussein.

But the grim reality is strategic defense is still not a reality. We still don't have the ability to defend against a missile attack. What happened during the Persian Gulf war? We used an air defense system to shoot down airplanes, and in the field, literally, as we shipped it from the United States to Israel and to Saudi Arabia and to Kuwait, made modifications in it so that we hoped it might work to shoot down some of the missiles that Saddam Hussein shot toward Saudi Arabia and Kuwait. In fact, some of those missiles—roughly a third of them—were intercepted by the Patriot. It was a crude weapon that was modified in the field. It had never been tested against other missiles. Yet we used what we had at the time because of the threat that existed.

The point I want to make today is this: The Soviet Union was brought to its knees because it believed President REAGAN when he said we are going to develop a means of countering your most effective weapon, so you might as well not even try to spend the money and the effort and the time to create this program because we will be able to defeat you; we are not kidding.

It has been over 20 years since President REAGAN made that announcement, and we still do not have the missiles in the ground. I am afraid some of our potential enemies are going to conclude that we were bluffing all along, that we do not have the will to spend the money and to put the program in place to provide this kind of defense.

The point of this defense is not just to be able to operationally test it and have it in the ground to stop a missile should one be launched against us, but to deter nations that might believe we are bluffing, to deter nations from spending the money to build these offensive weapons in the first place, to deter these leaders, these people in places such as North Korea and Iran, from concluding that if they will simply spend the money it will take to build the nuclear weaponry and the missiles to fire them, that we will somehow forget about developing missile defenses or conclude that it is too expensive, and the richest Nation on Earth, the Nation that has the financial capability of providing this kind of defense, will decide not to do it.

Now is the time for us to act. It is not the time for us to blink in the face of these dictatorial countries. Should we support the amendment that would cut the heart out of missile defense funding for this year, it would send a signal to these countries that the United States has been bluffing all along. We were not bluffing when RONALD REAGAN made that important announcement. The Soviet Union understood that. Can we do any less today than to make it crystal clear to our would-be enemies that we are not bluffing, that we mean what we say, that we intend to protect America, that we intend to protect others who are our allies, and that we will not permit an offensive ballistic missile to strike our land and kill our people? To do anything else would be morally irresponsible.

As President REAGAN said, if we have the capability of defending ourselves and preventing this kind of conflagration, should we not take advantage of that wonderful capability? I am optimistic about our ability, and I am confident about the American people, and I am sure they want us to confirm to the world that we mean what we say, just as RONALD REAGAN meant what he said.

Hon. Richard G. Lugar

OF INDIANA

Mr. President, I pay special tribute to Nancy Reagan who has been indispensable throughout the public life of the Reagans, and particularly during this past decade. It was my privilege to sit beside Mrs. Reagan during several White House and Republican Party events and to understand her strength and shared dream for America.

The service of President REAGAN to our country can only be approached by understanding how wide he cast the net of potential achievement, and fulfillment of dreams, hopes and visions.

President REAGAN actually believed and articulated that our country had a special destiny, that no barriers were insurmountable because we are Americans. He actually believed and said that the Soviet Union was an evil empire, that its political and economic institutions were disintegrating, and that if its leadership and people knew the alternatives which our country presented, they would choose democracy and market economics.

President REAGAN was prepared to invest an increasing portion of our national treasure in military defense with the certainty that we would negotiate successfully with our adversaries from a position of strength. He shocked foreign policy and defense specialists by proposing that all intermediate nuclear missiles be destroyed, a negotiating position labeled universally as a bizarre arms-control nonstarter.

He affirmed the staying power of NATO by deploying Pershing missiles to Germany and cruise missiles to Italy even after the Soviets declared that such deployment would end all arms control negotiations and stimulate Soviet nuclear buildup.

Add to this, President REAGAN's startling proposal that the United States should develop a Strategic Defense Initiative to protect our country against incoming missiles fired upon us. He contended that we should and could try to defend ourselves against the so-called balance of terror.

He proposed to President Gorbachev that the United States and the Soviet Union ban all nuclear weapons. In fact, he was confident that if he could take Gorbachev on an extended tour of America that Gorbachev would want to shape the Soviet Union into many of our successful traditions.

Meanwhile, President REAGAN knew that substantial new growth must occur in our domestic economy to pay for the special leadership role he had envisioned in foreign policy. He was confident that substantial cuts in individual marginal tax rates and a host of investment incentives would establish and sustain the longest peacetime prosperity we had ever enjoyed. Our prosperity underwrote the magnificent gains in free and fair trade which he championed and worldwide wealth grew abundantly.

When RONALD REAGAN stood on a balcony of the Reichstag in Berlin and challenged Gorbachev to tear down the Berlin Wall, he could see white crosses just below where courageous persons seeking freedom had lost their lives in that pursuit. Everything still appeared to be so locked up and grim, and sophisticated observers were barely patronizing in comment on his Berlin Wall challenge.

The evil empire crumbled, the Berlin Wall and other walls fell, all of the intermediate nuclear force weapons were destroyed in exactly 3 years as the INF Treaty provided, and the United States became the only superpower with the strongest economy and the ability, uniquely, to extend military authority around the world.

All of this occurred because President REAGAN persuaded the Congress and his countrymen to build our Armed Forces, to build our economy through the growth incentives termed "Reaganomics," to maintain the successful strategies of our NATO alliance, to utilize military force to support foreign policy as required, and to commence Strategic Defense Initiative research.

We now know that the Soviets were much weaker than experts estimated. We now know that they could not keep up the pace and that desperate attempts to do so led to the collapse of the Soviet empire and then to the collapse of the Soviet Union, itself.

President REAGAN advocated two more things which were inspiring and critically important in world history.

First, he rejected the Brezhnev doctrine, the idea that territory which socialism had occupied could never be reclaimed. When he advocated this rollback of the Iron Curtain, he created deep anxiety and alarm among most international foreign policy advisers who loved liberty a lot, but loved stability even more.

U.S. Stinger missiles shipped to the expert ministrations of the Mujahadin in Afghanistan were a major instrument of the Soviet rollback, and the world watched in awe as the Soviet troops withdrew to a smaller socialist world.

Second, President REAGAN enunciated a new policy in a statement sent to the Congress after the Philippine election and revolution. He stated that henceforth, we would oppose tyranny of the left and tyranny of the right, that we were for democracy developed by people who sought to know and enjoy democracy and human rights. This statement was severely criticized by experts who suggested that in the "real world" a good number of dictators were friendly to the United States and certainly useful in waging the cold war against communism.

In articulating his vision on the rollback of the Iron Curtain; in identifying with nations all over the world who applauded our passion for building democratic institutions; in celebrating human rights and free market principles; in all of these areas, RONALD REAGAN was far ahead of the prevailing wisdom. Yet he ultimately brought other leaders in America and around the world to his point of view in a relatively short interval.

President REAGAN was courageous and on the right side of history. He performed these deeds in a very public way which instructed and inspired others. Those of us in public service learned much from President REAGAN as we watched him speak and act. He was charismatic, he was determined and consistent, and he enjoyed a remarkable batting average of being right.

Hon. Charles E. Grassley

OF IOWA

Mr. President, at sunset last Friday, the 40th President of the United States was laid to rest on a hill overlooking the Pacific Ocean. The consummate optimist, who etched the promise of a "shining city upon a hill" into the Nation's conscience, leaves behind a legacy that beckons us to stay true to the American spirit.

Whether folks agree with his political philosophy or not, the actor-turned-politician-turned-statesman from the Midwest helped usher in the dawn of a new day for millions of jobless Americans and to those living in oppression behind the Iron Curtain.

Through bold, buoyant leadership, RONALD WILSON REAGAN, 1911–2004, persuaded his fellow citizens that it was "morning again in America" by restoring the promise of peace and prosperity.

The outpouring of support during last week's remembrance for the former President reflects REAGAN's ability to bring out the best in people and unite America.

The pageantry evoked patriotism. The solemnity of the events underscored the public's appreciation and respect for this leader who championed the cause of freedom all around the world. For 8 years, he served as a beacon of hope for those cast under the dark shadows of totalitarianism.

The Great Communicator arrived in the Oval Office when America was licking wounds left by Watergate and Vietnam. Stifled by a sinking economy, joblessness and sky-high inflation, the national mood also wavered under the uncertainty of the cold war. Americans yearned for brighter days.

Elected to his first term in November 1980, President REAGAN exuded optimism, charm and kinship with ordinary Americans. His good-natured disposition, self-deprecating humor and can-do attitude launched a new era in American politics. Like REAGAN, I won an upset victory over an incumbent in that election.

He and I shared a conservative political philosophy rooted in core beliefs spelled out by the Nation's Founders and agreed much more often than not. Now 24 years after the Reagan revolution, I am privileged to continue advancing our shared principles: Big ideas instead of big government. Deregulation to foster free enterprise. Tax relief that encourages productivity, growth and individual ingenuity. Self-reliance rather than self-pity.

REAGAN's policies proved that economic and political freedom bring about peace and prosperity. As REAGAN said in his 1989 farewell address to the Nation: "Democracy, the profoundly good, is also the profoundly productive."

Many people grossly underestimated the strength of REAGAN's convictions and the foot soldiers who helped sweep him into office. With a steely determination coupled with folksy charm, REAGAN masterminded the efforts that liberated Eastern Europe in 1989.

Eight years earlier, he had predicted the end of communism as the "sad, bizarre chapter in human history whose last pages are even now being written." REAGAN's leadership helped change the course of history for the better.

On June 5, 2004, REAGAN lost his 10-year battle with Alzheimer's disease. A decade earlier, in a handwritten note to the American people, REAGAN again looked on the bright side: "When the Lord calls me home, whenever that may be, I will leave with the greatest love for this country of ours and eternal optimism for its future."

President REAGAN valued the gift of life. He used his to expand human freedom. His legacy shapes America's character and lights our way as we continue the "march to freedom" against evil in the world.

Hon. Rick Santorum

OF PENNSYLVANIA

Mr. President, I rise today in great sadness, to speak on the passing of President RONALD WILSON REAGAN. It is a sad time for our Nation; a monumental figure in the history of the United States has gone to his rest. The response to his passing in our Nation's Capital and across this country has been overwhelming and a fitting tribute to this giant of 20th century politics.

First, I would like to offer my heartfelt condolences to Nancy and the Reagan family in this difficult time. Mrs. Reagan was not only an incredible role model for faithfulness to her spouse, but was always the rock that he leaned on when the entire world leaned on him.

In speeches on this floor, we have heard much about President REAGAN's vision and leadership on foreign and economic policy, which indeed continue to bear fruit. Yet, I come to the floor to speak about an aspect of the REAGAN Presidency that is less commented upon: President REAGAN's legacy on social policy, which stands still as a moral compass for our Nation's future.

As has been remarked, President REAGAN was a fabulous optimist. He worked to create a society where good and evil, life and death, are recognized for what they are, and are not obscured by the gray tones of moral relativism. After years of lingering malaise following Vietnam and Watergate, RONALD REAGAN came forward and proclaimed that America was "in the midst of a spiritual awakening and a moral renewal." That was a message of hope that America sorely needed to hear.

He believed that America's strength came not just from military might, but also from its moral superiority. As much of a priority as he made foreign and military policy, he strived just as hard to ensure that our Nation's roots as a people of faith, who value life and each other, was not diminished. It was that social foundation that made us different from the godless Soviet state that oppressed the Russian people.

President REAGAN spoke forcefully and brilliantly about the importance of family, the religious foundations of American democracy, and the tragedy of *Roe* v. *Wade*. He knew that strong families were a key to America's continued success as the land of opportunity. This conviction is clear in a proclamation he issued one Father's Day, where he asserted:

> There is no institution more vital to our Nation's survival than the American family. Here the seeds of personal character are planted, the roots of public virtue first nourished. Through love and instruction, discipline, guidance and example, we learn from our mothers and fathers the values that will shape our private lives and our public citizenship.

His political beliefs were greatly shaped by the sensible religion he grew up with in small-town Illinois, which permeated all aspects of daily life. He found the attempts of some to excise religion from the public square wrongheaded. He knew that Founding Fathers barred not only the government establishment of religion, but also any law "prohibiting the free exercise thereof."

As President REAGAN told those gathered at the Ecumenical Prayer Breakfast during the Republican National Convention in Dallas, TX:

> Without God, there is no virtue, because there's no prompting of the conscience. Without God, we're mired in the material, that flat world that tells us only what the senses perceive. Without God, there is a coarsening of the society. And without God, democracy will not and cannot long endure. If we ever forget that we're one nation under God, then we will be a nation gone under.

I began this speech by stating I would focus on President REAGAN's moral and social legacy rather than on the tremendous impact he had in bringing down the Iron Curtain and freeing Eastern Europe. But in truth, these different areas of policy all flowed from the same wellspring of faith and conscience.

In a particularly moving speech before the National Religious Broadcasters Convention in 1984, President REAGAN tied together these seemingly separate strands. He told listeners:

> Our mission stretches far beyond our borders; God's family knows no borders. In your life you face daily trials, but millions of believers in other lands face far worse. They are mocked and persecuted for the crime of loving God. To every religious dissident trapped in that cold, cruel existence, we send our love and support. Our message? You are not alone; you are not forgotten; do not lose your faith and hope because someday you, too, will be free.

Mr. President, I ask unanimous consent that a larger excerpt of this speech be printed in the *Record*.

REMARKS AT THE ANNUAL CONFERENCE OF THE NATIONAL RELIGIOUS BROADCASTERS CONVENTION, JANUARY, 30, 1984
"AMERICA IS HUNGRY FOR A SPIRITUAL REVIVAL..."

(By RONALD REAGAN)

I was pleased last year to proclaim 1983 the Year of the Bible. But, you know, a group called the ACLU severely criticized me for doing that. Well, I wear their indictment like a badge of honor. I believe I stand in pretty good company.

Abraham Lincoln called the Bible "the best gift God has given to man. But for it," he said, "we could not know right from wrong." Like that image of George Washington kneeling in prayer in the snow at Valley Forge, Lincoln described a people who knew it was not enough to depend on their own courage and goodness; they must also look to God their Father and Preserver. And their faith to walk with Him and trust in His word brought them the blessings of comfort, power, and peace that they sought.

The torch of their faith has been passed from generation to generation. "The grass withereth, the flower fadeth, but the word of our God shall stand forever."

More and more Americans believe that loving God in their hearts is the ultimate value. . . .

My experience in this office I hold has only deepened a belief I've held for many years: Within the covers of that single Book are all the answers to all the problems that face us today if we'd only read and believe.

Let's begin at the beginning. God is the center of our lives: the human family stands at the center of society: and our greatest hope for the future is in the faces of our children. . . .

God's most blessed gift to His family is the gift of life. He sent us the Prince of Peace as a babe in a manger. I've said that we must be cautious in claiming God is on our side. I think the real question we must answer is, are we on His side?

Our mission stretches far beyond our borders; God's family knows no borders. In your life you face daily trials, but millions of believers in other lands face far worse. They are mocked and persecuted for the crime of loving God. To every religious dissident trapped in that cold, cruel existence, we send our love and support. Our message? You are not alone; you are not forgotten; do not lose your faith and hope because someday you, too, will be free.

If the Lord is our light, our strength, and our salvation, whom shall we fear? Of whom shall we be afraid? No matter where we live, we have a promise . . . from Jesus {that can} soothe our sorrows, heal our hearts, and drive away our fears. He promised there will never be a dark night that does not end. Our weeping may endure for a night, but joy cometh in the morning. He promised if our hearts are true, His love will be as sure as sunlight. And, by dying for us, Jesus showed how far our love should be ready to go: all the way.

"For God so loved the world that He gave His only begotten Son, that whosoever believeth in Him should not perish but have everlasting life" . . . Helping each other, believing in Him, we need never be afraid. We will be part of something far more powerful, enduring, and good than all the forces here on Earth. We will be part of a paradise.

May God keep you always, and may you always keep God.

RONALD REAGAN was a champion of the pro-life movement and believed that abortion was a grave threat to the liberties we cherish as Americans. When President REAGAN came to office, the shock of *Roe* v. *Wade* was still fresh. It was commonly believed that the Supreme Court had had the final say on abortion, and that there was no hope in turning back the tide of the abortion-on-demand culture. The conventional wisdom was that enacting legislation to regulate abortion was politically impossible.

But President REAGAN chose to use the one tool that the Senate could not stall and the House could not block: his voice. His voice was strong and reassuring, and it reached the American people in their living rooms, bypassing those in Washington who thought they knew much better. Even his own advisors urged him not to speak out on abortion, yet he would not be silenced. He always spoke his conscience on the matters that weighed heavily on his heart, and no one could convince him to do otherwise.

On the tenth anniversary of *Roe* v. *Wade*, President REAGAN spoke from the heart against the abortion-on-demand culture, to poignant effect. That day, he said:

I, too, have always believed that God's greatest gift is human life and that we have a duty to protect the life of an unborn child. Until someone can prove the unborn child is not a life, shouldn't we give it the benefit of the doubt and assume it is?

Perhaps the only President to publish a book while in the Oval Office, President REAGAN's 1984 volume, entitled "Abortion and the Conscience of the Nation," stood as a thoughtful and moving essay that inspired the growing prolife movement. This message of this book was hopeful. "As a nation today, we have not rejected the sanctity of human life," he writes. "I am convinced that Americans do not want to play God with the value of human life."

Given his remarkable legacy on foreign and economic policy, I am not surprised that his moral agenda is less commented upon. Yet in his March 8, 1983, "Evil Empire" speech, President REAGAN devoted as much time talking about the sanctity of all human life as he did addressing foreign policy. On abortion, he told the audience, "Human life legislation ending this tragedy will some day pass the Congress, and you and I must never rest until it does."

Sadly, President REAGAN has gone to his rest without being able to see that glorious day when we again recognize the full and equal value of all human lives. But those of us who proudly follow in his footsteps will tirelessly continue the struggle until we correct this grievous wrong.

President REAGAN, that day, I know you will be smiling down on us from above.

Hon. John Ensign

OF NEVADA

Mr. President, I rise today to honor and remember the greatest President of the 20th century, RONALD WILSON REAGAN.

RONALD REAGAN is widely known for taking some of the most courageous stands on behalf of our Nation and for truly changing the course of the world, but RONALD REAGAN may have never known the impact that he had on so many individuals, including me.

I was in college when RONALD REAGAN swept through our country in 1980—on a mission to empower Americans by reducing taxes, shrinking the Federal bureaucracy, and instilling a sense of hope for the future. Until that point, I had always considered myself a Democrat. RONALD REAGAN's straight talk and emphasis on common sense and individual empowerment changed the way I looked at politics. As RONALD REAGAN used to say—and he would know—I became "a former Democrat who saw the light." He opened my eyes to a philosophy that I truly felt could change the direction of our country.

I was not alone. President REAGAN's popularity while in the Oval Office for two terms showed that Americans—Republicans, Democrats, and Independents—were inspired by him the way I was. More impressively, tens of thousands of Americans are mourning his death and reflecting on how he touched and changed their lives. The endless line of mourners, waiting for hours to walk past his coffin and pay final respects, is unparalleled. The most heartwarming for me is to see parents with their children, teaching them about the legacy of this great President and hopefully instilling a dose of REAGAN optimism in the next generation.

There are many lessons to teach our children about RONALD REAGAN. I know I will teach them to my own children.

Respect for others: Many of the stories that are being shared by those who knew RONALD REAGAN revolve around his respect for all people. Whether it was someone who washed dishes in the White House or the leader of another Nation, RONALD REAGAN treated each with the same amount of dignity and respect—and loving humor.

Commitment to principles: RONALD REAGAN never shied away from his principles. His steadfast commitment led to monumental changes in the world landscape—making it a better place for all of us. On Memorial Day 1986, President REAGAN said at Arlington National Cemetery:

> If we really care about peace, we must stay strong. If we really care about peace, we must, through our strength, demonstrate our unwillingness to accept an ending of the peace. We must be strong enough to create peace where it does not exist and strong enough to protect it where it does. That's the lesson of this century ...

And that is a lesson from our 40th President.

Mutual love and admiration: I would be remiss if I did not note the relationship that RONALD and Nancy REAGAN shared. Reading some of their old love letters, watching them together during his Presidency, and seeing her devotion over these most trying last 10 years, one cannot help but be touched by the feelings that emanated from their marriage. Nancy Reagan was every bit RONALD REAGAN's partner in the White House, and his legacy is theirs. Today Nancy Reagan grieves—she has lost her soulmate. And we grieve for her loss.

Optimism and hope for tomorrow: If nothing else, I hope that Americans today are inspired by RONALD REAGAN's eternal optimism. He believed in this country and its people with every fiber of his being. He once told a gathering of youth in 1985 that:

> True wealth, and the real hope for the future comes from the heart—from the treasure of ideas and spirit, from free people with a vision of the future, trust in their fellow men, and faith in God. The better future that we all yearn for will not be built by skeptics who spend their lives admiring the complexity of the problems. It'll be built by free men and women who believe in themselves.

I know RONALD REAGAN is in a better place today, and, from his view, he is rooting for us and believing in our future.

Leaders like RONALD REAGAN change the course of history with their vision and inspire a new generation. I serve Nevada in the U.S. Senate because I, too, was inspired by RONALD REAGAN. Today, I thank him from the bottom of my heart for his service to this Nation, for his unwavering leadership, and for his spirit that will always represent our greatness and remind us that we can achieve anything.

President REAGAN, may God bless you and watch over you. And may God continue to bless America.

MESSAGE FROM THE HOUSE—JUNE 9, 2004

At 9:33 a.m., a message from the House of Representatives, delivered by Mr. Hays, one of its reading clerks, announced that the House has agreed to House Resolution 663, expressing the profound regret and sorrow of the House of Representatives on the death of RONALD WILSON REAGAN, former President of the United States of America.

MESSAGE FROM THE HOUSE DURING ADJOURNMENT

At 3:26 p.m., a message from the House of Representatives, delivered by Ms. Niland, one of its reading clerks, announced that the House has agreed to the following concurrent resolution:

S. Con. Res. 115. Concurrent resolution authorizing the use of the rotunda of the Capitol for the lying in state of the remains of the late RONALD WILSON REAGAN, 40th President of the United States.

STATEMENTS ON INTRODUCED BILLS AND JOINT RESOLUTIONS

By Mr. CAMPBELL:

S. 2517. A bill to require the Secretary of the Treasury to mint coins in commemoration of RONALD WILSON REAGAN, the 40th President of the United States; to the Committee on Banking, Housing, and Urban Affairs.

Mr. CAMPBELL. Mr. President, today I introduce the "RONALD WILSON REAGAN Commemorative Coin Act of 2004."

This bill is the same as one I introduced in the 107th Congress, and would accomplish two worthy goals. First, it would help honor RONALD WILSON REAGAN, the 40th President of the United States, and the many worthy contributions he made to this Nation. Second, it would also help raise much needed resources to help families across the United States provide care for their loved ones who have been stricken by Alzheimer's disease.

This legislation's timeliness is obviously without question, as we as a Nation honor RONALD REAGAN this week and mourn his passing. The worthiness of the bill also goes without question. Most of us have seen Nancy Reagan discuss her husband's illness. Watching Mrs. Reagan as she has so openly and eloquently shared touching insights about their struggle with Alzheimer's disease has always been very moving. There is no doubt about the truly deep bonds that united RONALD and Nancy REAGAN and that we need to continue to do what we can to fight the disease that slowly took its terrible toll on the Reagans and so many other American families.

RONALD REAGAN wore many hats in his life, including endeavors as a sports announcer, actor, Governor and President of the United States. He was first elected President in 1980 and served two terms, becoming the first President to serve two full terms since Dwight Eisenhower.

His boundless optimism and deep-seated belief in the people of the United States and the American dream helped restore our Nation's pride in itself and brought about a new "morning in America." His challenge to Gorbachev to "tear down this wall!," his successful revival of our economic power, his determination to rebuild our Armed Forces in order to contain the spread of communism, and his international summitry skills as seen at Reykjavik, Iceland, combined to help bring an end to the cold war. RONALD REAGAN left our Nation in much better shape than it was in when he took office.

As Alzheimer's sets in, brain cells gradually deteriorate and die. People afflicted by the disease gradually lose their cognitive ability. Patients eventually become completely helpless and dependent on those around them for even the most basic daily needs. Each of the millions of Americans who is now affected will eventually, barring new discoveries in treatment, lose their ability to remember recent and past events, family and friends, even simple things like how to take a bath or turn on lights. RONALD REAGAN, one of the most courageous and optimistic Presidents in American history, was no exception.

Shortly after being shot in an assassination attempt, RONALD REAGAN's courage and good humor in the face of a life-threatening situation were evident when he famously apologized to his wife Nancy saying, "Sorry Honey, I forgot to duck." Unfortunately, once Alzheimer's disease takes hold, it delivers a slow mind destroying bullet that none of us can duck to avoid. As RONALD REAGAN wrote shortly after learning of his diagnosis "I only wish there was some way I could spare Nancy from this painful experience." From the moment of diagnosis, it's "a truly long, long, goodbye," Nancy Reagan said.

Fortunately for all of us, when RONALD REAGAN courageously announced in such an honest and public manner that he had Alzheimer's, rather than covering it up, he did a great deal to help alleviate the negative stigma that has long faced those suffering from this terrible disease. Much of the shame and pity traditionally associated with Alzheimer's was transformed almost overnight into sympathy and understanding as public awareness suddenly shot up and those suffering from Alzheimer's, and their families, knew that they were not alone.

While RONALD REAGAN's health didn't deteriorate right away, according to Mrs. Reagan, he had his good days and bad days, "just like everybody else." In recent years, however, REAGAN's condition completely deteriorated—and quickly. "It's frightening and it's cruel," Nancy said, speaking of the disease and what it has done to her husband and family. "It's sad to see somebody you love and have been married to for so long, with Alzheimer's, and you can't share memories," Mrs. Reagan said.

In the introduction to a recently released book based on the touching love letters exchanged between herself and REAGAN, Nancy elaborated on her sense of loss when she wrote, "You know that it's a progressive disease and that there's no place to go but down, no light at the end of the tunnel. You get tired and frustrated, because you have no control and you feel helpless." She also said, "There are so many memories that I can no longer share, which makes it very difficult."

Nancy Reagan has earned our Nation's admiration for her steadfast and loving dedication to her husband as she watched her beloved husband slowly fade away. Likewise, families all across our Nation, day in and day out, choose to personally provide care for their loved ones suffering from Alzheimer's, rather than putting them in institutions. They deserve our respect and support.

Fortunately, Mrs. Reagan has had access to vital resources that helped her care for her husband. This is how it should be. Unfortunately, there are many American families out there who do not have access to these resources. This bill will help alleviate that by raising money to help American families who are struggling while providing care for their loved ones.

Funding for Alzheimer's research has increased significantly over the past several years. RONALD REAGAN's courage in coming forward and publicly announcing his condition played an important role in raising public awareness of Alzheimer's and paved the way for the recent increases in research funding. But much more needs to be done and this bill would complement these efforts.

Once again, the legislation I am introducing today authorizes the U.S. Mint to produce commemorative coins honoring RONALD W. REAGAN while raising funds to help families care for their family members suffering from Alzheimer's disease. I urge my colleagues to support passage of this legislation.

RONALD REAGAN's eternal optimism and deep seated belief in an even better future for our Nation was underscored when he said. "I know that for America, there will always be a bright future ahead." In honoring him this week, and in honoring his struggle, this bill, in keeping with this quote's spirit, will help provide for a better future for many American families.

I ask unanimous consent that the text of the bill be printed in the *Record*.

There being no objection, the bill was ordered to be printed in the *Record*, as follows:

S. 2517

Be it enacted by the Senate and House of Representatives of the United States of America in Congress assembled,
SECTION 1. SHORT TITLE.
This Act may be cited as the "Ronald Reagan Commemorative Coin Act of 2004".
SEC. 2. COIN SPECIFICATIONS.
(a) DENOMINATIONS.—The Secretary of the Treasury (hereafter in this Act referred to as the "Secretary") shall mint and issue the following coins:
(1) $5 GOLD COINS.—Not more than 100,000 $5 coins, which shall—
(A) weigh 8.359 grams;
(B) have a diameter of 0.850 inches; and
(C) contain 90 percent gold and 10 percent alloy.
(2) $1 SILVER COINS.—Not more than 500,000 $1 coins, which shall—
(A) weigh 26.73 grams;
(B) have a diameter of 1.500 inches; and

(C) contain 90 percent silver and 10 percent copper.

(b) BIMETALLIC COINS.—The Secretary may mint and issue not more than 200,000 $10 bimetallic coins of gold and platinum instead of the gold coins required under subsection (a)(1), in accordance with such specifications as the Secretary determines to be appropriate.

(c) LEGAL TENDER.—The coins minted under this Act shall be legal tender, as provided in section 5103 of title 31, United States Code.

SEC. 3. SOURCES OF BULLION.

(a) PLATINUM AND GOLD.—The Secretary shall obtain platinum and gold for minting coins under this Act from available sources.

(b) SILVER.—The Secretary may obtain silver for minting coins under this Act from stockpiles established under the Strategic and Critical Materials Stock Piling Act and from other available sources.

SEC. 4. DESIGN OF COINS.

(a) DESIGN REQUIREMENTS.—

(1) IN GENERAL.—The design of the coins minted under this Act shall—

(A) be emblematic of the presidency and life of former President RONALD WILSON REAGAN;

(B) bear the likeness of former President RONALD REAGAN on the obverse side; and

(C) bear a design on the reverse side that is similar to the depiction of an American eagle carrying an olive branch, flying above a nest containing another eagle and hatchlings, as depicted on the 2001 American Eagle Gold Proof coins.

(2) DESIGNATION AND INSCRIPTIONS.—On each coin minted under this Act, there shall be—

(A) a designation of the value of the coin;

(B) an inscription of the year "2005"; and

(C) inscriptions of the words "Liberty", "In God We Trust", "United States of America", and "E Pluribus Unum".

(b) DESIGN SELECTION.—The design for the coins minted under this Act shall be—

(1) selected by the Secretary, after consultation with the Commission of Fine Arts; and

(2) reviewed by the Citizens Commemorative Coin Advisory Committee.

SEC. 5. ISSUANCE OF COINS.

(a) QUALITY OF COINS.—Coins minted under this Act shall be issued in uncirculated and proof qualities.

(b) MINT FACILITY.—Only one facility of the United States Mint may be used to strike any particular combination of denomination and quality of the coins minted under this Act.

(c) PERIOD FOR ISSUANCE.—The Secretary may issue coins minted under this Act only during the period beginning on January 1, 2005 and ending on December 31, 2005.

SEC. 6. SALE OF COINS.

(a) SALE PRICE.—The coins issued under this Act shall be sold by the Secretary at a price equal to the sum of—

(1) the face value of the coins;

(2) the surcharge provided in subsection (d) with respect to such coins; and

(3) the cost of designing and issuing the coins (including labor, materials, dies, use of machinery, overhead expenses, marketing, and shipping).

(b) BULK SALES.—The Secretary shall make bulk sales of the coins issued under this Act at a reasonable discount.

(c) PREPAID ORDERS.—

(1) IN GENERAL.—The Secretary shall accept prepaid orders for the coins minted under this Act before the issuance of such coins.

(2) DISCOUNT.—Sale prices with respect to prepaid orders under paragraph (1) shall be at a reasonable discount.

(d) SURCHARGES.—All sales of coins issued under this Act shall include a surcharge established by the Secretary, in an amount equal to not more than—

(1) $50 per coin for the $10 coin or $35 per coin for the $5 coin; and

(2) $10 per coin for the $1 coin.

SEC. 7. DISTRIBUTION OF SURCHARGES.

(a) IN GENERAL.—Subject to section 5134(f) of title 31, United States Code, the proceeds from the surcharges received by the Secretary from the sale of coins issued under this Act shall be paid promptly by the Secretary to the Department of Health and Human Services to be used by the Secretary of Health and Human Services for the purposes of—

(1) providing grants to charitable organizations that assist families in their efforts to provide care at home to a family member with Alzheimer's disease; and

(2) increasing awareness and educational outreach regarding Alzheimer's disease.

(b) AUDITS.—Any organization or entity that receives funds from the Secretary of Health and Human Services under subsection (a) shall be subject to the audit requirements of section 5134(f)(2) of title 31, United States Code, with regard to such funds.

SEC. 8. FINANCIAL ASSURANCES.

(a) NO NET COST TO THE GOVERNMENT.—The Secretary shall take such actions as may be necessary to ensure that minting and issuing coins under this Act will not result in any net cost to the United States Government.

(b) PAYMENT FOR COINS.—A coin shall not be issued under this Act unless the Secretary has received—

(1) full payment for the coin;

(2) security satisfactory to the Secretary to indemnify the United States for full payment; or

(3) a guarantee of full payment satisfactory to the Secretary from a depository institution, the deposits of which are insured by the Federal Deposit Insurance Corporation or the National Credit Union Administration Board.

Hon. Richard J. Durbin

ILLINOIS

As we mourn the passing of President RONALD REAGAN, we should recall his vision of America as a "shining city upon a hill"—a model of democracy, freedom and the rule of law that people around the world look to for inspiration. As President REAGAN said in his farewell address to the Nation:

> After 200 years, two centuries, {America} still stands strong and true on the granite ridge, and her glow has held steady no matter what storm. And she's still a beacon, still a magnet for all who must have freedom.

President REAGAN was right. Our "city upon a hill" must hold steady in defense of our principles no matter what storm. Despite the threat of terrorism, we must stand by our opposition to torture and other cruel treatment.

In fact, it was President REAGAN who first transmitted the Convention against Torture and Other Cruel, Inhuman or Degrading Treatment or Punishment to the Senate with his recommendation that the Senate ratify the treaty.

As President REAGAN reminded us, our "city upon a hill" must stand firm. The eyes of the world are upon us.

Hon. Patrick J. Leahy

OF VERMONT

Mr. President, we have come to the close of several days of tribute to our late President, RONALD REAGAN. So much has been said about President REAGAN's buoyant spirit and about the contributions he made to our Nation, and these tributes have helped millions of Americans with the healing process that comes with the death of so popular and beloved a leader.

Though much has already been said about President REAGAN, I do want to pay special tribute today to our former First Lady, Nancy Reagan.

For me—and, I suspect, for millions of other Americans—some of the most stirring images of this memorable week have been of Nancy Reagan and her family. We saw again, and so clearly, her strength, her compassion and her deep love for her husband.

Ever since President REAGAN's deeply moving announcement to his fellow citizens and to the world that he was suffering from Alzheimer's disease, I have watched Mrs. Reagan conduct herself with compassion, loyalty, competence and caring that have been an inspiration to the thousands of family members who every day struggle to cope with loved ones suffering from this disease or from any of the long variety of other disorders that can come upon us in our older ages—and sometimes far earlier than that.

The Alzheimer's Association estimates that 4.5 million Americans today suffer from this debilitating disease. Often, family members and especially, spouses—end up as primary caregivers to their partners or other family members. Along with the emotional pain and heartbreak of watching the mind of a loved one slowly fade away, many caregivers are ill equipped to handle the many facets of the illness that present themselves over the duration of this mental and physical struggle. Their own physical health suffers. Managing a job or any other activity outside the home becomes almost impossible.

I believe Nancy Reagan is an inspiration to so many Americans. The love that she and her husband so clearly showed to each other comforted and sustained their marriage in sickness, as it did in health.

Marcelle and I extend our best wishes to Mrs. Reagan and to the entire Reagan family.

Hon. Jon Kyl

OF ARIZONA

Mr. President, I ask unanimous consent that the column "Empty Words" by Frank Gaffney, which appears in today's *Washington Times*, be printed in the *Record*. I believe that this piece appropriately emphasizes the crucial role continued research plays in maintaining the credible nuclear deterrent of the United States. As more information becomes available regarding covert nuclear programs in North Korea and Iran, the sustainability and credibility of America's nuclear arsenal is of paramount concern.

There being no objection, the material was ordered to be printed in the *Record*, as follows:

{From the *Washington Times*, June 15, 2004}
EMPTY WORDS

(By Frank J. Gaffney, Jr.)

The U.S. Senate gets back to work today after a week of bipartisan mourning of RONALD REAGAN and tributes to his security policy legacy. It is fitting that the first orders of business will be votes on amendments to repudiate two of the initiatives most central to the GIPPER's foreign and defense policy success: the maintenance of a credible and safe nuclear deterrent, and protection of Americans against missile attack.

The first effort to reduce last week's Reagan endorsements to empty words will be led by some of the Senate's most liberal Democrats, notably Sens. Edward Kennedy of Massachusetts and Dianne Feinstein of California. They seek to preclude the United States from even researching new nuclear weapons, let alone testing or deploying them.

RONALD REAGAN hated nuclear weapons as much as anybody. What is more, he seriously worked to rid the world of them. Yet, unlike these legislators, President REAGAN understood—until that day—this country must have effective nuclear forces. He was convinced there was no better way to discourage the hostile use of nuclear weapons against us than by ensuring a ready and credible deterrent.

Toward that end, Mr. REAGAN comprehensively modernized America's strategic forces, involving both new weapons and an array of delivery systems. He built two types of intermediate-range nuclear missiles and deployed them to five Western European countries. And, not least, he recognized our deterrent posture depended critically upon a human and physical infrastructure that could design, test, build and maintain the nation's nuclear arsenal. Without such support, America would inexorably be disarmed.

In fact, it is no exaggeration to say that, but for Mr. REAGAN's nuclear modernization efforts—most of them over the strenuous objections of senators like Mr. Kennedy and John Kerry—we may well not have a viable nuclear deterrent today. Even with his legacy, 15 years of policies more in keeping with the anti-nuclear "freeze" movement's nostrums than Mr. REAGAN's philosophy of "peace through strength" have undermined the deterrent by creeping obsolescence, growing uncertainty about its reliability and safety and loss of infrastructure to ensure its future effectiveness.

This is especially worrisome since some of the research in question would explore whether a Robust Nuclear Earth Penetrator (RNEP) could be developed to penetrate deep underground before detonating. Such a capability would allow us to hold at risk some of the 10,000 concealed and hardened command-and-control bunkers, weapons of mass destruction (WMD) production and storage facilities and other buried high-value targets built by potential adversaries.

If anything, the absence of a credible American capability to attack such targets may have contributed to rogue states' massive investment in these facilities over the past 15 years. One thing is clear: Our restraint in taking even modest steps to modernize our nuclear deterrent—for example, by designing an RNEP or new, low-yield weapons—has certainly not prevented others from trying to "get the Bomb."

There is no more reason—Sens. Kennedy, Kerry and Feinstein's arguments to the contrary notwithstanding—to believe continuing our unilateral restraint will discourage our prospective enemies' proliferation in the future.

Last September, the Senate recognized this reality, rejecting an earlier Feinstein-Kennedy amendment by a vote of 53–41. Five Democrats—Sens. Evan Bayh of Indiana, Fritz Hollings of South Carolina, Zell Miller of Georgia, Ben Nelson of Nebraska and Bill Nelson of Florida—joined virtually every Republican in permitting nuclear weapons research, with the proviso further congressional approval would be required prior to development and production. The prudence of this is even more evident today in light of revelations of covert Iranian and North Korean nuclear activity since last fall.

The other assault on the REAGAN legacy will be led by Democratic Sens. Carl Levin of Michigan and Jack Reed of Rhode Island. They hope to strip more than $500 million from defense authorization legislation that would buy anti-missile interceptors, the direct descendant of Ronald Reagan's Strategic Defense Initiative (SDI).

Just last week, former Gorbachev spokesman Gennadi Gerasimov, reminded the world how mistaken those like Sen. Carl Levin, Michigan Democrat, were when they ridiculed and tried to undermine the Reagan missile defense program: "I see President REAGAN as a gravedigger of the Soviet Union and the spade that he used to prepare this grave was SDI."

Today, there are published reports the U.N. Security Council has been briefed by its inspectors that ballistic missiles and WMD components were slipped out of Iraq before Saddam Hussein was toppled. Such weapons, like some of the thousands of other short-range missiles in arsenals around the world, could find their way into terrorists hands and be launched at this country from ships off our shores.

Can there be any doubt but that RONALD REAGAN—faced with today's threat of missile attack and the proliferation of nuclear and other weapons of mass destruction—would have been any less resolute in building missile defenses and maintaining our nuclear deterrent than he was in the 1980s? If last week's praise for his visionary leadership two decades ago was not dishonest rhetoric, it should inspire, and guide us all now.

Wednesday, June 16, 2004

Hon. Barbara A. Mikulski

OF MARYLAND

Mr. President, I rise today to announce the introduction of the Ronald Reagan Alzheimer's Breakthrough Act of 2004. I believe the greatest tribute to President REAGAN and the Reagan family is a living memorial. That is why I am introducing this legislation with my colleague, Senator Kit Bond. Our legislation makes an all-out effort to spark and accelerate breakthroughs for Alzheimer's. The legislation supports research on how to prevent the disease, how to care for people who have it, and initiatives to support those who are caregivers. Let's celebrate President REAGAN's life of vigor by attacking Alzheimer's with vigor.

The time to act for real breakthroughs is now. Just last month, Senator Bond and I held a hearing on Alzheimer's research. Expert after expert told us: We are on the verge of amazing breakthroughs; we will lose opportunities if we don't move quickly; we are at a crucial point where NIH funding can make a real difference. Researchers, families, and advocates all said the same thing, we need to do more, and we need to do better. I believe that the answer to that call is passing the Ronald Reagan Alzheimer's Breakthrough Act of 2004.

We are truly on the brink of something that can make a huge difference for American families. We know that families face great difficulties when a loved one has Alzheimer's. There is great emotional cost as well as financial cost. We know that for our public investment we could get new treatments that would prolong a patient's cognitive abilities. Each month we delay admission to a long-term care facility is important to the family and to the taxpayer. Everybody wants a cure; that is our ultimate goal. But even if we keep people at home for 1 or 2 more years, to help them with their memory, and their activities of daily living, it would be an incredible breakthrough.

Our bill would do three things. First, it would strengthen our national commitment to Alzheimer's research. The legislation doubles the funding for Alzheimer's research at the National Institutes of Health from $700 million to $1.4 billion. We need to give researchers the resources they need to make breakthroughs that are on the horizon in diagnosis, prevention and intervention. Also, our bill calls for a national summit on Alzheimer's that would bring together the best minds to look at priorities for research moving forward.

Second, our bill provides critical support for caregivers. The family is always the first caregiver. The Nation saw what a family of prestige and means went through; imagine what other American families are going through. The legislation creates a tax credit for families caring for a loved one with a chronic condition, like Alzheimer's, that would help them pay for prescription drugs, home health care and specialized day care. Also, it helps create one-stop shops across the country so families can find services like respite care, adult day care and training for caregivers.

Third, our legislation promotes "News You Can Use" for families and physicians. Incredible advances are being made every day. We need to get the word out so families and doctors know the most current information. The Alzheimer's Association has been doing a great job with their "Maintain Your Brain" campaign; however, philanthropic efforts of advocacy groups are not a substitute for public policy. Our bill builds on these efforts to create an effective public education strategy.

It is amazing how far we have come. Back in the early eighties, Alzheimer's was a catchall term for any kind of memory loss. Today, doctors diagnose Alzheimer's with 90-percent accuracy. Every day NIH is making progress to identify risks, looking at new kinds of brain scans for appropriate detection, and understanding what this disease does to the brain.

How did we get this far, this fast? With a bipartisan commitment of the authorizers and appropriators. Together, we have been working to increase the funding for the National Institute on Aging. In 1998 the National Institute on

Aging was funded at approximately $500 million. Thanks to our bipartisan effort, it is at $1 billion. Now is the time to do more.

My own dear father had Alzheimer's. I remember when I would go to visit him. It didn't matter that I was a U.S. Senator; it didn't matter that I could get Nobel Prize winners on the phone. The research and treatments didn't exist for my father, for President REAGAN, or for more than 4 million families. Alzheimer's is an all-American disease that affected an all-American President. Now we need an all-American effort to speed up the breakthroughs so no family has to go through the long goodbye.

I urge my colleagues to support this bill and move swiftly to enact it into law.

Hon. Christopher S. Bond
OF MISSOURI

Mr. President, I rise today to speak of the life, leadership and the truly remarkable legacy of the 40th President of the United States, RONALD REAGAN.

President REAGAN was a great communicator with a powerful message. He preached the gospel of hope, freedom and opportunity not just for America but for the world. REAGAN was a genuinely optimistic person who brought that spirit of optimism and hope to the American people and to enslaved peoples around the world. He was a man who took disappointment and moved on. He was a man of unfailing good humor, care and thoughtfulness. Even people who disagreed with his policies across the board could not help but like him.

In the United States, his policies encouraged the return of more tax dollars to average Americans and unfettered entrepreneurship to create jobs and build the economy. REAGAN's strong military opposition to the Soviet Union helped bring down the walls that harbored communism and tyranny throughout Eastern Europe and much of the world.

In a letter to the American people in 1994 RONALD REAGAN announced he was one of the millions of Americans with Alzheimer's disease. One of the most courageous things RONALD and Nancy REAGAN did was to announce publicly that he had Alzheimer's disease. Through their courage and commitment, the former President and his wife, Nancy, changed the face of Alzheimer's disease by increasing public awareness of the disease and of the need for research into its causes and prevention.

In honor of RONALD REAGAN, today my colleague Senator Mikulski and I are introducing the Ronald Reagan Alzheimer's Breakthrough Act of 2004. This bill will increase research for Alzheimer's and increase assistance to Alzheimer's patients and their families. This bill will serve as a living tribute to President REAGAN and will: (1) double funding for Alzheimer's research at the National Institutes of Health; (2) increase funding for the National Family Caregiver Support Program from $153 million to $250 million; (3) reauthorize the Alzheimer's Demonstration Grant Program that provides grants to States to fill in gaps in Alzheimer's services such as respite care, home health care, and day care; (4) authorize $1 million for the Safe Return Program to assist in the identification and safe, timely return of individuals with Alzheimer's disease and related dementias who wander off from their caregivers; (5) Establish a public education campaign to educate members of the public about prevention techniques that can maintain their brain as they age, based on the current research being undertaken by NIH; (6) establish a $3,000 tax credit for caregivers to help with the high health costs of caring for a loved one at home; and (7) encourage families to prepare for their long-term needs by providing an above-the-line tax deduction for the purchase of long-term care insurance.

Ironically it was President REAGAN who drew national attention to Alzheimer's for the very first time when he launched a national campaign against Alzheimer's disease some 22 years ago.

In 1983 President REAGAN proclaimed November as National Alzheimer's Disease Month. In his proclamation President REAGAN said:

> The emotional, financial and social consequences of Alzheimer's disease are so devastating that it deserves special attention. Science and clinical medicine are striving to improve our understanding of what causes Alzheimer's disease and how to treat it successfully. Right now, research is the only hope for victims and families.

Today, approximately 4.5 million Americans have Alzheimer's, with annual costs for this disease estimated to exceed $100 billion. Today there are more than 4.5 million people in the United States with Alzheimer's, and that number is expected to grow by 70 percent by 2030 as baby boomers age.

In my home State of Missouri alone, there are over 110,000 people with Alzheimer's disease. Based on population growth, unless science finds a way to prevent or delay the onset of this disease, that number will increase to over 130,000 by 2025—that is an 18-percent increase.

In large part due to President REAGAN, there has been enormous progress in Alzheimer's research—95 percent of what we know we discovered during the past 15 years. There is real potential for major breakthroughs in the next 10 years. Baby boomers could be the first generation to face a future without Alzheimer's disease if we act now to achieve breakthroughs in science.

President and Mrs. REAGAN have been leading advocates in the fight against Alzheimer's for more than 20 years, and millions of Americans have been helped by their dedication, compassion and effort to support caregivers, raise public awareness about Alzheimer's disease and increase the Nation's commitment to Alzheimer's research.

This bill will serve as a living tribute to President REAGAN and will offer hope to all those suffering from the disease today. As we celebrate the life and legacy of RONALD REAGAN, we are inspired by his legendary optimism and hope, and today we move forward to confront this expanding public health crisis with renewed vigor, passion, and compassion.

Thursday, June 17, 2004

Hon. Jeff Sessions

OF ALABAMA

Mr. President, I thank Chairman Allard for his leadership and his expertise. He is becoming perhaps the most authoritative Member of the Senate on this issue. He has worked on national missile defense since he has been in the Senate. It is great to work with him.

We do need to do the right thing. We have committed as a country to deploy a national missile defense system. We voted to deploy that system as soon as technologically feasible. That was back in the nineties, and President Clinton signed the statute we passed. I believe it got 90-plus votes in the Senate. Although there were a lot of people who were opposed to it until the very end, in the end everybody realized that we needed to defend America, and we had the capability of doing so.

There has been a cottage industry of skeptics out there that has made fun of President REAGAN. They called his vision for national missile defense star wars. Then when President REAGAN said no to Gorbachev's proposal in Reykjavik, which accepted so many of the things President REAGAN wanted so badly but told President REAGAN he would have to stop national missile defense, he thought about that very hard on the eve of the reelection campaign. He knew he would be criticized, but he said, No; national missile defense is important to America. It was important to peace in the world because, instead of worrying about how many of the enemy we could kill, we could begin focusing on how to protect our people from being killed by missile attacks. It was a defining moment in the cold war. One expert recently said that was the moment that signaled the end of the Soviet Union.

Hon. William H. Frist

OF TENNESSEE

Mr. President, I would like to take a moment to thank all of the dedicated members of the Senate family who poured their hearts into making President REAGAN's final journey to the Nation's Capitol a dignified and fitting tribute.

Lawmakers and dignitaries from all corners of the globe, Supreme Court justices, Federal officials and hundreds of thousands of citizens made their way to the rotunda last week to pay their final respects to our 40th President.

It was a solemn and stately event. Each moment radiated a sense of history. I would like to thank some of the Senate individuals whose hard work made last week possible: (1) Sergeant at Arms Bill Pickle; his deputy, Keith Kennedy; protocol officer, Becky Daugherty; Capitol information officer, Laura Parker; and the Sergeant at Arms staff; (2) Alan Hantman, the Architect of the Capitol, and the Capitol Superintendent, Carlos Elias; (3) Terry Gainer and the Capitol Police who, under extraordinary pressure, maintained security with discretion and consideration; (4) Emily Reynolds, the Secretary of the Senate; her deputy, Mary Suit Jones; and their hard-working staff; (5) The Senate Chaplain, Pastor Barry C. Black whose sonorous and reflective tributes captured the public's love for President REAGAN; (6) All of the volunteers who handed out bereavement cards to the public, manned the condolence booths, and handed out water to the thousands of visitors waiting patiently to see the President; and (7) The Capitol Guide service which worked round the clock.

My sincere thanks also go to Chairman Lott and Senator Dodd. Their steady leadership over the proceedings was crucial.

Likewise, the President of the Senate and the President pro tempore presided over the Senate on this momentous occasion with dignity and distinction.

I also wish to extend my thanks to my colleagues in the House of Representatives. Throughout, both Chambers worked closely and patiently to carry out a tribute that I think all would agree properly reflected and celebrated President REAGAN's extraordinary legacy.

I specifically thank: (1) The Speaker and his dedicated staff; (2) The House Sergeant at Arms and Doorkeeper, Bill Livingood; (3) The House chief administrative officer, Jay Eagen; (4) The Clerk of the House, Jeff Trandahl; and (5) The House Chaplain, Reverend Daniel P. Coughlin. His stirring remarks are now a part of America's history.

Finally, to the Reagan family: Through a bleak and solemn weeklong procession, their love and respect for RONALD REAGAN was a beacon to us all. The Reagan family showed an uncommon dignity and grace that raised us up and touched our hearts.

We will never forget their love. And we will never forget how RONNIE loved his Nancy, and how hard it was for her, even at the very last, to let him go.

Thank you to the Reagan family. And thank you to the man who led us so well and loved his country so deeply—RONALD WILSON REAGAN, 40th President of the United States.

Monday, June 21, 2004

Hon. Jon Kyl

OF ARIZONA

Let me read what very recently, just before the Reagan funeral, Gennady Gerasimov, spokesman for the former Soviet leader Mikhail Gorbachev, had to say:

I see President REAGAN as a gravedigger of the Soviet Union and the spade that he used to prepare this grave was SDI, the Strategic Defense Initiative, so-called "star wars." The trick was that the Soviet leadership believed that this SDI defense is possible and then, because it's possible, then also we must catch up with the Americans. And this was an invitation to the arms race and the Soviet economy could not really afford it. In this way REAGAN really contributed to the demise of the Soviet Union.

It worked. President REAGAN was not bluffing. He meant to deploy this system. At Reykjavik, when Gorbachev said, "We can make this arms deal we have been talking about, if you will do one more thing. If you will stop development of your SDI Program, we have a deal."

President REAGAN thought about it overnight, came back the next morning and said, "I am sorry. The United States is going to proceed with missile defense."

Gorbachev knew at that moment it was over. They could not compete with us, and it wasn't obviously worth the effort to try to do so because they knew the technology of the United States could produce a defense against the only real weapon that the Soviet Union had that could defeat us, and that was the ballistic missile.

Thursday, June 24, 2004

Hon. William H. Frist

OF TENNESSEE

Mr. President, the hour is late, and I know we will be wrapping up in about 30 minutes or so. There is a lot of business with the recess tomorrow—and we will be in tomorrow—and we will be wrapping up tonight. It will take a while to wrap up.

Thus, I would like to take a few minutes to come to the floor and take advantage of the time to talk about the fascinating trip I had the opportunity and the privilege to take about 3 weeks ago. I had the privilege of traveling to Normandy, France, to celebrate the 60th anniversary of the D-day landings.

That same week, as my colleagues know, we suspended business on the floor of the Senate to pay tribute to President RONALD REAGAN—again, a wonderful week in that the messages were delivered and the tributes were shared.

In the midst of that, however, I did not have the opportunity to share with my colleagues some of my experiences from the D-day celebration in Normandy, France, and thus I would like to take this opportunity to do that.

I took this particular journey with two of our colleagues, Senator Bob Bennett and Senator John Ensign. The three of us had a truly extraordinary experience. We spent the previous 2 days in Baghdad, Iraq, and in Kuwait, and then flew from Baghdad to the United States-French binational ceremony at Omaha Beach.

Back in 1944, in the thick of war, Fortress Europe was the strongest at this point, reinforced with layers of obstacles, mines, and gun positions with hardened bunkers. Some of those structures are still there today. You can see the remnants of others. These remnants stand today almost as ghostly reminders of those battles that I had the opportunity to hear described first-hand by the veterans who had come back for the celebration.

At Normandy, Nazi forces were commanded, as we all know, by none other than Field Marshal Erwin Rommel, the "Desert Fox" of North Africa fame who was regarded as the finest, the very best field commander in the German Army. He won practically every battle he enjoined. His defenses were considered impenetrable.

In the early morning of June 6, 1944—of course, that was the day so many years later that we were there—American soldiers, mainly from the 1st Infantry Division and 29th Infantry Division, landed at that beach we visited now several weeks ago. They were supported by the Army Air Force flying over and naval gunfire. They struggled forward inch by inch, out of boats up the beach, as fellow soldiers were literally cut down one by one, wounded, and killed in this hail of enemy gunfire.

We have all read about what went on at that beach, but to have that opportunity to hear first-hand, as we walked along the ridge above that beach, from people who were there. Many of them had not talked a lot—at least they said they had not talked a lot about their experience. They seemed to open up as we were there. Many of them were there at the age of 16, 17, 18, or 19 years of age. And they all described the battle raging. Body counts swelled, and many expressed doubt that they would succeed—they described it as such—that every second seemed like an eternity.

It was clear that in spite of all this, soldiers, through boldness and through courage, persevered.

Further down the beach, the U.S. Army Rangers had scaled the cliffs at Pointe du Hoc and knocked out the German artillery positions that were there to disrupt any invasion force.

By the end of that blood-soaked day, our American boys had pierced that Atlantic wall. They seized their objectives. And, as history would prove, because we had the opportunity to celebrate, they launched the liberation of Europe.

Thousands of American soldiers perished in those few hours. Their heroism today is marked by the familiar pictures today with television and C–SPAN and video—the familiar pictures of all of those white crosses against that green grass and the stars of David, all in very neat rows. Wherever you stand, you see them lined up parallel, horizontally and vertically, or diagonally. Wherever you stand, the symmetry jumps out at you. It goes on for acres and acres. I have no idea how big it is. But these crosses go on for acres.

There is a little path where the beach is right below. You can walk along these winding paths of the cemetery. As you do so—especially, I think on this day, when the sky was bright blue, the white crosses, the green grass—there were veterans by the hundreds and, indeed, by the thousands with their family members, with, obviously, their daughters, sons, grandchildren, and great-grandchildren huddling around them as they walked along those paths. One could not help but admire their bravery, their boldness at a time in their life when they were very young, at a time they had to be uncertain; they were far away from home, fighting a ruthless enemy. Each cross and each star, obviously, represents a young man, a young person who died on June 6, 1944, defending his country.

The crowds would gather as we were there. A lot of people had come in. There was a lot of security at the gathering to hear President Bush and President Chirac. As the crowd gathered, we were seated amidst the sea of veterans. Usually they put the officials in one or two rows, separated, but, no, you would sit in the audience surrounded by scores and scores of veterans.

A few minutes ago I called Congressman Charlie Rangel to talk about another bill we will be talking about later tonight. In that conversation I was reminded of the fact that 2 weeks ago he was there. He called me over to meet several veterans from New York. There was another woman, Grace Bender, a neighbor of mine in Washington, DC. I had no idea I would see her there. She was there a few rows away with her father, of whom she was clearly so proud.

The veterans were gathering with their buddies and with their family members, with their shipmates, with their fellow crewmen. Even after 60 years, they clearly regarded these colleagues, these comrades in arms, as brothers, bonds forged over that period of a day, weeks, and those months in the midst of this war.

I vividly remember standing for the national anthem. As we all stood up, the first people on their feet were those veterans, the "greatest generation." They were the first to stand. I also noted, they were the ones who would be singing the loudest. They seemed to stand the tallest. Their love of country clearly had even grown over time.

President Bush spoke and delivered captivating remarks. President Chirac also delivered stirring remarks. They both recounted specific moments and acts of heroism on D-day. We honored those who gathered and we paid tribute to those who were no longer with us, the soldiers and the sailors and the airmen who had made that ultimate sacrifice for the cause of freedom.

The ceremony ended with a ceremony of honor guards. Again, my heart filled with awe and admiration to be able to walk with those veterans on that D-day celebration. They were then, and they clearly remain today, true heroes.

After the ceremony, my colleagues and I boarded a bus to the town of Bayeaux, a small French village that was spared the heavy fighting and bombing on D-day and of the weeks that followed. As we rode the bus through the countryside, we passed through beautiful green fields, hedgerows, and small towns of the French countryside that were showered in 1944 by the American paratroopers of the 101st and the 82d Airborne Divisions, the night before those Normandy landings.

I specifically mention the 101st because this past weekend I had the opportunity to be in Clarksville, TN, and Fort Campbell, KY, and had the opportunity to witness an air show in which the 101st Airborne participated. You can see dramatically their training exercises.

While I was in Kentucky last week, again, I was thinking back to what happened in 1944 when these paratroopers of the 101st and 82d Airborne Divisions paratrooped in the night before. Thousands of those paratroopers, as we all know, were killed. Many of them drowned. Many were wounded that night. Many were wounded on the jump itself. The mission was specifically to jump behind enemy lines to distract the Nazis and seize important strategic or key terrain and to disrupt the Nazi reinforcements. Their heroism and success were ultimately crucial to the allied victories at Omaha Beach, at Juno, at Sword, and at Gold.

When we arrived in Bayeaux, we were greeted by the president of the French senate. We had the opportunity to have lunch there with 33 members of their senate. We also met with the town mayor, and many of the town citizens came out to speak of this. I don't speak French, but as I went over to the side and shook hands and introduced myself to an interpreter, immediately a smile came on their faces with an expression of appreciation and thanks.

Among the people we had the opportunity to meet were many survivors of war who had been small children at the time of the occupation. They did recall D-day and the American GIs who liberated their villages.

They treated us to a wonderful luncheon that day and, once again, representing America as officials, U.S. Senators from America, we were showered with praise and thanks, as well as a promise of continued friendship and alliance. This was a group of French senators, so I did not expect that at the time, but that is what we received.

Our final event for the day was also very special. It was the multinational ceremony at Arromanches. We were joined by gatherings of heads of state from around the world, senior officials from countries around the world, and a number of our allied nations. We watched a whole range of demonstrations by various multinational military marching units. We had flyovers occur where a number of these nations demonstrated the very best of their aircraft in precision flights overhead. They had a wonderful multimedia presentation that combined the best of dance and video and audio to recount that history of World War II with a very special focus on Normandy.

During the final ceremony of the day, in which President Chirac delivered remarks, we did have the opportunity to reflect on those larger contours of the war and how America and her allies united to defeat tyranny and oppression.

As we sat among the survivors of D-day and as we listened to America's veterans recount their fears and exploits, I could not help but draw comparisons between the veterans of World War II and our proud troops serving abroad today, the very same troops which 2 days prior my colleagues and I had the opportunity to visit in Baghdad and Kuwait. The parallel is there, not just because of the temporal relationship, but because of both groups' commitment to freedom and democracy and to a better life for others.

America was blessed in World War II on that June 6, so long ago, yet so close, as it is now, to have the very same soldiers who have that strong character, who have that courage, that boldness, and that determination. Young patriots, then, as now, answered the call of duty, and through their bravery and through their selfless determination, they fought and they won the battle for freedom and security.

It was these traits that inspired a whole succession of American Presidents, including the late President REAGAN to whom we paid tribute 2 weeks ago. He believed in a Europe and a world whole and free of the shadow of communism. The "greatest generation" threat involved nazism and fascism. For nearly 50 years, America confronted another hegemonic ideology, that being communism. Under the leadership and vision of President REAGAN, we emerged from the cold war victorious and, as Margaret Thatcher rightly reminds us, without firing a single shot.

Today, we do fight a different enemy, but one that is no less ruthless, no less determined, no less uncompromising than our enemies of those wars past.

Once again, we must stay the course. Once again, we must have faith in our Armed Forces. Once again, we must hold tightly to the belief that freedom will prevail. That is our challenge. That is our calling. And I truly believe, like generations before us, we will look evil squarely in the eye, and we will not flinch, we will not run. We will gather up our courage to press forward and defeat the forces of terror and secure the blessings of democracy.

Friday, June 25, 2004

Hon. William H. Frist

OF TENNESSEE

Madam President, the Senate has been busy over the past 4 weeks. I thought I would take a few moments to look back and then look ahead a bit.

The 1 week I left out of the last 4 weeks is the week we spent in tribute to RONALD REAGAN, where we recognized the life and legacy of one of America's greatest Presidents. A little over 2 weeks ago, we paid our final respects to President RONALD WILSON REAGAN. Over the course of the week, we had the opportunity to mourn the passing of this great American leader but also to celebrate the values for which he stood. There were countless tributes paid to President REAGAN, his beloved wife Nancy, and to the entire REAGAN family. All of those tributes helped us celebrate the memory of this optimistic, bold, and compassionate President. World and national leaders filed through this building, the Nation's Capitol, down the hallway behind me, to pay respects as the President lay in state. We had the opportunity to welcome many of those world and national leaders, but what was truly remarkable to me was to be able to be in my office or in the hallway and see the hundreds and then the thousands and then the tens of thousands of ordinary, regular, hard-working Americans who came to the Nation's Capital from all around the country, people who would drive hundreds, indeed thousands, of miles. People would get on an airplane and arrive at 10 at night to stand in line for 4 or 5 hours to pay their respects.

Throughout the week, our shining Capital City united peoples throughout the world, both those who could be here, those who watched on television, those who read the newspapers, and those who heard it on the radio. It united the American people and the world peoples in a way that is very rare. Indeed, it is the sense of national and global community that embodied the legacy of the 40th President, and though we said goodbye to the man, we carry forward his relentless faith in those values of freedom and democracy.

Wednesday, July 20, 2004

Hon. Tom Daschle

OF SOUTH DAKOTA

Mr. President, 60 years ago Franklin Roosevelt gave one of the most memorable State of the Union speeches in our history.

As he spoke, Germany occupied all of Europe. Americans were dying in battle abroad and sacrificing for the war effort at home.

Total victory was uncertain. But that did not diminish President Roosevelt's optimism and vision.

In his address, he said the Nation had accepted a Second Bill of Rights that, he said, would create "a new basis of security" for all.

In this Second Bill of Rights, President Roosevelt cited the right to a decent home, a good education, and dependable health care; the right to fair prices for farmers and free competition for business; and the right to be free of the fears of hardship caused by old age. But first, and most fundamental, he called for the right to work for a fair wage.

Our country should be proud of the extraordinary progress we have made in many of these areas. Together we have made our country better, stronger, and more secure. There is, though, more work to be done, and today I want to focus on President Roosevelt's call for a fair wage.

No value is more fundamental to the American character than the value of work. No ideal is shared so widely or cherished so deeply.

No principle binds us more closely to the generations of Americans who built up our country, and the millions of new Americans who came to our shores to join in the effort. And no conviction so unites the conservative and liberal traditions of our Nation.

RONALD REAGAN once said that:

> People in America value family, work, and neighborhood. These are the things we have in common socially and politically. When it comes to the bottom line, all of us are striving for the same thing—a strong and healthy America and a fair shake for working people.

There is a fundamental American truth in those words—working people deserve a fair shake. It has always been the promise of our country, and as we debate legislation here in the Senate, we should do all we can to give life to that promise.

We should make certain that no American who works full time lives in poverty. Unfortunately, the gap between promise and reality is widening. Among full-time, year-round workers, poverty has doubled since the late seventies to 2.6 million workers. All told, the working poor are raising 9 million American children.

Moreover, as recent work by the Family Economic Self-Sufficiency Project shows, the level of income it now takes just to pay the basic bills is far above what we consider to be the poverty line. No working American wants a handout. These families are playing by the rules. But as hard as they work, they cannot escape the grip of poverty.

A few weeks ago a Sioux Falls family sent me a letter. The father works 56 hours a week as a skilled welder. His wife is a substitute teacher who only works part time so she can care for her son, who suffers from autism and diabetes. They live in a 20-year-old mobile home that has sinking floors and a leaking ceiling. They wrote:

> We are facing possible foreclosure. Lights, heat, phone, etc. are all 60-plus days past due and on the verge of disconnection.... Medical bills have been turned over to a collection agency.

Their final question was: "Now what?"

They feel trapped. Since they can't afford insurance, their son's medical bills have erased their savings and destroyed their credit. Without good credit, interest payments eat up much of their income. And without affordable child care, the family's mom can't shift to full-time work, which could help lift them out of poverty.

They are working as hard as they can and want to work even harder. But that doesn't seem to be enough. They are farther away from President Roosevelt's vision today than when they first wrote to me. It's in our national interest not to look away from this difficult problem, but to face it squarely and honestly.

If the people who work hard don't get a fair shake, then our Nation risks losing an essential value that has contributed to America's excellence and ongoing success. We cannot let that happen. We should not kid ourselves and pretend this is an easy problem. It is not. It is enormously complicated. But there are things we can and must do.

First, it is important that American business leaders live up to their responsibility as good corporate citizens and share the benefits of increased productivity with their workers, not just their shareholders. The chief economist at Merrill Lynch recently noted that there's been a notable "redistribution of income to the corporate sector." While salaries have remained flat over the past 4 years, corporate profits now occupy a greater share of our GDP than at any point since tracking began nearly 60 years ago. We are moving in the wrong direction, and leaders in the private sector have a responsibility to help us move back in the right direction.

Here in Congress, we also have a responsibility to address the problems confronting the working poor, and we should start by requiring a long overdue increase in the minimum wage. Today, the minimum wage of $5.15 per hour is worth $3 less than it was in 1968. Americans who work at the minimum wage for 40 hours a week, 52 weeks a year, still fall $5,000 short of the poverty line. That means, as the Sioux Falls family knows, that adequate housing, enough food to eat, health insurance, and college funds are the stuff of fantasy, not reality. In the time we have left this year, we should increase the minimum wage to $7. That won't solve all our problems, but it is a beginning.

We should also revisit the earned income tax credit. It was created 20 years ago as an incentive to help working families lift themselves out of poverty through hard work. President REAGAN called it the "best anti-poverty, the best pro-family, the best job creation measure to come out of Congress." I agree. Now we need to expand it, so that every American child grows up seeing that work is rewarded and respected.

We should also make sure all families receive their fair share of the child tax credit. Extending the credit to all working families would restore a basic level of fairness and offer millions of working families the same child tax credit given to those higher up the income ladder.

We must also acknowledge that despite the many benefits of globalization, it has placed downward pressure on low-income wages. We won't make progress if our wages fall faster than the prices for the products we need.

"What do the American people want more than anything else?" President Roosevelt asked in 1944.

This was his answer:

> To my mind, they want two things: work, with all the moral and spiritual values that go with it; and with work, a reasonable measure of security. ... Work and security. These are more than words. They are more than facts. They are the spiritual values, the true goal toward which our efforts should lead.

That was the challenge 60 years ago, and it remains a central challenge today. It is, as President Roosevelt said, "our duty."

I hope we can all join together to make that vision a reality for millions of hard-working and honest Americans.

Hon. Orrin G. Hatch

OF UTAH

In a July 1, 2004 article entitled "RONALD REAGAN, Sagebrush Rebel, Rest in Peace," William Pendley of the Mountain States Legal Foundation wrote: "I am, former Governor RONALD REAGAN proclaimed in 1980, 'a Sagebrush Rebel.'"

Now, at his hearing {to be nominated to be a U.S. circuit court judge for the Ninth Circuit}, Bill Myers was attacked merely for having used this same term, in an advocacy piece he wrote for his farming and ranching clients. In fact, he was mocked at this hearing, and after it, for merely channeling the concerns of his clients, who, like RONALD REAGAN, considered themselves "Sagebrush Rebels."

Mr. Pendley's article goes on:

> When RONALD REAGAN was sworn in, he became the first president since the birth of the modern environmental movement a decade before to have seen, first hand, the impact of excessive federal environmental regulation on the ability of state governments to perform their constitutional functions; of local governments to sustain healthy economies; and of private citizens to use their own property. ... REAGAN thought federal agencies in the West should be "good neighbors." Therefore, REAGAN returned control of western water

rights to the states, where they had been from the time gold was panned in California until Jimmy Carter took office. REAGAN sought to ensure that Western states received the lands that they had been guaranteed when they entered the Union. REAGAN responded to the desire of western governors that the people of their states be made a part of the environmental equation by being included in federal land use planning.

I would also like to note that REAGAN criticized "excessive" regulation, not any regulation at all—neither Bill Myers nor anyone else thinks there is no role for the Federal Government in environmental regulation. And Bill Myers emphasized this at his hearing, in response to very hostile questioning by Democratic Senators:

A centralized government—i.e. Congress—has an important role to play in environmental protection. And the Clean Water Act, the Clean Air Act—there are probably 70 environmental statutes that give evidence to that truth.

But the Reagan approach, which is also the Bush Interior Department's approach, which Bill Myers did his best to defend, is inimical to the environmental activist groups that oppose Mr. Myers' nomination. Any attempt to give the people who actually make their living on and around Western lands a stake in how those lands are regulated is violently opposed by these groups. And then these groups label their enemies "enemies of the environment," or "friends of polluters." It is unfortunate that such labels are uncritically accepted by some Senators, and because these liberal groups have similarly labeled Bill Myers, he won't get the up or down vote he deserves.

Thursday, July 22, 2004

Hon. Richard J. Durbin

OF ILLINOIS

As we mourn the passing of President RONALD REAGAN, all Americans should recall his vision of our Nation as a "shining city upon a hill." Here is what President REAGAN said about the shining city and immigration:

> If there have to be city walls, the walls have doors and the doors are open to anyone with the will and the heart to get here. ... The city is a beacon a magnet for all who must have freedom, for all pilgrims from all the lost places who are hurtling through the darkness, toward home.

Like me, President REAGAN was the son of an immigrant. We had very different political philosophies, but President REAGAN understood the importance of immigrants to our great country.

AUTHORIZING PRINTING OF A COMMEMORATIVE DOCUMENT

Mr. FRIST. Mr. President, I ask unanimous consent that the Senate proceed to the immediate consideration of S. Con. Res. 135, which is at the desk.

The PRESIDING OFFICER. The clerk will report the concurrent resolution by title.

The legislative clerk read as follows:

A concurrent resolution (S. Con. Res. 135) authorizing the printing of a commemorative document in memory of the late President of the United States, RONALD WILSON REAGAN.

There being no objection, the Senate proceeded to consider the concurrent resolution.

Hon. FRIST. Mr. President, I ask unanimous consent that the concurrent resolution be agreed to, the motion to reconsider be laid upon the table, and that any statements relating to the concurrent resolution be printed in the *Record*.

The PRESIDING OFFICER. Without objection, it is so ordered.

The concurrent resolution (S. Con. Res. 135) was agreed to, as follows:

S. CON. RES. 135

Resolved by the Senate (the House of Representatives concurring),
SECTION 1. COMMEMORATIVE DOCUMENT AUTHORIZED.

A commemorative document in memory of the late President of the United States, RONALD WILSON REAGAN, consisting of the eulogies and encomiums for RONALD WILSON REAGAN, as expressed in the Senate and the House of Representatives, together with the texts of the state funeral ceremony at the United States Capitol Rotunda, the national funeral service held at the Washington National Cathedral, Washington, District of Columbia, and the interment ceremony at the Ronald Reagan Presidential Library, Simi Valley, California, shall be printed as a Senate document, with illustrations and suitable binding.

SEC. 2. PRINTING OF DOCUMENT.

In addition to the usual number of copies printed, there shall be printed the lesser of—

(1) 32,500 copies of the commemorative document, of which 22,150 copies shall be for the use of the House of Representatives and 10,350 copies shall be for the use of the Senate; or

(2) such number of copies of the commemorative document that does not exceed a production and printing cost of $1,000,000, with distribution of the copies to be allocated in the same proportion as described in paragraph (1).

Wednesday, September 29, 2004

MESSAGES FROM THE HOUSE

At 3:56 p.m., a message from the House of Representatives, delivered by Ms. Niland, one of its reading clerks, announced that the House has passed the following bill, in which it requests the concurrence of the Senate:

S. Con. Res. 135. Concurrent resolution authorizing the printing of a commemorative document in memory of the late President of the United States, RONALD WILSON REAGAN.

Sunday, October 10, 2004

AUTHORIZING PRINTING OF COMMEMORATIVE DOCUMENT IN MEMORY OF LATE PRESIDENT RONALD WILSON REAGAN

Mr. FRIST. I ask that the Chair now lay before the Senate the House message to accompany S. Con. Res. 135, providing for the printing of a commemorative document honoring former President REAGAN.

The President pro tempore laid before the Senate a message from the House, as follows:

Resolved, That the resolution from the Senate (S. Con. Res. 135) entitled "Concurrent resolution authorizing the printing of a commemorative document in memory of the late President of the United States, RONALD WILSON REAGAN", do pass with the following amendment:

Page 1, beginning on line 13, strike {Senate document, with illustrations and suitable binding} and insert "House document, with illustrations and suitable binding, under the direction of the Joint Committee on Printing".

Mr. FRIST. I ask unanimous consent that the Senate concur in the House amendment and the motion to reconsider be laid upon the table, and any statements relating to the concurrent resolution be printed in the *Record*.

The PRESIDENT pro tempore. Without objection, it is so ordered.

INDEX

Memorial Tributes in the House of Representatives of the United States

Aderholt, Robert B., of Alabama:
  Address, 112
  Remarks
    Ronald Reagan at an Ecumenical Prayer Breakfast in Dallas, TX, August 23, 1984, 112
Akin, W. Todd, of Missouri, address, 117
Alexander, Rodney, of Louisiana, address, 19
Appointment of Members To Attend the Funeral, 159
Baca, Joe, of California, address, 50
Barrett, J. Gresham, of South Carolina, address, 94
Barton, Joe, of Texas, address, 32
Becerra, Xavier, of California, address, 149
Berkley, Shelley, of Nevada, address, 65
Biggert, Judy, of Illinois, address, 42
Bilirakis, Michael, of Florida, address, 134
Blackburn, Marsha, of Tennessee, address, 46
Blumenauer, Earl, of Oregon, address, 33
Blunt, Roy, of Missouri, address, 13
Boehlert, Sherwood, of New York, address, 31
Boehner, John A., of Ohio, addresses, 109, 175
Bonilla, Henry, of Texas:
  Addresses, 155, 160
  Letter from Robert L. DuPont, MD, et al., 160
Bonner, Jo, of Alabama, address, 156
Bono, Mary, of California, address, 127
Bordallo, Madeleine Z., of Guam, address, 48
Bradley, Jeb, of New Hampshire, address, 139
Brady, Kevin, of Texas, address, 125
Brown, Henry E., Jr., of South Carolina, address, 97
Brown-Waite, Ginny, of Florida, addresses, 52, 121
Burgess, Michael C., of Texas, addresses, 66, 88, 149
Burns, Max, of Georgia, address, 120
Burr, Richard, of North Carolina, address, 115
Burton, Dan, of Indiana, address, 101
Buyer, Steve, of Indiana, address, 103
Calvert, Ken, of California, address, 37
Cannon, Chris, of Utah, address, 145
Cantor, Eric, of Virginia, address, 117
Capito, Shelley Moore, of West Virginia, address, 110
Capps, Lois, of California, address, 154
Cardin, Benjamin L., of Maryland, address, 87
Carter, John R., of Texas, addresses, 93
Castle, Michael N., of Delaware, address, 157
Chocola, Chris, of Indiana, address, 38
Cole, Tom, of Oklahoma, address, 98
Collins, Mac, of Georgia, address, 135
Communication from the Clerk of the House, 6
Costello, Jerry F., of Illinois, address, 146
Cox, Christopher, of California, addresses, 71, 95, 123
Crane, Philip M., of Illinois, address, 111
Crenshaw, Ander, of Florida, address, 129
Cubin, Barbara, of Wyoming, address, 81
Cunningham, Randy "Duke," of California, addresses, 19, 57, 171
Davis, Artur, of Alabama, address, 105
Davis, Danny K., of Illinois, address, 13
Davis, Lincoln, of Tennessee, address, 81
Davis, Tom, of Virginia, address, 62
DeLay, Tom, of Texas, address, 7
Diaz-Balart, Lincoln, of Florida, addresses, 50, 94
Diaz-Balart, Mario, of Florida, address, 68
Dreier, David, of California:
  Addresses, 3, 24
  Tribute by George P. Shultz, 3
Duncan, John J., Jr., of Tennessee, address, 67
Ehlers, Vernon J., of Michigan, addresses, 67, 68
Emanuel, Rahm, of Illinois, address, 102
Emerson, Jo Ann, of Missouri, address, 84
Engel, Eliot L., of New York, address, 61
Etheridge, Bob, of North Carolina, address, 104
Everett, Terry, of Alabama, address, 90
Faleomavaega, Eni F.H., of American Samoa, address, 57
Feeney, Tom, of Florida, address, 88
Ferguson, Mike, of New Jersey, address, 105
Flake, Jeff, of Arizona, address, 109
Foley, Mark, of Florida, address, 64
Forbes, J. Randy, of Virginia, address, 93
Ford, Harold E., Jr., of Tennessee, address, 150
Franks, Trent, of Arizona, addresses, 46, 175
Frelinghuysen, Rodney P., of New Jersey, address, 150
Frost, Martin, of Texas, address, 81
Gallegly, Elton, of California, address, 14
Garrett, Scott, of New Jersey, address, 89
Gibbons, Jim, of Nevada, address, 92
Gilchrest, Wayne T., of Maryland, address, 87
Gingrey, Phil, of Georgia, address, 34
Goode, Virgil H., Jr., of Virginia, address, 44
Goodlatte, Bob, of Virginia, address, 30
Granger, Kay, of Texas, address, 45
Graves, Sam, of Missouri, address, 120
Green, Gene, of Texas, address, 49
Green, Mark, of Wisconsin, address, 88
Gutknecht, Gil, of Minnesota, address, 77
Hall, Ralph M., of Texas, address, 29
Harman, Jane, of California, address, 61
Harris, Katherine, of Florida, address, 91
Hart, Melissa A., of Pennsylvania, address, 28
Hastert, J. Dennis, of Illinois, address, 10
Hastings, Doc, of Washington, address, 91
Hayes, Robin, of North Carolina, addresses, 38, 164
Hayworth, J.D., of Arizona:
  Addresses, 77, 164
  Article from *Free Press*, 1997, 164
Hefley, Joel, of Colorado, address, 66
Hensarling, Jeb, of Texas, address, 41
Herger, Wally, of California, address, 23
Herseth, Stephanie, of South Dakota, 103
Hill, Baron P., of Indiana, address, 76
Hobson, David L., of Ohio, address, 138
Hoekstra, Peter, of Michigan, address, 59
Holden, Tim, of Pennsylvania, address, 50
Holt, Rush D., of New Jersey, address, 122
Hooley, Darlene, of Oregon, address, 82
Hostettler, John N., of Indiana, address, 120
House Concurrent Resolution 444, 68
House Resolution 663, 7
House Resolution 664, 11
Hoyer, Steny H., of Maryland, address, 16
Hunter, Duncan, of California, addresses, 39, 162, 164
Hyde, Henry J., of Illinois, address, 75
Isakson, Johnny, of Georgia, address, 92
Israel, Steve, of New York, address, 24
Issa, Darrell E., of California, addresses, 27, 51, 172
Istook, Ernest J., Jr., of Oklahoma, address, 129

Jackson-Lee, Sheila, of Texas, address, 20
Jenkins, William L., of Tennessee, address, 140
Johnson, Timothy V., of Illinois, address, 142
Kennedy, Mark R., of Minnesota, address, 104
Kildee, Dale E., of Michigan, address, 137
Kind, Ron, of Wisconsin, address, 111
King, Steve, of Iowa, address, 52
Kingston, Jack, of Georgia, address, 122
Kline, John, of Minnesota, address, 90
Kolbe, Jim, of Arizona, address, 58
Larson, John B., of Connecticut, address, 71
Latham, Tom, of Iowa, address, 132
Leach, James A., of Iowa, address, 147
Lewis, Jerry, of California, addresses, 11, 13, 23, 29, 31, 37, 41, 47
Lewis, Ron, of Kentucky, address, 119
Linder, John, of Georgia, address, 35
Lipinski, William O., of Illinois, address, 147
Matheson, Jim, of Utah, address, 75
McCarthy, Karen, of Missouri, address, 137
McCollum, Betty, of Minnesota, address, 153
McCotter, Thaddeus G., of Michigan, address, 114
McDermott, Jim, of Washington, address, 169
McGovern, James P., of Massachusetts, address, 119
McNulty, Michael R., of New York, address, 107
Meehan, Martin T., of Massachusetts, address, 145
Meek, Kendrick B., of Florida, address, 130
Menendez, Robert, of New Jersey, address, 159
Message from the President of the United States, 7
Michaud, Michael H., of Maine, address, 154
Millender-McDonald, Juanita, of California, address, 69
Miller, Candice S., of Michigan, address, 110
Miller, Gary G., of California, address, 152
Miller, Jeff, of Florida, address, 82
Moore, Dennis, of Kansas, addresses, 84, 121, 124
Moran, Jerry, of Kansas, address, 141
Murphy, Tim, of Pennsylvania, address, 114
Nethercutt, George R., Jr., of Washington, address, 116
Ney, Robert W., of Ohio, address, 73
Northup, Anne M., of Kentucky, address, 61
Norwood, Charlie, of Georgia, address, 80
Nunes, Devin, of California, address, 142
Nussle, Jim, of Iowa, address, 138
Ortiz, Solomon P., of Texas, address, 136
Osborne, Tom, of Nebraska, address, 34
Oxley, Michael G., of Ohio, address, 143
Paul, Ron, of Texas, addresses, 148, 174
Pearce, Stevan, of New Mexico, address, 122
Pelosi, Nancy, of California, address, 9
Pence, Mike, of Indiana, address, 80
Pitts, Joseph R., of Pennsylvania, addresses, 5, 65
Platts, Todd Russell, of Pennsylvania, address, 83
Pomeroy, Earl, of North Dakota, address, 158
Porter, Jon C., of Nevada, address, 133
Portman, Rob, of Ohio, address, 116
Prayer by Rev. John Boyles, 4
Pryce, Deborah, of Ohio, address, 115
Putnam, Adam H., of Florida, address, 108

Radanovich, George, of California, address, 79
Rahall, Nick J., II, of West Virginia, address, 146
Ramstad, Jim, of Minnesota, address, 108
Regula, Ralph, of Ohio, address, 156
Rehberg, Dennis R., of Montana, address, 131
Reyes, Silvestre, of Texas, address, 132
Rohrabacher, Dana, of California, addresses, 18
Ross, Mike, of Arkansas, address, 98
Royce, Edward R., of California, address, 78
Ryan, Paul, of Wisconsin, address, 144
Ryan, Tim, of Ohio, address, 97
Ryun, Jim, of Kansas, address, 4
Sandlin, Max, of Texas, address, 78
Saxton, Jim, of New Jersey, address, 47
Schrock, Edward L., of Virginia, address, 135
Scott, David, of Georgia, address, 15
Senate Concurrent Resolution 115, 74
Senate Concurrent Resolution 135, 173
Sensenbrenner, F. James, Jr., of Wisconsin, address, 76
Sessions, Pete, of Texas, address, 153
Shadegg, John B., of Arizona, address, 126
Shays, Christopher, of Connecticut:
    Addresses, 123, 170
    Tribute by Ambassador Joseph Verner Reed, 170
Shuster, Bill, of Pennsylvania, address, 67
Simmons, Rob, of Connecticut, address, 62
Simpson, Michael K., of Idaho, address, 161
Smith, Christopher H., of New Jersey, address, 139
Smith, Lamar S., of Texas, address, 130
Smith, Nick, of Michigan:
    Addresses, 6, 53, 168
    Poem by Albert Carey Caswell, 53
Souder, Mark E., of Indiana, address, 125
Stearns, Cliff, of Florida, address, 66
Stenholm, Charles W., of Texas, address, 26
Stupak, Bart, of Michigan, address, 151
Sullivan, John, of Oklahoma, address, 131
Tauzin, W.J. (Billy), of Louisiana, address, 147
Taylor, Charles H., of North Carolina, address, 128
Thomas, William M., of California, address, 15
Thornberry, Mac, of Texas, address, 86
Tiahrt, Todd, of Kansas, address, 133
Tiberi, Patrick J., of Ohio, address, 59
Turner, Michael R., of Ohio, address, 60
Udall, Tom, of New Mexico, address, 151
Upton, Fred, of Michigan, address, 94
Wamp, Zach, of Tennessee, address, 44
Waxman, Henry A., of California, address, 12
Weldon, Curt, of Pennsylvania, address, 106
Weldon, Dave, of Florida, address, 31
Weller, Jerry, of Illinois, address, 118
Wicker, Roger F., of Mississippi, address, 43
Wilson, Joe, of South Carolina, addresses, 36, 65, 163
Wolf, Frank R., of Virginia:
    Addresses, 5, 54
    Article from *Jerusalem Post*, June 6, 2004, 56
Wu, David, of Oregon, address, 101
Young, C.W. Bill, of Florida, address, 152

Memorial Tributes in the Senate of the United States

Alexander, Lamar, of Tennessee, address, 181
Allard, Wayne, of Colorado, address, 215
Allen, George, of Virginia, address, 205
Bennett, Robert F., of Utah, address, 244
Bond, Christopher S., of Missouri, addresses, 222, 312
Boxer, Barbara, of California, address, 193
Brownback, Sam, of Kansas, address, 211
Bunning, Jim, of Kentucky, address, 243
Burns, Conrad, of Montana, address, 186
Byrd, Robert C., of West Virginia:
    Address, 294
    Poem by an unknown author, 295
Carper, Thomas R., of Delaware, address, 276
Chafee, Lincoln D., of Rhode Island, address, 288
Cochran, Thad, of Mississippi, address, 184
Coleman, Norm, of Minnesota, address, 233
Collins, Susan M., of Maine, address, 284
Communication from the President, 240
Conrad, Kent, of North Dakota, address, 291
Cornyn, John, of Texas, address, 184
Corzine, Jon S., of New Jersey, address, 292
Craig, Larry E., of Idaho, address, 284
Daschle, Tom, of South Dakota, addresses, 202, 319
Dodd, Christopher J., of Connecticut, address, 288
Dole, Elizabeth, of North Carolina, address, 180
Domenici, Pete V., of New Mexico, address, 198
Dorgan, Byron L., of North Dakota, address, 213
Durbin, Richard J., of Illinois, addresses, 281, 309, 321
Edwards, John, of North Carolina, address, 293
Ensign, John, of Nevada, address, 305
Enzi, Mike, of Wyoming, address, 227
Feingold, Russell D., of Wisconsin, address, 238
Feinstein, Dianne, of California, address, 236
Fitzgerald, Peter G., of Illinois, address, 278
Frist, William H., of Tennessee:
    Addresses, 179, 241, 263, 298, 299, 313, 315, 318
    Authorizing Printing of Commemorative Document, 321, 322
Graham, Bob, of Florida, address, 254
Grassley, Charles E., of Iowa, address, 302
Gregg, Judd, of New Hampshire, address, 189
Hagel, Chuck, of Nebraska, address, 216
Harkin, Tom, of Iowa, address, 268
Hatch, Orrin G., of Utah, addresses, 255, 320
Hollings, Ernest F., of South Carolina, addresses, 235
Hutchison, Kay Bailey, of Texas, address, 269
Inhofe, James M., of Oklahoma, address, 230
Jeffords, James M., of Vermont, address, 289
Kennedy, Edward M., of Massachusetts, address, 242
Kyl, Jon, of Arizona:
    Addresses, 209, 292, 299, 309, 314
    Article from *Arizona Republic*, June 9, 2004, 293
    Article from *Washington Times*, June 15, 2004, 310
Lautenberg, Frank, of New Jersey, address, 287
Leahy, Patrick J., of Vermont, address, 309
Lieberman, Joseph I., of Connecticut, address, 296
Lincoln, Blanche L., of Arkansas, address, 290
Lott, Trent, of Mississippi:
    Address, 263
    Tribute by Senator Connie Mack, 263
Lugar, Richard G., of Indiana, address, 300
McCain, John, of Arizona, address, 235
McConnell, Mitch, of Kentucky, address, 265
Messages from the House of Representatives, 295, 306, 322
Mikulski, Barbara A., of Maryland, addresses, 220, 311
Murkowski, Lisa, of Alaska, address, 249
    Poem by Robert Service, 250
Nelson, Bill, of Florida, address, 229
Nickles, Don, of Oklahoma, address, 217
Prayers:
    Dr. Prentice Meador, 188
    Dr. Barry C. Black, Chaplain of the Senate, 179, 240
Pryor, Mark, of Arkansas, address, 239
Reid, Harry, of Nevada, address, 195
Santorum, Rick, of Pennsylvania:
    Address, 302
    Remarks
        Ronald Reagan at the Annual Conference of the National Religious Broadcasters Convention, January 30, 1984, 303
Senate 2517, 307
Senate Concurrent Resolution 115, 188
Senate Concurrent Resolution 118, 296
Senate Concurrent Resolution 135, 321
Senate Resolution 371, 188
Senate Resolution 373, 295
Senate Resolution 374, 295
Sessions, Jeff, of Alabama, addresses, 246, 313
Shelby, Richard C., of Alabama, address, 204
Smith, Gordon, of Oregon:
    Address, 224
    Remarks
        Ronald Reagan's Farewell Address, 224
Snowe, Olympia J., of Maine, address, 191
Specter, Arlen, of Pennsylvania, address, 200
Stabenow, Debbie, of Michigan, address, 290
Stevens, Ted, of Alaska, address, 207
Sununu, John E., of New Hampshire, address, 271
Talent, James M., of Missouri, address, 252
Thomas, Craig, of Wyoming, address, 249
Warner, John W., of Virginia:
    Address, 272
    Remarks
        Ronald Reagan's Speech at the U.S. Ranger Monument, Pointe du Hoc, Normandy, France, on the 40th Anniversary of D-Day, June 6, 1984, 274

www.ingramcontent.com/pod-product-compliance
Lightning Source LLC
Chambersburg PA
CBHW060334010526
44117CB00017B/2824